APPENDIX B: CONJUNCTIVE ADVERBS

Conjunctive adverbs are used at the beginning of sentences or clauses. We use conjunctive adverbs to show the connection between the sentence or clause they introduce and the information that came immediately before. Remember that before a conjunctive adverb, you need either a period (.) or a semi-colon (;). After a conjunctive adverb, you need a comma (,).

Conjunctive Adverb	Purpose	Example Sentences
in addition	to give more information	Chris volunteers at the art gallery; **in addition,** he is captain of the basketball team. Pollution in the river has lowered the fish population; **in addition,** it has killed plant life.
furthermore		The new mayor will lower taxes; **furthermore,** she will improve health services. Research into ghosts is a waste of time; **furthermore,** it's a waste of money.
moreover		The castle is a historical landmark; **moreover,** it's a popular tourist attraction. Small houses are cute; **moreover,** they are easy to keep clean.
besides		The Grand Hotel is too expensive; **besides,** it's too far away. Sociology 101 is not useful to my career; **besides,** it's boring!
for example	to give an example	Today's teenagers have many more gadgets than their parents did; **for example,** they have iPads and smartphones. Thai food is delicious; **for example,** Thai green curry is a tasty dish.
for instance		Why don't you take a language course? **For instance,** you could take Spanish or Russian. Hypnosis is often used to treat addictions; **for instance,** it is helpful for nicotine or alcohol addiction.
therefore	to show a result	We lost our semi-final match; **therefore,** we will not be in the final. Liz is allergic to cheese; **therefore,** she cannot eat pizza.
however	to show something unexpected	I thought I had done badly on the test; **however,** I got 85 percent! The weather forecast predicted rain; **however,** it was a nice, sunny day.
on the other hand	to show a contrast	The red coat is more stylish; **on the other hand,** the blue coat is warmer. The leather chair is more comfortable; **on the other hand,** the wooden chair is cheaper.
in contrast		Canada has very cold winters; **in contrast,** Arizona has warm and sunny winters. Susannah is good at science; **in contrast,** her brother Stuart is an excellent artist and musician.
in fact	to show emphasis	Nelson Mandela was a great leader; **in fact,** he was a hero to many people. Jenna is a good singer; **in fact,** she is the best singer in her choir.
actually	to correct someone	People sometimes say Ying is unfriendly; **actually,** she is just very shy. Some people think dragons are real animals; **actually,** they just appear in stories.

APPENDIX C: SUBORDINATING CONJUNCTIONS

We use subordinating conjunctions to connect dependent clauses to independent clauses. The order of the sentence can be IC + conjunction + DC, or it can be conjunction + DC + comma + IC.

The school bus is cancelled **whenever** it snows.

Whenever it snows, the school bus is cancelled.

Subordinating Conjunction	Purpose	Example Sentences
before after when whenever while until as soon as	to show a time relationship	Turn off the lights **before** you go to bed. **Before** you go to bed, turn off the lights. Jake backpacked in Europe **after** he graduated. **After** he graduated, Jake backpacked in Europe. They will text me **when** they are at the theatre. **When** they are at the theatre, they will text me. My basement floods **whenever** it rains. **Whenever** it rains, my basement floods. Mia hit a deer **while** she was driving home. **While** she was driving home, Mia hit a deer. You should stay here **until** you hear from him. **Until** you hear from him, you should stay here. I knew the news was bad **as soon as** I saw her face. **As soon as** I saw her face, I knew the news was bad.
so (that)	to show a purpose	Ami bought a cookbook **so (that)** she could learn to cook. **So (that)** she could learn to cook, Ami bought a cookbook.
because as	to show a reason	We're happy **because** it's Friday. **Because** it's Friday, we're happy. There is no school tomorrow **as** it's Canada Day. **As** it's Canada Day, there is no school tomorrow.
whereas while	to show a contrast	Biology 100 is easy, **whereas** Chemistry 101 is hard. **Whereas** Chemistry 101 is hard, Biology 100 is easy. China is a large country, **while** Singapore is small. **While** Singapore is a small country, China is large.
although even though	to show an unexpected event	Our flight is on time **although** it's foggy. **Although** it's foggy, our flight is on time. My plants died **even though** I watered them. **Even though** I watered my plants, they died.
if even if unless	to show a condition	We'll get a puppy **if** you promise to take care of it. **If** you promise to take care of it, we'll get a puppy. They won't make the playoffs, **even if** they win today. **Even if** they win today, they won't make the playoffs. We can't go skiing **unless** it snows tonight. **Unless** it snows tonight, we can't go skiing.

APPENDIX D: PHRASAL VERBS

Phrasal Verb	Example Sentence
break down	Our car **broke down** on the highway to Vancouver.
break up	I have sad news. Betsy and Roy have **broken up**.
bring up	The staff **brought up** some important points at the meeting.
call off	If she doesn't feel better by Saturday, we'll have to **call off** the party.
catch up on	He has to stay late and **catch up on** his work.
catch up with	You go on ahead. We'll **catch up with** you.
check out	There's a new bar in town; let's **check** it **out**.
come across	I don't know this word. I've never **come across** it before.
come back	When you **come back** to Canada, we'll go out for dinner.
fall through	Kai and I had planned to go backpacking, but our plans **fell through**.
fill out	To apply for a passport, you need to **fill out** some forms.
get along with	Ben didn't **get along with** his sister when they were children.
get behind in	Don't **get behind in** your work; it will be hard to catch up later.
get down	Children! **Get down** from that tree! You'll fall!
get in	Did you have a good time last night? What time did you **get in**?
get off	**Get off** the bus at River Street, then walk for 500 metres.
get on	Don't be afraid to **get on** the horse; it won't hurt you.
get out of	I have a previous commitment, but I can try to **get out of** it.
get over	It's taking me a long time to **get over** this cold.
get together	Shall we **get together** on the weekend and have coffee?
get up	I always **get up** at 6:00 in the morning.
give away	We **gave away** a lot of furniture when we moved to a smaller house.
give up	Meg worked hard to reach her goals; she never **gave up**.
go away	There's a strange dog in our front yard. I'll tell him to **go away**.
go over	Let's meet on the weekend and **go over** our travel plans.
grow up	The children are **growing up** so quickly!
keep on	We told them to be quiet, but they **kept on** singing and shouting.
leave out	When you write your essay, don't **leave out** that reference.
let down	Hannah promised to help me, but she **let** me **down**.
look away	She can't stand horror movies; she always **looks away**.
look after	My grandparents **looked after** me when I was a child.
look down on	Don't **look down on** me just because I am not good at math!
look for	I spend too much time **looking for** my glasses.
look forward to	The students are **looking forward to** the ski trip.
look in on	I **look in on** my children before I go to bed.
look out	When you're driving in the city, **look out** for cyclists.
look up	I don't know the capital of Nigeria. I'll **look** it **up**.
look up to	His children all admire him and **look up to** him.
make out	I can't **make out** what that street sign says. Can you read it?
make up (1)	Even as a young child, she loved to **make up** stories and poems.

Phrasal Verb	Example Sentence
make up (2)	If you miss the test, you can **make** it **up** at a later date.
make up (3)	I'm sorry we had an argument. Let's **make up** and be friends again.
pick up (1)	Don't drop garbage on the floor. Please **pick** it **up**.
pick up (2)	I'll **pick** you **up** in my car at a quarter to nine.
pick up (3)	Karen didn't take Chinese lessons, but she **picked up** some phrases.
point out	If you see George, please **point** him **out** to me.
put away	If you use my iPad charger, please **put** it **away** afterwards.
put down	That's a valuable piece of glass; you should **put** it **down**.
put off (1)	I need to see a dentist. I can't **put** it **off** any longer.
put off (2)	Don't let him **put** you **off**—you should apply for the job!
put on (1)	We're having dinner with Grandmother. **Put on** a nice skirt.
put on (2)	They aren't angry. They're **putting** it **on** to make you feel bad.
put out	Please **put out** your cigarette; you can't smoke here.
put up with	I'm not going to **put up with** his rudeness anymore!
run away	We used to have a small cat, but he **ran away**.
rule out	The house burned to the ground. The police have not **ruled out** arson.
run out of	I'm always **running out of** money! I need a part-time job.
see about	I'm meeting my professor to **see about** getting an extension.
show up	We invited Mike for dinner, but he didn't **show up**.
take after	The girl **takes after** her mother in appearance and personality.
take back	If you don't like your new TV set, **take** it **back** to the store.
take down	After the holidays, we'll have to **take down** the decorations.
take in (1)	She's lost weight, so she needs to **take in** all her clothes.
take in (2)	There was a stray cat in my neighbourhood, so I **took** him **in**.
take off (1)	The plane **takes off** at 3:15 and lands at 8:20.
take off (2)	If you're hot, why don't you **take off** your sweater?
take on	Roger has agreed to **take on** the organization of the project.
take up (1)	We never see Gerry, now that he's **taken up** golf.
take up (2)	Are we going to **take up** the answers in class tomorrow?
throw out	I'm so mad! My roommate **threw out** my important letter.
try on	This dress is pretty. Why don't you **try** it **on**?
turn down (1)	Henry was offered a job in Ottawa, but he **turned** it **down**.
turn down (2)	I can't stand this music! Can you **turn** it **down**, please?
turn off	We're going out. Let's **turn off** the television.
turn on	I can't **turn on** my computer—I hope it isn't broken.
turn up	**Turn up** the radio; I love this song!
write down	**Write** this information **down**, so you don't forget it.

GLOSSARY

Word or Term	Definition	Chapter	Page
absent-minded	forgetful	11	221
accessible	able to be reached or connected	6	114
accomplishment	an achievement	5	92
account for	explain	12	239
accountability	a state of being responsible to someone	12	239
achieve	gain something through hard work	1	15
acquaintance	someone with whom you are friendly, but whom you don't know well	7	144
addiction	a physical need for a substance such as tobacco, alcohol, coffee	10	203
adrenaline rush	a sudden burst of excitement	2	34
alien	a creature from outer space, an extraterrestrial	9	184
architect	a person who designs buildings	3	54
arena	a big place for an activity such as sports	5	92
attic	a small room in the top part of a house, under the roof	2	34
backpack (v.)	travel with a backpack, usually cheaply and for a long period of time	4	71
backslide	return to bad habits or bad ways	12	239
bilingualism	an ability to speak two languages	1	15
capture	catch	8	162
cautious	careful	9	184
cellar	a room underneath a house, often used for storage	2	34
cherished (adj.)	precious, much-loved	11	221
cold turkey (adv.)	all at once, not gradually	10	203
concept	an idea or thought	12	239
counterpart	someone with a similar role, somewhere else	5	91
criticize	make negative comments about	5	92
curiosity	an interest in finding out something	2	34
dynamic	full of life and energy	5	92
effective	giving the desired result	1	15
emphasize	draw particular attention to	5	92
encourage	support someone in doing something	5	92
encouragement	emotional support and confidence given by one person to another	1	15
endurance	the ability to continue to carry out a task over a long period of time	8	162
enforce	make something happen using power or force	1	15
engrave	cut words or a design into metal or wood	2	35
enthusiastic	interested and excited by something	4	71
erode	become worn away over time such as by wind or other weather conditions	3	55
evolve	develop and change over time	7	143
exotic	from a faraway place or a culturally different place	7	143
expectation	a vision of what should be achieved or done	5	92
fluid	liquid	10	203
goofy	silly	11	222
hostel	cheap accommodation, often for backpackers	4	72
hypnosis	mental state of being in a trance	10	203
illegible	impossible to read	4	72
inappropriate	not good or acceptable for the circumstance or place	5	92
inkling	a feeling about something	11	221

Word or Term	Definition	Chapter	Page
inspire	give someone ideas for creative work	3	55
intensify	become stronger	5	92
invisible	impossible to see	10	203
maintain	keep in good condition	3	55
mansion	a very large and possibly luxurious house	3	55
means (n.)	financial ability	6	114
meditation	deep thinking, often in a religious setting	8	162
mesmerize	hold someone's attention; put someone in a state of hypnosis	2, 10	34, 203
messy	not organized; untidy	11	221
official	connected with the government or other authority	1	14
opportunity	a chance to do exciting things	5	92
optimistic	having a positive outlook or opinion	6	114
orphan	a child without parents	3	54
outrageous	out of the ordinary, shocking	8	162
pace (v.)	walk in continuous steps, often back and forth, while thinking	11	222
panic	sudden fear, sometimes irrational	11	222
patience	the ability to wait without being nervous or anxious	2	34
phobia	an irrational and uncontrollable fear of something	10	203
pile (n.)	a stack of flat objects on top of each other	11	221
professional (adj.)	doing something as a job, not as a hobby	4	72
purchase	buy	3	54
quality	how good or valuable something is	7	143
quantity	the number or amount of something	7	143
real-estate agent	a person who helps you to buy or sell a house	3	54
reminisce	remember happily	4	72
rerun (n.)	a television program repeated from past seasons	9	184
researcher	a person who carries out academic studies	1	15
retirement	terminating your profession due to being older (e.g., 65 years of age)	3	54
schedule (n.)	a formal plan stating when things must happen (e.g., with transportation)	4	71
seal (v.)	close off	2	35
shrug	raise the shoulders in a gesture to say, "I don't know" or "I don't understand"	4	72
sibling	a brother or sister	11	222
sigh of relief	a breath taken after learning that there is no longer a need for fear	11	222
simultaneously	at the same time	8	162
sitcom	a situation comedy: a television program based on funny everyday events	9	184
skeptical	having doubts about the existence or effectiveness of something	10	203
social network	an online social site like Facebook or Twitter	7	143
sound barrier	the point at which the speed of a spacecraft is the same as the speed of sound	6	114
stamina	the ability to do something physical for a long time	5	92
stunning (adj.)	extremely beautiful	6	114
support (n.)	emotional or financial help	1	15
sustain	suffer (e.g., an injury)	5	92
Swiss ball	a big, soft ball, often used in physical exercise	8	162
trance	in a half sleep or conscious state, hypnotized	10	203
transgression	an act that is socially unacceptable or unlawful	12	239
unforgettable	always remembered	6	114
viable	able to live or survive	5	92
withered	dried up, aged, looking old	2	34

SOMETHING ABOUT THE AUTHOR®

Something about
the Author *was named
an "Outstanding
Reference Source,"
the highest honor given
by the American
Library Association
Reference and Adult
Services Division.*

ISSN 0276-816X

SOMETHING ABOUT THE AUTHOR®

**Facts and Pictures about Authors
and Illustrators of Books for Young People**

volume 166

THOMSON

GALE

Detroit • New York • San Francisco • San Diego • New Haven, Conn. • Waterville, Maine • London • Munich

THOMSON
GALE
™

Something About the Author, Volume 166

Project Editor
Lisa Kumar

Editorial
Michelle Kazensky, Joshua Kondek, Tracey
Matthews, Julie Mellors, Mary Ruby, Mark
Rzeszutek

Permissions
Ronald D. Montgomery, Jessica Schultz,
Shalice Shah-Caldwell

Imaging and Multimedia
Leitha Etheridge-Sims, Lezlie Light

Composition and Electronic Capture
Carolyn Roney

Manufacturing
Drew Kalasky

Product Manager
Chris Nasso

LIBRARY OF CONGRESS CATALOG CARD NUMBER 62-52046

ISBN 0-7876-8790-1
ISSN 0276-816X

This title is also available as an e-book.
ISBN 1-4144-1067-0
Contact your Thomson Gale sales representative for ordering information.

Printed in the United States of America
10 9 8 7 6 5 4 3 2 1

Contents

Authors in Forthcoming Volumes

Below are some of the authors and illustrators that will be featured in upcoming volumes of *SATA*. These include new entries on the swiftly rising stars of the field, as well as completely revised and updated entries (indicated with *) on some of the most notable and best-loved creators of books for children.

N.M. Browne ∎ While writing books for younger readers under the pen name Nicola Matthews, this British writer has also earned a following among teen fantasy fans through novels such as *Warriors of Alavana* and *Basilisk.* Within a world where outcasts are banished below ground and chaos erupts above, Browne weaves mythic beasts, shapeshifting, and suspense into her adventurous tales.

Anthony Eaton ∎ Making his publishing debut with the 2000 suspense novel *The Darkness,* former college English teacher Eaton also presents a humorous take on his own teen years in the semi-autobiographical *Nathan Nuttboard Hits the Beach.* History and time travel coincide in Eaton's novel *Fireshadow,* a further example of the Aussie author's versatility.

*Elizabeth Hand ∎ Hand is known for her science-fiction novels for adult readers, although she often casts adolescents as her main protagonists. In *Winterlong* teen twins travel across a barren future Earth to reunite, while *Black Light* features young woman battling her godfather's surreal plot to control humanity. In addition to original fiction, Hand has also contributed to novelizations of the "Star Wars" saga and other popular films.

Kimberley Heuston ∎ In addition to working as an English teacher, Heuston pens historic fiction for young adults. Her novel *The Shakeress* follows the experiences of a young orphan living in the 1820s as she finds a refuge in a close-knit Shaker community, while *Dante's Daughter* moves further back in time, bringing to life the world of the famous Italian poet and his teen daughter. Heuston's novels have been praised for their detailed research and engaging young-adult protagonists.

*Guy Gavriel Kay ∎ Kay began his writing career while training for a career in the law. Still in college, he worked with the son of British writer J.R.R. Tolkien to complete *The Silmarillion,* a book left unfinished at the elder Tolkien's death. Kay's fiction combines fantasy and history in an appealing mix that has won him a large readership and critical praise. Among his many works are the "Fionavar Tapastry" and "Sarantine Mosaic" novels, the latter set in the Mediterranean during the sixth century.

Sonia Manzano ∎ Best known for her groundbreaking role as Maria in the perennially popular *Sesame Street* television series, Manzano has become a role model for generations of Hispanic chil-dren—particularly young girls. In addition to her acting career and her work for public-service organizations, she adds "author" to her credits with the publication of *No Dogs Allowed!* Featuring pictures by John J. Muth, the story follows a family's trip to a city park, only to discover that their family dog is not permitted inside the park gates. As told by its upbeat young narrator, Manzano's book presents young children with a familiar quandary and a sunny solution.

*Joe Nickell ∎ Teens with a fascination with magic, the supernatural, and the otherwise unexplained are a natural audience for the books by paranormal investigator Nickell. The hidden tricks of magicians' sleight of hand are revealed in books such as *The Magic Detectives,* while *Secrets of the Supernatural* presents the results of Nickell's work as a research fellow for the New York-based Committee for the Scientific Investigation of Claims of the Paranormal. Moving to more temporal matters, books such as his *Crime Science: Methods of Forensic Detection* allow readers to investigate for themselves the technology fictionalized on popular television shows such as *CSI.*

Chloe Rayban ∎ Rayban introduced her popular teen protagonist Justine Duval in the 1991 novel *Wild Child,* and she has gone on to create several more fiction series with a similar appeal for trend-conscious teen readers. Sometimes mixing in fantasy elements, such as time travel, the "Justine" books, as well as Rayban's "Models Move On" series, follow the life of an affluent modern teen growing up amid London's shopaholic, celebrity-conscious culture.

Linda Strachan ∎ Beginning her career admittedly "by accident," Strachan has become a prolific author of nonfiction books for younger children. Bringing to life the natural surroundings of her native Scotland in books like *Walk in the Woods* and *Who Lives Here?,* she has also penned readers for the early elementary grades. A picture-book series featuring fictional hero Hamish McHaggis reflects Strachan's interest in her Scottish heritage as well as her entertaining wit.

Leonard Wise ∎ The Canadian city of Toronto is the focus of much of Wise's writing for adults, and he has gained a reputation as an expert in the city's history and points of interest. While writing nonfiction takes a back seat to his time-consuming legal career, Wise's natural curiosity and love of writing has also inspired him to write *The Way Cool License Plate Book,* a treasure trove of trivia for back-seat travelers forced to log long hours on North American road trips.

Introduction

Something about the Author (*SATA*) is an ongoing reference series that examines the lives and works of authors and illustrators of books for children. *SATA* includes not only well-known writers and artists but also less prominent individuals whose works are just coming to be recognized. This series is often the only readily available information source on emerging authors and illustrators. You'll find *SATA* informative and entertaining, whether you are a student, a librarian, an English teacher, a parent, or simply an adult who enjoys children's literature.

What's Inside *SATA*

SATA provides detailed information about authors and illustrators who span the full time range of children's literature, from early figures like John Newbery and L. Frank Baum to contemporary figures like Judy Blume and Richard Peck. Authors in the series represent primarily English-speaking countries, particularly the United States, Canada, and the United Kingdom. Also included, however, are authors from around the world whose works are available in English translation. The writings represented in *SATA* include those created intentionally for children and young adults as well as those written for a general audience and known to interest younger readers. These writings cover the entire spectrum of children's literature, including picture books, humor, folk and fairy tales, animal stories, mystery and adventure, science fiction and fantasy, historical fiction, poetry and nonsense verse, drama, biography, and nonfiction. Obituaries are also included in *SATA* and are intended not only as death notices but also as concise overviews of people's lives and work. Additionally, each edition features newly revised and updated entries for a selection of *SATA* listees who remain of interest to today's readers and who have been active enough to require extensive revisions of their earlier biographies.

Autobiography Feature

Beginning with Volume 103, *SATA* features one or more specially commissioned autobiographical essays in each volume. These unique essays, averaging about ten thousand words in length and illustrated with an abundance of personal photos, present an entertaining and informative first-person perspective on the lives and careers of prominent authors and illustrators profiled in *SATA*.

Two Convenient Indexes

In response to suggestions from librarians, *SATA* indexes no longer appear in every volume but are included in alternate (odd-numbered) volumes of the series, beginning with Volume 57.

SATA continues to include two indexes that cumulate with each alternate volume: the Illustrations Index, arranged by the name of the illustrator, gives the number of the volume and page where the illustrator's work appears in the current volume as well as all preceding volumes in the series; the Author Index gives the number of the volume in which a person's biographical sketch, autobiographical essay, or obituary appears in the current volume as well as all preceding volumes in the series.

These indexes also include references to authors and illustrators who appear in *Gale's Yesterday's Authors of Books for Children, Children's Literature Review,* and *Something about the Author Autobiography Series.*

Easy-to-Use Entry Format

Whether you're already familiar with the *SATA* series or just getting acquainted, you will want to be aware of the kind of information that an entry provides. In every *SATA* entry the editors attempt to give as complete a picture of the person's life and work as possible. A typical entry in *SATA* includes the following clearly labeled information sections:

PERSONAL: date and place of birth and death, parents' names and occupations, name of spouse, date of marriage, names of children, educational institutions attended, degrees received, religious and political affiliations, hobbies and other interests.

ADDRESSES: complete home, office, electronic mail, and agent addresses, whenever available.

CAREER: name of employer, position, and dates for each career post; art exhibitions; military service; memberships and offices held in professional and civic organizations.

MEMBER: professional, civic, and other association memberships and any official posts held.

AWARDS, HONORS: literary and professional awards received.

WRITINGS: title-by-title chronological bibliography of books written and/or illustrated, listed by genre when known; lists of other notable publications, such as plays, screenplays, and periodical contributions.

ADAPTATIONS: a list of films, television programs, plays, CD-ROMs, recordings, and other media presentations that have been adapted from the author's work.

WORK IN PROGRESS: description of projects in progress.

SIDELIGHTS: a biographical portrait of the author or illustrator's development, either directly from the biographee—and often written specifically for the *SATA* entry—or gathered from diaries, letters, interviews, or other published sources.

BIOGRAPHICAL AND CRITICAL SOURCES: cites sources quoted in "Sidelights" along with references for further reading.

EXTENSIVE ILLUSTRATIONS: photographs, movie stills, book illustrations, and other interesting visual materials supplement the text.

How a *SATA* Entry Is Compiled

A *SATA* entry progresses through a series of steps. If the biographee is living, the *SATA* editors try to secure information directly from him or her through a questionnaire. From the information that the biographee supplies, the editors prepare an entry, filling in any essential missing details with research and/or telephone interviews. If possible, the author or illustrator is sent a copy of the entry to check for accuracy and completeness.

If the biographee is deceased or cannot be reached by questionnaire, the *SATA* editors examine a wide variety of published sources to gather information for an entry. Biographical and bibliographic sources are consulted, as are book reviews, feature articles, published interviews, and material sometimes obtained from the biographee's family, publishers, agent, or other associates.

Entries that have not been verified by the biographees or their representatives are marked with an asterisk (*).

Contact the Editor

We encourage our readers to examine the entire *SATA* series. Please write and tell us if we can make *SATA* even more helpful to you. Give your comments and suggestions to the editor:

Editor
Something about the Author
Thomson Gale
27500 Drake Rd.
Farmington Hills MI 48331-3535

Toll-free: 800-877-GALE
Fax: 248-699-8070

Something about the Author Product Advisory Board

The editors of *Something about the Author* are dedicated to maintaining a high standard of excellence by publishing comprehensive, accurate, and highly readable entries on a wide array of writers for children and young adults. In addition to the quality of the content, the editors take pride in the graphic design of the series, which is intended to be orderly yet inviting, allowing readers to utilize the pages of *SATA* easily and with efficiency. Despite the longevity of the *SATA* print series, and the success of its format, we are mindful that the vitality of a literary reference product is dependent on its ability to serve its users over time. As literature, and attitudes about literature, constantly evolve, so do the reference needs of students, teachers, scholars, journalists, researchers, and book club members. To be certain that we continue to keep pace with the expectations of our customers, the editors of *SATA* listen carefully to their comments regarding the value, utility, and quality of the series. Librarians, who have firsthand knowledge of the needs of library users, are a valuable resource for us. The *Something about the Author* Product Advisory Board, made up of school, public, and academic librarians, is a forum to promote focused feedback about *SATA* on a regular basis. The nine-member advisory board includes the following individuals, whom the editors wish to thank for sharing their expertise:

Eva M. Davis
Youth Department Manager,
Ann Arbor District Library,
Ann Arbor, Michigan

Joan B. Eisenberg
Lower School Librarian,
Milton Academy,
Milton, Massachusetts

Francisca Goldsmith
Teen Services Librarian,
Berkeley Public Library,
Berkeley, California

Susan Dove Lempke
Children's Services Supervisor,
Niles Public Library District,
Niles, Illinois

Robyn Lupa
Head of Children's Services,
Jefferson County Public Library,
Lakewood, Colorado

Victor L. Schill
Assistant Branch Librarian/Children's Librarian,
Harris County Public Library/Fairbanks Branch,
Houston, Texas

Caryn Sipos
Community Librarian,
Three Creeks Community Library,
Vancouver, Washington

Steven Weiner
Director,
Maynard Public Library,
Maynard, Massachusetts

Acknowledgments

Grateful acknowledgment is made to the following publishers, authors, and artists whose works appear in this volume.

ANDREW, IAN ∎ Andrew, Ian, illustrator. From an illustration in *Black Beauty,* by Anna Sewell. Kingfisher, 2001. Illustrations copyright © Ian Andrew 2001. All rights reserved. Reproduced by permission of Larousse Kingfisher Chambers, New York.

ASHABRANNER, BRENT ∎ Ashabranner, Brent, photograph by Jennifer Ashabranner. Photo courtesy of Brent Ashabranner. Reproduced by permission./ Ashabranner, Dudley, and Rose Cotton, parents of Brent Ashabranner, photograph. Photo courtesy of Brent Ashabranner. Reproduced by permission./ Ashabranner, Brent with brother Gerard, photograph. Photo courtesy of Brent Ashabranner. Reproduced by permission./ White, Martha, Brent Ashabranner's wife-to-be, photograph. Photo courtesy of Brent Ashabranner. Reproduced by permission./ White, Martha, teaching home economics at Empress Menen School, Addis Ababa, Ethiopia, 1956, photograph. Photo courtesy of Brent Ashabranner. Reproduced by permission./ Ashabranner, Brent with family, 1959, photograph. Photo courtesy of Brent Ashabranner. Reproduced by permission./ Ashabranner, Brent, with Jack Vaughn, director of the Peace Corps, India, 1965, photograph. Photo courtesy of Brent Ashabranner. Reproduced by permission./ Ashabranner, Brent, being sworn in as deputy director of the Peace Corps by Hubert Humphrey, 1967, photograph. Photo courtesy of Brent Ashabranner. Reproduced by permission./ Ashabranner, Brent, with daughter Melissa, Washington D.C., 1988, photograph. Photo courtesy of Brent Ashabranner. Reproduced by permission./ Ashabranner, Brent, with daughter Jennifer, Williamsburg, Virginia, 1989, photograph. Photo courtesy of Brent Ashabranner. Reproduced by permission./ Ashabranner, Brent, with granddaughter Olivia-Jené, photograph. Photo courtesy of Brent Ashabranner. Reproduced by permission./ Ashabranner, Brent, standing at the Vietnam Veterans Memorial, photograph. Photo courtesy of Brent Ashabranner. Reproduced by permission./ Ashabranner, Brent, outside Castillo de San Marcos Fort, St. Augustine, Florida, photograph. Photo courtesy of Brent Ashabranner. Reproduced by permission./ Ashabranner, Brent, standing behind daughter Jennifer, photograph. Photo courtesy of Brent Ashabranner. Reproduced by permission.

AUSEON, ANDREW ∎ Gallery, Louis K. Meisel, illustrator. From a cover of *Funny Little Monkey,* by Andrew Auseon. Harcourt Inc., 2005. Jacket art copyright © Louis K. Meisel Gallery, Inc./Corbis.

BLUE, ROSE ∎ From an illustration in *Belle Starr,* by Rose Blue. Blackbirch Press, Inc.,2000. Reproduced by permission of Thomson Gale./ Blue, Rose, photograph. Reproduced by permission

BRACKETT, VIRGINIA ∎ From a cover of *Restless Genius: The Story of Virginia Woolf,* by Virginia Brackett. Morgan Reynolds Publishing, Inc., 2004. Reproduced by permission./ Brackett, Virginia, photograph. Reproduced by permission of Virginia Brackett

BRUEL, NICK ∎ From an illustration in *Boing,* by Nick Bruel. Roaring Brook Press, 2004. Illustrations copyright 2004 by Nick Bruel. Reprinted by permission of Henry Holt and Company, LLC.

CARRIER, ROCH ∎ Cohen, Sheldon, illustrator. From an illustration in *The Basketball Player,* by Roch Carrier. Tundra Books, 1996. Copyright © 1996 by Roch Carrier, illustrations by Sheldon Cohen, published in Canada by Tundra Books and in the United States by Tundra Books of Northern New York. Reproduced by permission./ Cohen, Sheldon, illustrator. From an illustration in *The Flying Canoe,* by Roch Carrier. Tundra Books, 2004. Copyright © 2004 by Roch Carrier, illustrations by Sheldon Cohen, published in Canada by Tundra Books and in the United States by Tundra Books of Northern New York. Reproduced by permission./ Carrier, Roch, 1991, photograph by Randy Velocci. *The Globe and Mail,* Toronto. Reproduced by permission of the Randy Velocci.

CLIMO, SHIRLEY ∎ Florczak, Robert, illustrator. From a cover of *The Persian Cinderella,* by Shirley Climo. HarperCollins Publishers, 1999. Illustrations copyright © 1999 by Robert Florczak. Used by permission of HarperCollins Publishers./ Brooks, Erik, illustrator. From an illustration in *Monkey Business: Stories from around the World,* by Shirley Climo. Henry Holt and Company, 2005. Illustrations copyright 2005 by Erik Brooks. All rights reserved. Reprinted by permission of Henry Holt and Company, LLC./ Climo, Shirley, photograph. Reproduced by permission of Shirley Climo.

COLLIER, JAMES LINCOLN ∎ Di Cesare, Joe, illustrator. From a cover of *My Brother Sam Is Dead,* by James Lincoln Collier and Christopher Collier. A Point book published by Scholastic Inc., 1974. Copyright © 1974 by James Lincoln Collier and Christopher Collier. Cover Illustration copyright © 1985 by Scholastic Inc. All rights reserved. Reprinted by permission of Scholastic Inc./ Hunter, Oliver, photographer. From a cover of *The Empty Mirror,* by James Lincoln Collier. Oliver Hunter/PHOTONICA/Getty Images./ Collier, James Lincoln, with brother Christopher, Connecticut, photograph. Reproduced by permission.

ECHLIN, KIM ∎ Chomica, Gloria H., and George Calef/Masterfile, photographers. From a cover of *Elephant Winter,* by Kim Echlin. Penguin Books, 1997. Copyright © Kim Echlin, 1997. Reproduced by permission of Masterfile and Penguin Group (Canada)./ Wolfsgruber, Linda, illustrator. From an illustration in *Inanna: From the Myth of Ancient Sumer,* by Kim Echlin. Groundwoods Books, 2003. Illustrations copyright © 2003 Linda Wolfsgruber. Reproduced by permission of Groundwood Books Ltd./ Echlin, Kim, photograph. Reproduced by permission of Groundwood Books Ltd.

EDENS, COOPER ∎ Day, Alexandra, illustrator. From an illustration in *Special Deliveries,* by Cooper Edens. HarperCollins Publishers, 2001. Illustrations copyright © 2001 by Alexandra Day. Used by permission of HarperCollins Publishers.

ETCHEMENDY, NANCY ▮ Koetsch, Mike, illustrator. From a cover of *The Power of Un,* by Nancy Etchemendy. Scholastic Apple Paperback, 2002. Reprinted by permission of Scholastic, Inc.

FORRESTER, SANDRA ▮ Colón, Raúl, illustrator. From a cover of *My Home Is Over Jordan,* by Sandra Forrester. Dutton Children's Books, 1997. Cover copyright © 1997 Raúl Colón. All rights reserved. Used by permission of Dutton Children's Books, A Division of Penguin Young Readers Group, A Member of Penguin Group (USA) Inc./ Lane, Nancy, illustrator. From a cover of *The Everyday Witch,* by Sandra Forrester. Barrons, 2002. Illustrations © copyright 2002 by Barron's Educational Series, Inc. All rights reserved. Reproduced by permission./ From a cover of *The Witches of Friar's Lantern,* by Sandra Forrester. Barrons, 2003. Illustrations © copyright 2003 by Barron's Educational Series, Inc. All rights reserved. Reproduced by permission./ Forrester, Sandra, photograph by Bob Boyd. Reproduced by permission

FRANK, LUCY ▮ Mayforth, Hal, illustrator. From a cover of *The Annoyance Bureau,* by Lucy Frank. Atheneum, 2002. Jacket design by Russell Gordon (NY, 2002). Jacket illustrations and hand-lettering copyright © 2002 by Hal Mayforth. Reprinted with permission of Atheneum Books for Young Readers, an imprint of Simon & Schuster Children's Publishing Division and Hal Mayforth./ Frank, Lucy, photograph. Reproduced by permission of Lucy Frank

GEAR, KATHLEEN O'NEAL ▮ From a cover of *People of the Owl,* by Kathleen O'Neal Gear. Forge, 2003. Reproduced by permission./ Natale, Vince, illustrator. From a cover of *It Sleeps in Me,* by Kathleen O'Neal Gear. Forge, 2005. Reproduced by permission.

GEAR, W. MICHAEL ▮ From a cover of *The Athena Factor,* by W. Michael Gear. Tor, 2005. Reproduced by permission./ From a cover of *Bone Walker,* by Kathleen O'Neal Gear and W. Michael Gear. Forge, 2001. Reproduced by permission./ Royo, illustrator.

GRALLEY, JEAN ▮ Gralley, Jean. From an illustration in *Very Boring Alligator,* by Jean Gralley. Henry Holt Company, 2001. Illustrations copyright 2005 by Jean Gralley. All rights reserved. Reprinted by permission of Henry Holt and Company, LLC./ Gralley, Jean, illustrator. From an illustration in *The Moon Came Down on Milk Street,* by Jean Gralley. Henry Holt and Company, 2004. Illustrations copyright 2005 by Jean Gralley. All rights reserved. Reprinted by permission of Henry Holt and Company, LLC./ Gralley, Jean, photograph. Photo courtesy of Jean Gralley. Reproduced by permission.

GREY, MINI ▮ From an illustration in *The Very Smart Pea and the Princess-to-Be,* by Mini Grey. Alfred A. Knopf, 2003. Copyright © 2003 by Mini Grey. Published in the UK as *The Pea and the Princess,* by Mini Grey, published by Jonathan Cape. Used by permission of Random House Children's Books, a division of Random House, Inc. In the UK by The Random House Group Ltd./ From an illustration in *Traction Man is Here!,* by Mini Grey. Alfred A. Knopf, 2005. Copyright © 2005 by Mini Grey. Used by permission of Alfred A. Knopf, a division of Random House, Inc. In the UK by The Random House Group Ltd.

HALL, FRANCIE ▮ Hall, Francie, photograph by Jim Foreman Creative Photography. Courtesy of Francie Hall. Reproduced by permission.

HOBBS, LEIGH ▮ Hobbs, Leigh, illustrator. From an illustration in *Old Tom, Man of Mystery,* by Leigh Hobbs. Peachtree, 2003. Text and illustrations © 2003 by Leigh Hobbs. Reproduced by permission./ Hobbs, Leigh, photograph by Peter Grey. Courtesy of Leigh Hobbs. Reproduced by permission.

HOLLINGSWORTH, MARY ▮ Hollingsworth, Mary, photograph. Courtesy of Mary Hollingsworth. Reproduced by permission.

INGPEN, ROBERT ▮ Ingpen, Robert, illustrator. From an illustration in *Shakespeare: His Work and His World,* by Michael Rosen. Candlewick Press, 2001. Text copyright © 2001 Michael Rosen. Illustrations copyright © 2001 Robert Ingpen. Reproduced by permission of Candlewick Press, Inc., Cambridge, MA., on behalf of Walker Books Ltd., London.

JOHNSON, SYLVIA A. ▮ "Die Nüw Welt," 1544, map from *Cosmographia,* by Sebastian Munster. Image from the collection of the James Ford Bell Library, University of Minnesota, Minneapolis, MN, US. Used with permission./ Melton, Charles W., photographer. From a photograph in *Songbirds: The Language of Song,* by Sylvia A. Johnson. Carolrhoda Books, Inc. 2001. Reproduced by permission./ Fink, Kenneth W., photographer. From a photograph in *Crows,* by Sylvia A. Johnson. Carolrhoda Books, 2005. Reproduced by permission.

KIRK, HEATHER ▮ Kirk, Heather, photograph by Steingard Photography. Courtesy of Heather Kirk. Reproduced by permission.

KNAAK, RICHARD A. ▮ Didier, Sam, illustrator. From a cover of *Day of the Dragon,* by Richard A. Knaak. Pocket Books, 2001. Copyright © 2001 Blizzard Entertainment. All rights reserved. Warcraft® provided courtesy of Blizzard Entertainment, Inc. Reproduced by permission.

LANE, DAKOTA ▮ Joern, James, and Michel Legrou, illustrators. From a cover of *Johnny Voodoo,* by Dakota Lane. Laurel-Leaf Books, 1996. Used by permission of Random House Children's Books, a division of Random House, Inc./ From a cover of *The Orpheus Obsession,* by Dakota Lane. Katherine Tegen Books, 2005. Text and photographs copyright © 2005 by Dakota Lane. Used by permission of HarperCollins Publishers./ Lane, Dakota, photograph by Alex Kamin. Reproduced by permission of Dakota Lane.

LAVALLEE, BARBARA ▮ Lavallee, Barbara, illustrator. From an illustration in *Uno, Dos, Tres; One, Two, Three,* by Pat Mora. Clarion Books, 1996. Illustrations copyright © 1996 by Barbara Lavallee. Reproduced by permission of Houghton Mifflin Company./ Lavallee, Barbara, illustrator. From an illustration in *All You Need for a Beach,* by Alice Schertle. Silver Whistle/Harcourt, Inc., 2004. Illustrations copyright © 2004 by Barbara Lavallee. Reproduced by permission of Harcourt, Inc.

LEVITHAN, DAVID ▮ From a cover of *Boy Meets Boy,* by David Levithan. Alfred A. Knopf, 2003. Copyright © 2003 by David Levithan. Reproduced by permission of Random House Children's Books, a division of Random House, Inc./ From a cover of *The Realm of Possibility,* by David Levithan. Alfred A. Knopf, 2004. Copyright © 2004 by David Levithan. Used by permission of Alfred A. Knopf, an imprint of Random House Children's Books, a division of Random House, Inc./ From a cover of *Are We There Yet?,* by David Levithan. Alfred A. Knopf, 2005. Copyright © 2005 by David Levithan. Used by permission of Alfred A. Knopf, an imprint of Random House Children's Books, a division of Random House, Inc.

LUDWIG, TRUDY ▮ Ludwig, Trudy, photograph. Courtesy of Trudy Ludwig. Reproduced by permission.

MADDERN, ERIC ▮ Hess, Paul, illustrator. From an illustration in *Death in a Nut,* by Eric Maddern. Frances Lincoln Children's Books, 2005. Illustration copyright © Paul Hess 2005. Reproduced by permission of Frances Lincoln Ltd, www.frances-lincoln.com. Distributed in the USA by Publishers Group West.

MANUSHKIN, FRAN ▮ Shulevitz, Uri, illustrator. From an illustration in *Daughters of Fire: Heroines of the Bible,* by Fran Manushkin. Silver Whistle/Harcourt, Inc., 2001. Illustrations copyright © 2001 by Uri Shulevitz. Reproduced by permission of Harcourt, Inc./ Gore, Leonid, illustrator. From an illustration in *The Little Sleepy-*

head, by Fran Manushkin. Dutton Children's Books, 2004. Illustrations copyright © 2004 Leonid Gore. All rights reserved. Used by permission of Dutton Children's Books, A Division of Penguin Young Readers Group, A Member of Penguin Group (USA) Inc./ Martin, Whitney, illustrator. From an illustration in *Let George Do It!,* by George Foreman with Fran Manushkin. Simon & Schuster Books for Young Readers, 2005. Illustrations copyright © 2005 by Whitney Martin. Reprinted with the permission of Simon & Schuster Books for Young Readers, an imprint of Simon & Schuster Children's Publishing Division./ Manushkin, Fran, photograph. Reproduced by permission.

MOORCOCK, MICHAEL ▌ Gould, Robert, illustrator. From a cover of *The Dreamthief's Daughter,* by Michael Moorcock. Aspect ,2001. Copyright (c) 2001 by Michael Moorcock and Linda Moorcock. All rights reserved. Reproduced by permission of Warner Books, Inc./ Atkins, Marc, photographer. From a cover of *King of the City,* by Michael Moorcock. William Morrow, 2002. Copyright (c) 2000 by Michael Moorcock and Linda Moorcock. Cover photograph by Marc Atikins/Panoptika. Reprinted by permission of HarperCollins Publishers./ Gold, Robert, illustrator. From a cover of *The White Wolf's Son,* by Michael Moorcock. Aspect, 2005. Copyright (c) 2005 by Michael Moorcock and Linda Moorcock. All rights reserved. Reproduced by permission of Warner Books, Inc./ Moorcock, Michael, photograph by Jerry Bauer. © Jerry Bauer. Reproduced by permission.

NIELDS, NERISSA ▌ Neumann, Horst, photographer. From a cover of *Plastic Angel,* by Nerissa Nields. Horst Neumann/PHOTONICA/ Getty Images.

NOLAN, DENNIS ▌ Nolan, Dennis, illustrator. From an illustration in *Dinosaur Dream,* by Dennis Nolan. Aladdin, 1990. Copyright © 1990 Dennis Nolan. Reprinted with the permission of Simon & Schuster Books for Young Readers, an imprint of Simon & Schuster Children's Publishing Division.

NORAC, CARL ▌ Godon, Ingrid, illustrator. From an illustration in *My Daddy Is A Giant,* by Carl Norac. Clarion Books, 2004. Illustrations copyright © 2004 by Ingrid Godon. Reproduced by permission of Houghton Mifflin Company.

O'MARA, CARMEL ▌ O'Mara-Horwitz, Carmel, photograph. Photo courtesy of Carmel O'Mara-Horwitz.

PEARSON, SUSAN ▌ Fiammenghi, Gioia, illustrator. From an illustration in *Eagle-Eye Ernie Comes to Town,* by Susan Pearson. Aladdin, 1990. Illustrations copyright © 1990 Gioia Fiammenghi. Reprinted with the permission of Simon & Schuster Books for Young Readers, an imprint of Simon & Schuster Children's Publishing Division./ Slonim, David, illustrator. From an illustration in *Squeal and Squawk: Barnyard Talk,* by Susan Pearson. Marshall Cavendish, 2004. Text copyright © 2004 by Susan Pearson. Illustrations copyright © 2004 by David Slonim. All rights reserved. Reproduced by permission./ Slonim, David, illustrator. From an illustration in *Who Swallowed Harold?,* by Susan Pearson. Marshall Cavendish, 2005. Text copyright © 2005 by Susan Pearson. Illustrations copyright © 2005 by David Slonim. All rights reserved. Reproduced by permission.

PILKEY, DAV ▌ Pilkey, Dav, illustrator. From an illustration in *The Adventures of Captain Underpants,* by Dav Pilkey. The Blue Sky Press/Scholastic, Inc., 1997. Copyright © 1997 by Dav Pilkey. Reprinted by permission of Scholastic Inc./ Beard, George, and Harold Hutchins, illustrators. From an illustration in *The Adventures of Super Diaper Baby,* by Dav Pilkey. Scholastic, Inc., 2002. Copyright © 2002 by Dav Pilkey. Reprinted by permission of Scholastic Inc./ Ontiveros, Martin, illustrator. From an illustration in *Ricky Riocotta's Mighty Robot vs. the Stupid Stinkbugs from Saturn,* by Dav Pilkey. Illustration copyright © 2003 by Martin Ontiveros. Scholastic Inc., 2003. Reprinted by permission of Scholastic, Inc./ Pilkey, Dav, photograph by Karen Carpenter. Copyright © 2001. Reproduced with permission.

PLATT, RICHARD ▌ Riddell, Chris, illustrator. From an illustration in *Pirate Diary: The Journal of Jake Carpenter,* by Richard Platt. Candlewick Press, 2001. Text copyright © 2001 Richard Platt. Illustrations copyright © 2001 by Chris Riddell. Reproduced by permission of Candlewick Press, Inc., Cambridge, MA., on behalf of Walker Books Ltd., London./ Buckley, Mike, illustrator. From a cover of *Eureka!,* by Richard Platt. Kingfisher, 2003. Reproduced by permission of Larousse Kingfisher Chambers, New York./ Platt, Richard, photograph. © Mary Platt 2003. Reproduced by permission.

PRATT, PIERRE ▌ Pratt, Pierre, illustrator. From a cover of *Where's Pup?,* by Dayle Ann Dodds. Dial Books for Young Readers, 2003. Pictures copyright © 2003 Pierre Pratt. All rights reserved. Used by permission of Dial Books for Young Readers, A Division of Penguin Young Readers Group, A Member of Penguin Group (USA) Inc.

RASCHKA, CHRISTOPHER ▌ From an illustration in *Waffle,* by Chris Raschka. Atheneum Books for Young Readers, 2001. Copyright © 2001 Chris Raschka. Reprinted with permission of Atheneum Books for Young Readers, an imprint of Simon & Schuster Children's Publishing Division./ Raschka, Chris, illustrator. From an illustration in *Be Boy Buzz,* by bell hooks. Jump at the Sun/ Hyperion Paperbacks for Children, 2002. Copyright © 2002. Reprinted by permission of Hyperion Books For Children.

ROBINS, DERI ▌ Buchanan, George, illustrator. From an illustration in *The Great Pirate Activity Book,* by Deri Robins. Kingfisher, 1995. Reproduced by permission of Larousse Kingfisher Chambers, New York.

SALLEY, COLEEN ▌ Stevens, Janet, illustrator. From an illustration in *Epossumondas,* by Coleen Salley. Harcourt, Inc., 2002. Illustrations copyright © 2002 by Janet Stevens. Reproduced by permission of Harcourt, Inc.

SINGLETON, LINDA JOY ▌ Novak, Lisa, illustrator. From a cover of *Last Dance,* by Linda Joy Singleton. Llewellyn Worldwide, Ltd., 2143 Wooddale Drive, Woodbury, MN 55125-2989, 2005. Copyright © 2005 by Linda Joy Singleton. All rights reserved. Used by permission of the publisher./ Singleton, Linda Joy, photograph. Courtesy of Linda Joy Singleton. Reproduced by permission.

STONE, DAVID LEE ▌ Lea, Bob, illustrator. From an illustration in *The Illmore Chronicles: The Ratastrophe Catastrophe,* by David Lee Stone. Hyperion Books for Children, 2004. Copyright © 2004. Reprinted by permission of Hyperion Books For Children.

TURTLEDOVE, HARRY ▌ Keegan, Charles, illustrator. From a cover of *Alternate Generals,* by Harry Turtledove. Baen Publishing, 1998. Reproduced by permission./ Stone, Steve, illustrator. From a cover of *Ruled Britannia,* by Harry Turtledove. ROC Book, 2002. Copyright © 2002 by Harry Turtledove. Used by permission of Dutton Signet, a division of Penguin Group (USA) Inc./ Eggleton, Bob, illustrator. From a cover of *Jaws of Darkness,* by Harry Turtledove. Tom Doherty Associates, 2003. Reproduced by permission.

WARNES, TIM ▌ Chapman, Jane, illustrator. From an illustration in *Mommy Mine,* by Tim Warnes. HarperCollins Publishers, 2005. Illustrations copyright © 2005 by Jane Chapman. Used by permission of HarperCollins Publishers.

WHITELAW, NANCY ▌ From an illustration in *Bram Stoker: Author of Dracula,* by Nancy Whitelaw. Morgan Reynolds, Inc., 1998. Reproduced by permission.

WISHINSKY, FRIEDA ▌ McCallum, Stephen, illustrator. From an illustration in *Just Call Me Joe,* by Frieda Wishinsky. Orca Book Publishers, 2003. Reproduced by permission./ Lamontagne, Jacques, illustrator. From an illustration in *Manya's Dream: A Story of Marie Curie,* by Frieda Wishinsky. Maple Tree Press Inc., 2003. Illustrations © 2003 by Jacques Lamontagne. Reproduced by permission.

WOODING, CHRIS ▌ Hidalgo, Francisco, photographer. From a cover of *The Haunting of Alaizabel Cray,* by Chris Wooding. Francisco Hidalgo/The Image Bank/Getty Images./ Kramer, Mya, and Chris Ferebee, photographers. From a cover of *Kerosene,* by Chris Wooding. Mya Kramer/Photonica (boy) and Chris Ferebee/Photonica (flames)/Getty Images.

YAMANAKA, LOIS-ANN ▌ Yee, Cora, illustrator. From "Like a Leopard on Ecstasy," on the cover of *Wild Meat and the Bully Burgers,* by Lois-Ann Yamanaka. Farrar, Straus & Giroux, 1996. Jacket design copyright © 1996 by Michael Ian Kaye. Jacket art © by Cora Yee. Reprinted by permission of Farrar, Straus & Giroux, LLC./ Lambase, Barbara, illustrator. From a cover of *Heads by Harry,* by Lois-Ann Yamanaka. Avon Books, Inc., 1999. Copyright © 1999 by Lois-Ann Yamanaka. Reprinted by permission of HarperCollins Publishers.

SOMETHING ABOUT THE AUTHOR

ANDREW, Ian 1962-
(Ian Peter Andrew)

Personal

Born August 8, 1962, in Beckenham, Kent, England; son of Frederick James Henry (an electrical engineer) and Eileen Christine (a nurse; maiden name, O'Connor) Andrew. *Education:* Attended Croydon College of Art; Camberwell, B.A. (with honors); Croydon Intermedia, Certificate in Animation; Royal College of Art, M.A. *Hobbies and other interests:* Collecting rubber stamps, exhibitions, live music concerts, comedy, cinema, theater, cycling, human rights activities, writing letters, "mysteries and the unknown."

Addresses

Office—300 Fortuneswell, The Isle of Portland, Dorset DT5 1LZ, England.

Career

Freelance animator, London, England, 1989-94; Len Lewis-Shootsey Animation, London, England, illustrator of backgrounds and renderer of models; worked as animator for TVC, Grand Slamm, Stuart Books, Alison de Vere, and Cinexa.

Member

Society of Authors, Association of Illustrators, Institute of Contemporary Arts.

Awards, Honors

First Bite Award, Bristol Festival, and Best Newcomer award, Zagreb Animation Festival, 1989, both for film *Dolphins;* shortlisted for Mother Goose Award, 1996, for *The Lion and the Mouse,* and for Carnegie Medal, 1999, for *The Kin;* shortlisted for Kate Greenaway Medal, British Library Association, 2005, for *The Boat* by Helen Ward.

Illustrator

Amanda Jane Wood, *The Lion and the Mouse: An Aesop's Fable,* Millbrook Press (Brookfield, CT), 1995.

Julia Derek Parker, *The Complete Book of Dreams,* Dorling Kindersley (New York, NY), 1995.

Rumer Godden, *Premlata and the Festival of Lights,* Greenwillow (New York, NY), 1996.

Caroline Repchuk, *The Forgotten Garden* (based on an idea by Mike Jolley), Millbrook Press (New York, NY), 1997.

Robert Louis Stevenson, *The Strange Case of Dr. Jekyll and Mr. Hyde,* adapted by Michael Lawrence, DK Publishing, 1997.

Virginia McKenna, *Back to the Blue,* Millbrook Press (New York, NY), 1998.

Berlie Doherty, *The Midnight Man,* Candlewick Press (Cambridge, MA), 1998.

Peter Dickinson, *The Kin,* 4 volumes, Macmillan (London, England), 1998, published in one volume, Putnam (New York, NY), 2003.

Charles Dickens, *Oliver Twist,* adapted by Naia Bray-Moffatt, DK Publishing (New York, NY), 1999.

Michael Morpurgo, *Colly's Barn,* Mammoth (London, England), 1999, Crabtree Publishing (New York, NY), 2002.

Penelope Lively, *In Search of a Homeland: The Story of the Aeneid,* Frances Lincoln (London, England), 2001.

Russell Hoban, *Jim's Lion,* Candlewick Press (Cambridge, MA), 2001.

Anna Sewell, *Black Beauty: His Grooms and Companions: The Autobiography of London,* Kingfisher (New York, NY), 2001.

Joan Aiken, *The Scream,* Macmillan (London, England), 2002.

Peter Dickinson, *The Tears of the Salamander,* Macmillan (London, England), 2003.

Rudyard Kipling, *The Jungle Book,* Templar (Dorking, England), 2003.

Tom Pow, *Tell Me One Thing, Dad,* Candlewick Press (Cambridge, MA), 2004.

Helen Ward, *The Boat,* Templar (Dorking, England), 2004.

(With Nick Harris and Helen Ward) *Egyptology: Search for the Tomb of Osiris: Being the Journal of Miss Emily Sands, November, 1926,* Candlewick Press (Cambridge, MA), 2004.

Peter Dickinson, *The Gift Boat,* Macmillan (London, England), 2004.

Also creator of short animation film called *Dolphins.* Contributor of illustration to *Greenpeace Book of Dolphins,* 1990; illustrator of books, including *Exploring Australia, Exploring China,* and *Exploring India,* all for Belitha Press.

Work in Progress

Illustrations for *Waterboy* and *Piratology: The Bible.*

Sidelights

British artist Ian Andrew began his career as an animator, moving into children's-book illustration with 1995's *The Lion and the Mouse: An Aesop's Fable.* Praising Andrew's black-and-white artwork for this book, a *Publishers Weekly* reviewer noted that the artist's "gossamer soft" illustrations imbue Aesop's classic text with "visual rhythms often missing from monochromatic art," while Janice Del Negro, writing in *Booklist,* called the work "rich in tone and intriguing in composition." In addition to providing illustrations for the works of other traditional children's books, such as Anna Sewall's *Black Beauty* and Rudyard Kipling's *The Jungle Book,* Andrew has also worked with contemporary writers such as Russell Hoban, Rumer Godden, and Berlie Doherty. His illustrations for *The Boat,* Helen Ward's retelling of the story of Noah and the ark, was shortlisted for the prestigious Kate Greenaway Award in 2005.

Praising Doherty's picture book *The Midnight Man,* *Booklist* contributor GraceAnne A. DeCandido dubbed Doherty's story about a boy and his dog who are drawn into dreamland by a mysterious man on horseback a "magical tale." Andrew's "colored-pencil illustrations

Andrew's evocative, sensitive illustrations bring new life to a 2001 edition of Anna Sewell's classic children's novel **Black Beauty,** *which was first published in 1877.*

are the stuff of dreams," noted DeCandido of the companion artwork, while a *Publishers Weekly* reviewer wrote that the "velvety world" created by the artist reflects the reassuring safety of home, making the dreamworld on "the vast moors at the edge of the world" more threatening by comparison. In *Jim's Lion,* Hoban's story about a frightened young invalid who fights for his life with the help of an inspiring nurse, Andrew's drawings "perfectly match the gentle, soft tone" of Hoban's story, in the opinion of a *Kirkus Reviews* writer. The artist's colored pencil and pastel art, in shades of blue, green, and earthy beige, "accentuate[s] the warmth" between the boy and his nurse, a *Publishers Weekly* writer commented, while in *School Library Journal* Faith Brautigam wrote that the "breathtaking" illustrations "perfectly match the quiet courage of the boy depicted" in Hoban's story.

As Andrew once told *SATA:* "It's important to grab opportunities with both hands, which is probably why I was at college for much longer than I intended. I was originally trained as an illustrator, but I found my obsession with animation growing, as I had a desire to work with sound and had always been inspired by film. This transition has always seemed to be a natural one. It was a move that proved invaluable, allowing experimentation and thinking on a completely different scale, with total awareness of time, producing hundreds and hundreds of drawings for just a few seconds of screen time. Your drawing becomes looser, and the process opens you to use media you wouldn't have considered before just to save time.

"When I finished at the Royal College of Art, I had completed a short animation called *Dolphins.* It was inspired by a lone dolphin off the west coast of Ireland in Dingle Bay, where I spent many of my summers during that time. Even though the film is really a study of dolphins in motion, it makes reference to the use of drift nets, which, sadly, cause many to drown when they become entangled. To my delight, Greenpeace saw the film on an animation program and asked to use it as part of a campaign in response to concerns over the status of small cetaceans around the coasts of Britain and Ireland. The Greenpeace vessel *Moby Dick* visited Cardigan Bay in Wales and Moray Firth in Scotland; these two habitats are home to virtually the entire British semi-resident coastal population of bottlenose dolphins. The tour was used to make people aware, locally and nationally, that there were dolphins in these particular areas and that they were under threat. My liaison with Greenpeace culminated in frames of the film and commissioned illustrations appearing in the *Greenpeace Book of Dolphins* in 1990.

"In the same year I ventured to Berlin to try to get work on a production of *The Little Prince,* but it turned out to be a fruitless venture. So I turned my attention to the National Film Board of Canada in Montreal. I went to see the 'pinscreen' housed there. Created by Alexandre Alexieff and Claire Parker, it enables you to animate with light, using hundreds of retractable pins. The quality is just beautiful, and some moments in their films *Night on Bare Mountain* and *The Nose* greatly influenced me. I became very aware of the drama achieved in the use of black and white. Someone at Candlewick Press asked me where I found the inspiration for the illustrations in *The Midnight Man.* I replied that the book grew out of 'my love of black and white films of the 1930s with their use of dramatic lights and shadows.' I try to capture on paper the luminous feel of those films.

"Seeing the pinscreen was a defining moment, and it inspired my black-and-white drawings for *The Lion and the Mouse,* which were intended for an animated film. I did manage to get them on to film for the Annecy animation festival, but the project was later shelved. That is why I owe so much to Templar and Millbrook Press, who saw the box of black and white drawings, chose the ones they liked, and added a text by Amanda Jane Wood. It was a real gamble for them, and it was my first published picture book.

"So, in full circle in 1996, they came back to me with *Back to the Blue.* I used the same techniques used in the animated film on dolphins—pencil and pastel. I knew the story well, having followed the jubilation at the closure of the last 'dolphinariums.' It was incredible to be able to work with Virginia McKenna, whose work with Bill Travers through the Born Free Foundation showed unparalleled conviction to saving animals in appalling situations. It was one of the most rewarding projects to be involved with. The publicity was like nothing I'd seen before—celebrities lending their support, attending signings with Virginia, a poster produced with my drawing on it, and quite wonderful feedback, from children especially, but also from readers of all ages—a joyous experience.

"I hope at some point I am destined to renew my acquaintance with such incredible subject matter as the dolphins, with their musicality, their easy sensuality and evident intelligence, but most of all their ability to call our assumed dominion over nature into question."

Biographical and Critical Sources

PERIODICALS

Booklist, February 1, 1996, Janice Del Negro, review of *The Lion and the Mouse,* p. 936; August, 1998, p. 2007; February 15, 1999, GraceAnne A. DeCandido, review of *The Midnight Man,* p. 1074; January 1, 2002, Cynthia Turnquest, review of *Jim's Lion,* p. 865.

Horn Book, May-June, 1997, Mary M. Burns, review of *Premlata and the Festival of Lights,* p. 320.

Kirkus Reviews, November 15, 2001, review of *Jim's Lion,* p. 1611.

Publishers Weekly, November 13, 1995, review of *The Lion and the Mouse,* p. 60; January 27, 1997, review of *Premlata and the Festival of Lights,* p. 107; December 14, 1998, review of *The Midnight Man,* p. 75; November 12, 2001, review of *Jim's Lion,* p. 59.

School Library Journal, September, 1997, p. 191; March, 1998, p. 184; January, 2002, Faith Brautigam, review of *Jim's Lion,* p. 101.

ONLINE

Templar Publishing Web site, http://www.templar publishing.co.uk/ (November 18, 2005), "Ian Andrew."

*   *   *

ANDREW, Ian Peter
See ANDREW, Ian

*   *   *

ASHABRANNER, Brent 1921-
(Brent Kenneth Ashabranner)

Personal

Born November 3, 1921, in Shawnee, OK; son of Dudley (a pharmacist) and Rose Thelma (Cotton) Ashabran-

Brent Ashabranner

ner; married Martha White, August 9, 1941; children: Melissa Lynn, Jennifer Ann. *Education:* Oklahoma State University, B.S., 1948, M.A., 1951; additional study at University of Michigan, 1955, and Boston University and Oxford University, 1959-60. *Hobbies and other interests:* Tennis, African and Asian traditional art.

Addresses

Home—15 Spring W., Williamsburg, VA 23188.

Career

Oklahoma State University, Stillwater, instructor in English, 1952-55; Ministry of Education, Technical Cooperation Administration, Addis Ababa, Ethiopia, educational materials adviser, 1955-57; U.S. International Cooperation Administration, Tripoli, Libya, chief of Education Materials Development division, 1957-59; U.S. Agency for International Development, Lagos, Nigeria, education program officer, 1960-61; Peace Corps, Washington, DC, acting director of program in Nigeria, 1961-62, deputy director of program in India, 1962-64, director of program in India, 1964-66, director of Office of Training, 1966-67, deputy director of Peace Corps, 1967-69; Harvard University Center for Studies in Education and Development, Cambridge, MA, research associate, 1969-70; Pathfinder Fund, Boston, MA, director of Near East-South Asia Population Program, 1970-

71; Planned Parenthood, director of project development for World Population International Assistance division, 1971-72; Ford Foundation, New York, NY, associate representative and population program officer, 1972-80, deputy representative to Philippines, 1972-75, deputy representative to Indonesia, 1975-80; writer, 1980—. *Military service:* U.S. Navy, 1942-45.

Awards, Honors

National Civil Service League career service award, 1968; Notable Children's Trade Book in the Field of Social Studies, 1982, and Carter G. Woodson Book Award, National Council for the Social Studies, 1983, both for *Morning Star, Black Sun: The Northern Cheyenne Indians and America's Energy Crisis;* Notable Children's Trade Book in the Field of Social Studies, American Library Association (ALA) Notable Book, and Books for the Teen Age, New York Public Library, all 1983, all for *The New Americans: Changing Patterns in U.S. Immigration;* Notable Children's Trade Book in the Field of Social Studies, 1984, ALA Best Book for Young Adults, 1984, and Carter G. Woodson Book Award, 1985, all for *To Live in Two Worlds: American Indian Youth Today;* Notable Children's Book in the Field of Social Studies and ALA Notable Book, both 1984, both for *Gavriel and Jemal: Two Boys of Jerusalem;* ALA Notable Book, 1985, *Boston Globe-Horn Book* Honor Book, 1986, and Carter G. Woodson Book Award, 1986, all for *Dark Harvest: Migrant Farmworkers in America;* ALA Notable Book and *School Library Journal* Best Book of the Year, both 1986, both for *Children of the Maya: A Guatemalan Indian Odyssey;* Notable Children's Trade Book in the Field of Social Studies, *School Library Journal* Best Book of the Year, ALA Notable Book, and Christopher Award, all 1987, all for *Into a Strange Land: Unaccompanied Refugee Youth in America;* Notable Children's Trade Book in the Field of Social Studies, 1987, for *The Vanishing Border: A Photographic Journey along Our Frontier with Mexico;* ALA Notable Book and Best Book for Young Adults designations, both 1988, both for *Always to Remember: The Story of the Vietnam Veterans Memorial; Born to the Land: An American Portrait, Counting America: The Story of the United States Census, People Who Make a Difference,* and *The Times of My Life: A Memoir* named Books for the Teen Age by New York Public Library. *Morning Star, Black Sun, The New Americans, To Live in Two Worlds, Gavriel and Jemal, Into a Strange Land, The Vanishing Border, Born to the Land, Counting America, A Grateful Nation: The Story of Arlington National Cemetery, A Memorial for Mr. Lincoln,* and *A New Frontier: The Peace Corps in Eastern Europe* were all Junior Literary Guild selections.

Writings

FOR CHILDREN

(With Russell Davis) *The Lion's Whiskers,* Little, Brown (Boston, MA), 1959, and editor, *The Lion's Whiskers and Other Ethiopian Tales,* revised edition, illustrated by Helen Siegl, Linnet Books (Hamden, CT), 1997.

(With Russell Davis) *Point Four Assignment: Stories from the Records of Those Who Work in Foreign Fields for the Mutual Security of Free Nations,* Little, Brown (Boston, MA), 1959.

(With Russell Davis) *Ten Thousand Desert Swords,* Little, Brown (Boston, MA), 1960.

(With Russell Davis) *The Choctaw Code,* McGraw (New York, NY), 1961, reprinted, Linnet Books, 1994.

(With Russell Davis) *Chief Joseph: War Chief of the Nez Percé,* McGraw (New York, NY), 1962.

(With Russell Davis) *Land in the Sun: The Story of West Africa,* Little, Brown (Boston, MA), 1963.

(With Russell Davis) *Strangers in Africa,* McGraw (New York, NY), 1963.

Morning Star, Black Sun: The Northern Cheyenne Indians and America's Energy Crisis, photographs by Paul Conklin, Dodd (New York, NY), 1982.

The New Americans: Changing Patterns in U.S. Immigration, Dodd (New York, NY), 1983.

To Live in Two Worlds: American Indian Youth Today, photographs by Paul Conklin, Dodd (New York, NY), 1984.

Gavriel and Jemal: Two Boys of Jerusalem, photographs by Paul Conklin, Dodd (New York, NY), 1984.

Dark Harvest: Migrant Farmworkers in America, photographys by Paul Conklin, Dodd (New York, NY), 1985, reissued, Linnet Books, 1993.

Children of the Maya: A Guatemalan Indian Odyssey, photographs by Paul Conklin, Dodd (New York, NY), 1986.

(With daughter, Melissa Ashabranner) *Into a Strange Land: Unaccompanied Refugee Youth in America,* Dodd (New York, NY), 1987.

The Vanishing Border: A Photographic Journey along Our Frontier with Mexico, photographys by Paul Conklin, Dodd (New York, NY), 1987.

Always to Remember: The Story of the Vietnam Veterans Memorial, photographs by daughter, Jennifer Ashabranner, Dodd (New York, NY), 1988.

Born to the Land: An American Portrait, photographs by Paul Conklin, Putnam (New York, NY), 1989.

I'm in the Zoo, Too!, illustrated by Janet Stevens, Cobblehill Books (New York, NY), 1989.

(With Melissa Ashabranner) *Counting America: The Story of the United States Census,* Putnam (New York, NY), 1989.

People Who Make a Difference, photographs by Paul Conklin, Cobblehill Books (New York, NY), 1989.

A Grateful Nation: The Story of Arlington National Cemetery, photographs by Jennifer Ashabranner, Putnam (New York, NY), 1990.

The Times of My Life: A Memoir, Dutton (New York, NY), 1990.

Crazy about German Shepherds, photographs by Jennifer Ashabranner, Dutton (New York, NY), 1990.

An Ancient Heritage: The Arab-American Minority, photographs by Paul Conklin, Harper (New York, NY), 1991.

Land of Yesterday, Land of Tomorrow: Discovering Chinese Central Asia, photographs by Paul, David, and Peter Conklin, Cobblehill Books (New York, NY), 1992.

A Memorial for Mr. Lincoln, photographs by Jennifer Ashabranner, Putnam (New York, NY), 1992.

Still a Nation of Immigrants, photographs by Jennifer Ashabranner, Dutton (New York, NY), 1993.

A New Frontier: The Peace Corps in Eastern Europe, photographs by Peter Conklin, Dutton (New York, NY), 1994.

(With Stephen Chicoine) *Lithuania: The Nation That Would Be Free,* photographs by Stephen Chicoine, Cobblehill Books (New York, NY), 1996.

Our Beckoning Borders: Illegal Immigration to America, photographs by Peter Conklin, Cobblehill Books (New York, NY), 1996.

A Strange and Distant Shore: Indians of the Great Plains in Exile, Dutton (New York, NY), 1996.

To Seek a Better World: The Haitian Minority in America, photographs by Peter Conklin, Cobblehill Books (New York, NY), 1997.

Their Names to Live: What the Vietnam Veterans Memorial Means to America, photographs by Jennifer Ashabranner, Twenty-first Century Books (New York, NY), 1998.

The New African Americans, photographs by Jennifer Ashabranner, Linnet Books (Hamden, CT), 1999.

Badge of Valor: The National Law Enforcement Officers Memorial, photographs by Jennifer Ashabranner, Twenty-first Century Books (New York, NY), 2000.

A Date with Destiny: The Women in Military Service for America Memorial, photographs by Jennifer Ashabranner, Twenty-first Century Books (New York, NY), 2000.

No Better Hope: What the Lincoln Memorial Means to America, photographs by Jennifer Ashabranner, Twenty-first Century Books (New York, NY), 2001.

Remembering Korea: The Korean War Veterans Memorial, photographs by Jennifer Ashabranner, Twenty-first Century Books (New York, NY), 2001.

On the Mall in Washington, D.C.: A Visit to America's Front Yard, photographs by Jennifer Ashabranner, Twenty-first Century Books (New York, NY), 2002.

The Washington Monument: A Beacon for America, photographs by Jennifer Ashabranner, Twenty-first Century Books (New York, NY), 2002.

OTHER

(Editor) *The Stakes Are High,* Bantam (New York, NY), 1954.

(With Judson Milburn and Cecil B. Williams) *A First Course in College English* (textbook), Houghton (Boston, MA), 1962.

A Moment in History: The First Ten Years of the Peace Corps, Doubleday (New York, NY), 1971.

Also contributor of numerous articles and short stories to periodicals.

Sidelights

A former Peace Corps director, Brent Ashabranner writes informative books for children about the social issues facing a variety of cultures present in the United States as well as other countries. The author has been praised for his knowledge of the customs and lifestyles of many groups of people. He is delicate but frank in his treatment of a wide range of topics, including the plight of Native Americans and migrant workers. Ashabranner once commented about his collaboration with Russell Davis on such books as *The Choctaw Code* and *Land in the Sun: The Story of West Africa:* "Russ and I have lived and worked in many countries—Ethiopia, Libya, Nigeria, India, Nicaragua—and have traveled in dozens of others. Most of our books are about these countries, their people, their colorful legends, and about Americans who live and work overseas. In other words, we write about what we know and have experienced—which is good advice for anyone who wants to be an author."

Since his joint efforts with Davis, Ashabranner has penned young-adult books on his own for which he has won several awards. Among his titles are *To Live in Two Worlds: American Indian Youth Today,* which presents the concerns of Native Americans in the 1980s, and *Gavriel and Jemal: Two Boys of Jerusalem,* an account of the experiences of a Jewish boy and an Arab boy who each reside with their families in the ethnically diverse city of Jerusalem, Israel. The author also draws on the knowledge he gained as deputy director of the Peace Corps in the late 1960s in *A Moment in History: The First Ten Years of the Peace Corps,* a well-received chronicle of the inception and development of the organization.

In more recent years, the author's nonfiction works for children have continued to be praised by reviewers. For example, Ashabranner's *A Memorial for Mr. Lincoln* was described by *Horn Book* reviewer Margaret A. Bush as "an informative and inspiring tribute to this national treasure." A collaboration with his photographer daughter Jennifer Ashabranner, the book includes black-and-white photographs as well as black-and-white reproductions. *Booklist* reviewer Carolyn Phelan commended Ashabranner's *No Better Hope: What the Lincoln Memorial Means to America,* calling it "an example of a quality series" and appreciating Ashabranner's "conversational author's note."

Of Ashabranner's *Still a Nation of Immigrants,* Margaret A. Bush commented in *Horn Book* that the book "is generally upbeat about putting a human face on the contemporary immigrant groups." Bush also called the book "an ambitious discussion." According to Hazel Rochman, a reviewer for *Booklist,* "the words and portraits" in *To Seek a Better World: The Haitian Minority in America* "bring [the reader] close to all kinds of individuals behind the prevailing stereotype."

Many of Ashabranner's books, like *A Memorial for Mr. Lincoln,* feature photographs by his daughter and focus on monuments in the U.S. capital. These titles, such as *Remembering Korea: The Korean War Veterans Memorial,* give brief descriptions of the monuments and the area, suitable both for tourists and for readers wanting more information about the memorials. *Remembering Korea* also discusses the history of the Korean War, giving some background on why the building of the monument was important. "The writing is crisp and informative," Carolyn Phelan of *Booklist* said of the title, while Andrew Medlar, writing in *School Library Journal* noted that "this short book will meet the needs of a wide range of users." Ashabranner has also written books about such landmarks as the Washington Mall and the Washington Monument. In *On the Mall in Washington, D.C.: A Visit to America's Front Yard,* Ashabranner gives an overview of many of the memorials and museums that line the Mall. Considered "useful for first-time visitors or for those who simply want some basic information" by Margaret C. Howell in *School Library Journal, On the Mall in Washington D.C.* provides readers with a map, as well as notes on sculptures and gardens in the area and events that take place during the summer. *The Washington Monument: A Beacon for America* describes the process of building the Washington Monument, a project that took more than a hundred year following its initial proposal. Pamela K. Bomboy, in her review for *School Library Journal,* commented on the "absorbing blend of facts and commentary" featured in the book, while *Booklist* contributor Carolyn Phelan considered the title "a solid addition to a fine series."

"I started out as a fiction writer when I was eleven years old," Ashabranner once told *SATA.* "I loved to read adventure books set in foreign places. Under the spell of a novel called *Bomba the Jungle Boy* I started writing a novel called *Barbara the Jungle Girl.* That wasn't very original, but at least I was, like Robert Louis Stevenson, 'playing the sedulous ape' to a writer I admired. By page three, I was hopelessly bogged down in the plot of my jungle story and never finished it; but that was a start, and I never stopped writing after that. I sold my first story when I was twenty and went on to publish scores of magazine short stories.

"I began nonfiction writing during the 1950s and 1960s when I was working overseas in the foreign aid program and the Peace Corps. The experiences I was having in Ethiopia, India, and other countries seemed more interesting than anything I could invent. I liked the nonfiction medium and have stayed with it. I began writing for children and young adults during my overseas years. The things I felt I was learning about other cultures and about people of different cultures understanding each other seemed worth sharing with young readers. Before, I wrote only for adults. Now, I write almost exclusively for children and young adults.

"I write mostly about rather complex social issues and problems; finding ways to make these subjects interesting and understandable to young readers is a challenging task I never tire of. I firmly believe that we do our most important reading when we are young; to try to engage young minds on worthwhile subjects is a great satisfaction.

"I do a great deal of field research and library research. In most cases I cover a lot of territory, talking with and sometimes living with the people I'm writing about. I think there is no other way to make my subjects interesting to young readers. But library research is vital to my full understanding of a subject. In the course of writing a book, I will consult many books, articles, government reports, and scholarly studies. The most important of these I put in a bibliography. I live only three hours from the Library of Congress, and I spend a good deal of time there."

Biographical and Critical Sources

BOOKS

Abrahamson, Richard F., and Betty Carter, *From Delight to Wisdom: Nonfiction for Young Adults,* Oryx (Phoenix, AZ), 1990.

PERIODICALS

Booklist, May 15, 1997, Hazel Rochman, review of *To Seek a Better World: The Haitian Minority in America,* p. 1569; October 15, 1999, Hazel Rochman, review of *The New African Americans,* p. 425; March 1, 2001, Carolyn Phelan, review of *No Better Hope: What the Lincoln Memorial Means to America,* p. 1272; September 15, 2001, Carolyn Phelan, review of *Remembering Korea: The Korean War Veterans Memorial,* p. 217; March 15, 2002, Shelle Rosenfeld, review of *On the Mall in Washington, D.C.: A Visit to America's Front Yard,* p. 1252; September 1, 2002, Carolyn Phelan, review of *The Washington Monument: A Beacon for America,* p. 117.

Cobblestone, May, 2002, "Digging Deeper," p. 46.

Faces: People, Places, and Culture, November, 2004, review of *Land of Yesterday, Land of Tomorrow: Discovering Chinese Central Asia,* p. 46; December, 2004, review of *Gavriel and Jemal: Two Boys of Jerusalem,* p. 47.

Horn Book, September-October, 1984; September-October, 1986; March-April, 1993, Margaret A. Bush, review of *A Memorial for Mr. Lincoln,* p. 217; January-February, 1994, Margaret A. Bush, review of *Still a Nation of Immigrants,* p. 84.

Library Journal, August, 1971.

Los Angeles Times, October 17, 1987.

New York Times Book Review, August 5, 1962; April 4, 1971.

School Library Journal, January, 1985; June-July, 1987; July, 2001, Margaret C. Howell, review of *No Better Hope,* p. 118; December, 2001, review of *Remembering Korea,* p. 150; April, 2002, Margaret C. Howell, review of *On the Mall in Washington, D.C.,* p. 162; November, 2002, Pamela K. Bomboy, review of *The Washington Monument,* p. 182.

School Library Media Activities Monthly, April, 1991.

Voice of Youth Advocates, October, 1987.

Washington Post Book World, June 8, 1986.

ONLINE

Chidren's Book Guild of Washington, D.C. Web site, http://www.childrensbookguild.org/ (January 25, 2006).

Autobiography Feature

Brent Ashabrenner

Brent Ashabranner contributed the following autobiographical essay to *SATA:*

It is possible for a person to have more than one life as he makes his way through this world. At least I have found that to be true, and I am sure it is true for many people. I have had three lives in my seventy years, and I will not be in the least astonished if there should be a fourth.

My first life lasted thirty-five years, and all of it—except for three years in the U.S. Navy during World War II—was spent in Oklahoma. I was born there, went to school and college there, became a husband, parent, and teacher there. I was a happy, provincial Midwesterner.

My second life spanned twenty-five years during which I lived and worked in many African and Asian countries: Ethiopia, Libya, Nigeria, India, the Philippines, and Indonesia. Nine of those years were spent with the Peace Corps, one of the best and most imaginative international programs our country has ever had.

My third life—which I am still enjoying immensely—has been in progress for over ten years. After the years in Africa and Asia, my wife Martha and I settled in Williamsburg, Virginia; I have used this quiet and wonderfully rich cradle of American democracy as a base for writing about and interpreting the American experience for young readers. I have left my comfortable Williamsburg home to travel with migrant farm workers throughout the country and have told their story in *Dark Harvest*. I have recorded the experiences of young Vietnamese and Cambodian refugees who have come to America in *Into a Strange Land*. I have driven our frontier with Mexico from San Diego to Brownsville, Texas, in order to explore the melding of U.S. and Mexican cultures; I wrote about that journey in *The Vanishing Border*. These are but a few of the books I have written about life in America today since returning to live in the United States. I think my years of living in other cultures around the world have helped me to be a better writer about my own country.

It all started for me in Shawnee, Oklahoma, where I was born in 1921 and where my father was a pharmacist. Shawnee was named for the Shawnee Indian tribe, one of the many tribes moved west by the government over the Trail of Tears to Indian Territory during the early part of the nineteenth century. President Andrew Jackson promised the Indians that the land would be theirs "as long as the grass grows or the water runs," but it didn't work out that way. Land-hungry white settlers wanted the good Indian land and got it; the result was Oklahoma, which became the forty-sixth state in 1907. I never learned the tragic story of Indian removal and broken treaties until I studied Oklahoma history in high school. It was history told from the white man's point of view, but I could read between the lines and understand something of the shameful treatment of the Indians and their struggle against hopeless odds.

My family moved from Shawnee when I was five years old, but I have always felt that the early glimpses I had of Indians in and around Shawnee worked their way into my unconscious memory and were the start of my lifelong interest in Native Americans.

Our new home was in El Reno, a town of about twelve thousand in central Oklahoma, where my father and mother bought a drugstore. The purchase had been made possible by oil royalties my mother received from family land. There was lots of oil money in Oklahoma and Texas in the 1920s. Throughout most of America, the twenties—until the very end of the decade—were years of prosperity, optimism, and unbounded confidence in the financial future of the country.

We were a small family, just my father, mother, brother Gerard—four years my senior—and I, and our life in El Reno was good. We lived in a spacious white house on a quiet, tree-lined street with other nice houses and lots of kids my age. My parents rented the house instead of buying it because they had put all their money into buying the drugstore, but we were well off. Our family car was a good, dependable Nash. We had a

Parents, Dudley and Rose Cotton Ashabranner, 1916

large console radio when many homes in the mid-' Twenties had no radio at all. Home television, of course, was still in the realm of fantasy.

Books were a part of our home. I learned to read early, but before that my mother read fairy tales and other classic stories to me. Ruskin's *King of the Golden River* was my favorite. We had a full set of the *Book of Knowledge,* and I spent many rainy-day hours browsing through them. Every time my mother visited friends in Oklahoma City, she brought me back a book in a long series about a boy named Jerry Todd and his pal Poppy Ott. The books had such intriguing titles as *Jerry Todd and Purring Egg* and *Poppy Ott and the Stuttering Parrot.* Even today I have fond memories of the adventures of Jerry, Poppy, and their friends in an Illinois town called Tutter.

My town, El Reno, was an interesting place. It had grown up in Indian Territory days near Fort Reno, one of a string of U.S. Army forts that extended from Texas to Montana. The purpose of these frontier forts had been to provide protection for white settlers by containing Plains Indian tribes on their newly assigned reservations; in theory at least, the forts were also to protect the Indians from land-hungry ranchers, farmers, and frontier adventurers selling whisky, guns, and other forbidden goods.

Fort Reno was located on land that had been assigned by the government to the Cheyenne and Arapaho tribes in 1867. All Indian reservations in Oklahoma were abolished by the Dawes Act of 1887, but many Cheyenne and Arapaho still lived around El Reno.

Fort Reno was still an active U.S. Army post, a cavalry remount station, when I lived in El Reno. A school friend of mine lived at the fort, and sometimes I would spend Friday or Saturday night at his house. His father, a captain with a finely waxed mustache, was a history buff and had turned their house into a virtual Indian wars museum. He had collected carbines, bows and arrows, lances, old maps and photographs, medicine pipes, buffalo robes, early uniforms, and scores of books on the Indian campaigns.

The captain loved to talk about Western history, and it was from him that I first heard about Chief Little Wolf and the Northern Cheyenne Indians, who lived in the Black Hills of South Dakota. In 1877 this branch of the Cheyenne tribe was forced by the army to move to the Darlington Agency near Fort Reno. From the beginning their life there was a disaster. There were too many people, no game to hunt, and nothing for the young men and women to do. The tribe lived on food handed out to them by the government.

One night, after a year of misery, Little Wolf led his people—over a thousand in number—out of the Darlington Agency. Ten thousand soldiers were stationed in forts along their escape route, but so skillful was Little Wolf in moving his people that the federal troops never caught them. After a homeward trek of fifteen hundred miles, they at last reached their beloved Black Hills. Once there, they were able to resist efforts to make them return to the Darlington Agency, and in 1884 the government finally gave the Northern Cheyenne a reservation on their traditional hunting grounds along the Tongue River in southeastern Montana.

I never forgot the story of Little Wolf that the captain at Fort Reno told me. It was one of the reasons, more than fifty years later, that I decided to write *Morning Star, Black Sun,* which is about the fight of the Northern Cheyenne tribe today to protect the sacred land of their reservation from big power companies that covet the immense quantities of coal that lie beneath the reservation.

My father was a quiet man who listened much more than he talked. I think that is why many Cheyenne and Arapaho came to his drugstore in El Reno to buy medicine. He would listen to their problems and offer his best advice, which was usually that they should go to a doctor. Whether they did or not, they still bought their medicine from him. One reason was that he would sell to them on credit if they didn't have cash. Not many stores would do that.

As a result of my father's rapport with the Indians, the Ashabranner family was sometimes invited to Cheyenne and Arapaho powwows and stomp dances. I was a fascinated onlooker, and I learned to like Indian food, especially fry bread, wild rice, and roasted beef with blackberry sauce. Sometimes they had venison, and that was a special treat.

During my six years of elementary school in El Reno, I had only one Indian friend. Indians were not barred from white public schools as blacks were in those days of segregation, but not many Indian children attended public schools. Indians were well aware of white prejudice, and they preferred to send their children to the few Indian schools still run by the government or not to send them to school at all. The Indian concept that education took place in the home and in nature was still very much alive in those days.

My friend was a Cheyenne boy whose name was Jimmy Red Fox. Some kids in school made fun of his name, but I thought it was great. I can't remember exactly how we became friends, but I do recall that one day I offered to trade him a banana for a piece of fry bread during our lunch break, and that broke the ice. We played together during recess, and sometimes I talked him into joining my dare base team. Dare base was a game where two members of opposing teams tried to grab a handkerchief and get back to their side without being touched by the other. Jimmy Red Fox was the fastest kid I ever saw, and we never lost when I could get him to play. Then one day his desk was empty, and he never came back to school. I don't know why. I looked for him at powwows and dances but never saw him again.

A few years ago—in my third life—I wrote a book called *To Live in Two Worlds,* which is about the desire of young American Indians today to retain their tribal heritage while at the same time succeeding in the dominant culture of the country. I don't know that my friendship with Jimmy Red Fox was part of the motivation for my writing the book, but it probably was. I remember being bothered as a boy that he was a friend I knew so little about.

By the time I was in third grade, Americans were no longer feeling optimistic about their financial future; the whole country was moving toward a frightening and demoralizing economic collapse that lasted more than ten years and became known as the Great Depression. It began with the Wall Street crash of 1929 when tens of thousands of investors were wiped out almost overnight; in the space of a few days millionaires became paupers, and small investors lost their life savings. A wave of suicides swept from coast to coast.

Before the economic disaster would run its course, sixty thousand businesses would fail; five thousand banks would close their doors permanently, causing ten million account holders to lose their money; hundreds of thousands of farms would be lost because farmers could not pay their bank loans or taxes. At the Depression's height, as many as twelve million job-seekers could find no work.

I did not know those grim statistics as I was growing up; but as the twenties turned into the thirties, I knew that something was wrong. We lived only a few blocks from the Rock Island Railroad tracks; several times a week shabbily dressed men, most of them young, would knock at our back door asking for food. These were the tramps of the Depression, unemployed men who rode in empty boxcars from town to town across the country looking for work that was seldom to be found. I don't remember my mother ever refusing a sandwich and coffee to these unfortunate men, even though she believed that they left some kind of mark on or near our house to let other tramps know that they had received food there.

There were other signs of evil times. When I listened to the radio, I tuned in mainly to my favorite programs such as "Little Orphan Annie" and "Jack Armstrong, All-American Boy," but I couldn't help hearing an often-played song which asked the sad question, "Brother, Can You Spare a Dime?" And when I went to the movies, the weekly newsreel always showed long lines of men and sometimes women at big-city soup kitchens.

The Depression hit home in a very real and personal way in 1932 when my father lost the drugstore. Business dropped off to the point that he couldn't make enough money to replenish stock, and he couldn't get another bank loan. One of his problems had been that he gave credit to people who simply couldn't pay their bills. That wasn't good business, but in those grim days he found it hard to say no to a person who needed medicine.

After the drugstore's debts were paid, only a few hundred dollars were left. My parents put that little bit of money in the bank, and a month later the bank closed its doors. They joined the ten million others who lost everything they had during the Depression.

But our family was more fortunate than many. My father's skill as a pharmacist was well known, and he was never out of work during the Depression years. He was hired to run the store he had once owned; his salary was a hundred dollars a month. A year later he was offered a job in a drugstore in Bristow, a small oil and agricultural town near Tulsa. We didn't want to leave El Reno, but there was no question that Dad had to take the job. He had been offered $125 a month, and he couldn't pass up the chance to increase the family income by 25 percent.

*

I began this essay by talking about the two lives I have lived and the third I am living now. One thread of continuity has run through all of these lives, and it is this: no matter where I was in the world, no matter what I was doing, I have always been a writer. Often the time I could give to writing was small, perhaps no more than five or six hours a week, but I always found some time.

I tried to write my first story in El Reno when I was eleven years old. Under the spell of an exciting book called *Bomba the Jungle Boy,* I began writing a story which I called "Barbara the Jungle Girl." That wasn't very original, I admit, but at least, like Robert Louis Stevenson, I "played the sedulous ape" to a writer I admired. I had yet to learn that a fresh idea, fresh material, or a different approach are what, in part, distinguish a good writer from a poor or mediocre one. In any case, by page three I was hopelessly bogged down in the plot, and "Barbara the Jungle Girl" was never finished. The only other story I remember trying to write in El Reno was about an Indian boy on his first buffalo hunt. That might have been a good idea, but I didn't finish that story either. I quickly discovered that I didn't know anything about buffalo, and I hadn't yet been introduced to something called research.

But the writing bug had somehow got in my blood, and I really never stopped writing after the beginning in El Reno. In the diary I began to keep when I was twelve years old there was a line asking what I wanted to be when I grew up. I recall very clearly that I wrote "Fiction Writer."

Both my reading and my writing continued unabated during my junior high school years in Bristow, and a small public library had enough fuel to stoke the fires of my imagination. More and more I became fascinated by books about foreign countries. I devoured Kipling, practically memorized *Beau Geste* and other French Foreign Legion books by P.C. Wren, and lived every moment with Richard Halliburton as he swam the Dardanelles in Turkey and cut through Guatemalan jungles in search of ancient Mayan treasures. A nonfiction book about the search for archeological treasures in Greece and Crete was a particular favorite. I read other things, of course. The wonderful dog stories of Albert Payson Terhune made me long for a collie; the library had a generous selection of Zane Grey's Western novels, and I read all of them.

My writing continued to be a mirror of my reading. I wrote stories about jewel smugglers in Bangkok, scientists hunting rare orchids in the Amazon jungles, British soldiers in India fighting rebellious Sikhs. No matter that I knew nothing about these subjects except what I read; my imagination was getting a terrific workout. I wrote the stories laboriously in longhand on yellow tablet paper and put them in a box under my bed. It would be fun for me to read some of those stories today, but someplace through the years the box was lost or thrown away.

In high school I had the great good fortune of having English teachers who took a genuine interest in me and my writing. Mrs. Arthurs stretched the limits in writing assignments to let me write on subjects I was interested in and even to let me write stories when a theme was called for. She made me pay attention to grammar and punctuation, and her red pencil always showed me where I was awkward or unclear. But a "Good!" beside a passage she liked and a thoughtful comment about my story as a whole always inspired me to do better next time.

Mrs. Arthurs did something else: she introduced me to American writers who wrote about the world around them. One of the books she gave me was McKinley Kantor's *The Voice of Bugle Ann,* the story of a hunting dog in the Missouri hill country. Another was Marjorie Kinnan Rawlings's *The Yearling,* about a rural family in Florida. She thought I was ready for some John Steinbeck, and I was. I thoroughly enjoyed everything she recommended, and I think Mrs. Arthurs was subtly suggesting that I might want to look around my own world and try writing about what I saw.

When I was a junior, the Bristow High School English teachers persuaded the principal to let them set up a creative-writing course. The course consisted of just four students, me and three of my friends who were also interested in writing. Creative-writing courses are commonplace today, but in 1938 such a course in high school—with only four students!—was rare indeed. The four of us sat in a classroom by ourselves for a semester just writing. There was no formal instruction, though Mrs. Covey, who was our supervising teacher, read everything we wrote and went over every story, poem, or essay with us.

It was Mrs. Covey who encouraged me to begin to write about things that I knew something about. After the reading direction that Mrs. Arthurs had given me, that did not seem to be such a strange idea. One of the stories I wrote during the creative-writing class was about a boxer whose fighting name was Samson, and that was the name of the story. My brother, Gerard, was a skillful amateur boxer, a district Golden Gloves lightweight champion. After high school he had begun to fight professional bouts in a little Depression-era, small-town boxing circuit that included Bristow. I went to all of Gerard's fights and sometimes reported on the whole fight card for our local newspaper, the *Bristow Daily Record.*

Mrs. Covey liked "Samson" and had me work on it and rewrite it until we were both sure I couldn't make it any better. Then she entered it in a national short-story competition sponsored by *Scholastic Magazine.* "Samson" won fourth prize and was later printed along with other prize winners in a book called *Saplings.* "Samson" was my first published story; seeing it in the book confirmed what I had known for a long time—that I truly wanted to be a writer.

I have never forgotten Mrs. Arthurs, Mrs. Covey, and Mrs. Shaw, who taught me journalism and introduced me to research in writing. I have never forgotten the difference they made in my life.

Perhaps I sound as if I spent all my time in Bristow reading and writing. Hardly. I had some good friends, and we filled many long summer days and nights fishing and camping along the Little Deep Fork of the Canadian River. I loved sports. I went out for track and was pretty good in the 100-yard dash and the 220. I made the tennis team when I was a senior and earned my high school athletic letter. I went with girls, not many, but they were on my mind a lot.

I grew up in the heart of the Depression years, and I know that the Depression left its lasting imprint on me—in my sympathy for people fighting poverty both in the United States and overseas, in my lifelong support of social programs designed to help people in difficult times and to prevent another Depression: Social Security, unemployment insurance, national health insurance, banking controls, and others.

It wasn't that my family or I suffered. We rarely had an extra dollar, but Dad was never out of work. We always had food, clothes, and a decent roof over us. I was well aware, however, that the blight of Depression lay on the land. I saw hitchhikers on the highways, moving from town to town, looking for work. I sometimes helped in our church's busy welfare program of food boxes and used clothing for the poor.

In addition to all the other economic ills, Oklahoma was now in the grip of a terrible drought, the Dust Bowl era. Many times I saw farmers, their land lost, heading down the highway in dilapidated trucks filled with family and a few household goods; usually they were moving west in the false hope that California was the promised land. In 1939, the year I graduated from high school, John Steinbeck told the story of these unfortunate but tough-spirited migrants in *The Grapes of Wrath.* They were often in my mind when I wrote *Dark Harvest* in 1984.

In those hard Depression times in Bristow I hated to ask my father for money, especially money for dates. I did have to ask him sometimes, and he always gave it; but I tried to keep a little money in my pocket through my own efforts. I delivered newspapers; I did janitorial work at our church; I worked for a year as delivery boy at the drugstore where Dad worked. I cleared land of brush and trees one summer and the next year did manual work at the natural gas plant. It took the influence of friends even to get low-paying, short-term jobs like these.

Somehow, though, Dad could find a way to do something special for us. I had learned to type in high school, and I yearned for a typewriter for writing stories. One night after work Dad came home with a secondhand, reconditioned Underwood standard typewriter and gave it to me. I was overjoyed. Now I was a real writer! I knew the typewriter had cost Dad thirty-five dollars because I had looked at it in the business-machine store on Main Street. He would be a long time paying for it at a few dollars a month, but he couldn't have bought me anything that would have meant more to me. He knew that, and I am sure that seeing my happiness made him feel good.

When my brother graduated from high school in Bristow, he had no prospects of a job and no way to go to college. There was no money to help him even if he could find a job in a college town to pay part of his expenses. What he did instead was decide to read law in a lawyer's office and then take the state bar examination to try to get a license to practice law. In Oklahoma in the 1930s a person could become a lawyer that way,

Brent with older brother, Gerard, about 1925

though hardly anyone ever tried to do it. It was just too lonely and uncertain a way to spend your time.

With Dad's help Gerard found a lawyer who agreed to let him read his law books. In return Gerard would answer the telephone and be receptionist; that would give him a desk and a reason for being in the office. The lawyer was Herbert Arthurs, the husband of my English teacher. With Mr. Arthurs's help, Gerard made out a plan of study and submitted it to the Oklahoma State Bar Association; it was approved.

Gerard read Herb Arthurs's law books for three years, going in every morning two hours before the office opened so he could get a good start on his study. I couldn't understand then and I never have really been able to understand how my brother did it. I can scarcely imagine the will power that must have been required for him to sit there day after day, month after month, year after year reading those law books without any guidance from a professor, without any tests to tell him whether he was learning what he had to know to pass the bar. He would be taking an examination made to test the graduates of the best law schools in the country, and he had never set foot in a college classroom.

When the time came, he went to Oklahoma City for the three-day examination and passed it with flying colors on his first try. My brother gave me the only lesson I ever needed about what sheer guts and determination can accomplish.

*

In my reading I traveled all over the globe, but curiously Bristow was where I had my first look at the real world beyond Oklahoma. As soon as I started seventh grade, I discovered that several of my classmates had surnames that sounded strange to my Midwestern ear—names such as Khoury, Dajani, and Naifeh. Other last names had a biblical sound to them: Abraham and Joseph. Most of these boys and girls had light brown skin that reminded me of the few Mexicans I had seen in my life.

But they weren't Mexicans, I soon learned. Their parents or grandparents had come from a country named Syria. I had never heard of Syria; but when I looked it up on a map, I saw some names that I did know: Palestine, which bordered on Syria, and Jerusalem and Bethlehem, cities in Palestine. My new classmates were Arabs—or, more properly since they lived in the United States, Arab Americans.

Little by little I pieced together the story of how they happened to be living in a small Oklahoma town. An Arab peddler named Joseph Abraham had come through Bristow in 1899 when it was still in Indian Territory. Bristow was thriving because of oil activity, and Abraham decided to settle there and become a merchant. In time he became wealthy by branching into real estate. He brought over his relatives and friends from Syria, who brought over their relatives and friends. By the time my family moved to Bristow in 1933 at least five hundred Arab Americans lived there, a substantial and prosperous part of the community.

Several of the Arab-American kids quickly became my friends; and if they were different from my Anglo friends, I never noticed. Some of their grandparents and occasionally their parents had accents, but my friends didn't. We talked the same, did the same things, even had the same religion. I knew something about Islam and Muslims because of my reading, but all the Arab Americans in Bristow were Christians, mostly Catholic but some Protestants.

I went to Boy Scout camp with Malik Khoury, played golf with Ed Naifeh, had fun on cookouts with Paul Joseph and his friends, wrote about the football heroics of Warren Shibley when I was editor of the school newspaper. My friends came out of an Arab background, but they were as American as anyone I ever knew.

One difference I did notice was that the Arab-American families tended to be larger and somehow closer together than Anglo families. A difference that meant more to me, however, was their food. When I ate at my Arab-American friends' houses, I might get meat loaf and hot dogs just as I would at home; but if I was lucky, I would be there on a day when they were having Syrian food. Then I would eat *kibbeh*—a tasty meat patty with bulgur and pine nuts—a delicious stuffed chicken called *djaaj mahshi,* grape leaf rolls, and *hummu*s, a wonderful chick-pea dish. And we might have *baklava* or *ma'amoul,* a cookie they baked mostly at

Easter, for dessert. In a small town in Oklahoma I acquired a love of Arabic food that has only grown through the years.

I have written here about the Arab-American community in Bristow for two reasons. One reason is that I am sure getting to know a different ethnic group early in life, and seeing how much we were the same made my own entry into foreign work and living easier.

The second reason is that in the late 1980s I wrote a book titled *An Ancient Heritage: The Arab-American Minority*. In my "second life" I lived and worked for several years in Arab North Africa and the Middle East. I learned a great deal about Arabs from those experiences, and my desire to write *An Ancient Heritage* stemmed partly from what I learned. But the seeds of that book, I have no doubt, were planted in my head fifty years earlier when I was growing up in Oklahoma with my Arab-American friends like Ed Naifeh and Malik Khoury.

*

After I graduated from high school, I enrolled at Oklahoma Agricultural and Mechanical College in Stillwater. The Depression was still very much with us; but my brother was now supporting himself, so Dad had a few extra dollars. I found a job waiting tables at a restaurant called the College Shop in Stillwater; for this work I received my meals. My parents were able to pay for my room and my enrollment fees, which by today's standards were absurdly small.

So I was in college but on the flimsiest of shoestrings; I sometimes had loose change in my pocket but rarely a dollar bill. I signed up as an English major, though my freshman courses were standard first-year fare: English composition, American history, mathematics, college orientation. The good stuff—the American novel, the English novel, Chaucer, Shakespeare, professional writing—would come later.

I really remember almost nothing about my freshman courses; they seemed in some ways to be a retread of high school. What I do remember is the library at Oklahoma A&M. It contained all the latest novels and nonfiction by the best and most successful writers of the time. I spent more hours with those books than I did with my textbooks. I discovered Hemingway, Fitzgerald, John Dos Passos, Somerset Maugham, and others I was to read with pleasure for years to come. I did all right in my courses, but my heart was in the library.

Something much more important than the library happened to me the very first day of the fall semester—the most important thing that has ever happened in my life. Waiting in the long line to sign up for my first semester courses, I began a casual conversation with the slender, brown-haired girl standing in front of me. I learned that her name was Martha White, that she came from Roswell, New Mexico, and was at Oklahoma

Wife-to-be, Martha White, in 1940

A&M because her sister, a junior, was studying in the college's highly regarded School of Home Economics.

After about an hour an announcement came over the public-address system that all persons whose last name began with *N* through *Z* should leave and come back the next day. Those with *A* through *M* names were to stay and enroll. I don't know why, but something told me I wanted to know this girl from Roswell better. Although I was supposed to stay, I stepped out of line when she started to leave.

"I'm tired of standing here," I said. "Why don't we go get a Coke?"

She agreed, and afterward I walked her back to Murray Hall, the girls' dormitory where she lived. Before I left, I asked her to go to a movie with me the next night, and again she said yes. Fortunately, that was one of the few times I had an extra dollar in my pocket. From that moment on I never went with any girl but Martha, and she never went with any boy but me.

At the beginning of my sophomore year, a well-known teacher of professional writing, Thomas H. Uzzell, joined the Oklahoma A&M English faculty. I desperately wanted to get into his course, called Fundamentals of Fiction, but it was open only to seniors and graduate students. I went to see him, pled my case, and left him some of my stories, including "Samson." He read them and let me in; I was dizzy with excitement.

Except for meeting Martha, becoming a student of Tom Uzzell was the most important thing that happened to me in all my college years. He was a successful short-story writer and a great teacher. I learned about character development, plotting, conflict, atmosphere, unified emotional effect, and other elements of story writing that I had never dreamed of. I wrote my heart out for Mr. Uzzell, and he read everything I wrote carefully, giving me his patient, wise analysis of what I was doing wrong and what I was doing right.

I quit my job at the College Shop so that I could have more time for writing and was trying to live on the $25 a month that my parents sent me. Martha worked at a college cafeteria and sometimes brought me food after the evening meal. That helped but it wasn't enough. I told Mr. Uzzell I had to sell some stories because I was starving.

"Write pulp," he said.

At that time, before television took their place, many magazines printed a particular kind of story: detective stories, Western stories, sports stories, science fiction stories, and others. These magazines were called "pulps" because they were printed on inexpensive, coarse paper. Such magazines as the *Saturday Evening Post* and *Good Housekeeping* were printed on costly coated paper and were called "slicks." There were many more pulp magazines than slicks, and they used many more stories. They were easier to sell to than the slicks but paid much less.

I chose the Western pulps because I was, after all, an Oklahoman and knew something about the West; also the Oklahoma A&M library had a fine section of Western Americana where I could do research. After a number of stories that brought printed rejection slips, I began to sell. The pulps paid only a penny a word, but a five-thousand-word story would bring a check for $50. In those days $50 seemed like a small fortune to me.

And then at the end of my sophomore year came another bombshell. Mr. Uzzell offered me a part-time job in his office doing routine tasks. I could still take courses on a reduced schedule, and I would earn $100 a month. With my story checks, my income would be at least $150 a month. I was rich!

Martha and I decided to get married and we did, just three months after I began working for Mr. Uzzell. Perhaps that was hurrying things, but we knew we were in love; and now that I was making enough money to support us, we saw no reason to wait. We were young and, despite the Depression, had the confidence of youth.

We got off to a great start. We had a nice little apartment, my work for Tom Uzzell was going well, my story sales were outnumbering rejections by a com-

fortable margin. What could stop us now? we asked. That question was soon answered. On December 7, 1941—five months after our marriage—the Japanese bombed Pearl Harbor. Within a week we were at war with both Japan and Germany.

*

The Depression disappeared overnight. Suddenly America was bursting with energy, and there were more jobs than workers to fill them. Everybody had money to spend. Did it really take a war to put the country back to work? I am sure it did not, but during the Depression the enemy had been vague and shapeless: lack of confidence, demoralization, uncertainty, fear. Now the enemy was very clear and had a huge headstart that we had to overcome.

I enlisted in the U.S. Navy, opting for a newly established unit called the Seabees, which stood for Construction Battalions (the initials CB being the basis for the nickname). The Seabees would operate in the Pacific, and their job would be to build airstrips, docks, fuel tanks, barracks, hospitals, and other necessities for holding onto islands that we would win back from the Japanese. I liked the idea of being in this new unit with such a specific purpose, and—always thinking about writing—I imagined the great story material my experiences would yield.

I reported to Camp Peary in Virginia for training, and Martha took a job with the Douglas Aircraft factory in Tulsa. Parting was hard. We had seldom been away from each other since we had met in line at Oklahoma A&M. Now we had no way of knowing when we would see each other again; it might be years.

As I was soon to learn, war takes strange twists for the individuals involved in it. After only a few days at Camp Peary, I was called into the personnel office. Someone there, examining the records of new recruits, discovered that I had over two years of college, was an English major, and had published stories. The personnel officer decided that I could be useful drafting letters, reports, and doing other paper work required by the camp's personnel office.

That was the end of my idea of serving in the Pacific with a Seabee battalion. I was assigned to Camp Peary's "ship's company," the men selected to run the camp, and I was there for two years. I would be untruthful if I said that I was unhappy at being assigned to Camp Peary, but it was a shock. I was doing useful war work but certainly not the kind I had expected to do.

After it became clear that I would be at Camp Peary for some time, Martha quit her job at Douglas Aircraft and came to live in Williamsburg, the town nearest the camp. Housing was very tight, but she was able to find a room in the home of an old Virginia family. I couldn't always get away from camp, but I was able to spend quite a bit of time with her, and on short leaves and weekends we explored Richmond, Washington, DC, and other nearby cities. On a trip to New York, I was able to visit some of my editors whom I had known only from their letters.

After two years Camp Peary's ship's company was cut down, and I was transferred out. To my considerable disappointment I was not assigned to a Seabee battalion but rather to the naval amphibious forces, where I suppose the need for men was greater. The war was moving inexorably toward an invasion of Japan itself, and massive amphibious forces would be needed to establish beachheads. I was assigned to an LST, which stood for Landing Ship (Tank). It was the largest and slowest of all the navy's amphibious vessels, but it could carry large amounts of war equipment in its huge hold. Battle-hardened oldtimers said that LST actually stood for Large Slow Target, but in months in the Pacific my ship never came under fire. We made one beachhead landing on the island of Borneo, but the Japanese had already been beaten back by aerial attacks and the guns of our big ships that prepared the way for us.

My LST covered much of the Pacific: the Philippines, New Guinea, and the Dutch East Indies (now Indonesia). We were moving material and sometimes men, and the rumors grew ever stronger that the invasion of Japan would come soon. Projections—these were not rumors—were that a million U.S. soldiers, Marines, and sailors might be casualties in this invasion. But there was no invasion. In early August 1945, the U.S. dropped atomic bombs on Hiroshima and Nagasaki, and a few days later the Japanese surrendered. The war was over.

In my memoir *The Times of My Life,* published in 1990, I have written more fully of my World War II experiences. But if I had to boil down to the barest essentials what I learned from those years, this is what I would say:

Our nation working together can accomplish almost anything.

The world is a big, exciting place.

Martha worked at the post office in Roswell while I was in the Pacific. After I was discharged from the navy, we returned to Stillwater in 1946 and easily picked up the threads of our former life. We enrolled once more at Oklahoma A&M, and a benign government's GI Bill of Rights for veterans helped with educational expenses. I had not published during the war; but I had kept a journal, so my writing was not too rusty. I began to sell stories again with little difficulty.

I had learned a great deal from writing for the pulp magazines: the importance of a fresh idea, putting my characters in lots of conflict, catching the reader's interest early, keeping the story moving. I continued to sell some Western stories, but my old mentor, Tom Uzzell, told me not to stay in the pulps too long. "You've learned all you can there," he said. "Branch out." So I graduated from the pulps and found that I could sell stories to other kinds of magazines. But my interest in

the West persisted, and I even placed one scholarly article with the University of California's *Western Folklore.*

We finished our undergraduate degrees—Martha taking hers in home economics—and I went on to take a master's degree in English. I was offered an appointment as instructor in the Oklahoma A&M English department and took it. As an instructor a large part of my teaching duties was freshman composition, but occasionally I was given a plum such as creative writing or the survey course in American literature. I liked teaching from the beginning, but I quickly saw how much I had to learn to be a good teacher. And I wanted to be good. Like the teacher in Chaucer's tale, I would gladly "lerne and gladly teche."

Life in Stillwater moved crisply and happily for Martha and me; ten years went by in a hurry. We built a small but pleasant house with redwood siding, a fireplace, and a big picture window. Our two daughters were born in the hospital just a block from our house, Melissa in 1950, Jennifer in 1952—two lovely redheads who brightened our days from the moments of their arrivals. It seemed that we were settling down to comfortable lives in an Oklahoma college town and that I was settling into a career as a teacher and writer.

*

Then in 1955, completely out of the blue, I had a chance to go to Africa as a worker in the United States' new program of technical assistance to developing countries. The United States had emerged from World War II as the richest and most powerful country in the world. Instead of sinking back into the isolationism, the fear of foreign entanglements, that had prevailed throughout most of the nation's history, America now took a leading role on the world stage.

The U.S. Marshall Plan helped the war-ravaged countries of Europe back to economic health. President Harry Truman started a Technical Cooperation Administration through which American technicians would help the poor countries of Africa, Asia, and Latin America improve their standards of agriculture, education, and health. This type of foreign aid quickly became known as the Point Four Program simply because President Truman had proposed it in the fourth point of his inaugural address.

Because of its fine agricultural department, Oklahoma A&M was asked by Point Four officials in Washington to help the African country of Ethiopia build an agricultural college and train its faculty. A&M agreed and had been sending agricultural experts to Ethiopia for several years. Now the Ethiopian Ministry of Education wanted Point Four advisors to help in the creation of books and other reading material for their elementary, middle, and secondary schools. Oklahoma A&M was asked to recruit the education advisors.

Because of my writing experience, I was offered one of the jobs. I could scarcely believe it. A chance to go to Africa! Ethiopia, the country of towering mountains and "valleys of dreadful depth" that I had read about years ago. Until then I don't believe I had ever thought about the great importance of the reading we do when we are young. All those books, fiction and nonfiction, that I had read about Africa and Asia as a boy were still in my conscious and unconscious memory. I could practically hear some inner voice whispering, "Come on! Now's your chance. Don't pass it up."

The decision to take the job was easy to make. Martha and our daughters would go with me, of course. The assignment was for two years, after which time we would return to Stillwater, and I would rejoin the A&M English department. Martha was as eager as I was to take advantage of this opportunity to see some more of the world; Melissa was five and Jennifer was three, both young enough to adapt easily to the change. As described to me, the work in Ethiopia sounded worthwhile and interesting; but in truth I'm sure I was thinking more about the rich lode of story material this remote African country would yield.

So we leased our house, packed our bags, and set out for a two-year adventure. We thought. What we were really doing was beginning our second life which would last twenty-five years and take us over much of Africa and Asia.

*

Ethiopia, located in the horn of Africa, was a strange new world, beautiful in some ways, far from beautiful in others. We lived in Addis Ababa, the capital city of the country. Addis sits almost on the equator, but at an elevation of eight thousand feet, the climate is splendid most of the time. The beauty was in the encircling mountains, the tall eucalyptus trees growing everywhere, the people in their shammas—long white wraparound clothes with colorful edgings worn by both men and women. The ugliness was in the open sewers, the poverty, the sight of too many thin, sickly children.

We had a nice house in a fenced-in compound, and before long the girls had acquired a black goat and a little brown monkey whom they named Chip; he was gentle, smart, and loved everyone in our family. Melissa went to first grade in a primary school organized by wives of American embassy and foreign aid workers. The only nursery school in Addis was run by the small French community, and we enrolled Jennifer in it even though she didn't know a word of French. But she learned, soon had a French friend named Monique she traded home visits with, and before long started dropping French words and phrases around the house, to Melissa's considerable annoyance. Martha enjoyed learning to shop in the big open-air vegetable market. Vegetables, fruits, and melons were plentiful and delicious; but any meat besides tough, stringy beef and small, tough chickens was not to be found—unless we acquired a taste for goat.

From the first day I found my work in Ethiopia absorbing. I met Russell Davis, who would be my Point Four partner for the next two years, and our tasks were explained to us by the head of the Point Four education program and the director-general of the Ethiopian Ministry of Education. Ethiopian schools, we were told, were desperate for teaching materials, particularly materials in Amharic, the national language of Ethiopia, and materials which would teach Ethiopian students about their own country and its history.

In order to get reading materials into the schools quickly, my job was to start two magazines along the lines of the American school magazines, *My Weekly Reader* and *Junior Scholastic*. One of the magazines, for elementary grades, would be published in Amharic; the other, for middle and secondary schools, would be in English, the language of education after the elementary level. Russ Davis was to work on a series of readers and math books in Amharic. We would have young Ethiopian counterparts working with us to learn and carry on the work after we were gone.

Russ and I said that was fine. We thought we could do what the director-general wanted, but first we would have to learn something about Ethiopia, its people, its languages. Russ was a gifted language learner; by the time he had been in Ethiopia for a few weeks, he was speaking Amharic, as well as writing it. I struggled with the language the whole time I was in Ethiopia; I never got really good with it, but I never gave up.

After our talk with the director-general, Russ and I loaded a Land Rover with sleeping bags and extra gas cans and, with our Ethiopian counterparts, Amara Worku and Million Neqneq, traveled Ethiopia's sometimes almost-nonexistent roads for a month. We slept on the ground, on classroom floors, and occasionally in a lumpy hotel bed. We learned to eat and enjoy *wat,* the Ethiopian national dish, and to soak up the fiery red sauce with a slightly sour gray bread called *injera* that we also grew to like.

We talked with headmasters and teachers and saw that the need for teaching materials really was desperate. In one school we visited, the students were struggling with a few copies of *The Vicar of Wakefield* that had been donated by a British publisher. I had read Oliver Goldsmith's novel in a graduate course in English literature and had found it hard going. It must have been almost meaningless to ninth-grade students in Ethiopia.

We visited Aksum, the holy city, where the kingdom of Ethiopia had its beginnings almost three thousand years ago. It is called Ethiopia's holy city because in the fourth century one of the Aksumite kings became a believer in the teachings of Jesus and spread Christianity throughout the area. Thus Ethiopia was one of the first Christian countries in Africa.

We became acquainted with the many different culture groups of Ethiopia: the Amharas, Gallas, Guragies, and others. We stayed for a few days with the Falasha

Martha teaching home economics at Empress Mene School in Addis Ababa, Ethiopia, 1956

people, who are often called the "black Jews" of Ethiopia because they practice the Judaic religion. The Falasha believe they came to Ethiopia in the time of King Solomon. They say they came with the Queen of Sheba when she returned to Ethiopia from a trip to Israel. In fact, some biblical scholars believe that Ethiopia may have been the home of the Queen of Sheba. The legend of Sheba and Solomon is one of the most ancient and best-loved stories in Ethiopia.

Russ and I discovered that every Ethiopian culture group had its own rich store of legends and folk stories. As we traveled throughout the country during our two-year assignment, we recorded many of them for use in the books and magazines we published for Ethiopian schools. The greatest storyteller we met in all our months in Ethiopia was an old Somali man named Zor who lived in the ancient town of Harar. We had heard that many people considered Zor a wizard because he could do a strange, inexplicable thing: he could charm the wildest and most untamable of all African animals, the hyena, and make them take food from his hand.

Zor's home was a one-room mud hut called a *tukal* near the *Budaber* (Gate of the Evil-eyed People), and we went there one night and asked him if he would

show us how he charmed wild hyenas. If Zor was surprised to see two Americans appear at his door, he did not show it. He invited us into his grassroofed *tukal,* which was partially lighted by a feebly flickering kerosene lantern. Zor asked us to sit in the shadows; he then took some bloody sheep bones from a basket and sat down cross-legged in the middle of the dirt floor.

We expected him to chant or beat a drum or use some other magic device, but instead he began to talk just as if he were speaking to people outside. "Abdullah," he called, "are you out there? Maymoonah, I have a nice bone for you. Zachariah, are you hungry tonight?"

He called other names, and in less than a minute we began to hear the soft padding of feet and low, deep-throated growls from the darkness outside. And then we saw them—more than a dozen huge, shaggy-coated hyenas moving restlessly back and forth in front of the *tukal* door. Occasionally, one would stop and peer inside, then suddenly jump back into the darkness.

"Maymoonah," the old man called, "I know you are there. Come in or I will give this bone to another."

That seemed to do the trick. One of the hyenas, a big, buff-colored beast, halted in the doorway and finally put her head into the hut. Zor held a meaty bone out to her and coaxed her softly. The hyena's eyes blazed toward the shadows where we sat, and she backed up a step. But her hunger seemed to conquer her fear; she slunk into the room, snatched the bone from Zor's hand, and bolted through the door. We could hear her crunching the bone in her powerful jaws, and the growls of the other hyenas grew louder.

Maymoonah's bravery seemed to give courage to the rest of the pack. The giant called Abdullah came in at once when his name was called. After that they came in eagerly, and sometimes there were three hyenas in the room at once; but as soon as they had their bone, they scrambled frantically through the door.

When the last bone was gone, Zor called out, "Enough. Be gone." Instantly the sounds of growling and of padding feet were gone from the yard outside. The night was eerily quiet.

Russ and I told Zor that we were amazed at what we had seen. Zor waved his hand and said it hadn't been good because the hyenas were frightened by our presence. Usually, he said, he made the hyenas sit down in front of him, take the bone from his hand, and eat it in the hut. We asked Zor if he could tell us how he came to have this strange power over hyenas.

Instead of answering us directly, Zor told us a story. There was a woman named Bizunesh who was newly married to a man with a young son named Segab. Bizunesh loved Segab, but he seemed to hate his new stepmother. She tried every way she could to please him, but nothing worked. Finally, Bizunesh went to a wizard and asked him to make her a love potion to put in Segab's food so that he would love her. The wizard said he could make a love potion, but in order to make it he would have to have three whiskers from a fierce lion that lived in the nearby black-rock desert. How she got the whiskers, the wizard said, was her problem, not his.

The heart of the story tells how Bizunesh slowly wins the lion's confidence by bringing him food, each day getting a little closer until the lion comes close enough for her to clip some whiskers from his face. When Bizunesh runs to the wizard with the whiskers, he tells her that she doesn't need a love potion. "You learned how to approach the lion—slowly, a little at a time. Do the same with your stepson, and he will surely love you."

The best folk stories from all countries have a meaning or point, and that is the kind of Ethiopian stories that Russ and I used in our books and magazines for the country's schools. My counterpart, Amara Worku, and I started two magazines, one in English for middle schools and high schools called *Time to Read* and one in Amharic for the elementary grades called *Yemambeb Gize,* which means "time to read." Both magazines contained folktales, history, and current events—all Ethiopian. Sometimes we used easy-to-understand articles on health, nutrition, and other useful subjects. We printed twenty-five thousand copies of *Yemambeb* Gize and ten thousand copies of *Time to Read.* Those numbers couldn't begin to meet the need for the whole country, but it was a start. After a few trial issues paid for by Point Four, the cost of publication was built into the Ministry of Education budget.

Some of my warmest memories from years of working in developing countries are those of being at an Ethiopian school on a day when *Yemambeb Gize* or *Time to Read* was being passed out to the students. That truly was "time to read," and read the students did, quietly and with complete concentration on stories they could understand and that had been written just for them. A few days later, after they had been over everything with the teacher, they would take their copy home. More than once I saw a student reading his magazine to his parents or grandparents.

Martha, Melissa, and Jennifer traveled with me a number of times on my trips around Ethiopia and got a real feeling for the beauty and variety of the country. Martha herself became involved in Ethiopian education in a special way. When the headmistress of Empress Menen School for Girls in Addis discovered that Martha had a degree in home economics, she asked her to teach machine sewing, cooking, and nutrition. Martha had never taught school, even practice teaching, but she felt she should try. I am sure Martha worked far harder on her lesson preparations than any of her students worked, but her hard work had its reward. I heard from many Empress Menen staff members that Martha was a good and well-liked teacher.

Two years passed with unbelievable swiftness; suddenly the time had come for us to return to Stillwater and resume our life in Oklahoma. The head of the English department wrote me that I would be promoted to assistant professor. But Point Four asked me to stay in overseas work; the agency wanted me to go to the newly independent North African country of Libya where a large Point Four program was taking shape.

This time Martha and I pondered our decision long and hard. We knew we were at a crossroads. Going to Libya with Point Four would mean severing our ties with Oklahoma A&M (which had recently been renamed Oklahoma State University). More important, if we stayed overseas, Jennifer and Melissa would miss all that American schools had to offer, at least in the early years of their education.

On the other hand, they were having rare and valuable experiences in seeing other parts of the world, getting to know other peoples, hearing other languages and experimenting with using them. We decided those were good educational trade-offs for our daughters; and after our two years in Ethiopia, Martha and I were sure we wanted to stay in foreign life and work. I resigned from Oklahoma State University, and we went to Libya.

*

Ethiopia was immensely important to me as a writer. I had never written for children or young adults; but I felt the things I had learned in Ethiopia about understanding other cultures and about people of different cultures understanding each other seemed worth sharing with young readers. My Point Four buddy, Russ Davis, felt the same way, so we decided to write our first children's book together. We called it *The Lion's Whiskers,* and in it we looked at the people of Ethiopia through their folk stories. We began our book with our visit to Zor, the hyena man, and his story about Bizunesh and what she learned from getting the lion's whiskers. *The Lion's Whiskers* is out of print now, but in its day it went through several printings and had an edition in Great Britain.

After *The Lion's Whiskers* the greatest part of my writing time overseas was devoted to books for young readers. My experiences in Libya and later in Nigeria and India were yielding material that I thought would be of interest to children and young adults. And I found that I enjoyed writing for a younger audience. Perhaps the reason was that I still remembered the pleasure I received as a boy from the books I read. I know that I enjoyed taking a subject and shaping it in a way that would make it most enjoyable and most meaningful to young readers.

Russ Davis and I discovered that we liked writing together just as we had liked working together in Ethiopia. Although he returned to America and became a teacher and then a professor at Harvard University and I continued overseas, we found that we could write together. We worked in a variety of ways. Sometimes I would write the entire first draft of a book, and he would edit and revise; sometimes it was the other way around. Sometimes a subject called for library research, which from his Harvard base Russ could do better. Often I collected material for our books in the country I was in. In some cases Russ wrote part of a book and I wrote part. The subject dictated the way we divided the tasks. But the collaboration worked. In all, we wrote seven books together while I was overseas, and we learned a lot from each other.

Libya gave the Ashabranner family a chance to experience an Arab culture. In our two years there, I pieced together the legend of an ancient bedouin tribe called the Bani Hilal, which means the sons of Hilal. In its time the tribe roamed over much of the Middle East and North Africa; literally hundreds of stories had been told about the Bani Hilal. Russ and I retold the best of them in a book we called *Ten Thousand Desert Swords.*

Our next assignment was in the West African country of Nigeria. Melissa and Jennifer had gone to an American school at Wheelus Air Base, a U.S. installation in Libya, and they would go to a small private British school in Lagos, the city in which we would live in Nigeria. We knew they would get good instruction in the fundamentals of reading, writing, and arithmetic.

The Ashabranner family leaving Libya after a two-year stint, 1959

The year was 1960, and I was excited about going to Nigeria. For more than a century a colony of Great Britain, Nigeria was about to receive its independence. The most populous country in Africa, rich in oil and other resources, it was certain to become a leader on the African continent. For me, the time to be working with the Ministry of Education couldn't be better.

Two things of great importance in my life and career happened during our two years in Nigeria. The first was that John F. Kennedy created the Peace Corps in 1961 as one of his first acts as president. Sargent Shriver, the first Peace Corps director, came to Nigeria to see if that country might be interested in receiving Peace Corps volunteers; although I was with the Agency for International Development (the new name for the U.S. foreign aid program), I was assigned to be Shriver's escort officer while he was in Nigeria. I liked everything I heard about the Peace Corps, and apparently Shriver liked me. Nigeria wanted the Peace Corps, and Shriver appointed me to set up the country's first program. That was the beginning of my nine years as a Peace Corps staff member in Nigeria, India, and Washington.

The second important thing that happened to me in Nigeria was that I became a nonfiction writer. Although I had written a few nonfiction pieces over the years, I had always thought of myself as a fiction writer. During my first year in Nigeria, I wrote a young adult novel entitled *Strangers in Africa.* Helen Jones, a wonderful editor at the publishing firm of Little, Brown in Boston, was my first children's book editor. She coaxed me into nonfiction. The year was 1962, and she said the time was right for an up-to-date book about West Africa because black Americans were becoming increasingly interested in their historic roots. I was a storyteller, I reminded Helen, not a geographer.

"Tell the story of West Africa," Helen said.

I tried. I really tried. I had a good title, *Land in the Sun,* but I hated that manuscript from the beginning. It seemed plodding and dull, and I couldn't get over the idea that I was writing nonfiction. I had to be able to document everything I wrote. What fiction writer could tolerate such a restriction?

I was setting up the first Peace Corps program for Nigeria while I was trying to write *Land in the Sun.* I dragged that wretched manuscript all over the country, writing in the back of Jeeps and at night in government rest houses. No matter where I was, it didn't sound any better.

Sargent Shriver called me to Washington for consultation. I put what I had written of *Land in the Sun* in my briefcase, thinking of the long in-flight hours and nights in hotel rooms. When I returned to Lagos and unpacked my briefcase, the manuscript was missing. I had left it on a plane or in a hotel room, and there was no copy. Strangely, I felt relieved.

After a few days, I wrote Helen and told her there would be no *Land in the Sun.* On the way to post the letter, I stopped at my office. A large brown manila envelope was on my desk; the return address was the Algonquin Hotel in New York, where I had last stayed. Inside was my manuscript and a letter from the hotel's assistant manager saying a maid had found it in the desk of the room I had occupied. He said he was sure I would be happy to get it back.

I wasn't happy. I had decided that I just wasn't a nonfiction writer and that I now could go happily back to writing fiction. But I sat down and read the pages again. In the days I had been separated from the manuscript something had happened; I seemed to be reading it for the first time. The opening chapter about Nigeria's independence celebrations at the end of British rule—which I had witnessed personally—was interesting and full of colorful detail. So were the chapters on the Yoruba, Fulani, and Ibo people—people I had come to know at firsthand.

I was cautiously optimistic. I added two more chapters, gave the manuscript a subtitle, *The Story of West Africa,* and sent it to Russ Davis. He liked it, did some editing, and sent the manuscript to Helen Jones. She liked it and didn't ask for any changes. I must have done something right. *Land in the Sun* stayed in print for years and was the best-selling book that Russ and I had as a writing team.

Our collaboration came to an end with *Land in the Sun.* Russ became so involved with his Harvard teaching and I with the Peace Corps that we couldn't stay in the close touch needed for successful collaborative work. But we had fun writing together and learning together; we remain close friends to this day.

I have written very little fiction since *Land in the Sun* was published. While I was working on *A Moment in History,* my book about the Peace Corps, I became

"With Jack Vaughn, director of the Peace Corps, on Vaughn's first trip to India," 1965

increasingly comfortable with the nonfiction form. And I felt that the experiences my family and I had had and were still having in Africa and Asia could be written about particularly well as nonfiction.

*

After I got the Peace Corps program in Nigeria underway, Sargent Shriver asked me to move to India to help with the program there. I am often asked which foreign country, of all I have lived in, is my favorite. I always hedge my answer. Because it was our first foreign assignment, Ethiopia perhaps seemed most exciting and exotic. But in Libya we experienced the vast Sahara Desert and lived beside the beautiful Mediterranean Sea. Nigeria gave us the opportunity to learn about and develop a deep appreciation for African art, which at its best has an emotional power that can scarcely be equaled. In every country we had good friends.

So I have no favorite country; at the same time I know that India made the deepest impression on me and left me with the warmest memories. We lived there nearly four years. We formed deep friendships; after thirty years, some of our Indian friends still visit us in the United States. Martha became an excellent cook of Indian food, learning from her many friends. Melissa and Jennifer were older and could experience the culture more fully; India is the country they have chosen to return to for visits.

India was most special to me because of the Peace Corps volunteers. The Peace Corps program in India became the largest in the world in 1965 while I was director, with over seven hundred volunteers serving all over the country. I had transferred to India before I had a chance to get to know the Nigeria Peace Corps volunteers well. India was different; I traveled the country for four years visiting volunteers at their work. Not all were successful; a few quit before their assignments were finished. But most stayed, did valuable work, and made a real contribution in their two years of service.

Their lives were not easy. Without exception they faced times of frustration and loneliness; but, also without exception, every volunteer I talked with at the end of his or her tour was glad to have been in India. Some were teachers in isolated schools; others worked in villages helping poor farmers raise better poultry and crops; volunteer nurses trained young Indian student nurses in poorly equipped hospitals; volunteers taught health and nutrition to villagers. These young Americans worked closely with the people in dozens of useful activities, and in doing so came to know India in a deep and personal way.

I have written about my Peace Corps experiences— rich beyond measure—in *A Moment in History,* out of print for some years, and more recently in *The Times of My Life.*

*

In 1966, I was called back to Washington by Jack Vaughn, who replaced Shriver as director of the Peace Corps. Vaughn asked me to be director of training and then deputy director of the Peace Corps. As far as Martha and I were concerned, the timing was perfect for returning to America. Our daughters could finish high school in their own country; and we could help them get started on their lives beyond high school before we returned overseas, which we were sure we wanted to do.

Things do not always turn out as planned or hoped for, but for us this time they did. We bought a house in the Maryland suburbs of Washington, and Melissa and Jennifer graduated from Walter Johnson High School there. Melissa went on to take a bachelor's degree in anthropology at Temple University and a master's degree in public and private management at Yale University. Today she is executive editor and part owner of a very good community newspaper on Capitol Hill in Washington.

Jennifer took some college courses but decided that her interests lay elsewhere. She had always loved pets and had for years been interested in photography. She took professional training in small pet grooming and studied photography in special programs at Northern Virginia Community College and at the Smithsonian Institution. Today she grooms dogs and cats (and occasionally a guinea pig and rabbit!), takes pet photographs for doting owners, and has other professional photography assignments. She lives in Alexandria, Virginia, less than half an hour from Melissa's home in Washington.

Being sworn in as deputy directory of the Peace Corps by Vice President Hubert Humphrey, 1967

After our daughters were well started on the tracks I have just described, Martha and I returned overseas. I joined the Ford Foundation and became officer-in-charge of their Philippine program. The Ford Foundation is one of the largest private philanthropic foundations in the world, with many programs in the United States and developing countries. Essentially, its work is to give financial assistance to organizations that are carrying out innovative programs in education, agriculture, health, and other fields concerned with the quality of life.

My work with the Ford Foundation was a continuation of foreign assistance activity I had begun with Point Four and carried on with the Peace Corps. Giving financial assistance to worthy organizations may sound like an ideal job, and in many ways it is. But it is harder than it might seem to choose between many applications, to research the soundness of the organization to which you may give money, and to monitor its use of the money.

In 1976 I was transferred from the Philippines to the Ford Foundation's program in Indonesia, and Martha and I lived in Jakarta, the capital city, for four years. We found our lives in the island nations of Southeast Asia fascinating and sailing "the shallow seas" between the islands reminded me of all the Joseph Conrad novels I had read.

Both the Philippines and Indonesia have a rich heritage of traditional arts—textiles, basketry, brass casting, figure carving—the arts of the people. My work called for me to travel a great deal in both countries, and Martha and I had ample opportunity to study the village arts, an interest of ours since our days in Africa and India. While we were in the Philippines and Indonesia, we published a series of articles about the arts of the Southeast Asian islands in the magazine *Arts of Asia.* Martha did much of the research and took the photographs, and I supplied the words. Working together this way gave our stay in the Philippines and Indonesia an added dimension and, besides, was just plain fun.

*

In 1980 Martha and I began our third life; we decided the time had come to conclude our overseas work and return to America to stay. We wanted to be nearer Jennifer and Melissa, and I wanted at last to devote all of my working time to writing. This I have done except for occasionally making room in my schedule to talk with students, teachers, and librarians.

I have concentrated on nonfiction for upper elementary, middle school, and high school students; and about half of my books have dealt with immigrants and growing ethnic groups in America, including Native Americans. I think that years of living in other cultures have made me better able to write about the hopes, fears, frustrations and achievements of immigrants and ethnic minorities.

Although I now write only nonfiction, I have not forgotten the tools of the fiction writer, which took me so long to learn. I will always be a storyteller. But per-

haps the hardest task of the nonfiction writer is to find the story and its proper form in his material. Speaking of his work, the great English sculptor Henry Moore wrote, "You begin with a block and you have to find the sculpture that's inside it. You have to overcome the resistance of the material by sheer determination and hard work."

Moore might have been talking about the nonfiction writer's task. You have collected a tremendous amount of material on your subject: stacks of interview and field notes, books, reports, newspaper and periodical clippings. They are stacked on your desk, your worktable, the shelves around you. That is your block, and you must find the story that is somewhere inside. You have to keep searching no matter how long it takes.

I wanted to write a book about refugees and asked Melissa to work on it with me. We interviewed refugees and collected refugee material for two years before we found the way to tell our story through the voices of refugee children from Vietnam, Cambodia, and other countries, children who had been set adrift in the world alone, without parents, family, or loved ones. Here was the story inside the great amount of material we had collected, the story that would touch young readers and

With older daughter, Melissa, in Washington, DC, 1988

make them think deeply and feel deeply about the plight of refugees. We called our book *Into a Strange Land.*

Many of my books deal with serious social issues and problems. I think I can make these issues and problems interesting to readers of all ages by keeping the focus on the people who are caught up in them. In *Gavriel and Jemal: Two Boys of Jerusalem* I explored the gulf separating Arabs and Jews in the Middle East by comparing and contrasting the lives of an Israeli Jewish boy and a Palestinian Arab boy who live almost side by side in the Old City of Jerusalem. In *Born to the Land: An American Portrait* I examined the great environmental and economic problems of farmers and ranchers in America today by telling the stories of people in one Southwestern community who are determined that the way of life they know and love will endure.

No matter what social issues or problems my books may deal with, I have one overriding hope for each of them: that the people I write about will emerge as human beings whose lives are real and valuable and who have a right to strive for decent lives. If I can get that truth across, young readers will hear it and know what I am talking about.

*

Paul Conklin's photographs illustrate most of my recent books. Good illustrations are essential to young readers' nonfiction today. Properly done, they expand the text and contribute to a more interesting, more readable, more informative book. In Paul I have a master who sets the highest standards for himself. We first met in Nigeria when I was starting the Peace Corps program, and Paul was an adventurous young freelance photographer learning to make a living with his camera. Later he joined the Peace Corps as a staff photographer and visited me in India.

I can't imagine writing a book and then hiring a photographer to take some pictures for it. Paul and I care about the same things, and we usually develop a book idea together; as often as possible we travel together, sharing the experiences of talking to people and taking pictures. When the time comes for me to lock myself in my study and write, I have Paul's pictures to help keep mood and memory alive.

Nothing pleases me more, though, than the fact that Jennifer has become the photographer for several of my books. Our first book together was *Always to Remember,* which is the story of the Vietnam Veterans Memorial, and I think no book has meant more to me. In it I tried to tell the human story of the memorial. *Always to Remember* is the story of Jan Scruggs, a Vietnam veteran determined that every American man and woman who died in the Vietnam War would have his or her name on a national memorial. It is the story of Maya Ying Lin, an architectural student at Yale, who in a magic half hour at the memorial site envisioned a design that would be chosen over designs by some of America's best-known architects and artists. But more

With daughter Jennifer in Williamsburg, Virginia, 1989

than anything I wanted the book to be the story of millions of Americans who have found in the memorial an emotional meeting ground that has helped to bring a divided nation together.

Jennifer's photographs complemented my text perfectly and helped to convey the powerful emotional quality of the memorial. Some of her photographs from the book have been reprinted in the *New York Times, USA Today, Parenting,* and in several textbooks. *Always to Remember* was selected as both an American Library Association Notable Children's Book and a Best Book for Young Adults. What a start for Jennifer as a book photographer! I cautioned her not to expect that kind of reception for every book.

Our next book together was *Crazy about German Shepherds,* something very different for me and a book that used Jennifer's expertise with dogs. It is the story of a friend of Jennifer's, Peggy O'Callaghan, who has made a career for herself raising and caring for dogs. Working on this book was fun for both of us, and we want to do another dog book sometime.

Our third book was *A Grateful Nation: The Story of Arlington National Cemetery,* which I think contains some of Jennifer's best photography; several reviewers complimented her work. We are now finishing a book about the Lincoln Memorial.

The author with his soccer-star granddaughter, Olivia-Jené Fagon, 2005

Into a Strange Land, my first collaboration with Melissa, was also selected as an American Library Association Notable Children's Book and in addition received a Christopher Award. We wrote another book, *Counting America,* about the United States census, and we would like to collaborate on more books. Perhaps we will, but Melissa is very busy now with the newspaper, a husband, and two energetic young children.

And what of a fourth life? Martha says that we should stay with this one for a while longer, and I am sure she is right. Williamsburg is a wonderful place to live; there are many more books I want to write; and Martha is busy with our house and with community projects such as recycling waste materials.

But, still, thinking ahead is fun.

Brent Ashabranner contributed the following update to *SATA* in 2006:

In my 1992 autobiographical essay for *SATA,* I wrote about the "three lives" that I had enjoyed to that point in the twentieth century. My first life covered thirty-five years of growing up in Oklahoma and becoming a husband, father, writer, and teacher there—a happy, provincial midwesterner. My second life spanned twenty-five years of living and working in Ethiopia, Libya, Nigeria, India, the Philippines, and Indonesia. My third life began in 1980 when my wife Martha and I returned to the United States, settled in Williamsburg, Virginia, and I devoted full time to writing. I remember that in 1992, after twelve years in Williamsburg, I was beginning to wonder what my fourth life would be and when it would begin.

Well, I am still wondering. I knew after years of living in Africa and Asia and writing about those parts of the world that I wanted to write about my own country. What I did not know was how much there would be to say! With one deeply sad exception, the years since my autobiography in 1992 have been rich and reward-

ing. Our grandson, Giancarlo, now a high school senior, is pondering his college choice. Our fourteen-year-old granddaughter, Olivia-Jené, is a star on her soccer league team. Our daughter, Melissa, and her husband, Jean-Keith, now publish three community newspapers that have important places in Washington, DC. Our daughter, Jennifer, is thriving as a photographer and pet-care specialist. I have written sixteen more books, mostly about America and American life.

The one exception to this happy flow of life was the death from cancer of my longtime friend and photographer colleague Paul Conklin in 2003. Altogether, Paul and I collaborated on fourteen books. Four of them were American Library Association notables, one was an ALA best book for young adults, and three received the Carter G. Woodson Book Award.

Two of our last books had a special meaning for us. One was *Our Beckoning Borders: Illegal Immigration in America.* In a sense it was the capstone of our series of books about immigrants and immigration because it took a close and hard look at what a great many Americans consider one of our most serious national problems: the almost one million people who come into the country illegally every year, most with the intention of staying permanently.

The other book with special meaning for us was *A New Frontier: The Peace Corps in Eastern Europe.* Both Paul and I served on the Peace Corps staff during the 1960s, Paul as a photographer, I as country director in India and administrator elsewhere. The Peace Corps had been important in our lives and was still very much in our blood. When the Peace Corps made a major decision in the early 1990s to accept an invitation to work in Eastern European countries that had thrown off the yoke of communism, Paul and I wanted to tell that story. We told it by following the adventures of Peace Corps volunteers in Poland, the Czech Republic, Bulgaria, and Romania.

Paul was so unassuming that it was easy to forget how good a photographer he was. But when he died, *Time,* the *New York Times,* the *Washington Post,* and other prominent news media carried his obituary detailing the importance of his work: the *New York Times* mentioned one of his most famous photographs showing a young woman, protesting the Vietnam War, placing a flower in the barrel of a National Guardsman's rifle during an anti-war demonstration at the Pentagon. One of his most dramatic pictures of a terrible earthquake in Mexico City appeared on the cover of *Time.*

After Paul became ill, Sargent Shriver, first director of the Peace Corps, wrote him a letter that said: "You were the one who gave the world a look at the Peace Corps in action. Your sensitivity, compassion, intelligence, and humanity came through with every photograph you took."

My good friend was a quiet man who let his camera speak for him. It spoke beautifully.

Even while I was working with Paul, my collaboration with my photographer daughter Jennifer began and continued crisply. Our first book together, *Always to Remember: The Story of the Vietnam Veterans Memorial,* was published in 1988. A committee organized by the American Library Association in 2000 selected it as one of the one hundred best nonfiction books for young adults published between 1966 and 1999.

In the late 1990s, I was approached by Twenty-first Century Books about doing a book for them. Jennifer and I ended up doing seven!

Partly because of the success of *Always to Remember* we had been thinking of writing about some of our country's other national memorials. In fact, our next book after *Always to Remember* was *A Memorial for Mr. Lincoln.* It was inevitable that, while working on *Always to Remember,* we would fall under the spell of the beautiful Lincoln Memorial that seems to hover protectively over the Vietnam Veterans Memorial only a few hundred feet away.

The other reason I wanted to write about our national memorials was that each one tells a story about some great American or group of Americans and about some period of American history that has shaped the kind of nation we are today. I have always thought of myself as a storyteller, and each of our national memorials contains two important stories—the story of the building of the memorial itself and the story of what it stands for.

Six of our books for Twenty-first Century became the "Great American Memorials" series. For a long time I had wanted to write a second book about the Vietnam Veterans Memorial, this time putting more emphasis on the names on the great black granite wall. The first book in our series became *Their Names to Live: What the Vietnam Veterans Memorial Means to America,* and I found the perfect title for the book in Ecclesiasticus XLIV 14: "Their bodies are buried in peace, but their names liveth for evermore."

I am particularly pleased that we were able to include two impressive new memorials in our series. *Badge of Valor* tells of the creation of the National Law Enforcement Officers Memorial, located in downtown Washington, DC, and dedicated in 1991. *A Date with Destiny* is about the Women in Military Service for America Memorial, dedicated in 1997, which stands at the entrance to Arlington National Cemetery. Both of these memorials, in their own special way, tell the story of the many thousands of courageous men and women who have served our nation since its very beginning and who continue to do so.

I think that for us the most challenging book in our "Great American Memorials" series was *Remembering Korea: The Korean War Veterans Memorial.* Together with the Lincoln Memorial and the Vietnam Veterans Memorial, the Korean War Veterans Memorial forms a triangle of historic beauty at the western end of the National Mall in our nation's capital. The Lincoln Memo-

Ashabranner experiencing the haunting reflective power of the Vietnam Veterans Memorial, 1998

rial and the Vietnam Veterans Memorial are well known to almost all Americans. The Korean War Veterans Memorial, however, is still relatively unknown. And the Korean War itself has often been called the Forgotten War.

In words and pictures, we tried to convey the message of the memorial that "freedom is not free" and that the sacrifice of the thirty-five-thousand American servicemen and women who fought and died in the war should not be forgotten.

President Bill Clinton spoke at a ceremony at the memorial commemorating the fiftieth anniversary of the war. "Korea was war at its worst," he said, "but it was America at its best. I submit to you today that looking back through the long lens of history, it is clear that the stand America took in Korea was indispensable to our ultimate victory in the cold war."

The president's words were with us every day as we wrote and photographed *Remembering Korea.*

Of all the books I have written since my 1992 autobiography, I am sure that the one most closely connected to a part of my life is *A Strange and Distant Shore: Indians of the Great Plains in Exile.* Curiously, my writing it came as a complete surprise to me. In 1995 I had gone to visit a relative in Florida. I had never been to the nearby small historic city of St. Augustine and spent an extra day to enjoy it.

One of the main city attractions is the massive old Spanish stone fort Castillo de San Marcos, which overlooks Matanzas Bay and the Atlantic Ocean. When I went inside the fort and saw the grim old rooms, called casemates, I was suddenly taken back to my days as a boy in central Oklahoma. I had grown up hearing stories of how, in the late nineteenth century, some of the leading chiefs and warriors of defeated Indian tribes— Arapaho, Cheyenne, Comanche, Kiowa—had been locked up in Fort Reno, near where we lived, and then as punishment and to weaken the tribes had been exiled to Castillo de San Marcos in Florida. It was a cruel, tragic chapter in American history.

As I looked at those dark, stifling stone-walled rooms, I thought about the Indians crowded in there and how they must have dreamed of the wind-swept plains where they had once roamed freely. They were kept in those casemates, in leg irons, for months. Finally a courageous army officer, Captain Richard Henry Pratt, was able to make their life in the fort more livable and even arranged for them to sometimes leave the fort in work or exercise groups, but they were still held in exile.

Out of their longing for their life on the Great Plains, some of the exiled Indians began to draw and paint pictures of their lost life—hunting scenes, fighting or playing games on horseback, details of camp life, religious ceremonies, much more. Captain Pratt supplied materials for their art. Some of the more accomplished

artists were Boy Hunting, Bear's Heart, Koba, Little Chief, Zotom, and Soaring Eagle. Their pictures became famous and much sought after. They were in fact the beginning of modern Native American art.

That day—that moment—when I stood inside the fort and saw where they had lived as exiles, I knew I had to tell their story for young readers today. I told it in *A Strange and Distant Shore* and brought my theme into focus with a line from the Greek tragedy *Agamemnon:* "I know how men in exile feed on dreams."

In addition to the sixteen books I have written since 1992, I have had the great satisfaction of editing a new edition of *The Lion's Whiskers.* Written in collaboration with my old friend and colleague Russell Davis, *The Lion's Whiskers,* published in 1959, was my first book for young readers and had been out of print for many years. For the new edition, published by Linnet Books in 1997 under the title *The Lion's Whiskers and Other Ethiopian Tales,* I selected the sixteen most popular stories from the original edition. I added a new introduction explaining how we collected the stories and an afterword describing Ethiopia today. The new edition was very well received and rated a star *School Library Journal.* I can say with no sense of bragging that a few of the stories in the book are among Africa's great folk tales. They are, after all, not really my stories; they belong to the first storytellers who told them around Ethio-

Outside Castillo de San Marcos fort in St. Augustine, Florida, 1996

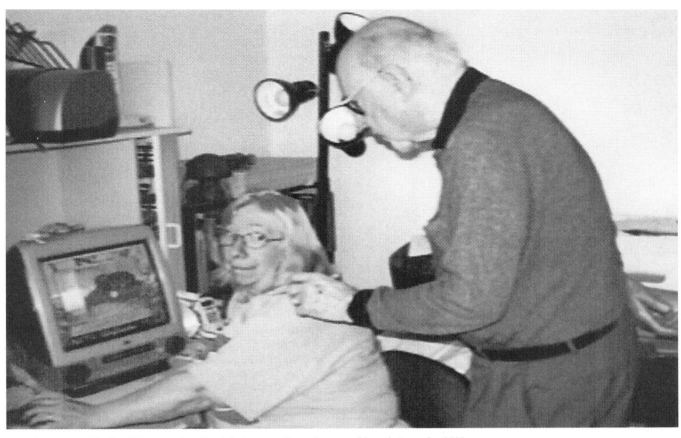

With daughter and book collaborator, Jennifer Ashabranner, discussing one of her photographs, 2005

pian campfires centuries ago. And what of the future? There may be another immigration book. Jennifer and I certainly had something worth saying in our book about recent African immigrants in *The New African Americans,* published in 1999. We are still a nation of immigrants with a new opportunity to be taken advantage of or a new problem to be solved every day. And in this age of terrorist threats and impending bird flu and other pandemics, I am sure we need a book about the work of our most important public health agency, Centers for Disease Control and Prevention. Jennifer wants us to do a book about the cats and dogs she has come to know

so well as a pet-care specialist over the past twenty years. She would like to call it *My One Thousand Best Friends.*

Recently I went for my regular six-month checkup by my primary-health-care physician. During the exam my doctor asked casually, "Are you still writing?" And I asked him, "Am I still breathing?"

My doctor smiled. "I see," he said. "As long as you are breathing, you'll be writing."

"Doctor, you got that right,"I said.

ASHABRANNER, Brent Kenneth
See ASHABRANNER, Brent

*   *   *

AUSEON, Andrew 1976-

Personal

Born 1976, in Columbus, OH; married Sarah Zogby; children: Samara Ruth. *Education:* Ohio University,

B.A. (creative writing); Vermont College, M.F.A. (creative writing for children and young adults). *Hobbies and other interests:* Travel.

Addresses

Home—Baltimore, MD. *Agent*—c/o Author Mail, Harcourt International, 6277 Sea Harbor Dr., Orlando, FL 32887.

Career

Writer. PhotoAssist, Inc., photo editor, 1999-2003; The History Factory, senior researcher, 2002-04; Words & Numbers, Baltimore, MD, currently editor and staff writer.

Member

Society of Children's Book Writers and Illustrators.

Writings

Funny Little Monkey, Harcourt (Orlando, FL), 2005.

Sidelights

An M.F.A. graduate of Vermont College who has traveled to over twenty countries, Andrew Auseon published his first book, the young-adult novel *Funny Little Monkey,* in 2005. In what a *Publishers Weekly* reviewer called a "darkly comic debut," Auseon introduces readers to mild-mannered main character Arty Moore. Arty is a mere shadow in contrast to his much-larger and quite intimidating twin brother Kurt. Raised by a single mother, and with a father who serves as a poor role model due to his career as a bank robber, the boys have always found themselves at odds. Now, as a freshman at Millard Fillmore High, Arty's luck seems to be changing when he makes two new friends: the beautiful, wealthy overachiever Leslie Dermott and Kerouac, the ringleader of a rebellious group of kids. With his friends' help, Arty is able to finally put his bullying brother in his place, while at the same time adjusting to life in high school. The *Publishers Weekly* critic wrote that Auseon "taps into the painful experience of high school, leavened with healthy doses of hyperbole, hope and wry humor," while Susan W. Hunter noted in *School Library Journal* that Arty "steps up and uses an outrageous fabrication to resolve the final crisis in this offbeat coming-of-age story."

Biographical and Critical Sources

PERIODICALS

Booklist, April 15, 2005, Jennifer Hubert, review of *Funny Little Monkey,* p. 1447.
Columbus Dispatch, November 6, 2005, Nancy Gilson, "Novel Explores Sophomoric Cruelty of High School."
Kirkus Reviews, June 1, 2005, review of *Funny Little Monkey,* p. 632.
Publishers Weekly, July 11, 2005, review of *Funny Little Monkey,* p. 94.
School Library Journal, June, 2005, Susan W. Hunter, review of *Funny Little Monkey,* p. 147.
Voice of Youth Advocates, June, 2005, Jazmine Nazek, review of *Funny Little Monkey,* p. 133.

ONLINE

Andrew Auseon Home Page, http://www.andrewauseon. com (November 6, 2005).

A short-of-stature fourteen year old decides to stand up to his much-taller twin, but finds that enlisting the help of a group of school misfits and a brainy new friend scales the heights of bad judgement in Auseon's 2005 novel. (Cover designed by Vaughn Andrews.)

* * *

AYTO, Russell 1960-

Personal

Born July 10, 1960, in Chichester, Sussex, England; son of Glyn Melvyn (a groundskeeper) and Christina Pearl (a postal clerk) Ayto; married Alyx Mary Louise Bennett (a secretary), March 3, 1990; children: Greta, Emilio, Loveday. *Education:* Attended Oxford Polytechnic; Exeter College of Art and Design, B.A. (graphic design; with honors). *Hobbies and other interests:* Collecting books on art and illustration.

Addresses

Home—Penzance, Cornwall, England. *Agent*—c/o Author Mail, Walker Books, 87 Vauxhall Walk, London SE11 5HJ, England.

Career

Illustrator. John Radcliffe II Hospital, medical laboratory scientific officer in department of histopathology, 1979-80.

Awards, Honors

Smartie's Book Prize Gold medal in under-five category, 2003, for *The Witch's Children and the Queen,* by Ursula Jones; Kate Greenaway Award shortlist, 2004, for *One More Sheep* by Mij Kelly.

Illustrator

Ian Whybrow, *Quacky Quack-Quack!,* Four Winds (New York, NY), 1991.

Vivian French, reteller, *Lazy Jack,* Candlewick Press (Cambridge, MA), 1995.

Anne Cottringer, *Ella and the Naughty Lion,* Houghton (Boston, MA), 1996.

Phyllis Root, *Mrs. Potter's Pig,* Candlewick Press (Cambridge, MA), 1996.

Joyce Dunbar, *The Baby Bird,* Candlewick Press (Cambridge, MA), 1998.

Ian Whybrow, *Whiff,* Barron's (Hauppauge, NY), 1999.

Ian Whybrow, *Where's Tim's Ted?,* Barron's (Hauppauge, NY), 2000.

Andrea Shavick, *You'll Grow Soon, Alex,* Walker (New York, NY), 2000.

James Sage, *Fat Cat,* HarperCollins (London, England), 2001, published as *Farmer Smart's Fat Cat,* Chronicle Books (San Francisco, CA), 2002.

Ursula Jones, *The Witch's Children,* Henry Holt (New York, NY), 2003.

James Sage, *Mr. Beast,* Henry Holt (New York, NY), 2005.

Giles Andreae, *Captain Flinn and the Pirate Dinosaurs,* Margaret K. McElderry Books (New York, NY), 2005.

Adaptations

Parts of the book *Quacky Quack-Quack!* have been animated for a videotape featuring various children's books.

Sidelights

Award-winning children's book illustrator Russell Ayto worked at a number of magazines and even held a position as a part-time postman prior to turning to the field of freelance illustration. As Ayto once told *SATA:* "I've always liked painting and drawing and have really just ended up illustrating children's books! I never had an idea where or what I might have ended up doing. I just love the process of bringing characters and stories to life visually, adding something extra to the books. The most important thing for me, when illustrating, is to try and bring visual surprises to a book, so that, when you turn a page, you never know quite what is coming."

Critics have praised Ayto's gentle watercolor-and-ink illustrations in books such as *Mrs. Potter's Pig* by Phyllis Root, *Ella and the Naughty Lion* by Anne Cottringer, and *The Witch's Children* by Ursula Jones. The first title concerns a fastidious mother and her extremely messy baby, Ermajean. Worried Mother admonishes Ermajean that if she is not more tidy, one day she will turn into an actual pig, and when Ermajean and a little piglet actually switch places, surprises abound. *Booklist* reviewer Susan Dove Lempke applauded the "ingenious interplay between text and pictures," calling Ayto "a master of framing and white space." A contributor to *Kirkus Reviews* also noted that the "illustrations are a perfect complement for the rollicking text, imbuing every character with lots of personality."

A jealous sibling protests the arrival of a new baby and welcomes the simultaneous appearance of a troublesome lion in *Ella and the Naughty Lion.* At first Ella does not care for her new brother, Jasper, and the lion shows his equal distaste for the infant by chewing up Jasper's teddy bear and pulling off his blanket. As Ella gradually warms to her new little brother, the lion magically fades away and disappears. A contributor to *Publishers Weekly* observed that Ayto's color-washed "imprecise squiggles of ink" lend a "stuffed-animal softness to the imagery," and *Booklist* critic Ilene Cooper stated that Ayto's illustrations propel "a rather pedestrian story to a book with so many amusing visual details that young listeners will take a second look."

In *The Witch's Children* animals and people alike attempt to steer clear of the three mischievous witch's children, as they head out for a day of spells and shenanigans in their neighborhood park. After casting a variety of spells, they realize they do not know how to undo their own magic and must put their minds to the test to correct their mishaps. "Ayto's characters are wonderfully expressive," commented *Horn Book* critic Joanna Rudge Long. *School Library Journal* reviewer Maryann H. Owen also enjoyed Ayto's illustrations, noting that "small details in the drawings add to the humor." A *Publishers Weekly* reviewer believed that Ayto's artwork adds depth to the amusing storyline, writing that, "kinetic and creatively skewed, these illustrations make the most of the slender tale."

Biographical and Critical Sources

PERIODICALS

Booklist, September 1, 1995, Hazel Rochman, review of *Lazy Jack,* p. 73; August, 1996, Susan Dove Lempke, review of *Mrs. Potter's Pig,* p. 1905; September 1, 1996, Ilene Cooper, review of *Ella and the Naughty Lion,* p. 141; June 1, 1998, Helen Rosenberg, review of *Baby Bird,* p. 1778; October 15, 2000, Shelley Townsend-Hudson, review of *You'll Grow Soon, Alex,* p. 447; July 2002, GraceAnne A. DeCandido, review of *Farmer Smart's Fat Cat,* p. 1860.

Bookseller, December 5, 2003, "Smarties Success," p. 29.

Horn Book, July-August, 2003, Joanna Rudge Long, review of *The Witch's Children,* p. 443.

Kirkus Reviews, May 15, 1996, p. 749; July 15, 1996, review of *Mrs. Potter's Pig,* p. 1046; April 1, 2003, review of *The Witch's Children,* p. 535.

Publishers Weekly, July 10, 1995, review of *Lazy Jack,* p. 57; September 2, 1996, review of *Ella and the Naughty Lion,* p. 130; March 17, 2003, review of *The Witch's Children,* p. 75; June 30, 2003, "A Moveable Feast for Preschoolers," p. 82.

School Library Journal, October, 1995, p. 125; July, 1996, Wendy Lukehart, review of *Mrs. Potter's Pig,* p. 71; July, 1998, Paula A. Kiely, review of *Baby Bird,* p. 73; October, 2000, Kathleen Whalin, review of *You'll Grow Soon, Alex,* p. 136; July, 2002, Marlene Gawron, review of *Farmer Smart's Fat Cat,* p. 98; July, 2003, Marann H. Owen, review of *The Witch's Children,* p. 99.

ONLINE

British Broadcasting Web site, http://www.bbc.co.uk/ (November 6, 2005), *Blast* interview with Ayto.

PFD Web site, http://www.pfd.co.uk/ (November 6, 2005), "Russell Ayto."

Walker Books Web site, http://www.walkerbooks.co.uk/ (November 6, 2005), "Russell Ayto."*

B

BAKER, Rosalie F. 1945-

Personal
Born February 8, 1945; married Charles F. Baker III (a writer and publisher); children: one son.

Addresses
Home—150 Page St., New Bedford, MA 02740. *E-mail*—cfbakeriii@meganet.net.

Career
Author, editor, and publisher. Formerly worked as a teacher; Ivy Close Publishing Company, cofounder with husband, Charles F. Baker III, beginning 1980; *Classical Calliope* (now *Calliope* magazine), co-editor and writer, beginning 1981.

Awards, Honors
(All with Charles F. Baker III; for *Calliope* magazine) Best New Magazine designation, *Library Journal*, 1991; EdPress Golden Lamp Award, 1998.

Writings

In a Word: 750 Words and Their Fascinating Stories and Origins, illustrated by Tom Lopes, Cobblestone (Peterborough, NH), 2003.

WITH HUSBAND, CHARLES F. BAKER III, EXCEPT WHERE NOTED

The Classical Companion, 1988.
Myths and Legends of Mount Olympos, illustrated by Joyce Audy Zarins, Cobblestone (Peterborough, NH), 1992.
Classical Ingenuity: The Legacy of the Ancient Greek and Roman Architects, Artists, and Inventors, 1992.
Ancient Greeks: Creating the Classical Tradition, Oxford University Press (New York, NY), 1997.

Ancient Romans: Expanding the Classical Tradition, Oxford University Press (New York, NY), 1998.
Ancient Egyptians: People of the Pyramids, Oxford University Press (New York, NY), 2001.
(Coauthor with Charles F. Baker III and Winfred Rembert) *Don't Hold Me Back: My Life and Art,* Cricket Books (Chicago, IL), 2003.
Companion to Ancient Greece, Oxford University Press (New York, NY), 2005.

Work anthologized in *Of Cabbages and Kings 1991: The Year's Best Magazine Writing for Kids,* Bowker, 1991. Contributor to educational materials, including textbooks for Harcourt Brace and Cobblestone Publishing; contributor of articles to numerous publications, including *Cricket, Calliope, Odyssey,* and *Boston Globe.*

Sidelights
Writer, teacher, and editor Rosalie F. Baker, together with her husband Charles F. Baker III, co-founded *Classical Calliope* magazine in 1981. Now simply known as *Calliope,* the magazine fulfills Baker's goal as a publisher: to heighten awareness among middle-school and high-school students of the importance and influence of Greek and Roman civilizations on modern society. In addition to her work on the award-winning magazine, Baker is also the author of several nonfiction titles focusing on ancient civilizations, among them *Ancient Egyptians: People of the Pyramids* and *Ancient Romans: Expanding the Classical Tradition.* In addition to each of these books, which have been coauthored with her husband, Baker has also penned *In a Word: 750 Words and Their Fascinating Stories and Origins,* an illustrated guide to etymology.

In *Ancient Egyptians* the coauthors chronicle the lives of twenty-eight famous Egyptians, organizing these subjects by historical period. In addition to the biographies—largely of ancient ruling kings and queens—Baker includes three appendices outlining the five names of each ruler, a list of foreign rulers other than native Egyptians, and lastly, a conclusive time line of the Egyptian civilization. "The text is readable and should be accessible to most students," commented a *Booklist* reviewer, while Cynthia M. Sturgis wrote in *School Library Journal* that *Ancient Egyptians* should serve as "a useful addition for report writers and subject enthusiasts."

Ancient Romans adopts a similar format, this time exploring forty individuals, including: emperors, high-ranking state officials, writers, and generals throughout Rome. Noting that the Bakers describe Roman society and culture "without sensationalizing its brutal aspects," *Booklist* contributor Randy Meyer added that the volume "admits the violent legacy of warfare and assassination while affirming the political and academic achievements that laid the foundation for our own culture."

Baker told *SATA:* "When my husband and I founded the magazine *Classical Calliope* (now *Calliope*) in 1981, a chief goal was to heighten awareness among young people of the importance and merits of studying Greek and Roman civilization. We felt that one of the ways to accomplish this goal would be to include a department that focused on the origins of English words derived from Greek and Latin. Since the first *Calliope* issue in January of 1981, we have done just that—even after we expanded the scope of *Calliope* from classical civilizations to world history. Today, the department is called 'Fun with Words.'

For years, we considered a book that would take all the word origins and expressions we had included in *Calliope* and arrange them somehow in book form. Our son, Chip and his friend, Jennifer Parker, took on the project when they worked for us as college interns. They created a mock-up of the potential designs, chose the words to include, and presented their idea of introducing fun facts to complement words, at spaced intervals, throughout the book. Everyone loved their ideas—and so, the work of collating and editing, as well as researching the facts, began. It was a great family project!"

Biographical and Critical Sources

PERIODICALS

Booklist, August, 1997, Karen Hutt, review of *Ancient Greeks: Creating the Classic Tradition,* p. 1889; September 15, 1997, review of *Ancient Greeks,* p. 262; May 1, 1998, Mary Ellen Quinn, review of *Ancient Romans: Expanding the Classical Tradition,* p. 1550; June 1, 1998, Randy Meyer, review of *Ancient Romans,* p. 1738; February 1, 2002, review of *Ancient Egyptians: People of the Pyramids,* p. 958.
Bulletin of the Center for Children's Books, December, 2001, review of *Ancient Egyptians,* p. 129.
Reference and Research Book News, February, 1998, review of *Ancient Greeks,* p. 21; August, 1998, review of *Ancient Romans,* p. 27.

School Library Journal, September, 1997, Cynthia M. Sturgis, review of *Ancient Greeks,* p. 228; August, 1998, David N. Pauli, review of *Ancient Romans,* p. 169; November, 2001, Cynthia M. Sturgis, review of *Ancient Egyptians,* p. 168; November, 2001, review of *Ancient Egyptians,* p. 168.

ONLINE

Oxford University Press Web site, http://www.oup.com/ (November 6, 2005).*

*　　*　　*

BARCLAY, Bill
See MOORCOCK, Michael

*　　*　　*

BARCLAY, William Ewert
See MOORCOCK, Michael

*　　*　　*

BARRINGTON, Michael
See MOORCOCK, Michael

*　　*　　*

BLUE, Rose 1931-

Personal

Surname originally Bluestone; born 1931, in New York, NY; daughter of Irving (a pharmacist) and Frieda (Rosenberg) Bluestone. *Education:* Brooklyn College (now Brooklyn College of the City University of New York), B.A.; Bank Street College of Education, M.A. *Politics:* Democrat.

Addresses

Home—1320 51st St., Brooklyn, NY 11219. *Agent*—c/o Author Mail, Millbrook Press, Simon & Schuster, 1230 Avenue of the Americas, New York, NY 10020.

Career

Writer. Former teacher in public schools in New York, NY; former teacher for Bedford Stuyvesant Headstart program. Lyricist of songs performed by Damita Jo, Jodie Sands, and the Exciters; member of Broadcast Music, Inc.

Member

Authors Guild, Authors League of America, Mensa, Professional Women's Caucus.

Rose Blue

Awards, Honors

Best Books, National Council for the Social Studies/ Children's Book Council, 1979, for *Cold Rain on the Water;* Red Ribbon Award, American Film Festival, 1982, for teleplay *Grandma Didn't Wave Back.*

Writings

FICTION; FOR CHILDREN

A Quiet Place, illustrated by Tom Feelings, Franklin Watts (New York, NY), 1969.

Black, Black, Beautiful Black, illustrations by Emmett Wigglesworth, Franklin Watts (New York, NY), 1969.

How Many Blocks Is the World?, illustrated by Harold James, Franklin Watts (New York, NY), 1970.

Bed-Stuy Beat, illustrated by Harold James, Franklin Watts (New York, NY), 1970.

I Am Here—Yo Estoy Aqui, illustrated by Moneta Barnett, Franklin Watts (New York, NY), 1971.

Grandma Didn't Wave Back, illustrated by Ted Lewin, Franklin Watts (New York, NY), 1972.

A Month of Sundays, illustrated by Ted Lewin, Franklin Watts (New York, NY), 1972.

Nikki 108, illustrated by Ted Lewin, Franklin Watts (New York, NY), 1973.

We Are Chicano, illustrated by Bob Alcorn, Franklin Watts (New York, NY), 1973.

The Preacher's Kid, illustrated by Ted Lewin, Franklin Watts (New York, NY), 1975.

Seven Years from Home, illustrated by Barbara Ericksen, Raintree (Austin, TX), 1976.

The Yo-Yo Kid, illustrated by Barbara Ericksen, Raintree (Austin, TX), 1976.

The Thirteenth Year: A Bar Mitzvah Story, Franklin Watts (New York, NY), 1977.

Cold Rain on the Water, McGraw-Hill, 1979.

Me and Einstein: Breaking through the Reading Barrier, illustrated by Peggy Luks, Human Sciences Press, 1979.

Wishful Lying, illustrated by Laura Hartman, Human Sciences Press, 1980.

My Mother the Witch, illustrated by Ted Lewin, McGraw-Hill, 1981.

Everybody's Evy, Berkley (New York, NY), 1983.

Bring Me a Memory, DIMI Press (Salem, OR), 1995.

Also author of *Goodbye Forever Tree,* New American Library; *Heart to Heart,* Tempo; *The Secret Papers of Camp Get-Around,* New American Library; and "Honey Bear" series books (with recording), Modern Publishing.

"SANDY'S WORLD" SERIES

First Day of School Blues (includes recording), illustrated by Vala Kondo, Caedmon, 1986.

Happy Birthday and All That Jazz (includes recording), illustrated by Vala Kondo, Caedmon, 1986.

Clean up Your Room Rag (includes recording), illustrated by Vala Kondo, Caedmon, 1986.

Rock-a-New Baby Rock (includes recording), illustrated by Vala Kondo, Caedmon, 1986.

TELEPLAYS

Grandma Didn't Wave Back (broadcast on NBC-TV, 1982), Multimedia Entertainment, 1982.

My Mother the Witch, NBC-TV, 1984.

JUVENILE NONFICTION

(With Corinne J. Naden) *The U.S. Air Force,* Millbrook Press (Brookfield, CT), 1993.

(With Corinne J. Naden) *The U.S. Coast Guard,* Millbrook Press (Brookfield, CT), 1993.

(With Corinne J. Naden) *The U.S. Navy,* Millbrook Press (Brookfield, CT), 1993.

(With Corinne J. Naden) *Working Together against Hate Groups,* Rosen (New York, NY), 1994.

(With Corinne J. Naden) *Black Sea,* Raintree (Austin, TX), 1995.

(With Corinne J. Naden) *Andes Mountains,* Raintree (Austin, TX), 1995.

Good Yontif: A Picture Book of the Jewish Year, illustrated by Lynne Feldman, Millbrook Press (Brookfield, CT), 1997.

(With Corinne J. Naden) *Staying out of Trouble in a Troubled Family,* Twenty-first Century Books (Brookfield, CT), 1998.

(With Corinne J. Naden) *You're the Boss: Positive Attitude and Work Ethics,* Peoples Publishing Group (Maywood, NJ), 1999.

(With Corinne J. Naden) *Why Fight?: The Causes of the American Civil War,* Raintree (Austin, TX), 2000.

(With Corinne J. Naden) *The Duty to Rescue,* Chelsea House (Philadelphia, PA), 2000.

(With Corinne J. Naden) *Punishment and Rehabilitation,* Chelsea House (Philadelphia, PA), 2001.

(With Corinne J. Naden) *The History of Gospel Music,* Chelsea House (Philadelphia, PA), 2001.

(With Corinne J. Naden) *New York* ("States" series), MyReportLinks.com (Berkeley Heights, NJ), 2002.

(With Corinne J. Naden) *Mississippi* ("States" series), MyReportLinks.com (Berkeley Heights, NJ), 2003.

(With Corinne J. Naden) *Massachusetts* ("States" series), MyReportLinks.com (Berkeley Heights, NJ), 2003.

(With Corinne J. Naden) *Marbury v. Madison: The Court's Foundation* ("Supreme Court Milestones" series), Benchmark Books (Tarrytown, NY), 2005.

(With Corinne J. Naden) *Dred Scott: Person or Property?* ("Supreme Court Milestones" series), Benchmark Books (Tarrytown, NY), 2005.

JUVENILE BIOGRAPHIES

(With Joanne E. Bernstein) *Diane Sawyer: Super Newswoman,* Enslow (Hillside, NJ), 1990.

(With Joanne E. Bernstein and Alan Jay Gerber) *Judith Resnik: Challenger Astronaut,* Lodestar Books (New York, NY), 1990.

(With Corinne J. Naden) *Christa McAuliffe: Teacher in Space,* Millbrook Press (Brookfield, CT), 1991.

(With Corinne J. Naden) *Barbara Bush: First Lady,* Enslow (Hillside, NJ), 1991.

(With Corinne J. Naden) *Colin Powell: Straight to the Top,* Millbrook Press (Brookfield, CT), 1991.

(With Corinne J. Naden) *Barbara Jordan,* Chelsea House (Philadelphia, PA), 1992.

(With Corinne J. Naden) *John Muir: Saving the Wilderness,* Millbrook Press (Brookfield, CT), 1992.

(With Corinne J. Naden) *People of Peace,* Millbrook Press (Brookfield, CT), 1994.

(With Corinne J. Naden) *Jerry Rice,* Chelsea House (New York, NY), 1994.

(With Corinne J. Naden) *Whoopi Goldberg: Entertainer,* Chelsea House (Philadelphia, PA), 1994.

(With Corinne J. Naden) *The White House Kids,* Millbrook Press (Brookfield, CT), 1995.

(With Corinne J. Naden) *Madeleine Albright: U.S. Secretary of State,* Blackbirch Press (Woodbridge, CT), 1999.

(With Corinne J. Naden) *Belle Starr and the Wild West,* Blackbirch Press (Woodbridge, CT), 2000.

(With Corinne J. Naden) *Chris Rock,* Chelsea House (Philadelphia, PA), 2000.

(With Corinne J. Naden) *Jonas Salk: Polio Pioneer,* Millbrook Press (Brookfield, CT), 2001.

(With Corinne J. Naden) *Benjamin Banneker: Mathematician and Stargazer,* Millbrook Press (Brookfield, CT), 2001.

(With Corinne J. Naden) *Cleopatra,* Chelsea House (Philadelphia, PA), 2001.

(With Corinne J. Naden) *Wesley Snipes,* Chelsea House (Philadelphia, PA), 2002.

(With Corinne J. Naden) *Halle Berry,* Chelsea House (Philadelphia, PA), 2002.

(With Corinne J. Naden) *Dian Fossey: At Home with the Giant Gorillas,* Millbrook Press (Brookfield, CT), 2002.

(With Corinne J. Naden) *Monica Seles,* Chelsea House (Philadelphia, PA), 2002.

(With Corinne J. Naden) *Harriet Tubman: Riding the Freedom Train,* Millbrook Press (Brookfield, CT), 2003.

(With Corinne J. Naden) *Tony Blair,* Lucent Books (San Diego, CA), 2003.

(With Corinne J. Naden) *Nicholas Cage,* Lucent Books (San Diego, CA), 2003.

(With Corinne J. Naden) *Mae Jemison: Out of This World,* Millbrook Press (Brookfield, CT), 2003.

(With Corinne J. Naden) *John Travolta,* Lucent Books (San Diego, CA), 2003.

(With Corinne J. Naden) *Wilma Rudolph,* Raintree (Chicago, IL), 2004.

(With Corinne J. Naden) *Lenin,* Lucent Books (San Diego, CA), 2004.

(With Corinne J. Naden) *George W. Bush,* Lucent Books (San Diego, CA), 2004.

(With Corinne J. Naden) *Muammar Qaddafi,* Lucent Books (San Diego, CA), 2005.

(With Corinne J. Naden) *Maya Angelou,* Raintree (Chicago, IL), 2005.

(With Corinne J. Naden) *Henry Louis Gates, Jr.,* Raintree (Chicago, IL), 2005.

(With Corinne J. Naden) *Cornel West,* Raintree (Chicago, IL), 2005.

(With Corinne J. Naden) *Condoleezza Rice,* Raintree (Chicago, IL), 2005.

Also author (with Corinne J. Naden) of *Heroes Just Don't Happen,* five volumes, 1996.

NONFICTION; "WHO'S THAT IN THE WHITE HOUSE" SERIES; COAUTHOR WITH CORRINE J. NADEN

The Founding Years: 1789 to 1829, Raintree (Austin, TX), 1998.

The Formative Years: 1829 to 1857, Raintree (Austin, TX), 1998.

The Expansive Years: 1857 to 1901, Raintree (Austin, TX), 1998.

The Progressive Years: 1901 to 1933, Raintree (Austin, TX), 1998.

The Turbulent Years: 1933 to 1969, Raintree (Austin, TX), 1998.

The Modern Years: 1969 to 2001, Raintree (Austin, TX), 1998.

NONFICTION; "HOUSE DIVIDED" SERIES; COAUTHOR WITH CORINNE J. NADEN

The Bloodiest Days: The Battles of 1861 and 1862, Raintree (Austin, TX), 2000.

Chancellorsville to Appomattox: The Battles of 1863 to 1865, Raintree (Austin, TX), 2000.

Civil War Ends: Assassination, Reconstruction, and the Aftermath, Raintree (Austin, TX), 2000.

NONFICTION; "GREAT PEOPLES AND THEIR CLAIM TO FAME" SERIES; COAUTHOR WITH CORINNE J. NADEN

The Aztecs and Tenochtitlan, Lake Street (Minneapolis, MN), 2003.

Ancient Romans and the Colosseum, Lake Street (Minneapolis, MN), 2003.

Ancient Maya and Tikal, Lake Street (Minneapolis, MN), 2003.

Ancient Greeks and the Parthenon, Lake Street (Minneapolis, MN), 2003.

Ancient Egyptians and the Pyramids, Lake Street (Minneapolis, MN), 2003.

NONFICTION; "EXPLORING THE AMERICAS" SERIES; COAUTHOR WITH CORINNE J. NADEN

Exploring the Southeastern United States, Raintree (Chicago, IL), 2003.

Exploring the Pacific Northwest, Raintree (Chicago, IL), 2003.

Exploring the Mississippi River Valley, Raintree (Chicago, IL), 2003.

Exploring Northeastern America, Raintree (Chicago, IL), 2003.

Exploring the St. Lawrence River Region, Raintree (Chicago, IL), 2004.

Exploring the Western Mountains, Raintree (Chicago, IL), 2004.

Exploring the Southwestern United States, Raintree (Chicago, IL), 2004.

Exploring the Arctic, Raintree (Chicago, IL), 2004.

Exploring South America, Raintree (Chicago, IL), 2004.

Exploring Central America, Mexico, and the Caribbean, Raintree (Chicago, IL), 2004.

OTHER

Author of reading series for Scholastic and reading workbooks and other materials for Brooklyn College School of Education and Communications Skill Builders. Coauthor, with Corinne J. Naden, of "Heroes Don't Just Happen" multicultural biography series. Feature writer for *Teacher, Day Care,* and *Action.* Contributor of short stories to Magazine Management and Sterling Group. Contributing editor to *Teacher.* Author of lyrics for popular songs, including "Drama of Love," "Let's Face It," "My Heartstrings Keep Me Tied to You," "Give Me a Break," and "Homecoming Party."

Adaptations

I Am Here—Yo Estoy Aqui was adapted as a filmstrip, Listening Library, 1980.

Sidelights

A former teacher and Headstart program worker in New York City who began her writing career penning fiction for young readers, Rose Blue has become a prolific author of nonfiction written with collaborator Corinne J.

Naden that includes biographies of contemporary newsmakers and U.S. state and regional profiles, as well as books that span American social and political history. Reviewing two of Blue and Naden's books on the U.S. armed services—*U.S. Air Force* and *U.S. Navy*—*Booklist* contributor Janice Del Negro called these volumes "well made, high-interest, and filled with easy-to-access information." Other nonfiction titles include *Dred Scott: Person or Property?,* which discusses the early eighteenth-century U.S. Supreme Court case that upheld slavery, and *Mae Jemison: Out of This World,* a profile of the first black American woman in space that *Booklist* contributor Carolyn Phelan dubbed "inviting" as well as "readable and colorful."

Blue and Naden's biographies examine the lives of individuals prominent in a wide spectrum of human endeavors: scientist Jonah Salk, First Lady Barbara Bush, politicians George W. Bush, Vladimir Lenin, Tony Blair, and Muammar Qaadafi, environmentalist John Muir, athletes Wilma Rudolph and Jerry Rice, and actors Nicholas Cage, Halle Berry, and Whoopi Goldberg are among the many individuals profiled for young report-writers. Reviewing *Lenin, Booklist* reviewer Gillian Engberg praised the coauthors' "clear, accessible language" and efforts to provide the background information necessary to a full understanding of the Soviet leader's life and communist ideology. In addition to profiling a sitting U.S. president and his wife, the collaborators also offer a unique view of day-to-day life at the White House, describing it from the perspective of the children who have lived in that historic building. *The White House Kids,* according to *School Library Journal* contributor Melissa Gross, features a "readable, chronological text [that] allows youngsters to contemplate antics such as roller skating down the halls of the White House or star gazing from the roof, as well as the realities of waiting to get an appointment to see the president and dating under the surveillance of the Secret Service." *Booklist* reviewer Carolyn Phelan called *The White House Kids* "an intriguing sidelight on presidential history."

In addition to biographies, Naden and Blue provide an overview of regional U.S. history in their contributions to the "Exploring the Americas" series, which provides young armchair travelers with maps, histories, descriptions, and a who's who inhabiting various regions of the Americas. Titles in the series include *Exploring the Western Mountains,* which describes the harsh terrain encountered by the explorers who traveled in the Rocky Mountain region of North America, and *Exploring South America, Exploring the Mississippi River Valley,* and *Exploring the Arctic.* Praising *Exploring the Arctic* in *School Library Journal,* Eldon Younce noted that the coauthors present a resource that is "serviceable" and "accurate."

Often featuring young protagonists growing up in the inner city, Blue's many works of fiction focus on "children burdened by difficulties they can't understand," ac-

Blue and coauthor Corine J. Naden put the life of a well-known Wild West outlaw into its historic context in their nonfiction title **Belle Star.**

cording to a *Publishers Weekly* contributor. Her stories—most published during the 1970s and 1980s—cover a wide range of topics—from illiteracy, gang violence, and racial intolerance to interfamily issues of divorce and dealing with elderly relatives' senility. Blue's 1979 novel *Cold Rain on the Water,* a story of Russian immigrants, was selected a best book of the year by the National Council for the Social Studies.

"I knew I wanted to be a writer since Miss Higgens called on me to read my stories to the first grade while she marked papers," Blue once told *SATA.* "I attended Bank Street College of Education in order to earn a master's degree and teaching license—after all, the rent must be paid. One instructor, a well-known scholar, gave a wonderful course in children's literature. After diligently reading an assignment, I said, 'When do we get to read the really good, realistic children's books?' She replied, 'We've read nearly everything ever writ-

ten.' I said, 'I can do better than that.' I wrote *A Quiet Place,* and 'the rest is history.'"

A Quiet Place focuses on an African-American boy who loves to read. When the library in Matthew's ghetto neighborhood is replaced by a book mobile, the boy must search for a new quiet place to read. Reading is also central to *Me and Einstein: Breaking through the Reading Barrier,* about a boy named Bobby who has dyslexia. Bobby is taunted by his school friends and put in a class for mentally handicapped and emotionally disturbed students until the boy's problem is diagnosed and his educational needs are met.

Dealing with family problems, *A Month of Sundays* follows Jeffrey, a boy whose parents have recently divorced, as he moves to a new home in the city. His mother now works and has little time for him, and Jeffrey sees his father only on Sundays. Making new friends and talking things over with his father, Jeffrey eventually learns to adjust to his new situation. Parental problems can also lead to more serious troubles for children, as Blue shows in her story, *The Yo-Yo Kid*, about teenager Jim, whose alcoholic mother keeps moving the family from home to home. In an attempt to gain stability, Jim joins a gang and is ultimately pushed to commit violence. Zena Sutherland, reviewing *A Month of Sundays* for the *Bulletin of the Center for Children's Books*, called the work "sensible and realistic in its evaluation of adjustment to change," while Lael Scott wrote in the *New York Times Book Review* that Jeffrey is "a believable child with whom most children can easily identify."

In *Grandma Didn't Wave Back* a girl named Debbie tries to cope with the fact that her grandmother is becoming senile. Debbie remembers fondly how her grandmother would always wave to her from the window whenever she returned from school and would give her and her friends treats. But now Grandma stares off into space more and more and doesn't seem to be herself. Debbie's parents talk about putting Grandma in an assisted living home, and her friends start calling the woman a crazy old lady. In the end, it is Grandma who is able to explain best what is happening to her and help Debbie accept and understand what sometimes happens when people age. A *Booklist* contributor called *Grandma Didn't Wave Back* a "moving story," one that treats its subject "with honesty and understanding," and a reviewer for *Publishers Weekly* deemed the novel a "well-told" tale about "believable people."

Biographical and Critical Sources

PERIODICALS

Appraisal: Science Books for Young People, spring-summer, 1995, pp. 83-84.

Booklist, March 15, 1973, review of *Grandma Didn't Wave Back,* p. 711; June 1, 1995, Carolyn Phelan, review of *The White House Kids,* p. 1755, and Janice Del Negro, review of *The U.S. Air Force* and *The U.S. Navy,* p. 1817; December 15, 1994, p. 747; April 15, 1995, pp. 1488-1489; December 1, 1998, Ilene Cooper, review of *Madeleine Albright: U.S. Secretary of State,* p. 663; June 1, 2004, Gillian Engberg, review of *Lenin,* p. 1751; February 1, 2005, John Peters, review of *Dred Scott: Person or Property?,* p. 976.

Bulletin of the Center for Children's Books, September, 1972, Zena Sutherland, review of *A Month of Sundays,* p. 3; March, 1974, Zena Sutherland, review of *We Are Chicano,* p. 106; October, 1975, Zena Sutherland, review of *The Preacher's Kid,* p. 22; December, 1976, Zena Sutherland, review of *The Yo-Yo Kid,* p. 54.

Kirkus Reviews, October 1, 1973, review of *We Are Chicano,* p. 1094; June 1, 1991, p. 727; December 15, 1991, p. 1588.

Kliatt, January, 2002, review of *Wesley Snipes,* p. 23.

New York Times Book Review, September 3, 1972, Lael Scott, "Divorce Juvenile-Style," p. 8.

Publishers Weekly, September 4, 1972, review of *Grandma Didn't Wave Back,* p. 51; December 27, 1976, review of *The Yo-Yo Kid,* p. 60; July 5, 1985, p. 68; January 13, 1997, review of *Good Yontif: A Picture Book of the New Year,* p. 71.

School Library Journal, September, 1979, p. 152; January, 1986, p. 30; December, 1991, p. 139; May, 1992, p. 97; July, 1993, Rick Moesch, review of *The U.S. Air Force* and *The U.S. Navy,* p. 88; August, 1995, Melissa Gross, review of *The White House Kids,* p. 146; January, 1995, p. 112; February, 1995, p. 104; June, 1995, p. 116; January, 1998, Marilyn Fairbanks, review of *Colin Powell,* p. 119; June, 1999, Sylvia V. Meisner, review of *Staying out of Trouble in a Troubled Family,* p. 140; January, 2000, Mary Mueller, review of "House Divided" series, p. 150; January, 2001, Patricia Ann Owens, review of *Belle Starr and the Wild West,* p. 152; September, 2001, Edith Ching, review of *Banjamin Banneker,* p. 239; January, 2002, Sue Sherif, review of *Jonas Salk,* p. 162; June, 2003, Shauna Yusko, review of *Harriet Tubman,* p. 124; November, 2004, Deanna Romriell, review of *Mormonism,* p. 170; February, 2005, reviewing *Exploring the Arctic* and *Exploring the Western Mountains,* p. 145; May, 2005, review of *Muammar Qaddafi,* p. 154.*

*   *   *

BRACKETT, Virginia 1950-
(Virginia Roberts Meredith Brackett)

Personal

Born April 7, 1950, in Fort Riley, KS; daughter of Edmund Condon Roberts (in the military) and Helen Kost Roberts Ferranti (a teacher); married William R. Meredith, (a physician; divorced); married Edmund Charles Brackett (an educational administrator), July 26, 1991; children: (first marriage) Lisa Paige Meredith Lamb, Shandra Renee Meredith Chapman, William Wade Meredith; (second marriage) Marcus A. Brackett (stepson). *Education:* University of Arkansas Medical Center, B.S.M.T. (medical technology), 1973; Missouri Southern State College, B.S. (marketing and management), 1989; Pittsburgh State University, M.A. (English), 1991; University of Kansas, Ph.D. (English), 1998. *Politics:* Democrat. *Religion:* Protestant. *Hobbies and other interests:* Gardening, research on women writers, puzzles.

Addresses

Agent—c/o Author Mail, Morgan Reynolds Publishing, 620 South Elm St., Greensboro, NC 27406. *E-mail*—gingerbrackett@hotmail.com.

Career

Medical technologist in Little Rock, AR, and Denver, CO, 1973-78; manager and co-owner of ophthalmology

Virginia Brackett

practice, Joplin, MO, 1978-89. Institute of Children's Literature, West Redding, CT, correspondence instructor, 1993-99; East Central University, Ada, OK, English instructor and professor, 1994-99; Triton College, River Grove, IL, English instructor, beginning 1999.

Member

Society of Children's Book Writers and Illustrators, Modern Language Association, International Shakespeare Association, National Council of Teachers of English.

Awards, Honors

University of Kansas Merrill Research Award, 1994; included in catalog of recommended reading for teens, New York Public Library, 1996, for *Elizabeth Cary: Writer of Conscience;* East Central University research grants, 1997, 1998, for *Early Women Writers: Voices from the Margins;* Oklahoma Humanities Foundation research grant and East Central University grant, both 1999, both for "Angie Debo: American Indian Champion"; named an Illinois author, Illinois Library Association, 2004; recommended feminist books for youth,

Amelia Bloomer Project/American Library Association Feminist Task Force of the Social Responsibilities Round Table, and Tristate Series of Note designation, both 2005, both for *Restless Genius;* Tristate Book of Note designation, 2005, for *A Home in the Heart.*

Writings

FOR YOUNG ADULTS

Elizabeth Cary: Writer of Conscience (biography), Morgan Reynolds (Greensboro, NC), 1996.

Charles Dickens's David Copperfield, Edcon Publishing, 1998.

Jeff Bezos (juvenile biography), Chelsea House (Philadelphia, PA), 2000.

John Brown: Abolitionist (juvenile biography), Chelsea House (Philadelphia, PA), 2001.

F. Scott Fitzgerald: A Biography, Morgan Reynolds (Greensboro, NC), 2001.

F. Scott Fitzgerald: Writer of the Jazz Age, Morgan Reynolds (Greensboro, NC), 2002.

Menachem Begin, Chelsea House (Philadelphia, PA), 2003.
Steve Jobs: Computer Genius of Apple, Enslow Publishers (Berkeley Heights, NJ), 2003.
Restless Genius: The Story of Virginia Woolf, Morgan Reynolds (Greensboro, NC), 2004.
A Home in the Heart: The Story of Sandra Cisneros, Morgan Reynolds (Greensboro, NC), 2005.

OTHER

Classic Love and Romance Literature: An Encyclopedia of Works, Characters, Authors, and Themes (nonfiction), ABC-Clio (Santa Barbara, CA), 1999.
The Contingent Self: One Reading Life (adult nonfiction), Purdue University Press (West Lafayette, IN), 2001.

Contributor to books, including *Catholic Women Writers,* Greenwood Publishing (Westport, CT), 2001; *Absolutism and the Scientific Revolution 1600-1720,* Greenwood Publishing, 2002; *Encyclopedia of Catholic Culture,* edited by Mary R. Reichardt, Greenwood Publishing, 2004; *Facts on File Companion to British Literature: Beginnings through Nineteenth Centuries,* Facts on File, 2005; and *Facts on File Companion to British Poetry: Seventeenth and Eighteenth Centuries,* 2007. Contributor of more than one hundred stories and articles, juvenile and adult, to periodicals, including *Children's Writer, Byline, Write Now, Children's Digest, Turtle, Today's Family,* and *Today's Christian Woman.* Contributor of articles to academic journals, including *Notes & Queries, Mosaic,* and *Women and Language.*

Sidelights

A teacher at the college level, Virginia Brackett also inspires younger students through her writing. She has published several biographies that relate the life stories of interesting individuals, including writers F. Scott Fitzgerald, Virginia Woolf, Sandra Cisneros, and Elizabeth Cary; former Israeli Prime Minister Menachem Begin; notorious abolitionist John Brown; and entrepreneurs Steve Jobs and Jeff Bezos. Designed for students, each of her biographies includes photographs and other illustrations, as well as time lines that help put the subject's life into its historical context.

A Home in the Heart: The Story of Sandra Cisneros follows the Chicana writer through her Chicago childhood through her adult years in San Antonio, Texas, as she attempts to straddle both American culture and her Mexican heritage. Through her autobiographical works such as *The House on Mango Street,* Cisneros has added a strong Latina voice to the growing body of American literature. Noting that Cisneros is "a compelling contemporary figure with significant YA appeal," *Bulletin of the Center for Children's Books* reviewer Karen Coates wrote that *A Home in the Heart* will "provide a starting place for interested readers," while *Booklist* critic Hazel Rochman deemed Brackett's biography a "lively account" that covers both Cisneros's writing and her work as an activist.

Nineteenth-century British writer Virginia Woolf led a complex personal life that haunted her until her suicide in middle age. Woolf's writing, while sometimes tackled in high school English classes, is sophisticated as well as autobiographical, and Brackett's *Restless Genius: The Story of Virginia Woolf* helps to make works such as *Mrs. Dalloway* and *To the Lighthouse* more approachable to teen readers. Praising Brackett's book as "short" and "well-organized," Carolyn Phelan added in *Booklist* that the work discusses Woolf's life, relationships, and work, combining these elements in "an involving story of an unusual woman" who, while little understood by her contemporaries, came to be considered one of the foremost writers of her day. Noting that Brackett also discusses the social and intellectual movements that influenced Woolf's work and life, *School Library Journal* reviewer Lori Matthews added that *Restless Genius* is an "accessible, engaging biography" that is both "a quick read and a good resource for reports."

Brackett once told *SATA:* "I did not begin writing for publication until I was almost forty years old. The article that jumpstarted my career featured my mother and my father, who was killed in Korea, and I over-

In this 2004 biography for younger readers, Brackett profiles the life of a writer whose personal life was as complex as her writing was innovative.

came my hesitance to write through a creative writing course at a local university. Although I had enjoyed writing in high school (I wrote most of the scripts for our high school assemblies during my senior year), I ended up pursuing a career in medical technology, then business, and also helped to raise three children. I used all of these activities as an excuse not to write. Following a critical life change, I rediscovered the great nurturing effect of writing, and I returned to college in 1989 to obtain a graduate degree in English, believing that a serious study of literature would help my writing abilities. It certainly did that, but it also did more. Along the way, I discovered a love for teaching, which became my third vocation. I also decided that I wanted to mold what many readers might consider the 'esoteric' subject matter of academia for popular readers, including a young audience.

"My academic studies of early women writers (1500s-1800s) ignited a tremendous excitement over a group of courageous individuals about whom little was known. This led to the writing and publication of two of my books, *Elizabeth Cary: Writer of Conscience* and *Early Women Writers: Voices from the Margins*. All of the women discussed in these books wrote, and some even published, during an extremely difficult time for women to be heard. Their pursuit of creative goals I found astounding, and I wanted to share that with an audience [that seems] to most need that motivation and inspiration: young readers. No one can read of Elizabeth Cary, writing while separated from her children and rejected by her husband due to her religious beliefs, and fail to think 'Wow—if she can do it, so can I,' whatever that 'it' happens to be.

"I would say to aspiring writers that the particular date on which you begin writing remains unimportant. What is important is the fact that you may, indeed, incorporate your personal passions into your writing. You simply must share those things you love the best with others."

Biographical and Critical Sources

PERIODICALS

Booklist, September 15, 1999, J.E. Sheets, review of *Classic Love and Romance Literature,* p. 301; September 15, 2004, Carolyn Phelan, review of *Restless Genius: The Story of Virginia Woolf,* p. 229; December 1, 2004, Hazel Rochman, review of *A Home in the Heart: The Story of Sandra Cisneros,* p. 645.
Book Notes, December, 2004, review of *A Home in the Heart.*
Bulletin of the Center for Children's Books,, November, 2004, Karen Coates, review of *Restless Genius: The Story of Virginia Woolf;* May, 2005, Karen Coates, review of *A Home in the Heart.*
Choice, January, 2000, review of *Classic Love and Romance Literature,* p. 894.
Library Journal, August, 1999, Peter A. Dollard, review of *Classic Love and Romance Literature,* p. 74.
School Library Journal, Maru H. Cole, review of *Classic Love and Romance Literature,* p. 77; May, 2002, Trisha Stevenson Medeiros, review of *F. Scott Fitzgerald,* p. 165; February, 2003, Jack Forman, review of *Menachem Begin,* p. 154; November, 2004, Lori Matthews, review of *Restless Genius,* p. 159; March, 2005, Joel Banglian, review of *A Home in the Heart,* p. 224.
Voice of Youth Advocates, April, 2002, review of *Jeff Bezos,* p. 58; May, 2002, Patricia Ann Owens, review of *John Brown: Abolitionist,* p. 165; August, 2002, review of *F. Scott Fitzgerald,* p. 216.

* * *

BRACKETT, Virginia Roberts Meredith
See BRACKETT, Virginia

* * *

BRADBURY, Edward P.
See MOORCOCK, Michael

* * *

BRUEL, Nick

Personal

Married; wife's name Carina.

Addresses

Home—Tarrytown, NY. *Agent*—c/o Author Mail, Roaring Brook Press, 2 Old New Milford Rd., Brookfield, CT 06804. *E-mail*—nick@nickbruel.com.

Career

Cartoonist and children's book author.

Awards, Honors

Top-ten finalist, Dr. Seuss Picture-Book Contest, 1993.

Writings

Boing, Roaring Brook Press (Brookfield, CT), 2004.
Bad Kitty, Roaring Brook Press (New Milford, CT), 2005.

Also author of *How to Be a Real Good Cartoonist,* 2003. Contributor to *Syncopated Comics.*

Sidelights

Author and cartoonist Nick Bruel brings his quirky sense of humor to bear on children's literature in the picture books *Boing* and *Bad Kitty.* Dubbed a "bouncy solo debut" by a *Kirkus Reviews* contributor, *Boing* fol-

A young joey gets a lesson in leaping from his enthusiastic animal friends in Bruel's encouraging self-illustrated picture book, Boing.

lows a young kangaroo as he learns how to jump from his mother. Despite being cheered on by his animal friends rabbit, frog, koala, and grasshopper, the young kanga's hop turns into a flop every time, until it is discovered that he has stuffed his pouch too full of treasures to become sufficiently airborne. Praising the book for its "sunny watercolor and ink cartoons" and its toddler appeal, *Horn Book* contributor Christine Heppermann added that *Boing* "is an accomplishment designed to have preschoolers springing from their seats." A *Publishers Weekly* writer agreed, noting that because "Bruel's cartoons brim with energy and emotion," *Boing* is "not a book for bedtime."

A delightful romp disguised as an alphabet book, *Bad Kitty* finds the family cat perplexed when she realizes that her owners have run out of cat food, and when she learns that the only edibles around are both healthy and nutritious, her mood quickly goes from bad to worse. Kitty turns her nose up at the alphabetical array of foods, ranging from asparagus to zucchini, and retaliates with typical bad-cat abandon. Finally her repentant owners restock the kitchen with her favorites, including anchovies, shark sushi, and baked zebra ziti, and bad kitty is transformed into a very, very good kitty. "Even readers who've mastered their ABCs will laugh at Bruel's gleefully composed litanies and the can-you-top-this spirit that animates every page," commented a *Publishers Weekly* critic, while *School Library Journal* reviewer Maura Bresnahan concluded that *Bad Kitty* "will appeal to youngsters who like their stories more naughty than nice." In *Kirkus Reviews* a contributor predicted that "Even the alphabet-experienced will love this bad, bad kitty!," while *Bookpage.com* reviewer Lynn Beckwith observed that "Bruel has created a joyfully silly portrait of a picky eater with attitude."

Biographical and Critical Sources

PERIODICALS

Horn Book, January-February, 2005, Christina M. Heppermann, review of *Boing,* p. 72.

Kirkus Reviews, October 15, 2004, review of *Boing!,* p. 1002; September 15, 2005, review of *Bad Kitty,* p. 1022.
Publishers Weekly, August 30, 2004, review of *Boing,* p. 53; October 17, 2005, review of *Bad Kitty,* p. 66.
School Library Journal, October, 2005, Maura Bresnahan, review of *Bad Kitty,* p. 109.

ONLINE

Nick Bruel Web site, http://www.nickbruel.com/ (January 24, 2006).*

*   *   *

BUCKLEY, James, Jr. 1963-

Personal

Born January 25, 1963, in Washington, DC; son of James F. and Alice Buckley; married Patricia Kelley (a graphic designer), 1992; children: Conor, Katie. *Education:* University of California, Berkeley, B.A. (English), 1985; Radcliffe Publishing Course, certificate, 1985. *Religion:* Roman Catholic.

Addresses

Office—Shoreline Publishing Group, 125 Santa Rosa Pl., Santa Barbara, CA 93109. *E-mail*—jbuckley@ shorelinepublishing.com.

Career

East West Network, New York, NY, senior editor, 1988-89; *Sports Illustrated,* New York, NY, editorial project manager, 1989-93; *Santa Barbara Independent,* Santa Barbara, CA, columnist, 1993-94; NFL Publishing, Los Angeles, CA, associate editor, then senior editor, 1994-99; Shoreline Publishing Group, president and editorial director, 1999—. Member of boards of directors of Santa Barbara Foresters Baseball and Transition House (homeless shelter).

Member

American Book Producers Association (member of board).

Awards, Honors

Sports Story of the Year, California Newspaper Publishers Association, 1994; Top-Ten Sports Books for Children designation, *Booklist,* 1998, for *America's Greatest Game.*

Writings

The Lost Cowboy Ghost, Scholastic (New York, NY), 1996.
America's Greatest Game: The Real Story of Football and the NFL, Hyperion (New York, NY), 1998.

NFL Rules!, Hyperion (New York, NY), 1998.

Football ("Eyewitness" series), Dorling Kindersley (New York, NY), 1999.

Baseball ("Eyewitness" series), Dorling Kindersley (New York, NY), 2000.

Rumbling Running Backs, Dorling Kindersley (New York, NY), 2001.

Spider-Man's Amazing Powers, Dorling Kindersley (New York, NY), 2001.

Strikeout Kings, Dorling Kindersley (New York, NY), 2001.

Super Shortstops: Nomar, A-Rod, and Jeter, Dorling Kindersley (New York, NY), 2001.

The Visual Dictionary of Baseball, Dorling Kindersley (New York, NY), 2001.

Home Run Heroes, Dorling Kindersley (New York, NY), 2001.

Monster Jam: The Amazing Guide, Dorling Kindersley (New York, NY), 2001.

NBA All-Time Super Scorers, Scholastic (New York, NY), 2001.

Peyton Manning, Dorling Kindersley (New York, NY), 2001.

Roberto Clemente, Dorling Kindersley (New York, NY), 2001.

(With Jim Gigliotti) *Baseball: A Celebration!,* Dorling Kindersley (New York, NY), 2001.

Play Ball!: The Official Major League Baseball Guide for Young Players, photographs by Mike Eliason, Dorling Kindersley (New York, NY), 2002.

NBA Superstars, Scholastic (New York, NY), 2002.

Bill Bradley, Rosen Publishing (New York, NY), 2002.

Great Moments in Football, World Almanac (Milwaukee, WI), 2002.

Great Moments in Hockey, World Almanac (Milwaukee, WI), 2002.

(With David Fischer) *Baseball Top Ten,* Dorling Kindersley (New York, NY), 2002, 2nd edition, 2004.

(With Jim Platt) *Sports Immortals: Stories of Inspiration and Achievement,* photographs by Matt Silk, Triumph Books (Chicago, IL), 2002.

Perfect: The Story of Baseball's Sixteen Perfect Games, Triumph Books (Chicago, IL), 2002, expanded as *Perfect: The Story of Baseball's Seventeen Perfect Games,* 2005.

(With Robert Stremme) *Scholastic Book of Lists,* Scholastic (New York, NY), 2003.

The World of Baseball (reader), Dorling Kindersley (New York, NY), 2003.

Super Bowl, 2nd edition, Dorling Kindersley (New York, NY), 2003.

Venus and Serena Williams, World Almanac (Milwaukee, WI), 2003.

The Incredible Hulk's Book of Strength, Dorling Kindersley (New York, NY), 2003.

Life in the Pits: Twenty Seconds That Make the Difference, Tradition Books (Excelsior, MN), 2003.

(With David Fischer) *Ice Skating Stars,* Dorling Kindersley (New York, NY), 2004.

Speedway Superstars, Readers' Digest Children's Publishing (Pleasantville, NY), 2004.

World Series Heroes, Dorling Kindersley (New York, NY), 2004.

One Thousand and One Facts about Hitters, statistics compiled by Matt Marini, Dorling Kindersley (New York, NY), 2004.

(With John Walters) *Sports in America: 1900-1919* (first volume in 8-volume series), Facts on File (New York, NY), 2004.

Space Heroes: Amazing Astronauts, Dorling Kindersley (New York, NY), 2004.

The Starting Line: Life as a NASCAR Rookie, Child's World (Chanhassen, MN), 2004.

(With Phil Pepe) *Unhittable: Reliving the Magic and Drama of Baseball's Best-Pitched Games,* Triumph Books (Chicago, IL), 2004.

NASCAR: Speedway Superstars, Reader's Digest Children's Books (Pleasantville, NY), 2004.

Muhammad Ali, World Almanac Library (Milwaukee, WI), 2004.

American Football Conference North: The Baltimore Ravens, the Cincinnati Bengals, the Cleveland Browns, and the Pittsburgh Steelers, Child's World (Chanhassen, MN), 2004.

American Football Conference South: The Houston Texans, the Indianapolis Colts, the Jacksonville Jaguars, and the Tennessee Titans, Child's World (Chanhassen, MN), 2004.

American Football Conference East, Child's World (Chanhassen, MN), 2005.

Scholastic Book of Firsts, Scholastic (New York, NY), 2005.

The Bathroom Companion, Quirk, 2005.

NASCAR ("Eyewitness" series), Dorling Kindersley (New York, NY), 2005.

A Batboy's Day, Dorling Kindersley (New York, NY), 2005.

(With David Fischer) *Greatest Sports Rivalries,* Barnes & Noble (New York, NY), 2005.

Let's Go to the Ballpark, Dorling Kindersley (New York, NY), 2005.

World's Biggest Everything, Time Inc. Home Entertainment (New York, NY), 2006.

Sidelights

In addition to his work as a professional editor, James Buckley, Jr., is also the author of many books on American sports that are geared toward young fans and budding athletes. Focusing on baseball, he has produced *Play Ball!: The Official Major League Baseball Guide for Young Players, Baseball: A Celebration!,* and *A Batboy's Day,* the last the profile of a teen who helps set up batting cages and makes game-day preparations for the Anaheim Angels. Buckley's books on football include *America's Greatest Game: The Real Story of Football and the NFL* and *Football,* the latter part of Dorling Kindersley's "Eyewitness" series. *School Library Journal* reviewer Richard Luzer noted that *America's Greatest Game,* which features full-color photographs of players ranging from little league to professional, is "certain to be a popular browsing item for young football fans." Other books composed primarily of photographs includes *Baseball: A Celebration!*, which contains 800 memorable images from the history of the game. While also fully illustrated, *Play Ball!* serves as a primer for budding players, covering warm-ups, the responsibilities of each position on the field, and batting techniques, all geared for elementary-aged readers. Reviewing *Play Ball!* in *Booklist*, GraceAnne A. DeCandido noted that Buckley's prose is "lively, the language nonsexist . . . , and the advice sagely rendered."

Buckley, who has founded a company called Shoreline Publishing Group to produce books for reluctant readers, maintains that sports are far more than simple hobbies or ways to burn off excess energy. In fact, well-known athletes frequently serve as role models for young children, and in his biographies of athletes such as basketball player Bill Bradley and baseball player Roberto Clemente, as well as in *Sports Immortals: Stories of Inspiration and Achievement,* he fosters that influential role. Dubbing the book "a marvel" due to its photographs and layout, *Booklist* reviewer Bill Ott further described *Sports Immortals* as "a browsing bonanza for all sports fans." Together with several other writers, Buckley and Shoreline Publishing Group have also produced an eight-volume history of American athletics titled "Sports in America," which follows the influence of sports on both U.S. culture and history on a year-by-year basis. *Sports in America: 1900-1919,* Buckley's contribution to the series, profiles such high-profile events as the notorious 1904 Olympic Games held in St. Louis, as well as developments in professional sports and individual human achievements in everything from swimming to running. Noting that the volumes in the series "face controversies head on," Michael McCullough wrote in *School Library Journal* that the books provide students and general readers with a "well-written, well-researched" resource.

Buckley once told *SATA:* "For as long as I can remember, sports have been central to my life, whether as a player, a fan, or a coach. Since high school, I've known that I wanted to be a writer, and I've been able to combine my love for sports and writing.

"I sort of fell into writing for children, and enjoyed it immensely from the start. And through a variety of adventures in the publishing trade on both coasts, I have arrived at a point where I seem to be doing nothing but writing about sports for kids.

"But shouldn't I be writing about something more serious for kids, something that will help them develop as members of twenty-first-century society? Is sports something kids should read about when there are more important things out there? To people who think that, I

say 'Lighten up.' When presented in the right way (and I hope readers and parents agree that our books are done in that 'right way'), sports can teach as many lessons as a lecture from a teacher. History, character, perseverance, style, physical fitness, goal-setting and goal-achieving—all these are part of the story of sports in the books I've been lucky enough to write or help create.

"Are there things wrong with sport? Sure, but why focus on the bad things and ignore the good things? My books focus on the good things. Let kids learn the bad stuff later. When they read the books I've written about sports, they're having fun. Do we teach them some things too? Well, sure.

"But don't tell them that.

"Through my own writing and through books produced by my company, the Shoreline Publishing Group, I'm working to disprove the theory that 'boys don't read,'" Buckley more recently added. "The vast majority of our products are aimed at young boys with a love of sports. We've had nothing but success with combining exciting sports action and facts with great design to make books that boys not only read . . . but love!"

Biographical and Critical Sources

PERIODICALS

Booklist, November 15, 1998, p. 582; October 1, 2001, Isabel Schon, review of *Roberto Clemente,* p. 328; November 15, 2001, Wes Lukowsky, review of *Baseball: A Celebration!,* p. 539; March 1, 2002, Wes Lukowsky, review of *Perfect: The Inside Story of Baseball's Sixteen Perfect Games,* p. 1077; May 15, 2002, GraceAnne A. DeCandido, review of *Play Ball! The Official Major League Baseball Guide for Young Players,* p. 1593; September 1, 2002, Bill Ott, review of *Sports Immortals: Stories of Inspiration and Achievement,* p. 44, and Roger Leslie, review of *Bill Bradley,* p. 129.

Library Journal, February 1, 2002, Robert C. Cottrell, review of *Perfect,* p. 103.

Natural History, April, 2002, George Gmelch, review of *Baseball: A Celebration!,* p. 94.

School Library Journal, February, 1999, Richard Luzer, review of *America's Greatest Game,* p. 114; February, 2005, Michael McCullough, review of "Sports in America," series, p. 82; July, 2002, Blair Christolon, review of *Play Ball!,* p. 104.

Voice of Youth Advocates, August, 2002, review of *Bill Bradley,* p. 213.

C

CARRIER, Roch 1937-

Personal
Born May 13, 1937, in Sainte-Justine-de-Dorchester, Quebec, Canada; son of Georges (in sales) and Marie-Anna (Tanguay) Carrier; married Diane Gosselin, 1959; children: two daughters. *Education:* Attended College Saint-Louis; University of Montreal, B.A., M.A., 1961; further study at Sorbonne, University of Paris, 1961-64.

Addresses
Home—Montreal, Quebec, Canada. *Agent*—c/o Author Mail, Tundra Books/Livres Toundra, 75 Sherbourne St., 5th Floor, Toronto, Ontario M5A 2P9, Canada.

Career
Novelist, poet, dramatist, screenwriter, and author of short fiction. Has held teaching positions at College Militaire Royal de Saint-Jean, Quebec, and at University of Montreal, Montreal, Quebec; lecturer. Theatre du Nouveau Monde, Quebec, secretary-general, 1970—; chair, Salon du Livre, Montreal; Canada Council, Ottawa, director, 1994—; appointed national librarian of Canada, 1999-2004.

Awards, Honors
Prix Litteraire de la Province de Quebec, 1964, for *Jolis deuils: Petites tragedies pour adultes;* Grand Prix Litteraire, City of Montreal, 1981; Stephen Leacock Prize for humor, 1991, for *Prayers of a Very Wise Child;* named officer, Order of Canada.

Roch Carrier

Writings

FOR CHILDREN

Les enfants du bonhomme dans la lune, illustrated by Sheldon Cohen, Stanké (Montreal, Quebec, Canada), 1979, reprinted, 1998, translation by Sheila Fischman published as *The Hockey Sweater, and Other Stories,* Anansi (Toronto, Ontario, Canada), 1979, reprinted, 1999.

Ne faites pas mal a l'avenir, Editions Paulinas, 1984.

Un champion, illustrated by Sheldon Cohen, Livres Toundra (Toronto, Ontario, Canada), 1991, translation by

Sheila Fischman published as *The Boxing Champion,* Tundra Books (Plattsburgh, NY), 1991.

Un bonne et heureuse année, illustrated by Gilles Pelletier, Livres Toundra (Toronto, Ontario, Canada), 1991, published as *A Happy New Year's Day,* Tundra Books (Plattsburgh, NY), 1991.

Canada je t'aime—I Love You, illustrated by Miyuki Tanobe, Tundra Books (Plattsburgh, NY), 1991.

Le plus long circuit, illustrated by Sheldon Cohen, Livres Toundra (Toronto, Ontario, Canada), 1993, translation by Sheila Fischman published as *The Longest Home Run,* Tundra Books (Plattsburgh, NY), 1993.

Joueur de basket-ball, illustrated by Sheldon Cohen, Livres Toundra (Toronto, Ontario, Canada), 1996, translation by Sheila Fischman published as *The Basketball Player,* Tundra Books (Plattsburgh, NY), 1996.

Le chandail de hockey, illustrated by Sheldon Cohen, Livres Toundra (Toronto, Ontario, Canada), 1999.

La chasse-galerie, illustrated by Sheldon Cohen, Livres Toundra (Toronto, Ontario, Canada), 2004, translated by Sheila Fischman as *The Flying Canoe,* Tundra Books (Plattsburgh, NY), 2004.

NOVELS; FOR ADULTS

La guerre, Yes Sir! (also see below), Editions du Jour (Montreal, Quebec, Canada), 1968, translation by Sheila Fischman published under the same title, Anansi (Toronto, Ontario, Canada), 1970.

Floralie, où es-tu? (also see below), Editions du Jour (Montreal, Quebec, Canada), 1969, translation by Sheila Fischman published as *Floralie, Where Are You?,* Anansi (Toronto, Ontario, Canada), 1971.

Il est par là, le soleil (also see below), Editions du Jour (Montreal, Quebec, Canada), 1970, translation by Sheila Fischman published as *Is It the Sun, Philibert?,* Anansi (Toronto, Ontario, Canada), 1972.

Le deux-millième étage, Editions du Jour (Montreal, Quebec, Canada), 1973, translation by Sheila Fischman published as *They Won't Demolish Me!,* Anansi (Toronto, Ontario, Canada), 1974.

Le jardin des délices, Editions la Press (Montreal, Quebec, Canada), 1975, translation by Sheila Fischman published as *The Garden of Delights,* Anansi (Toronto, Ontario, Canada), 1978.

Il n'y a pas de pays sans grand-père, Stanké (Montreal, Quebec, Canada), 1979, translation by Sheila Fischman published as *No Country without Grandfathers,* Anansi (Toronto, Ontario, Canada, 1981.

Les fleurs vivent-elles ailleurs que sur la terre, Stanké (Montreal, Quebec, Canada), 1980.

La trilogie de l'âge sombre (contains *La guerre, Yes Sir!, Floralie, où es-tu?,* and *Il est par là, le soleil*), Stanké (Montreal, Quebec, Canada), 1981.

La dame qui avait des chaînes aux chevilles, Stanké (Montreal, Quebec, Canada), 1981, translation by Sheila Fischman published as *Lady with Chains,* Anansi, 1984.

De l'amour dans la ferraille, Stanké (Montreal, Quebec, Canada), 1984, translation by Sheila Fischman published as *Heartbreaks along the Road,* Anansi (Toronto, Ontario, Canada), 1987.

L'ours et le kangourou, Stanké (Montreal, Quebec, Canada), 1986.

Un chameau en jordanie, Stanké (Montreal, Quebec, Canada), 1988.

Prières d'un enfant très très sage, Stanké (Montreal, Quebec, Canada), 1988, translation by Sheila Fischman published as *Prayers of a Very Wise Child,* Penguin (Toronto, Ontario, Canada), 1991.

L'homme dans le placard (mystery), Stanké (Montreal, Quebec, Canada), 1991, translation by Sheila Fischman published as *The Man in the Closet,* Viking (Toronto, Ontario, Canada), 1993.

Fin, Stanké (Montreal, Quebec, Canada), 1992, translation by Sheila Fischman published as *The End,* Viking (Toronto, Ontario, Canada), 1994.

Petit homme tornade, Stanké (Montreal, Quebec, Canada), 1996, translation by Sheila Fischman published as *The Lament of Charlie Longsong,* Viking, 1998.

Un chaise, Stanké (Montreal, Quebec, Canada), 1999.

Les moines dans la tour, XYZ Éditeur (Montreal, Quebec, Canada), 2004.

PLAYS

La guerre, Yes Sir! (four-act; adapted from Carrier's novel; produced in Montreal, 1970; English-language version produced in Stratford, Ontario, 1972), Editions du Jour (Montreal, Quebec, Canada), 1970, revised edition, 1973.

Floralie (adapted from Carrier's novel *Floralie, où es-tu?;* produced in Montreal, 1974), Editions du Jour (Montreal, Quebec, Canada), 1974.

Il n'y a pas de pays sans grand-père (adapted from Carrier's novel), produced in Montreal, Quebec, 1978.

La celeste bicyclette (produced in Montreal, 1979; translation produced in Toronto as *The Celestial Bicycle,* 1982), Stanke (Montreal, Quebec, Canada), 1980.

SCREENPLAYS

Le martien de Noël, National Film Board of Canada, 1970.

The Ungrateful Land, National Film Board of Canada, 1972.

The Hockey Sweater (short subject), animated by Sheldon Cohen, National Film Board of Canada, 1980.

OTHER

Les jeux incompris (poetry), Editions Nocturne (Montreal, Quebec, Canada), 1956.

Cherche tes mots, cherche tes pas (poetry), Editions Nocturne (Montreal, Quebec, Canada), 1958.

Jolis deuils: petites tragedies pour adultes (stories), Editions du Jour, 1964, reprinted, Stanké (Montreal, Quebec, Canada), 1999.

L'aube d'acier (poem), illustrated by Maurice Savoie, Auteurs Reunis, 1971.

Les voyageurs de l'arc-en-ciel, illustrations by François Olivier, Stanké (Montreal, Quebec, Canada), 1980.

Le cirque noir, Stanké (Montreal, Quebec, Canada), 1982.

Enfants de la planete, Paulines, 1989.

Le rocket (biography), Stanké (Montreal, Quebec, Canada), 2000, translated as *Our Life with the Rocket: The Maurice Richard Story,* Viking (New York, NY), 2001.

Le petit bonhomme rond qui avait des plume à son chapeau melon (stories), Éditions du Lilas (Vallée-Jonction, Quebec, Canada), 2001.

(Author of introduction) *626 by 9: A Goal-by-Goal Timeline of Maurice "The Rocket" Richard's Scoring Career in Pictures, Stats, and Stories,* Canadian Museum of Civilization (Gatineau, Quebec, Canada), 2004.

Contributor of short stories to periodicals, including *Études françaises* and *Ellipse.* Contributor of articles to periodicals, including *Écrits du Canada français.*

Sidelights

Honored as national librarian of Canada from 1999 to 2004, Quebec-based writer Roch Carrier has been cited among French Canada's most important novelists. With the translation of many of his works into English, Carrier is also widely known among American and British readers, where his adult novels such as *La Guerre, Yes Sir!* and *No Country without Grandfathers.* Earning recognition in the early 1970s with a trio of adult novels that focus on a half-century of Quebec history, he has established a reputation for his sensitive portrayal of the often-turbulent misunderstandings that exist between French-and English-speaking Canadians. A multi-talented writer, Carrier has also adapted several of his novels for the stage, and has promoted Canadian children's literature through both his own books for children and his work as Canada's national librarian from 1999 to 2004. Carrier's children's book *The Hockey Sweater* is considered a classic, and his other books for young readers, including *A Happy New Year's Day, The Longest Home Run,* and *The Flying Canoe,* have also received positive recognition.

Illustrated by Carrier's frequent collaborator Sheldon Cohen and written for elementary-grade readers, *The Hockey Sweater* draws on the author's youth and also reflects Carrier's personal views on topics ranging from French-Canadian nationalism to the English-French language barrier. In the story, "a disastrous boyhood episode is fondly recreated," according to *Horn Book* reviewer Ethel L. Heins. Growing up in Sainte-Justine, a small town in rural Quebec, Carrier was something of an oddity: a boy who wanted to be a writer while most of his friends aspired to become lumberjacks. However, the boys were united by their idolization of the beloved Montreal Canadiens. In the story, the young Roch is understandably mortified when his mother presents him with a new jersey—that of the hated rival Toronto Maple Leafs. To make matters worse, Roch is expected to wear the dreaded blue-and-white in public. "*The Hockey Sweater* is a funny story," asserted *School Library Journal* contributor Joan McGrath, "but it is the fun of an adult looking indulgently back to remember a horrible childhood humiliation from the tranquil plateau of adulthood."

Originally published in French, **The Basketball Player** *focuses on a young boy who learns that the things he fears are usually not as bad as they seem at first glance. (Illustration by Sheldon Cohen.)*

A sequel to *The Hockey Sweater, The Boxing Champion* again follows the life of young Roch as he strives to become a winning boxer despite the fact that his athletic talents are no match for those of the more durable Côte brothers. The boy appears again in *A Happy New Year's Day*, which features the author's recollections of New Year's Day 1941, including numerous details about his large extended family. "Carrier has filled his story with humour and an eye for the sort of clever details that many think children miss," remarked Linda Granfield in a review of the last-named title for *Quill & Quire*. Patricia L.M. Butler, writing in the *Canadian Review of Materials*, called *A Happy New Year's Day* "a story full of wonder, hope, joy and promise that should be felt by all each New Year's Day." Praising *The Boxing Champion* as a "humorously self-deprecating" tale, Norma Charles also cited Carrier's text for its "wit, lilt, and cadence" in a *Canadian Review of Materials* appraisal.

In *The Basketball Player* Roch reluctantly attends a seminary boarding school. Although he tries to make the best of it, after he is dealt with harshly by one of the school's priests and is forced to play basketball, a sport he despises, he runs away. On his own out in the dark, Roch experiences some fearsome realities that prompt his hasty return, and by accepting the encouragement of his new coach he finally makes his first basket. Welwyn Wilton Katz, reviewing *The Basketball Player* for *Books in Canada*, described the work as "a book about fear, and cold, and loneliness, about saying goodbye, about death," while *Quill & Quire* contributor Barbara Greenwood observed that Carrier's tale "ends on a wry note" featuring one of the author's "trademark subversive twists."

Carrier leaves his young alter-ego in several of his stories for younger readers but continues to infuses these seemingly simple tales with complex, adult-oriented themes. Set in 1940s Quebec, *The Longest Home Run* finds a boys' pick-up baseball game interrupted when a girl named Adeline asks to play. Accepted by the boys, she promptly hits the longest home run that any of the young players have ever witnessed; when asked who she is, Adeline gives her name and divulges that she is a magician associated with a traveling theater act visiting the area. The boys later attend the magic show, watch Adeline's father make her "disappear," and then are not allowed to see her anymore. Jetske Sybesma, writing in *Canadian Children's Literature*, commented on the story's wry commentary on the "older generation's stereotypical opinion about a girl's abilities which results in denying a talented child . . . the opportunity to develop her potential." A *Kirkus Reviews* critic, who called *The Longest Home Run* "another offbeat sports story" combining the talents of Carrier and illustrator Sheldon Cohen, concluded: "There's no real plot here, but the incidents are lively and amusing, while the near-surreal illustrations glow with energetic perspectives and intriguing comical details."

A group of lumberjacks stranded at a remote logging camp during Christmas find a way to return to their families with the help of a magic canoe in **The Flying Canoe.** *(Illustration by Sheldon Cohen.)*

Based on a French-Canadian folk tale, *The Flying Canoe* brings readers back to the mid-nineteenth century and introduces eleven-year-old Baptiste, who is working as a lumberjack in a remote logging camp. It is winter, and the loggers, homesick for their families due to the upcoming New Christmas holidays, use their dreams to fuel a plan whereby a canoe will magically transport them to their homes in time to celebrate the arrival of the New Year. Dubbing Carrier "a master storyteller," *Resource Links* contributor Nancy Ryan praised the tale, noting that the author's retelling of "an enchanted space ride" will leave young listeners "enthralled." In *School Library Journal* Corrina Austin was also enthusiastic, writing that all the Canadian author's stories are praiseworthy vehicles capable of "transporting readers back in time to colorful historical settings and wonderful childhood perspectives."

Carrier's award-winning *Prayers of a Very Wise Child*, while not written explicitly for children, has as its basis the prayers of a seven-year-old narrator. Once again set in rural Quebec, this autobiographical work portrays a child's pious simplicity, his puzzlement at the presence of evil—the child wonders why God "kills" little children and allows wars to happen—and his growing awareness of the differences between boys and girls. "The simplicity of [a] child's prayers belies the complexities of life and one's ability to grasp them," maintained Theo Hersh in the *Canadian Review of Materials.* Hersh added that "one of the beauties of Carrier's writing" is that the author "softens the blow of growing up with tender and poignant—and funny—remembrances of childhood." *Quill & Quire* commentator Daniel Jones asserted that *Prayers of a Very Wise Child* "succeeds by its richly comic invention," and in *Canadian Literature* reviewer John Lennox called the author "skilled at underlining the characteristics of human community and in using the child to illustrate the potential and limitations of human understanding."

Throughout his writing career, Carrier has been a strong supporter of a truly Canadian literature. In his role as national librarian of Canada, he advocated strongly for the preservation of a Canadian-centered literature; as David Kemper reported in the *McGill University Graduate School of Library and Information Studies Web site,* Carrier noted in a speech that if Canadians "do not preserve their own cultural and historical identity, other individuals, namely heavily funded Americans and their vast institutions, will record, perhaps incorrectly, Canada's past." He has extended this concern to the realm of Canadian children's literature, remarking to interviewers Alison Blackburn and Meagan Morash on the same Web site: "Why should the Americans always be the heroes?," referencing the books made available to young readers in Canadian public libraries. In a review with Diane Turbide for *Maclean's,* Carrier explained that, despite the lack of government funding for new artists, he nonetheless remains optimistic about the future of Canada's arts. "There would be no planes today if there hadn't been somebody, somewhere, who was dreaming of flying. It always starts with a dream. And artists are the ones who are dreaming. We need dreams. . . . Because dreams are vision, and people need vision."

Biographical and Critical Sources

BOOKS

Cameron, Donald, *Conversations with Canadian Novelists,* Macmillan of Canada (Toronto, Ontario, Canada), 1973, pp. 13-29.

Dictionary of Literary Biography, Volume 53: *Canadian Writers since 1960, First Series,* Thomson Gale (Detroit, MI), 1986.

Carrier, Roch, *Prayers of a Very Wise Child,* Penguin (Toronto, Ontario, Canada), 1991.

PERIODICALS

Books in Canada, April, 1997, Welwyn Wilton Katz, review of *The Basketball Player,* p. 34.

Bulletin of the Center for Children's Books, February, 1985, p. 102.

Canadian Children's Literature, Volume 69, 1993, p. 74; fall, 1994, pp. 77-79; winter, 1995, Jetske Sybesma, review of *The Longest Home Run,* pp. 90-91.

Canadian Literature, autumn-winter, 1989, pp. 209-211.

Canadian Review of Materials, March, 1992, Theo Hersh, review of *Prayers of a Very Wise Child,* p. 100.

Horn Book, March, 1985, p. 174; autumn, 1992, John Lennox, review of *Prayers of a Very Wise Child,* pp. 174-176; May, 1992, Ethel L. Heins, review of *The Hockey Sweater,* p. 371.

Kirkus Reviews, June 1, 1993, review of *The Longest Home Run,* p. 716.

Maclean's, April 22, 1996, Diane Turbide, "People Need a Vision," pp. 81-82.

Quill & Quire, March, 1991, p. 20; March, 1993, p. 46; October, 1991, Daniel Jones, review of *Prayers of a Very Wise Child,* pp. 27, 30; November, 1991, Linda Granfield, review of *A Happy New Year's Day,* p. 26; March, 1992, Patricia L.M. Butler, review of *A Happy New Year's Day,* p. 78; June, 1994, p. 45; December, 1996, Barbara Greenwood, review of *The Basketball Player,* p. 36; February, 2000, Anita Lahey, "National Library Ushers in Change," pp. 12-13.

Resource Links, October, 2000, review of *The Lament of Charlie Longsong,* p. 49; February, 2005, Nancy Ryan, review of *The Flying Canoe,* p. 12.

School Library Journal, March, 1985, Joan McGrath, review of *The Hockey Sweater,* p. 164; July, 1991, pp. 54-55; February, 1992, pp. 71-72; April, 2005, Corrina Austin, review of *The Flying Canoe,* p. 120.

ONLINE

Canadian Review of Materials, http://www.umanitoba.ca/cm/ (September, 1991), Norma Charles, review of *The Boxing Champion.*

McGill University Graduate School of Library and Information Studies Web site, http://www.gslis.mcgill/ca/ (November 18, 2005), David Kemper, "Author Becomes National Librarian," and Alison Blackburn and Meagan Morash, interview with Carrier.*

*   *   *

CASSIDY, Anne 1952-

Personal

Born 1952, in London, England; married; children: one son.

Addresses

Agent—c/o Author Mail, Scholastic, Ltd., 1-19 New Oxford St., London WC1A 1NU, England.

Career

Writer. Worked as a teacher in London, England for nineteen years; also worked in a bank.

Awards, Honors

British Book Trust Teenage Book of the Year designation, and Whitbread Children's Book of the Year shortlist, both 2004, and Carnegie Children's Book Award shortlist, 2005, all for *Looking for JJ.*

Writings

FOR CHILDREN

Talking to Strangers, Adlib (Tarporley, England), 1994.

Spider Pie, illustrated by Bee Willey, Hamish Hamilton (London, England), 1995.

The Hidden Child (young-adult novel), Scholastic (London, England) 1997.

The Crying Princess, illustrated by Colin Paine, Franklin Watts (London, England), 2000, Picture Window Books (Minneapolis, MN), 2003.

Pippa and Poppa, illustrated by Philip Norman, Franklin Watts (London, England), 2000.

Cheeky Monkey, illustrated by Lisa Smith, Franklin Watts (London, England) 2000, published as *The Sassy Monkey,* Picture Window Books (Minneapolis, MN), 2005.

Jasper and Jess, illustrated by François Hall, Franklin Watts (London, England), 2001, Picture Window Books (Minneapolis, MN), 2003.

Tough Love (young-adult novel), Scholastic (London, England), 2001.

Naughty Nancy, illustrated by Desideria Guicciardini, Franklin Watts (London, England), 2002, Picture Window Books (Minneapolis, MN), 2005.

Missing Judy (young-adult novel), Scholastic (London, England), 2002.

Love Letters (young-adult novel), Scholastic (London, England), 2003.

Blood Money (young-adult novel), Hodder Children's (London, England), 2003.

Cleo and Leo, illustrated by Philip Norman, Picture Windows Books (Minneapolis, MN), 2003.

Looking for JJ, Scholastic (London, England), 2004.

Toby's Trousers, illustrated by Jan Lewis, Franklin Watts (London, England), 2004, Sea to Sea (North Mankato, MN), 2005.

The Best Den Ever, illustrated by Deborah Allwright, Franklin Watts (London, England), 2004.

(Reteller) *Snow White,* illustrated by Melanie Sharp, Franklin Watts (London, England), 2005.

Birthday Blues (young-adult novel), Scholastic (London, England), 2005.

The Queen's Dragon, illustrated by Gwyneth Williamson, Picture Window Books (Minneapolis, MN), 2005.

Jumping Josie, Sea to Sea (North Mankato, MN), 2005.

CRIME NOVELS

Big Girl's Shoes, Lion Tracks (London, England), 1990.

Driven to Death, Scholastic (London, England), 1994.

"EAST END MURDERS" SERIES; NOVELS

A Family Affair, Scholastic (London, England), 1995.

End of the Line, Scholastic (London, England), 1996.

No Through Roads, Scholastic (London, England), 1996.

Accidental Death, Scholastic (London, England), 1996.

Brotherly Love, Scholastic (London, England), 1997.

Death by Drowning, Scholastic (London, England), 1999.

Dead Quiet, Scholastic (London, England), 2000.

Sidelights

The author of several teen thrillers in the "East End Murders" series as well as other young-adult novels known for their troubled protagonists and compelling plots, British writer Anne Cassidy explained to Madelyn Travis on the *Book Trust Web site* that she is attracted to "dark subjects." "I'm not interested only in whodunit, but in why something's done and how something's done and what effect it has on the people who did it," Cassidy added, in a discussion of her acclaimed novel *Looking for JJ.* In addition to her books for teens, Cassidy has also authored a number of books for entry-level readers.

Based on an actual incident that attracted worldwide attention—the murder of a young toddler by two ten-year-old British boys—*Looking for JJ* introduces another ten year old. Jennifer Jones is a lonely girl whose single mother focuses attention on her job rather than her daughter. Left with little supervision, JJ is drawn to the wrong sort: one of her two friends is a bully who ultimately eggs JJ and her equally weak-willed second friend into an act that has tragic consequences. Through the perspective of its three main characters, *Looking for JJ* focuses on "the power games that are going on, if you're at all soft or lonely or needy," Cassidy explained to Travis, adding of JJ and her friend that the two girls endure their friend's increasingly cruel behavior "just to fit in." Freed following a jail sentence for her participation in a horrific murder, JJ attempts to live life under a new name, but remains haunted by her past.

Other novels by Cassidy include *Tough Love,* which finds Gina falling for an older boy who seems to have his act together until he engages in gang violence and leaves Gina with an important choice to make. *Missing Judy* focuses on the aftermath of a young woman's abduction, as family and friends are left haunted by questions and inner terrors. While a teen is first flattered by the anonymous notes she receives, as *Love Letters* continues she realizes that she is actually being stalked, and *Blood Money* follows three teens who, after discovering a bag of cash and realizing that it is the lost property of a local drug dealer, are now faced with a moral dilemma in which several options could result in violence. Cassidy attempts to understand the thoughts of a young woman who abandons her newborn infant in *Birthday Blues,* another novel inspired by a prominent news story.

A devotee of crime fiction—particularly the novels of Ruth Rendell, Sue Grafton, John Harvey, and Scott Turow—Cassidy has also contributed several books to the detective genre with her "East Side Murders" series. Including the novels *Death by Drowning, No Through Road,* and *Dead Quiet,* these books feature teen sleuth Patsy Kelly, an eighteen year old who works for her uncle's detective agency. "There's a lot more to these books than you'd think," Cassidy noted of crime fiction on her home page. "I love them. At their best they're thrilling and puzzling and—if they're well written—they tell you a lot about human nature and a darker side of life."

Biographical and Critical Sources

PERIODICALS

Magpies, May, 2002, review of *Naughty Nancy,* p. 29; September, 2005, review of *Birthday Blues,* p. 41.
School Librarian, May, 1995, review of *Talking to Strangers,* p. 76; May, 1996, review of *End of the Line,* p. 71; February, 1997, review of *Accidental Death,* p. 44; August, 1997, review of *The Hidden Child,* p. 157; spring, 2000, review of *Death by Drowning,* p. 43; autumn, 2002, review of *The Queen's Dragon,* p. 129, and *Missing Judy,* p. 154; winter, 2003, review of *Blood Money,* p. 207; spring, 2005, Rudolf Lowewnstein, review of *The Best Den Ever,* p. 19; summer, 2005, review of *Looking for JJ,* p. 99.
School Library Journal, November, 2004, Mary Elam, review of *Naughty Nancy,* p. 94; February, 2005, Melinda Piehler, review of *The Queen's Dragon,* p. 94.

ONLINE

Anne Cassidy Home Page, http://www.anne.cassidy4.users.btopenworld.com (October 6, 2005).
British Book Trust Web site, http://www.booktrusted.co.uk/ (November 6, 2005), Madelyn Travis, "No Hiding Place."

*   *   *

CLIMO, Shirley 1928-

Personal

Born November 25, 1928, in Cleveland, OH; daughter of Morton J. (a paving contractor) and Aldarilla (a writer; maiden name, Shipley) Beistle; married George F. Climo (a corporate historian), June 17, 1950; children: Robert, Susan, Lisa. *Education:* Attended DePauw University, 1946-49. *Politics:* "Variable." *Religion:* Protestant.

Addresses

Home—24821 Prospect Ave., Los Altos Hills, CA 94022.

Career

WGAR-Radio, Cleveland, OH, scriptwriter for weekly juvenile series. "Fairytale Theatre," 1949-53; freelance writer, 1976—. President, Los Altos Morning Forum, 1971-73.

Shirley Climo

Member

Authors Guild, Society of Children's Book Writers and Illustrators.

Writings

(Reteller) *Piskies, Spriggans, and Other Magical Beings: Tales from the Droll-Teller* (juvenile), illustrated by Joyce Audy dos Santos, Crowell (New York, NY), 1981.
The Cobweb Christmas (picture book), illustrated by Joe Lasker, Crowell (New York, NY), 1982, published with illustrations by Jane Manning as *Cobweb Christmas,* HarperCollins (New York, NY), 2001.
Gopher, Tanker, and the Admiral (juvenile), illustrated by Eileen McKeating, Crowell (New York, NY), 1984.
Someone Saw a Spider (juvenile) illustrated by Dirk Zimmer, Harper (New York, NY), 1985.
A Month of Seven Days (juvenile historical novel), Crowell (New York, NY), 1987.
King of the Birds (picture book), illustrated by Ruth Heller, Harper (New York, NY), 1988.
The Egyptian Cinderella (picture book), illustrated by Ruth Heller, Crowell (New York, NY), 1989.
T. J.'s Ghost (juvenile), Crowell (New York, NY), 1989.
City! New York (juvenile history), photographs by George Ancona, Macmillan (New York, NY), 1990.

City! San Francisco (juvenile history), photographs by George Ancona, Macmillan (New York, NY), 1990.

City! Washington, D.C. (juvenile history), photographs by George Ancona, Macmillan (New York, NY), 1991.

The Match between the Winds (picture book), illustrated by Roni Shepherd, Macmillan (New York, NY), 1991.

The Korean Cinderella (picture book), illustrated by Ruth Heller, HarperCollins (New York, NY), 1993.

Stolen Thunder (picture book), illustrated by Alexander Koshkin, Clarion (New York, NY), 1994.

The Little Red Ant and the Big Crumb (picture book), illustrated by Francisco X. Mora, Clarion (New York, NY), 1995.

Atalanta's Race (picture book), illustrated by Alexander Koshkin, Clarion (New York, NY), 1995.

The Irish Cinderlad (picture book), illustrated by Loretta Krupinski, HarperCollins (New York, NY), 1996.

(Collector and reteller) *A Treasury of Princesses: Princess Tales from around the World,* illustrated by Ruth Sanderson, HarperCollins (New York, NY), 1996, published as *A Pride of Princesses: Princess Tales from around the World,* illustrated by Angelo Tillery, HarperCollins (New York, NY), 1999.

(Collector and reteller) *A Treasury of Mermaids: Mermaid Tales from around the World,* illustrated by Jean and Mou-sien Tseng, HarperCollins (New York, NY), 1997, published as *A Serenade of Mermaids: Mermaid Tales from around the World,* illustrated by Lisa Falkenstern, HarperTrophy (New York, NY), 1999.

(Reteller) *Magic and Mischief: Tales from Cornwall,* illustrated by Anthony Bacon Venti, Clarion (New York, NY), 1999.

The Persian Cinderella (picture book), illustrated by Robert Florczak, HarperCollins (New York, NY), 1999.

Monkey Business (picture book), illustrated by Erik Brooks, Holt (New York, NY), 2005.

Contributor to books, including Sylvia K. Burack, editor, *Writing and Selling Fillers, Light Verse, and Short Humor,* Writer, Inc. (Boston, MA), 1982; contributor to magazines, including *Family Weekly, Writer, Cricket, Ranger Rick,* and *Seventeen,* and to newspapers.

Sidelights

Shirley Climo's works are often inspired by traditional folk tales and legends; she has compiled collections of folk tales, retold traditional stories as picture books, and woven mythology into her own original stories. In her first children's story book, *Piskies, Spriggans, and Other Magical Beings: Tales from the Droll-Teller,* Climo selects and adapts nine Cornish folk tales filled with magical creatures, surrounding the stories with informative introductions and humorous codas that explain the dialect used and the superstitions presented. In a review for the *New York Times Book Review,* Selma G. Lanes commented on Climo's "lean, no-nonsense prose, which will give her credibility with today's possibly skeptical children." A *Publishers Weekly* contributor called the collection "a folklore aficionado's paradise."

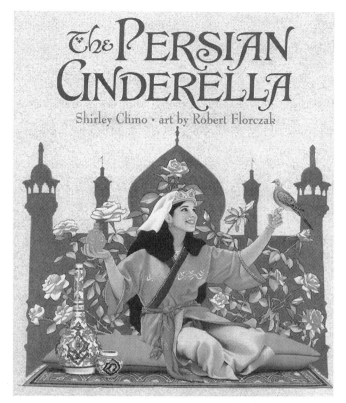

Based on a story from the classic **Arabian Nights,** *Climo's picture book finds a beautiful young girl helped by a genie in her effort to attend a royal ball.* (Cover illustration by Robert Florczak.)

For her next project, Climo retells a 300-year-old German legend that explains the tradition of hanging tinsel on Christmas trees. *The Cobweb Christmas* tells the story of Cristkindel, who takes pity on the cold spiders which have been ejected from a newly cleaned house on Christmas Eve by bringing them inside with him. The spiders cover the Christmas tree in cobwebs which Cristkindel turns to silver and gold. A reviewer for the *Bulletin of the Center for Children's Books* called *The Cobweb Christmas* a "pleasant but rather sedate modern example of a 'why' story." *Cobweb Christmas* was published with new illustrations in 2001.

King of the Birds is another picture book in the "why" genre of children's books. In this work, Climo retells the ancient legend that places the homely wren as king of the birds due to his clever decision to hop aboard an eagle and thereby fly higher and longer than any other bird in the animal kingdom. A *Publishers Weekly* critic remarked, "Climo has created a lively, elegant version of an ancient legend." Richard Peck, reviewing *King of the Birds* in the *Los Angeles Times Book Review,* concluded that the combination of Climo's text and illustrator Ruth Heller's pictures is nearly ideal: "When the birds take wing across a double-page spread, the soul soars." With *The Match between the Winds,* Climo produces another picture book based on legend that has been praised for its evocative setting and the charm of the author's rendering.

In *The Egyptian Cinderella* Climo blended ancient Egyptian folklore and fact in the picture-book story of a young Greek slave girl who marries an Egyptian pharaoh with the help of a pair of magic slippers. While some reviewers perceived an element of racism in the tale's depiction of the fair-haired protagonist's triumph over the darker servant girls, most found the story an exotic take on the traditional and much-loved Cinderella tale. Martha Rosen, reviewing this work for *School Library Journal,* called *The Egyptian Cinderella* "a stunning combination of fluent prose and exquisitely wrought illustrations. Climo has woven this ancient tale . . . with clarity and eloquence." Climo has penned several other variations of the "Cinderella" story, including *The Korean Cinderella, The Irish Cinderlad,* and *The Persian Cinderella.* Of the last title, a *Publishers Weekly* reviewer commented, "Historical details in both the verse and illustrations readily transport readers to 15th-century Persia."

For *Someone Saw a Spider: Spider Facts and Folktales,* Climo retells legends and facts about these creatures, including a bibliography of further sources for the enterprising young reader. Although some reviewers found the book's value to be as a source for storytelling, a *Kirkus Reviews* critic remarked that Climo's "fact-filled and fun" volume "is to be praised for her sparkling retellings." Using *Someone Saw a Spider* as a model,

Monkey lore, monkey facts, and monkey hijinks abound in Climo's **Monkey Business: Stories from around the World.** *(Illustration by Erik Brooks.)*

Climo authored *Monkey Business: Stories from around the World.* This title includes fourteen tales about monkeys in three regions of the world: Africa and Madagascar, the Americas, and Asia. "While staying true to the originals, she adds engaging details and dialogue," wrote Suzanne Myers Harold of Climo's retellings in *School Library Journal.* Like the bibliography in *Someone Saw a Spider, Monkey Business* contains "an extensive, annotated bibliography," according to a critic for *Kirkus Reviews.* The stories in the book are complimented by "facts, sayings, and carefully researched illustrations," noted Eliza Ridgeway, reviewing *Monkey Business* for the *Los Altos Town Crier.*

With *Atalanta's Race,* Climo teams up with Alexander Koshkin, the illustrator she worked with in *Stolen Thunder,* her retelling of a Norse myth. *Atalanta's Race* introduces young readers to the Greek tale of Atalanta, an athlete raised by bears who refuses to marry a man unless he can beat her in a race. With some help from the goddess Aphrodite, Atalanta meets her true love. Along with her retelling of the myth, Climo includes an afterword "that links the heroine to the modern Olympics," as a *Publishers Weekly* reviewer noted.

Climo collects stories of princesses and mermaids in her collections *A Treasury of Princesses* and *A Treasury of Mermaids* (more recently published in paperback as *A Pride of Princesses* and *A Serenade of Mermaids,* respectively). In a review of *A Treasury of Mermaids,* *Booklist* critic Karen Morgan praised Climo's "lyrical use of language."

With her collection *Magic and Mischief* Climo returns to the stories of Cornwall. Like her book *Piskies, Spriggans, and Other Magical Beings, Magic and Mischief* contains tales of Cornish fairies and creatures, and uses Cornish words and phrases to give readers a sense of setting. "Climo's retellings are fresh and creative," noted Shelle Rosenfeld in her *Booklist* review.

Beyond her picture books, Climo has also authored a number of novels for middle-grade readers. The first of these novels, *Gopher, Tanker, and the Admiral,* pairs a young boy nicknamed Gopher with the cranky retired admiral who is his neighbor. Together, the unlikely duo solve the mystery behind the rash of burglaries on their block. A *School Library Journal* reviewer praised the humorous elements in Climo's short novel, and in *Bulletin of the Center for Children's Books* a contributor remarked: "There's appeal in the bridging of a generation gap."

T.J.'s Ghost is Climo's second mystery for middle-grade readers. Set on the California coast, this story focuses on a young girl who expects a dull time when she stays with her aunt and uncle while her parents vacation in Hawaii. Instead she meets a ghost and helps the spectre find the ring that keeps it linked to the material world. Critics praised the evocative setting of Climo's novel more than its plot, but Margaret Mary Ptacek, reviewing *T. J.'s Ghost* in the *Voice of Youth Advocates* concluded: "This isn't a great adventure but a pleasant tale."

A Month of Seven Days is an historical novel for middle-grade readers that is set during the American Civil War. The novel's heroine, twelve-year-old Zoe, and Zoe's mother, are terrified when their home is commandeered by Yankee troops just as Zoe's father is expected home on leave from the Confederate army. Zoe attempts to protect her father by scaring away the superstitious Yankee captain, and in the process learns that even the enemy is human. In *Publishers Weekly* a contributor stated that Zoe's emerging self-confidence, her teasing of the Northern soldiers, and her perception that her enemies are not monsters but human beings "are just a few of the tantalizing issues that are brought to light but never satisfactorily resolved." Taking a more favorable view, a *Kirkus Reviews* writer remarked that "Zoe is believable; her anger and bewilderment are well portrayed, as is the experience of being part of an occupied country."

In a departure from fiction, Climo has also published three travel guides for young tourists that are illustrated with photographs by George Ancona. Comprising *City! New York, City! San Francisco,* and *City! Washington, D.C.,* this series has been commended for its entertainment value as well as for containing suggestions for activities and sights to see in each of the cities featured. Elizabeth S. Watson, reviewing the volume on San Francisco for *Horn Book,* commented that Climo has "produce[d] a superbly clear picture of the city."

"To be a children's book writer always seemed the most wonderful aspiration in the world to me . . . and the most natural," Climo once told *SATA*. "My earliest memory is of being rocked in a creaky wicker carriage while my mother, a children's author, recited her stories. Long before I could read, I'd begun telling my own tales to myself and to anyone else willing to listen." When asked by *Los Altos Town Crier* interviewer Ridgeway what she finds difficult about the writing life, Climo answered: "having to be a self-starter." Discussing her career as a children's book author in a *Writer* article, she also noted: "When I talk to fifth-and six-grade students about writing, most of them want to write for adults, even before they've grown up themselves. When I speak to adult groups, most of them want to write for children. I encourage all of them. For while fewer picture books get into print now than a decade or so ago, today's books are better than ever. Editors are still willing to stop, look, and listen to a good picture book."

Biographical and Critical Sources

PERIODICALS

Booklist, April 15, 1995, Carolyn Phelan, review of *Atalanta's Race,* p. 1494; November 15, 1997, Karen Morgan, review of *A Treasury of Mermaids,* p. 554; July, 1999, Susan Dove Lempke, review of *The Persian Cinderella,* p. 1948; August, 1999, Shelle Rosenfeld, review of *Magic and Mischief,* p. 2048.

Bulletin of the Center for Children's Books, October, 1982, review of *The Cobweb Christmas,* p. 23; September, 1984, review of *Gopher, Tanker, and the Admiral*; March, 1986; October, 1987; February, 1988; October, 1999, review of *Magic and Mischief,* p. 49.

Horn Book, May-June, 1990, Elizabeth S. Watson, review of *City! San Francisco,* p. 346; January-February, 1991, p. 94; July-August, 2005, Margaret A. Bush, review of *Monkey Business,* p. 481.

Kirkus Reviews, November 15, 1985, review of *Someone Saw a Spider: Spider Facts and Folktales,* p. 1266; November 15, 1987, review of *A Month of Seven Days,* p. 1625; March 15, 1989, pp. 460-461; May 15, 2005, review of *Monkey Business,* p. 585.

Los Altos Town Crier, October 19, 2005, Eliza Ridgeway, "Local Author Shirley Climo Visits Linden Tree."

Los Angeles Times Book Review, March 27, 1988, Richard Peck, review of *King of the Birds.*

New York Times Book Review, July 5, 1981, Selma G. Lanes, review of *Piskies, Spriggans, and Other Magical Beings: Tales from the Droll-Teller*; December 11, 1987, review of *A Month of Seven Days,* p. 66; January 15, 1988, review of *King of the Birds,* p. 94; November 12, 1989, p. 50.

Publishers Weekly, March 20, 1981, review of *Piskies, Spriggans, and Other Magical Beings: Tales from the Droll-Teller*; August 6, 1982, p. 70; September 29, 1989, p. 67; May 10, 1991, p. 256; April 10, 1995, review of *Atalanta's Race,* p. 62; May 10, 1999, review of *A Pride of Princesses,* p. 69; June 7, 1999, review of *The Persian Cinderella,* p. 82; August 23, 1999, review of *Magic and Mischief,* p. 61; July 3, 2000, review of *Atalanta's Race,* p. 73; August 27, 2001, review of *The Persian Cinderella,* p. 87.

School Library Journal, February, 1981; May, 1984, p. 101; December, 1985, review of *Gopher, Tanker, and the Admiral,* p. 87; December, 1987, p. 84; August, 1988, p. 79; October, 1989, Martha Rosen, review of *The Egyptian Cinderella*; November, 1989, p. 105; March, 1991; December, 1991; April, 1995, Patricia Lothrop Green, review of *Atalanta's Race,* p. 140; June, 1999, Tina Hudak, review of *A Serenaid of Mermaids* and *A Pride of Princesses,* p. 112; August, 1999, Connie C. Rockman, review of *Magic and Mischief,* p. 167; March, 2004, Andrew Medlar, review of *Atalanta's Race,* p. 68; June, 2005, Suzanne Myers Harold, review of *Monkey Business,* p. 133.

Teacher Librarian, December, 1999, review of *The Persian Cinderella,* p. 50.

Voice of Youth Advocates, August, 1989, Margaret Mary Ptacek, review of *T.J.'s Ghost,* p. 156.

Writer, July, 1983, Shirley Climo, "Creating a Picture Book," pp. 18-20, 44.

ONLINE

Humboldt Children's Author Festival Web site, http://www.authorfest.org/ (November 30, 2005), "Shirley Climo."

COLLIER, James Lincoln 1928-
(Charles Williams)

Personal

Born June 27, 1928, in New York, NY; son of Edmund and Katharine (Brown) Collier; married Carol Burrows, September 2, 1952 (divorced); married Ida Karen Potash, July 22, 1983; children: (first marriage) Geoffrey Lincoln, Andrew Kemp. *Education:* Hamilton College, A.B., 1950. *Hobbies and other interests:* "I have been deeply involved in jazz from youth and continue to work as a jazz musician regularly."

Addresses

Home—71 Barrow St., New York, NY 10014. *Agent*—c/o William Deiss, John Hawkins and Associates, 71 W. 23rd St., New York, NY 10010.

Career

Writer. Magazine editor, 1952-58. *Military service:* U.S. Army, 1950-51; became private.

Writings

FICTION; FOR CHILDREN

The Teddy Bear Habit; or, How I Became a Winner, illustrations by Lee Lorenz, Norton (New York, NY), 1967.

Rock Star, Four Winds (Bristol, FL), 1970.

Why Does Everybody Think I'm Nutty?, Grosset (New York, NY), 1971.

It's Murder at St. Basket's, Grosset (New York, NY), 1972.

Rich and Famous: The Further Adventures of George Stable, Four Winds (Bristol, FL), 1975.

Give Dad My Best, Four Winds (Bristol, FL), 1976.

Planet out of the Past, Macmillan (New York, NY), 1983.

When the Stars Begin to Fall, Delacorte (New York, NY), 1986.

Outside Looking In, Macmillan (New York, NY), 1987.

The Winchesters, Macmillan (New York, NY), 1988.

My Crooked Family, Simon & Schuster (New York, NY), 1991.

The Jazz Kid, Puffin (New York, NY), 1996.

The Corn Raid: A Story of the Jamestown Settlement, Jamestown Publishers (Lincolnwood, IL), 2000.

The Worst of Times: A Story of the Great Depression, Jamestown Publishers (Lincolnwood, IL), 2000.

Chipper, Marshall Cavendish/Benchmark Books (New York, NY), 2001.

Wild Boy, Marshall Cavendish (New York, NY), 2002.

Me and Billy, Marshall Cavendish (New York, NY), 2004.

The Empty Mirror, Bloomsbury (New York, NY), 2004.

HISTORICAL NOVELS FOR CHILDREN; WITH BROTHER, CHRISTOPHER COLLIER

My Brother Sam Is Dead, Four Winds (Bristol, FL), 1974.

The Bloody Country, Four Winds (Bristol, FL), 1976.

The Winter Hero, Four Winds (Bristol, FL), 1978.

James Lincoln Collier

Jump Ship to Freedom, Delacorte (New York, NY), 1981.

War Comes to Willy Freeman, Delacorte (New York, NY), 1983.

Who Is Carrie?, Delacorte (New York, NY), 1984.

The Clock, Delacorte (New York, NY), 1991.

With Every Drop of Blood, Delacorte (New York, NY), 1994.

NONFICTION; FOR CHILDREN

Battleground: The United States Army in World War II, Norton (New York, NY), 1965.

A Visit to the Fire House, photographs by Yale Joel, Norton (New York, NY), 1967.

Which Musical Instrument Shall I Play?, photographs by Yale Joel, Norton (New York, NY), 1969.

Danny Goes to the Hospital, photographs by Yale Joel, Norton (New York, NY), 1970.

Practical Music Theory: How Music Is Put Together from Bach to Rock, Norton (New York, NY), 1970.

The Hard Life of the Teenager, Four Winds (Bristol, FL), 1972.

Inside Jazz, Four Winds (Bristol, FL), 1973.

Jug Bands and Hand-Made Music, Grosset (New York, NY), 1973.

The Making of Man: The Story of Our Ancient Ancestors, Four Winds (Bristol, FL), 1974.

Making Music for Money, F. Watts (New York, NY), 1976.

CB, F. Watts (New York, NY), 1977.

The Great Jazz Artists, illustrations by Robert Andrew Parker, Four Winds (Bristol, FL), 1977.

Louis Armstrong: An American Success Story, Macmillan (New York, NY), 1985.

Duke Ellington, Macmillan (New York, NY), 1991.

Jazz: An American Saga, Holt (New York, NY), 1997.

The Sitting Bull You Never Knew, illustrated by Greg Copeland, Children's Press (New York, NY), 2003.

The George Washington You Never Knew, illustrated by Greg Copeland, Children's Press (New York, NY), 2003.

The Frederick Douglass You Never Knew, illustrated by Greg Copeland, Children's Press (New York, NY), 2003.

The Clara Barton You Never Knew, illustrated by Greg Copeland, Children's Press (New York, NY), 2003.

The Alexander Hamilton You Never Knew, illustrated by Greg Copeland, Children's Press (New York, NY), 2003.

The Abraham Lincoln You Never Knew, illustrated by Greg Copeland, Children's Press (New York, NY), 2003.

The Tecumseh You Never Knew, illustrated by Greg Copeland, Children's Press (New York, NY), 2004.

The Susan B. Anthony You Never Knew, illustrated by Greg Copeland, Children's Press (New York, NY), 2004.

The Mark Twain You Never Knew, illustrated by Greg Copeland, Children's Press (New York, NY), 2004.

The Louis Armstrong You Never Knew, illustrated by Greg Copeland, Children's Press (New York, NY), 2004.

The Eleanor Roosevelt You Never Knew, illustrated by Greg Copeland, Children's Press (New York, NY), 2004.

The Benjamin Franklin You Never Knew, illustrated by Greg Copeland, Children's Press (New York, NY), 2004.

Gunpowder and Weaponry, Benchmark Books (New York, NY), 2004.

Vaccines, Benchmark Books (New York, NY), 2004.

Clocks, Benchmark Books (New York, NY), 2004.

Steam Engines, Benchmark Books (New York, NY), 2005.

Electricity and the Light Bulb, Marshall Cavendish Benchmark (New York, NY), 2005.

The Automobile, Marshall Cavendish Benchmark (New York, NY), 2005.

NONFICTION; "DRAMA OF AMERICAN HISTORY" SERIES; WITH CHRISTOPHER COLLIER

Clash of Cultures: Prehistory to 1638, Benchmark Books (New York, NY), 1998.

The Paradox of Jamestown, 1585 to 1700, Benchmark Books (New York, NY), 1998.

The French and Indian War, 1660 to 1763, Benchmark Books (New York, NY), 1998.

The American Revolution, 1763 to 1783, Benchmark Books (New York, NY), 1998.

Pilgrims and Puritans, 1620 to 1676, Benchmark Books (New York, NY), 1998.

Creating the Constitution, 1787, Benchmark Books (New York, NY), 1998.

Building a New Nation, 1789 to 1803, Benchmark Books (New York, NY), 1998.

Andrew Jackson's America, 1821 to 1850, Benchmark Books (New York, NY), 1998.

The Cotton South and the Mexican War, 1835 to 1850, Benchmark Books (New York, NY), 1998.

The Jeffersonian Republicans, 1800 to 1820, Benchmark Books (New York, NY), 1998.

The Civil War, 1860 to 1866, Benchmark Books (New York, NY), 1998.

The Road to the Civil War, 1831 to 1861, Benchmark Books (New York, NY), 1998.

Reconstruction and the Rise of Jim Crow, Benchmark Books (New York, NY), 1998.

The Rise of Industry: 1860 to 1900, Marshall Cavendish (New York, NY), 1999.

A Century of Immigration: 1820 to 1924, Marshall Cavendish/Benchmark Books (Tarrytown, NY), 1999.

Indians, Cowboys, and Farmers and the Battle for the Great Plains, 1865 to 1910, Benchmark Books (New York, NY), 2000.

The United States Enters the World Stage: From Alaska through World War I, 1867 to 1919, Benchmark Books (New York, NY), 2000.

Progressivism, the Great Depression, and the New Deal, 1901 to 1941, Benchmark/Cavendish (Tarrytown, NY), 2000.

The Rise of the Cities, Cavendish/Benchmark (Tarrytown, NY), 2000.

World War II, Benchmark Books (New York, NY), 2001.

The Changing Face of America, 1945 to 2000, Benchmark Books (New York, NY), 2001.

The United States in the Cold War, Benchmark/Cavendish (Tarrytown, NY), 2002.

The Middle Road: American Politics, 1945 to 2000, Benchmark Books (New York, NY), 2002.

FOR ADULTS

Cheers (nonfiction), Avon (New York, NY), 1960.

Somebody up There Hates Me (humor), Macfadden, 1962.

The Hypocritical American: An Essay on Sex Attitudes in America, Bobbs-Merrill, 1964.

(With others) *Sex Education U.S.A.: A Community Approach,* Sex Information and Education Council of the United States, 1968.

The Making of Jazz: A Comprehensive History, Houghton (Boston, MA), 1978.

Louis Armstrong: An American Genius, Oxford University Press (New York, NY), 1983, published as *Louis Armstrong: A Biography,* Michael Joseph (London, England), 1984.

(With brother, Christopher Collier) *Decision in Philadelphia: The Constitutional Convention of 1787,* Random House (New York, NY), 1986.

Duke Ellington, Oxford University Press (New York, NY), 1987.

Benny Goodman and the Swing Era, Oxford University Press (New York, NY), 1989.

The Rise of Selfishness in the United States, Oxford University Press (New York, NY), 1991.

Jazz: The American Theme Song, Oxford University Press (New York, NY), 1993.

Also author, under pseudonym Charles Williams, of *Fires of Youth.* Contributor of numerous articles to periodicals, including *Reader's Digest, New York Times Magazine, Village Voice,* and *Esquire.*

Adaptations

My Brother Sam Is Dead was adapted as a record, a cassette, and a filmstrip with cassette.

Sidelights

James Lincoln Collier is a prolific writer of fiction and nonfiction for both adults and children. Notable among his works for young people are volumes of nonfiction informed by his background in music and his interest in American history, fictional works portraying young male narrators, and historical novels and nonfiction written in

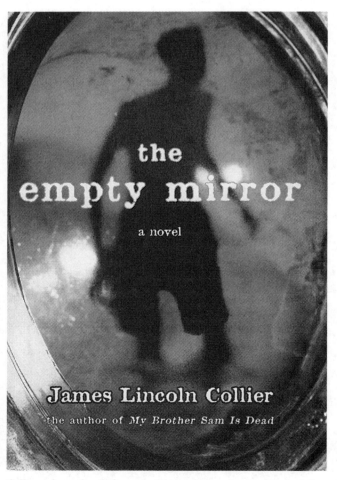

Collier takes a break from straight-up history to pen this haunting story of an orphaned teen who discovers that his troublemaking twin is haunting the cemetery of his small New England town. (Cover illustration by Oliver Hunter/Photonica.)

collaboration with his brother, historian Christopher Collier. While Collier's nonfiction has been hailed as educational and well written, his novels are often lauded for their exciting, fast-paced plots and their depiction of characters who grapple with moral dilemmas and unpleasant parental figures. Praising *Me and Billy,* which focuses on two orphans who survive by their wits during the American Gold Rush of the mid-1800s, *School Library Journal* reviewer Douglas P. Davey praised the book as "a small gem from an award-winning author."

Collier was born in 1928, into a family of writers. After serving in the U.S. Army from 1950 to 1951, he moved to New York City, and supported himself as a magazine editor while he focused on eventually earning a living from his writing. He sold articles to magazines and in 1960 had the first of several books for adults published. In the mid-1960s Collier decided to try his hand at children's literature, "a choice," according to Hughes Moir in *Language Arts,* "he has never regretted."

Collier's first book for a young audience, *Battleground: The United States Army in World War II,* is a nonfiction work that discusses the military maneuvers conducted in Europe during World War II. Many other nonfiction works have followed during his career, with music and musicians among his favorite topics. Discussing *Practical Music Theory: How Music Is Put Together from Bach to Rock, School Library Journal* reviewer Loretta B. Jones wrote that Collier has created a "lucid, step-by-step exposition of musical theory for dedicated music students." The writer has also earned praise for *Inside Jazz,* a 1973 book that Loraine Alterman in the *New York Times Book Review* called "as good a verbal explanation as I've seen about jazz and its distinguishing features." The author's other books on music include the historical overview *Jazz: An American Saga* as well as the biographies *The Great Jazz Artists, Louis Armstrong: An American Success Story,* and *Duke Ellington.*

In addition to producing musician biographies, Collier has authored a number of books on notable Americans from history in a related collection that includes *The Abraham Lincoln You Never Knew, The Eleanor Roosevelt You Never Knew,* and *The Frederick Douglass You Never Knew.* Noting in *School Library Journal* that the series addresses and debunks several popular myths that have grown up about the individuals covered, Rita Soltan added that Collier's "free-flowing style . . . elicits compassion, understanding, and awareness" by humanizing his subject. While writing that the books are geared for readers who know little about their subjects, *Booklist* contributor Carolyn Phelan explained that in his biography of Alexander Hamilton Collier focuses on the fact that Hamilton was "born poor and orphaned as a child," adding that the story of Hamilton's rise to prominence as a father of the new republic is "readable and informative."

Collier has also joined his brother, Christopher Collier, in creating a number of nonfiction titles in the "Drama of American History" series, which traces U.S. history from the settling of the Americas and the American Revolution through the U.S. Civil War, the cold war, and into the twenty-first century. In this multi-volume overview the coauthors focus on an array of historical topics, including the French and Indian War, the settling of Jamestown, the framing of the U.S. Constitution, the importance of cotton in the Southern economy, the rise of American industry, the situation of Native Americans, U.S. involvement in the two world wars, immigration, and the impact of political movements such as Progressivism. Reviewing one of the first titles in the series, *Building a New Nation, 1789-1801, Booklist* reviewer Carolyn Phelan called the entire series "well-written." Of *The Rise of Industry, 1860-1900,* Phelan noted this volume, like other books in the series, has "the visual appeal of colorful graphics and good layout." Writing in *School Library Journal,* Patricia Ann Owens found *Indians, Cowboys, and Farmers and the Battle for the Great Plains, 1865-1910* to be "American history at its most basic," and dubbed *The Rise of the Cities, 1820-1920* a work "that focuses on the broad themes of history rather than facts and dates."

Collier's list of writings includes fiction as well as nonfiction, and his first effort, *The Teddy Bear Habit; or, How I Became a Winner,* details how teenager George Stable's obsession with his teddy bear leads to his involvement in a jewel theft. The book's suspenseful plot and comic scenes of adventure prompted Jerome Beatty, Jr., writing in the *New York Times Book Review* to call *The Teddy Bear Habit* "a heck of an exciting story." A sequel, *Rich and Famous: The Further Adventures of George Stable,* also earned high marks from reviewers. "George is . . . consistently perceptive, and often humorous, [in his] observations of people and situations," wrote Donald A. Colberg in *School Library Journal.*

While his first fiction works were humorous, many of Collier's more recent novels concern young people struggling to overcome adversity, which often appears in the form of an unsavory parent. *Give Dad My Best* finds a boy forced to care for his family because his father is a down-and-out musician, while in *The Winchesters* Collier presents a boy caught in the middle of a dispute between his wealthy relatives and a town in economic peril. In *My Crooked Family,* set in 1910, Collier depicts a young boy's efforts to triumph over poverty and negligent parents, while a young teen living New England several decades later finds himself haunted by ghosts from his delinquent past in *The Empty Mirror. The Jazz Kid* tells the story of Paulie Horvath and how his love of jazz transforms his life from a dead-end, blue-collar existence to the fulfillment of a career in music.

In *The Corn Raid: A Story of the Jamestown Settlement* Collier offers up the story of twelve-year-old Richard's

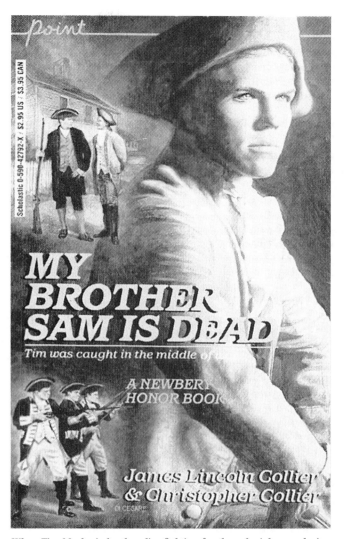

When Tim Meeker's brother dies fighting for the colonial army during the Revolutionary War, Tim is forced to chose between his brother's cause and the pro-British views of his distraught parents.

efforts to overcome the harsh realities of colonial life. Richard is an indentured servant living in fear of the master who continually beats him. Discovering that the English are planning a raid on a local Indian tribe, Richard warns the natives, but feels guilty enough later to admit to his master what he has done. When the angry man begins to beat the boy, Richard finally stands up to such brutal treatment and begins to plan for the day when he will be free. Also set in the past, *Me and Billy* follows twelve-year-old Possum and his best friend Billy after they run away from an orphanage and encounter a variety of people on their way to California in the hopes of striking it rich during the gold rush. Reviewing *The Corn Raid* in *School Library Journal,* Shawn Brommer judged that "history takes precedence over story." Lighter in tone, *Me and Billy* "packs a wallop of exciting adventures and plot twists," noted a *Kirkus Reviews* critic, while *Booklist* reviewer GraceAnne A. DeCandido predicted that the novel will appeal to older preteens because "elements of tall tale abound and the language is fast and funny." Noting

Possum's growth as a person when he realizes that his life choices differ from those of his less-honest friend, Davey concluded in his *School Library Journal* review of *Me and Billy* that Collier's "wonderful use of vernacular and the friendship/tension" that develops between Possum and Billy make the novel stand out.

Collier has collaborated on several highly esteemed books of historical fiction with his brother Christopher, a distinguished historian. Most popular among their novels set in the Revolutionary War era is *My Brother Sam Is Dead;* other books include *The Winter Hero, War Comes to Willy Freeman,* and *Who Is Carrie?* The success of these books rests, according to Moir in *Language Arts,* on both Christopher's ability to provide the story with historically accurate data and James's talent for fashioning "out of raw events a story that is fast-moving and highly readable." In the 1992 novel *The Clock,* set in Connecticut in the early nineteenth century, fifteen-year-old Annie Steele is sent by her father to work in a woolen mill in order to pay off the man's chronic debts. The story involves Annie's dealings with the villainous mill boss, and it touches on historical issues such as patriarchal power and the country's gradual change from agrarian to industrial modes of production. Reviewing the title in *Publishers Weekly,* a contributor concluded that *The Clock* "succeeds not only as historical fiction, but also as a riveting story of the tragic romance and hard-won victory of one teenaged girl." A further fiction title coauthored with Christopher Collier is *With Every Drop of Blood,* a Civil War tale about a Southern youth captured by Northern forces who comes to respect and like the black Union soldier guarding him. *Booklist* contributor Hazel Rochman noted that the theme of "my enemy, my friend is at the core of this docu-novel of the Civil War." Rochman further noted that it is "the large canvas that will draw readers to the story."

Collier professes a deep appreciation of children's literature. Expressing his fondness for the craft, he was quoted by Moir as noting: "The 'real' books written today are written for children. . . . The author [of children's books] can deliver more than just a good read, but also a view of the world."

Biographical and Critical Sources

BOOKS

Authors and Artists for Young Adults, Volume 13, Thomson Gale (Detroit, MI), 1994.
Beacham's Guide to Literature for Young Adults, Volume 2, Beacham Publishing (Osprey, FL), 1998.
Children's Literature Review, Volume 3, Thomson Gale (Detroit, MI), 1978.
Contemporary Literary Criticism, Volume 30, Thomson Gale (Detroit, MI), 1984.

Fifth Book of Junior Authors and Illustrators, edited by Sally Holmes Holtze, H.W. Wilson (New York, NY), 1983.

PERIODICALS

Booklist, February 15, 1966, p. 582; June 1, 1976, p. 1403; February 1, 1992, p. 1026; July, 1994, Hazel Rochman, review of *With Every Drop of Blood,* pp. 1935-1936; April 15, 1998, p. 1442; February 15, 1999, Carolyn Phelan, review of *Building a New Nation, 1789-1801,* p. 1061; February 15, 2000, Carolyn Phelan, review of *The Rise of Industry, 1860-1900,* p. 1106; March 15, 2001, Carolyn Phelan, review of *The Rise of the Cities, 1820-1920,* p. 1396; November 1, 2002, Todd Morning, review of *Wild Boy,* p. 490; October 15, 2003, Carolyn Phelan, review of *The Alexander Hamilton You Never Knew,* p. 423; September 15, 2004, GraceAnne A. DeCandido, review of *Me and Billy,* p. 231; October 15, 2004, Linda Perkins, review of *The Empty Mirror,* p. 403.
English Journal, September, 1992, p. 95.
Horn Book, April, 1975, p. 152; February, 1976, p. 48; March-April, 1992, p. 203; January-February, 1995, pp. 57-58.
Kirkus Reviews, August 15, 2004, review of *The Empty Mirror,* p. 803; September 15, 2004, review of *Me and Billy,* p. 912.
Language Arts, March, 1978, Hughes Moir, "Profile: James and Christopher Collier—More than Just a Good Read," p. 373.
Library Journal,.
New York Times Book Review, March 12, 1967, Jerome Beatty, Jr., review of *The Teddy Bear Habit; or, How I Became a Winner,* p. 28; October 25, 1970, p. 38; February 25, 1973, p. 10; December 30, 1973, Loraine Alterman, review of *Inside Jazz,* p. 10; November 3, 1974, p. 26; May 2, 1976, p. 26; February 13, 1977, p. 25; February 14, 1982, p. 28; May 8, 1983, p. 37; March 2, 1986, p. 19.
Publishers Weekly, March 8, 1971, p. 71; October 16, 1972, p. 49; November 7, 1977, p. 83; May 25, 1984, p. 59; July 5, 1985, p. 67; November 28, 1986, p. 77; March 13, 1987, p. 86; October 28, 1988, p. 82; July 25, 1991, p. 55; January 1, 1992, review of *The Clock,* p. 56; July 11, 1994, p. 79; June 17, 1996, p. 33.
School Library Journal, December, 1970, Loretta B. Jones, review of *Practical Music Theory: How Music Is Put Together from Bach to Rock,* p. 58; November, 1975, Donald A. Colberg, review of *Rich and Famous: The Further Adventures of George Stable,* p. 72; March, 1976, p. 111; December, 1976, p. 53; September, 1977, p. 142; November, 1977, p. 68; September, 1978, p. 132; January, 1984, p. 73; October, 1985, p. 169; November, 1986, p. 98; January, 1989, p. 92; October, 1991, p. 142; August, 1994, p. 168; April, 1999, p. 145; April, 2000, Shawn Brommer, review of *The Corn Raid: A Story of the Jamestown Settlement,* p. 130; July, 2001, Patricia Ann Owens, review of *Indians, Cowboys, and Farmers and the Battle for the Great Plains,1865-1910,* p. 120; April, 2002, Kathleen

Simonetta, review of *The Changing Face of American Society, 1945-2000,* p. 168; November, 2002, Lee Bock, review of *Wild Boy,* p. 160; January, 2004, Rita Soltan, review of *The Abraham Lincoln You Never Knew,* p. 143; March, 2004, Lynn Evarts, review of *Vaccines,* p. 228.

Teaching K-8, January, 1988, p. 35; October, 2004, Connie Tyrrell Burns, review of *The Empty Mirror,* p. 159; January, 2005, Douglas P. Davey, review of *Me and Billy,* p. 126.

ONLINE

Balkin Buddies Web site, http://www.balkinbuddies.com/ (December 1, 2005), "James Lincoln Collier."

*   *   *

COLVIN, James
See MOORCOCK, Michael

D-E

DENIM, Sue
    See PILKEY, Dav

* * *

ECHLIN, Kim 1955-

Personal

Born June 12, 1955, in Toronto, Ontario, Canada; daughter of Robert Edward (a dentist) and Madeleine Lillian Echlin; married Ross Edward Grant Upshur, June 2, 1990. *Education:* McGill University, B.A. (English; with honors), 1976; York University, M.A. (English), 1977, Ph.D. (English), 1982; studied French at Sorbonne, University of Paris, 1979.

Addresses

Home—Toronto, Ontario, Canada. *Agent*—c/o Westwood Creative Artists, 94 Harbord St., Toronto, Ontario M5S 1G6, Canada.

Career

Writer, journalist, and educator. Canadian Broadcasting Corporation, producer of *The Journal* (arts documentary), 1985-90; *Ottawa Citizen,* fiction editor, 1999-2003; freelance writer and editor. University of Toronto School for Continuing Studies, Toronto, Ontario, Canada, instructor in creative writing, 1997-2005; teacher at Ryerson School of Journalism, University of Guelph, and York University. Editor, Banff Centre for the Arts creative nonfiction workshop.

Awards, Honors

McGeachy scholarship, United Church of Canada, 1999-2000; Canada Council for the Arts Award, 1998-99; Torgi Award; Chapters/Books in Canada First Novel Award nomination; National Magazine Award nomination.

Kim Echlin

Writings

(Translator and editor with Nie Zhixiong) Yuan Ke, *Dragons and Dynasties: An Introduction to Chinese Mythology,* Penguin (London, England), 1991.
Elephant Winter (novel), Viking (New York, NY), 1997.

(Editor) *To Arrive Where You Are: Literary Journalism from the Banff Centre for the Arts,* Banff Centre Press (Banff, Alberta, Canada), 1999.

Dagmar's Daughter (novel), Viking (New York, NY), 2001.

Inanna: From the Myth of Ancient Sumer (for children), illustrated by Linda Wolfsgruber, Groundwood Books (Toronto, Ontario, Canada), 2003.

Elizabeth Smart: A Fugue Essay on Women and Creativity, Women's Press, 2004.

Contributor to books, including *Best Canadian Essays,* Fifth House Publishers, 1989; *Up and Doing: Canadian Women and Peace,* Women's Press, 1989; *Taking Risks,* Banff Centre Press, 1998; and *Living Sideways: Trickster in American Indian Oral Traditions,* University of Oklahoma Press, 2004. Contributor to periodicals, including *Canadian Fiction* and *Studies in American Indian Literatures.* Scriptwriter for television, including *Life and Times* series.

Sidelights

Canadian author, translator, editor, and teacher Kim Echlin has written two novels for adults as well as literary nonfiction and the illustrated storybook *Inanna: From the Myth of Ancient Sumer.* Echlin, who has taught creative writing at several Canadian universities, is also a literary scholar who has made a study of Ojibway trickster tales.

Associated with the planet Venus, Inanna is an ancient goddess that figured prominently in the civilization that existed in the location of modern-day Iraq over four thousand years ago. Although lost for centuries, her stories, carved on stone tablets, were recently recovered by archeologists. Sister to Gilgamesh, Inanna grows to maturity and through her determination, wisdom, and ambition she learns the extent of her own destructive and creative powers. In *Inanna* Echlin relates the warrior goddess's story in poetic form, from her birth as the daughter of the Moon god to her growing desire for her handsome shepherd brother Dumuzi (an Adonis-like character), her death and descent into the underworld, and her fight to regain her place on Earth as well as her power within the pantheon of Sumerian gods. Noting that the book, which is illustrated by European artist Linda Wolfsgruber, would be most valuable to young-adult readers, Patricia D. Lothrop wrote in *School Library Journal* that *Inanna* "could be an enticing introduction to a little-known figure from ancient Near East myth." In crafting her book-length story, Echlin positions traditional stories about the goddess "in chronological order, following Inanna's development from an eager, ambitious goddess to the position of the all-powerful queen whose 'light shines through everything,'" according to *Resource Links* contributor Joan Marshall. Marshall dubbed the book a "fascinating tale of a young goddess who knows how to get the power she wants."

Echlin's novels for adult readers, which include *Elephant Winter* and *Dagmar's Daughter,* are critically respected. *Elephant Winter,* the story of a young woman who returns to her rural Ontario home to tend to her dying mother and finds her life altered due to a romantic relationship with a wildlife caretaker at a neighboring safari park, was described as "enormously engaging" by Maureen Garvie in *Quill & Quire.* Frank Moher further observed in a *Saturday Night* review of the novel that Sophie's growing empathy is reflected by "prose that is as extravagant in feeling as it is in expression." Echlin draws on the ancient myths of Demeter and Persephone, as well as on the story of Inanna, in *Dagmar's Daughter,* in which a motherless teen is almost drowned before finding safety on a small island. The woman's story is interwoven with those of three generations of gifted Gaelic-speaking women into a novel that, although difficult, "rewards the effort," according to *Canadian Woman Studies* reviewer Clara Thomas. Noting that the novel's plot moves at a brisk pace, Elaine Jones added in *Resource Links* that *Dagmar's Daughter* relates "a powerful and intriguing story."

In **Inanna: From the Myth of Ancient Sumer** *Echlin collects the many stories featuring the ancient Sumerian warrior goddess who was worshiped for her wisdom, beauty, and power, as well as for her constant quest for knowledge. (Illustration by Linda Wolfsgruber.)*

Biographical and Critical Sources

PERIODICALS

Books in Canada, April, 1997, p. 37.

Canadian Woman Studies, summer-fall, 2001, Clara Thomas, review of *Dagmar's Daughter,* p. 150.

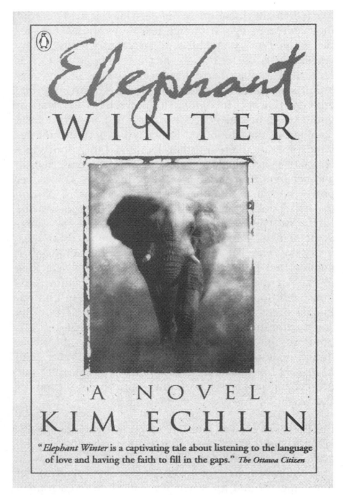

In Echlin's 1997 novel a woman nursing her dying mother is reminded of life's joys when she spends time with a group of Asian elephants pasturing in the tourist park near her mother's home.

Quill & Quire, January, 1997, Maureen Garvie, review of Elephant Winter, p. 35; February, 2001, review of *Dagmar's Daughter,* p. 29.

Resource Links, October, 2002, Elaine Jones, review of *Dagmar's Daughter,* p. 55; December, 2003, Joan Marshall, review of *Inanna,* p. 36.

Saturday Night, March, 1997, Frank Moher, review of *Elephant Winter,* p. 14.

School Library Journal, March, 2004, Patricia D. Lothrop, review of *Inanna,* p. 299.

ONLINE

Groundwood Books Web site, http://www.groundwood books.com/ (December 1, 2005), "*Inanna.*"

*   *   *

EDENS, Cooper 1945-

Personal

Born Gary Drager, September 25, 1945, in WA; son of Otto (an electrical engineer) and Garnet (Cooper) Drager; married Louise Arnold, March 3, 1979; children: David, Emily. *Education:* University of Washington, B.A., 1970. *Politics:* "Universalist." *Religion:* "Universalist."

Addresses

Home—4204 NE 11th Ave. No. 15, Seattle, WA 98105. *Agent*—c/o Green Tiger Press/Laughing Elephant, 3645 Interlake Avenue N., Seattle, WA 98103.

Career

Author and illustrator, 1978—. Participant in programs of Children's Museum of the Museum of Seattle, WA. *Exhibitions:* Foster-White Gallery, Seattle, 1970—.

Awards, Honors

Children's Critic Award, Bologna International Children's Book Fair, 1980, for *The Starcleaner Reunion;* American nominee for Golden Apple Award (Prague, Czechoslovakia), 1983, for *Caretakers of Wonder.*

Writings

SELF-ILLUSTRATED

If You're Afraid of the Dark, Remember the Night Rainbow, Green Tiger Press (San Diego, CA), 1978, 2nd edition, 1984, reprinted, Chronicle Books (New York, NY), 2002.

The Starcleaner Reunion, Green Tiger Press (San Diego, CA), 1979.

Caretakers of Wonder, Green Tiger Press (San Diego, CA) 1980.

With Secret Friends, Green Tiger Press (San Diego, CA), 1981.

Inevitable Papers, Green Tiger Press (San Diego, CA), 1982.

(With others) *Paradise of Ads,* Green Tiger Press (San Diego, CA), 1987.

Now Is the Moon's Eyebrow, Green Tiger Press (San Diego, CA), 1987.

Hugh's Hues, Green Tiger Press (San Diego, CA), 1988.

Nineteen Hats, Ten Teacups, an Empty Birdcage, and the Art of Longing, Green Tiger Press (San Diego, CA), 1992.

The Little World, Blue Lantern Books, 1994.

If You're Still Afraid of the Dark, Add One More Star to the Night, Simon & Schuster (New York, NY), 1998.

FOR CHILDREN

Emily and the Shadow Shop, illustrated by Patrick Dowers, Green Tiger Press (San Diego, CA), 1982.

A Phenomenal Alphabet Book, illustrated by Joyce Eide, 1982.

The Prince of the Rabbits, illustrated by Felix Meroux, Green Tiger Press (San Diego, CA), 1984.

Santa Cows, illustrated by Daniel Lane, Green Tiger Press (San Diego, CA), 1991.

The Story Cloud, illustrated by Kenneth LeRoy Grant, Green Tiger Press (San Diego, CA), 1991.

A Present for Rose, illustrated by Molly Hashimoto, Sasquatch Books, 1993.

Shawnee Bill's Enchanted Five-Ride Carousel, illustrated by Daniel Lane, Green Tiger Press (San Diego, CA), 1994.

Santa Cow Island, illustrated by Daniel Lane, Green Tiger Press (San Diego, CA), 1994.

How Many Bears?, illustrated by Marjett Schille, Atheneum (New York, NY), 1994.

The Wonderful Counting Clock, illustrated by Kathleen Kimball, Simon & Schuster (New York, NY), 1995.

Santa Cow Studios, illustrated by Daniel Lane, Simon & Schuster (New York, NY), 1995.

Nicholi, illustrated by A. Scott Banfill, Simon & Schuster (New York, NY), 1996.

(With Alexandra Day) *The Christmas We Moved to the Barn,* illustrated by Alexandra Day, HarperCollins (New York, NY), 1997.

(With Alexandra Day) *Taffy's Family,* HarperCollins (New York, NY), 1997.

(With Harold Darling and Richard Kehl) *Invisible Art,* Blue Lantern Studio (Seattle, WA), 1999.

(With Daniel Lane) *The Animal Mall,* illustrated by Edward Miller, Dial (New York, NY), 2000.

(With Alexandra Day) *Special Deliveries,* illustrated by Alexandra Day, HarperCollins (New York, NY), 2001.

How Many Bears? has been translated into Spanish.

ILLUSTRATOR

Alexandra Day, *Helping the Sun,* Green Tiger Press (San Diego, CA), 1987.

Alexandra Day, *Helping the Flowers and Trees,* Green Tiger Press (San Diego, CA), 1987.

Alexandra Day, *Helping the Night,* Green Tiger Press (San Diego, CA), 1987.

Alexandra Day, *Helping the Animals,* Green Tiger Press (San Diego, CA), 1987.

OTHER

(With Alexandra Day and Welleran Poltarnees) *Children from the Golden Age, 1880-1930,* Green Tiger Press (San Diego, CA), 1987.

(Compiler) *The Glorious Mother Goose,* illustrated by various artists, Atheneum (New York, NY), 1988.

(Compiler) Lewis Carroll, *Alice's Adventures in Wonderland: The Ultimate Illustrated Edition,* Bantam (New York, NY), 1989.

(Compiler) *Beauty and the Beast,* Green Tiger Press (New York, NY), 1989.

(Compiler) *Goldilocks and the Three Bears,* illustrated by various artists, Green Tiger Press (New York, NY), 1989.

(Compiler) *Little Red Riding Hood,* illustrated by various artists, Green Tiger Press (New York, NY), 1989.

(Compiler) *The Glorious ABC,* illustrated by various artists, Atheneum (New York, NY), 1990.

(Compiler) *Day and Night and Other Dreams,* Green Tiger Press (New York, NY), 1990.

(Compiler) *Hansel and Gretel,* illustrated by various artists, Green Tiger Press (New York, NY), 1990.

(Compiler) *Jack and the Beanstalk,* illustrated by various artists, Green Tiger Press (New York, NY), 1990.

(Compiler with Harold Darling) *Favorite Fairy Tales,* illustrated by various artists, Chronicle Books (San Francisco, CA), 1991.

(Compiler) *The Three Princesses,* illustrated by various artists, Bantam (New York, NY), 1991.

(With Alexandra Day and Welleran Poltarnees) *An ABC of Fashionable Animals,* Green Tiger Press (New York, NY), 1991.

(Compiler with Richard Kehl) *The Flower Shop,* illustrated by various artists, Blue Lantern Books (Seattle, WA), 1992.

(Compiler with Richard Kehl) *The Heart Shop,* illustrated by various artists, Blue Lantern Books (Seattle, WA), 1992.

(Compiler with Harold Darling), Clement Moore, *The Night before Christmas,* illustrated by various artists, Chronicle Books (San Francisco, CA), 1998.

(Compiler) Carlo Collodi, *Pinocchio,* illustrated by various artists, Chronicle Books (San Francisco, CA), 2001.

(Compiler) E. Charles Vivian, *Robin Hood,* illustrated by various artists, Chronicle Books (San Francisco, CA), 2002.

(Compiler) *'Tis the Season: A Classic Illustrated Christmas Treasury,* illustrated by various artists, Chronicle Books (San Francisco, CA), 2003.

(Compiler) Robert Louis Stevenson, *A Child's Garden of Verses,* illustrated by various artists, Chronicle Books (San Francisco, CA), 2004.

(Compiler) *Princess Stories,* illustrated by various artists, Chronicle Books (San Francisco, CA), 2004.

(Compiler) *The Glorious American Songbook,* illustrated by various artists, Chronicle Books (San Francisco, CA), 2005.

Adaptations

The Starcleaner Reunion was adapted as a ballet.

Sidelights

Author and illustrator Cooper Edens is noted for his quirky plots, colorful illustrations, and his long affiliation with Green Tiger Press, a San Diego-based small publisher founded by Harold and Sandra Day that first gained a reputation for reproducing the work of nineteenth-century illustrators during the 1970s. Himself an aficionado of the works of the "Golden Age of Illustration," Edens had written and illustrated a number of books for young children, and has shared the imaginative visions of artists from the era that produced Edmund Dulac, Arthur Rackham, Jesse Willcox Smith, Kay Nielsen, and others by compiling volumes that collect the artwork of various artists that illustrate the same classic children's text. Edens' earliest self-illustrated picture books, *If You're Afraid of the Dark, Add One More Star to the Night* and *The Starcleaner Reunion,* remained in publication for over three decades after first appearing in the late 1970s.

Raised in Washington state on the shore of Lake Washington, Edens once told *SATA:* "A huge highway separated me from prospective playmates who might otherwise have come to visit. Consequently, I spent many hours alone by the lake, daydreaming. I would imagine the island in the lake to be a pirate ship, or another world altogether. It seems to me that many artists are, or were in childhood, enchanted by bodies of water—the sea, a lake, a creek or a pond. This was certainly true for me. I had a rowboat which I repainted again and again; first it was a giraffe, then a zebra.

"I tended to miss quite a bit of school. I don't remember whether this was for some legitimate reason, or simply because I didn't want to go. My earliest 'textbooks' were coloring books which I would color in peculiar ways, changing the words as I went along. I cut up and reorganized comic strips from the newspaper, superimposing, say, Felix the Cat into the alien world of another comic strip character.

"On very hot days I would invite friends to watch me draw on the walls of my tent, listening to nonsensical recitations of my own stories. I guess my storytelling actually began in those strange tent proceedings. I also wrote songs. My art work began by coloring over other people's drawings. My uncle campaigned for mayor and when he lost the election, I inherited all of his posters. I colored them, and then began to design my own, inspired by such television shows as *Hopalong Cassidy.* In fourth grade, when my attendance in school became more regular, I was put in charge of the bulletin board, changing it for each holiday and season. It could be said in relation to my work today that I am *still* doing the bulletin board! "My confidence grew out of these coloring book and bulletin board escapades. I considered myself master of color. In junior high school, I was regarded the 'art guy,' who was always hanging out in the 'art room.'

"Philosophically I hold that everyone comes into the world with something great to share. The first authority figure we encounter, be it parent or teacher, encourages or stifles the gift. Our early creativity is fragile and can be easily crushed. As luck had it, I was encouraged in school."

Edens' first self-illustrated picture book, *The Starcleaner Reunion,* had an interesting genesis. As its creator once recalled to *SATA:* "When I began to exhibit my work, I noted that some of the characters in my paintings tended to recur. One day I randomly laid the paintings on the floor and began to lace the images together with titles. I wrote a story around the paintings, which became *The Starcleaner Reunion.* So my first book was about tying images together with words. Since then, however, I write the story first and then illustrate it.

"My original Starcleaners, as I was to discover, were oversized for standard publishing practice. I put these giant cardboard figures in a suitcase—the combined weight of which was over two hundred pounds—and carried them to New York in the middle of the summer, sweating profusely as I made the rounds of New York publishers. I had visions of publishers occupying grand rooms, where all of an illustrator's art work was hung on white, spotlighted gallery walls. In fact, the offices of these prominent people were often smaller than my suitcase! I often set up my gigantic Starcleaners on top of someone's bologna sandwich. Everyone responded favorably to my work, but felt that it was too expensive to reproduce. This was in 1978, before four-color printing was feasible for large publishers.

"Several editors suggested that I contact Green Tiger Press, which had a reputation for being eccentric. I went to Green Tiger, and they were willing to invest in my work, although they published my second book, *If You're Afraid of the Dark, Remember the Night Rainbow,* first. *Night Rainbow* was a song I had many times attempted to have recorded. I submitted the song as a text and Green Tiger okayed it, but they didn't know that I could draw. They had already submitted the book to several well-known illustrators, but liked my work and decided to accept my illustrations. Green Tiger put up the money to make four-color separation and we came out with a soft-cover first edition, which was very unusual because there weren't many soft-covered children's books. An advantage is that they can be easily mailed as gifts and are, therefore, sold in gift shops. *If You're Afraid of the Dark, Remember the Night Rainbow* was often the only book sold in such shops. These outside markets helped get 200,000 copies of the book sold because it never had to compete with other children's books."

In creating the many unique picture books he has written since, Edens sometimes joins with other illustrators, such as Sandra Darling, who under the pen name Alexandra Day, has collaborated with Edens on books such as *Darby, the Special-Order Pup, The Christmas We Moved to the Barn,* and *Special Deliveries,* all which feature Day's watercolor illustrations. In *Darby, the Special-Order Pup* the chewing habit that results in the ouster of a young English bull terrier from the Bell family home ultimately saves the day in a "sparse but effective text" that *Booklist* contributor Ellen Mandel praised for its surprise ending. Calling *Special Deliveries* "delightful" and "imaginative," Mandel also enjoyed Edens and Day's story about a group of animals that, with their owner, take over a rural postal route and pen letters for lonely neighbors who miss receiving letters. In *Publishers Weekly* a reviewer also praised the picture book, calling it "beguilingly and deceptively straightforward," but with "imaginative pleasures at every turn."

Edens and coauthor Alexandra Day introduce a caring family of animal lovers who create special letters for neighbors with empty mailboxes in **Special Deliveries.** *(Illustration by Alexandra Day.)*

Edens joins illustrator Daniel Lane in *Santa Cows,* a spoof of the Santa Claus myth that was described as "a preposterous yarn that plays havoc with Clement Clarke Moore's famous Christmas rhyme and attacks our fast-food, video-driven culture," by Stephanie Zvirin in *Booklist.* In *Santa Cows,* the nine members of a modern family are enjoying their microwaved Christmas dinners when they are visited by a herd of cows bearing decorations for the house and equipment for a Christmas-day game of baseball. The result is a "wacky fantasy" that a reviewer for *Publishers Weekly* predicted "will leave readers who appreciate its irreverent humor wanting more."

Lane also teams up with Edens for *Shawnee Bill's Enchanted Five-Ride Carousel.* In this story, Shawnee Bill, "summertime's answer to Saint Nick," according to a reviewer for *Publishers Weekly,* provides the town's toddlers with a special ride on his carousel's animals. Freed from the carousel, the cavorting animals carry the babies through fields of wildflowers.

In *Nicholi,* illustrated by A. Scott Banfill, Edens returned to the theme of Christmas, this time in the story

of an annual snow-sculpting event at which a stranger appears and carves out a sleigh and a team of reindeer that magically come to life. The stranger, named Nicholi, then offers the townspeople a ride on the sleigh, which sails over the earth and meets up with the other ice sculptures in the show, all magically come to life. "Edens's first-person text bespeaks genuine childlike exhilaration," wrote a *Publishers Weekly* critic, adding that the storyline provides a large part of the enjoyment to be gleaned from this "brightly wrapped holiday fantasy."

In more recent years Edens has devoted much of his time to creating a series of volumes celebrating the history of children's book illustration. In these books, Edens reprints one version of a classic children's story, such as *Hansel and Gretel, Little Red Riding Hood, Pinocchio,* or *Beauty and the Beast,* together with illustrations from a number of artists who have adapted the tales since the nineteenth century. In *The Three Princesses: Cinderella, Sleeping Beauty, Snow White,* Edens presents three traditional tales about princesses, each accompanied by splendid colored artwork. The great asset of such work "for anyone interested in the history of book illustration," attested Michael Dirda in the *Washington Post Book World,* is Edens' selection of more than 150 illustrations from artists of the past. As a "sampler" in the history of children's book illustration, *The Three Princesses* is "tantalizing," Dirda concluded, and should inspire readers to seek out the original books Edens drew upon as his sources. Edens takes a similar approach with *The Glorious American Songbook,* studding over fifty songs by Cole Porter, Irving Berlin, and other composers with vintage illustrations dating from each song's original publication.

As an author, Edens' general philosophical approach to children's literature is a departure from traditional precepts. "*Alice in Wonderland, Peter Pan, The Wizard of Oz,* and Sendak's *Where the Wild Things Are* are the classic big four stories in my opinion, and they all work in a similar way. Essentially these stories transport us to the world of dreams from which we must return. In essence these books are saying, 'You must be home for dinner.' They present a dualistic vision: there is a dream world, and there is a real world to which you must return. I'm trying to break the dualism of the classic tale. My stories embrace the philosophy that these two worlds exist simultaneously—the real world is a dream and the dream world is real. Because of this, there are no classic quests in my books. I don't have people going away to the dream world and returning to reality.

"In *Caretakers of Wonder,* for example, the characters are real people doing such surreal things as balancing rainbows or mending clouds. My characters are in a real world doing dream things or in a dream doing real things. It isn't a voyage through a door to some strange and secret place. After all, the only real secret is that when you're awake you're in a dream and when you are asleep you're in reality. . . . Many schools use *Caretakers of Wonder* to teach children about ecology. This feels good because it means I'm not sending a completed work into the world, but a catalyst. I want my readers to have the necessary room for a creative response to my work."

Edens offers the following encouragement to young artists: "The hardest step is to admit that you want to do it," he once explained. "But the second you start, something will come back to you—call it God or nature or mystery. I'm a witness to the fact that if you participate you will be joined by some other energy or spirit or friend; then, you're instantly a team, a couplement, and once this happens, everything is easy. When people submit their books to me I always say, 'The one thing that separates you from most people is that you *want* to do it; the minute you want to do it, you're a very select person.' There aren't that many people who consistently work at something, who consistently show up. . . .

"There is craft involved in any art. You'll have to know the brushes and paints eventually. But there are victories before you learn the right brush. You can make a lot of spills and still find a reason to show up again. After all, you're with friends. As a philosopher once said, 'The planet exists because life needs it.' It isn't the earth that makes life possible, it's life that makes the earth what it is. That's the way it is with art. It exists because you want it to."

Biographical and Critical Sources

PERIODICALS

Booklist, November 1, 1991, Stephanie Zvirin, review of *Santa Cows,* p. 531; November 1, 2000, Ellen Mandel, review of *Darby, the Special-Order Pup,* p. 547; May 1, 2001, Ellen Mandel, review of *Special Deliveries,* p. 1668; November 15, 2003, Ilene Cooper, review of *'Tis the Season,* p. 596; October 14, 2004, Jennifer Mattson, review of *Princess Stories,* p. 402.

Kirkus Reviews, September 1, 1997, p. 1387.

Newsweek, November, 1979, p. 64; December 5, 1983, p. 111.

Publishers Weekly, September 20, 1991, review of *Santa Cows,* p. 133; May 30, 1994, review of *Shawnee Bill's Enchanted Five-Ride Carousel,* p. 54; October 6, 1997, review of *Nicholi,* p. 55; June 4, 2001, review of *Special Deliveries,* p. 79; September 22, 2003, review of *'Tis the Season,* p. 73; May 30, 2005, review of *The Glorious American Songbook,* p. 63.

School Library Journal, October, 1979, p. 138; May, 2001, Holly Belli, review of *Special Deliveries,* p. 114; December, 2001, Heide Piehler, review of *Pinocchio,* p. 133; October, 2003, Eva Mitnick, review of *'Tis the Season,* p. 62; January, 2005, Harriett Fargnoli, review of *Princess Stories,* p. 109; August, 2005, Mary Elam, review of *The Glorious American Songbook,* p. 144.

Washington Post Book World, January 12, 1992, Michael Dirda, review of *The Three Princesses,* p. 8.*

*   *   *

ETCHEMENDY, Nancy 1952-
(Nancy Elise Howell Etchemendy)

Personal

Born 1952, in Reno, NV; married John William Etchemendy (a professor of philosophy), 1973; children: Matthew Xavier. *Education:* University of Nevada, B.A., 1974. *Politics:* Democrat. *Hobbies and other interests:* Gardening, travel, cooking; "I'm a dedicated dabbler . . . particularly in anthropology, archaeology, and paleontology. In addition, I like to spend time in the deserts of the North American West."

Addresses

Home—Northern California. *Agent*—Virginia Knowlton, Curtis Brown, Ltd., 10 Astor Pl., New York, NY 10003. *E-mail*—etchemendy@sff.net.

Career

Western Industrial Parts, Reno, NV, lithographer, 1970-75; Sutherland Printing, Reno, NV, worked in art, stripping, and camera, 1975-76; W.H. Barth Corp., Sunnyvale, CA, art director, 1976-79; Etchemendy Commercial Graphics, Palo Alto, CA, sole proprietor, 1979-81; writer, 1981—.

Member

Authors Guild, PEN USA, Society of Children's Book Writers and Illustrators, Science Fiction Writers of America, Horror Writers Association.

Awards, Honors

Bram Stoker Award, 1998, for short story "Bigger than Death"; Bram Stoker Award finalist, 2001, for short story "Demolition"; Bram Stoker Award, Golden Duck Award for Excellence in Children's Science-Fiction Literature, Georgia Children's Book Award, Anne Spencer Lindbergh Prize Silver Medal, Nautilus Award finalist, PEN USA West Award finalist, and Dorothy Canfield Fisher Master List, all 2002, an Volunteer State Award Master Reading list inclusion, 2003-04, all for *The Power of Un;* Bram Stoker Award, Horror Writers Association, 2004, for short story "Nimitseahpah."

Writings

JUVENILE SCIENCE-FICTION NOVELS

The Watchers of Space, Avon (New York, NY), 1980.
Stranger from the Stars, Avon (New York, NY), 1982.
The Crystal City, Avon (New York, NY), 1985.
The Power of Un, Cricket Books (Chicago, IL), 2000.

OTHER

Cat in Glass, and Other Tales of the Unnatural (young adult), Cricket Books (Chicago, IL), 2002.

Works have appeared in anthologies, including *Shadows 8,* edited by Charles Grant, Doubleday, 1985; *The Year's Best Fantasy and Horror,* St. Martin's Press, 1990; *Mysterious Cat Stories,* edited by John Richard Stephens, Carroll & Graf, 1993; *Bruce Coville's Book of Ghosts,* edited by Bruce Coville, Scholastic, 1994; *Xanadu Three,* edited by Jane Yolen, Tor Books, 1995; *The Armless Maiden, and Other Tales for Childhood's Survivors,* edited by Terri Windling, Tor Books, 1995; *Enchanted Forests,* edited by Katherine Kerr and Martin Greenberg, DAW Books, 1995; *American Gothic Tales,* edited by Joyce Carol Oates, Dutton-Signet, 1996; *Bruce Coville's Book of Aliens 2,* Scholastic, 1996; *New Altars,* edited by Dawn Albright and Sandra Hutchinson, Angelus Press, 1997; *One Hundred Fiendish Little Frightmares,* edited by Stefan Dziemianowicz and Rob-

ert Weinberg, Barnes & Noble Books, 1997; *Bruce Coville's UFOs,* Avon, 2000; *Bram Stoker Award Winners: That's Ghosts for You,* edited by Marianne Carus, Front Street/Cricket Books, 2000; *Be Afraid,* edited by Edo van Belkom, Tundra Books, 2000; and *Personal Demons,* edited by Brian A. Hopkins and Garrett Peck, Lone Wolf Publications, 2001. Contributor of fiction and poetry to periodicals, including *Fantasy and Science Fiction, Asimov's Science Fiction, Twilight Zone, Cricket, Quantum,* and *Fantastyka.*

Work in Progress

A lengthy fantasy novel for children, tentatively titled *The Harrilore;* short stories and poetry.

Sidelights

Beginning her career as a graphic designer, Nancy Etchemendy has shaped a career rooted in her longtime love of writing. She is the author of several science-fiction books for young readers as well as of a collection of horror tales for teens, and her short fiction and poetry has appeared in both magazines and anthologies. In addition to other honors, Etchemendy has won Bram Stoker awards for her short story "Bigger than Death," as well as for her 2000 novel *The Power of Un.*

In *The Power of Un* Etchemendy addresses the philosophical problems that can result from time travel. The novel's protagonist, Gib, a middle-school student, is faced with this issue when a mysterious stranger gives him an "unner" capable of sending him back in time. Shortly after he receives the device, Gib learns that his younger sister has been hit by a truck and is now in a coma. While using his new unner might be a solution to saving his sister's life, Gib also realizes that there is a risk: the interconnectedness of events and people may unravel in unexpected ways if he does not use the time-travel device correctly. "Gib tackles free will, memory, the bending of time, and contradictory impulses in a way that will sound fairly logical to middle-schoolers," commented GraceAnne A. DeCandido in a review of *The Power of Un* for *Booklist.* While *School Library Journal* contributor Susan L. Rogers wrote that Etchemendy's characterizations are rather two-dimensional, she appreciated the story's suspense, noting that it "builds to a surprising and satisfying conclusion."

Widely known for her short fiction, Etchemendy has also received praise for the short-story collection *Cat in Glass, and Other Tales of the Unnatural.* The subjects of the stories in this collection range from wicked felines to alternate realities and from haunting dreams to a post-apocalyptic world. The assembled works were described by *Booklist* contributor Anne O'Malley as "rather dark tales [that] will appeal mostly to horror fans," while Catherine Threadgill, writing in the *School Library Journal,* noted that although Etchemendy sometimes utilizes "coarse language and disturbingly graphic description," such elements ultimately enhance her "masterfully rendered, absorbing tales."

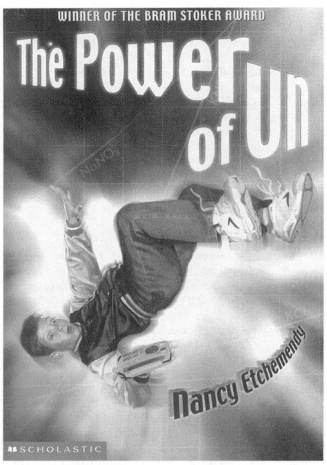

WINNER OF THE BRAM STOKER AWARD

The Power of Un

Nancy Etchemendy

SCHOLASTIC

When Gib Finney finds the Unner, a machine that undoes all his mess-ups, he thinks his luck has turned, but soon learns that not all things can be fixed by a quick "unning." (Cover illustration by Mike Koetsch.)

Etchemendy once told *SATA:* "From the time my sister and I were four or five years old until we were teenagers, my dad used to read to us on a regular basis. He always had a passion for science fiction, so we heard a lot of it during our evening story time. Tom Swift, the 'Tom Corbett' series, and even judicious amounts of Jules Verne and Ray Bradbury all found places on Dad's reading list. By the time I was eight years old, I knew that I was going to live in space when I grew up. Other little girls talked about becoming nurses or stewardesses or mommies when they grew up. But I wanted to be an astronaut, or a brave settler on some far-flung and mysterious world.

"At the same time, I was rapidly discovering a second love—the love of words, and the thrill of making them leap and dance to a tune of my own. I learned the alphabet; I discovered the miraculous connection between marks on a sheet of paper and the thoughts inside my head; and I began to write stories and poems. All of that happened to me at once in Miss Elcano's first-grade class.

"For a long time I hoped I could be a writer and an astronaut. It didn't seem too farfetched. Surely they were going to need somebody to chronicle all those adventures we were going to have. But then several things happened. [U.S. President] John Kennedy died. We found ourselves in a seemingly endless war in Southeast Asia. And our social priorities began to change. People started saying things like, 'Why are we spending all this money on the moon when the masses are starving right here on Earth?' and 'Look at the mess we've made of this planet. Do you want the same thing to happen to the other planets?' and 'Why don't we solve the problems of this world before we worry about solving the problems of space travel?'

"Feeling very bleak indeed, I watched the space program fizzle to a smoldering stump, like a big Roman candle that turned out to be a dud. To make matters worse, I was getting old. And I knew that sooner or later I was going to have to find a way to pay the rent and keep potatoes in the pot. Writing was fun, but you couldn't rely on the income. So, basically, I chickened out. I went to work in a print shop, and that's how I came to be a graphic designer writing science-fiction novels on my lunch hours.

"Eventually it became clear to me that no matter what happened, I was going to be dead or too old to make the trip by the time the call went out for space colonists. But I was never able to shake the conviction that mankind belongs in space; that it is in fact our best hope for civilized survival in a dangerous age."

Discussing her work as a children's book writer, Etchemendy once noted: "It's a joy to write for kids. As a group they're more sincere and concise about things than any other people I can think of. If you've missed the mark, they'll tell you so—plainly and candidly, without any intention of either sparing you or hurting you. But if you're on target, and a child somewhere begins to think about what you've said, then in a small way you've really affected eternity." In answer to the question "Why write science fiction?," she added: "It's a lot of fun to consider scientific possibilities. It's important for people to think about all the different things science means to us, and how it might affect our lives. That's partly because scientific inventions can be very dangerous if we use them without thinking about them. I believe it's especially important for today's kids to think about science, particularly space science, because I think that space is the future home of mankind and that we should start exploring it as soon and as fast as possible. People your age will probably be able to live in space if we just hurry up a little."

Biographical and Critical Sources

PERIODICALS

Booklist, May 1, 2000, GraceAnne A. DeCandido, review of *The Power of Un,* p. 1665; November 15, 2002, Anne O'Malley, review of *Cat in Glass, and Other Tales of the Unnatural,* p. 588.

Instructor, January, 1981, Allan Yeager, review of *The Watchers of Space,* p. 113.

Magazine of Fantasy and Science Fiction, September, 1987, Orson Scott Card, review of *The Watchers of Space* and *The Crystal City,* p. 24.

School Library Journal, September, 1980, Margaret L. Chatham, review of *The Watchers of Space,* p. 69; April, 1984, Marilyn C. Kihl, review of *Stranger from the Stars,* p. 113; June, 2000, Susan L. Rogers, review of *The Power of Un,* p. 144; December, 2002, Catherine Threadgill, review of *Cat in Glass, and Other Tales of the Unnatural,* p. 137.

Voice of Youth Advocates, April, 2003, review of *Cat in Glass, and Other Tales of the Unnatural,* p. 62.

ONLINE

Nancy Etchemendy Home Page, http://www.sff.net/people/ etchemendy/ (December 1, 2005).*

*   *   *

ETCHEMENDY, Nancy Elise Howell
See ETCHEMENDY, Nancy

F

FLAKE, Sharon G.

Personal
Born in Pittsburgh, PA; children: Brittney.

Addresses
Home—Pittsburgh, PA. *Agent*—c/o Author Mail, Hyperion, 77 W. 66th St., 11th Fl., New York, NY 10023. *E-mail*—ShrFla9@aol.com.

Career
Center for the Assessment and Treatment of Youth in Philadelphia, Philadelphia, PA, youth counselor; Katz Business School, University of Pittsburgh, Pittsburgh, PA, director of publications.

Awards, Honors
August Wilson Short Story Contest winner; *Highlights for Children* writers' conference scholarship; Best Book for Young-Adult Readers selection, and Quick Pick for Reluctant Readers selection, both American Library Association (ALA), Top-Ten Books for Youth selection, *Booklist,* Best Children's Book selection, Bank Street College of Education, Coretta Scott King/John Steptoe Award for new authors, and New York Public Library Book for the Teen Age selection, all 1999, all for *The Skin I'm In;* Coretta Scott King Honor Book designation, 2002, for *Money Hungry;* Coretta Scott King Honor Award, YALSA Best Books for Young Adults designation, and ALA Quick Pick for Reluctant Readers selection, all 2006, and Missouri Gateway Readers Award nomination, 2006-07, all for *Who Am I without Him?*

Writings
The Skin I'm In, Jump at the Sun (New York, NY), 1998.
Money Hungry, Jump at the Sun (New York, NY), 2001.

Begging for Change (sequel to *Money Hungry*), Jump at the Sun (New York, NY), 2003.
Who Am I without Him?: Short Stories about Girls and the Boys in Their Lives, Jump at the Sun (New York, NY), 2004.
Bang!, Jump at the Sun (New York, NY), 2005.

Adaptations
The Skin I'm In was adapted for audio, Recorded Books, 2004.

Sidelights
Beginning her writing career while working in public relations, Sharon G. Flake has become noted for her novels geared for African-American teens, particularly teen girls. In *The Skin I'm In,* thirteen-year-old Maleeka Madison is a bright student who is taunted for her excellent grades, her dark complexion, and the fact that her clothes are handmade rather than in-fashion clothes from the mall. Although Maleeka tries to fit in by hanging out with Charlese, the toughest girl in the school, the teen's life changes after Ms. Saunders becomes her new English teacher. Although Maleeka at first joins in the taunts that are directed toward the woman, whose face is disfigured by a large birthmark, she rethinks her actions when Ms. Saunders publicly praises Maleeka's writing and encourages the girl to enter a writing contest. *Booklist* reviewer Hazel Rochman noted that Flake's "characters are complex," while a *Publishers Weekly* contributor wrote that "those identifying with the heroine's struggle to feel comfortable inside the skin she's in will find inspiration here."

Money Hungry focuses on thirteen-year-old Raspberry Hill, who lives with her always-working mother in a housing project. The family's situation has been bordering on desperate: until recently, Raspberry and her mother had lived on the street and crashed on friends' couches after leaving Raspberry's drug-addicted father. Determined to move into a better neighborhood, Raspberry will do just about anything to earn money; anything except illegal things, like selling dope or shoplifting. She sells pencils and candy, cleans houses, and washes cars. Rather than eat, she even adds her lunch money to her hoard. Her hyper-stinginess eventually causes problems when her mother finds the bankroll and, believing that the money is stolen, throws it out the window. Ironically, everything they own is stolen shortly thereafter, and Raspberry and her mom once again find themselves living on the street, buoyed by the support of caring neighbors. A *Publishers Weekly* contributor wrote that Flake "candidly expresses the difficulty in breaking the cycle of poverty and leaves it up to the reader to judge Raspberry's acts," while *School Library Journal* reviewer Gail Richmond praised Flake for doing "a stunning job of intertwining Raspberry's story with daily urban scenes"; "she writes smoothly and knowingly of teen problems." In another enthusiastic review of *Money Hungry*, Gillian Engberg commented in *Booklist* that Flake's "razor-sharp dialogue and unerring details evoke characters, rooms, and neighborhoods with economy and precision, creating a story that's immediate, vivid, and unsensationalized."

Begging for Change again focuses on Raspberry, as she works to rebuild her nest egg. She is a far more desperate girl than she was in *Money Hungry;* now Raspberry steals cash from friends, raising issues of trust. Her motives are pressing, however: her mother has been hospitalized after being hit with a pipe. In keeping with her character, the desperate teen also continues to earn much of her money honorably, although most of her earnings are taken by her homeless father. When Raspberry and her mother finally move to a better neighborhood, the girl confesses her crimes and begins to repair her ways. A *Publishers Weekly* writer felt that, "touching upon issues of prejudice, street violence, homelessness, and identity crises, this poignant novel sustains a delicate balance between gritty reality and dream fulfillment." Engberg wrote that, "although vivid images of urban poverty, violence, and drug addiction clearly illustrate why Raspberry is so afraid, Flake never sensationalizes."

Flake's *Who Am I without Him?: Short Stories about Girls and the Boys in Their Lives* contains ten stories that address relationships between young people dealing with a variety of issues, most often from a girl's point of view. Flake's stories contain no obscenity or sex, and as Rochman noted, while "there are messages, . . . the narrative is never preachy or uplifting; it's honest about the pain." Class is the central issue in one story about a boy who steals clothes so that he can dress well for a date with a suburban girl, while race figures in another tale in which Erika, a black girl from the ghetto, develops crushes on white boys. In yet a another tale a girl tolerates the abusive behavior of a handsome boy just to be with him.

A *Kirkus Reviews* critic, reviewing *Who Am I without Him?*, wrote that Flake's fiction "shines with an awareness of the real-life social, emotional, and physical pressures that teens feel about dating." Describing one particular story, in which a father writes a letter to his daughter, telling her not to settle for someone like him, Mary N. Oluonye commented in a *School Library Journal* review that the tale "is sad, poignant, and loving," adding that, in her fiction, "Flake has a way of teaching a lesson without seeming to do so."

In the novel *Bang!* Flake tells her story through the experiences of a male teen whose family is devastated following the murder of his little brother. Thirteen-year-old Mann and his friends become fatalistic, believing that it is only a matter of time before they, too, become statistics reflecting the violence of their inner-city community. When Mann's father decides to take his son and friend Keelee on a survival adventure disguised as a camping trip in the hopes that the experience will "toughen up" the young teens, the results change Mann's life forever. The events of the story "will spark as much controversy among readers as it does among characters" in Flake's novel, noted a *Publishers Weekly* reviewer, praising *Bang!* as a "hard-hitting survival tale." In *Booklist* Jennifer Mattson wrote that "the complicated relationship" between father and son "represents a welcome investigation of African American manhood," while in *Kirkus Reviews* a contriutor deemed the novel a "powerful—and disturbing" depiction of "teens struggling to deal with a world that is out of control."

Biographical and Critical Sources

PERIODICALS

Booklist, September 1, 1998, Hazel Rochman, review of *The Skin I'm In,* p. 110; June 1, 2001, Gillian Engberg, review of *Money Hungry,* p. 1880; August, 2003, Gillian Engberg, review of *Begging for Change,* p. 1980; April 15, 2004, Hazel Rochman, review of *Who Am I without Him?: Short Stories about Girls and the Boys in Their Lives,* p. 1440; July, 2005, Jennifer Mattson, review of *Bang!,* p. 1916.

Kirkus Reviews, June 1, 2003, review of *Begging for Change,* p. 803; April 15, 2004, review of *Who Am I without Him?,* p. 393; July 15, 2005, review of *Bang!,* p. 788.

Kliatt, November, 2004, Samantha Musher, review of *Begging for Change,* p. 16.

Publishers Weekly, November 9, 1998, review of *The Skin I'm In,* p. 78; December 21, 1998, "Flying Starts," p. 28; June 18, 2001, review of *Money Hungry,* p. 82; June 9, 2003, review of *Begging for Change,* p. 52; October 24, 2005, review of *Bang!,* p. 59.

School Library Journal, July, 2001, Gail Richmond, review of *Money Hungry,* p. 107; July, 2003, Sunny Shore, review of *Begging for Change,* p. 129; May, 2004, Mary N. Oluonye, review of *Who Am I without Him?,* p. 147; October, 2005, Ginny Gustin, review of *Bang!,* p. 160.

ONLINE

New York Public Library Web site, http://www.nypl.org/ (July 18, 2002), transcript of live chat with Flake.
Sharon G. Flake Home Page, http://www.sharongflake. com (December 1, 2005).*

*   *   *

FORRESTER, Sandra 1949-

Personal

Born April 8, 1949, in Cullman, AL; daughter of Robert Martin (a transportation specialist) and Dorothy (a government employee; maiden name, Fine) Forrester. *Education:* Judson College, B.A., 1970; attended University of Virginia, 1972; University of North Carolina at Greensboro, M.L.I.S., 1996. *Hobbies and other interests:* Reading ("everything from mysteries to poetry to history"), restoring old doll houses, beachcombing, researching, collecting nineteenth-and early twentieth-century children's books, Majolica pottery, and Santa Clauses.

Addresses

Office—National Institute of Environmental Health Sciences, 101 Alexander Dr., Research Triangle Park, NC 27709. *Agent*—Barbara S. Kouts, P.O. Box 558, Bellport, NY 11713.

Career

Department of the Army, Alexandria, VA, occupational analyst, 1974-85, Falls Church, VA, management analyst, 1985-92; National Institute of Environmental Health Sciences, Research Triangle Park, NC, management analyst, 1992—.

Member

American Library Association, Society of Children's Book Writers and Illustrators, American Society for the Prevention of Cruelty to Animals.

Awards, Honors

Notable Children's Trade Book in the Field of Social Studies designation, and Bank Street College Children's Book of the Year designation, both 1996, both for *Sound the Jubilee.*

Writings

Sound the Jubilee (young-adult novel), Dutton (New York, NY), 1995.
My Home Is over Jordan (sequel to *Sound the Jubilee*), Dutton (New York, NY), 1997.

Sandra Forrester

Dust from Old Bones, Morrow (New York, NY), 1999.
Wheel of the Moon, HarperCollins (New York, NY), 2000.

"BEATRICE BAILEY" SERIES

The Everyday Witch, Barron's (Hauppauge, NY), 2002.
The Witches of Friar's Lantern, Barron's (Hauppauge, NY), 2003.
The Witches of Sea-Dragon Bay, Barron's (Hauppauge, NY), 2003.
The Witches of Winged-Horse Mountain, Barron's (Hauppauge, NY), 2004.
The Witches of Bailiwick, Barron's (Hauppauge, NY), 2005.

Work in Progress

A sixth book in the "Beatrice Bailey" series, working title *The Witches of Widdershins Academy;* an historical novel for young adults, set in a small town in Alabama during the Depression, working title *Leo and the Lesser Lion.*

Sidelights

Sandra Forrester is the author of several novels for young adults, among them her lighthearted "Beatrice Bailey" series, which follows young witch Beatrice as she tries to receive the "Classical Witch" rating so she can learn important magic. Forrester's first novel was not related to fantasy at all, however; *Sound the Jubilee* and its sequel, *My Home Is over Jordan,* tell the story of Maddie, a runaway slave living during the U.S. Civil War. As Forrester once told *SATA,* "*Sound the Jubilee* is based on actual events that occurred on the Outer Banks during the Civil War. After the Union Army captured Roanoke Island in February 1862, runaway slaves began to arrive almost immediately seeking sanctuary. Their numbers grew rapidly, until there were more than three thousand people living on the island in what was called the 'Contraband Camp.' The federal government gave each family an acre of land upon which to build a house and plant a garden . . . and the result was the largest, most prosperous community on the Outer Banks up to that time. *Sound the Jubilee* is the story of a young girl named Maddie who fled to Roanoke Island with her family in search of freedom. The reality of their lives on the island was often difficult and quite different from what they had envisioned." Laura J. Mikowski wrote in *Voice of Youth Advocates* that "the beauty of the book lies in two things: Maddie's growth and Forrester's balancing of the realities of the Civil War." Elizabeth M. Reardon stated in *School Library Journal* that "the author's use of a modified dialect adds substance to her characterization."

"I learned about the Contraband Camp several years ago when I was vacationing on 'The Banks' and came across a brief reference to the camp's residents in a book on Outer Banks history," Forrester explained of writing her book. "I searched for more information on these people but found that practically nothing had been written about them. Eventually I located letters that had been written by some of the camp's men when they were serving in the Union Army, as well as journals and privately printed memoirs of Union soldiers who were stationed on Roanoke Island during the war. Many of the incidents experienced by Maddie and her friends and family are based on these first-hand accounts. Sadly, nothing remains on the island to remind us that a thriving business and residential community once stood there. The buildings were destroyed long ago, and the land has reverted to forest and undergrowth. I wrote *Sound the Jubilee* because I was inspired by the courage of these self-freed slaves and moved by the poignancy of their experience. . . . The many hours spent in libraries and archives researching Maddie's story rekindled a childhood aspiration," Forrester once recalled to *SATA.* "When I was growing up I loved libraries and always wanted to work in one. My . . . collaborative efforts with librarians, who were as excited by my research as I was, convinced me to return to school for a degree in library studies."

My Home Is over Jordan follows Maddie's life after the Civil War is over, and she has to decide between pursuing her dream of a college education and supporting her family. Maddie becomes the assistant to a local young black school teacher, and though things begin very well for Maddie and her family in their new life, racial tensions soon rise in the community. Ultimately, an attack on the teacher occurs, followed by the departure of a member of Maddie's family north. Calling *My Home Is*

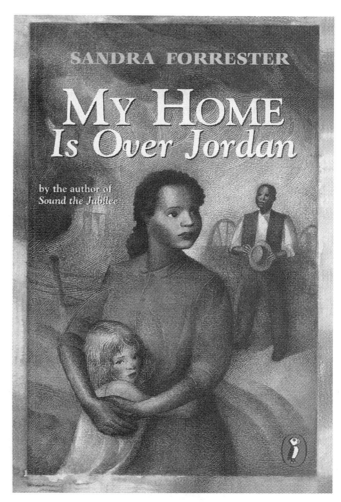

No longer a slave as the Civil War ends, teenager Maddie hopes to follow her dream of becoming a teacher; now she learns that freedom comes with its own obstacles. (Cover illustration by Raul Colón.)

over Jordan a "docunovel," Hazel Rochman noted in *Booklist* that "Forrester sets Maddie's personal story of strength and integrity against the harsh historical truth."

Set in New Orleans, *Dust from Old Bones* describes the social structure of the free people of color living in that Southern city during the years leading up to the Civil War. Young Simone wants to be like her beautiful cousin Claire-Marie, and when Tante Madelon comes from Paris for a visit, Simone views the European woman as an ideal role model. When Tante Madelon betrays Simone to help Claire-Marie, however, Simone finds herself looking beyond appearances to find truth, and begins to fight for the freedom of her aunt's slaves. John Peters of *Booklist* called the novel "a diaristic tale of a thirteen year old losing some illusions."

Forrester explores another little-known part of history in *Wheel of the Moon,* which tells the story of orphans from London who are captured and sent to Virginia as indentured servants. Life in the colonies is better than life on the streets for Pen, the narrator of the tale, but the same is not true for all of her friends: some die during the sea passage, and others find themselves indentured to cruel masters. When Pen's friends Rose and Bram decide to escape, Pen must choose to embrace her new life or make a run for freedom. "The facts are authentic . . . and Forrester's style is clear and direct," noted Hazel Rochman in her *Booklist* review. Lisa Prolman, writing in *School Library Journal*, considered the novel "a good, clear story about a time period not generally mentioned in history texts."

Along with her historical fiction, Forrester has created a series of tales featuring Beatrice Bailey, a young witch who wants nothing more that to receive her magic-rating on her twelfth birthday. She will either be rated as "Everyday" or as "Classical," the more prestigious of the two titles. When her birthday comes, however, the Witches' Executive Council give her a Noble Quest instead, telling Beatrice that her success at the task of rescuing a sorcerer and his daughters will earn her a rating. With her three best friends, Beatrice travels to the mythical land of Bailiwick to begin her quest. Elaine E. Knight, writing in *School Library Journal*, found that the first volume of the series, *The Everyday Witch*, is filled with characters who "are a cohesive group and

In this sequel to **The Witches of Friar's Lantern** *Beatrice continues her efforts to perfect her magic, braving ghosts, swamps, and quirky cats while also learning a bit about her past.*

Hoping to gain the top witch rating when she turns twelve years old, Beatrice finds she must prove her powers by breaking a sorcerer's spell or be ranked as a not-so-special Everyday Witch in Forrester's engaging fantasy. (Cover illustration by Nancy Lane.)

there is a nice emphasis on cooperation and individual efforts." Of another novel in the series, *The Witches of Friar's Lantern,* Catherine Threadgill wrote in *School Library Journal* that "this fun, easy read is a satisfactory option for die-hard Potter fans." A critic for *Curriculum Review* commented on the "mix of humor, magic, and spooky adventure" in the series, while Heidi Hauser Green, writing in *Kliatt,* noted that the "Beatrice Bailey" books also contain a "satisfying blend" of magical elements and mystery.

"My passion for books is rivaled only by my love for animals," Forrester once explained. "I have been active in animal rescue for years because I believe strongly that all animals, wild and domesticated, deserve our respect and protection. Unfortunately, a majority of cats and dogs born in this country are 'throwaways' who never know the comforts of a secure home and a loving family. I can only hope that we will someday learn to value the lives of these innocents, who require so little and give so much. I currently live with two cats, Oliver and Cayenne, who have taught me to worry less, to play more, and to never sit in the cats' chair wearing my good navy suit."

Biographical and Critical Sources

PERIODICALS

Booklist, October 1, 1997, Hazel Rochman, review of *My Home Is Over Jordan,* p. 319; August, 1999, John Peters, review of *Dust from Old Bones,* p. 205; November 15, 2000, Hazel Rochman, review of *Wheel of the Moon,* p. 641.

Bulletin of the Center for Children's Books, December, 1997, review of *My Home Is over Jordan,* p. 125.

Curriculum Review, October, 2003, "Another Day for the Everyday Witch," p. 12.

Kliatt, May, 2005, Heidi Hauser Green, review of *The Witches of Bailiwick,* p. 34.

Publishers Weekly, October 20, 1997, review of *My Home Is over Jordan,* p. 77; February 21, 2000, review of *My Home Is over Jordan,* p. 89.

School Library Journal, May, 1995, Elizabeth M. Reardon, review of *Sound the Jubilee,* p. 118; October, 1999, Starr E. Smith, review of *Dust from Old Bones,* p. 150; October, 2000, Lisa Prolman, review of *Wheel of the Moon,* p. 156; October, 2002, Elaine E. Knight, review of *The Everyday Witch,* p. 163; July, 2003, Catherine Threadgill, review of *The Witches of Friar's Lantern,* p. 130; March, 2004, Elaine E. Knight, review of *The Witches of SeaDragon Bay,* p. 210.

Voice of Youth Advocates, August, 1995, Laura J. Mikowski, review of *Sound the Jubilee,* p. 158.

*   *   *

FRANK, Lucy 1947-

Personal

Born March 22, 1947, in New York, NY; daughter of Sidney (a dentist) and Viola (a teacher and photographer; maiden name, Sobol) Kantrowitz; married Peter C. Frank (a film editor), September 30, 1978; children: Michael. *Education:* Barnard College, A.B., 1968. *Hobbies and other interests:* Reading, gardening, nature study, music.

Addresses

Home—New York, NY. *Agent*—c/o Curtis Brown, Ltd., 10 Astor Place, New York, NY 10003. *E-mail*—info@lucyfrank.com.

Career

Author of books for young adults. Assistant portfolio manager and marketing manager for a major mutual fund company, New York, NY, 1986-96; placement counselor for temporary employment service, New York, NY, beginning 1996; worked variously as a vitamin pill shipping clerk, an editorial assistant, a children's clothing designer, a low-income housing program administrator, a placement counselor, and an administrator for a neurobiology lab.

Lucy Frank

Member

Society of Children's Book Writers and Illustrators, Authors Guild, Authors League of America.

Awards, Honors

Children's Literature Choice listee, 1995, and New York Public Library Books for the Teen Age selection, 1996, both for *I Am an Artichoke;* New York Public Library Books for the Teen Age selection, 2001, for *Just Ask Iris.*

Writings

I Am an Artichoke, Holiday House (New York, NY), 1995.

Will You Be My Brussels Sprout?, Holiday House (New York, NY), 1996.

Oy, Joy!, Dorling Kindersley (New York, NY), 1999.

Just Ask Iris, Atheneum (New York, NY), 2001.

The Annoyance Bureau, Atheneum (New York, NY), 2002.

Lucky Stars, Atheneum (New York, NY), 2005.

Sidelights

Lucy Frank is a young-adult author whose tales of adolescent angst center on intelligent and funny characters going through realistic problems. Frank's own son was struggling through early adolescence while she was writing her first published book, *I Am an Artichoke,* and she relied on her son's input; "I figured if he laughed we were OK," Frank told Bella Stander in a *Publishers Weekly* interview. Frank also drew on her observations of people she saw on the street and on buses in her hometown of Manhattan. "Part of getting the voice right is listening to kids," the author told Stander, "and part of it is just letting my imagination rip." The draw of writing for young adults is that "the teenage point is where a lot is changing fast and emotions are running high," Frank continued. "Kids have a highly developed sense of the ridiculous or weird, which appeals to me."

In *I Am an Artichoke* fifteen-year-old Sarah is bored with her dull suburban existence and decides that working in Manhattan as a mother's helper over the summer will be lots more exciting. Thus begins her association with the dysfunctional Friedman family. Florence Friedman, a flamboyant magazine writer who is "presented with a vividness that has a fingernail-across-the-chalk board effect," according to Dolores J. Sarafinski in *Voice of Youth Advocates,* hires Sarah in the hope that the girl will be able to cure twelve-year-old daughter Emily's anorexia. Florence's agenda becomes painfully obvious only after Sarah accepts the job; "as the story evolves," explained Elizabeth S. Watson in *Horn Book,* "it becomes clear that, while Sarah can make a difference, she will not cure Emily or the myriad problems in the family."

Frank's "accomplished first novel sparkles with deliciously wry humor," enthused a reviewer in *Publishers Weekly,* reviewing *I Am an Artichoke.* The novel was warmly received by other critics as well, and Frank was praised for consistent characterization, solid pacing, and thoughtful treatment of issues such as self-esteem, family, and friendship, as well as for her sense of humor. Susan Dove Lempke concluded her review in the *Bulletin of the Center for Children's Books* by writing: "Tart, witty narration, strong characterization, and well-paced, realistic plot development make this writer's initial entry into fiction bode well for her future work."

In *Will You Be My Brussels Sprout?,* the sequel to *I Am an Artichoke,* Sarah meets and falls in love with Emily's older brother David on one of her weekly trips to Manhattan to take cello lessons at the New York Conservatory of Music. Frank's account of first love is "punctuated with humor and witty dialogue and filled with all the angst any teen could ever want," remarked Lauren Peterson in *Booklist.* Other reviewers were less enthusiastic, however, complaining, like Alice Casey Smith in *School Library Journal,* that Frank's conclusion is "disappointingly open-ended." Although reviewers generally commended the author's treatment of sex as responsible and age-appropriate, a critic for *Kirkus Reviews* concluded that Sarah's inability to break up with David, who pressures her for sex and undermines her musical ambitions, may leave some readers with the feeling that "all the sexual stereotypes they've been taught to recognize and resist have just been reinforced—in spades." Nevertheless, like *I Am an Arti-*

choke, *Will You Be My Brussels Sprout?* garnered praise as a "well-paced [novel] with fresh characters and an appealing plot," from *Voice of Youth Advocates* reviewer Judy Sasges.

Oy, Joy! introduces readers to freshman Joy, Joy's younger brother Nathan, and their mother's Uncle Max, who moves in with Joy's family while he is recovering from a stroke. Joy wants to have a boyfriend, but she isn't at all enthusiastic about her uncle's desire to help her find one. "It's the scenes with Joy and Uncle Max cooking, playing cards, or taking walks wherein the true lessons . . . and laughs . . . lay," wrote a reviewer for *Publishers Weekly.* Michael Cart, writing in *Booklist,* called the novel "a funny, downright joyful story about first love, family feelings, and . . . cross-generational friendship."

In *Just Ask Iris* Iris Pinkowitz needs a bra. She is twelve years old and boys are beginning to notice her, but her mother resists buying Iris a bra because she does not want to acknowledge that her daughter is growing up. Iris, who is half-Jewish and half-Latina, decides to take matters into her own hands and, to earn the money for her first brassiere, begins a business called "Just Ask Iris." While doing odd jobs for the neighbors in her new building, she develops a friendship with Willy, who is confined to a wheel-chair and is unable to leave the building until the elevator is fixed, and the Cat Lady, a woman who lives on the top floor and has more cats than the health code allows. Willy and Iris help keep the Cat Lady from being evicted, and eventually, Iris takes on the building manager herself, making it her quest to get the old elevator fixed. She also manages, in the process, to raise enough money to buy the coveted undergarment. "This slice of urban life is thoroughly entertaining," according to a reviewer for *Publishers Weekly,* while Paula Rohrlick, writing in *Kliatt,* noted that "Iris is a spunky and believable heroine, and the multiethnic characters are skillfully portrayed." Terrie Dorio commented in *School Library Journal* that "Frank tells this appealing contemporary story with a light touch and plenty of humorous dialogue."

The Annoyance Bureau is a holiday story with a twist; twelve-year-old Lucas is forced to spend his Christmas in New York with his father and step-family, including his obnoxious stepsister. Although Lucas is geared up to have a miserable time, he soon discovers that he can see people walking around New York that other people do not seem to notice. One of them is Izzy Gribitz, a man dressed like Santa Claus and stationed outside a bookstore who reveals to Lucas that he is actually a member of the Annoyance Bureau, a secret organization developed to control all the world's annoyances. Rohrlick, again writing in *Kliatt,* called the novel "a fun romp, with an underlying message about standing up for oneself and speaking out." Michael Cart, in *Booklist,* deemed *The Annoyance Bureau* a "genial, funny, goodhearted, and hopelessly illogical portrait of contemporary urban life."

What started as a boring visit with his city-dwelling father becomes an adventure when twelve-year-old Lucas crosses paths with Izzy Gribitz, a strange man whose job is to rid the world of small pests of the non-insect variety. (Cover illustration by Hal Mayforth.)

Returning from the fantastic and illogical to a contemporary fiction title, Frank penned *Lucky Stars,* a tale of three middle-school outcasts who become friends due to their shared love of music. Kira is mortified to discover that her father and step-siblings have been making money by singing in the city subway. Although Kira has a beautiful voice, she refuses to sing with them because she finds it humiliating. Jake has a stutter, and although he is very smart, he skips class so he will not be embarrassed by his speech. Eugene is a class clown and Jake's best friend. The three teens are first brought together by a stray duck stranded in a snowstorm, and later through their love of music. "Readers will thank their lucky stars when they meet this trio," commented a contributor to *Kirkus Reviews.* Marie Orlando, writing in *School Library Journal,* noted that "deft characterization, an authentic sense of place, and a good mix of serious and funny scenes make this a better-than-average novel." A *Publishers Weekly* critic concluded of *Lucky Stars* that "Readers can't help but applaud."

In an interview on her home page, Frank explained that her books "aren't about me. They're about what's on my mind. For example, feeling fat even when you're not, feeling as if there is almost nothing in your life that you can control, and if you could only lose weight, or find a boyfriend, it would change things. . . . And I write about all the infuriatingly stupid, irritating, wrong things, and life feeling so hard and annoying that a kid might want to jump out of his world into an imaginary one with magical devices. And of course I love writing about love."

Biographical and Critical Sources

PERIODICALS

Booklist, February 1, 1995, p. 999; April 15, 1996, Lauren Peterson, review of *Will You Be My Brussels Sprout?,* p. 1433; January 1, 2000, Michael Cart, review of *Oy, Joy!,* p. 902; September 15, 2000, Stephanie Zvirin, review of *Oy, Joy!,* p. 234; November 15, 2001, Ilene Cooper, review of *Just Ask Iris,* p. 570; November 1, 2002, Michael Cart, review of *The Annoyance Bureau,* p. 491.

Bulletin of the Center for Children's Books, June, 1995, Susan Dove Lempke, review of *I Am an Artichoke,* pp. 342-343.

Horn Book, September, 1995, Elizabeth S. Watson, review of *I Am an Artichoke,* p. 609; January-February, 2002, Christine M. Hepperman, review of *Just Ask Iris,* p. 77.

Kirkus Reviews, January 15, 1996, review of *Will You Be My Brussels Sprout?,* p. 133; September 15, 2002, review of *The Annoyance Bureau,* p. 1389; May 15, 2005, review of *Lucky Stars,* p. 588.

Kliatt, November, 2002, Paula Rohrlick, review of *The Annoyance Bureau,* p. 9; May, 2003, Paula Rohrlick, review of *Just Ask Iris,* p. 16.

Publishers Weekly, March 27, 1995, review of *I Am an Artichoke,* p. 86; July 3, 1995, Bella Stander, "Flying Starts," pp. 31-32; April 15, 1996, p. 70; November 18, 1996, review of *I Am an Artichoke,* p. 78; December 13, 1999, review of *Oy, Joy!,* p. 84; July 23, 2001, review of *Oy, Joy!,* p. 79; November 19, 2001, review of *Just Ask Iris,* p. 68; November 11, 2002, review of *The Annoyance Bureau,* p. 64; July 18, 2005, review of *Lucky Stars,* p. 207.

School Library Journal, March, 1995, p. 222; April, 1996, Alice Casey Smith, review of *Will You Be My Brussels Sprout?,* p. 154; December, 2001, Terrie Dorio, review of *Just Ask Iris,* p. 133; October, 2002, Susan Patron, review of *The Annoyance Bureau,* p. 59; July, 2005, Marie Orlando, review of *Lucky Stars,* p. 102.

Voice of Youth Advocates, August, 1995, Dolores J. Sarafinski, review of *I Am an Artichoke,* p. 158; October, 1996, Judy Sages, review of *Will You Be My Brussels Sprout?,* pp. 208-209; June, 2005, Amanda MacGregor, review of *Lucky Stars,* p. 129.

ONLINE

Lucy Frank Home Page, http://www.lucyfrank.com (November 30, 2005).

G

GEAR, Kathleen M. O'Neal
See GEAR, Kathleen O'Neal

*   *   *

GEAR, Kathleen O'Neal 1954-
(Kathleen M. O'Neal Gear)

Personal

Born October 29, 1954, in Tulare, CA; daughter of Harold (a farmer and writer) and Wanda Lillie (a journalist; maiden name, Buckner) O'Neal; married W. Michael Gear (a writer), October 1, 1982. *Education:* California State University—Bakersfield, B.A. (cum laude); California State University—Chico, M.A. (summa cum laude); Attended University of California—Los Angeles; Attended Hebrew University of Jerusalem, Israel. *Religion:* "Native American." *Hobbies and other interests:* Hunting, fishing, hiking.

Addresses

Home—P.O. Box 1329, Thermopolis, WY 82443. *Agent*—Matthew Bialer, Sanford J. Greenburger & Associates, 55 5th Ave., New York, NY 10003.

Career

Archaeologist and writer. Museum of Cultural History, Los Angeles, CA, senior museum preparator, 1979-80; City of Cheyenne, Cheyenne, WY, city historian, 1980-81; U.S. Department of the Interior, Cheyenne, state historian, 1981-82, Casper, WY, archaeologist, 1982-86; Wind River Archaeological Consultants, Thermopolis, WY, archaeologist, beginning 1986; Timescribes, Thermopolis, writer, beginning 1986; Red Canyon Buffalo Ranch, co-owner, beginning 1992.

Member

Science Fiction & Fantasy Writers of America, American Association of Physical Anthropologists, National Bison Association, Archaeological Conservancy, Nature Conservancy, Society for Historical Archaeology, Western Bison Association, Wisconsin Bison Producers Association, Western Writers of America, Center for Desert Archaeology, Wyoming Writers Incorporated.

Awards, Honors

Special Achievement Awards, U.S. Department of the Interior, 1984 and 1985, for archaeological work; Spur Award for best novel of the West (with W. Michale Gear), Western Writers of America, 2005, for *People of the Raven*.

Writings

NOVELS

Sand in the Wind, Tor (New York, NY), 1990.
This Widowed Land, Tor (New York, NY), 1993.
Thin Moon and Cold Mist, Forge (New York, NY), 1995.
(With husband, W. Michael Gear) *Dark Inheritance,* Warner Books (New York, NY), 2001.
(With W. Michael Gear) *Raising Abel,* Warner Books (New York, NY), 2002.
It Sleeps in Me, Forge (New York, NY), 2005.

"POWERS OF LIGHT" NOVEL SERIES

An Abyss of Light, DAW Books (New York, NY), 1990.
Treasure of Light, DAW Books (New York, NY), 1990.
Redemption of Light, DAW Books (New York, NY), 1991.

"FIRST NORTH AMERICANS" NOVEL SERIES; WITH W. MICHAEL GEAR

People of the Wolf, Tor Books (New York, NY), 1990.
People of the Light, DAW Books (New York, NY), 1991.
People of the Fire, Tor Books (New York, NY), 1991.
People of the Earth, Tor Books (New York, NY), 1992.

People of the River, Tor Books (New York, NY), 1992.
People of the Sea, Tor Books (New York, NY), 1993.
People of the Lakes, Tor Books (New York, NY), 1994.
People of the Lightning, Tor Books (New York, NY), 1995.
People of the Silence, Tor Books (New York, NY), 1996.
People of the Mist, Tor Books (New York, NY), 1997.
People of the Masks, Tor Books (New York, NY), 1998.
People of the Owl, Tor Books (New York, NY), 2003.
People of the Raven, Tor Books (New York, NY), 2004.
People of the Moon, Tor Books (New York, NY), 2005.

"ANASAZI MYSTERY" NOVEL SERIES; WITH W. MICHAEL GEAR

The Visitant, Forge (New York, NY), 1999.
The Summoning God, Forge (New York, NY), 2000.
Bone Walker, Forge (New York, NY), 2001.

Adaptations

Several of the Gears's novels have been adapted as audiobooks, including *People of the Owl,* Books on Tape, 2003; and *It Sleeps in Me,* Books on Tape, 2005.

Work in Progress

Research into exotic healing rituals among Native American tribes and on Mississippian archaeological sites in the southern United States.

Sidelights

Kathleen O'Neal Gear and her husband, W. Michael Gear, are the coauthors of a popular series of novels that follow the tribes of prehistoric North America. Their "First North Americans" series, which includes the novels *People of the Wolf, People of the Fire, People of the Sea,* and *People of the Owl,* have been praised for their detailed description of an ancient way of life, descriptions enhanced by Kathleen O'Neal Gear's training as an archeologist. Praising the series in *Booklist,* Brad Hooper wrote that the "First North Americans" novels "are, indeed, lessons in life past, and all the facts they marshal are well integrated into a smoothly flowing story line."

The Gears began their "First North Americans" novel series in 1990 with *People of the Wolf.* The novel centers on the power struggle between two brothers, the visionary Wolf Dreamer and the warrior Raven Hunter, as they each follow their natures and ultimately divide their tribe. *People of the Fire* focuses on Little Dancer, a dreamer who is befriended by an outcast named Two Smokes and trained as a visionary. In *People of the River* the Gears bring to life the earth-mound-builder culture that lived in southern Illinois between 700 A.D. and 1500 A.D. The Mississippians, as they were known, cultivated corn, knew astronomy, and disappeared before European explorers reached the area. "Fast-paced and engrossing," *People of the Fire* "has the ring of authenticity as well," stated a contributor to *Publishers Weekly.*

People of the Sea is set in a coastal California Native American community around 10,000 B.C., as an Ice Age period is ending and rising water levels are wreaking havoc on the area's ecosystem. Large animals are disappearing, portending starvation for the populace. A religious leader, Sunchaser the Dreamer, worries about these changes that he cannot explain, but a mysterious woman comes to see him, and he runs away with her. He gains understanding regarding the fate of his own community along the way. A *Publishers Weekly* contributor praised the authors for "integrating a tremendous amount of natural and anthropological research into a satisfactory narrative," and called the book "a vivid and fascinating portrait."

The eighth book in the series, *People of the Lightning,* is set in prehistoric Florida's Windover community, a group that is not related to other Native American groups. The Standing Hollow Horn clan is led by a tyrant, Cottonmouth, who kidnaps members of a rival clan, among them a warrior woman named Musselwhite who had killed Cottonmouth's son in a previous skirmish. Musselwhite believes her husband, Diver, has been killed, and she is married off in captivity to an albino. When she learns that Diver is alive, she flees to find him. "A wealth of rich historical detail once again bolsters a pulsing narrative set in a turbulent time," noted a reviewer for *Publishers Weekly.*

People of the Silence is set amid the Anasazi culture in New Mexico around 1000 A.D., while *People of the Mist* takes place inside a matrilineal society in the Chesapeake Bay region and finds a young woman named Red Knot facing an arranged marriage to Copper Thunder, chieftain of a neighboring clan. The match is a political alliance, negotiated in part by Red Knot's grandmother, but Red Knot is slain on her wedding day, and more than one potential culprit surfaces. "Suffused with suspense, [the Gears'] . . . imaginative story offers a fascinating portrait of an ancient matrilineal culture," noted *Library Journal* contributor Mary Ellen Elsbernd in a review of *People of the Mist,* while a *Publishers Weekly* critic termed it a "fluid, suspenseful mix of anthropological research and character-driven mystery" with "a solid, satisfying resolution."

People of the Masks is set in long-ago New York State, where the Earth Thunderer clan, part of the Iroquois' Turtle Nation, rejoices when a dwarf is born to one of its members. According to tribal beliefs, a dwarf has the power to perform miracles, and the child, named Rumbler, is appropriately indulged and occupies a place of high honor in Paint Rock village. Neighboring villages, however, panic when they learn of his arrival, for it will give the Earth Thunderers an advantage. As a young child, Rumbler has a premonition of his own kidnaping, and this proves true when a warrior from a neighboring clan abducts the boy. The Walksalong villagers fear the child and attempt to kill him, but Rumbler is ultimately saved by orphan child Little Wren, who leads the boy away from the Walksalong people. *Booklist* reviewer

Diana Tixier Herald termed *People of the Masks* "prehistoric epic at its finest," commending the "gripping plot, lots of action, [and] well-developed characters." A *Publishers Weekly* commentator also enjoyed the novel, describing it as "fast-paced, fluid, rich with smoothly integrated background detail and softened by a touch of romanticism that deflects the violence and brutality."

People of the Owl features fifteen-year-old Mud Puppy, a visionary juvenile warrior who is given the responsible for his entire clan after being christened Salamander at his initiation ceremony. With three disloyal wives and a reputation for being the village idiot, Salamander must weather assaults from hidden enemies within his tribe while also battling the warring spirits of good and evil. A *Publishers Weekly* reviewer noted that *People of the Owl* is "propelled by the Gears' spry storytelling," while Brad Hooper commented in *Booklist* that the Gears "provide fascinating information on the customs of past times."

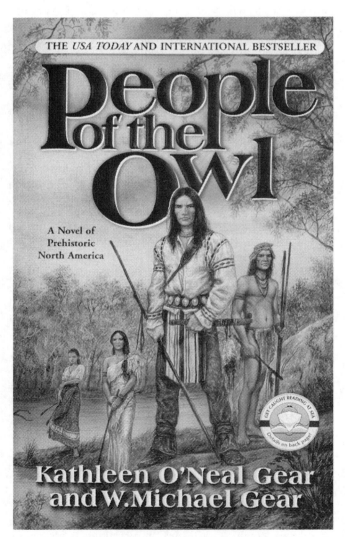

Part of the Gears' popular series set in prehistoric North America, this 2003 novel finds a young teen forced to become leader of his people after his brother is killed. (Cover illustration by Royo.)

The Visitant, a novel in the Gears' "Anasazi Mystery" series, alternates between the past and present in telling the story of archeologist Dusty Stewart and anthropologist Maureen Cole. Looking for clues as to why the Chaco Anasazi Indians disappeared from northwestern New Mexico centuries before, the two discover several mass graves of young women whose skulls have been smashed. Meanwhile, after Anasazi war chief Browser's wife winds up dead and several other deaths of young women in the tribe follow, Browser's uncle Stone Ghost is called upon to deal with the situation. As the two situations converge, Stewart and Cole bring in the office of the Native American Graves Protection and Repatriation Act and a holy woman named Hail arrives to sort out the mystery. "Readers will enjoy the wide range of characters and thick suspense," predicted Susan A. Zappia in *Library Journal*. Praising the "breathtaking descriptions [that] evoke the harsh beauty of the desert in both winter and summer," a *Publishers Weekly* reviewer commended the Gears' "lucid, erudite historical perspectives," and Herald wrote that "the vividly depicted characters and settings are satisfying."

The Summoning God, the second book in the "Anasazi Mystery" series, centers upon the Katsinas people in the 1200s and explains the mystery of the Anasazi extinction. An afterword cautions that the fate of this people may befall human civilization as well. A *Publishers Weekly* contributor called *The Summoning God* a "memorable novel" and stated that while it is a book "not for the squeamish . . . the Gears offer unusual insight into Anasazi culture and history."

In addition to novels set in North America's past, the Gears have also penned contemporary works. *Dark Inheritance* centers upon the efforts of British pharmaceutical manufacturer Smyth-Archer Chemicals (SAC) to create a "smart" chimpanzee. To do so, the company has placed apes with scientists and their families, among them single father Jim Dutton and his daughter, Brett. Umber, a bonobo ape—a variety of chimpanzee—has been raised alongside Brett, and the pair are as close as human sisters. Umber communicates with Brett and Jim via sign language and a hand-held computer, and Jim discovers that she can do math as well. She even asks about a higher being, which prompts Jim to grow suspicious about her origins. Meanwhile, questions are raised regarding SAC's experiments and the fact that certain chimps who do not achieve some level of intellectual advancement may become violent. *Booklist* critic William Beatty called *Dark Inheritance* a "lively, thought-provoking, and convincing story."

In addition to collaborations with her husband, Kathleen O'Neal Gear has published a number of novels for adult readers, including her "Powers of Light" series and several standalone novels. Set in seventeenth-century Quebec, *This Widowed Land* features Jesuit ministers who clash with Huron Indians, until one of the Europeans falls in love with a Huron woman named Andiora. *Publishers Weekly* reviewer Sybil S. Steinberg

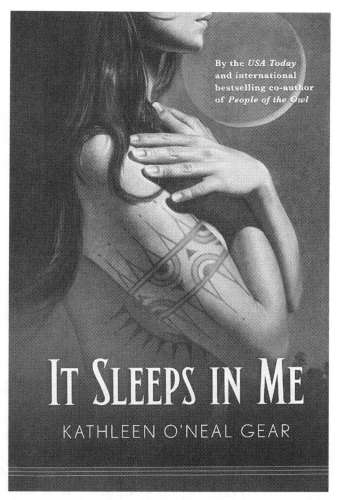

Haunted by the memory of the husband who abandoned her, a high chieftess builds a new life while guiding her clan until a stranger unlocks old emotions and threatens her ability to rule during a time of war in this 2005 novel. (Cover illustration by Vince Natale.)

called Gear's characters "static and two-dimensional" but noted that "her use of period detail breathes life into daily events at the Huron village."

Thin Moon and Cold Mist is set during the U.S. Civil War and features Robin Walkingstick Heatherton, a female spy who masquerades as a black male soldier in order to infiltrate the Union army and spy for the Confederacy. When Robin finds herself on the run from a Union major who blames her for his brother's death, she flees to Colorado with her five-year-old son, Jeremy, and there falls in love with another Union soldier. *It Sleeps in Me* finds the leadership of Black Falcon high chieftess Sora threatened by duplicitous allies and haunted by the shadow soul of her dead husband while attempting to lead her people and sustain her life. Again writing in *Publishers Weekly,* Steinberg noted that Gear imbues *Thin Moon and Cold Mist* "with historical detail and intriguing plot twists, delivered in lively prose," and *Library Journal* reviewer Mary Ellen Elsbernd wrote that in *It Sleeps in Me* Gear "spins her magic . . . in a saga peppered with murder, intrigue, and . . . love scenes."

Biographical and Critical Sources

PERIODICALS

Booklist, January 1, 1996, Kathleen Hughes, review of *People of the Lightning,* p. 786; January 1, 1997, Margaret Flanagan, review of *People of the Silence,* p. 818; February 1, 1998, Eric Robbins, review of *People of the Mist,* p. 898; October 15, 1998, Diana Tixier Herald, review of *People of the Masks,* p. 401; January 1, 1999, review of *People of the Mist,* p. 781; July, 1999, Diana Tixier Herald, review of *The Visitant,* p. 1893; December 1, 2000, William Beatty, review of *Dark Inheritance,* p. 675; May 15, 2003, Brad Hooper, review of *People of the Owl,* p. 1619.

Gazette (Colorado Springs, CO), April 22, 2001, Linda DuVal, "Defining Humanity," p. B6.

Kirkus Reviews, June 1, 2002, review of *Raising Abel,* p. 756; August 1, 2005, review of *People of the Moon,* p. 821.

Library Journal, February 1, 1998, Mary Ellen Elsbernd, review of *People of the Mist,* p. 110; November 1, 1998, Mary Ellen Eisbernd, review of *People of the Masks,* p. 125; August, 1999, Susan A. Zappia, review of *The Visitant,* p. 139; May 15, 2003, Mary Ellen Elsbernd, review of *People of the Owl,* p. 123; April 15, 2005, Mary Ellen Elsbernd, review of *It Sleeps in Me,* p. 72.

Post and Courier (Charleston, SC), January 14, 2001, Michael A. Green, review of *The Summoning God,* p. 3.

Publishers Weekly, May 3, 1991, review of *People of the Wolf* (sound recording), p. 50; June 1, 1992, review of *People of the River,* p. 51; January 18, 1993, Sybil S. Steinberg, review of *This Widowed Land,* p. 448; September 13, 1993, review of *People of the Sea,* p. 89; June 12, 1995, Sybil S. Steinberg, review of *Thin Moon and Cold Mist,* p. 47; October 30, 1995, review of *People of the Lightning,* p. 46; June 3, 1996, review of *The Morning River,* p. 61; December 2, 1996, review of *People of the Silence,* p. 42; November 24, 1997, review of *People of the Mist,* p. 52; November 2, 1998, review of *People of the Masks,* p. 71; July 5, 1999, review of *The Visitant,* p. 62; June 26, 2000, review of *The Summoning God,* p. 53; February 5, 2001, review of *Dark Inheritance,* p. 65; July 1, 2002, review of *Raising Abel,* p. 55; May 26, 2003, review of *People of the Owl,* p. 49.

St. Louis Post-Dispatch, March 23, 1997, Dick Richmond, "Rise and Fall of Ancient Civilization," p. T9.

ONLINE

W. Michael Gear and Kathleen O'Neal Gear Web site, http://www.gear-gear.com (December 25, 2005).*

*   *   *

GEAR, W. Michael 1955-

Personal

Born May 20, 1955, in Colorado Springs, CO; son of William Gear (a television anchor) and Katherine Perry

Cook (an artist); married Kathleen O'Neal (an historian and writer), October 20, 1982. *Education:* Colorado State University, B.A., 1976, M.A., 1979. *Politics:* "Libertarian/Republican." *Religion:* "Native American." *Hobbies and other interests:* Hunting, shooting, reloading, motorcycle touring, bison, travel.

Addresses

Home—P.O. Box 1329, Thermopolis, WY 82443. *Office*—415 Park St., Thermopolis, WY 82443. *Agent*—Owen Laster, William Morris Literary Agency, 1325 Avenue of the Americas, New York, NY 10019. *E-mail*—Wmgear1@aol.com.

Career

Western Wyoming College, Rock Springs, archaeologist, 1979-81; Metcalf-Zier Archaeologists, Inc., Eagle, CO, archaeologist, 1981; Pronghorn Anthropological Association, Casper, WY, owner and principal investigator, 1982-84; Wind River Archaeological Consultants, owner and principal investigator, 1988-2000.

Member

American Anthropological Association, American Association of Physical Anthropology, Society of American Archaeology, Paleopathology Association, National Bison Association, Western Writers of America, Wyoming Writers.

Awards, Honors

Spur Award for best novel of the West (with Kathleen O'Neal Gear), Western Writers of America, 2005, for *People of the Raven.*

Writings

NOVELS

Long Ride Home, Tor Books (New York, NY), 1988.
Big Horn Legacy, Pinnacle (New York, NY), 1988.
The Warriors of Spider, DAW (New York, NY), 1988.
The Way of Spider, DAW (New York, NY), 1989.
The Web of Spider, DAW (New York, NY), 1989.
The Artifact, DAW (New York, NY), 1990.
Starstrike, DAW (New York, NY), 1990.
Requiem for the Conqueror, DAW (New York, NY), 1991.
Relic of Empire, DAW (New York, NY), 1992.
Countermeasures, DAW (New York, NY), 1993.
The Morning River, Forge (New York, NY), 1996.
Coyote Summer, Forge (New York, NY), 1997.
The Athena Factor, Forge (New York, NY), 2005.

"FIRST NORTH AMERICANS" NOVEL SERIES; WITH WIFE, KATHLEEN O'NEAL GEAR

People of the Wolf, Tor Books (New York, NY), 1990.
People of the Light, DAW Books (New York, NY), 1991.
People of the Fire, Tor Books (New York, NY), 1991.

People of the Earth, Tor Books (New York, NY), 1992.
People of the River, Tor Books (New York, NY), 1992.
People of the Sea, Tor Books (New York, NY), 1993.
People of the Lakes, Tor Books (New York, NY), 1994.
People of the Lightning, Tor Books (New York, NY), 1995.
People of the Silence, Tor Books (New York, NY), 1996.
People of the Mist, Tor Books (New York, NY), 1997.
People of the Masks, Tor Books (New York, NY), 1998.
People of the Owl, Tor Books (New York, NY), 2003.
People of the Raven, Tor Books (New York, NY), 2004.
People of the Moon, Tor Books (New York, NY), 2005.

"ANASAZI MYSTERY" NOVEL SERIES; WITH KATHLEEN O'NEAL GEAR

The Visitant, Forge (New York, NY), 1999.
The Summoning God, Forge (New York, NY), 2000.
Bone Walker, Forge (New York, NY), 2001.

Adaptations

Several of the Gears' novels have been adapted as audiobooks, including *People of the Owl,* Books on Tape, 2003.

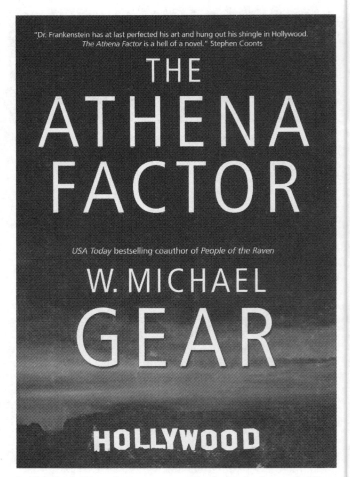

"Dr. Frankenstein has at last perfected his art and hung out his shingle in Hollywood. *The Athena Factor* is a hell of a novel." Stephen Coonts

THE ATHENA FACTOR

USA Today bestselling coauthor of *People of the Raven*

W. MICHAEL GEAR

HOLLYWOOD

In Gear's thriller, after top actress Sheela Marks is attacked by a syringe-wielding assailant, she puts her ex-Marine bodyguard and former FBI agent Christal Anaya on the case, and the pair unearth a plot involving a wealthy potentate, a megacorporation, and a threat to Hollywood.

Sidelights

Frequently working with his wife, writer Kathleen O'Neal Gear, W. Michael Gear began his writing career penning western novels in the late 1980s and has gone on to write modern thrillers like *The Athena Factor* and several books that mix the historical western with a science-fiction edge. The Gears, who are both trained archeologists, are best known for their novels centered on the native people of prehistoric North America. The "First North Americans" series, which includes titles such as *People of the Wolf, People of the Mist,* and *People of the Moon,* blend whodunit suspense, historical romance, compelling characters, and a wealth of anthropological details in stories focusing on primitive native tribes. Calling Gear "a vigorous writer," a *Publishers Weekly* contributor noted in a review of Gear's *The Morning River* that the author "writes a superbly rolling prose with flair, confidence, wit, an ear for sounds and an eye for details."

A fourth-generation Coloradoan, Gear earned an advanced anthropology degree in 1979 and worked as a field archaeologist and archaeological consultant for a number of years. The seasonal nature of the profession freed him during the long winter months, and he began writing during one such break. He had little success finding a publisher for his first manuscripts, but in 1982 he married archeologist O'Neal, and four years later the pair decided to devote their energies to writing on a full-time basis. They moved to a remote mountain cabin built by Gear's great-uncle near Empire, Colorado, and lived there for three years with no running water and only a pair of stoves to provide heat. The determination, however, proved worthwhile; Gear's first book, a western novel titled *Long Ride Home,* was accepted by Tor Books in early 1987.

Gear penned the western novel *Big Horn Legacy* before beginning *The Warriors of Spider,* which blends science fiction and Native American beliefs in a story that finds a lost colony of Native American and Hispanic descendants "discovered" by an advanced civilization. After continuing the story though two subsequent books, Gear devised the premise for a new series. He imagined an educated, early nineteenth-century Bostonian lost in the wilderness of the American west in the 1820s. The idea became *The Morning River,* published in 1996.

The Morning River centers on Richard Hamilton, a pretentious Harvard University philosophy student whose father decides to send Richard west on business as a way to teach the young man a bit about the world. Hamilton lands in trouble soon after arriving at his destination: he is assaulted and robbed of his money, then sold as an indentured servant on a trade boat heading into Indian Territory. Help comes in the form of a boat passenger named Travis Hartman, a mountain man who knows several Native-American languages and teaches the Bostonian to appreciate Native customs. A young Shoshone woman, Heals like the Willow, is also being held as a slave, and her life and Hamilton's soon inter-

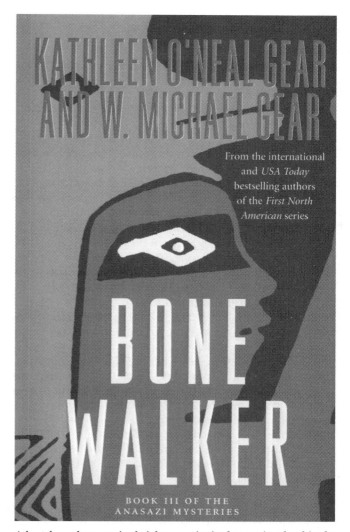

A brutal murder committed eight centuries in the past is echoed in the present as two modern archeologists find that the death of one of their colleagues seems to echo the ancient evil responsible.

sect. Hamilton's saga continues in *Coyote Summer,* as he and Heals like the Willow fall in love, battle various enemies, and begin a family. A writer for *Publishers Weekly* faulted the novel's prose, but stated that Gear nevertheless produces "a well-plotted page-turner that distinguishes itself from other westerns in the depth and quality of its historical reconstruction."

Gear and his wife began their "First North Americans" series in 1990 with *People of the Wolf.* The saga presents an ancient people who purportedly traveled from Asia across an ice bridge to North America during the Ice Age. The plot centers upon the power struggle between two brothers, Wolf Dreamer and Raven Hunter. In the fourth novel of the series, *People of the River,* the Gears imagine events among the earth-mound builder culture that lived in southern Illinois between 700 A.D. and 1500 A.D., while *People of the Sea* is set among a coastal California Native American community around 10,000 B.C., as an Ice Age period is ending and rising water levels are wreaking havoc for the area's ecosystem. "Fast-paced and engrossing, the novel has the ring of authenticity as well," stated a contributor to *Publishers Weekly* in reviewing *People of the Sea,* and a *Publishers Weekly* reviewer praised the Gears for "integrating a tremendous amount of natural and anthropological research into a satisfactory narrative." The reviewer went on to call *People of the Sea* "a vivid and fascinating portrait."

People of the Lightning is set in the Windover community in prehistoric Florida, where the Standing Hollow Horn clan is led by a tyrant named Cottonmouth. During a kidnapping raid on a rival clan, Cottonmouth captures Musselwhite, a warrior woman who had killed Cottonmouth's son in a previous skirmish. "A wealth of rich historical detail once again bolsters a pulsing narrative set in a turbulent time," noted a reviewer for *Publishers Weekly. People of the Silence* is set among the Anasazi culture in New Mexico around 1000 A.D., while *People of the Mist* takes place inside a matrilineal society in the Chesapeake Bay region. *People of the Mist* involves an arranged marriage between two neighboring clans, but this political alliance goes awry when the bride is slain on her wedding day and more than one potential culprit surfaces. "Suffused with suspense, their imaginative story offers a fascinating portrait of an ancient matrilineal culture," noted *Library Journal* reviewer Mary Ellen Eisbernd of the Gears' work, while a *Publishers Weekly* critic termed *People of the Mist* a "fluid, suspenseful mix of anthropological research and character-driven mystery" with "a solid, satisfying resolution."

People of the Masks, set in long-ago New York State, finds a dwarf born to a member of the Earth Thunderer clan and fated to be both revered and feared. In *Booklist,* Diana Tixier Herald termed *People of the Masks* "prehistoric epic at its finest," and commended the Gears for their "gripping plot, lots of action, [and] well-developed characters."

The first volume in the Gears' "Anasazi" series, *The Visitant,* focuses on archeologist Dusty Stewart and anthropologist Maureen Cole as they pair up to determine why the Chaco Anasazi Indians once disappeared in northwestern New Mexico but find themselves embroiled in murder when mass graves are discovered. The series continues in *The Summoning God* and *Bone Walker,* the latter which finds Dusty embroiled in the ritual murder of his uncle, a murder that has links to the history of the Chaco Canyon excavation site. "Readers will enjoy the wide range of characters and thick suspense," predicted Susan A. Zappia in *Library Journal.* Herald, writing for *Booklist,* praised "the vividly depicted characters and settings are satisfying and leave the reader hoping for more titles in this promising series." The coauthors also address modern technology in *Dark Inheritance,* which centers upon a British pharmaceutical maker and its attempt to create a "smart" chimpanzee through biological engineering, then raising

treated animals with staff-members and their families. *Booklist* critic William Beatty called *Dark Inheritance* a "lively, thought-provoking, and convincing story."

As Gear told Dale L. Walker in an interview with the *Rocky Mountain News,* he always strives to depict history from a balanced perspective in his books. "We've created a great many myths about our history," he explained. "I appreciate the myths, but I think people like to read about the way it really was. Kathy and I both struggle to write that kind of book."

Biographical and Critical Sources

PERIODICALS

Booklist, January 1, 1996, Kathleen Hughes, review of *People of the Lightning,* p. 786; January 1, 1997, Margaret Flanagan, review of *People of the Silence,* p. 818; February 1, 1998, Eric Robbins, review of *People of the Mist,* p. 898; October 15, 1998, Diana Tixier Herald, review of *People of the Masks,* p. 401; January 1, 1999, review of *People of the Mist,* p. 781; July, 1999, Diana Tixier Herald, review of *The Visitant,* p. 1893; December 1, 2000, William Beatty, review of *Dark Inheritance,* p. 675; May 15, 2003, Brad Hooper, review of *People of the Owl,* p. 1619.

Gazette (Colorado Springs, CO), April 22, 2001, Linda DuVal, "Defining Humanity," p. B6.

Kirkus Reviews, November 15, 2001, review of *Bone Walker,* p. 1582; June 1, 2002, review of *Raising Abel,* p. 756; May 15, 2005, review of *The Athena Factor,* p. 557; August 1, 2005, review of *People of the Moon,* p. 821.

Library Journal, February 1, 1998, Mary Ellen Elsbernd, review of *People of the Mist,* p. 110; November 1, 1998, Mary Ellen Eisbernd, review of *People of the Masks,* p. 125; August, 1999, Susan A. Zappia, review of *The Visitant,* p. 139; May 15, 2003, Mary Ellen Elsbernd, review of *People of the Owl,* p. 123.

Post and Courier (Charleston, SC), January 14, 2001, Michael A. Green, review of *The Summoning God,* p. 3.

Publishers Weekly, May 3, 1991, review of *People of the Wolf* (sound recording), p. 50; June 1, 1992, review of *People of the River,* p. 51; September 13, 1993, review of *People of the Sea,* p. 89; October 30, 1995, review of *People of the Lightning,* p. 46; June 3, 1996, review of *The Morning River,* p. 61; December 2, 1996, review of *People of the Silence,* p. 42; July 14, 1997, review of *Coyote Summer,* p. 66; November 24, 1997, review of *People of the Mist,* p. 52; November 2, 1998, review of *People of the Masks,* p. 71; July 5, 1999, review of *The Visitant,* p. 62; June 26, 2000, review of *The Summoning God,* p. 53; February 5, 2001, review of *Dark Inheritance,* p. 65; July 1, 2002, review of *Raising Abel,* p. 55; May 26, 2003, review of *People of the Owl,* p. 49.

Rocky Mountain News, June 16, 1996, Dale L. Walker, "Young Man Comes of Age in the Wild West," p. D30.

St. Louis Post-Dispatch, March 23, 1997, Dick Richmond, "Rise and Fall of Ancient Civilization," p. T9.

ONLINE

W. Michael Gear and Kathleen O'Neal Gear Web site, http://www.gear-gear.com (December 25, 2005).*

* * *

GRALLEY, Jean

Personal

Born in New York, NY. *Education:* Parsons New School for Design, graduated; studied at Wayne State University and Harvard University.

Addresses

Agent—c/o Author Mail, Philomel, Putnam Berkley Group, 200 Madison Ave., New York, NY 10016. *E-mail*—jeangralley@aol.com.

Career

Writer and illustrator. *Cricket* magazine, staff artist for fourteen years; freelance illustrator and writer. Also creates plays, music, cartoons, and experimental multimedia. Picture-book commentator on National Public Radio's *Looseleaf Notebook* program.

Member

Society of Children's Book Writers and Illustrators, Children's Book Guild of Washington, DC, Picture Book Artists Association.

Awards, Honors

Don Freeman Memorial grant; Ezra Jack Keates fellowship for book illustration; Best Books designation, Children's Book Council, for *Very Boring Alligator*.

Writings

(Illustrator) Jane Yolen, *And Twelve Chinese Acrobats,* Philomel Books (New York, NY), 1994.
(Self-illustrated) *Hogula, Dread Pig of Night,* Henry Holt (New York, NY), 1999.
(Self-illustrated) *Very Boring Alligator,* Henry Holt (New York, NY), 2001.
(Self-illustrated) *The Moon Came down on Milk Street,* Henry Holt (New York, NY), 2004.

Contributor to periodicals, including the *New York Times, Detroit Free Press,* and *Horn Book.*

Sidelights

Jean Gralley had a brief, doomed career in conservatory where she spent more time drawing on her music than practicing until she got a clue and left for Parson's

Jean Gralley

School of Design in New York City. There she studied with noted illustrator Maurice Sendak, who spoke of the spirit of music in picture books and "the light went on," as she told *SATA.* Now she loves everything about this art form, including speaking about it, as she often has for writers' and illustrators' conferences and for National Public Radio. A new interest of hers is the digital future of the picture book.

Beginning her career as staff artist for *Cricket* magazine, author and illustrator Jean Gralley has created several picture books for young readers in addition to exploring the evolution of illustrated books in digitized media. Her books includes *Hogula, Dread Pig of Night* and *Very Boring Alligator,* as well as the *The Moon Came down on Milk Street,* a book that some critics have compared to Maurice Sendak's classic *The Night Kitchen.* The comparison is apt; as a student at Parsons School of Design Gralley studied under Sendak, and the noted author/illustrator has been one of her strong influences. She has also illustrated for the *New York Times.*

The Moon Came down on Milk Street is "a gentle, heartfelt tribute to those who work together in emergencies," according to a *Kirkus Reviews* critic. In this subtle story Gralley presents readers with a look at how ordinary individuals react in times of crisis through a rhyming text that brings to life fantastical and non-threatening emergencies. On one particular evening, for example, the moon suddenly falls softy from the sky and breaks into pieces in a large city. Shocked city residents all pitch in to put the pieces back together and raise the moon back into its proper place in the sky. Gralley enhances her text with large illustrations that emphasize the importance of teamwork as a group of children work together as a cohesive unit to accomplish their goal of restoring the moon properly. Joanna Rudge Long, writing in *Horn Book,* described Gralley's artwork as "simple, expressive drawings washed in saturated, slightly muted colors that enhance the dreamlike quality." *The Moon Came down on Milk Street* was also cited by the State Library of Louisiana as one of the books that could be helpful to young evacuees of 2005's Hurricane Katrina.

In *Very Boring Alligator* Gralley relates the story of a very little redheaded girl with a very large problem, once again utilizing a rhyming text. When the little girl realizes that the very boring alligator that lounges around all day on her purple couch, talking, has no intention of leaving she does everything she can think of to get him to go. Finally the resourceful girl calls the Gator Cops in hopes that they can remove the boring alligator from her house. However, upon their arrival the Gator Cops fall under the alligator's spell; becoming boring themselves, they too refuse to leave! It is only when the girl finally decides to clearly and emphatically say what she means that she gets her wish. The gator is allowed back only under the condition that he absolutely must leave when asked. Praising the text with its "simple, humorously thumping rhymes," Connie Fletcher wrote in *Booklist* that *Very Boring Alligator* is an "age-appropriate take on empowerment, managing moods, and controlling nerve-wracking situations." A *Kirkus Reviews* critic stated that, while a lazy alligator seems a strange star in a jaunty tale, "Gralley pulls it off with flair, investing the little girl with all the energy the dullard alligator lacks."

In The Moon Came down on Milk Street *author/illustrator Gralley tells a reassuring tale about how people come together in times of trouble to put things right.*

In a rhyming text, Gralley tells a quirky tale about a little girl's efforts to deal with an overbearing and slow-to-leave houseguest in Very Boring Alligator.

Biographical and Critical Sources

PERIODICALS

Booklist, November 15, 1999, Ilene Cooper, review of *Hogula, Dread Pig of Night,* p. 635; September 15, 2001, Connie Fletcher, review of *Very Boring Alligator,* p. 231.

Bulletin of the Center for Children's Books, October, 1999, review of *Hogula, Dread Pig of Night,* p. 54.

Faces: People, Places, and Cultures, March, 2002, p. 46.

Horn Book, January-February, 2005, Joanna Rudge Long, review of *The Moon Came down on Milk Street,* p. 76.

Kirkus Reviews, August 15, 2001, review of *Very Boring Alligator,* p. 1213; October 15, 2004, review of *The Moon Came down on Milk Street,* p. 1006.

Parents, October, 1999, review of *Hogula, Dread Pig of Night,* p. 40.

Publishers Weekly, July 23, 2001, review of *Very Boring Alligator,* p. 75.

Reading Teacher, October, 2000, review of *Hogula, Dread Pig of Night,* p. 197.

School Library Journal, June, 1995, Carolyn Noah, review of *And Twelve Chinese Acrobats,* p. 115; November, 1999, Judith Constantinides, review of *Hogula, Dread Pig of Night,* p. 116; October, 2001, Maryann H. Owen, review of *Very Boring Alligator,* p. 118; November, 2004, Bethany L.W. Hankinson, review of *The Moon Came down on Milk Street,* p. 104.

Washington Post Book World, November 7, 2004, Elizabeth Ward, review of *The Moon Came down on Milk Street,* p. 12.

ONLINE

Jean Gralley Home Page, http://www.jeangralley.com (November 6, 2005).

*   *   *

GRAVELLE, Karen 1942-

Personal

Born July 22, 1942, in Alexandria, VA; daughter of Gordon Karl (an urban traffic commissioner) and Aileen (a homemaker; maiden name, Clark) Gravelle. *Education:* University of Oregon, B.A., 1965; Catholic University of America, M.S.W., 1969; City University of New York, Ph.D., 1981.

Addresses

Home—New York, NY; eastern VA. *Office*—55 W. 70th St., New York, NY 10023.

Career

Hospital for Special Surgery, New York, NY, medical social worker, 1969-70; Greenwich House Counseling Center, New York, NY, therapist, 1970-75; Hunter College of the City University of New York, adjunct lecturer, 1978-81, visiting assistant professor of psychology, 1982; Hamilton College, Clinton, NY, visiting assistant professor of psychology, 1981; Cancer Research Institute, New York, NY, director of public information, 1983-84; Fox Chase Cancer Center, Philadelphia, PA, senior science editor, 1985-86; Renaissance Medical Group, New York, NY, supervisor of behavioral modification support program for obese patients, 1986-87. Freelance writer, editor, and photographer, 1982—.

Member

Authors Guild, Authors League of America.

Awards, Honors

Best Book Award, Young Adult Library Services Association/American Library Association, 1993, for *Teenage Fathers: An Inside View;* New York Public Library's Books for the Teen Age citation, 1999, for *What's Going on down There?*

Writings

FOR CHILDREN

Feather (fiction), Weekly Reader (Stamford, CT), 1985.

Fun Facts about Creatures, Weekly Reader (Stamford, CT), 1986.

(With Ann Squire) *Animal Talk,* Messner (New York, NY), 1988.

Lizards, Franklin Watts (New York, NY), 1991.

Animal Societies, Franklin Watts (New York, NY), 1993.

Growing up in a Holler in the Mountains: An Appalachian Childhood, Franklin Watts (New York, NY), 1997.

Growing up Where the Partridge Drums Its Wings: A Mohawk Childhood, photographs by Stephen R. Poole, Franklin Watts (New York, NY), 1997.

(With Sylviane A. Diouf) *Growing up in Crawfish Country: A Cajun Childhood,* Franklin Watts (New York, NY), 1998.

FOR YOUNG ADULTS

(With Bertram A. John) *Teenagers Face to Face with Cancer,* Messner (New York, NY), 1989.

(With Charles Haskins) *Teenagers Face to Face with Bereavement,* Messner (New York, NY), 1989.

Understanding Birth Defects, Franklin Watts (New York, NY), 1990.

(With Leslie Peterson) *Teenage Fathers: An Inside View,* Messner (New York, NY), 1992.

(With Susan H. Fischer) *Where Are My Birth Parents?: A Guide for Teenage Adoptees,* Walker (New York, NY), 1993.

Soaring Spirits: Conversations with Native American Teens, Franklin Watts (New York, NY), 1995.

(With Jennifer Gravelle) *The Period Book: Everything You Don't Want to Ask (But Need to Know),* illustrated by Debbie Palen, Walker (New York, NY), 1996.

(With Nick and Chava Castro) *What's Going on down There?: Answers to Questions Boys Find Hard to Ask,* illustrated by Robert Leighton, Walker (New York, NY), 1998.

Five Ways to Know about You, illustrated by Mary Lynn Blasutta, Walker (New York, NY), 2001.

The Driving Book: Everything New Drivers Need to Know but Don't Know to Ask, illustrated by Helen Flook, Walker (New York, NY), 2005.

OTHER

(With Robert Rivlin) *Deciphering the Senses: The Expanding World of Human Perception* (adult nonfiction), Simon & Schuster (New York, NY), 1984.

Contributor of articles to scholarly journals, including *Animal Behavior* and *Sociobiology.*

Sidelights

Many of Karen Gravelle's books are written for young children and teens experiencing the confusing and turbulent years of adolescence. Dealing with issues such as grief, disease, puberty, and racial discrimination, often through interviews with young people, Gravelle provides information and new perspectives that help young adults understand basic issues that affect their lives. In writing several of her books, Gravelle has worked with teen coauthors as a way to help her focus on what modern teens really want to know.

Gravelle's first book for young adults, *Teenagers Face to Face with Cancer,* is based on interviews with sixteen adolescents who were then battling cancer. Gravelle and coauthor John A. Bertram grouped the adolescents' stories by theme to provide answers to questions teens with cancer often ask, including the difficult question: "What if I die?" Types of cancer, treatments, doctors, family matters, and coping techniques are also discussed by both interviewees and coauthors. A *Kirkus Reviews* writer concluded that this "honest treatment" of cancer would "help and reassure other teenage cancer patients, as well as their friends and relatives."

Teenagers Face to Face with Bereavement, written by Gravelle and Charles Haskins, utilizes an interview structure similar to *Teenagers Face to Face with Cancer* to provide information about death and the loss of loved ones. In the book seventeen teenagers comment on their relationships with parents, siblings, and friends, their feelings at the time of death and at the funeral, and the emotions they experience at later stages of grief. The authors provide guidance and advice while highlighting positive activities teenagers can take on to help them rebuild their lives after the death of a loved one. As Libby K. White pointed out in the *School Library Journal,* "Both interviewees and compilers offer hope and comfort. The compilers endorse survivor counseling and point to successful outcomes of peer group therapy."

After publishing *Understanding Birth Defects,* another book for young adults, Gravelle went on to write *Teenage Fathers: An Inside View* with Leslie Peterson. The third book in Simon & Schuster's interview-based series, the book presents in-depth discussions with thirteen teenage fathers and was designated a 1993 Young Adult Library Services Association/American Library Association best book. Described as "well laid out and informative" by a writer for *Kirkus Reviews, Teenage Fathers* allows readers to examine the diverse situations, backgrounds, and characteristics of these fathers as well as to understand the challenges presented by fatherhood. *Booklist* contributor Stephanie Zvirin characterized the interviews as "filled with disillusionment, fear, anger, and occasionally real joy," the young men's words presenting a "dramatic, eye-opening portrayal of what teen fathers face when their desires and expectations collide with reality." In *Voice of Youth Advocates,* Mary Veronica advised that young men should listen to the advice of teen fathers, suggesting: "Wait, don't rush into a relationship which could change your life and all of your dreams."

Gravelle provides another important resource for young people in *Where Are My Birth Parents?: A Guide for Teenage Adoptees.* Co-written with Susan Fischer, this book describes the process of and problems with searching for birth parents. The authors present advice on what to expect from birth mothers as well as adoptive parents throughout the search. A list of search and support groups is also included.

Soaring Spirits: Conversations with Native American Teens focuses on the issues of growing up in contemporary society as a young Native American. Gravelle interviewed seventeen teens from five different tribes who lived on Indian reservations across the United States. "We need more contemporary books like this to go with the historical fiction and the shelves of great folklore," commented Hazel Rochman in a *Booklist* review.

Gravelle's two prominent books on puberty, *The Period Book: Everything You Don't Want to Ask (But Need to Know)* and *What's Going on down There?: Answers to Questions Boys Find Hard to Ask,* were co-written by young teens. Gravelle's niece, Jennifer, contributes insight into girl questions about periods in *The Period Book,* while Nick and Chava Castro, two brothers from Los Angeles, aided Gravelle in selecting the subject matter for *What's Going on down There?* Most of the issues in *The Period Book* revolve around menstruation, but also feature topics such as what to expect from a gynecologist, how to handle strong emotions, and ways of dealing with cramps and pimples. A *Publishers Weekly* contributor considered *The Period Book* to be an "accessible guide for adolescent girls." *What's Going on down There?* deals with puberty issues and changes in the body, as well as sex, masturbation, and STDs. "The tone is candid and the advice objective," noted Roger Sutton in a review of Gralley's book for *Horn Book.*

In addition to books on puberty, Gravelle is the author of the teen personality guide *Five Ways to Know about You,* which introduces readers to numerology, astrology (both Western and Chinese), palm reading, and handwriting analysis. Many critics cited the greatest value of the book as the combination of the five types of personality analysis; most books that cover these topics for teens only feature one of the five. Ann G. Brouse, writing in *School Library Journal,* commented of the book, "More than just a taste, this is a satisfying first course." *Kliatt* reviewer Tricia Finch considered *Five Ways to Know about You* "a teen-friendly publication" that features an "accessible" text.

Gravelle covers a teen rite of passage in *The Driving Book: Everything New Drivers Need to Know but Don't Know to Ask.* The guide covers not only driving issues, but also describes general car maintenance and deals with road rage and the use of cell phones in cases of emergency. Gravelle also covers topics such as peer-pressure situations that affect driving, as well as how the use of drugs or medication can affect a driver's judgment, perception, and abilities. "Every new driver needs to read this book," proclaimed *Booklist* reviewer Ilene Cooper, who commented that the volume's size makes it convenient to carry in the glove compartment.

Kathleen E. Gruver commented in *School Library Journal* that "the book is clearly written and well organized, but it is also humorous and appealing."

Gravelle's books for younger readers include *Fun Facts about Creatures,* which provides interesting information about reptiles and insects. *Animal Talk,* written with Ann Squire, discusses animal communication both with other animals and with humans, and was described by Beth Ames Herbert in *Booklist* as a "fascinating" work. *Lizards* describes the differences and similarities between the lives of humans and lizards, while *Feather,* Gravelle's first work of fiction, is the story of a convalescent girl and a trapped pigeon.

Gravelle is also the author of the "Growing up in America" series, featuring such titles as *Growing up in a Holler in the Mountain* and *Growing up Where the Partridge Drums Its Wings.* These books allow young readers to peek into the everyday lives of children who have quite different experiences while growing up. Hazel Rochman wrote in *Booklist* that the titles in the series will aid readers in seeing beyond assumptions about people from specific regions; "The tone is very positive," Rochman wrote, "hitting hard at stereotypes of the poor and uneducated."

Biographical and Critical Sources

PERIODICALS

Booklist, October 15, 1988, Beth Ames Herbert, review of *Animal Talk,* p. 408; October 15, 1992, Stephanie Zvirin, review of *Teenage Fathers,* p. 413; March 15, 1996, Hazel Rochman, review of *Soaring Spirits: Conversations with Native American Teens,* and Stephanie Zvirin, review of *The Period Book: Everything You Don't Want to Ask (But Need to Know),* p. 1258; January 1, 1998, Hazel Rochman, review of *Growing Up in a Holler in the Mountains: An Appalachian Childhood* and *Growing up Where the Partridge Drums Its Wings: A Mohawk Childhood,* p. 804; November 1, 1998, Stephanie Zvirin, review of *What's Going on down There?: Answers to Questions Boys Find Hard to Ask,* p. 481; December 1, 1998, Ilene Cooper, review of *Growing up in Crawfish Country: A Cajun Childhood,* p. 663; March 1, 2005, Ilene Cooper, review of *The Driving Book: Everything New Drivers Need to Know but Don't Know to Ask,* p. 150.
Bulletin of the Center for Children's Books, July 1996, review of *The Period Book,* p. 373.
Canadian Journal of Human Sexuality, winter, 2000, Ann Barrett, review of *What's Going on down There?,* p. 278.
Horn Book, January, 1999, Roger Sutton, review of *What's Going on down There?,* p. 70.
Kirkus Reviews, December 1, 1986, review of *Teenagers Face to Face with Cancer,* p. 1800; June 1, 1989, p. 836; June 15, 1993, p. 785; August 15, 1992, review of *Teenage Fathers,* p. 1061.
Kliatt, May, 2002, Tricia Finch, review of *Five Ways to Know about You,* p. 35.
Publishers Weekly, February, 1996, review of *The Period Book,* p. 217.
School Library Journal, February, 1987, p. 90; July, 1989, Libby K. White, review of *Teenagers Face to Face with Bereavement,* p. 95; January, 2002, Ann G. Brouse, review of *Five Ways to Know about You,* p. 156; May, 2005, Kathleen E. Gruver, review of *The Driving Book,* p. 150.
Voice of Youth Advocates, December, 1992, Mary Veronica, review of *Teenage Fathers,* p. 307; June, 1996, review of *The Period Book,* p. 116; December, 2001, review of *Five Ways to Know about You,* p. 380.

ONLINE

Karen Gravelle Web site, http://www.karengravelle.com (November 30, 2005).*

*   *   *

GREY, Mini

Personal

Born in Wales; partner's name Tony. *Education:* University College, London, B.A. (English); studied theatre design; University of Brighton, M.A. (sequential design). *Hobbies and other interests:* Running, cycling, playing electric piano.

Addresses

Home—Oxford, England. *Agent*—c/o Author Mail, Jonathan Cape, Random House, 20 Vauxhall Bridge Rd., London SW1V 2SA, England.

Career

Author and illustrator. Formerly worked as a puppet maker; teacher in South London for six years.

Awards, Honors

Kate Greenaway Award shortlist, 2004, for *The Pea and the Princess;* Smarties Prize, 2004, for *Biscuit Bear.*

Writings

SELF-ILLUSTRATED

Egg Drop, Jonathan Cape (London, England), 2002.
The Pea and the Princess, Jonathan Cape (London, England), 2003, published as *The Very Smart Pea and the Princess-to-Be,* Knopf (New York, NY), 2003.
Biscuit Bear, Jonathan Cape (London, England), 2004, Knopf (New York, NY), 2005.

Traction Man Is Here, Cape Children's (London, England), 2005.

The Adventures of the Dish and the Spoon, Knopf (New York, NY), 2006.

Sidelights

Author and illustrator Mini Grey has combined a degree in English, training in both theatre arts and fine arts, a job as a puppet-maker, and six years' experience working as a teacher in South London schools to fashion a career as an award-winning creator of children's picture books. In addition to her titles *The Pea and the Princess*—published in the United States as *The Very Smart Pea and the Princess-to-Be*—and *Biscuit Bear,* Grey is the author and illustrator of *Traction Man Is Here!,* the chronicle of a young boy's adventures while putting his brand new, camouflage-wearing action figure through its high-adventure paces. Told through the boy's eyes, the story follows Traction Man as he battles household horrors such as the Poisonous Dishcloth and rises above the indignity of wearing a green sweater knitted up by a loving grandma, creating a story that *School Library Journal* reviewer Marge Loch-Wouters dubbed an "imaginative and very funny romp."

A well-known tale is turned topsy-turvy in *The Very Smart Pea and the Princess-to-Be,* as Grey recounts the classic test for princess-hood from the poor pea's point of view. Raised in a pod in the palace garden, this particular pea knows it has a higher purpose than the royal dining table, and sure enough, it is plucked by the queen and used as a way to test potential wives for her son, the prince. Realizing that the test is flawed after a number of highly qualified princesses have slept like babies atop the pile of mattresses under which the small pea has been placed, the pea decides to intervene; when the pretty young gardener who once tended it is tested for princess-hood, the pea climbs the mattress mountain and whispers relentlessly about the lump in the girl's mattress. A *Kirkus Reviews* critic described the story as a "rib-tickling" tale, adding that Grey's illustrations contain "plenty of sight gags" that pair with her "chatty narrative." Susan Dove Lempke also praised the story

The true story of a girl so sensitive that she can feel the lump a tiny pea makes under a stack of twenty mattresses is told from the veggie's viewpoint in The Very Smart Pea and the Princess-to-Be.

in *Horn Book,* citing its "visual wit" and commenting on the "vegetable and fruit motifs" that appear in the painted illustrations.

Biscuit Bear, which features a mix of photography and digital art, finds a bear-shaped cookie coming magically to life and escaping its fate—being eaten—by making a nighttime journey to the display window of a nearby city bakery. Other books by Grey include *Egg Drop,* about an egg that knows its destiny is to fly, and *The Adventures of the Dish and the Spoon,* a saga that follows the famed Dish and Spoon of "Hey Diddle Diddle" fame as they make their way in the world during the Great Depression. *Biscuit Bear* won the Smarties Prize in 2004, a special achievement considering it was Grey's third picture book.

Biographical and Critical Sources

PERIODICALS

Booklist, March 1, 2005, Carolyn Phelan, review of *Traction Man Is Here!,* p. 1203.

Horn Book, November-December, 2003, Susan Dove Lempke, review of *The Very Smart Pea and the Princess-to-Be,* p. 730; March-April, 2005, Christine M. Heppermann, review of *Traction Man Is Here!,* p. 188.

Kirkus Reviews, August 15, 2003, review of *The Very Smart Pea and the Princess-to-Be,* p. 1073; March 15, 2005, review of *Traction Man Is Here!,* p. 352.

Publishers Weekly, March 7, 2005, review of *Traction Man Is Here!,* p. 67.

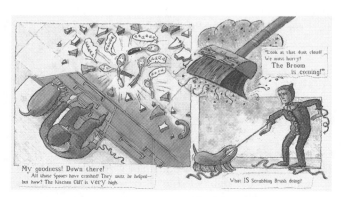

Grey opens a window into the imagination of a child at play in a world chock full of exciting make-believe adventures in her self-illustrated picture book Traction Man Is Here!

School Librarian, winter, 2002, review of *Egg Drop,* p. 186; autumn, 2003, review of *The Princess and the Pea,* p. 130.

School Library Journal, September, 2003, Wendy Wood-fill, review of *The Very Smart Pea and the Princess-to-Be,* p. 179; June, 2005, Marge Loch-Wouters, review of *Traction Man Is Here!,* p. 115.

ONLINE

Book Trust Web site, http://www.booktrusted.co.uk/ (December 1, 2005), Madelyn Travis, "Bear-faced Biscuit."

Random House Canada Web site, http://www.www.randomhouse.ca/ (December 1, 2005), "Mini Grey."*

H

HALL, Francie 1940-

Personal

Born December 23, 1940, in Canton, OH; daughter of Lambert (owner of an advertising/broadcasting company) and Burdette (an accountant and musician; maiden name Cattell) Huffman; married Robert Bowman (deceased); married Ralph G. Hall (an attorney and graduate school professor), 1992; children: (first marriage) Miriam, Gregory, Alicia. *Education:* Attended University of Illinois; California State University, Los Angeles, B.A.; Appalachian State University, M.A. *Hobbies and other interests:* Travel, entertaining and cooking for guests, writing, reading, swimming, walking.

Addresses

Home and office—1545 Watauga River Rd., Sugar Grove, NC 28679. *Agent*—c/o Publicity Director, Overmountain Press, Box 1261, Johnson City, TN 37605. *E-mail*—franciehall@mac.com.

Career

Writer. Jungle Aircraft, Suriname, South Africa, radio control operator, 1965; writer and producer in Nairobi, Kenya, 1972-80; teacher and administrator in Watauga County, NC, schools, 1982-2000; currently supervising student teachers.

Writings

Appalachian ABC's, illustrated by Kent Oehm, Overmountain Press (Johnson City, TN), 1998.
Scottish Highland Games, illustrated by Kent Oehm, Overmountain Press (Johnson City, TN), 2002.

Author of scripts for slide presentations for non-profit organizations.

Francie Hall

Sidelights

Francie Hall told *SATA:* "My writing career began at age ten when I wrote my own scripts for a weekly radio program titled 'Kiddie Koncert.' *Pagent Magazine* wrote an article about me titled 'World's Youngest Disc Jockey' in 1950."

"At age twelve I spent three months traveling in thirteen European countries, visiting a school in each country. I wrote human-interest stories about my experience that were published in a series of twelve articles in *Junior Scholastic* magazine and what was then *International News Service.* I spoke to civic groups and was interviewed on the *Today Show* as well as Italian television networks. I wrote and produced a weekly educational television show for a government television station in Nairobi, Kenya for about eight years.

"As an educator, I taught and encouraged children to write. I have presented workshops on writing for teachers and students. My primary interest is to entertain and inform children about cultural surroundings and events. I also am focusing some current writing on virtues and inspiration.

"With my expansive experiences having lived overseas for thirteen years, I would like to extend my writings to chapter books for children and an adult novel (or series) based on my life experiences. The themes of these books would definitely include cross-cultural experiences and coming-of-age experiences with adventures and a certain amount of intrigue."

*   *   *

HINTON, Nigel 1941-

Personal

Born September 28, 1941, in London, England; son of Raymond George (a builder) and Eva (Blatchley) Hinton. *Education:* College of St. Mark and St. John, London, B.A., 1966; University of Kent at Canterbury, M.A., 1975.

Addresses

Home and office—1 Hillside Cottages, Mardens Hill, Crowborough, East Sussex TN19 7JN, England. *E-mail*—info@nigelhinton.net.

Career

Author and actor. Lintas Ltd., London, England, executive trainee in advertising, 1960-62; Kent Education Committee, Kent, England, English teacher and department head, 1966-74; professional actor, 1974—; appeared in television plays, including *The Reaper,* Thames TV, 1979; and *Burning the Boat,* Thames TV.

Writings

FOR CHILDREN

Collision Course, Thomas Nelson (London, England), 1976.
Getting Free, Thomas Nelson (London, England), 1978.

Buddy (also see below), J. Dent (London, England), 1982.
Buddy's Song (also see below), J. Dent (London, England), 1987.
The Finders, Viking (London, England), 1993.
Buddy's Blues, Viking (London, England), 1995.
Out of the Darkness, Puffin (London, England), 1998.
Ship of Ghosts, illustrated by Anthony Lewis, Barrington Stoke (Edinburgh, Scotland), 1999.
Partners in Crime, Barrington Stoke (Edinburgh, Scotland), 2003.
Time Bomb, Puffin (London, England), 2005, Tricycle Press (Berkeley, CA), 2006.
Until Proven Guilty, Barrington Stoke (Edinburgh, Scotland), 2006.

"BEAVER TOWERS" SERIES; FOR CHILDREN

Beaver Towers, illustrated by Peter Rush, Abelard-Schuman (London, England), 1980.
The Witch's Revenge, illustrated by Peter Rush, Abelard-Schuman (London, England), 1981.
Run to Beaver Towers, illustrated by Susan Varley, Andersen (London, England), 1986, published as *The Dangerous Journey,* Puffin (London, England), 1997.
The Dark Dream, illustrated by Anne Sharp, Puffin (London, England), 1997.

OTHER

The Heart of the Valley (adult novel), Harper & Row (New York, NY), 1986.
The TV Script of Buddy (series; produced on BBC-TV), edited by Ray Speakman, Heinemann Education (London, England), 1987.
Buddy's Song (television film; based on Hinton's novel), produced 1990.
Le café des Reves (television series), BBC Educational Publishing/Longman (London, England), 1994.
The Play of Buddy's Song, Heinemann (Oxford, England), 1994.
Clementine (television series), British Broadcasting Corporation, 1995.
Isabel (television series), British Broadcasting Corporation, 1997.

Contributor to books, including *Peel's Men,* Hamlyn, 1978; and *The Book of Numbers,* Random House, 1979.

Sidelights

British writer Nigel Hinton once told *SATA:* "My first novel was written while I was still a teacher. I wanted to write something better for the kind of pupils I was teaching than what was generally available. When I received a letter about the book from a young American reader who signed himself 'Your new friend,' I found the urge to go on irresistible. I write for children and young adults because their world still has the dramatic clash between their personalities and social conventions (largely absent in adult Western society)."

Biographical and Critical Sources

PERIODICALS

Guardian (London, England), February 5, 2005, Jan Mark, review of *Time Bomb.*

ONLINE

Nigel Hinton Home Page, http://www.nigelhinton.net (November 6, 2005).

* * *

HOBBS, Leigh 1953-

Personal
Born April 18, 1953, in Melbourne, Victoria, Australia. *Education:* Attended art school.

Addresses
Home—Australia. *Agent*—c/o Author Mail, Penguin Books Australia, P.O. Box 701, Hawthorn 3122, Victoria, Australia.

Career
Illustrator, writer, sculptor, cartoonist, and painter. Art teacher until 2002. *Exhibitions:* Work exhibited widely, including at UWA Perth International Arts Festival, 2005; has exhibited drawings, paintings, and sculpture in galleries throughout Australia and England.

Awards, Honors
Shortlisted, Children's Book Council of Australia Picture Book of the Year award, 2002, for *Horrible Harriet,* and 2003, for *Old Tom's Holiday;* KOALA Award, 2004, for *Old Tom, Man of Mystery.*

Writings

SELF-ILLUSTRATED

Old Tom, Puffin Books (Ringwood, Victoria, Australia), 1994.
Old Tom at the Beach, Puffin Books (Ringwood, Victoria, New South Wales), 1995.
Old Tom Goes to Mars, Puffin Books (Ringwood, Victoria, Australia), 1997.
Old Tom's Guide to Being Good, Puffin Books (Ringwood, Victoria, Australia), 1998.
Itsy-Bitsy, Puffin Books (Ringwood, Victoria, Australia), 2000.
Old Tom's Holiday, ABC Books (Sydney, New South Wales, Australia), 2002, Peachtree (Atlanta, GA), 2004.
Horrible Harriet, Allen & Unwin (Crows Nest, New South Wales, Australia), 2003.

Leigh Hobbs

Old Tom, Man of Mystery, ABC Books (Sydney, New South Wales, Australia), 2003, Peachtree (Atlanta, GA), 2005.
Fiona the Pig, Running Press Kids (Philadelphia, PA), 2004.
Hooray for Horrible Harriet, Allen & Unwin (Crows Nest, New South Wales, Australia), 2005.
4F for Freaks, Allen & Unwin (Crows Nest, New South Wales, Australia), 2006.
Fiona the Pig's Big Day, Penguin/Viking (Sydney, New South Wales, Australia), 2006.

ILLUSTRATOR

Judy Tuer, *Cheer up, Jessie,* Collins Dove (Blackburn, Victoria, Australia), 1987.
Emily Dunt, *Supersleuth's Brief: An Open and Shut Case,* Martin Education (Cammeray, New South Wales, Australia), 1988.
Pippa MacPherson, *Caro's Croc Café,* Oxford University Press (Melbourne, Victoria, Australia), 1991.
Kathleen J. Hill, *Ding Dong Daily: Ideas for Writing in the Classroom,* Rigby Jeinemann (Port Melbourne, Victoria, Australia), 1991.

Else Edwards, *Issues & Responses,* Macmillan (South Melbourne, Victoria, Australia), 1991.

Mike Dumbleton, *Mr Knuckles,* Allen & Unwin (St. Leonards, New South Wales, Australia), 1993.

Dianne Bates, *Belly Busters,* Red Fox (Milsons Point, New South Wales, Australia), 1994.

Valerie Thomas, *Around the World with Miss Jones and Miss Brown,* Hodder Headline (Rydalmere, New South Wales, Australia), 1996.

Jim Howes, *Fish for Sale,* Longman Australia (Melbourne, Victoria, Australia), 1996, Sundance (Littleton, CO), 1997.

Gretel Killeen, *My Sister's an Alien,* Random House (Milsons Point, New South Wales, Australia), 1998.

Gary Crew, *Leo the Lion Tamer,* Lothian Books (Port Melbourne, Victoria, Australia), 1999.

Meredith Costain, *Get a Life with Freddy and Fifi,* Puffin Books (Ringwood, Victoria, Australia), 1999.

Meg Caraher, *Second Story Sally,* Sundance (Littleton, MA), 1999.

Jen McVeity, *Green with Red Spots Horrible,* Sundance (Littleton, MA), 1999.

James Moloney, *Blue Hair Day,* Puffin Books (Ringwood, Victoria, Australia), 2000.

Christine Harris, *Hairy Legs,* Random House Australia (Milsons Point, New South Wales, Australia), 2001.

Gretel Killeen, *My Sister's Yo-Yo,* Red Fox (London, England), 2002.

Sofie Laguna, *Bad Buster,* Penguin Books (Camberwell, Victoria, Australia), 2003.

Diana Lawrenson, *It's True! Your Hair Grows Fifteen Kilometres Each Year,* Allen & Unwin (East Melbourne, Victoria, Australia), 2004.

OTHER

Cartoonist for Melbourne, Australia newspaper the *Age.*

Adaptations

Hobbs's "Old Tom" series was adapted as a cartoon television series that aired in Australia, Europe, and the United States beginning in 2002.

Sidelights

Australian children's book author and illustrator Leigh Hobbs began writing and illustrating stories while still in primary school. Working in a range of mediums, he became a freelance cartoonist following art school, and has become well known for the books he writes and illustrates for children. Among Hobbs's self-illustrated books are those in the "Old Tom" series, a sequence featuring a scraggly, curmudgeonly feline that includes *Old Tom, Man of Mystery* and *Old Tom's Holiday.* Other books by Hobbs include *Horrible Harriet,* which introduces a girl that would be hard to top as a school bully, and *Fiona the Pig,* about a perfectionist pig who cares more about a chance to go on stage than she does a roll in the mud.

When a wily house cat is threatened with performing cleaning chores around the house, he devises an alter ego that distracts his housemate Angela while also adding spice to the neighborhood in Hobbs's quirky **Old Tom, Man of Mystery.**

Old Tom made his first appearance in *Old Tom,* published in the fall of 1994, and the adventures of the trouble-making cat continue in books such as *Old Tom, Man of Mystery*, *Old Tom's Holiday,* and *Old Tom at the Beach.* In *Old Tom, Man of Mystery* Old Tom pretends he has fallen ill in order to get out of performing the chores his keeper, tidy Angela Throgmorton, has assigned him. Taken in by the feline's clever ruse, Angela dotes on the ill kitty, tucking Tom into bed and doting on him throughout the day, while also doing the chores originally designated for Old Tom. A *Kirkus Reviews* critic praised Hobbs for his amusing story, noting that "the deadpan delivery and squiggly, almost drunken illustration are back, and fans who loved the first [Old Tom story] will enjoy this." In *School Library Journal,* Shawn Brommer also praised the book, commenting that Hobbs's "wacky artwork" features a "quirky child-like quality" and characters drawn with "angular, exaggerated features" in a variety of media.

Old Tom's Holiday finds Angela once again displeased with her lazy cat. She decides to leave Old Tom at home while she goes on a holiday trip. Upon arriving at her hotel and unpacking her suitcase, Angela does not realize—as do observant readers—that Old Tom has secretly stowed away in his keeper's luggage. While Angela enjoys her holiday activities, Old Tom can be seen following her about, loitering, lurking in the shrubbery, and even hanging from chandeliers. "The humor in this book is sure to appeal to children" commented Shawn Brommer, reviewing *Old Tom's Holiday* for *School Library Journal.*

Biographical and Critical Sources

PERIODICALS

Age (Melbourne, Victoria, Australia), June 19, 2002, Anne Crawford, "Leigh's Leap of Fame."

Kirkus Reviews, August 15, 2004, review of *Old Tom's Holiday,* p. 807; August 1, 2005, review of *Old Tom, Man of Mystery,* p. 849.

Magpies, March, 1996, review of *Old Tom at the Beach,* p. 30; March 1997, review of *Old Tom Goes to Mars,* 30; November, 2001, review of *Horrible Harriet,* p. 30; May, 2002, review of *Old Tom's Holiday,* p. 30; September, 2003, review of *Old Tom, Man of Mystery,* p. 29; March, 2004, Liz Derouet, review of *Fiona the Pig,* p. 27; March, 2005, Moira Robinson, review of *Hooray for Horrible Harriet,* p. 30.

Publishers Weekly, July 19, 2004, review of *Fiona the Pig,* p. 160.

School Librarian, summer, 1998, review of *Old Tom Goes to Mars,* p. 79.

School Library Journal, November, 2004, Shawn Brommer, review of *Old Tom's Holiday,* p. 107.

ONLINE

Leigh Hobbs Home Page, http://www.leighhobbs.com.au/ (November 6, 2005).

Mary Hollingsworth

* * *

HOLLINGSWORTH, Mary 1947-
(Professor Scribbler, Mary Shrode)

Personal

Born October 18, 1947, in Dallas, TX; daughter of Clyde E. (a minister) and Thelma G. (a homemaker; maiden name, Hargrave) Shrode. *Education:* Abilene Christian University, B.S.Ed., 1970. *Politics:* "Independent." *Religion:* Christian. *Hobbies and other interests:* Singing, travel, collecting Hummel figurines and miniature and rare books.

Addresses

Office—Shady Oaks Studio, 1507 Shirley Way, Bedford, TX, 76022-6737.

Career

Sweet Publishing, Fort Worth, TX, managing editor, 1984-95; Shady Oaks Studio, Bedford, TX, owner, author, editor, and consultant, 1988—; A Capella Junction (mail-order music distributor), owner, 1991—. Special music ministry leader, Richland Hills Church of Christ, 1985-2002; president, Richland Hills Singers, 1985-94; member of Infinity (a capella jazz ensemble), 1985-2002.

Member

Christian Booksellers Association, Society of Children's Book Writers and Illustrators, Christian Education Association (member of board of directors, 1993-96).

Awards, Honors

Matrix Award, Women in Advertising Association, for *Just Imagine! with Barney;* Gold Award, Evangelical Christian Publishers Association, 1995, for *My Little Bible;* gold Award, Evangelical Christian Publishers Association (ECPA), for *International Children's Story Bible;* Platinum Award, ECPA, for *My Little Bible;* books included on Christian best-seller lists over 100 times.

Writings

JUVENILE

International Children's Story Bible, Word Inc. (Dallas, TX), 1991.

(Reteller) *My Little Bible,* Wordkids (Dallas, TX), 1991.

The Captain, the Countess, and Cobby the Swabby: A Book about Honor, illustrated by Daniel J. Hochstatter, Chariot Family Publishing (Elgin, IL), 1992.

Parrots, Pirates, and Walking the Plank: A Book about Obeying, illustrated by Daniel J. Hochstatter, Chariot Family Publishing (Elgin, IL), 1992.

A Girl's Diary of Prayers, illustrated by Lois Rosio Sprague, Thomas Nelson (Nashville, TN), 1992.

A Boy's Book of Prayers, illustrated by Lois Rosio Sprague, Thomas Nelson (Nashville, TN), 1992.

(Under name Mary Shrode) *Just Imagine! with Barney,* illustrated by Mary Grace Eubank, Lyons Group, 1992.

Journey to Jesus: A Four-in-One Story, illustrated by Mary Grace Eubank, Baker Book House (Grand Rapids, MI), 1993.

The Kids-Life Bible Storybook, illustrated by Rick Incrocci, Chariot Family Publishing (Colorado Springs, CO), 1994, published as *The Kids-Life Bible,* 1998.

The Children's Topical Bible (with activity package), Honor Books (Rapid City, SD), 1994.

Bumper and Noah, Chariot Family Publishing, 1994.

Songs and Rhymes for Wiggle Worms, Questar Publishers (Sisters, OR), 1995.

Who Is Jesus?, Questar Publishers (Sisters, OR), 1995.

What Does Jesus Say?, Questar Publishers (Sisters, OR), 1995.

The Story of Jesus, Questar Publishers (Sisters, OR), 1995.

Bumper the Dinosaur, Chariot Family Publishing, 1996.

Into My Heart: A Treasury of Songs and Rhymes, Questar Publishers (Sisters, OR), 1996.

The Preschooler's Picture-Reading Bible, Baker Book House (Grand Rapis, MI), 1997.

The Time Trax Bible, Baker Book House (Grand Rapids, MI), 1997.

The Amazing Expedition Bible: Linking God's Word to the World, illustrated by Christopher Gray and Daniel J. Hochstatter, New Kids Media (Grand Rapids, MI), 1997.

Hugs for Kids: Stories, Sayings, and Scripture to Encourage and Inspire, Howard Pub. (West Monroe, LA), 2000.

Bible Fun Facts, illustrated by Rick Incrocci, Honor Kidz (Tulsa OK), 2001.

Bible Heroes, illustrated by Rick Incrocci, Honor Kidz (Tulsa, OK), 2001.

Bible Lessons, illustrated by Rick Incrocci, Honor Kidz (Tulsa, OK), 2001.

Bible Questions, illustrated by Rick Incrocci, Honor Kidz (Tulsa, OK), 2001.

Bible Words, illustrated by Rick Incrocci, Honor Kidz (Tulsa, OK), 2001.

God, illustrated by Rick Incrocci, Honor Kidz (Tulsa, OK), 2001.

God's Animals, illustrated by Rick Incrocci, Honor Kidz (Tulsa, OK), 2001.

Also author of numerous stories, plays, poetry, and songs; also author of video scripts based on her children's books.

"CHILDREN OF THE KING" SERIES

The King's Alphabet: A Bible Book about Letters, Worthy Publications (Fort Worth, TX), 1988.

The King's Numbers: A Bible Book about Counting, Worthy Publications (Fort Worth, TX), 1988.

The King's Workers: A Bible Book about Serving, Word Inc. (Dallas, TX), 1990.

The King's Manners: A Bible Book about Courtesy, Word Inc. (Dallas, TX), 1990.

The King's Animals: A Bible Book about God's Creatures, Word Inc. (Dallas, TX), 1991.

The King's Children: A Bible Book about God's People, Word Inc. (Dallas, TX), 1991.

"GOD'S HAPPY FOREST" SERIES

Polka Dots, Stripes, Humps, 'n' Hatracks: How God Created Happy Forest, illustrated by Mary Grace Eubank, Brownlow (Fort Worth, TX), 1990.

Twizzler, the Unlikely Hero: Bigger Is Not Always Better, illustrated by Mary Grace Eubank, Brownlow (Fort Worth, TX), 1990.

Christmas in Happy Forest: Love Is the Greatest Gift, illustrated by Mary Grace Eubank, Brownlow (Fort Worth, TX), 1990.

"MY VERY FIRST BOOK" SERIES

My Very First Book of Bible Heroes, illustrated by Rick Incrocci, Thomas Nelson (Nashville, TN), 1993.

My Very First Book of Bible Lessons, illustrated by Rick Incrocci, Thomas Nelson (Nashville, TN), 1993.

My Very First Book of Bible Words, illustrated by Rick Incrocci, Thomas Nelson (Nashville, TN), 1993.

My Very First Book of Prayers, illustrated by Rick Incrocci, Thomas Nelson (Nashville, TN), 1993.

My Very First Book on God, illustrated by Rick Incrocci, Thomas Nelson (Nashville, TN), 1994.

My Very First Book of God's Animals—and Other Creatures, illustrated by Rick Incrocci, Thomas Nelson (Nashville, TN), 1994.

My Very First Book of Bible Questions, illustrated by Rick Incrocci, Thomas Nelson (Nashville, TN), 1994.

My Very First Book of Bible Fun Facts, illustrated by Rick Incrocci, Thomas Nelson (Nashville, TN), 1994.

UNDER PSEUDONYM PROFESSOR SCRIBBLER

Charlie and the Shabby Tabby: Learning How to Be a Real Friend, illustrated by Dan Peeler, Brownlow (Fort Worth, TX), 1989.

Charlie and the Missing Music: Learning about God's Concern for the Lost, illustrated by Dan Peeler, Brownlow (Fort Worth, TX), 1989.

Charlie and the Jinglemouse: Learning about God's Forgiveness, illustrated by Dan Peeler, Brownlow (Fort Worth, TX), 1989.

Charlie and the Gold Mine: Learning What's Really Valuable in Life, illustrated by Dan Peeler, Brownlow (Fort Worth, TX), 1989.

OTHER

Help! I Need a Bulletin Board, Quality Publications (Abilene, TX), 1975.
(Coeditor) *The International Children's Bible,* Worthy Books, 1985.
For Mom with Love, Brownlow (Fort Worth, TX), 1987.
A Few Hallelujahs for Your Ho-Hums: A Lighthearted Look at Life, Brownlow (Fort Worth, TX), 1988.
Just between Friends, Brownlow (Fort Worth, TX), 1988.
It's a One-derful Life! A Single's Celebration, Brownlow (Fort Worth, TX), 1989.
Rainbows, C. R. Gibson (Norwalk, CT), 1989.
Apple Blossoms: A Tribute to Teachers, C. R. Gibson (Norwalk, CT), 1990.
(With Charlotte A. Greeson and Michael Washburn) *The Grief Adjustment Guide: A Pathway through Pain,* Questar Publishers (Sisters, OR), 1990.
(With Charlotte A. Greeson and Michael Washburn) *The Divorce Recovery Guide,* Questar Publishers (Sisters, OR), 1991.
(Compiler) *Together Forever: Reflections on the Joys of Marriage,* Word Inc. (Dallas, TX), 1993.
(Compiler) *On Raising Children: Lessons on Love and Limits,* Word Inc. (Dallas, TX), 1993.
(With Fred and Anna Kendall) *Speaking of Love,* Thomas Nelson (Nashville, TN), 1995.
Reborn! (play), produced in Fort Worth, TX, 1995.
Living Lights, Shining Stars: Ten Secrets to Becoming the Light of the World, Howard Pub. (West Monroe, LA), 1997.
Hugs for Women: Stories, Sayings, and Scriptures to Encourage and Inspire, Howard Pub. (West Monroe, LA), 1998.
Fireside Stories: Heartwarming Tales of Life, Love, and Laughter, Word Pub. (Nashville, TN), 2000.
Fireside Stories: Heartwarming Tales of Faith, Family, and Friendship, Word Pub. (Nashville, TN), 2001.
Little Taps on the Shoulder from God, Andrews McMeel (Kansas City, MO), 2002.
Mary Hollingsworth's Love Notes from God, Tyndale House (Wheaton, IL), 2003.
Mary Hollingsworth's Love Notes from God for Busy Moms, Tyndale House (Wheaton, IL), 2003.
Contagious Joy (Women of Faith devotional), W. Publishing Group (Nashville, TN), 2006.

Editorial director, *The Everyday Study Bible: New Century Version,* Word, 1996; editor of other books. General editor, "Let There Be Laughter" series, Guidepost Books (New York, NY), 2005-06. Executive editor, *TEACH Newsletter,* 1985-95. Contributor of articles to periodicals.

Some of Hollingsworth's works have been translated into other languages.

Sidelights

Mary Hollingsworth once told *SATA:* "As a preschooler I was coaxed into taking a nap by my mom, who took turns with me making up stories and telling them to each other. I'm sure Mom had no idea what long-range impact that little creative ritual would have on me. No doubt, my storytelling career began with my mom, my teddy bear, and my nap blankie.

"Today writing is not only my living but also my life. I can't survive without it, financially or emotionally. I cannot *not* write any more than happy children cannot *not* play. My writing is the essence of me. If you want to know my heart and mind, read my writing.

"I write in various areas and genres—adult nonfiction, gift books, children's nonfiction, children's fiction, plays, songs, articles, scripts, cover copy for books, study guides, and whatever else comes my way. The writing market changes often, and I must be flexible enough to go with the flow, or the flow will simply go without me. Besides, I enjoy the variety.

"The most significant book I've ever worked on, or ever hope to work on, was the first translation of the Bible ever done for children—*The International Children's Bible.* The task was both humbling and exhilarating. While that book certainly does not carry my name, the experience of working on God's Word changed my career goal and writing style forever. It made me painfully aware that the reader's being able to understand the message far outweighs the importance of my being able to show off my vocabulary and writing flair. It simplified my style, my message, and my life.

"The greatest thrill for me as a writer is to hear children giggling at something funny I wrote, or to have a mother tell me she cried all the way through *For Mom with Love.* One little four-year-old boy came running up to me and said, 'Hi, Professor Scribbler! I can say your book.' Thinking he had made a mistake, I said, 'You mean you can *read* my book?' 'No,' he said, 'I can *say* your 'book.' And he proceeded to recite from memory the entire text of *The King's Numbers.* I was astounded and so humbled by that incident. What an incredible responsibility I have as a children's author. They trust me; they learn from me; they believe anything I write. It's a fearful and wonderful thing to write for children.

"My right brain loves the freedom to be out of control, but my left brain likes my carefully orchestrated rut. I'm normally at my desk by nine o'clock and work consistently until about five or six. It's a habit developed through the years of working for major corporations and other people. It fits me; it works; I like it. I won't deny a few midnight inspirations and three a.m. creative storms, but those are not the norm for me. My rut is carpeted, draped, and air-conditioned. It's me.

"A glorious parade of writers, poets, composers, playwrights, and others have influenced my work so far. Among them are my all-time favorites: Dr. Seuss, Beatrix Potter, Dr. V. Gilbert Beers, C.S. Lewis, and Calvin Miller. Illustrators who delight me the most are Mary

Grace Eubank, Peter Spier, the Nick Butterworth and Mick Inkpen team, the Disney animators, and many others. I love the ones whose little kids inside them are obviously alive and well; they're the best.

"Every person alive has a legitimate story to tell, and most of us believe our stories deserve book status. Unfortunately, most aspiring writers are unwilling to devote the time, money, and effort to really learn the trade, to do their homework, to become the best in the industry in order to compete with the professionals. Most of the published authors and illustrators I know didn't just 'luck into it.' They are educated, trained, and experienced people, who continually study and upgrade their skills and abilities. They know they have to earn their place in the industry, and they don't expect a handout from publishers and other professionals. Writing and illustrating are careers, not just hobbies. If they are not your career, then you shouldn't expect to make a living at it. If you want to make them your living, then they must become your life.

"If I can make one life a little brighter: if one sentence I write strikes a note of hope, if one poem or song I write lives after I'm gone to encourage other people or make a child laugh, then I will consider myself a successful writer. In truth, I write for God and for me. If other people happen to listen in and are blessed, that's good. If no one ever sees a word I write, I am no less a writer in the eyes of God or when I look in the mirror. Writing is life; mine will stop simultaneously."

Biographical and Critical Sources

ONLINE

Abilene Christian University Web site, http://www.acu.edu/ alumni/career_connections/ (November 6, 2005), "Mary Hollingsworth '70."

Crescent Blues Book Views Online, http://www.crescent blues.com/ (November 6, 2005), Dawn Goldsmith, review of *Hugs for Women.*

Mary Hollingsworth Web site, http://www.mary hollingsworth.com (February 28, 2006).

Tyndale House Publishers Web site, http://www.tyndale. com/ (November 6, 2005), "Mary Hollingsworth."

I

INGPEN, Robert 1936-
(Robert Roger Ingpen)

Personal

Born October 13, 1936, in Geelong, Victoria, Australia; son of Thomas Roger (a manufacturer's agent) and Vida Ingpen; married Angela Mary Salmon, May 8, 1959; children: Katrina Arch, Susan, Sophie, Tom. *Education:* Attended Geelong College; Royal Melbourne Technical College (now Royal Melbourne Institute of Technology), Diploma of Art (graphic arts), 1957.

Addresses

Home and office—29 Parker St., Anglesea, Victoria, Australia 3230.

Career

Commonwealth Scientific and Industrial Research Organization, Australia, senior artist, 1959-68. Freelance author, illustrator, and designer, 1968—. Deakin University, Geelong, Victoria, Australia, foundation councillor; Dromkeen Children's Literature Foundation, governor. *Exhibitions:* Ingpen's illustrated works have been exhibited in Europe and the United States.

Awards, Honors

Award for illustration, Children's Book Council of Australia, 1975, for *Storm-Boy;* award for illustration, International Board on Books for Young People, 1978, for *The Runaway Punt;* Hans Christian Andersen Medal, 1986; Dromkeen Medal, 1989; honorary doctorate of arts, Royal Melbourne Institute of Technology, 2005.

Writings

SELF-ILLUSTRATED

Pioneers of Wool, Rigby (Adelaide, South Australia, Australia), 1972.

Pioneer Settlement in Australia, Rigby (Adelaide, South Australia, Australia), 1972.

Robe: A Portrait of the Past, Rigby (Adelaide, South Australia, Australia), 1975.

Marking Time: Australia's Abandoned Buildings, Rigby (Adelaide, South Australia, Australia), 1979.

Australian Gnomes, Rigby (Adelaide, South Australia, Australia), 1979.

The Voyage of the Poppykettle, Rigby (Adelaide, South Australia, Australia), 1980, Minedition (New York, NY), 2005.

Australia's Heritage Watch: An Overview of Australian Conservation, Rigby (Adelaide, South Australia, Australia), 1981.

The Unchosen Land, Rigby (Adelaide, South Australia, Australia), 1981.

(With Sally Carruthers and others) *Australian Inventions and Innovations,* Rigby (Adelaide, South Australia, Australia), 1982.

(With Graham Pizzey) *Churchill Island,* Victoria Conservation Trust (East Melbourne, Victoria, Australia), 1982.

(With Mellonie Bryan) *Beginnings and Endings with Lifetimes in Between,* Hill of Content (Melbourne, Victoria, Australia), 1983, published as *Lifetimes: A Beautiful Way to Explain Death to Children,* Bantam (New York, NY), 1983.

Click Go the Shears, Collins (Sydney, New South Wales, Australia), 1984.

The Idle Bear, Lothian (Melbourne, Victoria, Australia), 1986, revised as *The Miniature Idle Bear,* NTC, 1989.

(With Margaret Dunkle) *Conservation,* Hill of Content (Melbourne, Victoria, Australia), 1987.

The Age of Acorns, Lothian (South Melbourne, Victoria, Victoria, Australia), 1988, Bedrick/Blackie (New York, NY), 1990.

The Dreamkeeper: A Letter from Robert Ingpen to His Granddaughter Alice Elizabeth, Lothian (South Melbourne, Victoria, Australia), 1995.

The Afternoon Treehouse, Lothian (South Melbourne, Victoria, Australia), 1996.

(With Ted Egan) *The Drover's Boy,* Lothian (South Melbourne, Victoria, Australia), 1997.

(With Michael Lawrence) *The Poppykettle Papers* (graphic novel), Pavilion (London, England), 1999.

Once upon a Place, Lothian (South Melbourne, Victoria, Australia), 1999.

A Robert Ingpen Compendium, Lothian (Port Melbourne, Victoria, Australia), 1999.

A Bear Tale, Lothian (Port Melbourne, Victoria, Australia), 2000.

Pictures Telling Stories: The Art of Robert Ingpen, commentary by Sarah Mayor Cox, Lothian (South Melbourne, Victoria, Australia), 2004, Minedition (New York, NY), 2005.

The Rare Bear, Lothian (Melbourne, Victoria, Australia), 2004.

(With Gary Crew) *In the Wake of the Mary Celeste,* Lothian (South Melbourne, Victoria, Australia), 2004.

(With Bryan Mellonie) *Beginnings and Endings with Lifetimes in Between,* Puffin (Ringwood, Victoria, Australia), 2005.

(With Rosanne Hawke) *Mustara,* Lothian (South Melbourne, Victoria, Australia), 2006.

Also author of a series of Chinese-language books for Grimm Press, Taiwan.

Author's works have been translated into German, French, Japanese, and Swedish.

Ingpen's papers are collected at the National Library of Australia.

SELF-ILLUSTRATED; WITH MICHAEL F. PAGE

Aussie Battlers, Rigby (Adelaide, South Australia, Australia), 1982.

The Great Bullocky Race, Hill of Content (Melbourne, Victoria, Australia), 1984, Dodd, Mead (New York, NY), 1988.

Encyclopedia of Things That Never Were: Creatures, Places, and People, Paper Tiger (Limpsfield, England), 1985, Viking (New York, NY), 1987.

Out of This World: The Complete Book of Fantasy, Lansdowne Press (Sydney, New South Wales, Australia), 1986.

The Making of Australians, Dent (Knoxfield, Australia), 1987, Houghton (Boston, MA), 1990.

Worldly Dogs, Lothian (South Melbourne, Victoria, Australia), 1988.

SELF-ILLUSTRATED; WITH PHILIP WILKINSON

The Encyclopedia of Mysterious Places: The Life and Legends of Ancient Sites around the World, Viking (New York, NY), 1990.

Encyclopedia of World Events: Eighty Turning Points in History, Viking (New York, NY), 1991.

Encyclopedia of Ideas That Changed the World: The Greatest Discoveries and Inventions of Human History, Viking (New York, NY), 1993.

A Celebration of Customs and Rituals of the World, Dragon's World (Limpsfield, England), 1994, Facts on File (New York, NY), 1996.

SELF-ILLUSTRATED; WITH BARBARA HAYES

Folk Tales and Fables of Asia and Australia, Dragon's World (Limpsfield, England), 1992, Chelsea House (New York, NY), 1994.

Folk Tales and Fables of Europe, Dragon's World (Limpsfield, England), 1992, Chelsea House (New York, NY), 1994.

Folk Tales and Fables of the Americas and the Pacific, Dragon's World (Limpsfield, England), 1992, Chelsea House (New York, NY), 1994.

Folk Tales and Fables of the Middle East and Africa, Dragon's World (Limpsfield, England), 1992, Chelsea House (New York, NY), 1994.

SELF-ILLUSTRATED; WITH MOLLY PERHAM

Ghouls and Monsters, Dragon's World (Limpsfield, England), 1995, Chelsea House (New York, NY), 1996.

Gods and Goddesses, Dragon's World (Limpsfield, England), 1995, Chelsea House (New York, NY), 1996.

Heroes and Heroines, Dragon's World (Limpsfield, England), 1995, Chelsea House (New York, NY), 1996.

Magicians and Fairies, Dragon's World (Limpsfield, England), 1995, Chelsea House (New York, NY), 1996.

ILLUSTRATOR

Colin Thiele, *Storm-Boy,* Rigby (Adelaide, South Australia, Australia), 1974.

Michael F. Page, *The Runaway Punt,* Rigby (Adelaide, South Australia, Australia), 1976.

Don Dunstan, *Don Dunstan's Cookbook,* Rigby (Adelaide, South Australia, Australia), 1976.

Andrew McKay, *Surprise and Enterprise: Fifty Years of Science for Australia,* edited by Frederick White and David Krimpton, Commonwealth Scientific Industrial Research Organization, 1976.

The Australian Countrywoman's Cookbook, photographs by Peter Gower, Rigby (Adelaide, South Australia, Australia), 1976.

Colin Thiele, *Lincoln's Place,* Rigby (Adelaide, South Australia, Australia), 1978.

Nick Evers, *Paradise and Beyond: Tasmania,* Rigby (Adelaide, South Australia, Australia), 1978.

Colin Thiele, *Chadwick's Chimney,* Ashton Scholastic (Sydney, New South Wales, Australia), 1979.

Colin Thiele, *River Murray Mary,* Rigby (Adelaide, South Australia, Australia), 1979.

Colin Stone, *Running the Brumbies: True Adventures of a Modern Bushman,* Rigby (Adelaide, South Australia, Australia), 1979.

Michael F. Page, *Turning Points in the Making of Australia,* Rigby (Adelaide, South Australia, Australia), 1980.

Michael F. Page, *Robert Ingpen,* compiled by Angela Ingpen, Macmillan (South Melbourne, Victoria, Australia), 1980.

Ronald Rose, *This Peculiar Colony,* Rigby (Adelaide, South Australia, Australia), 1981.

Mary Small, *Night of the Muttonbirds,* Methuen (Sydney, New South Wales, Australia), 1981.

A.B. Paterson, *Clancy of the Overflow,* Rigby (Adelaide, South Australia, Australia), 1982, reprinted, Lansdowne (The Rocks, New South Wales, Australia), 2000.

Max Charlesworth, *Religious Worlds,* Hill of Content (Melbourne, Victoria, Australia), 1985.

Michael F. Page, *Colonial South Australia: Its People and Buildings,* J. M. Dent (South Melbourne, Victoria, Australia), 1985.

Barbara Hayes, reteller, *Folk Tales and Fables of the World,* Paper Tiger (Limpsfield, England), 1987.

Mark Twain, *The Stolen White Elephant,* Ashton Scholastic (Sydney, New South Wales, Australia), 1987.

Mark Twain, *A Strange Expedition,* Ashton Scholastic (Sydney, New South Wales, Australia), 1988.

Charles Dickens, *A Christmas Tree,* Ashton Scholastic (Sydney, New South Wales, Australia), 1988.

Charles Dickens, *The Child's Story,* Ashton Scholastic (Sydney, New South Wales, Australia), 1988.

Patricia Wrightson, *The Nargun and the Stars,* Hutchinson (Hawthorn, Victoria, Australia), 1988.

Maurice Saxby, reteller, *The Great Deeds of Superheroes,* Millennium (Newtown, New South Wales, Australia), 1989, P. Bedrick (New York, NY), 1990.

Maurice Saxby, reteller, *The Great Deeds of Heroic Women,* Dragon's World (Limpsfield, England), 1989, P. Bedrick (New York, NY), 1990.

Katherine Scholes, *Peacetimes,* Hill of Content (Melbourne, Victoria, Australia), 1989, published as *Peace Begins with You,* Little, Brown (Boston, MA), 1990.

Robert Louis Stevenson, *Treasure Island,* Viking (New York, NY), 1992.

Philip Steele, *River through the Ages,* Eagle (London, England), 1993, Troll (Mahwah, NJ), 1994.

Colin Thiele, *Brahminy: The Story of a Boy and a Sea Eagle,* Lothian (South Melbourne, Victoria, Australia), 1995.

Jacqueline Dineen, *Hunting, Harvesting, and Home,* Chelsea House (New York, NY), 1998.

Jacqueline Dineen, *Feasts and Festivals,* Chelsea House (New York, NY), 1998.

Michael Cave, *Fabulous Places of Myth: A Journey with Robert Ingpen to Camelot, Atlantis, Valhalla, and the Tower of Babel,* Lothian (South Melbourne, Victoria, Australia), 1998.

Ejnar Agertoft, *Jacob, the Boy from Nuremberg,* Lothian (South Melbourne, Victoria, Australia), 1998.

Jacqueline Dineen, *Rites of Passage,* Chelsea House (New York, NY), 1999.

Jacqueline Dineen, *Living with the Gods,* Chelsea House (New York, NY), 1999.

Tom Pow, *Who Is the World For?,* Candlewick (Cambridge, MA), 2000.

Michael Rosen, *Shakespeare: His Work and His World,* Candlewick (Cambridge, MA), 2001.

Anna Carew-Miller, *Chief Seattle: Great Chief,* Mason Crest (Broomhall, PA), 2002.

Charise Neugebauer, *Halloween Circus at the Graveyard,* North-South Books (London, England), 2003, published as *Halloween Circus,* North-South Books (New York, NY), 2003.

Anne Marie Sullivan, *Mother Theresa,* Mason Crest (Broomhall, PA), 2003.

John Riddle, *Robert F. Scott: British Explorer of the South Pole,* Mason Crest (Broomhall, PA), 2003.

John Riddle, *Marco Polo,* Mason Crest (Broomhall, PA), 2003.

Beatrice Phillpotts, *The Wizard's Book of Spells,* Viking (Camberwell, Victoria, Australia), 2003.

Keith Dunstan, *The Tapestry Story: Celebrating 150 Years of the Melbourne Cricket Ground,* Lothian (South Melbourne, Victoria, Australia), 2003.

J.M. Barrie, *Peter Pan and Wendy,* Orchard (New York, NY), 2004.

Brigitte Weninger, *The Magic Crystal,* Minedition (New York, NY), 2005.

Werner Thuswaldner, *Silent Night, Holy Night: A Song for the World,* Minedition (New York, NY), 2005.

Michael Rosen, *Dickens: His Work and His World,* Candlewick (Cambridge, MA), 2005.

Hans Christian Andersen, *The Ugly Duckling,* Minedition (New York, NY), 2005.

ILLUSTRATOR

Philip Wilkinson and Jacqueline Dineen, *The Lands of the Bible,* Dragon's World (Limpsfield, England), 1992, Chelsea House (New York, NY), 1994.

Philip Wilkinson and Michael Pollard, *The Magical East,* Angus & Robertson (Pymble, New South Wales, Australia), 1992, Chelsea House (New York, NY), 1994.

Philip Wilkinson and Jacqueline Dineen, *The Mediterranean,* Angus & Robertson (Pymble, New South Wales, Australia), 1992, Chelsea House (New York, NY), 1994.

Philip Wilkinson and Michael Pollard, *The Master Builders,* Angus & Robertson (Pymble, New South Wales, Australia), 1992, Chelsea House (New York, NY), 1994.

Philip Wilkinson and Jacqueline Dineen, *People Who Changed the World,* Chelsea House (New York, NY), 1994.

Philip Wilkinson and Jacqueline Dineen, *Statesmen Who Changed the World,* Chelsea House (New York, NY), 1994.

Philip Wilkinson and Jacqueline Dineen, *Scrolls to Computers,* Dragon's World (Limpsfield, England), 1994.

Philip Wilkinson and Jacqueline Dineen, *Caves to Cathedrals,* Dragon's World (Limpsfield, England), 1994.

Philip Wilkinson and Michael Pollard, *Science and Power,* Dragon's World (Limpsfield, England), 1994.

Philip Wilkinson and Michael Pollard, *Scientists Who Changed the World,* Chelsea House (New York, NY), 1994.

Philip Wilkinson and Michael Pollard, *Wheels to Rockets: Innovations in Transport,* Dragon's World (Limpsfield, England), 1994.

Philip Wilkinson and Michael Pollard, *Generals Who Changed the World,* Chelsea House (New York, NY), 1994.

Philip Wilkinson and Michael Pollard, *Transportation,* Chelsea House (New York, NY), 1995.

Philip Wilkinson and Michael Pollard, *The Industrial Revolution,* Chelsea House (New York, NY), 1995.

Philip Wilkinson and Jacqueline Dineen, *The Early Inventions,* Chelsea House (New York, NY), 1995.

Philip Wilkinson and Jacqueline Dineen, *Art and Technology through the Ages,* Chelsea House (New York, NY), 1995.

Also illustrator of maps, brochures, and other visual materials.

Sidelights

Robert Ingpen is an Australian author and illustrator who has captured the natural beauty and cultural quirks of his native country within his books. Elements of the supernatural weave through the pages of many of his titles, including *Australian Gnomes* and *The Voyage of the Poppykettle,* as well as a series Ingpen coauthored with Molly Perham that includes such titles as *Ghouls and Monsters* and *Magicians and Fairies.* Ingpen's interest in not only the supernatural but also in folklore, technology, and the history of ideas and politics is worldwide in scope. This wide-ranging interest is evident in the many nonfiction books he has coauthored with others and which include his award-winning artwork. Ingpen is the only Australian to ever be awarded the Hans Christian Andersen Medal for Illustration.

Born in 1936, Ingpen was raised in Geelong, Victoria, Australia. Trained in art at the Royal Melbourne Institute of Technology, he began his publishing career by writing and illustrating several books recording the history of Australia's lesser-known locales. His first illustration project for young people was the book *Storm-Boy,* written by Colin Thiele and published in 1974. Awarded several prestigious honors, including the 1986 Hans Christian Andersen medal, Ingpen's artwork has been compared to that of U.S. ilustrator N.C. Wyeth due to his realistic approach. Although Ingpen uses a variety of media, including watercolor, pencil, and pastel, his work is distinctive in its detail and its adherence to historical accuracy. Ingpen has been praised for his style, his choice of earthen hues, and his unique approach to light and shadow.

Among the fictional works penned and illustrated by Ingpen are *The Idle Bear* and *The Age of Acorns.* Teddy bears figure prominently in both works; in *The Idle Bear,* two worn teddies who have watched their owners grow up and leave them try to make sense of their place in the world, while in *The Age of Acorns,* a younger bear is accidentally left outdoors by the child he belongs to. Called both humorous and poignant, *The Idle Bear* drew praise from reviewers, including a *Publishers Weekly* commentator who concluded that "such wide-eyed bears, in dire need of family, should find a home in any reader's heart." Although a *Kirkus Reviews* contributor praised the dialogue in *The Idle Bear* as "deceptively aimless yet cadenced and philosophical," Zena Sutherland of *Bulletin of the Center for Children's Books* questioned its appropriateness for a young

audience. However, Sutherland went on to praise Ingpen's illustrations as "remarkable for their textural quality and their deftness in depiction of light and shade." Sutherland also praised *The Age of Acorns* in a *Bulletin of the Center for Children's Books* review, noting that "the colors are quiet, reflecting the poignant wistfulness of the story."

The Dreamkeeper: A Letter from Robert Ingpen to His Granddaughter Alice Elizabeth was published in Australia in 1995. Interweaving elements of reality and fantasy, he explains how the beings conjured up by human imaginations during dreams are kept from invading reality by a Dreamkeeper, who with the use of imaginative and intricately engineered traps and other tools, returns all dream beings to their proper home in the Dreamtree. Storybook characters, as well as scarier creatures, live within the dreams of imaginative young people, and characters from Aladdin to Long John Silver to the entire cast of *Alice in Wonderland* are among those caught by the ever-vigilant Dreamkeeper. "Myth and lore collide to create a promising fantasy" in Ingpen's unique work, according to a *Publishers Weekly* contributor who noted that the book, hand-lettered by the illustrator to resemble a letter to Alice, is by turns "mystical, dreamlike and occasionally nightmarish."

In 1999 Ingpen revisited his picture book *The Voyage of the Poppykettle* and teamed up with Michael Lawrence to adapt the work as a graphic novel, *The Poppykettle*

Ingpen captures the essence of plays such as The Tempest *in his illustrations for Michael Rosen's* Shakespeare: His Work and His World.

Papers, about the Hairy Peruvians featured in the original story. Like *The Voyage of the Poppykettle,* the graphic novel tells the story of the journey of a group of tiny people across the ocean. Two young boys discover a bundle of papers translated by an archeologist that reveals the dangers the Hairy Peruvians had in their crossing. According to Barbara Buckley in a review for *School Library Journal,* "Ingpen's illustrations are painterly, giving the impression of danger and excitement without scariness." The original tale was published in the United States in 2005; a *Kirkus Reviews* contributor commented, "Ingpen captures the voyage with engrossing drama."

In keeping with his penchant for myth and fantasy, Ingpen has collaborated with Barbara Hayes to create a series of collections of folk tales and fables from around the world, including *Folk Tales & Fables of Asia and Australia* and *Folk Tales and Fables of the Middle East and Africa.* Of the latter title, *Booklist* reviewer Julie Corsaro noted that Ingpen's "full-page paintings are meticulously detailed, warmly colored and strikingly composed." Ingpen has collaborated with Michael Page on other fantastic titles, including *Encyclopedia of Things That Never Were: Creatures, Places, and People.* Richard K. Burns, in *Library Journal,* considered the book "a significant contribution to all collection in fantasy and allied genres," and noted: "the illustrations are extraordinary."

Ingpen has illustrated books for many children's authors, and two published compilations of his work have been published to showcase his art: *A Robert Ingpen Compendium* and *Pictures Telling Stories: The Art of Robert Ingpen.* Noting that the latter title contains sketches and storyboards as well as full-color prints of Ingpen's work, Heather E. Miller, in *School Library Journal,* commented that "the reproductions are the obvious stars of this book." Of his illustrations for Tom Pow's *Who Is the World For?,* a *Publishers Weekly* contributor noted that "the visual cadence of Ingpen's . . . artwork reflects the graceful nuances of the text." Wendy Lukehart, writing in *School Library Journal,* noted that the same text features "a safe and aesthetically pleasing world." Reviewing in the same periodical, Nancy Menaldi-Scanlan dubbed Ingpen's contribution to Michael Rosen's *Shakespeare: His Work and His World* "detailed, realistic illustrations."

While many of Ingpen's subjects come not from the world of dreams and the imagination but from the factual, real world of history, technology, and science, he is able to transform the commonplace and everyday into the marvelous, sparking the curiosity of his young fans. Describing Ingpen's work in *Children's Books and Their Creators,* essayist Suzy Schmidt cited the author/illustrator's ultimate goal as "to engage young people's imaginations both with his art and with the stories he chooses to illustrate."

Biographical and Critical Sources

BOOKS

Silvey, Anita, editor, *Children's Books and Their Creators,* Houghton (Boston, MA), 1995.

PERIODICALS

Booklist, November 15, 1994, Julie Corsaro, review of *Folk Tales and Fables of the Middle East and Africa,* p. 596.
Bulletin of the Center for Children's Books, December, 1987, Zena Sutherland, review of *The Idle Bear,* pp. 66-67; December, 1990, Zena Sutherland, review of *The Age of Acorns,* p. 88.
Horn Book, May, 1999, Karen Jameyson, review of *The Drover's Boy,* p. 364.
Kirkus Reviews, October 15, 1987, review of *The Idle Bear,* p. 1516; May 1, 2005, review of *The Voyage of the Poppykettle,* p. 539.
Library Journal, January, 1999, Richard K. Burns, review of *Encyclopedia of Things That Never Were: Creatures, Places, and People,* p. 86.
Magpies, March, 2005, Maurice Saxby, review of *Pictures Telling Stories: The Art of Robert Ingpen,* p. 14.
Publishers Weekly, October 9, 1987, review of *The Idle Bear,* p. 84; June 3, 1996, review of *The Dreamkeeper,* p. 84; October 30, 2000, review of *Who Is the World For?,* p. 75.
School Librarian, February, 1996, p. 20.
School Library Journal, March, 1988, p. 167; March, 2000, Barbara Buckley, review of *The Poppykettle Papers,* p. 240; January, 2001, Wendy Lukehart, review of *Who Is the World For?,* p. 107; February, 2004, Nancy Menaldi-Scanlan, review of *Shakespeare: His Work and His World,* p. 82; May, 2005, Heather E. Miller, review of *Pictures Telling Stories: The Art of Robert Ingpen,* p. 152.
Voice of Youth Advocates, February, 1996, p. 403.

ONLINE

Royal Melbourne Institute of Technology Alumni Web site, http://www.alumni.rmit.edu.au/ (December 1, 2005), "Robert Ingpen."*

*   *   *

INGPEN, Robert Roger
See INGPEN, Robert

*   *   *

IVERSON, Eric G.
See TURTLEDOVE, Harry

J-K

JAMES, Philip
See MOORCOCK, Michael

*   *   *

JOHNSON, Sylvia A.

Personal
Born in Indianapolis, IN. *Education:* Marian College (IN), graduate; University of Illinois, M.A.

Addresses
Agent—c/o Author Mail, Lerner Publishing Group, 1251 Washington Ave. N, Minneapolis, MN 55401.

Career
Writer and freelance children's book editor.

Awards, Honors
New York Academy of Sciences special award, 1983, for *Apple Trees, Beetles, Crabs, Frogs and Toads, Inside an Egg, Ladybugs, Mosses, Mushrooms, Penguins, Potatoes, Silkworms,* and *Snails.*

Writings

FOR YOUNG PEOPLE

(With Jim Hargrove) *Mountain Climbing,* photographs by John Yaworsky, Lerner (Minneapolis, MN), 1983.

(With Alice Aamodt) *Wolf Pack: Tracking Wolves in the Wild,* Lerner (Minneapolis, MN), 1985.

(With Louis B. Casagrande) *Focus on Mexico: Modern Life in an Ancient Land,* photographs by Phillips Bourns, Lerner (Minneapolis, MN), 1986.

Albatrosses of Midway Island ("Nature Watch" series), photographs by Frans Lanting, Carolrhoda Books (Minneapolis, MN), 1990.

Roses Red, Violets Blue: Why Flowers Have Colors, photographs by Yuko Sato, Lerner (Minneapolis, MN), 1991.

A Beekeeper's Year, photographs by Nick Von Ohlen, Little, Brown (Boston, MA), 1994.

Raptor Rescue!: An Eagle Flies Free, photographs by Ron Winch, Dutton (New York, NY), 1995.

Ferrets ("Nature Watch" series), Carolrhoda Books (Minneapolis, MN), 1996.

Tomatoes, Potatoes, Corn, and Beans: How the Foods of the Americas Changed Eating around the World, Atheneum (New York, NY), 1997.

Mapping the World, Atheneum (New York, NY), 1999.

(Editor) Denise Burt, *Koalas,* Carolrhoda (Minneapolis, MN), 1999.

(Editor) Denise Burt, *Kangaroos,* Carolrhoda (Minneapolis, MN), 2000.

(Editor) Becka Anders, *Mae: A Peregrine Falcon's True Story,* Northern States Power Company (Minneapolis, MN), 2000.

Songbirds: The Language of Song ("Nature Watch" series), Carolrhoda (Minneapolis, MN), 2001.

Crows ("Nature Watch" series), Carolrhoda (Minneapolis, MN), 2005.

"LERNER WILDLIFE LIBRARY" SERIES

Animals of the Deserts, illustrated by Alcuin C. Dornisch, Lerner (Minneapolis, MN), 1976.

Animals of the Grasslands, illustrated by Alcuin C. Dornisch, Lerner (Minneapolis, MN), 1976.

Animals of the Mountains, illustrated by Alcuin C. Dornisch, Lerner (Minneapolis, MN), 1976.

Animals of the Polar Regions, illustrated by Alcuin C. Dornisch, Lerner (Minneapolis, MN), 1976.

Animals of the Temperate Forests, illustrated by Alcuin C. Dornisch, Lerner (Minneapolis, MN), 1976.

Animals of the Tropical Forests, illustrated by Alcuin C. Dornisch, Lerner (Minneapolis, MN), 1976.

The Wildlife Atlas (series compilation), Lerner (Minneapolis, MN), 1997.

"DISCOVERING DINOSAURS" SERIES

(With Kunihiko Hisa) *The Dinosaur Family Tree,* Lerner (Minneapolis, MN), 1990.

(With Kunihiko Hisa) *How Did Dinosaurs Live?,* Lerner (Minneapolis, MN), 1990.

(With Kunihiko Hisa) *What Were Dinosaurs?,* Lerner (Minneapolis, MN), 1990.

"NATURAL SCIENCE" SERIES

Penguins, Lerner (Minneapolis, MN), 1981.

Beetles, photographs by Isao Kishida, Lerner (Minneapolis, MN), 1982.

Crabs, photographs by Atsushi Sakurai, Lerner (Minneapolis, MN), 1982.

(With Jane Dallinger) *Frogs and Toads,* photographs by Hiroshi Tanemura, Lerner (Minneapolis, MN), 1982.

Inside an Egg, photographs by Kiyoshi Shimuzi, Lerner (Minneapolis, MN), 1982.

Ladybugs, photographs by Yuko Sato, Lerner (Minneapolis, MN), 1982.

Mushrooms, photographs by Masana Izawa, Lerner (Minneapolis, MN), 1982.

Silkworms, photographs by Isao Kishida, Lerner (Minneapolis, MN), 1982.

Snails, photographs by Modoki Masuda, Lerner (Minneapolis, MN), 1982.

Mosses, photographs by Masana Izawa, Lerner (Minneapolis, MN), 1983.

Apple Trees, photographs by Hiroo Koike, Lerner (Minneapolis, MN), 1983.

Potatoes, photographs by Masaharu Suzuki, Lerner (Minneapolis, MN), 1984.

Coral Reefs, photographs by Shohei Shirai, Lerner (Minneapolis, MN), 1984.

Mantises, photographs by Satoshi Kuribayashi, Lerner (Minneapolis, MN), 1984.

Wasps, photographs by Hiroshi Ogawa, Lerner (Minneapolis, MN), 1984.

Bats, photographs by Modoki Masuda, Lerner (Minneapolis, MN), 1985.

Rice, photographs by Noburo Moriya, Lerner (Minneapolis, MN), 1985.

Morning Glories, photographs by Yuko Sato, Lerner (Minneapolis, MN), 1985.

Snakes, photographs by Modoki Masuda, Lerner (Minneapolis, MN), 1986.

Tree Frogs, photographs by Modoki Masuda, Lerner (Minneapolis, MN), 1986.

Chirping Insects, photographs by Yuko Sato, Lerner (Minneapolis, MN), 1986.

How Leaves Change, photographs by Yuko Sato, Lerner (Minneapolis, MN), 1986.

Fireflies, photographs by Satoshi Kuribayashi, Lerner, Lerner (Minneapolis, MN), 1986.

Elephant Seals, photographs by Frans Lanting, Lerner (Minneapolis, MN), 1989.

Hermit Crabs, photographs by Kazunari Kawashima, Lerner (Minneapolis, MN), 1989.

Water Insects, photographs by Modoki Masuda, Lerner (Minneapolis, MN), 1989.

Wheat, photographs by Masaharu Suzuki, Lerner (Minneapolis, MN), 1990.

Johnson has also adapted books from translation for "The Animal Friends" series, Carolrhoda Books, and co-authored, with Karlind T. Moller and Clark D. Starr, *A Parent's Guide to Cleft Lip and Palate,* University of Minnesota Press, 1990.

Sidelights

Sylvia A. Johnson, a prolific author of science and nature books, delves into topics ranging from wolves to mushrooms. Praised for her ability to simplify complex topics, Johnson has written many well-received titles in Lerner's "Natural Science" series and has also produced standalone nonfiction titles such as *A Beekeeper's Year, Wolf Pack: Tracking Wolves in the Wild,* and *Tomatoes, Potatoes, Corn, and Beans: How the Food of the Americas Changed Eating around the World.* Reviewing *Wolf Pack* for the *Bulletin of the Center for Children's Books,* a reviewer called Johnson's work "scientific without being pedantic" and "full of engrossing, well-selected information." Called a "handsome and informative resource" by *School Library Journal* contributor Joy Fleishhacker, Johnson's *Mapping the World* follows the history of human efforts to create visual representations of the multidimensional Earth, from the clay tablets created by the Babylonians to the satellite images of the late twentieth century. The work is of special interest to students due to the author's approach; she presents each development in the history of cartography in terms of "the particular mapmaker's knowledge and view of the world," as *Booklist* reviewer Ilene Cooper noted.

Johnson, who has also worked as a freelance book editor in Minnesota, has done most of her writing for the Minneapolis-based Lerner Publications. Her first published work comprises six titles in the "Lerner Wildlife Library" series: *Animals of the Deserts, Animals of the Grasslands, Animals of the Mountains, Animals of the Polar Regions, Animals of the Temperate Forests,* and *Animals of the Tropical Forests.* Each book briefly describes a specific geographic region, discussing climatic conditions as well as flora and fauna. Johnson also includes one-page descriptions of the ten animals that best represent each region, from the giant panda in the mountain regions to the anteater in the tropical forests. Noting the brief text, Barbara Elleman wrote in *Booklist* that the author's focus "is limited to the physical characteristics, such as camouflage or eating habits, which enable the animal to survive in its particular environment." Reviewing *Animals of the Deserts* for *Appraisal,* Marjorie E. Smith praised the book as "an easy way to introduce a study of the desert, animals, conservation, the effects of lack of water on plant and animal life, and much more." Linda L. Mills, reviewing the "Lerner Wildlife Library" overall, maintained in *School Library*

In **Mapping the World** *Johnson explains the history of map-making, and shows how the work of cartographers tells more about their personal world view than it does about the almost-unchanged Earth.*

Journal that the books are "unusual for their division of animals by climate" and useful for both "the older intermediate grades" and "advanced third graders." Johnsons's wildlife series has more recently been published in a single volume as *The Wildlife Atlas.*

The bulk of Johnson's work has been for Lerner's "Natural Science Book" series, each volume which features scientific terminology in boldface type along with appended glossaries that further define words. Series' installments focus on a particular life form ranging from penguins to mosses, and illustrations include diagrams and close-up color photographs. In addition to providing original texts, Johnson has also adapted the translation of writings by Japanese authors for English-speaking readers.

Johnson's first contribution to the series, *Penguins,* features a text that "should appeal not only to budding naturalists but to all children (and grownups) who are captivated by the unique birds at home in the icy Antarctic," according to a reviewer for *Publishers Weekly.* The reviewer went on to praise *Penguins* as an "outstanding addition" to the series. "I hope this series goes

on forever," Terry Lawhead exclaimed, reviewing Johnson's *Beetles* and *Silkworms* for *School Library Journal.* Noting the "lovely writing," Lawhead added that the author's "attention to highly accurate anatomy, life cycles and detailed close-up photographs never ceases to amaze me." Elisabeth LeBris praised *Bats* in *School Library Journal,* calling it an "excellent book" and one which "no library should be without," while Martha T. Kane wrote in *Appraisal* that *Bats* is "a beautiful book" that "will hold its readers spellbound." The lumbering amphibians of California's Año Nuevo Island are examined in *Elephant Seals,* another of Johnson's "winning addition" to the Lerner series, according to *School Library Journal* contributor Kathryn Weisman. "Johnson's book will appeal to browsers as well as report writers and should be a part of most natural history collections," Weisman concluded.

Plants also have their place in the "Natural Science" series, and Johnson has contributed many titles with a horticultural focus. Reviewing *Mosses* for *Horn Book,* Sarah S. Gagne observed that the "reproductive cycle of moss . . . is so well illustrated that one can form mental images of the structures and so readily follow the cycle." William D. Perkins commented in *Appraisal* that Johnson "has done an excellent job of packaging information in manageable bits which build upon one another to give the reader a solid sense of what is important about these fascinating plants." Nancy Curtin observed in *School Library Journal* that Johnson's *Apple Trees* offers fine detail on the fertilization and development of the apple, and that though other books have looked at the same topic, "none cover the subject better." Other plants Johnson examines in the series include potatoes, rice, and wheat. "Here is everything anyone always wanted to know about potatoes, but didn't even know enough to ask," wrote Eldon Younce in a *School Library Journal* review of *Potatoes.* "The text is well written and the color photography is excellent," Younce concluded, calling the volume "an informative book about a very versatile vegetable." Summing up the series in general, *Booklist* reviewer Elleman called it "lucid" and "handsomely photographed," while Althea L. Phillips deemed the series as a whole "extremely attractive and well-written" in *Appraisal.*

Johnson has also expanded Carolrhoda's "Nature Watch" series with the volumes *Albatrosses of Midway Island* and *Ferrets.* The former title captures "the mystery of the world's largest flighted bird," according to a *Kirkus Reviews* critic who called the book "informative, funny," and "a delight for nature browser or bird lover."

The possibility of keeping ferrets as pets is explored in the second volume. Ellen M. Riordan, writing in *School Library Journal,* noted that "good quality, full-color photographs accompany a clear, readable text in this comprehensive book." A *Kirkus Reviews* contributor concluded a review of *Ferrets* by stating that the "presentation of information is straightforward and easy to follow," while *Booklist* reviewer Irene Wood cited the balanced discussion of "these furry, stubby-legged, energetic creatures."

One of Johnson's individual titles, *Wolf Pack* explains that wolves, essentially wild dogs, display all the traits generally associated with domesticated dogs, including loyalty and social cohesion. Like dogs, who are related to them, wolves structure themselves socially in packs and mate for life. Lee Jeffers Brami, writing in *Appraisal,* remarked that *Wolf Pack* "conveys these facts and many others through simple, flowing prose and superb color photographs." Cynthia M. Sturgis observed in *School Library Journal* that Johnson's text is "well-written" and the combination of text, diagrams, and photographs provided in the volume "make this an excellent candidate for school or public library collections."

A Beekeeper's Year focuses on the work of a Minnesota beekeeper, tracing the man's labors through the seasons

What do bird songs mean? Do birds have more than one song? These and other questions are the subject of Johnson's Songbirds: The Language of Song.

Most people see crows every day, and almost everywhere, but these common birds have several interesting habits, as Johnson explains in **Crows,** *part of the "Nature Watch" series.*

from the time he removes the protective winter trappings on the hives in April until he seals them up again in autumn. "From the arresting jacket photograph to the recipes on the last page of the text, this is a most intriguing book," commented Stephanie Zvirin in a *Booklist* review; "Pair this with books on honeybee behavior and physiology, and you may find a few budding apiarists in your midst." *Horn Book* reviewer Margaret A. Bush called *A Beekeeper's Year* "informative" and "useful," commenting particularly on Johnson's descriptions of the extracting and packaging of the honey as well as what happens following the introduction of a foreign queen bee to the hive.

Birds of a different feather are the focus of several other books by Johnson, among them *Songbirds: The Language of Song* and *Crows.* Part of the "Nature Watch" series, *Songbirds* discusses the way ornithologists approached the process of describing, recording, and studying bird song, and also presents several theories that attempt to reveal its meaning. In *Crows* a bird unique to the Americas is profiled, along with the myths surrounding the genus Corvidae and its involvement in the spread of the West Nile virus. *School Library Journal* writer Cynde Marcengill praised *Songbirds* as a "factual . . . peek into a fascinating phenomenon,"

while Nancy Call maintained in her review of *Crows* for the same periodical that in Johnson's "interesting text," young "report writers will get all the information they need" regarding the ubiquitous bird and its life cycle.

Johnson tells the story of a bald eagle, patient S-137, at an animal rescue center in St. Paul, Minnesota, in *Raptor Rescue! An Eagle Flies Free.* The victim of a gunshot wound, this bald eagle recovered and was ultimately released back into nature. Along with this true tale, the author also related the story of raptors in general and how they have become endangered due to the spread of human settlements. "Flowing text and striking close-ups present the rehabilitation of a bald eagle," commented Tippen McDaniel in *Appraisal,* while Susan Dove Lempke noted in *Booklist* that *Raptor Rescue!* combines "the appeal of an animal book, a veterinary career book, and a conservation book."

With *Tomatoes, Potatoes, Corn, and Beans* Johnson shows how the eating habits of people all over the world changed as a consequence of the discovery and exportation of foods from the Americas. She "blends history, botany, geography, folklore, cookery, and art in a fascinating account of how Columbus' 'discovery' in 1492 began an exchange of foods between the Americas and the Old World that improved the lives of millions," Hazel Rochman explained in *Booklist*. Ironically, these foodstuffs from the Americas turned out to be of ultimately greater value to Europe than the gold and silver for which Columbus and other explorers were searching. Johnson also includes peppers and peanuts in her informational stew, creating a book that Lois McCulley described in *School Library Journal* as "useful for social-history collections as well as any library needing information about the history of foodstuffs." Writing in *Voice of Youth Advocates*, Joyce Hamilton observed that *Tomatoes, Potatoes, Corn, and Beans* "contains information that will be difficult to find elsewhere," and also noted that "the numerous anecdotes, such as those on the origination of peanut butter and potato chips, are entertaining."

Biographical and Critical Sources

PERIODICALS

Appraisal, winter, 1977, Marjorie E. Smith, review of *Animals of the Deserts,* pp. 24-25; winter, 1983, Althea L. Phillips, review of "Natural Science" series, pp. 65-66; spring-summer, 1984, William D. Perkins, review of *Mosses,* pp. 52-53; summer, 1986, Lee Jeffers Brami, review of *Wolf Pack,* p. 39; fall, 1986, Martha T. Kane, review of *Bats,* pp. 58-59; summer, 1989, p. 46; summer, 1990, pp. 70-71; winter, 1992, pp. 35-36; winter, 1996, Tippen McDaniel, review of *Raptor Rescue!,* pp. 31-32; July, 1997, Irene Wood, review of *Ferrets,* p. 1814.

Booklist, September 1, 1976, Barbara Elleman, review of "Lerner Wildlife Library" series, p. 39; September 1, 1981, Barbara Elleman, review of "Natural Science" series, p. 43; December 1, 1991, p. 693; March 15, 1994, Stephanie Zvirin, review of *A Beekeeper's Year,* p. 1348; September 15, 1995, Susan Dove Lempke, review of *Raptor Rescue!,* p. 155; April 15, 1997, Hazel Rochman, review of *Tomatoes, Potatoes, Corn, and Beans,* p. 1415; December 1, 1999, Hazel Rochman, review of *Mapping the World,* p. 700.

Bulletin of the Center for Children's Books, December, 1985, review of *Wolf Pack,* pp. 69-70; December, 1991, p. 94; July-August, 1994, pp. 361-362; July-August, 1997, p. 399; November, 1999, review of *Mapping the World,* p. 97.

Horn Book, June, 1984, Sarah S. Gagne, "Views on Science Books," p. 370; September-October, 1994, Margaret A. Bush, review of *A Beekeeper's Year,* p. 612; January-February, 1996, p. 91.

Kirkus Reviews, November 15, 1986, p. 1730; January 1, 1990, review of *Albatrosses of Midway Island,* p. 47; September 15, 1991, p. 1223; February 15, 1997, p. 301; June 1, 1997, review of *Ferrets,* p. 874.

Publishers Weekly, May 22, 1981, review of *Penguins,* p. 76.

School Library Journal, September, 1976, Linda L. Mills, review of "Lerner Wildlife Library" series, p. 118; November, 1982, Terry Lawhead, review of *Beetles* and *Silkworms,* p. 80; April, 1984, Nancy Curtin, review of *Apple Trees,* pp. 115-116; November, 1984, Eldon Younce, review of *Potatoes,* p. 126; January, 1986, Cynthia M. Sturgis, review of *Wolf Pack,* p. 69; February, 1986, Elisabeth LeBris, review of *Bats,* p. 86; March, 1987, p. 160; July, 1990, p. 80; March, 1989, Kathryn Weisman, review of *Elephant Seals,* p. 192; October, 1995, p. 148; May, 1997, Lois McCulley, review of *Tomatoes, Potatoes, Corn, and Beans,* p. 146; August, 1997, Ellen M. Riordan, review of *Ferrets,* p. 148; December, 1999, Donna L. Scanlan, review of *Mapping the World,* p. 152; April, 2001, Cynde Marcengill, review of *Songbirds,* p. 162; January, 2004, Joy Fleishhacker, review of *Mapping the World,* p. 78; April, 2005, Nancy Call, review of *Crows,* p. 152.

Voice of Youth Advocates, December, 1997, Joyce Hamilton, review of *Tomatoes, Potatoes, Corn, and Beans,* pp. 334-335.*

* * *

JONES, Volcano
See MITCHELL, Adrian

* * *

KELLY, Mij

Personal

Born in Edinburgh, Scotland; children: two. *Education:* Attended York University and Stirling University.

Addresses

Home—Yorkshire, England. *Agent*—c/o PFD, Drury House, 34-43 Russell St., London WC2B 5HA, England. *E-mail*—mijinyork@dsl.pipex.com.

Career

Writer, editor, and journalist.

Awards, Honors

Kathleen Fidler Award, 1993, for *48 Hours with Franklin;* White Ravens selection, International Youth Library, 2002, for *William and the Night Train.*

Writings

FOR CHILDREN

48 Hours with Franklin (novel), Blackie (London, England), 1993.

Franklin Falls Apart, Dutton (London, England), 1995.

I Hate Everyone, illustrated by Ruth Palmer, David Bennett Books (St. Albans, England), 2000.

William and the Night Train, illustrated by Alison Jay, Hodder Headline (London, England), 2000, Farrar, Straus & Giroux (New York, NY), 2001.

One More Sheep, illustrated by Russell Ayto, Hodder Headline (London, England), 2004.

Sweet Pea and Boogaloo, Hodder (London, England), 2004.

Where's My Darling Daughter?, illustrated by Katharine McEwen, Oxford University Press (Oxford, England), 2005.

Potty Thieves, Hodder (London, England), 2006.

OTHER

(Editor with Tim Edensor) *Moving Worlds,* Polygon (Edinburgh, Scotland), 1989.

Sidelights

At age five British children's book author Mij Kelly just knew writing was her destiny; as Kelly explained on her home page, her grandma predicted it would be so. The author of picture books such as *William and the Night Train, One More Sheep,* and *Where's My Darling Daughter?,* Kelly spins her simple stories in verse because, as she explained, "writing in rhyme makes it much easier to control the rhythm and therefore the way the story ultimately sounds. It doesn't matter whether it's a teacher, parent or older sibling who's going to be doing the reading, you want them to read with expression—you want them to declaim your story like an orator." In her review of *One More Sheep* for the London *Guardian,* Julia Eccleshare wrote that "Kelly's rhyming text has terrific panache."

Illustrated by Alison Jay and released in both Kelly's native England and the United States, *William and the Night Train* centers around a young boy who, like so many children, has difficulty falling asleep. Using subtle imagery, Kelly portrays sleep as a midnight locomotive, its passengers boarding as they close their eyes, then traveling through the nighttime toward Tomorrow. William's family joins many other people as well as a diverse group of animals, boarding the train in Jay's illustrations. Although the young boy is eager for tomorrow to come, he is too excited to fall asleep on the train, and his restlessness disrupts his sleepy fellow passengers and postpones the train's departure. Ultimately, the boy's mother finally convinces him that shutting his eyes will allow tomorrow to come. "This is the kind of book that children and adults will pore over together," commented Connie Fletcher in a *Booklist* review, while a *Publishers Weekly* critic praised Jay's "soothing illustrations, bathed in muted earth tones," and added that "Kelly's poetic text unspools in a seamless strand, twining scrumptious rhymes . . . with nimble worldplay."

Biographical and Critical Sources

PERIODICALS

Booklist, February 15, 2001, Connie Fletcher, review of *William and the Night Train,* p. 1135.

Bulletin of the Center for Children's Books, June, 2001, review of *William and the Night Train,* p. 376.

Guardian (London, England), July 10, 2004, Julia Eccleshare, review of *One More Sheep.*

New Statesman and Society, August 18, 1989, Nancee Oku Bright, "Moving Worlds: Personal Recollections of 21 Immigrants to Edinburgh," p. 29.

Publishers Weekly, December 18, 2000, review of *William and the Night Train,* p. 77.

School Librarian, February, 1994, review of *48 Hours with Franklin,* p. 21; May, 1996, review of *Franklin Falls Apart,* p. 62.

School Library Journal, March, 2001, Rosalyn Pierini, review of *William and the Night Train,* p. 213.

Teacher Librarian, December, 2001, review of *William and the Night Train,* p. 12; February, 2002, review of *William and the Night Train,* p. 50.

Today's Parent, August, 2005, Stephanie Simpson McLellan, review of *One More Sheep,* p. 26.

ONLINE

Mij Kelly Home Page, http://www.mijinyork.dsl.pipex.com/ (November 6, 2005).

PFD Web site, http://www.pfd.co.uk/ (November 6, 2005), "Mij Kelly."*

*   *   *

KIRK, Heather 1949-

Personal

Born October 17, 1949, in London, Ontario, Canada; daughter of Jack Willsie (a civil engineer) and Gwendolyn Lundy (a homemaker; maiden name Pearson) Kirk; married John Ernest Winzer (a engineering professor), 1984. *Education:* Dalhousie University, B.A., 1973; University of Toronto, M.A., 1975; York University, M.A., 1989. *Hobbies and other interests:* Long-distance swimming, dog walking.

Addresses

Home—155 Owen St., Barrie, Ontario L4M 3H8, Canada. *E-mail*—shall-be@rogers.com.

Career

Writer, teacher, and editor. Freelance writer and editor; University of Alberta, Edmonton, Alberta, Canada, lecturer, 1975-77; University of Warsaw, Warsaw, Poland, instructor, 1977-79; Grande Prairie R. College, Grande Prairie, Alberta, instructor, 1980-84; Georgian College, Barrie, Ontario, Canada, part-time instructor, 1990-2005.

Member

Canadian Society of Authors, Illustrators, and Performers; Writers' Union of Canada.

Heather Kirk

Awards, Honors

Second prize, L.F. Brannan Memorial Essay Competition, 1987, for *Negative Capability;* Frank E. Thomas Award, 1988, for nonfiction prose in *Cross-Canada Writers'* magazine; nonfiction prize, *Grain,* 1999; finalist, Writers' Union of Canada Writing for Children Competition, 2000.

Writings

Warsaw Spring, Napoleon Pub. (Toronto, Ontario, Canada), 2001.
A Drop of Rain (sequel to *Warsaw Spring*), Napoleon Publishing (Toronto, Ontario, Canada), 2004.
Wacousta (based on the novel by John Richardson), Winding Trail Press (Embrun, Ontario, Canada), 2005.

Contributor to periodicals, including *Canadian Literature 84, Grain, Beaver, Bookbird, Books in Canada, Canadian Author, Canadian Children's Literature, Canadian Review of Materials, Canadian Women's Studies, Contemporary Verse II, Cross-Canada Writers, Literary Review of Canada, Poetry Toronto, Quill & Quire, Scrivener, Wascana Review,* and *Western People.* Author of radio scripts for Canadian stations, including Canadian Broadcasting Corporation.

Work in Progress

A novel for young adults; a humorous grammar book; a junior biography, *Mazo de la Roche: Rich and Famous Writer,* for XYZ Publishing, 2006.

Sidelights

Heather Kirk told *SATA:* "I wrote the novels *Warsaw Spring* and *Drop of Rain* because I admire modern Poland. The Polish solidarity uprising was one of the greatest passive-resistance movements of the twentieth century, if not the greatest!

"I rewrote the classic Canadian novel *Wacousta,* by John Richardson, because I am fascinated with the early history of Canada. *Wacousta* illuminates the early conflicts between aboriginals and Europeans, and it is fair to both sides."

Biographical and Critical Sources

PERIODICALS

Books in Canada, April, 2003, Clara Thomas, review of *Warsaw Spring.*
Midwestern Book Review, October, 2004, review of *A Drop of Rain.*
Resource Links, October 2, 2004, Margaret Mackey, review of *A Drop of Rain.*

ONLINE

Canadian Society of Children's Authors, Illustrators, and Performers Web site, http://www.canscaip.org/ (November 6, 2005), "Heather Kirk."
Writers Union of Canada Web site, http://www.writers union.ca/ (November 6, 2005), "Heather Kirk."

*   *   *

KNAAK, Richard A. 1961-
(Richard Allen Knaak)

Personal

Surname pronounced "Nack"; born May 28, 1961, in Chicago, IL; son of James Richard and Anna Maria Knaak. *Education:* University of Illinois at Urbana-Champaign, B.A. (rhetoric), 1984.

Addresses

Home and office—P.O. Box 8151, Bartlett, IL 60103. *Agent*—Peekner Literary Agency, 3418 Shelton Ave., Bethlehem, PA 18017. *E-mail*—rknaak@centurytel.net.

Career

Writer.

Member

Science Fiction Writers of America.

Writings

FANTASY NOVELS

King of the Grey, Warner/Questar, 1993.
Frostwing, Warner/Questar (New York, NY), 1995.
The Janus Mask, Warner/Questar (New York, NY), 1995.
Dutchman, Warner (New York, NY), 1996.
Ruby Flames ("Shattered Light" series), Simon & Schuster (New York, NY), 1999.

"DRAGONLANCE" SAGA

The Legend of Huma ("Heroes" series), TSR (Renton, WA), 1988.
Kaz, the Minotaur ("Heroes" series), TSR (Renton, WA), 1990.
Land of the Minotaurs ("Lost Histories" series), TSR (Renton, WA), 1990.
Reavers of the Blood Sea "Chaos War" series), TSR (Renton, WA), 1999.
The Citadel ("Classics" series), Wizards Publishing (Renton, WA), 2000.
Night of Blood ("Minotaur Wars" series), Wizards of the Coast (Renton, WA), 2003.
Tides of Blood ("Minotaur Wars" series), Wizards of the Coast (Renton, WA), 2004.
Empire of Blood ("Minotaur Wars" series), Wizards of the Coast (Renton, WA), 2005.

"DRAGONREALM" SERIES

Firedrake, Warner/Questar (New York, NY), 1989, reprinted, iUniverse.com, 2000.
Ice Dragon, Warner/Questar (New York, NY), 1990, reprinted, iUniverse.com, 2000.
Wolfhelm, Warner/Questar (New York, NY), 1990.
Shadow Steed, Warner/Questar (New York, NY), 1990.
The Crystal Dragon, Warner/Questar (New York, NY), 1993.
The Dragon Crown, Warner/Questar (New York, NY), 1994.
The Horse King, Warner/Questar (New York, NY), 1997.

"DRAGONREALM ORIGINS" SERIES

The Shrouded Realm, Warner/Questar (New York, NY), 1991.
Children of the Drake, Warner/Questar (New York, NY), 1991.
Dragon Tome, Warner/Questar (New York, NY), 1992.

"DIABLO" SERIES

Legacy of Blood, Pocket Books (New York, NY), 2001.
The Kingdom of Shadow, Pocket Books (New York, NY), 2002.

Also author of *Moon of the Spider.*

"WARCRAFT" SERIES

Day of the Dragon, Pocket Books (New York, NY), 2001.
The Well of Eternity ("War of the Ancients" series), Pocket Books (New York, NY), 2004.
The Demon Soul ("War of the Ancients" series), Pocket Books (New York, NY), 2004.
The Sundering ("War of the Ancients" series), Pocket Books (New York, NY), 2005.

"RAGNAROK" SERIES; MANGA

Eve of Apocalypse, Tokyopop (Los Angeles, CA), 2002.
Day of Reckoning, Tokyopop (Los Angeles, CA), 2002.
Night of Blood, Tokyopop (Los Angeles, CA), 2002.
Twilight of Terror, Tokyopop (Los Angeles, CA), 2003.
Midnight's Masters, Tokyopop (Los Angeles, CA), 2003.

OTHER

Dragon Hunt (manga; "Warcraft: The Sunwell Trilogy" series), illustrated by Jae Hwan Kim, Tokyopop (Los Angeles, CA), 2005.

Author of short stories anthologized in *Dragonlance Tales,* Volumes 1-3, TSR, 1987; *Dragonlance Tales II,* Volumes 1-3, TSR, 1992; *The Dragons of Krynn,* TSR, 1994; *Superheroes,* Ace, 1995; *History of Dragonlance,* TSR, 1995; *Dragons of Chaos,* TSR, 1997; *Relics and Omens,* TSR, 1998; *Heroes and Fools,* TSR, 1999; *Rebels and Tyrants,* Wizards of the Coast, 2000; *The Best of Tales,* Wizards of the Coast, 2000; *Leaves of the Inn II,* Wizards of the Coast, 2001; *Tales from the War of Souls,* Wizards of the Coast, 2001; and *The Traveling Players of Gilean,* Wizards of the Coast, 2003.

Knaak's books have been translated into Czech, Danish, Finnish, French, German, Hungarian, Italian, Japanese, Polish, Russian, Spanish, and Turkish.

Sidelights

A prolific author, Richard A. Knaak specializes in the realms of both science fiction and fantasy as a contributor to the popular "Dragonlance" series of novels begun by Margaret Weis and Terry Hickman and based on a popular role-playing game originally produced by Washington-based company TSR. In addition to the "Dragonlance" books, which include story arcs such as "The Minotaur Wars" and "Chaos War," Knaak has also penned several standalone fantasy novels as well as the "Warcraft" novel series, based on a popular fantasy role-playing/computer game, has authored a number of short stories based in the "Dragonlance" world, and has more recently explored the manga format through both his work adapting the Korean manga series "Ragnarok" and his ongoing collaboration with illustrator Jae Hwan

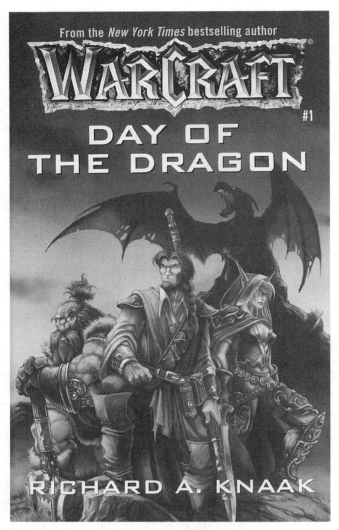

From the *New York Times* bestselling author

WARCRAFT

#1

DAY OF THE DRAGON

RICHARD A. KNAAK

Set in the mythic world of Azeroth, Knaak's novel follows a mage named Rhonin as he is sent into an Orc stronghold, there to join with untrustworthy ancient allies in order to foil a devious plan that threatens all. (Cover illustration by Sam Didier.)

Kim in adapting the "Warcraft" novel series into manga. Praising Knaak's novel *Frostwing,* about an immortal man who suddenly finds that dreams of a mysterious gargoyle are combining with a growing amnesia to destroy his identity, a *Publishers Weekly* contributor dubbed the book an "intriguing" modern-day fantasy.

The first manga volume in Knaak's "Warcraft: Sunwell Trilogy," *Dragon Hunt* takes place in the fantastical world of Azeroth, a peaceful human kingdom. Knaak first provides readers with the "Warcraft" backstory: Azeroth, a kingdom threatened by bloodthirsty orcs from another dimension, finds its safety compromised when its king, Arthas, decides to acquire an elvish artifact known as the Sunwell, which is known to attract dragons. He dispatches his servant, the evil elf Dar'Khan, to obtain the relic, and Dar'Khan orders a dwarf underling to complete the task. The dwarf and his band hunt down the blue dragon Kalec, hoping Kalec will lead them to the Sunwell; instead, Kalec shape-

shifts into a young man and is joined by peasant girl Anveena in a quest to save the coveted talisman. *Dragon Hunt* is filled with "betrayal, magic and, of course, pages and pages of sword fights," according to a *Publishers Weekly* contributor, while George Galuschak wrote in *Kliatt* that Knaak serves up "a fast read with plenty of action" that, despite its complicated plot, likely "makes total sense to people who enjoy role-playing games."

"I began writing when I was young, after I realized that I didn't have the patience to learn to draw but could put a decent story together," Knaak once commented. "My imagination has always been a strong part of me. I started reading mysteries but soon discovered science fiction and fantasy; I've been hooked since.

"If there is any theme running through my work, it is that one should never give up. There is always hope. You are the one who generally determines your own success or failure. This represents my personal view as well as my own experience. Many writers hope to sell someday. I went out and found my first sale and things have moved smoothly since then. In a nutshell, your only limits are the ones you form in your own mind."

Biographical and Critical Sources

PERIODICALS

Kliatt, July, 2005, George Galushak, review of *Dragon Hunt,* p. 32.
Publishers Weekly, November 14, 1994, review of *Frostwing,* p. 64; May 26, 2003, review of *Night of Blood,* p. 54; April 11, 2005, review of *Dragon Hunt,* p. 36.
School Library Journal, July, 2005, John Leighton, review of *Dragon Hunt,* p. 126.
Voice of Youth Advocates, December, 1988, review of *The Legend of Huma,* p. 246.

ONLINE

Dragon Lance Nexus Web site, http://www.d13e.com/ (April 7, 2003), interview with Knaak.
Richard Knaak Home Page, http://www.sff.net/people/knaak/ (November 6, 2005).
Wizards.com, http://www.wizards.com/ (November 6, 2006).*

*　　*　　*

KNAAK, Richard Allen
See KNAAK, Richard A.

*　　*　　*

KNUTSON, Barbara 1959-2005

Personal

Born 1959, in South Africa; immigrated to United States, 1971; died of an autoimmune deficiency, May 7,

2005; daughter of American missionaries; married Chris Jensen (a teacher), 1994. *Education:* St. Olaf College, University of Minnesota, B.A. (art education and French). *Hobbies and other interests:* Travel.

Career

Author and illustrator. Teacher in Nigeria for two years.

Awards, Honors

Minnesota Book Award, 1991, for *How the Guinea Fowl Got Its Spots,* and 1994, for *Sungura and Leopard;* Best of Issue designation, *Highlights for Children* magazine, 2002, for illustration; Notable Book designation, American Library Association, 2005, for *Love and Roast Chicken.*

Writings

SELF-ILLUSTRATED PICTURE BOOKS

Why the Crab Has No Head: An African Tale, Carolrhoda Books (Minneapolis, MN), 1987.
How the Guinea Fowl Got Her Spots: A Swahili Tale of Friendship, Carolrhoda Books (Minneapolis, MN), 1990.
Sungura and Leopard: A Swahili Trickster Tale, Little Brown (Boston, MA), 1993.
Love and Roast Chicken: A Trickster Tale from the Andes, Lerner Pub. Group (Minneapolis, MN), 2004.

ILLUSTRATOR

James Haskins, *Count Your Way through Africa,* Carolrhoda Books (Minneapolis, MN), 1989.
Pat McKissack, *From Heaven Above: The Story of Christmas Proclaimed by the Angels,* Augsburg (Minneapolis, MN), 1992.
Trish Marx, *Hanna's Cold Winter,* Carolrhoda Books (Minneapolis, MN), 1993.
April A. Brady, *Kwanzaa Karamu: Cooking and Crafts for a Kwanzaa Feast,* Carolrhoda Books (Minneapolis, MN), 1995.
Bridget Mary Meehan, *Heat Talks with Mother God,* Liturgical Press (Collegeville, MN), 1995.
Holly Littlefield, *Colors of Ghana,* Carolrhoda Books (Minneapolis, MN), 1999.
Linda Lowery Keep, *Day of the Dead,* Carolrhoda Books (Minneapolis, MN), 2004.
Linda L. McDunn, *The Color of Me,* Liturgical Press (Collegeville, MN), 2004.
Linda Lowery Keep, *Cinco de Mayo,* Carolrhoda Books (Minneapolis, MN), 2005.

Contributor of illustrations to periodicals, including *Cricket* and *Highlights for Children.*

Sidelights

Born in South African, picture-book author and illustrator Barbara Knutson moved to the United States with her missionary parents at age twelve. Although the United States remained her home, she continued to feed her curiosity about the world through travels to South America and Europe, also teaching school in Nigeria for two years and living in Peru while her husband, Chris Jensen, taught biology in Lima. Trained in art education and French, Knutson eventually put her skills to use as an illustrator, and created artwork for books by Pat McKissack, Trish Marks, and several other authors. She also created four original stories—*Why the Crab Has No Head: An African Tale, How the Guinea Fowl Got Its Spots: A Swahili Tale of Friendship, Sungura and Leopard: A Swahili Trickster Tale,* and *Love and Roast Chicken: A Trickster Tale from the Andes Mountains*—prior to her premature death at age forty-five in May of 2005. Praising the award-winning *Sungura and Leopard,* about a witty hare and sleek leopard who each build a home and discover that they have both been constructing the same building, *Horn Book* reviewer Margaret A. Bush wrote that the "vigorous humor" of Knutson's pen-and-ink and watercolor illustrations "and the broad comedy of a familiar story scheme are both delightful."

Based on a Peruvian folktale, *Love and Roast Chicken* is a playful tale about a guinea pig named Cuy (pronounced "Kwee," the Quechuan word for guinea pig) who tricks a wily fox named Tio Antonio several times and thus avoids becoming the fox's dinner. To avoid Tio's attention, Cuy disguises himself as a small man by donning a poncho and a hat; when he is hired by a farmer to tend a small alfalfa field, Cuy feels doubly in luck: he can work during the day and hide from the fox, then sneak back into the field at night and have an alfalfa dinner. However, the farmer is clever too, and has set a trap to catch alfalfa-stealing rodents. Caught in the trap, Cuy must quickly find a way out, while also tricking the gullible fox into taking his place in the farmer's trap. Knutson's "robust prints, characterized by heavy black lines and subdued colors, are remarkably effective in conveying expressions and humor," commented *Horn Book* critic Kitty Flynn, while Lee Bock wrote in *School Library Journal* that "observant children will delight in the visual and cultural details and in the energy" of the author/illustrator's woodcut illustrations."

Biographical and Critical Sources

PERIODICALS

Booklist, July, 1993, Quraysh Ali, review of *Sungura and Leopard: A Swahili Trickster Tale,* p. 1970; September 15, 2004, Hazel Rochman, review of *Love and Roast Chicken: A Trickster Tale from the Andes Mountains,* p. 247.
Bulletin of the Center for Children's Books, July, 1990, review of *How the Guinea Fowl Got Her Spots: A Swahili Tale of Friendship,* p. 270; December, 1993, re-

view of *Sungura and Leopard,* p. 126; October, 2004, Timnah Card, review of *Love and Roast Chicken,* p. 83.

Emergency Librarian, September, 1991, review of *How the Guinea Fowl Got Her Spots,* p. 50.

Five Owls, September, 1990, review of *How the Guinea Fowl Got Her Spots,* p. 9.

Horn Book, September-October, 1990, Ellen Fader, review of *How the Guinea Fowl Got Her Spots,* p. 611; September-October, 1993, Margaret A. Bush, review of *Sungura and Leopard,* p. 609; November-December, 2004, Kitty Flynn, review of *Love and Roast Chicken,* p. 720.

Kirkus Reviews, August 1, 2004, review of *Love and Roast Chicken,* p. 743.

Publishers Weekly, November 1, 1993, review of *Sungura and Leopard,* p. 78.

Quill and Quire, November, 1993, review of *Sungura and Leopard,* p. 40.

Reading Teacher, April, 1991, review of *How the Guinea Fowl Got Her Spots,* p. 587.

School Library Journal, September, 1990, Regina Pauly, review of *How the Guinea Fowl Got Her Spots,* p. 216; October, 1993, Lyn Miller-Lachmann, review of *Sungura and Leopard,* p. 119; November, 1993,

Sally R. Dow, review of *Hanna's Cold Winter,* p. 86; November, 2004, Lee Bock, review of *Love and Roast Chicken,* p. 126.

Social Education, April, 1991, review of *How the Guinea Fowl Got Her Spots,* p. 257.

ONLINE

Barbara Knutson Web site, http://www.barbaraknutson. com (November 6, 2005).

OBITUARIES

PERIODICALS

Los Angeles Times, May 13, 2005, p. 6.

ONLINE

Children's Literature Network, http://www.childrens literaturenetwork.org/ (November 6, 2005), "Barbara Knutson."*

L

LANE, Dakota 1959-

Personal
Born September 23, 1959, in Brooklyn, NY; children: Alex Kamin, Hailey Pearson. *Education:* Attended San Francisco State University.

Addresses
Home—P.O. Box 591, Woodstock, NY 12498. *Agent*—c/o Author Mail, HarperCollins Children's, 1350 Avenue of the Americas, New York, NY 10019. *E-mail*—love@orpheusobsession.com.

Career
Freelance writer, c. 1996—; creative writing instructor, 1996—.

Awards, Honors
American Library Association Best Books for Young Adults designation, 2006, for *The Orpheus Obsession.*

Writings

Johnny Voodoo, Delacorte (New York, NY), 1996.
The Orpheus Obsession, HarperTempest (New York, NY), 2005.

Contributor to periodicals, including *Village Voice, Entertainment Weekly, Interview,* and *Woodstock Times.*

Adaptations
Johnny Voodoo was adapted as an audiobook by Recorded Books, 1997.

Sidelights
Reflecting its author's familiarity with New York City and its urban culture, Dakota Lane's debut novel, *Johnny Voodoo,* focuses on Deirdre, a sixteen year old

Dakota Lane

who has just suffered the loss of her mother. As the story opens, Deirdre is uprooted by her artist father from her familiar home in New York City and taken to live with him in a rural community in Louisiana. Deirdre finds it hard to adjust to her new home and school and begins to rebel against her father. However, she soon meets the boy described by Lane's title, whose real name is Johnny Vouchamps. Johnny has a mysterious, exotic quality that attracts Deirdre, and he is rumored by the other students to be homeless. Deirdre's

Moving from New York City to rural Louisiana, a young woman feels like an outcast until a relationship with a mysterious young man gives her the confidence to deal with the realities of her life.

father tries to discourage the relationship, causing more tension between parent and child. As Johnny's behavior becomes increasingly strange, however, Deirdre begins to reconsider her father's advice more seriously. The story concludes with Deirdre becoming closer to her family and classmates. Deirdre decides that "the love she had for her mother and for Johnny will live forever in her heart," wrote *Voice of Youth Advocates* contributor Mary Hedge.

Lane drew on her own life experiences, as well as her knowledge of New York City, in penning her first novel. In a *Publishers Weekly* interview, she explained that, as a child, she attended some twenty-five schools. At one school, according to interviewer Cindi DiMarzo, Lane "was the only white girl" and "she experienced first-hand the intense bathroom scenes described in *Johnny Voodoo,* in which the popular girls try to intimidate anyone who dares to be different." Lane also incorporated other experiences from her childhood in the novel, including "stories about the bayou that were told to her by a babysitter," explained DiMarzo.

Critics responded favorably to *Johnny Voodoo.* Margaret Cole, writing in *School Library Journal,* hailed the novel as "a well-paced story filled with symbolism, emotion, and intriguing characters," while a *Publishers Weekly* commentator observed that the book's "mood is perfect." Deborah Stevenson, writing in the *Bulletin of the Center for Children's Books,* commended Lane's "incisive accuracy about various cliques and patterns in the high-school social world."

Another sixteen year old is the subject of Lane's second novel, *The Orpheus Obsession.* Stuck in upstate New York for the summer and looking for ways to avoid dealing with her mentally unstable and abusive mother, high schooler Anooshka Stargirl frequently travels south to visit her older sister, ZZ Moon, and spend the weekend in ZZ's Manhattan apartment. During these heady escapes to the city she becomes drawn to the music of a popular up-and-coming rocker known as Orpheus. After hearing his music during a performance at Brighton Beach, she begins to obsess over Orpheus's lyrics, which speak to her own feelings. Fixated, Annoshka discusses his music in online chats, and while following his blog on the Internet she begins to believe that she

To escape from a troubled home life, an upstate teen spends time with an older sister living in New York City and her obsession with a popular rock star soon draws her into a dark, alien world where tragedy takes root.

and the musician have a special connection. In typical groupie form, she pieces together Orpheus's day-to-day life from his blog entries, and sets about tracking him down, even when his path leads her to destructive behavior in a less-than-hospitable part of the city. Unlike most fans, Anooshka ultimately meets her idol, and the photographs she takes recording her summer journey are incorporated into Lane's compelling story.

Reviewing *The Orpheus Obsession,* critics found parallels both with Lane's debut novel and the fiction of West coast writer Francesca Lia Block. Contrasting the novel with *Johnny Voodoo, Booklist* reviewer Debbie Carton wrote that Lane's second novel "takes a fascinating premise and develops it with even more high crafted prose." A *Publishers Weekly* contributor also praised the novel, calling Anooshka a "brash, hip heroine" and noting that Lane's storyline will be "instantly recognizable to . . . anyone who has ever experienced the highs and lows of an obsessive crush." *Kliatt* critic Claire Rosser noted the references to the myth of Eurydice and Orpheus, god of the underworld, adding that *The Orpheus Obsession* "has a dreamlike quality to it." In *School Library Journal* Miranda Doyle praised Lane's "lyrical, angst-filled story" and predicted that sophisticated teen readers will "identify with Anooshka's intense emotions," brought to life through "highly descriptive, poetic language."

Biographical and Critical Sources

PERIODICALS

Booklist, September 15, 1996, p. 232; September 15, 2005, Debbie Carton, review of *The Orpheus Obsession,* p. 58.

Bulletin of the Center for Children's Books, January, 1997, Deborah Stevenson, review of *Johnny Voodoo,* p. 178; July-August, 2005, review of *The Orpheus Obsession.*

Kirkus Reviews, June 15, 2005, review of *The Orpheus Obsession,* p. 685.

Kliatt, July, 2005, Claire Rosser, review of *The Orpheus Obsession,* p. 12.

Publishers Weekly, November 18, 1996, review of *Johnny Voodoo,* pp. 76-77; December 16, 1996, Cindi DiMarzo, "Flying Starts," p. 32.

School Library Journal, November, 1996, Margaret Cole, review of *Johnny Voodoo,* p. 123; September, 2005, Miranda Doyle, review of *The Orpheus Obsession,* p. 205.

Teaching and Learning Literature, September-October, 1997, pp. 95-96.

Voice of Youth Advocates, October, 1996, Mary Hedge, review of *Johnny Voodoo,* p. 210.*

LANGLEY, Andrew 1949-

Personal

Born October 26, 1949, in Bath, England; son of Kenneth Edward (an engineer) and Mona Emily Francis (a homemaker) Langley; married Lois Ann Norah d'Esterre (an editor), April 19, 1975; children: Samuel Charles, Rose Alice. *Education:* London University, B.A. (English literature; with honors).

Addresses

Home—Bath, England. *Agent*—c/o Author Mail, Raintree/Heinemann, Halley Court, Jordan Hill, Oxford OX2 8EJ, England.

Career

Children's book author. Penguin Books, London, England, marketing assistant, 1974-78.

Writings

FOR CHILDREN

Explorers on the Nile ("In Profile" series), Silver Burdett (Upper Saddle River, NJ), 1981.

Working in the Army: A Guide for Young People, National Extension College, 1983.

The Superpowers, Wayland (London, England), 1983.

The First Men 'round the World, Silver Burdett (Upper Saddle River, NJ), 1983.

Ian Botham (biography), illustrated by Karen Heywood, Hamilton, 1983.

Cleopatra and the Egyptians ("Life and Times" series), illustrated by Gerry Wood, Wayland (London, England), 1985, Bookwright Press (New York, NY), 1986.

Doctor, photographs by Chris Fairclough, Franklin Watts (London, England), 1985.

Energy, Bookwright Press (New York, NY), 1985.

Passport to Great Britain, Franklin Watts (London, England), 1985, Bookwright Press (New York, NY), 1986.

John F. Kennedy (biography), illustrated by Richard Hook, Wayland (London, England), 1985, Bookwright Press (New York, NY), 1986.

Librarian, photographs by Chris Fairclough, Franklin Watts (London, England), 1985.

The Making of the Living Planet, Little, Brown (Boston, MA), 1985.

Peoples of the World, Wayland (London, England), 1985, Bookwright Press (New York, NY), 1986.

The Army, Wayland (London, England), 1986.

Combat Pilot, photographs by Chris Fairclough, Franklin Watts (London, England), 1986.

A Family in the Fifties ("How They Lived" series), illustrated by John James, Wayland (London, England), 1986.

The Search for Riches, Wayland (London, England), 1986, Raintree Steck-Vaughn (Austin, TX), 1997.

The Royal Air Force, Wayland (London, England), 1986.

The Royal Navy, Wayland (London, England), 1986.

Sailor, photographs by Chris Fairclough, Franklin Watts (London, England), 1986.

Airports, illustrated by James Dugdale and others, Franklin Watts (London, England), 1987.

Cars, Franklin Watts (London, England), 1987.

Genghis Kahn and the Mongols ("Life and Times" series), illustrated by Clyde Pearson, Wayland (London, England), 1987.

Travel Games for Kids, illustrated by Alisa Tingley, W. Foulsham, 1987, Berkshire House, 1992.

The World of Sharks, Wayland (London, England), 1987, Bookwright Press (New York, NY), 1988.

Twenty Names in Pop Music, illustrated by Gary Rees, Wayland (London, England), 1987, Marshall Cavendish (Tarrytown, NY), 1988.

Travel Quizzes for Kids, W. Foulsham, 1988.

Twenty Explorers, illustrated by Edward Mortelmans, Wayland (London, England), 1988, Marshall Cavendish (Tarrytown, NY), 1990.

Twenty Names in Crime, illustrated by Gary Rees, Wayland (London, England), 1988.

(With Maira Butterfield) *People,* illustrated by Norman Young, Gareth Stevens (Milwaukee, WI), 1989.

Sport, Wayland (London, England), 1989.

Sport and Politics, Wayland (London, England), 1989, Rourke Enterprises (Vero Beach, FL), 1990.

(With others) *World Issues,* two volumes, Bowker (New York, NY), 1990.

Trucks and Trailers, Puffin (Harmondsworth, England), 1991.

Young Sailor, illustrated by Robin Lawrie and Bob Mathias, Sheridan House (Dobbs Ferry, NY), 1993.

Grasslands, illustrated by Neil Bulpitt and others, J. Morris, 1993.

The Illustrated Book of Questions and Answers, Kibworth Books (Leicester, England), 1993, Facts on File (New York, NY), 1996.

Wetlands, illustrated by Neil Bulpitt and others, J. Morris, 1993.

The Industrial Revolution, Viking (New York, NY), 1994.

The Age of Industry ("See through History" series), Hamlyn (London, England), 1994.

Medieval Life, photographs by Geoff Brightling and Geoff Dann, Knopf (New York, NY), 1996, revised edition, Dorling Kindersley (New York, NY), 2004

(With Philip de Souza) *The Roman News,* Candlewick Press (Cambridge, MA), 1996.

Victorian Factories, illustrated by James Field, Heinemann (London, England), 1996.

Victorian Railways, illustrated by James Field, Heinemann (London, England), 1996.

(With Gerald Wood) *Life in a Victorian Steamship,* Heinemann (London, England), 1997.

Tudor Palaces, illustrated by Mark Bergin and James Field, Heinemann (London, England), 1997.

Food and Farming, Heinemann (London, England), 1997.

Hans Christian Andersen: The Dreamer of Fairy Tales, illustrated by Toni Morris, Oxford University Press (Oxford, England), 1997.

Alexander the Great: The Greatest Ruler of the Ancient World ("What's Their Story?" series), illustrated by Alan Marks, Oxford University Press (Oxford, England), 1997, Oxford University Press (New York, NY), 1998.

Amelia Earhart: The Pioneering Pilot ("What's Their Story?" series), illustrated by Alan Marks, Oxford University Press (Oxford, England), 1997.

Trade and Transport, illustrated by Mark Bergin, James Field, and John James, Heinemann (London, England), 1998.

Castle at War: The Story of a Siege ("Be an Eyewitness" series), illustrated by Peter Dennis, Dorling Kindersley (London, England), 1998.

Renaissance, Knopf (New York, NY), 1999.

(With Alan Brown) *What I Believe: A Young Person's Guide to the Religions of the World,* Millbrook Press (Brookfield, CT), 1999.

Leonardo, Dorling Kindersley (London, England), 1999, published with "treasure chest" materials, Running Press (Philadelphia, PA), 2001.

Shakespeare's Theatre, illustrated by June Everett, Oxford University Press (Oxford, England), 1999.

Shakespeare and the Elizabethan Age (published with "treasure chest" materials), Running Press (Philadelphia, PA), 2000.

One Hundred Things You Should Know about Pirates, Miles Kelly (Great Bardfield, England), 2000, Mason Crest (Broomall, PA), 2003.

You Wouldn't Want to Be a Viking Explorer: Voyages You'd Rather Not Make, Franklin Watts (New York, NY), 2001.

One Hundred Things You Should Know about the Wild West, Miles Kelly (Great Bardfield, England), 2001, Mason Crest (Broomall, PA), 2003.

(With Fiona Macdonald and Jane Walker) *Five Hundred Things You Should Know about History,* Miles Kelly (Great Bardfield, England), 2001.

First Fun Atlas, Miles Kelly (Great Bardfield, England), 2001, Mason Crest (Broomall, PA), 2003.

Pirates, Miles Kelly (Great Bardfield, England), 2002.

Barbara Hepworth ("Creative Lives" series), Heinemann (Oxford, England), 2002.

Mikhail Gorbachev ("Leading Lives" series), Heinemann (Oxford, England), 2002, Heinemann (Chicago, IL), 2003.

Pablo Picasso, Raintree (Chicago, IL), 2003.

Michelangelo, Raintree (Chicago, IL) 2003.

An International Rugby Union Star, Heinemann (Oxford, England), 2004.

"BEHIND THE SCENES" SERIES; FOR CHILDREN

Radio Station, photographs by Chris Fairclough, Franklin Watts (London, England), 1983.

Hotel, photographs by Chris Fairclough, Franklin Watts (London, England), 1983.

Car Ferry, photographs by Chris Fairclough, Franklin Watts (London, England), 1983.

Football Club, photographs by Chris Fairclough, Franklin Watts (London, England), 1983.

Supermarket, photographs by Chris Fairclough, Franklin Watts (London, England), 1983.

Police Station, photographs by Chris Fairclough, Franklin Watts (London, England), 1983.

Post Office, photographs by Chris Fairclough, Franklin Watts (London, England), 1985.

Newspapers, photographs by Chris Fairclough, Franklin Watts (London, England), 1985.

"ORIGINS" SERIES; FOR CHILDREN

A Cup of Tea, Wayland (London, England), 1982.

The Meat in Your Hamburger, Wayland (London, England), 1982.

The Paper in Your Home, Wayland (London, England), 1982.

"TOPICS" SERIES; FOR CHILDREN

Great Disasters, Wayland (London, England), 1985, Bookwright Press (New York, NY), 1986.

Under the Ground, Wayland (London, England), 1985, Bookwright Press (New York, NY), 1986.

Television, Wayland (London, England), 1986, Bookwright Press (New York, NY), 1987.

Jungles, Wayland (London, England), 1986, Bookwright Press (New York, NY), 1987.

"FOCUS ON" SERIES; FOR CHILDREN

Focus on Wool, Wayland (London, England), 1985.

Focus on Vegetables, Wayland (London, England), 1985.

Focus on Timber, Wayland (London, England), 1986, published as *Spotlight on Timber,* Rourke Enterprises (Vero Beach, FL), 1987.

"SPOTLIGHT ON" SERIES; FOR CHILDREN

Spotlight on Airports, Franklin Watts (London, England), 1987.

Spotlight on Aircraft, illustrated by Peter Bull, Franklin Watts (London, England), 1987, published as *Aircraft,* Bookwright Press (New York, NY), 1989.

Spotlight on Dinosaurs, Franklin Watts (London, England), 1987.

Spotlight on Spacecraft, illustrated by Christopher Forsey, Michael Roffe, and others, Franklin Watts (London, England), 1987.

Spotlight on the Moon, illustrated by Christopher Forsey, Franklin Watts (London, England), 1987, published as *The Moon,* 1988.

Spotlight on Trees, Franklin Watts (London, England), 1987.

"LET'S LOOK AT" SERIES; FOR CHILDREN

Let's Look at Bikes, Wayland (London, England), 1988, published as *Bikes and Motorcycles,* Bookwright Press (New York, NY), 1989.

Let's Look at Trucks, Wayland (London, England), 1988, published as *Trucks,* Bookwright Press (New York, NY), 1989.

Let's Look at Circuses, illustrated by D. Bowles, Wayland (London, England), 1989.

Let's Look at Aircraft, Wayland (London, England), 1989, published as *Aircraft,* Bookwright Press (New York, NY), 1989.

Let's Look at Trains, illustrated by Mike Turner, Wayland (London, England), 1989, published as *Trains,* Bookwright Press (New York, NY), 1989.

Let's Look at Racing Cars, illustrated by Mike Atkinson, Wayland (London, England), 1990, published as *Racing Cars,* Bookwright Press (New York, NY), 1990.

Let's Look at Monster Machines, illustrated by Mike Atkinson, Wayland (London, England), 1990, published as *Monster Machines,* Bookwright Press (New York, NY), 1990.

"THE STORY OF" SERIES; FOR CHILDREN

(With Stella Alcantara and Josefina Dalupan Hofilena) *The Story of the Philippines,* World Book International (Chicago, IL), 1989.

The Story of Singapore, World Book International (Chicago, IL), 1990.

(With Garry Bailey) *The Story of India,* World Book International (Chicago, IL), 1990.

"RESOURCES" SERIES; FOR CHILDREN

Copper, Wayland (London, England), 1981.

Paper, Wayland (London, England), 1991, Thomson Learning (Stamford, CT), 1993.

Steel, Wayland (London, England), 1992, Thomson Learning (Stamford, CT), 1993.

"HISTORY OF BRITAIN" SERIES; FOR CHILDREN

The Tudors, 1485 to 1603, Hamlyn (London, England), 1993.

The Stuarts, 1603 to 1714, Hamlyn (London, England), 1993.

Georgian Britain, 1714 to 1837, Hamlyn (London, England), 1994.

Victorian Britain, 1837 to 1901, Hamlyn (London, England), 1994.

Modern Britain, 1901 to the 1990s, Hamlyn (London, England), 1994.

Queen Victoria, illustrated by James Field, Hamlyn (London, England), 1995.

The Blitz, 1939-1945, illustrated by John James, Hamlyn (London, England), 1995.

The Home Front, Hamlyn (London, England), 1995.

Elizabeth I, illustrated by Mark Bergin, Heinemann (Oxford, England), 1996.

Shakespeare and the Theatre, illustrated by John James, Heinemann (Oxford, England), 1996.

"GREAT EXPLORERS" SERIES; FOR CHILDREN

Discovering the New World: The Voyages of Christopher Columbus, illustrated by Paul Crompton, Kibworth Books (Leicester, England), 1994.

Exploring the Pacific: The Expeditions of Captain Cook, illustrated by David McAllister, Kibworth Books (Leicester, England), 1994.

The Great Polar Adventure: The Journeys of Roald Amundsen, illustrated by Kevin Barnes, Kibworth Books (Leicester, England), 1994.

Journey into Space: The Missions of Neil Armstrong, illustrated by Alex Pang, Kibworth Books (Leicester, England), 1994.

"ONE HUNDRED GREATEST" SERIES; FOR CHILDREN

One Hundred Greatest Tyrants, Dragon's World Children's Books (Limpsfield, England), 1996.

One Hundred Greatest Inventions, Grolier (Danbury, CT), 1997.

One Hundred Greatest Men, Grolier (Danbury, CT), 1997.

One Hundred Greatest Women, Grolier (Danbury, CT), 1997.

One Hundred Greatest Sports Champions, Grolier (Danbury, CT), 1997.

One Hundred Greatest Manmade Wonders, Grolier (Danbury, CT), 1997.

One Hundred Greatest Medical Discoveries, Grolier (Danbury, CT), 1997.

One Hundred Greatest Explorers, Grolier (Danbury, CT), 1997.

One Hundred Greatest Disasters, Grolier (Danbury, CT), 1997.

One Hundred Greatest Natural Wonders, Grolier (Danbury, CT), 1997.

One Hundred Greatest Amazing Animals, Grolier (Danbury, CT), 1997.

One Hundred Greatest Archaeological Discoveries, Grolier (Danbury, CT), 1997.

"TIME TOURS" SERIES; FOR CHILDREN

Medieval Castle, illustrated by James Field and others, Victoria House (Bath, England), 1998.

Spanish Galleon, illustrated by Mark Bergin and others, Reader's Digest Children's Books (Bath, England), 1998.

Egyptian Tomb, illustrated by Mike Smith and others, Reader's Digest Children's Books (Bath, England), 1999.

Roman Arena, illustrated by Donald Harley and others, Reader's Digest Children's Books (Bath, England), 1999.

"OXFORD FIRST ENCYCLOPEDIA" SERIES; FOR CHILDREN

Oxford First Encyclopedia, Oxford University Press (Oxford, England), 1998.

Earth and the Universe, Oxford University Press (Oxford, England), 1999.

Science and Technology, Oxford University Press (Oxford, England), 1999.

People and Places, Oxford University Press (Oxford, England), 1999.

My Body, Oxford University Press (Oxford, England), 1999.

Animals and Plants, Oxford University Press (Oxford, England), 1999.

Oxford First Book of Space, Oxford University Press (Oxford, England), 1999, Oxford University Press (New York, NY), 2000.

"HISTORY IN ART" SERIES; FOR CHILDREN

Ancient Egypt, Raintree (Chicago, IL), 2005.

Victorian Britain, Raintree (Oxford, England), 2005.

Ancient Greece, Raintree (Chicago, IL), 2005.

"GREAT CITIES OF THE WORLD" SERIES; FOR CHILDREN

Cape Town, World Almanac Library (Milwaukee, WI), 2005.

St. Petersburg, World Almanac Library (Milwaukee, WI), 2005.

Athens, World Almanac Library (Milwaukee, WI), 2005.

"LIVE ACTION" SERIES; FOR CHILDREN

Swimming, Chrysalis (North Mankato, MN), 2004.

Running, Chrysalis (North Mankato, MN), 2004.

Walking, Chrysalis (North Mankato, MN), 2004.

OTHER

(Editor with John Utting) *The Village on the Hill: Aspects of Colerne History,* Colerne History Group, 1990.

Glenfiddich: Made without Compromise since 1887, photographs by Philip Sayer, Good Books (Melksham, England), 1995.

London Pride: 150 Years of Fuller, Smith, and Turner, 1845-1995, Good Books, 1995.

(With Adam Hargreaves) *Mr. Mean's Guide to Management,* Egmont World (Hanforth, England), 2000.

(With Adam Hargreaves) *Mr. Lazy's Guide to Fitness,* Egmont World (Hanforth, England), 2000.

(With Adam Hargreaves) *Mr. Greedy's Guide to Food,* Egmont World (Hanforth, England), 2000.

Rupert Murdoch: An Unauthorized Biography, Heinemann (Oxford, England), 2001.

Sidelights

British writer Andrew Langley has dedicated his career to penning educational books that meet the needs of young readers. Langley's first books were primarily straightforward works designed to explain day-to-day facts; in his "Behind the Scenes" series, for example, he explores what goes on at various familiar locations, such as a hotel, a police station, and a post office while his "Origins" series explains where things like as hamburger meat come from. As his career has progressed, Langley has increasingly focused on the subject that most interests him: namely history. Mining the world's past, he has produced biographies of a broad range of people from history as well as historic overviews such as *The Roman News, Medieval Life, Renaissance,* and *Ancient Egypt.* In addition to these fact-based works, Langley joined with author Alan Brown to write *What I Believe: A Young Person's Guide to the Religions of the World.* A comprehensive book, *What I Believe* provides readers with what *Booklist* reviewer Ilene Cooper praised as a "knowledgeable, friendly . . . overview of eight world religions." Told from the point of view of eight young people, the book discusses the history and practices at the core of Judaism, Christianity, Taoism, Shintoism, Hinduism, Islam, Buddhism, and Sikhism.

In his biographical work, Langley focuses on individuals from the broad historical spectrum. The ruler of Macedonia who conquered much of the ancient world is profiled in *Alexander the Great: The Greatest Ruler of the Ancient World,* while in *John F. Kennedy* he focuses on a popular U.S. president of the mid-twentieth century. Profiles of individuals who have chosen similar walks in life are the subject of such volumes as *Twenty Explorers, Twenty Names in Pop Music,* and *Twenty Names in Crime,* while in *Leonardo, Michelangelo,* and *Hans Christian Andersen: The Dreamer of Fairy Tales* delve into the life story of people who have contributed to the world's cultural fabric. In *Shakespeare's Theatre* Langley focuses on the life of a building rather than a person, creating what a *Publishers Weekly* contributor dubbed a "factual, focused and lively" history of the theatre in which William Shakespeare's famous plays were first produced. When the first structure burned down in 1613, it was rebuilt but survived only until 1644; it was finally rebuilt in a ten-year construction project that concluded in 1997, inspired by the vision of Shakespeare fan Sam Wanamaker.

Langley has received high praise for his "History of Britain" series, which covers the fifteenth century through modern times in titles such as *The Stuarts, 1603 to 1714, Modern Britain, 1901 to the 1990s,* and *The Blitz, 1939-1945.* In these works, the historian describes all aspects of British history—social, military, political—thoroughly and in a way that is understandable to young readers. Each book in the series contains illustrations as well an index, glossary, and time chart to help readers navigate Britain's past. A *Junior Bookshelf* critic called the "History of Britain" an "important" series that would be a useful library acquisition.

Langley's books range across the historical spectrum, and he delves into the increasingly distant past in *Medieval Life* and *The Roman News.* In sixty-four pages, *Medieval Life* provides readers with an overview of European life from the fifth through the fifteenth centuries.

While some reviewers felt that the overview approach does not present an adequate picture of medieval life and society for young students, others had high praise for the book, citing Langley's realistic portrayal of these interesting times. Norton Hodges, writing in *School Librarian,* praised in particular Langley's technique of giving credit to the roles played by women and the importance of Islamic cultural influences during the medieval era, and "wholeheartedly recommend[ed]" the book to "teachers, librarians and young readers."

Moving further back in time, *The Roman News,* which Langley co-wrote with Philip de Souza, represents a creative approach to teaching history to youngsters by covering historical events as if they were articles in a modern-day newspaper. Not only are far-reaching events such as the assassination of Julius Caesar and the Spartan invasion covered, but also items of social interest, such as slavery, sports, and clothing fashions. Advertisements and advice columns also appear, adding an element of fun and humor. For example, one article wryly suggests that you should always designate just one room in your home as a vomitorium. The book's "readable style, and interesting selection of subjects, makes it a good introduction to Roman history for older juniors and younger secondary children," suggested a *Junior Bookshelf* reviewer, while a *Booklist* contributor predicted that *The Roman News* will "encourage creative projects" and be useful to "students having difficulty with standard textual materials." Other ancient civilizations are covered in a more traditional fashion in books such as *Ancient Egypt,* which reveals Egyptian society through its artifacts. Part of the "History of Art" series, *Ancient Egypt* was praised by *School Arts* contributor Ken Maratz for its "clearly-written texts" and Langley's inclusion of timetables, index, and glossary.

Discussing his reason for dedicating his career to teaching young people about history, Langley once told *SATA:* "The study of history is endlessly fascinating and frequently enthralling, but an area of staggering ignorance for a huge number of people (especially Americans). Only by understanding the past can we hope to understand the present. I hope that my books—in a very modern way—aid that understanding."

Biographical and Critical Sources

PERIODICALS

Appraisal, winter, 1988, p. 67; summer, 1985, p. 49; fall, 1993, pp. 85-86.
Booklist, January 1, 1991, pp. 917, 919; October 1, 1996, review of *The Roman News,* p. 345; August, 1998, Carolyn Phelan, review of *Alexander the Great,* p. 1995; July, 1999, Randy Meyer, review of *Shakespeare's Theatre,* p. 1944; October 1, 1999, Ilene Cooper, review of *What I Believe: A Young Person's Guide to the Religions of the World,* p. 371.

Bulletin of the Center for Children's Books, October, 1988, p. 45.

Growing Point, January, 1988, p. 4919.

Junior Bookshelf, February, 1985, review of *Georgian Britain,* p. 38; August, 1994, p. 145; October, 1994, pp. 181-182; August, 1995, pp. 145-146; December, 1996, review of *The Roman News,* p. 270.

Kirkus Reviews, May 15, 1996, p. 746.

Publishers Weekly, August 12, 1996, p. 84; July 12, 1999, review of *Shakespeare's Theatre,* p. 94.

Resource Links, October, 1999, review of *Renaissance,* p. 19.

School Arts, March, 2005, Ken Marantz, review of *Michelangelo,* p. 72; April, 2005, Ken Marantz, review of *Ancient Egypt,* p. 47.

School Librarian, May, 1988, p. 60; August, 1996, Norton Hodges, review of *Medieval Life,* p. 112; autumn, 1999, review of *Animals and Plants,* p. 131, and *Shakespeare's Theatre,* p. 160l.

School Library Journal, February, 1990, p. 96; January, 1995, p. 127; July, 1996, p. 92; January, 1999, Esther C. Ball, review of *Hans Christian Andersen,* p. 117; April, 1999, Megan McGuire, review of *Castle of War,* p. 150; September, 1999, Barbara Buckley, review of *Renaissance,* p. 236; October, 1999, Sally Margolis, review of *Shakespeare's Theatre,* p. 171; February, 2000, Linda Beck, review of *What I Believe,* p. 108; February, 2001, John Peters, review of *The Oxford First Book of Space,* p. 113; August, 2003, Barbara Auerbach, review of *First Fun Atlas,* p. 110; January, 2004, Judith Constantinides, review of *Athens,* p. 150.

Science Books and Films, May, 1997, p. 120.

Times Educational Supplement, November 25, 1983, p. 29; March 9, 1984, p. 51; June 12, 1985, p. 21.*

*   *   *

LAVALLEE, Barbara 1941-

Personal

Born November 6, 1941, in Davenport, IA; daughter of Clarence H. (a Protestant minister) and Dorothy (a teacher; maiden name, Keeler) Koehler; married Thomas H. Lavallee (a teacher and counselor), October 22, 1965 (divorced, 1981); children: Charles, Mark. *Education:* Illinois Wesleyan University, B.F.A., 1964. *Hobbies and other interests:* "Travel: anytime, anywhere."

Addresses

Home—Anchorage, AK. *Office*—1026 W. 4th Ave., Anchorage, AK 99501. *Agent*—c/o Author Mail, Chronicle Books, 86 2nd St., 6th Fl., San Francisco, CA 94105.

Career

U.S. Army Service Club, Lenggries, Germany, recreational specialist, 1964-65; social worker in hospital for the mentally handicapped, 1965-66, and for an adoption agency, Portland, ME, 1966-67; Job Corps Center for

Women, Poland Spring, ME, counselor, 1967-69; art teacher for Bureau of Indian Affairs, on Navajo Reservation, 1969-70, and at Mount Edgecumbe native school, Sitka, AK, 1970-75; self-employed artist in Anchorage, AK, 1975—. Vice president of Girdwood Parent Teacher Association (PTA), 1983-84. *Exhibitions:* Work exhibited in galleries in Alaska, including Annie Kaill's Gallery, Juneau, AJm and Artique, Ltd., Anchorage.

Member

Society of Children's Book Writers and Illustrators.

Awards, Honors

Tomas Rivera Mexican-American Children's Book Award nomination, 1996, for *Uno, Dos, Tres = One, Two, Three,* by Pat Mora; Golden Kite Award, Society of Children's Book Writers and Illustrators, and National Association of Parenting Publications Award, both 1991, and ABC Children's Booksellers Choice Award, 1992, all for *Mama, Do You Love Me?,* by Barbara M. Joosse; Charlotte Zolotow Award Highly Commended designation, 2003, for *All You Need Is a Snowman* by Alice Schertle.

Illustrator

FOR CHILDREN

Freya Littledale, *The Snow Child,* Scholastic (New York, NY), 1989.

Barbara M. Joosse, *Mama, Do You Love Me?,* Chronicle Books (San Francisco, CA), 1991, tenth anniversary edition, 2000.

Pat Mora, *Uno, Dos, Tres = One, Two, Three,* Clarion Books (New York, NY), 1996.

Kristine L. Franklin, *The Gift,* Chronicle Books (San Francisco, CA), 1999.

Alice Schertle, *All You Need for a Snowman,* Harcourt (San Diego, CA), 2002.

Tricia Brown, *Groucho's Eyebrow,* Alaska Northwest Books (Anchorage, AK), 2003.

Alice Schertle, *All You Need for a Beach,* Silver Whistle (Orlando, FL), 2004.

Barbara M. Joosse, *Papa, Do You Love Me?,* Chronicle Books (San Francisco, CA), 2005.

"IMAGINE LIVING HERE"

Vicki Cobb, *This Place Is Cold: Alaska,* Walker (New York, NY), 1989.

Vicki Cobb, *This Place Is Dry: Arizona's Sonoran Desert,* Walker (New York, NY), 1989.

Vicki Cobb, *This Place Is Wet: The Brazilian Rain Forest,* Walker (New York, NY), 1990.

Vicki Cobb, *This Place Is High: The Andes Mountains of South America,* Walker (New York, NY), 1990.

Vicki Cobb, *This Place Is Lonely: Australia,* Walker (New York, NY), 1991.

Vicki Cobb, *This Place Is Crowded: Japan,* Walker (New York, NY), 1992.

Vicki Cobb, *This Place Is Wild: East Africa,* Walker (New York, NY), 1998.

OTHER

Cecilia Nibeck, *Salmon Recipes from Alaska* (cookbook), AK Enterprises, 1987.

Cecilia Nibeck, *Alaskan Halibut Recipes* (cookbook), AK Enterprises, 1989.

(With B.G. Olson) *Barbara Lavallee's Painted Ladies: And Other Celebrations,* Epicenter Press (Fairbanks, AK), 1995.

Sidelights

Barbara Lavallee is an award-winning illustrator who has received praise for her artistic collaborations with several picture-book authors. Together with Barbara M. Joosse, she produced *Mama, Do You Love Me?,* Joosse's story in which a young Inuit girl presents her mother with mischievous situations. The little girl is curious as to whether her mother would still love her if she were to carry out any of these troublemaking propositions. As Lavalle once told *SATA, Mama, Do You Love Me?* "was an illustrator's dream: a universal concept couched in the trappings of a culture and people that continue to fascinate me after over twenty years of living in Alaska." Noted for including the fine details of Inuit life in her illustrations, Lavallee's watercolor illustrations contribute to the book's sensitive portrait of a loving relationship between mother and daughter, and they won the Golden Kite Award in 1991.

In addition to working with Joosse on a follow-up work, *Papa, Do You Love Me,?* Lavallee has also teamed with friend and author Vicki Cobb for the "Imagine Living Here" series of books. Including titles such as *This Place Is Lonely: Australia, This Place Is Cold: Alaska, This Place Is Wet: The Brazilian Rain Forest,* these books relate what life is like in various countries and climates around the world.

"I am undeniably the product of my life's experiences," Lavallee once explained to *SATA:* "a 1950s Midwest childhood with three sisters and a strong, courageous mother who put our lives back together after the death of my father; an adventurous husband who encouraged me to sometimes go beyond the limits of comfort; my beloved sons, who shared their childhood with a single parent; and the roller coaster ride of making a living as a freelance artist. My family remains a strong influence on my life and work."

In describing how she came to her chosen profession, the artist recalled: "I have always known I wanted to 'do' art, but it was only after I moved to Alaska, fell in love with the land, its people, and fascinating native

Lavallee's round-cheeked characters move to the seashore, enjoying the sand and sun in Alice Schertle's 2004 picture book **All You Need for a Beach.**

cultures, that I knew I wanted to be an artist. I majored in art in college and had experience teaching art. When it became time to do my first book, I read Uri Schulevitz's book *Writing with Pictures* to get an idea of how to go about illustrating a book. I found it to be a wonderful resource, a worthy recommendation to anyone who is interested in illustrating."

Lavallee's first illustration projects were cookbooks, but she moved to children's books after teaming with Cobb to create the "Imagine Living Here" series. In fact, she credits Cobb as being a mentor of sorts: "I have worked closely with her throughout the "Imagine Living Here" series, and we have developed a working relationship in which we discuss the kinds of things each of us would like to include in our books. I love to travel and have had the opportunity to experience bits of Peru, Bolivia, Brazil, Australia, and Japan while researching books with Vicki."

Other books featuring Lavallee's artwork include *Groucho's Eyebrows,* a picture book by Tricia Brown that focuses on a beloved kitten who becomes lost in the snow while playing outside with her human companion, a young girl named Kristie. Reviewing the book, *ChildrensLit.com* contributor Laura Hummmel wrote that Lavallee's "soft, breezy watercolors . . . capture the loving emotions and wintry scenes." Collaborating with Alice Shertle, she has illustrated both *All You Need for a Snowman* and *All You Need for a Beach,* both of which find young children engaged in outdoor play that involves teamwork. *Horn Book* writer Joanna Rudge Long noted of the first book that, through her "ebullient" art, Lavallee "clearly understands the serious joys of making snowmen in superabundant snow," while Gillian Engberg commented in *Booklist* that Shertle's rhyming text in *All You Need for a Beach* is "nicely matched by [Lavallee's] sun-baked watercolors."

"Painting is so much a part of my life that it is impossible to separate art from lifestyle," Lavallee once explained, describing the steps necessary to complete each piece of art. "I find a book requires total concentration, so I clear my decks of any other work before starting on a new book. The first piece of work I do on a manuscript is research, so that authentic details can become part of the characters and story. Then a storyboard needs to be done. The storyboard breaks the text down into

pages and action concepts that will occur on each page. I never work on pages in sequence—I always do the one with the strongest, most well developed image (consequently, the easiest one) first. One of the aspects of illustrating I like most is the freedom I'm given by both the author and the editor to create the initial sketches without influence to do it the way either of them sees it."

"Alaska is a huge place, with a diverse and exotic history," Lavallee once noted, describing her rather unusual adopted home. "I have lived here for twenty-three years, and I am still overwhelmed by its staggering beauty. Visual overload is commonplace but never boring or plagued with sameness. The Alaskan native cultures are also extremely diverse, with many differences due to geographic placement within the state. The extraordinary arts practiced by each of these native groups symbolize universal concepts as well as the basic hu-

Lavallee's graphic, eye-catching illustrations for Pat Mora's Uno, Dos, Tres = One, Two, Three *introduce young readers to the Spanish language.*

man need to decorate those things that surround one's life. Most of all, the idea that a group of people have managed for generations to exist—and flourish—in a harsh and unforgiving environment, speaks of a culture that has conceptualized working together for the survival of the group. Because of modern life, much of these traditional concepts are changing and the dilemma of adapting to these changes is the greatest challenge to Alaska's natives. I believe that although a way of life may be lost, the art forms of these cultures will survive and continue to be practiced."

Lavallee enjoys the challenge of illustrating books that feature cultures that area unfamiliar to her, "because," as she once explained to *SATA,* "they frequently require travel and research, which in turn enriches my life and experiences." Her illustrations for one such work, Pat Mora's *Uno, Dos, Tres = One, Two, Three,* bring to life a Mexican marketplace in what *Booklist* writer Annie Ayers described as "luminous watercolors" that "vibrantly dance with the text." "My work has always reflected my interest in people," Lavallee added: "how they live, what they do. I prefer to portray the magnificence of man, his joy and humor, his tenacity, and his ability to overcome. I want my work to illustrate without being illustrative, something a viewer can 'get lost in' as well as relate to. . . . I feel it is the role of the illustration to enhance and enrich the text."

Biographical and Critical Sources

PERIODICALS

Booklist, June 1, 1996, Annie Ayers, review of *Uno Dos, Tres = One, Two, Three,* p. 1736; November 15, 1998, Isabel Schon, review of *Mama, Do You Love Me?,* p. 599; July, 2004, Gillian Engberg, review of *All You Need for a Beach,* p. 1848.

Horn Book, May-June, 1996, Maeve Visser Knoth, review of *Uno, Dos, Tres = One, Two, Three,* p. 327; November-December, 2002, Joanna Rudge Long, review of *All You Need for a Snowman,* p. 739.

Publishers Weekly, November 15, 1999, review of *The Gift,* p. 65; October 21, 2002, review of *All You Need for a Snowman,* p. 73.

ONLINE

ChildrensLit.com, http://www.childrenslit.com/ (April 28, 2005), Marilyn Courtot, "Barbara Lavallee."*

*   *   *

LEVITHAN, David 1972-

Personal

Born 1972, in Short Hills, NJ. *Education:* Brown University, B.A., 1994. *Hobbies and other interests:* Photography.

Addresses

Office—Scholastic, 557 Broadway, New York, NY 10012-3999. *E-mail*—david@davidlevithan.com.

Career

Writer; Scholastic, New York, NY, editorial director of Push imprint. New School University Graduate School of Creative Writing, New York, NY, professor of children's and teen literature.

Writings

(Editor) *You Are Here, This Is Now: The Best Young Writers and Artists in America: A Push Anthology,* Scholastic (New York, NY), 2002.

Boy Meets Boy, Knopf (New York, NY), 2003.

The Realm of Possibility, Random House (New York, NY), 2004.

Are We There Yet?, Knopf (New York, NY), 2005.

Marly's Ghost: A Remix of Charles Dickens' A Christmas Carol, illustrated by Brian Selznick, Dial (New York, NY), 2005.

(Editor, with Ann M. Martin) *Friends: Stories about New Friends, Old Friends, and Unexpectedly True Friends,* Scholastic (New York, NY), 2005.

(Editor) *When We Are, What We See: A Push Anthology,* Scholastic (New York, NY), 2005.

(With Rachel Cohn) *Nick and Norah's Infinite Playlist,* Knopf (New York, NY), 2006.

(Editor, with Billy Merrell) *The Full Spectrum: A New Generation of Writing about Gay, Lesbian, Bisexual, Transgender, Questioning, and Other Identities,* Knopf (New York, NY), 2006.

Wide Awake, Knopf (New York, NY), 2006.

Contributor to anthologies, including *Everything Man for Himself,* edited by Nancy Mercato; *Sixteen,* edited by Megan McCafferty, Three Rivers Press, 2004, and *What a Song Can Do,* edited by Jennifer Armstrong, Knopf, 2004.

MEDIA TIE-INS

The Mummy: A Junior Novelization (based on the motion picture by Stephen Sommers), Scholastic (New York, NY), 1999.

(With Anne Downey and James Preller) *The Mummy: Movie Scrapbook,* Scholastic (New York, NY), 1999.

101 Ways to Get away with Anything! (based on the television series *Malcolm in the Middle*), Scholastic (New York, NY), 2001.

101 Ways to Stop Being Bored (based on the television series *Malcolm in the Middle*), Scholastic (New York, NY), 2003.

Charlie's Angels: Full Throttle (based on the motion picture by John August), Aladdin (New York, NY), 2003.

The Perfect Score (based on the motion picture by Mark Hyman and Jon Zack), Simon Spotlight (New York, NY), 2004.

Also author of a novelization of the movie *Ten Things I Hate about You* and spin-off books based on the movie *The Sixth Sense.*

Work in Progress
More novels.

Sidelights
David Levithan has written several novels for teens and young adults, as well as novelizations of movies and television-show tie-ins. Several of his novels actually began as short stories written as Valentine's Day gifts for friends, a tradition he began many years ago; his novels *Boy Meets Boy*, *The Realm of Possibility,* and *Are We There Yet?* all got their start this way. Along with his work as a writer, Levithan works as editorial director and executive editor at Scholastic, where his responsibilities include editing the entire Push imprint. A line of books focusing on new voices and new authors in young-adult fiction, Push led to Levithan's editorship of the anthology *You Are Here, This Is Now:*

The voices of twenty teens dealing with life and love in a modern high school are woven into a compelling narrative in Levithan's 2004 work.

The Best Young Artists and Writers in America: A Push Anthology, which was the first book-length work to feature his name on its cover.

Levithan's first original novel, *Boy Meets Boy,* is set in a utopian high school where all students are tolerated, regardless of their sexual preference. At this high school, the football quarterback is also a drag queen, and narrator Paul is in the middle of a tricky romance. He has just broken up with Kyle and is beginning a new relationship with Noah, but Noah suspects Paul of being unfaithful, and Paul has to prove his feelings for Noah. According to Michael Rosen in the London *Guardian,* Levithan has "written a book that cunningly superimposes some previously unwritten-about feelings and behaviour on to a thoroughly familiar frame." Rosen went on to compare *Boy Meets Boy* to the popular teen romances set in the fictional Sweet Valley High, and television shows such as *Saved by the Bell* and concluded that the novel "is intimate, feel-good, and quick-fire." Michael Cart, writing in *Booklist,* considered *Boy Meets Boy* to be "the first upbeat gay novel for teens," while Johanna Lewis pointed out in *School Library Journal* that "Levithan's prophecy of a hate-free world in which everyone loves without persecution makes this a provocative and important read." *Lambda*

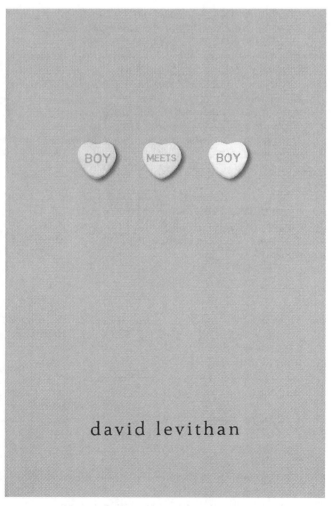

Adolescence is especially confusing for high-school sophomore Paul when he begins to realize that his friendship with Noah is more than just platonic in Levithan's highly acclaimed 2003 novel.

reviewer Nancy Garden saw the book less as prophetic than as an achievable goal: "We are treated to a glimpse of what life can and should be for GLBT kids, and what, in some enlightened parts of the country, it to a large extent already is."

The Realm of Possibility, Levithan's second novel, is a series of linked poems, taking the perspectives of twenty students from the same high school to create a communal picture of what their lives are like. The perspectives of a wide variety of teens, from the outsiders to the most popular, give details about friendship, relationships, and changes that happen during high school. The book begins with a poem by Daniel and wraps up with a poem by his boyfriend, Jed. Though initially, the poems seem to stand alone, connections can be drawn among them to form a narrative. Miranda Doyle, writing in *School Library Journal,* called *The Realm of Possibility* an "enchanting collection of linked poems that delve deep and go far beyond the original stereotypes." John Green, a contributor to *Booklist,* considered the book a "hugely ambitious novel in verse," noting that while some teen readers will be frustrated by the structure, "the distinct voices and plethora of poetic styles make for interesting reading."

The relationship between two brothers is the focus of Levithan's *Are We There Yet?* Seventeen-year-old Elijah and his older brother, Danny, an advertising executive, are tricked into taking a trip to Italy together by their parents. While their parents feel it will be good for the brothers to bond, Elijah and Danny believe they are so different that they share little common ground. When Elijah falls for a college dropout named Julia, it seems like true love, but Julia is interested in Danny as well. The story alternates point of view from Elijah to Danny, so that each brother's experience is fleshed out. Calling the novel "insightful and gently humorous," *School Library Journal* reviewer Susan Riley commented that Levithan "gets better and better with each book." A *Kirkus Reviews* contributor wrote that the author "works his magic creating two real and round narrators in a series of poetic vignettes."

When asked by an interviewer on the Barnes & Noble Web site to give his advice for writers waiting to be discovered, Levithan commented: "Don't write to be published. Write because it's something you want (or have) to write."

Biographical and Critical Sources

PERIODICALS

Booklist, August, 2003, Michael Cart, review of *Boy Meets Boy,* p. 1980; January 1, 2004, review of *Boy Meets Boy,* p. 779; September 1, 2004, John Green, review of *The Realm of Possibility,* p. 108.

Guardian (London, England), April 15, 2005, Michael Rosen, review of *Boy Meets Boy.*

Although Elijah and Danny are brothers, they can't be more different; at least, that's what the teens think until their parents send them on a trip to Italy, where their separate friendship with the same girl changes everything.

Horn Book, January-February, 2004, Roger Sutton, review of *Boy Meets Boy,* p. 83.

Kirkus Reviews, August 15, 2003, review of *Boy Meets Boy,* p. 1075; July 15, 2004, review of *The Realm of Possibility,* p. 689; July 1, 2005, review of *Are We There Yet?,* p. 738.

Lambda Book Report, March-April, 2004, Nancy Garden, "Brave New World," p. 32.

Publishers Weekly, October 6, 2003, review of *Boy Meets Boy,* p. 85; April 11, 2005, John F. Baker, "YA Stars Combine on Novel," p. 16; July 11, 2005, audiobook review of *Boy Meets Boy,* p. 97.

School Librarian, summer, 2005, Gerry McSourley, review of *Boy Meets Boy,* p. 103.

School Library Journal, September, 2003, Johanna Lewis, review of *Boy Meets Boy,* p. 216; June, 2004, Angela M. Boccuzzi, review of *The Perfect Score,* p. 145; September, 2004, Miranda Doyle, review of *The Realm of Possibility,* p. 211; April, 2005, review of *The Realm of Possibility,* p. S72; July, 2005, Susan Riley, review of *Are We There Yet?,* p. 105.

Voice of Youth Advocates, April, 2005, Nancy Zachary, review of *The Realm of Possibility,* p. 14.

ONLINE

Barnes & Noble Web site, http://www.bn.com/ (December 20, 2005), interview with Levithan.

David Levithan Home Page, http://www.davidlevithan.com (November 30, 2005).

Teen Reads.com, http://www.teenreads.com/ (November 30, 2005), "David Levithan."

*   *   *

LUDWIG, Trudy 1959-

Personal

Born June 29, 1959, in New Bedford, MA; daughter of Herbert (a construction consultant) and Ethyle (a marriage and family therapist; maiden name Kauffman) Ludwig; married Brad Long (a footwear project engineer) October 27, 1991; children: Allie, Bennett. *Education:* Attended University of New Hampshire, 1977-79; University of California, Santa Barbara, B.A. (communications and Spanish), 1981.

Addresses

Office—Ludwig Creative, Inc., P.O. Box 25505, Portland, OR 97298-0505. *E-mail*—trudy@trudyludwig.com.

Career

Children's author and lecturer. Bilingual immigration consultant, 1982-85; Carnegie Mellon University, Pittsburgh, PA, projects manager and editor of *Accent on Research,* 1985-88; senior advertising/marketing copywriter in Lynwood, WA, 1988-92; freelance copywriter and editor, 1992-2002. Volunteer and speaker for Full Esteem Ahead. Has appeared on television programs, including *Good Morning America* and *Keeping Kids Healthy.*

Member

Society of Children's Book Writers and Illustrators, Willamette Writers.

Awards, Honors

Phi Beta Kappa honors, University of New Hampshire, 1980; Silver CASE National Award, Council for the Advancement and Support of Education, and Women in Communications Matrix award honorable mention, both 1988, both for *Accent on Research;* CUNA Diamond Award of Merit, 2002.

Writings

My Secret Bully, illustrated by Abigail Marble, RiverWood Books (Ashland, OR), 2003.

Just Kidding, illustrated by Adam Gustavson, Tricycle Press (Berkeley, CA), 2005.

Sorry!, illustrated by Maurie Manning, Tricycle Press (Berkeley, CA), 2006.

Trudy Ludwig

Author's work has been translated into Spanish.

Sidelights

Trudy Ludwig told *SATA:* "Throughout my earlier career as an advertising/marketing copywriter, I never quite felt passionate about my craft. I knew I loved to write. I just didn't love what I was writing.

"My creative life turned around when my daughter, who was seven at the time, became the target of bullying friends. It was one of those experiences that had a profound impact on the both of us. I didn't want to fight my daughter's battles; I wanted to give her the social skills and tools she would need to fight her own battles in life.

"In my search for age-appropriate books to address the very real and rampant problem of social cruelty among peers, I came up empty-handed. Frustrated with this resource gap, I wrote *My Secret Bully,* my first children's book, to help empower my daughter and many children like her to make healthier friendship choices. It was such a rewarding and energizing experience for me that I quit my freelance copywriting career to focus on making a difference in kids' lives, one book at a time.

"Because the social world of today's children is very complex and difficult to navigate, I try to incorporate into my stories the wisdom and insights of young readers, so that my books resonate with the authenticity of real life experiences and views. I also have the added pleasure of tapping into my own inner child—letting her laugh, cry, and simply breathe. I've finally reached the point where I not only love to write, I truly love what I'm writing."

Biographical and Critical Sources

PERIODICALS

School Library Journal, January, 2004, Rosalyn Pierini, review of *My Secret Bully,* p. 100.

ONLINE

Books to Grow With Newsletter Online, http://www.lutra press.com/ (April, 2005).

Embracing the Child Web site, http://www.embracingthe child.com/ (March 24, 2004), interview with Ludwig.

My Secret Bully Web site, http://www.mysecretbully.com/ (November 6, 2005).

Ten Speed Press/Tricycle Press Web site, http://www. tenspeed press.com/ (November 6, 2005), "Trudy Ludwig."

Trudy Ludwig Web site, http://www.trudyludwig.com (December 12, 2005).

M

MADDERN, Eric 1950-

Personal

Born 1950, in Whyalla, South Australia, Australia; father a bricklayer. *Education:* University of Sheffield, degree (social psychology).

Addresses

Home and office—Cae Mabon, Fachwen, Llanberis, Gwynedd LL55 3HB, Wales. *E-mail*—eric@fachwen.org.

Career

Singer, songwriter, storyteller, and writer. Commonwealth Institute, former exhibition educational coordinator; business communication facilitator and communications consultant. Tutor at storytelling retreats; performer at storytelling festivals throughout the world.

Writings

Earth Story, illustrated by Leo Duff, Barron's (Hauppauge, NY), 1988.

Life Story, illustrated by Leo Duff, Barron's (Hauppauge, NY), 1988.

Curious Clownfish, illustrated by Adrienne Kennaway, Little, Brown (Boston, MA), 1990.

Rainbow Bird: An Aboriginal Folktale from Northern Australia, illustrated by Adrienne Kennaway, Francis Lincoln (London, England), 1996.

The Fire Children: A West African Creation Tale, pictures by Frané Lessac, Dial Books for Young Readers (New York, NY), 1993.

(With Helen East) *Spirit of the Forest: Tree Tales from around the World,* illustrated by Alan Marks, Francis Lincoln (London, England), 2003.

The King with Horse's Ears, illustrated by Paul Hess, Francis Lincoln (London, England), 2003.

Death in a Nut, illustrated by Paul Hess, Frances Lincoln (London, England), 2005.

The Cow on the Roof, illustrated by Paul Hess, Frances Lincoln (London, England), 2006.

Author of song lyrics performed on *Full of Life: Earth-Songs for All* (CD), produced by Calum MacColl, 2003.

Sidelights

Author, storyteller, songwriter, and performing artist Eric Maddern has entertained and educated children throughout the world. Spending his early childhood in Whyalla, South Australia, where his father worked as a bricklayer, Maddern moved at age eleven to Great Britain following his mother's death. After graduating from college, he spent a decade traveling the world and studying dance, voice, theatre, massage, yoga, and meditation. Becoming involved in community arts while working with Aboriginal people in central Australia, he eventually returned to London, where his job for the Commonwealth Institute as an exhibition coordinator developed into a career as a storyteller, songwriter, and speaker. Through his storytelling, Maddern has also turned to writing, and has produced such children's books as *The King with Horse's Ears, Rainbow Bird: An Aboriginal Folktale from Northern Australia,* and *The Fire Children: A West African Creation Tale.*

The Fire Children tells the story of man's arrival upon the earth. Aso Yaa and Kwaku Ananse were living happily inside the sky god Nyame, until one day when the great god sneezed, sending the pair flying down to Earth by accident. To aid in combating their loneliness, Aso Yaa decides to build children using the clay around them, but the couple hide these children when Nyame comes down from above to visit. One of their hiding spots is a fire, where they place the statues until the jealous god has left. After Nyame returns to the sky, the couple breath life into the clay statues, populating the world with children with skin of a variety of shades, depending on how long they had been hidden in the fire. "Perfect for sharing with a group, this book is an exciting addition to the growing list of multicultural resources for children," commented reviewer Ellen Fader in *Horn Book,* while a *Publishers Weekly* critic praised *The Fire Children* as "elegantly told, gorgeously illustrated and conveying a timely but unforced message."

In **Death in a Nut** *Maddern retells a traditional Scottish tale about a young man who rids the world of death, only to find that life loses meaning without balance. (Illustration by Paul Hess.)*

Other books by Maddern include *Death in a Nut,* a retelling of a Scottish story that finds a young boy who, worried over the health of his sickly mother, meets up with Death during a walk on the beach near his home. When Death asks for directions to his home, the boy captures the raggedy creature in a nut, then throws Death out to sea. Although his mother soon seems cured, other things act oddly, and the boy realizes that getting rid of Death means ending life as well.

A porquois tale from Australia, *Rainbow Bird* explains how man gained the use of fire. As the story opens, greedy Crocodile Man keeps all the firesticks for himself. When the covetous creature begins to fall asleep, watchful Bird Woman swoops down from a nearby tree and carries off the firesticks, distributing them to the rest of mankind. "Maddern's gracefully honed text makes this one for storytellers to cherish," noted Julie Corsaro in her review for *Booklist.*

Biographical and Critical Sources

PERIODICALS

Booklist, October 15, 1993, Julie Corsaro, review of *Rainbow Bird: An Aboriginal Folktale from Northern Australia,* p. 447; July, 1993, Janice Del Negro, review of *The Fire Children: A West African Creation Tale,* p. 1971.

Bulletin of the Center for Children's Books, June, 1993, review of *The Fire Children,* p. 322.

Horn Book, September-October, 1993, Ellen Fader, review of *The Fire Children,* p. 610.

Instructor, May, 1994, review of *The Fire Children,* p. 65; January, 1995, review of *The Fire Children,* p. 87.

Kirkus Reviews, December 15, 2004, review of *Death in a Nut,* p. 1205.

Language Arts, December, 1993, review of *The Fire Children,* p. 678.

Magpies, March, 2005, Barbara James, review of *Death in a Nut,* p. 32.

Publishers Weekly, February 14, 2005, review of *Death in a Nut,* p. 76; June 7, 1993, review of *The Fire Children,* p. 69.

Reading Teacher, March, 1995, review of *The Fire Children,* p. 513.

School Library Journal, March, 1994, Linda Boyles, review of *Rainbow Bird: An Aboriginal Folktale from Northern Australia,* p. 217; August, 1993, Lyn Miller-Lachmann, review of *The Fire Children,* p. 160; July, 1990, Jane Marino, review of *Curious Clownfish,* p. 61.

Wilson Library Bulletin, September, 1993, Donnarae Mac-Cann and Olga Richard, review of *The Fire Children,* p. 87.

ONLINE

Eric Maddern Home Page, http://www.ericmaddern.co.uk (November 6, 2005).

Northern Children's Book Festival Web site, http://www.ncbf.org.uk/ (November 6, 2005), "Eric Maddern."

* * *

MANUSHKIN, Fran 1942-
(Frances Manushkin)

Personal

Surname is pronounced "Ma-*nush*-kin"; born November 2, 1942, in Chicago, IL; daughter of Meyer (a furniture salesman) and Beatrice (Kessler) Manushkin. *Education:* Attended University of Illinois and Roosevelt University; Chicago Teachers College, North Campus (now Northeastern Illinois University), B.A., 1964. *Religion:* Jewish. *Hobbies and other interests:* Travel, travel, travel! Swimming, bird watching, cat watching, reading, book collecting, snorkeling, theatergoing.

Addresses

Home and office—121 E. 88th St., Apt. 4C, New York, NY 10128. *Agent*—Amy Berkower, Writers House, 21 W. 26th St., New York, NY 10010. *E-mail*—fran@franmanushkin.com.

Career

Writer. Elementary teacher in Chicago, IL, 1964-65; Lincoln Center for Performing Arts, New York, NY, tour guide, 1966; Holt, Rinehart & Winston, Inc., New York, NY, secretary to college psychology editor, 1967-68; Harper & Row Publishers, Inc., New York, NY, secretary, 1968-72, associate editor of Harper Junior Books, 1973-78; Random House Inc, New York, NY, editor of Clubhouse K-2 (student paperback-book club), 1978-80. Mentor to adult writers in Eastern Europe through International Step-by-Step Association.

Fran Manushkin

Member

PEN, Author's League of America, Author's Guild, Society of Children's Book Writers and Illustrators, National Audubon Society.

Awards, Honors

Notable Children's Book citation, Association of Jewish Libraries, 2000, for *Come Let Us Be Joyful: The Story of Hava Nagila.*

Writings

FOR CHILDREN

Baby, illustrated by Ronald Himler, Harper (New York, NY), 1972, published as *Baby, Come Out!,* 1984, reprinted, Star Bright Books (New York, NY), 2002.

Bubblebath!, illustrated by Ronald Himler, Harper (New York, NY), 1974.

Shirleybird, illustrated by Carl Stuart, Harper (New York, NY), 1975.

Swinging and Swinging, illustrated by Thomas DiGrazia, Harper (New York, NY), 1976.

The Perfect Christmas Picture, illustrated by Karen A. Weinhaus, Harper (New York, NY), 1980.

Annie Finds Sandy, illustrated by George Wildman, Random House (New York, NY), 1981.

Annie Goes to the Jungle, illustrated by George Wildman, Random House (New York, NY), 1981.

Annie and the Desert Treasure, illustrated by George Wildman, Random House (New York, NY), 1982.

Annie and the Party Thieves, illustrated by George Wildman, Random House (New York, NY), 1982.

Moon Dragon, illustrated by Geoffrey Hayes, Macmillan (New York, NY), 1982.

The Tickle Tree, illustrated by Yuri Salzman, Houghton (Boston, MA), 1982.

The Roller Coaster Ghost, illustrated by Dave Ross, Scholastic (New York, NY), 1983.

Hocus and Pocus at the Circus, illustrated by Geoffrey Hayes, Harper (New York, NY), 1983.

The Adventures of Cap'n O.G. Readmore: To the Tune of "The Cat Came Back," illustrated by Manny Campana, Scholastic (New York, NY), 1984.

Buster Loves Buttons, illustrated by Dirk Zimmer, Harper (New York, NY), 1985.

Jumping Jacky, illustrated by Carolyn Bracken, Golden Books (New York, NY), 1986.

(With Lucy Bate) *Little Rabbit's Baby Brother,* illustrated by Diane de Groat, Crown (New York, NY), 1986.

Ketchup, Catch Up!, illustrated by Julie Durrell, Golden Books (New York, NY), 1987.

Beach Day, illustrated by Kathy Wilburn, Western Publishing (Racine, WI), 1988.

Puppies and Kittens, illustrated by Ruth Sanderson, Golden Books (New York, NY), 1989.

Latkes and Applesauce: A Hanukkah Story, illustrated by Robin Spowart, Scholastic (New York, NY), 1990.

(Compiler) *Glow in the Dark Mother Goose,* illustrated by Mary Grace Eubank, Western Publishing (Racine, WI), 1990.

(With Lucy Bate) *Be Brave, Baby Rabbit,* illustrated by Diane de Groat, Crown (New York, NY), 1990.

(Adaptor) *Walt Disney Pictures Presents: The Prince and the Pauper* (based on the film), illustrated by Russell Schroeder and Don Williams, Western Publishing (Racine, WI), 1990.

Hello World: Travel along with Mickey and His Friends, illustrated by Juan Ortiz and Phil Bliss, Disney Press (New York, NY), 1991.

Walt Disney's 101 Dalmatians: A Counting Book, illustrated by Russell Hicks, Disney Press (New York, NY), 1991.

The Best Toy of All, illustrated by Robin Ballard, Dutton (New York, NY), 1992.

My Christmas Safari, illustrated by R. W. Alley, Dial (New York, NY), 1993.

(Compiler) *Somebody Loves You: Poems of Friendship and Love,* illustrated by Jeff Shelly, Disney Press (New York, NY), 1993.

Let's Go Riding in Our Strollers, illustrated by Benrei Huang, Hyperion (New York, NY), 1993.

Peeping and Sleeping, illustrated by Jennifer Plecas, Clarion (New York, NY), 1994.

The Matzah That Papa Brought Home, illustrated by Ned Bittinger, Scholastic (New York, NY), 1995.

Starlight and Candles: The Joys of the Sabbath, illustrated by Jacqueline Chwast, Simon & Schuster (New York, NY), 1995.

Miriam's Cup: A Passover Story, illustrated by Bob Dacey, Scholastic (New York, NY), 1998.

Come, Let Us Be Joyful!: The Story of Hava Nagilah, illustrated by Rosalind Charney Kaye, UAHC Press (New York, NY), 2000.

Sophie and the Shofar: A New Year's Story, illustrated by Rosalind Charney Kaye, UAHC Press (New York, NY), 2001.

Daughters of Fire: Heroines of the Bible, illustrated by Uri Shulevitz, Harcourt Brace (San Diego, CA), 2001.

Hooray for Hanukkah!, Random House (New York, NY), 2001.

The Little Sleepyhead, illustrated by Leonid Gore, Dutton (New York, NY), 2004.

(With George Foreman) *George Forman: Let George Do It!,* illustrated by Whitney Martin, Simon & Schuster (New York, NY), 2005.

NOVELS; "ANGEL CORNERS" SERIES; FOR CHILDREN

Rachel, Meet Your Angel, Puffin (New York, NY), 1995.
Toby Takes the Cake, Puffin (New York, NY), 1995.
Lulu's Mixed-Up Movie, Puffin (New York, NY), 1995.
Val McCall, Ace Reporter?, Puffin (New York, NY), 1995.

Work in Progress

"BRRR!" Said the Shivers, illustrated by Paul Zelinsky; *Grandma Beatrice Brings Sprink to Minsk,* illustrated by Holly Berry; and *The Tushy Book,* illustrated by Pascal Lemaitre.

Sidelights

Fran Manushkin is the author of numerous books for young readers. Noted for her whimsical imagination and her lovingly drawn characters, Manushkin's works range from such entertaining picture books as *Baby, Moon Dragon,* and *The Tickle Tree* to novels like *Lulu's Mixed-Up Movie* and *Val McCall, Ace Reporter?,* both part of her "Angel Corners" series for girls. In addition, she is the author of several books that portray children and their parents celebrating both Jewish and Christian holidays. In a writing career that has spanned over two decades, Manushkin provides young children with a window on a world where even the simplest things are transformed into joyous events.

Born in Chicago, Illinois, in 1942, Manushkin never thought she would grow up to be an author. Instead, upon graduating from high school, she went to college and earned a teaching certificate. After a four-month stint as a substitute teacher, however, Manushkin decided to abandon the idea of a career in teaching. What she really wanted was to live in New York City, and a job at the Illinois pavilion during the 1964 World's Fair got her there. After the fair ended, Manushkin remained in Manhattan and began a new career, this time in publishing. She worked for a series of book publishers, including Holt, Rinehart & Winston, Harper & Row, and Random House, where she met a host of people who inspired her to try her hand at writing books for children.

Manushkin's first book, *Baby,* was published in 1972; proving perennially popular with readers, it was reissued as *Baby, Come Out!* in 1984 and has been translated into eight other languages. *Baby* is the lighthearted story of a not-quite-yet-born baby who decides that Mom's tummy suits her just fine—until Daddy comes home promising kisses that she cannot feel. *Horn Book* reviewer Sidney D. Long praised Manushkin's first effort as a "special book for mothers-to-be to share with their other children."

"My stories tend to grow from a single image," Manushkin once told *SATA*. "*Baby*, for example, blossomed from an image I had in my head of a mother communicating with her newborn baby. That image metamorphosed into a mother communicating with the child she is carrying in her womb. When the child said, 'I don't want to be born,' it just happened. I did not plan it. I didn't have a plot in mind." Before she became a writer herself, Manushkin believed that books "existed in a pure state in author's heads," with their endings perfectly well thought out. "That simply isn't true," she explained. "Books develop according to their own time. You cannot dictate that a book be born; neither can you dictate to a book. Listen," she added, "really listen, and your book will speak."

Baby was the first of many imaginative books that Manushkin has written for children, each one evolving out of an image or idea. In *Swinging and Swinging* a young girl on a swing soon finds that she has passen-

gers; first a soft, puffy cloud, then the cheery sun, the moon, and a rain of stars join her. As she drifts into a drowsy half-sleep the moon and stars climb back up into the sky and night falls. In *The Tickle Tree* a young squirrel in the mood for a belly-grabbing tickle gets his friends to stack up and help him reach the top of a feather-leafed palm tree—which causes such a giggle that the animal tower soon topples like a laughing house of cards.

"Whether you know it or not, every book you write is about yourself," Manushkin explained. "*Hocus and Pocus at the Circus*, for example, is about my sister and myself—but I'm not telling who the nice sister is!" Geared for beginning readers, *Hocus and Pocus at the Circus* is about two witches—one mean, the other nice—who are busy laying plans for Halloween night. While Hocus plots to cause havoc at a circus, Pocus misspeaks her spells and ends up adding to the circus-goers' fun by turning rubber balls into puppies and her-

The Little Sleepyhead, a gentle story about a toddler who searches for a place to sleep in a newly created world, is brought to life through Leonid Gore's comforting pastel drawings.

self into a squealing baby pig, and ends the evening by shooting her sister out of a cannon (harmlessly, of course!). A world where magic is possible also figures in *Moon Dragon,* a trickster tale wherein a tiny mouse devises a way to fool a huge, fire-breathing dragon that has eaten everything in sight and now wants the mouse for dessert. Noting that the author's "magic touch invests all her stories," a *Publishers Weekly* reviewer wrote that *Moon Dragon* "is one of [Manushkin's] best."

Manushkin has also written a number of well-received picture books for preschoolers, including *Let's Go Riding in Our Strollers* and *Peeping and Sleeping.* Featuring a lively, rhyming verse text, *Let's Go Riding in Our Strollers* presents all of the excitement of the urban outdoors as seen through the eyes of toddlers in strollers on their adventurous trip to the park. *Booklist* reviewer Ilene Cooper praised Manushkin's "exuberant text" in *Let's Go Riding in Our Strollers,* concluding that the book is "fun to look at and to read." *Peeping and Sleeping* centers on a peeping noise that is keeping little Barry awake. Barry's father takes the young child out to the pond to investigate, and soon the boy's fears turn to curiosity and wonder at the busy activities of nocturnal creatures. *School Library Journal* contributor Lisa Wu Stowe praised "Manushkin's wonderfully realistic dialogue and evocative descriptions of a warm spring night's walk" in *Peeping and Sleeping.* A *Publishers Weekly* reviewer maintained: "Especially well captured is the trembling mixture of fear and giddiness that accompanies children's nighttime excursions." In another favorable estimation, *Booklist* reviewer Hazel Rochman asserted: "Although rooted in reality, the story with its gentle reversals creates a sense of hidden wonder, of magic and mischief in a hushed nighttime landscape."

Some of Manushkin's books for younger readers are designed as bedtime stories. *The Little Sleepyhead* features a young troublemaker who, after a day at play, wants to find a soft place to sleep. But grass tickles him, trees are too bumpy, and the bear snores. The child is eventually able to find a bed of feathers, and coaxes a lamb to snuggle with him as he drifts off to sleep. "The last sentence makes it perfect for the last story before bed," noted a critic for *Kirkus Reviews.* A *Publishers Weekly* contributor noted that Manushkin has created "an appealing toddler-size adventure, casting her spell from the opening words."

Manushkin also teamed up with celebrity George Foreman on a book for young readers, *Let George Do It!,* which recounts misadventures in the real-life Foreman family, where all the boys and their father are named George. "Youngsters will find plenty of laughs in the premise," promised a *Publishers Weekly* reviewer.

For older readers, Manushkin has created the "Angel Corners" series, which takes place in the town of Angel Corners and also has guardian angels as characters. In

Manushkin joins forces with boxing champion George Foreman in telling the lighthearted tale **Let George Do It!,** *about a father, Big George, who names each of his sons George. (Illustration by Whitney Martin.)*

Rachel, Meet Your Angel, the first book of the series, a lonely fifth grader who finds herself friendless after a move to a new town suddenly finds Merribel, a guardian-angel apprentice, looking over her shoulder. Things soon start to improve for Rachel; she meets three friends and together the girls find a way to raise the money needed to repair the town clock. "Middle-grade girls whose taste in novels runs to the fanciful will find the inaugural novel in the Angel Corners series a fun—if flighty—read," asserted a *Publishers Weekly* commentator. Other books in the series, each of which feature a different girl and her guardian angel, include *Toby Takes the Cake* and *Lulu's Mixed-Up Movie.*

In addition to her purely fictional tales, Manushkin has written several books that weave warm, joyous imagery into tradition-based religious holidays. Although Manushkin grew up in a Jewish home and is, herself, Jewish, her first holiday tales revolved around Christmas, including *My Christmas Safari,* a retelling of the "Twelve Days of Christmas" using African jungle motifs, and *The Perfect Christmas Picture.* The latter title, which tells the story of perplexed photographer Mr. Green attempting to get his whole family together for a holiday snapshot, "is about my family—the way I wish my family had been," the author explained to *SATA.* "I suppose the 'message' in that book has to do with acceptance in a rather odd, madcap family." The Green family is indeed madcap; the picture-taking process

In Daughters of Fire: Heroines of the Bible *Manushkin retells ten stories about courageous women who influenced Jewish history. (Illustration by Uri Shulevitz.)*

lasts a full nine months due to the fact that it is constantly thwarted by giggling, pinching, blinking eyes, and countless other minor disasters. *Horn Book* reviewer Mary M. Burns praised Manushkin for the "pleasant, unhackneyed lilt" she brings to the book's text.

Manushkin has written books about traditional Jewish holidays as well. Among these are *The Matzah That Papa Brought Home, Miriam's Cup,* and *Hooray for Hanukkah!* Reviews of *The Matzah That Papa Brought Home* characterize the favorable critical reception of these works. A cumulative Passover tale for preschoolers and beginning readers, the picture book was dubbed "a unique, lively offering" by *School Library Journal* contributor Marcia Posner. Stephanie Zvirin, in *Booklist,*

maintained that "what the book actually does best is convey the feeling of closeness and community engendered by the celebration." *Miriam's Cup* compares a young girl named Miriam to her Biblical namesake in a retelling of the story of Passover. A *Publishers Weekly* reviewer felt that the book is "likely to become a favorite holiday read-aloud." *Hooray for Hanukkah!* explains the traditions of the winter holiday from the perspective of the family menorah. A *School Library Journal* reviewer called the book "a sweetly old-fashioned story." Several of Manushkin's other titles also have Jewish themes; *Come Let Us Be Joyful: The Story of Hava Nagila* explains the history of a popular Jewish song, and *Sophie and the Shofar* is a tale of family, the High Holy Days, and the traditional blowing of the shofar.

Manushkin confessed in an interview with Kathleen O'Grady on the *Women's Studies Resources at the University of Iowa Web site* that she was, at first, nervous about writing picture books about Judaism; her anxieties came to a head when she began working on *Daughters of Fire*. "I was terrified to do this book," she told O'Grady. "I thought only men with grey beards were allowed to write Jewish books." Unlike Manushkin's previous stories of Jewish tradition, *Daughters of Fire* collects the stories of ten women of the Hebrew Bible, revealing for young readers the history of Judaism as told from a feminine point of view. The tales of Eve, Miriam, Hannah, Queen Esther, and others are fleshed out by combining scripture with Jewish legends and folklore, giving them "the richness and complexity of the wider Jewish traditions," according to a reviewer for *Publishers Weekly*. "This is the longest book I've ever written," Manushkin told O'Grady, and explained, "It took me so long to realize that I had as much right to write these stories as so many other people." Amy Lilien-Harper noted in *School Library Journal* that "the author's lyrical, slightly old-fashioned writing fits her topic," while GraceAnne A. DeCandido, writing for *Booklist*, felt that in *Daughters of Fire* Manushkin "adds a spirited freshness to the tales."

Manushkin once offered to *SATA* her advice for young writers-to-be: "In my years as a writer and editor I have learned a few things I would like to pass on: don't give up on a book even if lots of editors reject it, keep sending it around . . . and don't be nervous if you've started writing something but don't know where it is going—be willing to discover the book as it evolves."

Biographical and Critical Sources

PERIODICALS

Booklist, June 1, 1993, Ilene Cooper, review of *Let's Go Riding in Our Strollers*, p. 1858; July, 1993, p. 1971; June, 1994, Hazel Rochman, review of *Peeping and Sleeping*, p. 1841; January 15, 1995, Stephanie Zvirin, review of *The Matzah That Papa Brought Home*, p. 937; December 15, 2001, GraceAnne A. DeCandido, review of *Daughters of Fire: Heroines of the Bible*, p. 726; May 1, 2004, "Good Night, Sleep Tight," p. 1563.
Bulletin of the Center for Children's Books, April 1972, p. 127; September 1980, p. 16; September 1982, p. 16; February 1983, p. 113; November 1990, pp. 64-65; January, 2002, review of *Daughters of Fire*, p. 178.
Horn Book, June, 1972, Sidney D. Long, review of *Baby*, p. 261; December 1980, Mary M. Burns, review of *The Perfect Christmas Picture*, p. 626.
Junior Bookshelf, August, 1978, p. 188.
Kirkus Reviews, March 15, 1972, p. 321; May 1, 1974, p. 476; August 15, 1982, p. 935; October 15, 1993, p. 1332; July 15, 1995, p. 1028; September 1, 2001, review of *Daughters of Fire*, p. 1296; May 1, 2004, review of *The Little Sleepyhead*, p. 445; May 1, 2005, review of *Let George Do It!*, p. 538.

Publishers Weekly, April 30, 1982, review of *Moon Dragon*, p. 59; July 25, 1986, p. 186; September 14, 1990, p. 123; September 20, 1993, p. 34; April 25, 1994, review of *Peeping and Sleeping*, p. 77; February 6, 1995, review of *Rachel, Meet Your Angel!*, p. 86; December 22, 1997, review of *Miriam's Cup: A Passover Story*, p. 54; August 27, 2001, review of *Daughters of Fire*, p. 81; September 24, 2001, review of *Hooray for Hanukkah!*, p. 48; May 31, 2004, review of *The Little Sleepyhead*, p. 73; May 23, 2005, review of *Let George Do It!*, p. 77.
Quill & Quire, December, 1990, p. 19.
Reading Teacher, April, 1999, review of *Miriam's Cup*, p. 762.
School Library Journal, November, 1976, p. 50; June, 1992, p. 99; October, 1992, p. 46; June, 1994, Lisa Wu Stowe, review of *Peeping and Sleeping*, p. 110; February, 1995, Marcia Posner, review of *The Matzah That Papa Brought Home*, p. 76; February, 1998, Susan Pine, review of *Miriam's Cup*, p. 88; October, 2001, Amy Lilien-Harper, review of *Daughters of Fire*, p. 188; October, 2001, review of *Hooray for Hanukkah!*, p. 67; January, 2002, Linda R. Silver, review of *Sophie and the Shofar: A New Year's Story*, p. 106; September, 2004, Shelley B. Sutherland, review of *The Little Sleepyhead*, p. 173.
Social Education, May, 1999, review of *Miriam's Cup*, p. 14.

ONLINE

Fran Manushkin Home Page, http://www.franmanushkin.com (December 1, 2005).
Women's Studies Resources at the University of Iowa Web site, http://bailiwick.lib.uiowa.edu/wstudies/ (September 15, 2004), Kathleen O'Grady, interview with Manushkin.

*   *   *

MANUSHKIN, Frances
See MANUSHKIN, Fran

*   *   *

MITCHELL, Adrian 1932-
(Volcano Jones, Apeman Mudgeon, Gerald Stimpson)

Personal

Born October 24, 1932, in London, England; son of James (a research chemist) and Kathleen (a nursery school teacher; maiden name, Fabian) Mitchell; married second wife Celia Hewitt (an actress and bookseller); children: (first marriage) Alistair, Danny, Briony; (second marriage) Sasha, Beattie. *Education:* Studied at Christ Church, Oxford. *Politics:* Pacifist. *Religion:* "The arts."

Addresses

Agent—c/o PFD, Drury House, 34-43 Russell St., London WC2B 5HA, England.

Career

Poet, playwright, and fiction writer. *Oxford Mail,* Oxford, England, former reporter; *Evening Standard,* London, England, reporter; freelance journalist; freelance writer, beginning mid-1960s. University of Iowa, instructor at writers' workshop, 1963-67; University of Lancaster, Granada fellow in the arts, 1967-69; Wesleyan University Center for the Arts, fellow, 1972; Sherman Theatre, Cardiff, Wales, resident writer, 1974-75; Billericay Comprehensive School, visiting writer, 1974-75; Cambridge University Judith E. Wilson fellow, 1980-81; Unicorn Theatre for Children, resident writer, 1982-83; Nayang University, Singapore, fellow in drama, 1995; Dylan Thomas fellow, Swansea, 1995. *Military service:* Royal Air Force, compulsory service, c. 1950.

Member

Royal Society of Literature (fellow).

Awards, Honors

Eric Gregory Award, 1961; PEN Translation Prize (co-recipient), 1966, for *Marat/Sade;* Tokyo Festival television film award, 1971; Gold Medal of the Theatre of Poetry (Varna, Bulgaria); honorary doctorate, North London University, 1997; named *Red Pepper* magazine Shadow Poet laureate, 2002; Poetry Book Society Best Collection of Children's Poetry designation, 2004, and CLPE Poetry Award shortlist, 2005, both for *Daft as a Doughnut.*

Writings

FOR CHILDREN

Nothingmas Day, Allison & Busby (London, England), 1984.

The Baron Rides Out: The Adventures of Baron Munchausen as He Told Them to Adrian Mitchell, illustrated by Patrick Benson, Walker (London, England), 1985.

The Baron on the Island of Cheese: More Adventures of Baron Munchausen, illustrated by Patrick Benson, Walker (London, England), 1986.

The Baron All at Sea: More Adventures of Baron Munchausen, illustrated by Patrick Benson, Walker (London, England), 1987.

Our Mammoth, illustrated by Priscilla Lamont, Walker (London, England), 1987.

Our Mammoth Goes to School, illustrated by Priscilla Lamont, Walker (London, England), 1987.

Our Mammoth in the Snow, illustrated by Priscilla Lamont, Walker (London, England), 1987.

(Compiler) *Strawberry Drums: A Book of Poems with a Beat for You and All Your Friends to Keep,* illustrated by Frances Lloyd, Macdonald Children's (Hove, England), 1989, Delacorte (New York, NY), 1991.

All My Own Stuff (poems), illustrated by F. Lloyd, Simon & Schuster (New York, NY), 1991.

(Editor) *The Orchard Book of Poems,* Orchard Books (London, England), 1993.

(Compiler) *The Thirteen Secrets of Poetry,* Simon & Schuster (New York, NY), 1993.

(Reteller) Hans Christian Andersen, *The Ugly Duckling,* illustrated by Jonathan Heale, DK Publishing (London, England), 1994.

Gynormous!: The Ultimate Book of Giants, illustrated by Sally Gardner, Orion Children's Books (London, England), 1996.

Maudie and the Green Children, illustrated by Sigune Hamann, Tradewind, 1996.

(Reteller) Hans Christian Andersen, *The Steadfast Tin Soldier,* illustrated by Jonathan Heale, DK Publications (London, England), 1996.

Balloon Lagoon and Other Magic Islands of Poetry, illustrated by Tony Ross, Orchard Books (London, England), 1997.

(Reteller) *The Adventures of Robin Hood and Marian,* illustrated by Emma Chichester Clark, Orchard Books (London, England), 1998.

Twice My Size, illustrated by Daniel Pudles, Bloomsbury (London, England), 1998, Millbrook Press (Brookfield, CT), 1999.

My Cat, Mrs Christmas, illustrated by Sophy Williams, Orion Children's Books (London, England), 1998.

Dancing in the Street: A Poetry Party, illustrated by Tony Ross, Orchard Books (London, England), 1999.

Daft as a Doughnut, illustrated by Tony Ross, Orchard Books (London, England), 1999.

(Reteller) *The Odyssey,* illustrated by Stuart Robertson, Dorling Kindersley (New York, NY), 2000.

Nobody Rides the Unicorn, illustrated by Stephen Lambert, Arthur A. Levine Books (New York, NY), 2000.

(Reteller) *The Snow Queen,* illustrated by Nilesh Mistry, Dorling Kindersley (New York, NY), 2000.

(Selector) *A Poem a Day,* illustrations by Russell Ayto and others, Orchard Books (London, England), 2001.

(With Daisy) *Zoo of Dreams* (poetry), Orchard Books (London, England), 2001.

Poetry and lyrics recorded by Mitchell on *The Dogfather,* 57 Production (London, England), 2000; poems recorded for British Library Archives (London, England), 2005.

PLAYS; FOR CHILDREN

(Author of lyrics) *George Orwell's Animal Farm* (musical), adapted by Peter Hall, music by Richard Peaslee, Methuen (London, England), 1985.

(Adapter) *The Pied Piper,* Oberon (London, England), 1988.

(Adapter) *The Wild Animal Song Contest; and, Mowgli's Jungle,* introduction and activities by Alison Jenkins, Heinemann Educational (Oxford, England), 1993.

(Adapter) *The Snow Queen,* Oberon (London, England), 1998.

(Adapter) *The Lion, the Witch, and the Wardrobe* (based on the novel by C.S. Lewis), Oberon (London, England), 1998.

Tom Kitten and His Friends (musical; based on the work of Beatrix Potter), music by Stephen McNuff, Samuel French (London, England), 1998.

The Mammoth Sails Tonight! (musical), music by Peter Moser, Oberon (London, England), 1999.

(Adapter) Lewis Carroll, *Alice in Wonderland and Through the Looking Glass,* Oberon (London, England), 2001.

(Adapter) *Vasilisa the Fair* (based on *The Frog Princess and Other Russian Folk Tales,* by Sophia Prokofieva), Samuel French (New York, NY), 2003.

(Adapter) *Two Beatrix Potter Plays: Jemima Puddle-Duck and Her Friends; Peter Rabbit and His Friends,* Oberon (London, England), 2004.

Aladdin, produced in Belfast, Ireland, 2004.

Robin Hood and Marian (adapted from his children's book), produced in Troy, NY, 2005.

Also co-author, with Sasha Mitchell, of puppet-show adaptation of his children's book *Nobody Rides the Unicorn,* 2005. Author of puppet show *Perseus and the Gorgon's Head,* 2006.

POETRY; FOR ADULTS

[Poems] Fantasy Poets No. 24, Fantasy Press, 1955.

Poems, J. Cape (London, England), 1962.

Peace Is Milk, Housmans, 1966.

Out Loud, Cape Goliard (London, England), 1968, published as *The Annotated Out Loud,* Writers and Readers Publishing Cooperative, 1976.

Ride the Nightmare: Verse and Prose, J. Cape (London, England), 1971.

(With John Fuller and Peter Levi) *Penguin Modern Poets 22,* Penguin (Harmondsworth, England), 1973.

The Apeman Cometh: Poems, J. Cape (London, England), 1975.

For Beauty Douglas: Collected Poems 1953-1979, pictures by Ralph Steadman, Allison & Busby (London, England), 1982.

On the Beach at Cambridge: New Poems, Allison & Busby (London, England), 1984.

(Editor with Leonie Kramer) *The Oxford Anthology of Australian Literature,* Oxford University Press (Oxford, England), 1985.

Love Songs of World War Three, Allison & Busby (London, England), 1989.

Adrian Mitchell's Greatest Hits: His Forty Golden Greats, Bloodaxe (Newcastle on Tyne, England), 1991.

Blue Coffee: Poems 1985-1996, Bloodaxe (Newcastle on Tyne, England), 1996.

Heart on the Left: Poems, 1953-1984, illustrated by Ralph Steadman, Bloodaxe (Newcastle on Tyne, England), 1997.

All Shook Up: Poems 1997-2000, Dufour Editions (Chester Springs, PA), 2000.

(Editor with Andy Croft) *Red Sky at Night: An Anthology of British Socialist Poetry,* Five Leaves, 2003.

The Shadow Knows: Poems 2000-2004, Bloodaxe (Tarset, Northumberland, England), 2004.

Poems recorded on *Adrian Mitchell's Greatest Hits* (with Peter Mosher).

PLAYS; FOR ADULTS

(Translator and verse adaptor, with Geoffrey Skelton) Peter Weiss, *The Marat/Sade,* adapted by Peter Brooks, Atheneum (New York, NY), 1966.

Tyger: A Celebration Based on the Life and Work of William Blake, J. Cape (London, England), 1971.

Man Friday, music by Mike Westbrook; *Mind Your Head: A Return Trip with Songs,* music by Andy Roberts, Methuen (London, England), 1974.

(Adapter) Pedro Calderon de la Barca, *The Mayor of Zalamea; or, The Best Garrotting Ever Done,* Salamander Press (Edinburgh, Scotland), 1981 published in *Three Plays by Calderon: The Mayor of Zalamea, Life's a Dream,* and *The Great Theatre of the World,* Oberon (London, England), 1998.

(Editor) Dylan Thomas, *A Child's Christmas in Wales: Christmas Musical,* adapted by Jeremy Brooks, Dramatic Publishing Company (London, England), 1984.

(With Berta Freistadt and Deborah Levy) *Peace Plays,* Methuen (London, England), 1988.

(Adapter) Lope de Vega, *Fuente Ovejuna; Lost in a Mirror (It Serves Them Right),* Aris & Phillips, 1989, published in *Two Plays by Lope da Vega: Fuente Ovejuna* and *Lost in a Mirror,* Oberon (London, England), 1998.

(Adapter) Nikolai V. Gogol, *The Government Inspector,* Methuen (London, England), 1989.

The Patchwork Girl of Oz, Dramatic Publishing Company (London, England), 1994.

(Adapter) Pedro Calderon de la Barca, *The Great Theatre of the World,* Dramatic Publishing (London, England), 1994 published in *Three Plays by Calderon: The Mayor of Zalamea, Life's a Dream,* and *The Great Theatre of the World,* Oberon (London, England), 1998.

(Editor) Pedro Calderon de la Barca, *Life's a Dream,* adapted by John Barton, Dramatic Publishing (London, England), 1994 published in *Three Plays by Calderon: The Mayor of Zalamea, Life's a Dream,* and *The Great Theatre of the World,* Oberon (London, England), 1998.

Plays with Songs: Tyger Two, Man Friday, Satie Day/Night, In the Unlikely Event of an Emergency, Oberon (London, England), 1996.

The Siege: A Play with Songs, music by Andrew Dickson, Oberon (London, England), 1996.

Also author of libretti for operas, including *The Magic Flute,* 1966, and *Houdini,* 1977, for Netherlands Opera.

NOVELS; FOR ADULTS

If You See Me Comin', Macmillan (New York, NY), 1962.

The Bodyguard, J. Cape (London, England), 1970, Double-day (New York, NY), 1971.

Wartime, J. Cape (London, England), 1973, Doubleday (New York, NY), 1975.

OTHER

(Editor) *Blackbird Singing: Poems and Lyrics, 1965-1999,* W.W. Norton (New York, NY), 2001, revised as *Blackbird Singing: Poems and Lyrics, 1965-2001,* 2002.

Lyricist for play *US,* by Peter Brook. Translator and/or editor of various volumes of poems. Contributor of articles to the London *Guardian,* London *Daily Mail, New York Times, New Statesman, Observer, Sunday Times,* and *Peace News,* among other periodicals. Some works published under pseudonyms Volcano Jones, Apeman Mudgeon, and Gerald Stimpson.

Sidelights

British poet and playwright Adrian Mitchell gained notice in the 1960s as a performance poet whose works—including the verse collections *Peace Is Milk* and *Out Loud* and the plays *Tyger: A Celebration Based on the Life and Work of William Blake, Mind Your Head,* and *Man Friday*—resonate with pacifism and his belief in the empowerment of the common man amid the politicized artistic environment of the 1960s and 1970s. As Tony Silverman Zinman noted in the *Dictionary of Literary Biography,* all of Mitchell's works "express his idealistic socialism: his goal is not only to right the world's wrongs but also to establish contact with mass audiences." As Mitchell himself has said, "Most people ignore most poetry because most poetry ignores most people."

Increasingly, Mitchell's artistic efforts have turned toward children's literature, and specifically to drama, where his produced works include *The Pied Piper,* an adaptation of C.S. Lewis's *The Lion, the Witch, and the Wardrobe, Aladdin,* and *The Snow Queen.* As Mitchell explained to John-Paul Flintoff in the London *Financial Times,* he prefers writing plays for young people because "you get an audience without any theory or prejudice. And they're very easily bored, which they will show immediately. If they're hitting each other you know that part of the play needs fixing." Mitchell has also written volumes of poetry for young readers, has edited volumes of poetry, and has written several picture-book series, one about a prehistoric mammoth that shows up in the modern world and another retelling the adventures of German storyteller Baron Munchausen.

Mitchell was born in 1932 in London, the son of a research chemist and a teacher. Educated at Dauntsey's School in Wiltshire, he did one year of compulsory national service in the Royal Air Force before entering Christ Church, Oxford in 1952. At Oxford Mitchell originally planned to train as a teacher, he became heavily influenced by poets such as Alistair Elliott and during his third and last year there was literary editor of *Isis* magazine. An early pamphlet of Mitchell's poems appearing in 1955 and included "The Fox," a poem considered one of his best works. Mitchell was strongly influenced by nineteenth-century British poet William Blake, and eventually wrote a play about Blake's life.

After leaving Oxford, earning a living became paramount in Mitchell's life. He first found work as a reporter on the *Oxford Mail* and after a few years he moved to the London *Evening Standard.* Mitchell also wrote television and music reviews for other magazines and newspapers, all the while gaining a reputation for his poetry through readings and published poems. In his 1975 volume of poems, titled *The Apeman Cometh,* Mitchell first displayed his talent for writing for a youthful audience, including a section of fifteen poems headed "Mainly for Kids."

Mitchell's first volume of poetry for children, *Nothingmas Day,* appeared in 1984. Margery Fisher, writing in *Growing Point,* called these poems "entertaining verbal fireworks" that include puns, assonances, comic arrangement of lines and "inspired gobbledegook" such as the opening line from "My Last Nature Walk": "I strode among the clumihacken." In her review, Fisher concluded that Mitchell's work contains "space for the melancholy beneath nonsense, for innumerable individual reactions to ordinary matters." A *Junior Bookshelf* reviewer also praised *Nothingmas Day,* observing that Mitchell's poems have "that turn of phrase, that startling thought, that seductive sound . . . so attractive to the young child," and deeming the collection "a joy to handle, a delight to read, and a pleasure to look at."

In *All My Own Stuff* Mitchell assembles twenty-five poems "showing a variety of tones and moods," according to a writer in *Junior Bookshelf,* the critic adding that "the poetry is full of plays on words." Jocelyn Hanson commented in *School Librarian* that Mitchell's second collection for young readers ranges from "the silly to the profound," including "funny little verses and couplets, clever and amusing, quick to read and assimilate," and that "all demonstrate a love of the sound and shape of words." The poet's trademark playfulness can be found in lines such as "I am Boj/Organised Sludge and a Thunder-Wedge." Hanson concluded that *All My Own Stuff* "would be useful in demonstrating to children . . . how freely words can be used, manipulated and played with within the structures of poetry."

In addition to publishing his own poetry, Mitchell has collected and edited several poetry anthologies, among them *Strawberry Drums,* the teen poetry anthology *Dancing in the Street,* and *The Orchard Book of Poems. Strawberry Drums* was praised as "an engrossing and readable collection of poems" by a critic in *Junior Bookshelf.* In this work Mitchell collects poems from around the world, the poets included ranging from well-known British poets William Blake and Robert Graves to lyricists and former Beatles Paul McCartney and John Lennon to writings from the Navajo of the American Southwest, the Jakun of Malaysia. The *Junior Bookshelf* reviewer concluded that Mitchell's anthology projects "a freshness that is captivating," making it "a bubbly, effervescent anthology with golden oldies and new poems side by side." Jane Marino, writing in *School Library Journal,* found the collection to be a "far-flung, eclectic group of thirty poems that invites readers to celebrate words," while Pippa Rann called *Strawberry Drums* a "pleasingly varied collection," in *School Librarian.* Writing in the introduction to the volume, Mitchell commented: "I chose the poems . . . because they are bright and sweet like strawberries. And all of them have a beat—like drums." Rann noted in *School Librarian* that a central strength of the book is this introduction, in which Mitchell demonstrates for readers how to go about writing a poem.

The Orchard Book of Poems, a "fresh and beautifully produced collection," according to Pam Harwood in *Books for Keeps,* compiles poets ranging from John Keats to John Lennon, and organizes verses into sections such as "The Palace of People" and "The Dazzling City." Harwood called the anthology a "courageous blending of old favourites and new faces."

Mitchell's inventive word play and sense of the fantastic have also been channeled into picture books. In the "Baron" series, he adapts the tall tales about real-life eighteenth-century German adventurer Baron Munchausen, whose exploits were fictionalized by R.E. Raspe, to create his own version of events. *The Baron Rides Out,* which commenced the series, tells of the baron's forty-eight brothers and sisters, his magical horse, and his ship, which is drawn by seagulls. "Nobody need believe any of this," observed a reviewer for *Junior Bookshelf,* "but the stories are so fantastic that they are fun. Children accept them for what they are and enjoy them." Kenneth Marantz, writing in *School Library Journal,* concluded that, "for those who enjoy . . . [American folk hero] Paul Bunyan, this German teller of tall tales will be a special delight."

The Baron on the Island of Cheese provides "another series of ebullient adventures," according to a *Kirkus Reviews* critic, who concluded: "Mitchell embellishes the nonstop action with delicious asides. This may be the 18th-century verbal equivalent of the Saturday morning cartoons, but it's still fun." Reviewing this second title in the series, Constance A. Mellon noted in *School Library Journal* that "the book is clever, written in the clipped style typical of British humor." Mellon concluded that the book "would be a good extension of the folklore area, and, properly presented, would be of both literary and artistic value to children." Reviewing the third series installment, *The Baron All at Sea,* Nancy Palmer commented in *School Library Journal* that "Mitchell has cleaned up the original stories without sanitizing them; plenty of action remains, and nothing feels sapped or bowdlerized." In *The Baron All at Sea*

the baron heroically attempts to help a choir of 1,000 Africans return to Timbuktu, a feat that involves a shipwreck and confrontations with wolves and polar bears. "This will be a title of choice for check-out and for reading aloud," Palmer concluded.

Mitchell's second series of picture books includes *Our Mammoth, Our Mammoth Goes to School,* and *Our Mammoth in the Snow.* The Gumble twins are at the beach one day when a giant block of ice is washed ashore. As the ice melts, they discover that there is a mammoth inside. Awaking from its long deep-freeze, the mammoth becomes a giant, shaggy means of transport for the twins, carrying them to their house. The twins' unflappable mother accepts the beast into the household, preparing a buttercup pie for its sustenance. A *Publishers Weekly* critic noted that *Our Mammoth* "is both quirky and intriguing," and that "Mitchell's eloquent prose accentuates the story's deadpan humor."

The twins take their mastodon friend with them to school in *Our Mammoth Goes to School.* At first, the animal has a hard time, and is disliked by the headmaster because of its fleas, but soon the mammoth joins in a school outing and discovers kindred spirits in the elephants at the zoo. "This is another successful example of that familiar genre of the picture book, depicting the appearance of a monstrous monster who eventually becomes everybody's friend," observed William Edmonds in *School Librarian.* Margery Fisher maintained in *Growing Point* that *Our Mammoth Goes to School* pairs an "idiosyncratic text with explosive words and onomatopoeic phrases."

Among Mitchell's many books for children are retellings of stories by Hans Christian Andersen, such as *The Ugly Duckling* and *The Steadfast Tin Soldier.* Reviewing *The Ugly Duckling* for *School Librarian,* Jane Doonan declared, "Here's the art of the backward glance, in a handsome new edition of the old classic. . . . Mitchell's poetic retelling retains the sensuous quality of the original descriptions." Writing of *The Steadfast Tin Soldier* in the same periodical, Doonan noted that Mitchell retains the original intent of the noted Danish author while simplifying the text. "This is an illustrated book which could take today's children into a very different world," Doonan concluded, "although the theme, exploring the vulnerability of anyone who steadfastly loves another, is timeless." Janice M. Del Negro commented in the *Bulletin of the Center for Children's Books* that *The Steadfast Tin Soldier* "is a remarkably readable interpretation of Andersen's tragic fairy tale," and concluded: "It's sometimes difficult to make a case for yet another picture-book version of an often-retold fairy tale, but this unique interpretation is its own convincing argument."

Mitchell's imaginative flights have also take him to Sherwood Forest for *Adventures of Robin Hood and Marian,* as well as back in time to the ancient world for *The Odyssey,* a "smoothly written" version of the ancient story according to *School Library Journal* contributor Nancy Call. They have also inspired the poetry/ short-story compilation on giants titled *Gynormous!* as well as the collection *Daft as a Doughnut*, which was selected the best collection of children's poetry of 2004 by the Poetry Book Society. Another imaginative flight by Mitchell was recognized by the people voting in the 2004 National Poetry Day poll, which ranked the poet's "Human Beings" as the poem fans would most like to see launched into space as a way of communicating with other forms of life. A poem encouraging cultural tolerance and peace, "Human Beings" appeared in Mitchell's collection *The Shadow Knows: Poems 2000-2004* as well as being displayed at England's National Space Centre.

Whatever form Mitchell's work takes, be it poetry, drama, prose, or interstellar transmission, he retains his original conviction in the transformational power of words. His writing for children has been characterized as unpretentious and simple, and his empathy with young readers is apparent. For Mitchell, poetry and words are not just means of communication; they can change a reader's perception of the world.

Biographical and Critical Sources

BOOKS

The Cambridge Guide to Literature in English, Cambridge University Press (Cambridge, England), 1988.
Contemporary British Dramatists, St. James Press (Detroit, MI), 1994.
Contemporary Poets, 6th edition, St. James Press (Detroit, MI), 1996.
Dictionary of Literary Biography, Volume 40: Poets of Great Britain and Ireland since 1960, Thomson Gale (Detroit, MI), 1985, pp. 371-379.
Mitchell, Adrian, *All My Own Stuff,* Simon & Schuster (New York, NY), 1991.
Mitchell, Adrian, *Nothingmas Day,* Allison & Busby (London, England), 1984.
Mitchell, Adrian, *Strawberry Drums,* Delacorte (New York, NY), 1991.

PERIODICALS

Booklist, December 15, 1987, p. 711; March 15, 1992, p. 1330; November 1, 1996, p. 509; April 15, 2000, Lauren Peterson, review of *Twice My Size,* p. 1537.
Books for Keeps, January, 1997, Pam Harwood, review of *The Orchard Book of Poems,* p. 26.
Bulletin of the Center for Children's Books, January, 1988, p. 96; January, 1997, Janice M. Del Negro, review of *The Steadfast Tin Soldier,* p. 163; February, 2000, review of *Nobody Rides the Unicorn,* p. 216.
Financial Times (London, England), December 18, 2004, John-Paul Flintoff, "Adrien Mitchell Has Impressed and Offended with His Plays, Poems, and Opinions," p. 3.

Growing Point, January, 1985, Margery Fisher, "Sing, Perform or Just Listen," p. 4372; May, 1988, Margery Fisher, review of *Our Mammoth Goes to School,* p. 4993.
Junior Bookshelf, February, 1985, review of *Nothingmas Day,* p. 43; February, 1986, review of *The Baron Rides Out,* p. 17; October, 1986, p. 183; October, 1989, review of *Strawberry Drums,* pp. 229-230; October, 1991, review of *All My Own Stuff,* p. 226; February, 1997, Jane Doonan, review of *The Steadfast Tin Soldier,* p. 17.
Kirkus Reviews, September 15, 1986, review of *The Baron on the Island of Cheese,* p. 1451.
Magpies, March, 2002, review of *Zoo of Dreams,* p. 17, and *A Poem a Day,* p. 18.
Publishers Weekly, October 30, 1987, review of *Our Mammoth,* p. 68; April 24, 2000, review of *Nobody Rides the Unicorn,* p. 90.
School Librarian, November, 1987, pp. 323-324; February, 1992, p. 28; May, 1988, William Edmonds, review of *Our Mammoth Goes to School,* p. 54; November, 1989, Pippa Rann, review of *Strawberry Drums,* p. 158; November, 1991, Jocelyn Hanson, review of *All My Own Stuff,* p. 150; February, 1997, Jane Doonan, review of *The Steadfast Tin Soldier,* p. 17; autumn, 1999, review of *Dancing in the Street,* p. 152; spring, 2000, review of *Newbody Rides the Unicorn,* p. 19; winter, 2001, review of *A Poem a Day,* p. 209; summer, 2005, Sybill Hannavy, review of *Daft as a Doughnut,* p. 97.
School Library Journal, May, 1986, Kenneth Marantz, review of *The Baron Rides Out,* p. 82; January, 1987, Constance A. Mellon, review of *The Baron on the Island of Cheese,* p. 76; January, 1988, Nancy Palmer, review of *The Baron All at Sea,* pp. 67-68; March, 1988, pp. 171-172; August, 1988, p. 84; June, 1991, Jane Marino, review of *Strawberry Drums,* pp. 96-97; July, 1994, p. 73; January, 1997, p. 75; June, 1999, Sue Norris, review of *Twice My Size,* p. 103; September, 2000, Nancy Call, review of *The Odyssey,* p. 218; January, 2001, Carol Schene, review of *Nobody Rides the Unicorn,* p. 104.
Times Educational Supplement, May 12, 1989, p. B8; June 8, 1990, p. B16; August 20, 1993, p. 19; July 5, 1996, p. R2; October 3, 1997, p. B6.

ONLINE

British Council Web site, http://www.contemporarywriters.com/ (December 1, 2005), "Adrian Mitchell."
Ripping Yarns Web site, http://www.rippingyarns.com/ (December 1, 2005), "Adrian Mitchell."

*   *   *

MOON, Lily
See WARNES, Tim

MOORCOCK, Michael 1939-

(Bill Barclay, William Ewert Barclay, Michael Barrington, a joint pseudonym, Edward P. Bradbury, James Colvin, Philip James, a joint pseudonym, Michael John Moorcock, Desmond Reid, a house pseudonym)

Personal

Born December 18, 1939, in Mitcham, Surrey, England; son of Arthur and June (Taylor) Moorcock; married Hilary Bailey (a writer), September, 1962 (divorced, April, 1978); married Jill Riches, 1978 (divorced); married Linda Mullens Steele, September, 1983; children: (first marriage) Sophie, Katherine, Max. *Education:* Attended ten schools, including Michael Hall School, Sussex, and Pitman's College. *Hobbies and other interests:* Songwriting, performing in rock and roll bands.

Addresses

Home—Lost Pines, TX. *Agent*—c/o Howard Moreham, HML, 841 Broadway, New York, NY 10003.

Career

Writer and editor; has also worked as a singer/guitarist. Editor, *Tarzan Adventures* (juvenile magazine), 1956-58; Amalgamated Press, London, England, writer and editor for Sexton Blake Library and for comic strips and children's annuals, 1959-61; pamphleteer and editor, Liberal Party, 1962; *New Worlds* (science-fiction magazine), London, England, editor and publisher, 1964-70. Leader of rock band Michael Moorcock and the Deep Fix; also worked with bands Hawkwind and Blue Oyster Cult. *Military service:* Served in British Air Training Corps.

Member

Authors Guild, Fawcett Society, National Socialist Party for the Prevention of Cruelty to Children (council member), Royal Overseas League, SPLC (leadership council), Shelter.

Awards, Honors

Nebula Award, Science Fiction Writers of America, 1967, for *Behold the Man;* British Science Fiction Association Award, and Arts Council of Great Britain Award, both 1967, both for *New Worlds;* August Derleth Award, British Fantasy Society, 1972, for *The Knight of the Swords,* 1973, for *The King of the Swords,* 1974, for *The Jade Man's Eyes,* 1975, for *The Sword and the Stallion,* and 1976, for *The Hollow Lands;* International Fantasy Award, 1972, 1973, for fantasy novels; *Guardian* Fiction Prize, 1977, for *The Condition of Muzak;* John W. Campbell Memorial Award, 1978, and World Fantasy Award, World Fantasy Convention, 1979, both for *Gloriana; or, The Unfulfilled Queen;* Booker Prize nomination, for *Mother London;* Whitbread Award nomination, for *King of the City.*

Michael Moorcock

Writings

(With James Cawthorn, under house pseudonym Desmond Reid) *Caribbean Crisis,* Sexton Blake Library (London, England), 1962.

The Sundered Worlds, Compact Books (London, England), 1965, Paperback Library (New York, NY), 1966, published as *The Blood Red Game,* Sphere Books (London, England), 1970.

The Fireclown, Compact Books (London, England), 1965, Paperback Library (New York, NY), 1966, published as *The Winds of Limbo,* Sphere Books (London, England), 1970.

(Under pseudonym James Colvin) *The Deep Fix,* Compact Books (London, England), 1966.

The Wrecks of Time (bound with *Tramontane* by Emil Petaja), Ace (New York, NY), 1966, revised edition published separately as *The Rituals of Infinity,* Arrow Books (London, England), 1971.

The Twilight Man, Compact Books (London, England), 1966, Berkley Publishing (New York, NY), 1970, published as *The Shores of Death,* Sphere Books (London, England), 1970.

(Under pseudonym Bill Barclay) *Printer's Devil,* Compact Books (London, England), 1966, published under name Michael Moorcock as *The Russian Intelligence,* Savoy Books (Manchester, England), 1980.

(Under pseudonym Bill Barclay) *Somewhere in the Night,* Compact Books (London, England), 1966, revised edition published under name Michael Moorcock as *The Chinese Agent,* Macmillan (New York, NY), 1970.

(Co-author) Roger Harris, *The LSD Dossier,* Compact Books (London, England), 1966.

The Ice Schooner, Sphere Books (London, England), 1968, Berkley Publishing (New York, NY), 1969, revised edition, Harrap (Edinburgh, Scotland), 1985.

(With wife, Hilary Bailey) *The Black Corridor,* Ace (New York, NY), 1969.

The Time Dweller, Hart-Davis (London, England), 1969, Berkley Publishing (New York, NY), 1971.

(With James Cawthorn under joint pseudonym Philip James) *The Distant Suns,* Unicorn Bookshop (Brighton, England), 1975.

Moorcock's Book of Martyrs, Quartet Books (London, England), 1976, published as *Dying for Tomorrow,* DAW (New York, NY), 1978.

(With Michael Butterworth) *The Time of the Hawklords,* A. Ellis (Henley-on-Thames, England), 1976.

Sojan (juvenile), Savoy Books (Manchester, England), 1977.

Epic Pooh, British Fantasy Society, 1978.

Gloriana; or, The Unfulfilled Queen, Allison & Busby (London, England), 1978, Avon (New York, NY), 1979, reprinted, Aspect (New York, NY), 2004.

The Real Life of Mr. Newman, A.J. Callow, 1979.

The Golden Barge, DAW (New York, NY), 1980.

My Experiences in the Third World War, Savoy Books (Manchester, England), 1980.

The Retreat from Liberty: The Erosion of Democracy in Today's Britain, Zomba (London, England), 1983.

(With others) *Exploring Fantasy Worlds: Essays on Fantastic Literature,* edited by Darrell Schweitzer, Borgo Press (Rockville, MD), 1985.

Letters from Hollywood, Harrap (Edinburgh, Scotland), 1986.

(With James Cawthorn) *Fantasy: The One Hundred Best Books,* Carroll & Graf (New York, NY), 1988.

Mother London, Crown (New York, NY), 1989.

Wizardry and Wild Romance: A Study of Heroic Fantasy, Gollancz (London, England), 1989.

Casablanca, Gollancz (London, England), 1989.

Earl Aubec, and Other Stories, Millennium (London, England), 1993.

(Author of introduction) H.G. Wells, *The Time Machine* J.M. Dent (London, England), 1993.

Hawkmoon, White Wolf (Stone Mountain, GA), 1995.

(With Storm Constantine) *Silverheart* ("Eternal Champion" series), Simon & Schuster (New York, NY), 2000.

Blitz Kid (graphic novel), art by Walter Simonson and Bob Wiacek, DC Comics (New York, NY), 2001.

King of the City, William Morrow (New York, NY), 2000.

London Bone (short stories), Scribner (London, England), 2001.

(Author of afterword) Norman Spinrad, *Bug Jack Barron,* Overlook (Woodstock, NY), 2004.

Contributor, sometimes under pseudonyms, to *Punch, Ambit,* London *Times,* London *Guardian, New Statesman,* London *Daily Telegraph,* and other publications. Writer of comic strips for DC Comics and Dark Horse Comics, 1957-64, and with *Michael Moorcock's Multiverse,* DC Comics, 1997. Credited with providing ideas for books by Michael Butterworth, *Queens of Deliria* and *The Time of the Hawklords,* Collectors Guides, 1995.

"ELRIC" SERIES; "ETERNAL CHAMPION" BOOKS

The Stealer of Souls, and Other Stories (also see below), Neville Spearman (London, England), 1963, Lancer Books (New York, NY), 1967.

Stormbringer, Jenkins, 1965, Lancer Books (New York, NY), 1967.

The Singing Citadel (also see below), Berkley Publishing (New York, NY), 1970.

The Sleeping Sorceress, New English Library (London, England), 1971, Lancer Books (New York, NY), 1972, published as *The Vanishing Tower,* DAW (New York, NY), 1977.

The Dreaming City, Lancer Books (New York, NY), 1972, published as *Elric of Melnibone,* Hutchinson (London, England), 1972.

The Jade Man's Eyes, Unicorn Bookshop (Brighton, England), 1973.

Elric: The Return to Melnibone, Unicorn Bookshop (Brighton, England), 1973, published in graphic-novel format, Jayde Design (London, England), 1997, novel reprinted, Gollancz (London, England) 2001.

The Sailor on the Seas of Fate, DAW (New York, NY), 1976.

The Bane of the Black Sword, DAW (New York, NY), 1977.

The Weird of the White Wolf (contains some material from *The Stealer of Souls, and Other Stories* and *The Singing Citadel*), DAW (New York, NY), 1977.

Elric at the End of Time, DAW (New York, NY), 1985.

The Fortress of the Pearl, Ace (New York, NY), 1989.

The Revenge of the Rose, Ace (New York, NY), 1991.

Stormbringer (contains *The Sleeping Sorceress, The Revenge of the Rose, The Stealer of Souls and Other Stories, Kings in Darkness,* and *The Caravan of Forgotten Dreams*), Orion (London, England), 1997.

The Dreamthief's Daughter, Earthlight (London, England), 2001, published as *The Dreamthief's Daughter: A Tale of the Albino,* Warner (New York, NY), 2001.

The Skrayling Tree: The Albino in America, Warner (New York, NY), 2003.

The White Wolf's Son: The Albino Underground, Warner (New York, NY), 2005.

"MICHAEL KANE" SERIES; UNDER PSEUDONYM EDWARD P. BRADBURY

Warriors of Mars (also see below), Compact Books (London, England), 1965, published under name Michael Moorcock as *The City of the Beast,* Lancer Books (New York, NY), 1970.

Blades of Mars (also see below), Compact Books (London, England), 1965, published under name Michael Moorcock as *The Lord of the Spiders,* Lancer Books (New York, NY), 1971.

The Barbarians of Mars (also see below), Compact Books (London, England), 1965, published under name Michael Moorcock as *The Masters of the Pit,* Lancer Books (New York, NY), 1971.

Warrior of Mars (contains *Warriors of Mars, Blades of Mars,* and *The Barbarians of Mars*), New English Library (London, England), 1981.

"HISTORY OF THE RUNESTAFF" SERIES

The Jewel in the Skull (also see below), Lancer Books (New York, NY), 1967.

Sorcerer's Amulet (also see below), Lancer Books (New York, NY), 1968, published as *The Mad God's Amulet,* Mayflower Books (St. Albans, England), 1969.

Sword of the Dawn (also see below), Lancer Books (New York, NY), 1968.

The Secret of the Runestaff (also see below), Lancer Books (New York, NY), 1969, published as *The Runestaff,* Mayflower Books (St. Albans, England), 1969.

The History of the Runestaff (contains *The Jewel in the Skull, Sorcerer's Amulet, Sword of the Dawn,* and *The Secret of the Runestaff*), Granada (London, England), 1979, reprinted, Gollancz (London, England), 2003.

"JERRY CORNELIUS" SERIES

The Final Programme (also see below), Avon (New York, NY), 1968, revised edition, Allison & Busby (London, England), 1969.

A Cure for Cancer (also see below), Holt (New York, NY), 1971.

The English Assassin (also see below), Allison & Busby (London, England), 1972.

The Lives and Times of Jerry Cornelius (also see below), Allison & Busby (London, England), 1976, published as *The Lives and Times of Jerry Cornelius: Stories of the Comic Apocalypse,* Four Walls Eight Windows (New York, NY), 2003.

The Adventures of Una Persson and Catherine Cornelius in the Twentieth Century (also see below), Quartet Books (London, England), 1976.

The Condition of Muzak (also see below), Allison & Busby (London, England), 1977, Gregg, 1978.

The Cornelius Chronicles (contains *The Final Programme, A Cure for Cancer, The English Assassin,* and *The Condition of Muzak*), Avon (New York, NY), 1977.

The Great Rock 'n' Roll Swindle, Virgin Books, 1980.

The Entropy Tango (also see below), New English Library (London, England), 1981.

The Opium General (also see below), Harrap (Edinburgh, Scotland), 1985.

The Cornelius Chronicles, Volume 2 (contains *The Lives and Times of Jerry Cornelius* and *The Entropy Tango*), Avon (New York, NY), 1986.

The Cornelius Chronicles, Volume 3 (contains *The Adventures of Una Persson and Catherine Cornelius in the Twentieth Century* and *The Opium General*), Avon (New York, NY), 1987.

A Cornelius Calendar, Phoenix House, 1993.

The Cornelius Quartet (contains *The Final Programme, A Cure for Cancer, The English Assassin,* and *The Condition of Muzak*), Phoenix Books, 1993.

"KARL GLOGAUER" SERIES

Behold the Man, Allison & Busby (London, England), 1969, Avon (New York, NY), 1970, reprinted, Millennium (London, England), 1999.

Breakfast in the Ruins: A Novel of Inhumanity, New English Library (London, England), 1972, Random House (New York, NY), 1974.

"CORUM" SERIES; "ETERNAL CHAMPION" BOOKS

The Knight of the Swords (also see below), Mayflower Books (St. Albans, England), 1970, Berkley Publishing (New York, NY), 1971.

The Queen of the Swords (also see below), Berkley Publishing (New York, NY), 1971.

The King of the Swords (also see below), Berkley Publishing (New York, NY), 1971.

The Bull and the Spear (also see below), Berkley Publishing (New York, NY), 1973.

The Oak and the Ram (also see below), Berkley Publishing (New York, NY), 1973.

The Sword and the Stallion (also see below), Berkley Publishing (New York, NY), 1974.

The Swords Trilogy (contains *The Knight of the Swords, The Queen of the Swords,* and *The King of the Swords*), Berkley Publishing (New York, NY), 1977, published as *Corum, the Prince in the Scarlet Robe,* Gollancz (London, England), 2002.

The Chronicles of Corum (contains *The Bull and the Spear, The Oak and the Ram,* and *The Sword and the Stallion*), Berkley Publishing (New York, NY), 1978, published as *The Prince with the Silver Hand,* Orion (London, England), 1997.

"JOHN DAKER" SERIES; "ETERNAL CHAMPION" BOOKS

The Eternal Champion, Dell (New York, NY), 1970, revised edition, Harper (New York, NY), 1978.

Phoenix in Obsidian, Mayflower Books (St. Albans, England), 1970, published as *The Silver Warriors,* Dell (New York, NY), 1973.

The Dragon in the Sword, Granada (London, England), 1986.

"OSWALD BASTABLE" SERIES

The Warlord of the Air (also see below), Ace (New York, NY), 1971.

The Land Leviathan (also see below), Quartet Books (London, England), 1974.

The Steel Tsar (also see below), DAW (New York, NY), 1983.

The Nomad of Time (contains *The Warlord of the Air, The Land Leviathan,* and *The Steel Tsar*), Granada (London, England), 1984.

"DANCERS AT THE END OF TIME" SERIES

An Alien Heat (also see below), Harper (New York, NY), 1972.

The Hollow Lands (also see below), Harper (New York, NY), 1974.

The End of All Songs (also see below), Harper (New York, NY), 1976.

Legends from the End of Time, Harper (New York, NY), 1976.

The Transformations of Miss Mavis Ming, W.H. Allen (London, England), 1977, published as *A Messiah at the End of Time,* DAW (New York, NY), 1978.

The Dancers at the End of Time (contains *An Alien Heat, The Hollow Lands,* and *The End of All Songs*), Granada (London, England), 1981.

"CASTLE BRASS" SERIES; "ETERNAL CHAMPION" BOOKS

Count Brass (also see below), Mayflower Books (St. Albans, England), 1973, reprinted, Millennium (London, England), 1993.

The Champion of Garathorm (also see below), Mayflower Books (St. Albans, England), 1973.

The Quest for Tanelorn (also see below), Mayflower Books (St. Albans, England), 1975, Dell (New York, NY), 1976.

The Chronicles of Castle Brass (contains *Castle Brass, The Champion of Garathorm,* and *The Quest for Tanelorn*), Granada (London, England), 1985.

"VON BEK FAMILY" SERIES

The War Hound and the World's Pain, Timescape, 1981.

The Brothel in Rosenstrasse, New English Library (London, England), 1982, Tigerseye Press, 1986.

The City in the Autumn Stars, Ace (New York, NY), 1986.

Lunching with the Antichrist: A Family History: 1925-2015 (omnibus), Mark V. Ziesing (Shingleton, CA), 1995.

Von Beck (contains *The War Hound and the World's Pain, The City and the Autumn Stars, The Dragon in the Sword,* and *The Pleasure Garden of Felipe Sagittarius*), White Wolf (Stonemountain, GA), 1996.

"COLONEL PYAT" SERIES

Byzantium Endures, Secker & Warburg (London, England), 1981, Random House (New York, NY), 1982.

The Laughter of Carthage, Random House (New York, NY), 1984.

Jerusalem Commands, Secker & Warburg (London, England), 1992.

"BLOOD TRILOGY"

Blood: A Southern Fantasy, Morrow (New York, NY), 1994.

Fabulous Harbors: A Sequel to Blood, Avon (New York, NY), 1996.

The War amongst the Angels, Avon (New York, NY), 1997.

Michael Moorcock's Multiverse (graphic novel), art by Walter Simonson, Mark Reeve, and John Ridgway, DC Comics (New York, NY), 1999.

SCREENPLAYS

The Final Programme (based on his novel of the same title; removed name from credits after dispute with director), EMI, 1973.

The Land That Time Forgot, British Lion, 1975.

EDITOR

(And contributor under name Michael Moorcock and under pseudonym James Colvin) *The Best of "New Worlds,"* Compact Books (London, England), 1965.

Best SF Stories from "New Worlds," Panther Books, 1967, Berkley Publishing (New York, NY), 1968.

The Traps of Time, Rapp & Whiting, 1968.

(And contributor under pseudonym James Colvin) *The Best SF Stories from "New Worlds" 2,* Panther Books, 1968, Berkley Publishing (New York, NY), 1969.

(And contributor under pseudonym James Colvin) *The Best SF Stories from "New Worlds" 3,* Panther Books, 1968, Berkley Publishing (New York, NY), 1969.

The Best SF Stories from "New Worlds" 4, Panther Books, 1969, Berkley Publishing (New York, NY), 1971.

The Best SF Stories from "New Worlds" 5, Panther Books, 1969, Berkley Publishing (New York, NY), 1971.

(And contributor) *The Best SF Stories from "New Worlds" 6,* Panther Books, 1970, Berkley Publishing (New York, NY), 1971.

The Best SF Stories from "New Worlds" 7, Panther Books, 1971.

New Worlds Quarterly 1, Berkley Publishing (New York, NY), 1971.

New Worlds Quarterly 2, Berkley Publishing (New York, NY), 1971.

New Worlds Quarterly 3, Sphere Books (London, England), 1971.

(With Langdon Jones and contributor) *The Nature of the Catastrophe,* Hutchinson (London, England), 1971.

New Worlds Quarterly 4, Berkley Publishing (New York, NY), 1972.

New Worlds Quarterly 5, Sphere Books (London, England), 1973.

New Worlds Quarterly 6, Avon (New York, NY), 1973.

Before Armageddon: An Anthology of Victorian and Edwardian Imaginative Fiction Published before 1914, W.H. Allen (London, England), 1975.

England Invaded: A Collection of Fantasy Fiction, Ultramarine, 1977.

New Worlds: An Anthology, Fontana, 1983, revised edition, Thunders Mouth (New York, NY), 2004.

(With David Garnett) *New Worlds 1* (originally published in comic-book format), VGSF (London, England), 1991.

(With David Garnett and consultant editor) *New Worlds 2,* VGSF (London, England), 1992.

LYRICIST; RECORDINGS WITH MICHAEL MOORCOCK AND THE DEEP FIX

The New World's Fair, United Artists, 1975.
Dodgem Dude/Starcruiser (single), Flicknife, 1980.
The Brothel in Rosenstrasse/Time Centre (single), Flicknife, 1982.
(With others) *Hawkwind Friends and Relations,* Flicknife, 1982.
(With others) *Hawkwind & Co.,* Flicknife, 1983.

Composer of songs recorded by others, including *Sonic Attack, The Black Corridor, The Wizard Blew His Horn, Standing at the Edge, Warriors, Kings of Speed, Warrior at the End of Time, Psychosonia, Coded Languages, Lost Chances, Choose Your Masks,* and *Arrival in Utopia,* all recorded by Hawkwind; *The Great Sun Jester, Black Blade,* and *Veteran of the Psychic Wars,* all recorded by Blue Oyster Cult.

Adaptations

The character Elric was adapted for use in role-playing games from Avalon Hill Game Company and from Chaosium; featured in comic books published by Pacific Comics and by Star Reach Productions; and has been licensed for manufacture as miniature figures marketed by Citadel Miniatures. Moorcock's characters Elric and Oswald Bastable have been featured in computer games.

Sidelights

Michael Moorcock is considered among the most original and influential writers working as part of the so-called New Wave of science fiction, an international movement that brought a wide range of subjects and experimental literary styles to the genre beginning in the 1960. A prolific author with twelve series and many individual works to his credit, Moorcock has written comic novels, satires, high fantasy in the sword-and-sorcery vein, historical allegory, and nonfiction as well as science fiction; he has also written short stories and screenplays and has edited several science-fiction collections. As editor of the British science-fiction magazine *New Worlds,* Moorcock is credited with helping to spark the New Wave movement and for providing a showcase for some of its most talented practitioners. A writer, he is widely acknowledged as a gifted storyteller who is, in the words of *Booklist* reviewer Algis Budrys, one of "fantasy/sf's most uninhibited experimenters."

Many commentators praise Moorcock's books, which characteristically combine imaginative narratives with experimental literary structures, humor, and joyous wordplay, as thoughtful, inventive, literate, entertaining, and, on occasion, profound; several of his works, in fact, are considered tour de forces. Some critics have been less enthralled with Moorcock's books, calling them obscure, self-indulgent, and disturbing. Moorcock is well regarded, however, both for the quality of his writing and the sincerity of his approach. In an essay for the *Dictionary of Literary Biography,* Colin Greenland wrote that Moorcock's "editorial work and his own fiction together represent a titanic effort, often against great resistance from the establishments of magazine and book publishing, to reunite the highest literary values with the forms and vitality of popular culture." *Washington Post Book World* critic Gregory Feeley added that Moorcock "has long been Britain's quintessential novelist of urban life" and dubbed the writer "one of our very best novelists and a national treasure."

Although the author of only one book written specifically for children, the heroic fantasy *Sojan,* Moorcock's books have been popular with younger readers since the 1960s. Writing in *Science Fiction Studies,* Ralph Willett claimed that during the 1960s and early 1970s Moorcock became "that rare phenomenon, the popular novelist whose work has also become a cult among the young and avant-garde"; *Spectator* critic Paul Ableman called the author "the thinking hippy's bard." Several of Moorcock's books feature youthful protagonists who search for a sense of self, and as the author once commented, "All the characters in a Fantasy have to be childish or adolescent in order to function. Because they're larger than life their emotions are huge, their ambitions and their destinies are vast."

In one of his most prominent series, Moorcock describes the adventures of Elric of Melnibone, a young hero who differs vastly from the macho figures who often appear in fantasy stories. A fey albino who is dependent on his vampiric broadsword Stormbringer, Elric battles for his soul with the Lords of Order and Chaos; according to Greenland, Elric's "problems of identity and meaning, purpose and desire, battled out in a crude and violent universe ruled by ambiguous powers indifferent to his values, are essentially problems of adolescent frustration." The "Elric" books are among the most popular of Moorcock's titles among the young, and have inspired comic books and games as well as a line of miniature figures.

Early in his career, while writing and editing *Tarzan Adventures,* Moorcock created realistic short stories for adults. Attracted by both the freedom and the marketability of science fiction, he began contributing stories to magazines, including "The Stealer of Souls," which introduces his character Elric. Encouraged by E.J. Carnell, editor of *New Worlds* magazine and a man whom Moorcock has called "the single most influential figure in British sf," he wrote more "Elric" stories and began producing novellas and novelettes for *New Worlds, Science Fantasy,* and *Science Fiction Adventures.* After leaving *Tarzan Adventures,* Moorcock joined the Sexton Blake Library and Amalgamated Press, considered the longest-running detective series in the world, and wrote the Sexton Blake novel *Caribbean Crisis* with James Cawthorn under the house pseudonym Desmond Reid;

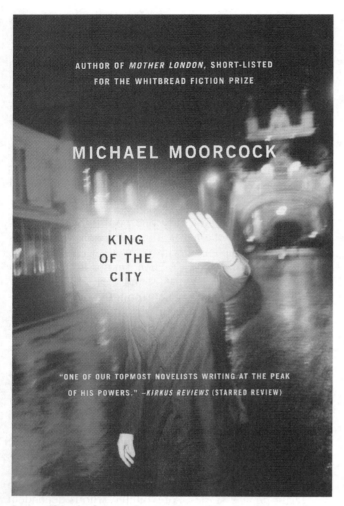

Immersed in the fast-paced, pop culture of London, former rock star Dennis Dover and cousin Rosie Beck have been best friends for years; now they must join forces to save their colorful world from a corrupt man whose goal is to destroy the city they love. (Cover design by Keenan.)

he also worked for several children's annuals and wrote comic strips featuring both real and imaginary heroes before becoming employed by the British Liberal Party.

During the early 1960s Moorcock published his first two books, *The Stealer of Souls and Other Stories* and *Stormbringer,* and became editor of *New Worlds* following Carnell's retirement. At the magazine, he encouraged content that was more socially and politically relevant. "I felt sf could become a genuine literary form whilst retaining its popular audience," he once explained. In this way, *New Worlds* became a keystone of the New Wave movement; it featured experimental stories by such writers as Jorge Luis Borges, William S. Burroughs, and J.G. Ballard and published the work of Brian Aldiss, Samuel R. Delany, and Thomas M. Disch, among others. In an interview with Ian Covell for *Science Fiction Review,* Moorcock noted of New Wave: "We were a generation of writers who had no nostalgic view of the pulp magazines, who had come to SF as a possible alternative to mainstream literature and had taken SF seriously. . . . We were trying to find a vi-

able literature for our time. A literature which took account of science, of modern social trends, and which was written . . . according to the personal requirements of the individuals who produced it."

Although *New Worlds,* under Moorcock's leadership, was an influential magazine in its field, it was never a financial success and was attacked for its inclusion of explicit sex and violence. As editor and publisher, Moorcock was often forced to write a quick novel to pay the bills. In his *Dream Makers: The Uncommon People Who Write Science Fiction,* Charles Platt recounted: "It was not unusual for the magazine's staff to be found cowering on the floor with the lights out, pretending not to be home, while some creditor rang the bell and called hopefully through the mail slot in the front door—to no avail." Ignored by British publishing distributors, *New Worlds* ceased publication in 1970; since then, Moorcock has edited several original anthologies of the magazine, both individually and with David Garnett.

As he did with *New Worlds,* Moorcock attempted to liberate his own writing from the traditional forms of fantasy and science fiction. *The Final Programme,* the ironic thriller that introduces popular protagonist Jerry Cornelius, is the first of Moorcock's books to accomplish this goal. Jerry Cornelius, a physicist turned adventurer, is the antihero of a multivolume series of darkly comic contemporary novels that are often considered Dickensian in their scope. Combining fantastic elements with James Bond-style adventures, the series marks Jerry as a symbol of 1960s values while lampooning his excesses. Described by his creator as "something of a modern Candide" and by Greenland as "an entirely new kind of fictional character," Jerry has no consistent gender, personality, or appearance; he/she changes sex and race and morphs into different characters in every volume. The landscape Jerry inhabits is just as flexible, containing a multitude of alternative histories, each contradictory and all peopled with characters who die and are resurrected as a matter of course. Jerry travels from one inconclusive adventure to another, trapped in an endless existence.

Throughout the "Jerry Cornelius" series, as with others in his oeuvre, Moorcock creates a "multiverse," a series of parallel universes each with their own reality, and he underscores these imaginative landscapes with the theme of how society's emphasis on power and war has led to its deterioration. The novels *The Condition of Muzak* and *The Great Rock and Roll Swindle* may be of special interest to young people: *The Condition of Muzak* casts Jerry as a working-class lad who dreams of becoming a rock star, while *The Great Rock and Roll Swindle* was written at the same time as the film that shares its name, about seminal punk band the Sex Pistols. Moorcock considers four "Jerry Cornelius" novels—*The Final Programme, A Cure for Cancer, The English Assassin,* and *The Condition of Muzak*—to be a single work. These books, more recently collected as *The Cornelius Chronicles,* were considered by Angus

Wilson in the *Washington Post Book World* to form "one of the most ambitious, illuminating, and enjoyable works of fiction published in English" during the late twentieth century.

Like the "Jerry Cornelius" books, several of Moorcock's other works comment on contemporary society; as John Clute noted in the *New Statesman,* the author has, in fact, written "the history of the modern world." For example, *Behold the Man,* a novel expanded from a Nebula award-winning novella of the same title, describes how Karl Glogauer, a modern-day Jew, time-travels to ancient Palestine to search for the truth about the Crucifixion and discovers Jesus Christ, in the words of Janice Elliott in *New Statesman,* as "a hunchbacked congenital imbecile." Assuming Christ's identity, Karl is finally crucified as Jesus, "leaving" as Greenland noted, "no opportunity for a second coming." *Behold the Man* is usually accepted as the novel through which critics began to recognize Moorcock as a serious writer.

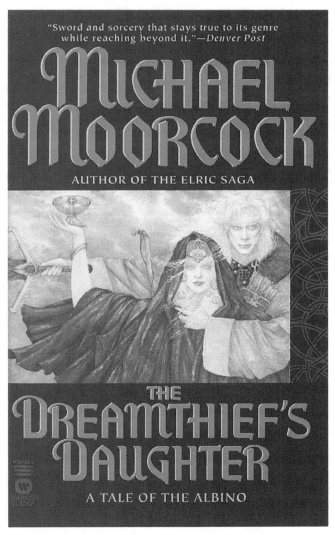

Part of Moorcock's "Eternal Champion" series, this 2001 novel finds Ulric von Bek forced to travel to the twentieth century to prevent Nazi leader Adolf Hitler and the Ahnenerbe SS from locating an ancient sword that harnesses a dark magic. (Cover illustration by Robert Gold.)

In the second "Glogauer" novel, *Breakfast in the Ruins,* Moorcock resurrects the character and presents accounts of his incarnations during times of catastrophe and torture—past, present, and future—in such cities as Capetown, Kiev, Shanghai, and Saigon.

Moorcock's literary reputation has also been enhanced by the publication of *Byzantium Endures* and *The Laughter of Carthage,* novels that are often considered among his finest contributions to more conventional fiction. Together, the books describe the autobiography of Russian emigre Colonel Maxim Arturovitch Pyatnitski (shortened to Pyat), born January 1, 1900, whose life mirrors the history of the twentieth century. A figure who first appeared peripherally in the "Jerry Cornelius" tetralogy, Pyat survives the Russian Revolution, travels throughout America and Europe, meets figures ranging from Dylan Thomas to Tom Mix, and participates in several important historical events. He is, however, a self-aggrandizing megalomaniac and cocaine addict who imagines himself to be a great engineer and inventor—the equal of Thomas Edison—and a major figure on the stage of world history. The illegitimate son of a Jewish father, Pyat is an anti-Semite who sees the truest form of Christianity, as embodied in the Russian Orthodox Church, in opposing the Jews, Asians, Bolsheviks, and other groups whom he considers destroyers of order; he likens Western Christianity to Byzantium, his enemies to Carthage.

In his review in the *Chicago Tribune Book World,* Robert Onopa called *Byzantium Endures* "utterly engrossing as narrative, historically pertinent, and told through characters so alive and detail so dense that it puts to shame all but a few writers who have been doing this kind of work all along." *Times Literary Supplement* reviewer Valentine Cunningham noted of *The Laughter of Carthage* that "this is epic writing," while Gregory Sandow observed in the *Village Voice:* "It's wonderful to see Moorcock grow from a genre writer into, simply, a writer. . . . [He] has had to come the long way to literary recognition. But now, with *The Laughter of Carthage,* he can surely no longer be denied his due; this enormous book . . . must establish him in the front rank of practising English novelists."

Moorcock's "Blood Trilogy," which includes *Blood, Fabulous Harbors,* and *The War amongst the Angels* and is accompanied by a graphic novel titled *Michael Moorcock's Multiverse,* features characters able to transport themselves from reality to a secondary world called the Second Ether until a fault in reality threatens to swallow the world into the "multiverse." The series includes theological speculations, philosophy, and alternate histories. Of *The War amongst the Angels,* Roland Green wrote in *Booklist:* "The pacing is brisk, [and] Moorcock's command of the language is quite up to his usual high standard." The author's alternate worlds intersect with the "Blood Trilogy," as well as with scenes from the author's own history. "Moorcock delights in the juxtaposition: the tone lurches and shifts enough to make the reader seasick, but Moorcock makes it work," wrote Robert K.J. Killheffer in a review for the *Magazine of Science Fiction and Fantasy*. Killheffer also noted, "It's devilishly hard to convey [the series'] substance in any kind of traditional summary."

After years between books in the saga of Elric the Eternal Man, Moorcock decided to return to his hero. He explained to an interviewer for *Crescent Blues Web site* that his reasons for doing so were threefold: "I was surprised that so many readers found the "Blood Trilogy" baffling and the Multiverse comic that goes along with it even more baffling. . . . When this happens, I feel I have to redeem myself with those readers who were disappointed *without* disappointing those readers who liked the more experimental stuff." His second reason was due to a crime perpetrated by a criminal who said he was compelled by the spirit of Elric. This act brought up a theme Moorcock has written about: the fascist elements of sword and sorcery. "Because I was troubled, I tried to produce an Elric sequence which would somehow address some of those troubling issues." The third reason was that "Nobody would buy *King of the City* unless I agreed to do more commercial fantasy as well." (*King of the City* is Moorcock's ambitious novel that *Guardian* essayist Iain Sinclair considered "a comprehensive encyclopedia of lost lives, uncelebrated loci, trashed cultural memory.")

The more recent "Elric" stories focus on Elric's parallel as he exists in a different reality: Count Ulric von Bek. Set during World War II, *The Dreamthief's Daughter* follows von Bek as he attempts to with Elric and Oona, the daughter of a magical woman known as the dreamthief, in order to defeat Gaynor von Minct, the otherworldly incarnation of Elric's eternal enemy. The entire balance of the multiverse is in peril, unless von Bek and Elric can use the forces of their two enchanted swords, Ravenbrand and Stormbringer, to overcome evil and balance the forces of Law and Chaos. Paula Luedtke, in *Booklist*, noted that the novel is "full of magic and mystery" and commented that the villains meet "satisfyingly gory ends." Luedtke recommended the book for a young-adult audience. *Library Journal* reviewer Jackie Cassada called the novel "fast-paced action with metaphysical adventure."

Oona and Ulric von Bek vacation in Nova Scotia in *The Skrayling Tree*, and after von Bek is kidnaped by Indian warriors, Oona joins a shaman called White Crow in order to rescue her husband from an alternate reality. Elric, in the meantime, has been asked by another force to defeat a giant named White Crow. As their forces oppose, the heroes begin to learn the truth of who is pulling the strings. "The tale's power stems largely from the astounding lyricism of the author's prose," noted a reviewer for *Publishers Weekly*. Roland Green, in *Booklist*, while noting that the second book might be confusing for newcomers to Moorcock's multiverse, wrote that the tale will "be eagerly embraced by serious followers of Moorcock's fictive cosmos."

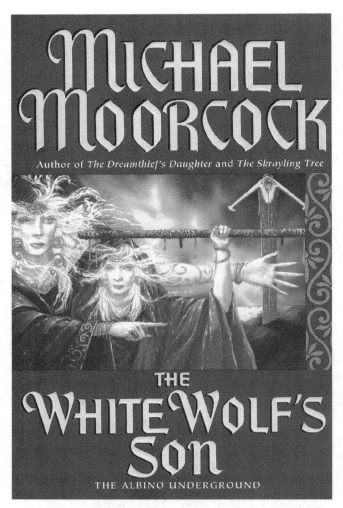

Drawing together many of the characters from the "Eternal Champion" novels, this 2005 work finds Elric facing the ultimate challenge as he unearths a plan to disrupt the cosmic balance and allow evil to rule. (Cover illustration by Robert Gold.)

The third and final book of the trilogy, *The White Wolf's Son,* tells the story of Oonagh von Bek, the daughter of Oona and Ulric. While her parents are away, Oonagh disappears into a series of caves and discovers a world peopled with talking animals and people. Transported from the past and now placed out of their time-line, these people include a young woman who is actually Oonagh's grandmother. "The author plays fascinating games with shifting realities," commented a critic for *Kirkus Reviews,* while a *Publishers Weekly* reviewer called the book a "triumph" for the "ever original, vastly influential Moorcock."

Evaluations of Moorcock's career often emphasize the sheer volume and variety of his work. "It is like trying to evaluate an industry," Philip Oakes explained in the London *Sunday Times Magazine*. Throughout his career, the author has been credited for his impressive ability to write consistently well within a wide range of genres and styles. As Oakes noted, "Moorcock strikes me as the most prolific, probably the most inventive and without doubt the most egalitarian writer practising today." In an interview with Ian Covell for *Science Fiction Review,* Moorcock spoke about his literary philosophy: "I'm attempting all the time to find equilibrium between unchecked Romanticism ("Chaos") and stifling Classicism ("Law"). . . . And in form I'm always looking for a combination (that will work) of the epic and the novel—or the romance and the novel. . . . I call very few of my books 'novels' because they are not, classically speaking, novels. They are romances. Scene and idea (allegorical concerns) in general take precedence over characters. . . . The same moral arguments are debated again and again from my earliest (*The Golden Barge*) to my latest. . . . The trick is to look at them from as many different ways as possible."

"Even my fantasy novels are inclined to deal with moral problems rather than magical ones," the writer added. "I'm turning more and more away from SF and fantasy and more toward a form of realism used in the context of what you might call an imaginative framework. Late Dickens would be the model I'd most like to emulate." Moorcock's writing process, however, leans more toward his beginnings in the comic book industry. "Pretty much everything I do has some sort of storyboard," he told Stephen Hunt of the *Science Fiction Crowsnest Web site,* concluding: "I don't know anyone else who does this."

In *Contemporary Authors Autobiography Series,* Moorcock wrote further about the writing life: "The job of a novelist has its own momentum, its own demands, its own horrible power over the practitioner. When I look back I wonder what I got myself into all those years ago when I realised I had a facility to put words down on paper and have people give me money in return. For ages the whole business seemed ludicrous. I couldn't believe my luck. Frequently, I still can't but it seems an unnatural way of earning a living. Of course, it's no longer easy. It's often a struggle. It spoils my health. . . . I suppose it must be an addiction. I'm pretty sure, though I deny it heartily, that I could now no longer give it up. I'm as possessed as any fool I used to mock." Moorcock, once nominally retired, told Paula Guran of *Publishers Weekly* about the works he still hoped to write. "I want to devote myself to shorter, more autobiographical books and any short fantasy I write will only be if I have an idea I feel strongly about and if it's commissioned, say, by an anthology or magazine."

Biographical and Critical Sources

BOOKS

Bilyeu, R., *Tanelorn Archives,* Pandora's Books, 1979.
Callow, A.J., compiler, *The Chronicles of Moorcock,* A.J. Callow, 1978.
Carter, Lin, *Imaginary Worlds,* Ballantine (New York, NY), 1973.

Contemporary Authors Autobiography Series, Volume 5, Thomson Gale (Detroit, MI), 1987.
Contemporary Literary Criticism, Thomson Gale (Detroit, MI), Volume 27, 1984, Volume 58, 1990.
Dictionary of Literary Biography, Volume 14: British Novelists since 1960, Thomson Gale (Detroit, MI), 1983.
Greenland, Colin, *The Entropy Exhibition: Michael Moorcock and the British "New Wave" in Science Fiction,* Routledge & Kegan Paul (London, England), 1983.
Harper, Andrew, and George McAulay, *Michael Moorcock: A Bibliography,* T-K Graphics, 1976.
Moorcock, Michael, and Colin Greenland, *Death Is No Obstacle* (interview), Savoy Books (Manchester, England), 1992.
Platt, Charles, *Dream Makers: The Uncommon People Who Write Science Fiction,* Berkley Publishing (New York, NY), 1980.
Walker, Paul, editor, *Speaking of Science Fiction: The Paul Walker Interviews,* Luna Publications, 1978.
Wollheim, Donald A., *The Universe Makers,* Harper (New York, NY), 1971.

PERIODICALS

Analog, February, 1970; March, 1990.
Booklist, September 1, 1979, Algis Budrys, review of *Gloriana,* p. 29; February 15, 1995, p. 1064; November 15, 1997, Roland Green, review of *The War amongst the Angels,* p. 548; March 15, 2001, Paula Luedtke, review of *The Dreamthief's Daughter,* p. 1361; February 15, 2003, Roland Green, review of *The Skrayling Tree,* p. 1060.
Books and Bookmen, June, 1971, p. 44; October, 1972, p. 72; May, 1974, p. 86; August, 1978, p. 44.
Chicago Tribune Book World, January 31, 1982; March 21, 1982, Robert Onopa, review of *Byzantium Endures,* p. 10; March 26, 1989.
Commonweal, August 1, 1975.
Encounter, November, 1981, p. 81.
Extrapolation, winter, 1989, p. 412.
Guardian (London, England), November 23, 2000, Iain Sinclair, "Crowning Glory: Michael Moorcock's London."
Guardian Weekly, April 10, 1969, p. 15.
Kirkus Reviews, October 1, 1995, p. 1387; October 15, 2004, review of *New Worlds: An Anthology,* p. 990; May 15, 2005, review of *The White Wolf's Son,* p. 568.
Library Journal, November 15, 1997, review of *The War amongst the Angels,* p. 79; April 15, 2001, Jackie Cassaca, review of *The Dreamthief's Daughter,* p. 137; August, 2001, Marc Kloszewski, review of *King of the City,* p. 163; February 15, 2003, Jackie Cassada, review of *The Skrayling Tree,* p. 172; November 15, 2004, Jackie Cassada, review of *New Worlds: An Anthology,* p. 55; June 15, 2005, Jackie Cassada, review of *The White Wolf's Son,* p. 66.
Listener, June 23, 1988, p. 31; January 18, 1990, p. 33.
Locus, November, 1989, p. 57; February, 1990, p. 15.
Magazine of Fantasy and Science Fiction, June, 1998, Robert K.J. Killheffer, review of *The War amongst the Angels,* p. 39.
New Republic, June 15, 1974.

New Statesman, April 4, 1969, Janice Elliott, "Present & Past," p. 486; June 18, 1976, p. 821; September 7, 1984, John Clute, "No Escape," pp. 31-32.

New York Times Book Review, April 5, 1970, p. 43; April 25, 1976, p. 46; February 21, 1982, p. 12; February 10, 1985, p. 24; November 23, 1986, p. 31.

Observer (London, England), April 4, 1976, p. 27; April 3, 1977, p. 26.

Publishers Weekly, January 16, 1995, p. 442; October 30, 1995; February 12, 2001, review of *The Dreamthief's Daughter,* p. 188; July 16, 2001, review of *King of the City,* p. 156; January 27, 2003, review of *The Skrayling Tree,* p. 241; September 22, 2003, review of *The Life and Times of Jerry Cornelius,* p. 89; May 23, 2005, review of *The White Wolf's Son,* p. 63, and Paula Guran, "A Busy Retirement," p. 64; July 25, 2005, review of *Silverheart,* p. 53.

Punch, January 16, 1985, p. 82.

Saturday Review, April 25, 1970. p. 61.

Science Fiction Review, July, 1979, interview with Moorcock, pp. 18-25.

Science Fiction Studies, March, 1976, Ralph Willett, "Moorcock's Achievement and Promise in the Jerry Cornelius Books," pp. 75-79.

Spectator, August 10, 1974, p. 182; April 9, 1977, p. 21; June 27, 1981, Paul Ableman, "Unagonising Saga," pp. 24-25; February 9, 1985, p. 24; May 13, 2000, D. J. Taylor, review of *King of the City,* p. 33; May 19, 2001, Miranda France, review of *London Bone,* p. 43.

Sunday Times Magazine, November 5, 1978, Philip Oakes, "Michael Moorcock," p. 100.

Time, January 28, 1985, p. 82.

Times Literary Supplement, May 31, 1974, p. 577; May 7, 1976, p. 561; June 30, 1978, p. 742; July 3, 1981, p. 747; September 7, 1984, Valentine Cunningham, "Incontinent Continents-Full," p. 1005; July 1, 1988, p. 731; February 23, 1990, p. 202.

Village Voice, March 2, 1982, Gregory Sandow, review of *Byzantium Endures,* pp. 42-43.

Washington Post Book World, December 23, 1984, Angus Wilson, "The Picaresque Imagination of Michael Moorcock," pp. 1, 13; May 14, 1989, Gregory Feeley, "In the Heart of the Heart of the City," p. 8.

Writer, September, 2003, "Michael Moorcock Believes That It May Be Time 'to Hang up My Pointy Fantasy Hat,'" p. 10.

ONLINE

Crescent Blues Web site, http://www.crescentblues.com/ (December 3, 2005), interview with Moorcock.

SFCrowsnest.com, http://www.sfcrowsnest.com/ (August, 2002), Stephen Hunt, interview with Moorcock.*

*   *   *

MOORCOCK, Michael John
See MOORCOCK, Michael

*   *   *

MUDGEON, Apeman
See MITCHELL, Adrian

N

NADEN, Corinne J. 1930-

Personal

Born June 20, 1930, in Park Ridge, NJ; daughter of Henry Edwin and Josephine (Peragallo) Naden. *Education:* New York University, B.S., 1959.

Addresses

Home and office—140 Clinton Ave., Dobbs Ferry, NY 10522.

Career

Children's author and editor. Franklin Watts (publisher), New York, NY, children's book editor, c. 1970s; R.R. Bowker (publisher), New York, NY, senior editor for reference and professional books, c. 1980s. *Military service:* U.S. Navy, journalist, 1951-55.

Writings

The First Book of Rivers, Franklin Watts (New York, NY), 1967.
Frank Lloyd Wright, Franklin Watts (New York, NY), 1968.
The Haymarket Affair, Franklin Watts (New York, NY), 1968.
The Chicago Fire, Franklin Watts (New York, NY), 1969.
Golf, Franklin Watts (New York, NY), 1970.
Grasslands around the World, Franklin Watts (New York, NY), 1970.
Let's Find out about Bears, Franklin Watts (New York, NY), 1971.
The Triangle Shirtwaist Fire, Franklin Watts (New York, NY), 1971.
Let's Find out about Frogs, Franklin Watts (New York, NY), 1972.
The Nile River, Franklin Watts (New York, NY), 1972.
Woodlands around the World, Franklin Watts (New York, NY), 1973.

The Colony of New Jersey, Franklin Watts (New York, NY), 1974.
The Mississippi, Franklin Watts (New York, NY), 1974.
Driving Your Bike Safely, Messner, 1979.
(With John T. Gillespie) *Junior Plots 3,* R.R. Bowker (New York, NY), 1987.
(With John T. Gillespie) *Seniorplots,* R.R. Bowker (New York, NY), 1989.
(With John T. Gillespie) *Best Books for Children,* 4th edition, R.R. Bowker (New York, NY), 1990.
Ronald McNair, Chelsea House (Philadelphia, PA), 1991.
Barbara Jordan, Chelsea House (Philadelphia, PA), 1992.
(With John T. Gillespie) *Junior Plots,* R.R. Bowker (New York, NY), 1993.
(With John T. Gillespie) *Middleplots 4,* R.R. Bowker (New York, NY), 1994.
(With John T. Gillespie) *Best Books for Children,* 5th edition, R.R. Bowker (New York, NY), 1994.
I Can Read about Sharks, illustrated by Paul Lopez, Troll Associates (Mahwah, NJ), 1996.
(With John T. Gillespie) *The Newbery Companion: Booktalk and Related Materials for Newbery Medal and Honor Books,* Libraries Unlimited (Englewood, CO), 1996, 2nd edition, 2001.
(Compiler with John T. Gillespie) *Characters in Young-Adult Literature,* Thomson Gale (Detroit, MI), 1997.
(With John T. Gillespie) *Teenplots: A Booktalk Guide to Use with Readers Ages 12-18,* Libraries Unlimited (Englewood, CO), 2003.

NONFICTION; COAUTHOR WITH ROSE BLUE

Barbara Bush: First Lady, Enslow (Hillside, NJ), 1991.
Christa McAuliffe: Teacher in Space, Millbrook Press (Brookfield, CT), 1991.
Colin Powell: Straight to the Top, Millbrook Press (Brookfield, CT), 1991.
John Muir: Saving the Wilderness, Millbrook Press (Brookfield, CT), 1992.
U.S. Navy, Millbrook Press (Brookfield, CT), 1993.
U.S. Air Force, Millbrook Press (Brookfield, CT), 1993.
U.S. Coast Guard, Millbrook Press (Brookfield, CT), 1993.

Whoopi Goldberg: Entertainer, Chelsea House (New York, NY), 1994.

People of Peace, Millbrook Press (Brookfield, CT), 1994.

Jerry Rice, Chelsea House (Philadelphia, PA), 1994.

Working Together against Hate Groups, Rosen (New York, NY), 1994.

Black Sea, Raintree (Austin, TX), 1995.

Andes Mountains, Raintree (Austin, TX), 1995.

The White House Kids, Millbrook Press (Brookfield, CT), 1995.

Staying out of Trouble in a Troubled Family, Twenty-first Century Books (Brookfield, CT), 1998.

You're the Boss: Positive Attitude and Work Ethics, Peoples Publishing Group (Maywood, NJ), 1999.

Madeleine Albright: U.S. Secretary of State, Blackbirch Press (Woodbridge, CT), 1999.

Why Fight?: The Causes of the American Civil War, Raintree (Austin, TX), 2000.

The Duty to Rescue, Chelsea House (Philadelphia, PA), 2000.

Belle Starr and the Wild West, Blackbirch Press (Woodbridge, CT), 2000.

Chris Rock, Chelsea House (Philadelphia, PA), 2000.

Jonas Salk: Polio Pioneer, Millbrook Press (Brookfield, CT), 2001.

Cleopatra, Chelsea House (Philadelphia, PA), 2001.

Punishment and Rehabilitation, Chelsea House (Philadelphia, PA), 2001.

The History of Gospel Music, Chelsea House (Philadelphia, PA), 2001.

Benjamin Banneker: Mathematician and Stargazer, Millbrook Press (Brookfield, CT), 2001.

Wesley Snipes, Chelsea House (Philadelphia, PA), 2002.

Halle Berry, Chelsea House (Philadelphia, PA), 2002.

Dian Fossey: At Home with the Giant Gorillas, Millbrook Press (Brookfield, CT), 2002.

New York ("States" series), MyReportLinks.com (Berkeley Heights, NJ), 2002.

Monica Seles, Chelsea House (Philadelphia, PA), 2002.

Harriet Tubman: Riding the Freedom Train, Millbrook Press (Brookfield, CT), 2003.

Tony Blair, Lucent Books (San Diego, CA), 2003.

Nicholas Cage, Lucent Books (San Diego, CA), 2003.

Mississippi ("States" series), MyReportLinks.com (Berkeley Heights, NJ), 2003.

Massachusetts ("States" series), MyReportLinks.com (Berkeley Heights, NJ), 2003.

Mae Jemison: Out of This World, Millbrook Press (Brookfield, CT), 2003.

John Travolta, Lucent Books (San Diego, CA), 2003.

Wilma Rudolph, Raintree (Chicago, IL), 2004.

Lenin, Lucent Books (San Diego, CA), 2004.

George W. Bush, Lucent Books (San Diego, CA), 2004.

Mormonism, Lucent Books (San Diego, CA), 2004.

Muammar Qaddafi, Lucent Books (San Diego, CA), 2005.

Maya Angelou, Raintree (Chicago, IL), 2005.

Henry Louis Gates, Jr., Raintree (Chicago, IL), 2005.

Cornel West, Raintree (Chicago, IL), 2005.

Condoleezza Rice, Raintree (Chicago, IL), 2005.

Marbury v. Madison: The Court's Foundation ("Supreme Court Milestones" series), Benchmark Books (Tarrytown, NY), 2005.

Dred Scott: Person or Property? ("Supreme Court Milestones" series), Benchmark Books (Tarrytown, NY), 2005.

Coauthor, with Blue, of "Heroes Don't Just Happen" multicultural biography series.

NONFICTION; "HOUSE DIVIDED" SERIES; COAUTHOR WITH ROSE BLUE

The Bloodiest Days: The Battles of 1861 and 1862, Raintree (Austin, TX), 2000.

Chancellorsville to Appomattox: The Battles of 1863 to 1865, Raintree (Austin, TX), 2000.

Civil War Ends: Assassination, Reconstruction, and the Aftermath, Raintree (Austin, TX), 2000.

NONFICTION; "WHO'S THAT IN THE WHITE HOUSE" SERIES; COAUTHOR WITH ROSE BLUE

The Founding Years: 1789 to 1829, Raintree (Austin, TX), 1998.

The Formative Years: 1829 to 1857, Raintree (Austin, TX), 1998.

The Expansive Years: 1857 to 1901, Raintree (Austin, TX), 1998.

The Progressive Years: 1901 to 1933, Raintree (Austin, TX), 1998.

The Turbulent Years: 1933 to 1969, Raintree (Austin, TX), 1998.

The Modern Years: 1969 to 2001, Raintree (Austin, TX), 1998.

NONFICTION; "GREAT PEOPLES AND THEIR CLAIM TO FAME" SERIES; COAUTHOR WITH ROSE BLUE

The Aztecs and Tenochtitlan, Lake Street (Minneapolis, MN), 2003.

Ancient Romans and the Colosseum, Lake Street (Minneapolis, MN), 2003.

Ancient Maya and Tikal, Lake Street (Minneapolis, MN), 2003.

Ancient Greeks and the Parthenon, Lake Street (Minneapolis, MN), 2003.

Ancient Egyptians and the Pyramids, Lake Street (Minneapolis, MN), 2003.

NONFICTION; "EXPLORING THE AMERICAS" SERIES; COAUTHOR WITH ROSE BLUE

Exploring the Southeastern United States, Raintree (Chicago, IL), 2003.

Exploring the Pacific Northwest, Raintree (Chicago, IL), 2003.

Exploring the Mississippi River Valley, Raintree (Chicago, IL), 2003.

Exploring Northeastern America, Raintree (Chicago, IL), 2003.

Exploring the St. Lawrence River Region, Raintree (Chicago, IL), 2004.

Exploring the Western Mountains, Raintree (Chicago, IL), 2004.

Exploring the Southwestern United States, Raintree (Chicago, IL), 2004.

Exploring the Arctic, Raintree (Chicago, IL), 2004.

Exploring South America, Raintree (Chicago, IL), 2004.

Exploring Central America, Mexico, and the Caribbean, Raintree (Chicago, IL), 2004.

Work in Progress

More works of nonfiction.

Sidelights

Together with frequent coauthor Rose Blue, Corine J. Naden is the author of numerous books for elementary-aged readers that focus on U.S. history and culture, as well as books detailing the lives of men and women who have achieved greatness in many areas, including polio vaccine creator Jonah Salk; political leaders George W. Bush, Vladimir Lenin, Tony Blair, and Muammar Qaadafi; athletes Wilma Rudolph and Jerry Rice; civil servants Madeleine Albright and Condolezza Rice; and actors Nicholas Cage, Halle Berry, and Whoopi Goldberg. Praising the coauthors for their "clear, accessible language" in _Lenin, Booklist_ reviewer Gillian Engberg added that Naden and Blue are careful to explain the terminology surrounding Lenin's rise to power in Russia following World War I, and also "offer plenty of historical background." In _Muammar Qaadafi_ their discussion of the life of the Libyan ruler was praised for being "up to date" and a "useful choice" for young researchers, according to _School Library Journal_ contributor Elizabeth Stumpf.

"Nonfiction fascinates me," Naden once told _SATA,_ "it always has. I remember the sense of anticipation I used to feel on the first day of a high school or college class, pen ready and blank notebook open to capture all the marvelous new information that was going to come my way. I get that same sense today when I sit in front of the computer with brand new materials spread all over the desk, but now I'm the one about to send out all that marvelous new information—perhaps to someone who'll receive it with the same thrill I did."

Biographical and Critical Sources

PERIODICALS

Booklist, March 1, 1997, Hazel Rochman, review of _The Newbery Companion,_ p. 1177; November 15, 1997, review of _Characters in Young-Adult Literature,_ p. 575; December 1, 1998, Ilene Cooper, review of _Madeleine Albright: U.S. Secretary of State,_ p. 663; February 15, 2003, Carolyn Phelan, review of _Mae Jemison: Out of This World,_ p. 1082; June 1, 2004, Gillian Engberg, review of _Lenin,_ p. 1751; February 1, 2005, John Peters, review of _Dred Scott: Person or Property?,_ p. 976.

Kliatt, January, 2002, review of _Wesley Snipes,_ p. 23; January, 2004, Paula Rohrlick, review of _Teenplots,_ p. 32.

School Library Journal, January, 1998, Marilyn Fairbanks, review of _Colin Powell,_ p. 119; June, 1999, Sylvia V. Meisner, review of _Staying out of Trouble in a Troubled Family,_ p. 140; January, 2000, Mary Mueller, review of "House Divided" series, p. 150; January, 2001, Patricia Ann Owens, review of _Belle Starr and the Wild West,_ p. 152; September, 2001, Edith Ching, review of _Banjamin Banneker,_ p. 239; January, 2002, Sue Sherif, review of _Jonas Salk,_ p. 162; June, 2003, Shauna Yusko, review of _Harriet Tubman,_ p. 124; February, 2004, Susan McCaffrey, review of _Teenplots,_ p. 175; November, 2004, Deanna Romriell, review of _Mormonism,_ p. 170; February, 2005, reviewing _Exploring the Arctic_ and _Exploring the Western Mountains,_ p. 145; May, 2005, review of _Muammar Qaddafi,_ p. 154.*

*   *   *

NIELDS, Nerissa 1967-

Personal

Born 1967, in New York, NY; married David Jones (a musician and teacher; divorced); married Tom Duffy (a writer), 2005. _Education:_ Yale University, B.A.

Addresses

Home—Northampton, MA. _Agent_—Ginger Knowlton, Curtis Brown Ltd., 10 Astor Place, New York, NY 10003. _E-mail_—NFNields@aol.com.

Career

Singer, songwriter, and writer. The Nields (musical group), performer beginning 1991; musician performing with sister, Katryna Nields, beginning 1998; writing workshop leader. Vocalist on recordings (with The Nields), including _66 Hoxsey Street,_ 1992; _Live at the Iron Horse Music Hall,_ 1993; _Bob on the Ceiling,_ 1994; _Abigail,_ 1995; _Gotta Get over Greta,_ 1996; _Mousse,_ 1998; _Play,_ 1998; _If You Lived Here, You'd Be Home Now,_ 2000; and _Live from Northampton,_ 2001. Vocalist on recordings with sister, Katryna Nields, including _Love and China,_ 2001; _This Town Is Wrong,_ 2004; and _Songs for Amelia_ (for children), 2004.

Writings

Plastic Angel (novel; includes CD of song "This Town Is Wrong" and "Glow-in-the-Dark Plastic Angel"), Orchard Books (New York, NY), 2005.

Work in Progress

The Big Idea, a novel; _How to Be an Adult,_ a memoir and self-help book.

Sidelights

A singer and songwriter, as well as one of the founding members of the musical group The Nields, Nerissa Nields has toured North America, had her music recorded on several major labels, and developed a following among folk-music fans in her native New England. In addition to continuing to perform as a musician, often in a duo with sister Katryna Nields—the two first appeared together in 1998 at Lilith Fair—Nields has broadened her creative horizons through her writing. In addition to launching into the field of children's literature with the novel *Plastic Angel,* she also conducts writing retreats and a workshop she calls "Writing It up in the Garden" from her home in western Massachusetts.

Released with a CD recording of two songs performed by the Nields, *Plastic Angel* was described as a "well-written and appealing story" by a *Kirkus Reviews* contributor. The novel focuses on two thirteen-year-old girls, their struggle with conformity in their upscale suburban community, and their ability to cope with family conflicts. It is through the eyes of Randi Rankin, the down-to-earth daughter of an indulgent musician, that readers meet Angela "Gellie" Riddle, Randi's best friend. A beautiful and talented model/actress, Gellie finds herself in a constant battle with her overbearing stage mother, who wants to dominate her daughter's life and career. Together Gellie and Randi decide to start a band, Plastic Angel. True to form, Gellie's mother rejects the idea, trying everything within her power to get her daughter to withdraw from the band. Gellie is then faced with a serious decision when she lands her first big acting role in a commercial film at the same time the band is scheduled to play its debut gig.

Plastic Angel "moves along well," noted the *Kirkus Reviews* contributor, "touching issues of family dissent and emerging individuality," while in *School Library Journal* Diane P. Tuccillo praised the two teen protagonists as "likeable" and cited "Randi's witty and perceptive point of view." *Booklist* contributor Debbie Carton also praised the "considerable charm" of Nields' teen characters, adding that the "pull between acceptance and self-expression" that these girls deal with in *Plastic Angel* "will resonate strongly with young teens."

Biographical and Critical Sources

PERIODICALS

Booklist, August, 2005, Debbie Carton, review of *Plastic Angel,* p. 2016.

Kirkus Reviews, May 15, 2005, review of *Plastic Angel,* p. 594.

People, January 26, 2004, Ralph Novak, review of *This Town Is Wrong: Nerissa and Katryna Nields,* p. 36.

School Library Journal, September, 2005, Diane P. Tuccillo, review of *Plastic Angel,* p. 209.

Sing Out, summer, 2002, review of *Love and China,* p. 130; spring, 2004, Daniele Dreilinger, review of *This Town Is Wrong,* p. 139.

ONLINE

Nerissa Nields Home Page, http://www.nerissanields.com (November 6, 2005).

The Nields Web site, http://www.nields.com/ (November 6, 2005).

Inspired by the lyrics to the CD This Town Is Wrong, *recorded by Nields and her sister, Katryna Nields, this 2005 novel finds two strong-minded, talented young teens determined to find their own path to adulthood. (Cover photograph by Horst Neumann/Photonica.)*

*   *   *

NOLAN, Dennis 1945-

Personal

Born October 19, 1945, in San Francisco, CA; son of Arthur Thomas (an opera singer) and Helen (Fortier) Nolan; married Susan Christine Ericksen, January 28, 1967 (marriage ended); married Lauren Ainsworth Mills (an author and artist), June 1, 1987; children: (first marriage) Andrew William; (second marriage) one daughter. *Education:* Attended College of San Mateo, 1963-65; San Jose State College (now University), B.A., 1967, M.A., 1968.

Addresses

Home—Westhampton, MA. *Agent*—c/o Author Mail, Hyperion Books, 114 5th Ave., New York, NY 10011.

Career

Author and illustrator. San Mateo County Library, Belmont, CA, graphic artist, 1970-77; Canada Junior College, Redwood City, CA, art instructor, 1979-86; University of Hartford, Bloomfield, CT, coordinator of illustration program in Hartford Art School, beginning 1986. Art instructor at College of San Mateo, 1982-86, and at San Jose State University, 1983-86. *Exhibitions:* Work exhibited in one-man shows and in group shows.

Awards, Honors

Outstanding Science Book Award, National Science Teachers Association, 1981, for *The Joy of Chickens,* and 1987, for *Step into the Night;* Pick of the List, American Booksellers, and, Top-Twelve Books designation, *Christian Science Monitor,* both 1987, and Prix de Zephyr (France), 1988, all for *The Castle Builder; Parents Choice* magazine Top-Fifteen Books designation, and Commonwealth Club of California award, both 1988, both for *Step into the Night;* Notable Social Studies Books selection, 1988, for *Legend of the White Doe;* Golden Kite Picture-Book Honor, 1990, for *Dinosaur Dream,* and 1995, for *Fairy Wings.*

Writings

FOR CHILDREN; SELF-ILLUSTRATED

Big Pig (picture book), Prentice-Hall (Englewood Cliffs, NJ), 1976.

Monster Bubbles: A Counting Book (picture book), Prentice-Hall (Englewood Cliffs, NJ), 1976.

Alphabrutes (picture book), Prentice-Hall (Englewood Cliffs, NJ), 1977.

Wizard McBean and His Flying Machine (picture book), Prentice-Hall (Englewood Cliffs, NJ), 1977.

Witch Bazooza (picture book), Prentice-Hall (Englewood Cliffs, NJ), 1979.

The Joy of Chickens (nonfiction), Prentice-Hall (Englewood Cliffs, NJ), 1981.

The Castle Builder (picture book), Macmillan (New York, NY), 1987.

Wolf Child (picture book), Macmillan (New York, NY), 1989.

Dinosaur Dream (picture book), Macmillan (New York, NY), 1990.

(Reteller) *Androcles and the Lion* (picture book), Harcourt (New York, NY), 1997.

Shadow of the Dinosaurs (picture book), Simon & Schuster (New York, NY), 2001.

ILLUSTRATOR

Charles Keller, compiler, *Llama Beans,* Prentice-Hall (Englewood Cliffs, NJ), 1979.

Bill Nygren, *Gnomes Color and Story Album,* Troubador Press, 1980.

Karen Schiller, *Bears Color and Story Album,* Troubador Press, 1982.

William Hooks, *The Legend of the White Doe,* Macmillan (New York, NY), 1988.

Joanne Ryder, *Step into the Night,* Four Winds (New York, NY), 1988.

Joanne Ryder, *Mockingbird Morning,* Four Winds (New York, NY), 1989.

Jane Yolen, *Dove Isabeau,* Harcourt (New York, NY), 1989.

Nancy Carlstrom, *Heather Hiding,* Macmillan (New York, NY), 1990.

Joanne Ryder, *Under Your Feet,* Four Winds (New York, NY), 1990.

Jane Yolen, *Wings,* Harcourt (New York, NY), 1991.

Nancy Carlstrom, *No Nap for Benjamin Badger,* Macmillan (New York, NY), 1991.

Ann Tompert, *Savina, the Gypsy Dancer,* Macmillan (New York, NY), 1991.

Maxinne Rhea Leighton, *An Ellis Island Christmas,* Viking (New York, NY), 1992.

T.H. White, *The Sword in the Stone,* Philomel Books (New York, NY), 1993.

Diane Stanley, *The Gentleman and the Kitchen Maid,* Dial Books for Young Readers (New York, NY), 1994.

Bruce Coville, reteller, *William Shakespeare's A Midsummer Night's Dream,* Dial Books (New York, NY), 1995.

Lauren A. Mills, *Fairy Wings* (picture book), Little, Brown (Boston, MA), 1995.

Lauren A. Mills, *The Dog Prince,* Little, Brown (Boston, MA), 1996.

Garry D. Schmidt, reteller, *The Blessing of the Lord: Stories from the Old and New Testaments,* W.B. Eerdmans (Grand Rapids, MI), 1997.

Bruce Coville, reteller, *William Shakespeare's Romeo and Juliet,* Dial Books (New York, NY), 1999.

Ann Warren Turner, *Red Flower Goes West,* Hyperion (New York, NY), 1999.

Jane Yolen, editor, *Sherwood: Original Stories from the World of Robin Hood,* Philomel Books (New York, NY), 2000.

Lauren A. Mills, *The Dog Prince: An Original Fairy Tale,* Little, Brown (Boston, MA), 2001.

Lauren A. Mills, *Fia and the Imp,* Little, Brown (Boston, MA), 2002.

Jane Yolen, *The Perfect Wizard: Hans Christian Andersen,* Dutton's Children's Book (New York, NY), 2004.

Robert F. Kennedy, Jr., *Saint Francis of Assisi: A Life of Joy,* Hyperion (New York, NY), 2005.

FOR ADULTS; ILLUSTRATOR

Jim Barrett and others, editors, *"Sunset" Homeowner's Guide to Wood Stoves,* Lane, 1979.

David E. Clark and others, editors, *Gardeners Answer Book,* Lane, 1983.

Sidelights

Award-winning author and illustrator Dennis Nolan is known for the highly realistic paintings he has created for both his own picture-book texts and the work of other writers. Although he works primarily in acrylics, Nolan has worked in water color to illustrate books such as Nancy Carlstrom's *No Nap for Benjamin Badger.* His detailed renderings delve into the fanciful, gaining comparison to the work of illustrator Arthur Rackham in the award-winning *Fairy Wings,* one of several works he has illustrated for his wife, writer and fellow artist Lauren A. Mills.

Born and raised in San Francisco, Nolan gained an interest in art due to his exposure to the opera, where his father performed as a tenor and Nolan was allowed to spend time backstage. After attending San Jose State University, he worked as a graphic artist and published his first self-illustrated picture book, *Big Pig,* in 1976. A silly poetic romp in which preschool readers can find all sorts of chubby animals—from stout trouts to blimpy chimps and, on every page, a fat pig—*Big Pig* was praised as "an ingenious but incongruous little book," by a *Booklist* reviewer, although the critic noted that some of the language may be too sophisticated for young readers. Works such as *Monster Bubbles: A Counting Book, Alphabrutes,* and *Wizard McBean and the Flying Machine* followed through the rest of the 1970s. In 1979 Nolan also began illustrating texts for other writers, beginning with Charles Keller's humorous anthology *Llama Beans.*

Nolan spent much of the early 1980s as an art instructor at a California junior college, and during this time he worked on only a few children's books. In 1986 he left teaching and also left the West Coast, moving to a position at a small Connecticut university that allowed him more time for book illustration. His first book to come from this increased attention to his art is *The Castle Builder,* which enters the world of childhood imagination as it tells of one young boy's day at the beach. The boy builds a sand castle and imagines himself to be its lord, Sir Christopher, a brave hero who defends his home against dragons and evil knights. When the tide comes in, however, the waves become a foe the boy cannot defeat. Undaunted, after his castle is washed away, he vows to return to the beach and build a new one. In a review of *The Castle Builder School Library Journal* contributor Shirley Wilton called it "a charming evocation of a child's world," while a *Publishers Weekly* critic wrote that Nolan's "photograph-like pictures in halftones . . . exhibit startling clarity." As Betsy Hearne noted in the *Bulletin of the Center for Children's Books,* "The duality of trompe l'oeil screened by a surface of dots serves the fantasy theme well."

The Castle Builder was followed by *Wolf Child,* a story set in prehistoric times about a little boy who befriends a wolf cub that later saves him from a charging mammoth. Although some critics called the story and characters uninspired, Nolan still received praise for his illustrations in this work, a *Kirkus Reviews* writer deeming *Wolf Child* an "unexceptional story" enhanced by "well-crafted paintings" rendered "in a formal style that recalls [noted nineteenth-century illustrator] N.C. Wyeth."

In 1990 Nolan won his first Golden Kite picture-book honor for *Dinosaur Dream.* Returning to the world of childhood imagination he captured in *The Castle Builder,* Nolan once again brings dreams to life in this story about a modern boy who helps a baby apatosaurus find its way home. Wilbur is awakened one night when Gideon the dinosaur taps at his window. The boy, knowing immediately what must be done, resolves to return Gideon to the Jurassic era. He manages to do this by the simple means of walking back through time, one step at a time, with Gideon following him like a obedient puppy. The two step past the Ice Age and back into the world of dinosaurs, while braving hazards like volcanoes and saber-tooth cats. Throughout the fanciful tale, the author/illustrator leaves it to the reader to decide whether the adventure is real or merely a dream Wilbur is having, inspired by reading a book about dinosaurs just prior to falling asleep.

Although Cathryn A. Camper, writing in *School Library Journal,* called the premise of *Dinosaur Dream* a "trite plot gimmick" and found the conclusion "cloying," *Booklist* contributor Leone McDermott praised the book as "a dinosaur lover's delight." A *Publishers Weekly* commentator found Nolan's story to be clever, especially the role reversal between Wilbur and Gideon that depicts the boy to be unexpectedly braver than his rather sheepish and cowardly dinosaur friend, and added that Gideon "ranks with the best of animal creations." Nolan reprises his dinosaur character for *Shadow of the Dinosaur,* which finds a modern-day Dachshund swept into the Jurassic past when he digs up a dino bone during a family camping trip. Dubbing the story a "prehistoric dreamscape" similar to *Dinosaur Dream,* John Peters noted in *Booklist* that Nolan weaves dinosaur facts into his tale and his renderings of prehistoric creatures are "sharp [and] precisely drawn."

Much of Nolan's creative work involves illustrating the stories of other authors, such as William Hooks, Joanne Ryder, Bruce Coville, Jane Yolen, Nancy Carlstrom, and Ann Tompert. In 1994 he provided the illustrations for Diane Stanley's *The Gentleman and the Kitchen Maid,* a very unique and well-received fantasy about the love between two figures in separate portraits hanging in a city art museum. A young art student who has come to copy the work of the Dutch masters becomes attuned to the plight of these unrequited lovers, and joins the two in a painting of her own making. "Hats off to Nolan for his thorough research and credible renderings of paintings in the style of artists ranging from Rembrandt to Picasso," commented a *Publishers Weekly* reviewer, while Carolyn Phelan, writing in *Booklist,* called *The Gentleman and the Kitchen Maid* "an original"; "Nolan's sensitive watercolor illustrations make

Falling asleep while reading about dinosaurs, a young boy rescues a baby apatosaurus and returns it to the Jurassic age, despite the dangers that dwell there in Nolan's self-illustrated **Dinosaur Dream.**

each portrait in the museum a definite character in the story." *School Library Journal* contributor Shirley Wilton also commented favorably on Stanley and Nolan's effort in this work, asserting that "this lighthearted story is deftly told and handsomely illustrated."

Other collaborations include *Red Flower Goes West,* a story by Ann Turner that focuses on a family traveling west along the Oregon Trail to make a new life in California. Along with their many possessions, Ma packs a red flowering plant, dug from her garden and potted up; as the trip becomes more challenging the family is cheered by the bright flower and knows that if the flower can survive, so can they. Recalling old-fashioned sepia-toned photographs, Nolan's "strong pictures" created by pencil and pastels reinforce the family's travels, according to *Booklist* reviewer Hazel Rochman. In *Publishers Weekly* a critic commented in particular on the illustrator's use of the red flower "as an emblem of the family's hope," its brilliant hue contrasting with Nolan's "finely etched portraits and landscapes."

Nolan joins his wife, Lauren A. Mills, on several projects, the first being *Fairy Wings,* a tale about a wingless, ridiculed fairy named Fia who saves her fellow fairies from a wicked troll. "Delicate, detailed watercolors add greatly to the book's appeal," noted *Booklist* reviewer Susan Dove Lempke, and *School Library Journal* contributor Lisa Dennis similarly praised the "lovely illustrations, reminiscent of Arthur Rackham's ethereal style." A sequel, *Fia and the Imp,* finds the wingless fairy working to save a pair of young woodkins—lowly forest creatures—after they are swept away on a river raft while the other fairies stand by and do nothing. *School Library Journal* reviewer Shelley B. Sutherland praised Nolan for depicting Fia's fantasy world in "ethereal watercolors" and also dubbed Mills' text "sophisticated." In *The Dog Prince* Mills and Nolan present a story about a boorish prince who finds everything in his royal life boring. The prince changes his attitude after a fairy, angered by his insulting treatment of a poor goat girl, transforms the spoiled young man into a scruffy bloodhound.

Nolan once told *SATA:* "As an illustrator I approach most of my projects with the visual problems foremost in my mind. The story generally moves along after the pictures have been visualized, at least in my mind if not on paper. Planning the illustrations for the lead-in, the climax, and the ending across a thirty-two-page format is also a major concern. Most of my books are humorous, and I plan them in storyboard form somewhat like an animated film. In this way I can control the timing of the punch lines, surprises, and build-ups. I have found that varying my style and technical approach has kept me fresh for each new project."

Biographical and Critical Sources

PERIODICALS

Booklist, April 15, 1976, review of *Big Pig,* p. 1192; February 15, 1978, p. 1010; December 1, 1989, p. 750; December 15, 1989, p. 834; March 15, 1990, p. 1443; October 15, 1990, Leone McDermott, review of *Dinosaur Dream,* p. 439; November 1, 1991, p. 330; January 15, 1994, Carolyn Phelan, review of *The Gentleman and the Kitchen Maid,* p. 939; November 1, 1995, Susan Dove Lempke, review of *Fairy Wings,* p. 478; May 1, 1999, Hazel Rochman, review of *Red Flower Goes West,* p. 1602; December 15, 2001, John Peters, review of *Shadow of the Dinosaurs,* p. 740.

Bulletin of the Center for Children's Books, July, 1977, p. 178; January, 1988, Betsy Hearne, review of *The Castle Builder,* p. 96; February, 1988, p. 110.

Horn Book, September, 1999, Mary A. Burns, review of *Red Flower Goes West,* p. 602.

Kirkus Reviews, March 1, 1976, p. 253; January 15, 1977, p. 43; January 1, 1978, p. 1; August 15, 1989, review of *Wolf Child,* p. 1248; October 1, 1989, p. 1483; February 15, 1990, p. 273; October 1, 1991, p. 1293.

Los Angeles Times Book Review, November 25, 1990, p. 18; December 16, 1990, p. 9.

Newsweek, December 3, 1990, p. 64.

Publishers Weekly, March 15, 1976, p. 57; January 17, 1977, p. 82; December 19, 1980, p. 52; August 14, 1987, review of *The Castle Builder,* p. 103; January 20, 1989, p. 147; July 28, 1989, p. 221; February 9, 1990, p. 60; October 26, 1990, review of *Dinosaur Dream,* p. 67; September 20, 1991, p. 132; November 22, 1993, review of *The Gentleman and the Kitchen Maid,* p. 63; November 6, 1995, p. 94; June 14, 1999, review of *Red Flower Goes West,* p. 69; October 8, 2001, review of *The Dog Prince,* p. 64.

School Library Journal, April, 1976, p. 62; May, 1977, p. 54; February, 1978, p. 49; January, 1980, p. 60; January, 1988, Shirley Wilton, review of *The Castle Builder,* p. 68; July, 1989, p. 75; December, 1989, p. 102; April, 1990, p. 110; July, 1990, p. 79; November, 1990, Cathryn A. Camper, review of *Dinosaur Dream,* p. 96; August, 1994, Shirley Wilton, review of *The Gentleman and the Kitchen Maid,* p. 146; January, 1996, Lisa Dennis, review of *Fairy Wings,* p. 9;

June, 1999, Steven Engelfried, review of *Red Flower Goes West,* p. 108; August, 2000, Nancy Call, review of *Sherwood,* p. 192; December, 2001, Steven Engelfried, review of *Shadow of the Dinosaur,* p. 108; December, 2002, Shelley B. Sutherland, review of *Fia and the Imp,* p. 102; February, 2004, Nancy Menaldi-Scanlon, review of *William Shakespeare's Romeo and Juliet,* p. 83.

ONLINE

Hyperion Publishers Web site, http://www.hyperionbooks forchildren.com/ (February 6, 2006) "Dennis Nolan."*

*   *   *

NORAC, Carl 1960-

Personal

Born 1960, in Mons, Belgium; son of a writer and puppet-theatre owner and an actress; children: Else.

Addresses

Home—269, rue de la Source 45160, Olivet, France. *E-mail*—carlnorac@wanadoo.fr.

Career

Children's book author and poet. Has also worked as a French teacher, television scriptwriter, and journalist. Hans Christian Andersen ambassador, 2005.

Awards, Honors

Literary prize, c. 1978; recipient of several other awards.

Writings

Le lion fanfaron, Casterman, 1991.

Romulus et Rémi, une fable à l'opèra, Pastel (Paris, France), 1994.

Dimanche aux Hespérides (poems), Editions de la Différence (Paris, France), 1994.

La semaine de Monsieur Gris, Altiora, 1994.

Coeur de singe, illustrated by Jean Claud Hubert, Pastel (Paris, France), 1995.

La candeur (poems), Editions de la Différence (Paris, France), 1996.

Les mots doux, illustrated by Claude K. Dubois, Pastel (Paris, France), 1996, translated as *I Love You So Much,* Random House (New York, NY), 1998.

Un loup dans la nuit bleue, illustrated by Louis Joos, Pastel (Paris, France), 1996.

Nemo et le volcan, illustrated by Louis Joos, Pastel (Paris, France), 1996.

Beau comme au cinéma, illustrated by Louis Joos, Pastel (Paris, France), 1997.

L'île aux câlins, illustrated by Claude K. Dubois, Pastel (Paris, France), 1998.

L'espoir pélican, illustrated by Louis Joos, Pastel (Paris, France), 1998.

Le sourire de Kiawak, illustrated by Louis Joos, Pastel (Paris, France), 1998.

La grande ourse, illustrated by Kitty Crowther, Pastel (Paris, France), 1999.

La carnival des animaux, Thèatre Royal de la Monnaie, 1999.

Bonjour mon petit coeur, illustrated by Claude K. Dubois, Pastel (Paris, France), 1999, translated as *Hello, Sweetie Pie,* Random House (New York, NY), 2000.

Marine et Louisa, illustrated by Claude K. Dubois, Pastel (Paris, France), 2000.

Le rêve de l'ours, illustrated by Louis Joos, Pastel (Paris, France), 2000.

Le message de la baleine, illustrated by Jean-Luc Englebert, Pastel (Paris, France), 2000.

La petite souris d'Halloween, illustrated by Stibane, Pastel (Paris, France), 2000.

Le père Noël m'a écrit, illustrated by Kitty Crowther, Pastel (Paris, France), 2001.

Un Bisou, c'est trop court, illustrated by Claude K. Dubois, Pastel (Paris, France), 2001.

Le dernier voyage de Saint-Exupéry, Renaissance du livre, 2001.

Kuli et le sorcier, illustrated by Dominiqu Mwankumi, Archimède, 2001.

Je veux un bisou!, illustrated by Claude K. Dubois, Pastel (Paris, France), 2001.

Je suis un amour, illustrated by Claude K. Dubois, Pastel (Paris, France), 2001.

Donne-moi un ours!, illustrated by Emile Jadoul, Pastel (Paris, France), 2001.

Zeppo, illustrated by Peter Elliott, Pastel (Paris, France), 2002.

Une visite chez la sorcière, illustrated by Sophie, Pastel (Paris, France), 2002.

Tu m'aimes ou tu m'aimes pas?, illustrated by Claude K. Dubois, Pastel (Paris, France), 2002.

Pierrot d'Amour, illustrated by Jean-Luc Englebert, Pastel (Paris, France), 2002.

Lettres du géant à l'enfante qui passé et autres poèmes, Labor (Brussels, Belgium), 2002.

Un secret pour grandir, illustrated by Carll Cneut, Pastel (Paris, France), 2003.

Tu es si gentil, mon ours, illustrated by Anne Isa le Touzé, Pastel (Paris, France), 2003.

Métrpolitaines: tentative de photographier avec le language, métro de Paris, hiver 1999-2000, Escampette (Paris, France), 2003.

Tout près de maman, illustrated by Catherin Pineur, Pastel (Paris, France), 2004.

Mon papa est un géant, illustrated by Ingrid Godon, Bayard Jeunesse (Paris, France), 2004, translated as *My Daddy Is a Giant,* Clarion Books (New York, NY), 2005.

I Love to Cuddle, illustrated by Claude K. Dubois, Dell Dragonfly Books (New York, NY), 2002.

Le petit sorcier de la pluie, illustrated by Anne-Cat de Boel, Pastel (Paris, France), 2004.

Coeur de papier, illustrated by Carll Cneut, Pastel (Paris, France), 2004.

Akli, prince du désert, illustrated by Anne-Cat de Boel, Pastel (Paris, France), 2004.

Angakkeg: la légende de l'oiseau, illustrated by Louis Joos, Pastel (Paris, France), 2004.

Le géant de la grande tour, Sarbacane, 2005.

Mon meilleur ami du monde, illustrated by Claude K. Dubois, Pastel (Paris, France), 2005.

Norac's works have been translated into eighteen languages.

Sidelights

Belgian-born author and poet Carl Norac discovered his passion for the arts at a young age, while writing poetry and acting out performances with his friends and family. Beginning his career as a children's book author in the mid-1990s, his books quickly gained popularity and are now read all over the world. Several of Norac's works have been translated into English, among them *My Daddy Is a Giant* as well as *I Love You So Much,* and *I Love to Cuddle,* both of which feature a young hamster

Belgian children's book author Carl Norac gained a legion of new fans when his book **My Daddy Is a Giant** *gained a place in U.S. storyhour circles.* (Illustration by Ingrid Godon.)

named Lola. Brought to life in pencil drawings by illustrator Claude K. Dubois, Lola experiences the same emotions as a loving child; she serves as an "affectionate" protagonist in *I Love to Cuddle,* which a *Publishers Weekly* dubbed a "winsome" book that "trumpets an uplifting and timeless theme."

Norac explores a child's love and admiration for his father in *My Daddy Is a Giant,* illustrated by Ingrid Godon. From the small child's close-to-the-ground perspective, his father is like a towering giant whose shoulders reach as high as the clouds and whose sneezes can blow back the tides of the seas. The story's simple text expresses "the child's belief that Daddy possesses extraordinary powers," noted a *Publishers Weekly* reviewer, adding that "Children may enjoy this story's gentle humor best from the warmth of Daddy's lap." Amy Lilien-Harper, writing in *School Library Journal,* stated that Godon's "slightly simplistic drawings depict the loving bond between father and son perfectly, bringing the relationship and text to life."

Biographical and Critical Sources

PERIODICALS

Bookbird (annual), 1999, review of *L'espoir pélican,* p. 62.

Booklist, April 1, 2000, Ilene Cooper, review of *Hello, Sweetie Pie,* p. 1470.

Horn Book, May-June, 2005, Joanna Rudge Long, review of *My Daddy Is a Giant,* p. 311.

Kirkus Reviews, May 15, 2005, review of *My Daddy Is a Giant,* p. 594

Publishers Weekly, January 5, 1998, review of *I Love You So Much,* p. 66; December 21, 1998, review of *I Love to Cuddle,* p. 66; July 31, 2000, review of *Hello, Sweetie Pie,* p. 97; January 14, 2002, review of *I Love You So Much,* p. 63; December 2, 2002, review of *I Love You So Much,* p. 54; December 16, 2002, review of *I Love to Cuddle,* p. 70; August 25, 2003, review of *Hello, Sweetie Pie,* p. 67; December 15, 2003, review of *I Love to Cuddle,* p. 75; June 6, 2005, review of *My Daddy Is a Giant,* p. 63.

Reviewer's Bookwatch, May, 2005, Lynne Marie Pisano, review of *My Daddy Is a Giant.*

School Library Journal, February, 1998, Jacke Kechtkopf, review of *I Love You So Much,* p. 89; March, 1999, Marcia Hupp, review of *I Love to Cuddle,* p. 183; August, 2000, Sally R. Dow, review of *Hello, Sweetie Pie,* p. 162; May, 2005, Amy Lilien-Harper, review of *My Daddy Is a Giant,* p. 94.

ONLINE

École des Loisirs Web site, http://www.ecoledesloisirs.fr/ (November 6, 2005), "Carl Norac."

Hans Christian Andersen Ambassadors 2005 Web site, http://www.hca2005.com/ (November 6, 2005), "Carl Norac."

Ricochet-Jeunes Web site, http://www.ricochet-jeunes.org/ (November 6, 2005), "Carl Norac."*

O-P

O'MARA, Carmel 1965-
(Carmel O'Mara-Horwitz)

Personal

Born April 17, 1965, in San Diego, CA; daughter of Michael Bond (an artist) and Allwyn (a fine-art book binder, teacher, and children's bookseller) O'Mara; married Charles Samuel Horwitz (a real estate broker), June 4, 1994; children: Julian, Lauren, Amber, Jeremy. *Education:* Long Beach State University, B.F.A., 1991.

Addresses

Office—2630 Bentley Ave., W. Los Angeles, CA 90064. *E-mail*—carmelhorwitz@comcast.net.

Career

Freelance artist and illustrator. Los Angeles Unified School District, Los Angeles, CA, part-time teacher; freelance toy designer for Small World Toys, Lakeshore Learning Materials, and Mattel. Volunteer elementary school teacher and gardener; volunteer at other community organizations.

Member

Society of Children's Book Writers and Illustrators.

Writings

SELF-ILLUSTRATED PICTURE BOOKS

Good Morning, Good Night, Harcourt Brace (San Diego, CA), 1997.
Good Morning, Harcourt Brace (San Diego, CA), 2000.
Good Night, Harcourt Brace (San Diego, CA), 2000.
Rainy Day, Harcourt Brace (San Diego, CA), 2001.
Sunny Day, Harcourt Brace (San Diego, CA), 2001.

Carmen O'Mara

Author's works have been translated into Hebrew.

Sidelights

Carmel O'Mara told *SATA:* "There are few things as wonderful to me as the moment my pictures smile back at me. When the story shows itself from page to page; and the characters emerge from scribbles. Or when the words dance in my mind stumbling and tripping till they waltz right off into the computer.

"I love to illustrate books. I love to write and illustrate books. I love to read books. There never seem to be enough books to keep my son (Julian now seven) and myself satisfied for our night time reading. So lets bring on more and more books.

"In many ways it was my destiny to work on children's books. My mother, Allwyn O'Mara, was a children's book buyer for many wonderful book stores as I grew up; and my father, Michael O'Mara, was an artist who taught me to draw, paint and print.

"I recall there was a moment when I was a child, where I realized I wanted to be a children's book author and illustrator. It was a beautiful summer day, my mother had put together an autograph party for several illustrators and authors at one of her book stores, John Cole's Books in La Jola, California. I was standing on the grass by a folding table watching James Marshall sign my *George and Martha* book. He drew me a picture next to his signature. It made me smile with awe and I thought 'I want to be able to make magic pictures and write stories like him.'

"Now I work on illustrations and stories everyday. My family still keeps me going. My sister, Kathleen Svetlik, a librarian, helps me research. Her husband, John Svetlik, helped me make a video about myself. My son Julian, husband Charles, cats, and dogs pose for me. My latest project is a pop-up book and what fun I'm having making my pictures move.

"Who knows what will be next, but what I know is there is always room in my life to make more books!"

Biographical and Critical Sources

PERIODICALS

Magpies, July, 1997, review of *Good Morning, Good Night,* p. 26.

Publishers Weekly, February 10, 1997, review of *Good Morning, Good Night,* p. 85; March 12, 2001, review of *Sunny Day,* p. 93; March 12, 2001, review of *Rainy Day,* p. 93; March 12, 2001, review of *Good Night,* p. 93; March 12, 2001, review of *Good Morning,* p. 93.

School Library Journal, July, 2001, Olga R. Kuharets, review of *Sunny Day,* p. 86; July, 2001, Olga R. Kuharets, review of *Rainy Day,* p. 86.*

*   *   *

O'MARA-HORWITZ, Carmel
See O'MARA, Carmel

PEARSON, Susan 1946-

Personal

Born December 21, 1946, in Boston, MA; daughter of Allen M. (a Swedish masseur) and Chloris (a secretary; maiden name, Horsman) Pearson. *Education:* St. Olaf College, Northfield, MN, B.A., 1968.

Addresses

Office—c/o Chronicle Books, 86 2nd St., 6th Fl., San Francisco, CA 94105.

Career

Author and editor. Volunteers in Service to America (VISTA), Columbia, SC, volunteer worker, 1968-69; Quaker Oats Co., Minneapolis, MN, sales representative, 1969-71; Viking Press, New York, NY, assistant editor, 1971-72; Dial Press, New York, NY, editor, 1972-78; Carolrhoda Books, Minneapolis, editorial director, 1978-85; freelance editor and writer, 1985-89; Lothrop, Lee & Shepherd, New York, NY, editorial director, 1989-99; Chronicle Books, San Francisco, CA, editor-at-large, 2000—.

Awards, Honors

New York Times Outstanding Books of the Year designation, and Child Study Association Children's Books of the Year designation, both 1975, both for *Izzie;* International Reading Association Children's Choice selection, 1982, for *Saturday I Ran Away.*

Writings

Izzie, illustrated by Robert Andrew Parker, Dial (New York, NY), 1975.

Monnie Hates Lydia, illustrated by Diane Paterson, Dial (New York, NY), 1975.

That's Enough for One Day, J.P.!, illustrated by Kay Chorao, Dial (New York, NY), 1977.

Everybody Knows That!, illustrated by Diane Paterson, Dial (New York, NY), 1978.

Monday I Was an Alligator, illustrated by Sal Murdocca, Lippincott (Philadelphia, PA), 1979.

Molly Moves Out, illustrated by Steven Kellogg, Dial (New York, NY), 1979.

Karin's Christmas Walk, illustrated by Trinka H. Noble, Dial (New York, NY), 1980.

Saturday I Ran Away, illustrated by Susan Jeschke, Lippincott (Philadelphia, PA), 1981.

Happy Birthday, Grampie, illustrated by Ronald Himler, Dial (New York, NY), 1987.

Baby and the Bear, illustrated by Nancy Carlson, Viking (New York, NY), 1987.

The Day Porkchop Climbed the Christmas Tree, illustrated by Rick Brown, Prentice Hall, 1987.

When Baby Went to Bed, illustrated by Nancy Carlson, Viking (New York, NY), 1987.

My Favorite Time of Year, illustrated by John Wallner, Harper & Row (New York, NY), 1988.

Porkchop's Halloween, illustrated by Rick Brown, Simon & Schuster (New York, NY), 1988.

(Reteller) *Jack and the Beanstalk,* illustrated by James Warhola, Simon & Schuster (New York, NY), 1989.

The Bogeyman Caper, illustrated by Gioia Fiammenghi, Simon & Schuster (New York, NY), 1990.

The Campfire Ghosts, illustrated by Gioia Fiammenghi, Simon & Schuster (New York, NY), 1990.

Eagle-Eye Ernie Comes to Town, illustrated by Gioia Fiammenghi, Simon & Schuster (New York, NY), 1990.

The Tap Dance Mystery, illustrated by Gioia Fiammenghi, Simon & Schuster (New York, NY), 1990.

Well, I Never, illustrated by James Warhola, Simon & Schuster (New York, NY), 1990.

The Green Magician Puzzle, illustrated by Gioia Fiammenghi, Simon & Schuster (New York, NY), 1991.

The 123 Zoo Mystery, illustrated by Gioia Fiammenghi, Simon & Schuster (New York, NY), 1991.

The Spooky Sleepover, illustrated by Gioia Fiammenghi, Simon & Schuster (New York, NY), 1991.

The Spy Code Caper, illustrated by Gioia Fiammenghi, Simon & Schuster (New York, NY), 1991.

Lenore's Big Break, illustrated by Nancy Carlson, Viking (New York, NY), 1992.

Silver Morning, illustrated by David Christiana, Harcourt (San Diego, CA), 1998.

(Selector) *The Drowsy Hours: Poems for Bedtime,* illustrated by Peter Malone, HarperCollins (New York, NY), 2002.

Squeal and Squawk: Barnyard Talk, illustrated by David Slonim, Marshall Cavendish (New York, NY), 2004.

Grimericks, illustrated by Gris Grimly, Marshall Cavendish (New York, NY), 2005.

Who Swallowed Harold?, and Other Poems about Pets, illustrated by David Slonim, Marshall Cavendish (New York, NY), 2005.

Hooray for Feet, illustrated by Roxanna Baer-Block, Chronicle Books (San Francisco, CA), 2005.

Slugs in Love, illustrated by Kevin O'Malley, Marshall Cavendish (New York, NY), 2006.

Adaptations

Everybody Knows That! was filmed and released as a video, directed by Chris Pelzer, Phoenix Films and Video, 1984.

Sidelights

In addition to serving in an editorial capacity at several major publishing houses, Susan Pearson has written dozens of books for beginning readers. Beginning with the picture book *Izzie,* she has also produced the highly praised illustrated books *Happy Birthday, Grampie* and *Silver Morning,* the second capturing "the magic of a foggy morning" in Person's "evocative text," according to Ilene Cooper in *Booklist.* A poet since childhood, Pearson has more recently begun to publish rhymes for children, serving as editor of *The Drowsy Hours: Poems for Bedtime* and serving up her original poems in

In the eighteen poems in **Who Swallowed Harold?, and Other Poems about Pets** *readers meet up with iguanas, guinea pigs, puppies, and snakes, all of which share special bonds with human friends. (Illustration by David Slonim.)*

Who Swallowed Harold? and *Squeal and Squawk: Barnyard Talk.* In *School Library Journal* Lee Bock praised *Squeal and Squawk* as "a clever, quick-reading collection with loads of child appeal," while a contributor to *Publishers Weekly* deemed the sixteen poems included in *The Drowsy Hours* "outstanding," citing in particular the collection's "layered, metaphoric language and equally textured illustrations" by artist Peter Malone.

Pearson's love of poetry—and of books in general—began during her "idyllic childhood," as she once described it to *SATA.* An only child, she was raised in Massachusetts, Virginia, and Minnesota. "Few restrictions were placed on me. I was never expected to play with dolls or to fit into a particular mold, and was encouraged in all my interests," she recalled. She started writing in the second grade, encouraged by a teacher who insisted that she create a booklet for each subject the class studied. "I decided I wanted my *own* booklet," she related. "The first thing I ever wrote was titled, 'My Booklet.' It consisted of drawings, very short stories, and some poems."

During Pearson's teen years her family moved to Minnesota. During high school she began to approach writing more seriously. "I think adolescence has something to do with that," the author maintained. "Many female writers I know started writing in earnest during their adolescence, when they were too embarrassed to tell people what they were really feeling."

Attending St. Olaf College in Northfield, Minnesota, Pearson majored in English. Lacking just a few credits for graduation, she convinced her advisors to let her write and illustrate a children's book as an independent study project. When she completed the book, which was illustrated with silkscreens, her professor was so impressed that he sent it out to several publishers. Though this early effort never saw print publication, Pearson once explained to *SATA* that its positive reception helped her believe that she could make writing her career. Her senior year "instilled in me a real feeling of confidence, a feeling that, 'Gee, maybe I really could. . . .'"

Following graduation, Pearson worked at a variety of office jobs. Each time she saved about 1,000 dollars, she would quit her job and concentrate on writing. She learned a great deal about the publishing industry while working as an editor at Dial Press in New York City, and it was during her tenure there that her first book, *Izzie,* was published in 1975. Three years later Pearson became editor-in-chief of Carolrhoda Books in Minneapolis, where she remained until leaving for several years in the late 1980s to write full time. Returning to publishing in 1989, she served as editorial director for Lothrop before moving to San Francisco-based Chronicle books as an editor-at-large in 2000.

Pearson received critical praise for her book *Happy Birthday, Grampie,* published in 1987. Every Sunday after church, young Martha accompanies her family to the nursing home to visit her beloved grandfather. She remembers Grampie when he was strong enough to push her on the swings, but now he is frail and blind and has reverted to speaking only his native Swedish. When his eighty-ninth birthday arrives, Martha makes a special card with raised letters that spell out "I love you, Grampie," hoping through her card to reconnect with him. A writer for *Kirkus Reviews* called *Happy Birthday, Grampie* "a lovely, realistic evocation of the American family at its best," while in *Horn Book* Hanna B. Zeiger noted that "this story of a strong Swedish-American family is a welcome addition to book collections."

Among Pearson's books for children are a series of books featuring child detective Ernestine Jones—nicknamed Eagle-Eye Ernie. In *Eagle-Eye Ernie Comes to Town* Ernie has just moved to Minnesota from Virginia and started classes at the local school. Several of Ernie's new classmates make fun of her clothes and the

Pearson collects a farm full of rambunctious poems that capture the lives of everything from chickens and geese to goats and farm cats in Squeal and Squawk: Barnyard Talk. *(Illustration by David Slonim.)*

Featuring a spunky young girl named Ernestine Jones, Pearson's easy-reading "Eagle-Eye Ernie" series was published in the 1990s. (Illustration from Eagle-Eye Ernie Comes to Town *by Gioia Fiammenghi.)*

way she talks, and they are quick to blame the new student when food mysteriously disappears from their lunches. Determined to solve the mystery, Ernie discovers that William, one of the nicest boys in her class, has been taking the food because an older bully has been stealing his lunch. A proactive girl, she helps William get revenge on the bully and earns her classmates' respect in the process. Lisa Smith, in a review for *School Library Journal,* predicted that "children will relate to both the situations and the characters, who are realistic and well drawn."

In *Lenore's Big Break* Pearson uses the plight of an unpopular adult to show children that there are positive aspects to being different. Nerdy Lenore is the object of much ridicule at her office job, but the only thing important to her is her secret dream of training birds. Every night she returns to her small apartment with bread, insects, worms, and small fish to feed the variety of birds who live with her. Among her many amazing feats, Lenore trains pelicans to tap dance, puffins to walk a tightrope, and flamingoes to perform a ballet. Before long, she appears with her performing feathered friends on television, gets her big break into show business, and becomes famous, leaving the snide remarks of her former co-workers far behind. A reviewer for *Publishers Weekly* noted that "Pearson's snappy text skillfully holds the reader's attention as Lenore's double life unfolds." Ilene Cooper, writing in *Booklist,* added that "there is a real message here for children who may need encouragement to follow a different drummer."

Describing her writing process, Pearson once told *SATA:* "I usually write in the morning. I have a separate room, and everything is there. It's a very cheerful room and I enjoy the sunlight and the company of my cats." She had the following advice for hopeful young writers: "To be a writer, you have to 'write.' You must believe that you can do it. If you want it badly enough, you can do it. But there is no point in wanting it for the glamour because writing isn't glamorous, it's a lot of hard work, and if you don't love words there's not much point in getting involved."

Biographical and Critical Sources

PERIODICALS

Booklist, January 15, 1989, p. 874; February 1, 1989, p. 936; June 15, 1989, p. 1826; November 15, 1990, p. 667; April, 1991, p. 101; January 15, 1992, Ilene Cooper, review of *Lenore's Big Break,* p. 949; March 15, 1998, Ilene Cooper, review of *Silver Morning,* p. 1250; October 15, 2002, Gillian Engberg, review of *The Drowsy Hours: Poems for Bedtime,* p. 402.

Horn Book, May-June, 1987, Hanna B. Zeiger, review of *Happy Birthday, Grampie,* pp. 333-334.

Kirkus Reviews, March 15, 1987, review of *Happy Birthday, Grampie,* p. 475; January 1, 1988, p. 59; August 15, 1990, p. 1178; May 15, 2002, review of *The Drowsy Hours,* p. 739.

Publishers Weekly, February 27, 1987, p. 161; January 15, 1988, p. 94; May 19, 1989, p. 82; December 13, 1991, review of *Lenore's Big Break,* p. 55; May 13, 2002, review of *The Drowsy Hours,* p. 69; March 8, 2004, review of *Squeal and Squawk,* p. 74.

School Library Journal, April, 1987, p. 88; March, 1989, p. 168; February, 1991, p. 73; April, 1991, Lisa Smith, review of *Eagle-Eye Ernie Comes to Town,* p. 101; December, 1991, p. 99; February, 1992, p. 76; March, 1992, p. 223; June, 1992, p. 100; April, 1998, Martha Topol, review of *Silver Morning,* p. 108; June, 2002, Kathleen Whalin, review of *The Drowsy Hours,* p. 124; June, 2004, Lee Bock, review of *Squeal and Squawk,* p. 131; April, 2005, Linda Staskus, review of *Who Swallowed Harold?,* p. 124.

Wilson Library Bulletin, April, 1987, pp. 54-55.

ONLINE

Balkin Buddies Web site, http://www.balkinbuddies.com/ (August 1, 2005), "Susan Pearson."*

* * *

PILKEY, Dav 1966-
(Sue Denim, David Murray Pilkey, Jr.)

Personal

First name is pronounced "Dave"; born David Murray Pilkey, Jr., March 4, 1966, in Cleveland, OH; son of

Dav Pilkey

David Murray (a sales manager) and Barbara (an organist; maiden name, Pembridge) Pilkey; married 2005; wife's name Sayuri. *Education:* Kent State University, A.A.

Addresses

Home—Western WA. *Agent*—c/o Author Mail, Blue Sky Press/Scholastic, Inc., 557 Broadway, New York, NY 10012.

Career

Freelance writer and illustrator, 1986—.

Awards, Honors

Caldecott Honor Book, American Library Association, 1997, for *The Paperboy*.

Writings

CHILDREN'S BOOKS; PICTURE BOOKS AND PRIMARY-GRADE FICTION; SELF-ILLUSTRATED, EXCEPT AS NOTED

World War Won, Landmark Editions (Kansas City, MO), 1987.
'Twas the Night before Thanksgiving, Orchard Books (New York, NY), 1990.
When Cats Dream, Orchard Books (New York, NY), 1992.
Dogzilla: Starring Flash, Rabies, and Dwayne and Introducing Leia as the Monster, Harcourt (New York, NY), 1993.

Kat Kong: Starring Flash, Rabies, and Dwayne and Introducing Blueberry as the Monster, Harcourt (New York, NY), 1993.
Dog Breath! The Horrible Trouble with Hally Tosis, Blue Sky Press (New York, NY), 1994.
The Moonglow Roll-o-Rama, Orchard Books (New York, NY), 1995.
The Hallo-Wiener, Blue Sky Press (New York, NY), 1995.
The Paperboy, Orchard Books (New York, NY), 1996.
God Bless the Gargoyles, Harcourt (New York, NY), 1996.
'Twas the Night before Christmas 2: The Wrath of Mrs. Claus, Blue Sky Press (New York, NY), 1998.
The Silly Gooses, Blue Sky Press (New York, NY), 1998.
The Silly Gooses Build a House, Blue Sky Press (New York, NY), 1998.

"DRAGON" SERIES; BEGINNING READERS

A Friend for Dragon, Orchard Books (New York, NY), 1991.
Dragon Gets By, Orchard Books (New York, NY), 1991.
Dragon's Merry Christmas: Dragon's Third Tale, Orchard Books (New York, NY), 1991.
Dragon's Fat Cat: Dragon's Fourth Tale, Orchard Books (New York, NY), 1992.
Dragon's Halloween: Dragon's Fifth Tale, Orchard Books (New York, NY), 1993.

"DUMB BUNNIES" SERIES; PICTURE BOOKS; UNDER PSEUDONYM SUE DENIM

The Dumb Bunnies, Blue Sky Press (New York, NY), 1994.
The Dumb Bunnies' Easter, Blue Sky Press (New York, NY), 1995.
Make Way for Dumb Bunnies, 1996.
The Dumb Bunnies Go to the Zoo, Blue Sky Press (New York, NY), 1997.

"BIG DOG AND LITTLE DOG" SERIES; BOARD BOOKS

Big Dog and Little Dog, Harcourt (New York, NY), 1997.
Big Dog and Little Dog Getting in Trouble, Harcourt (New York, NY), 1997.
Big Dog and Little Dog Going for a Walk, Harcourt (New York, NY), 1997.
Big Dog and Little Dog Wearing Sweaters, Harcourt (New York, NY), 1998.
Big Dog and Little Dog Guarding the Picnic, Harcourt (New York, NY), 1998.
Big Dog and Little Dog Making a Mistake, Harcourt (New York, NY), 1999.
The Complete Adventures of Big Dog and Little Dog, Harcourt (San Diego, CA), 2003.

"CAPTAIN UNDERPANTS" SERIES; MIDDLE-GRADE FICTION

The Adventures of Captain Underpants: An Epic Novel, Blue Sky Press (New York, NY), 1997.

Captain Underpants and the Attack of the Talking Toilets: Another Epic Novel, Blue Sky Press (New York, NY), 1999.

Captain Underpants and the Invasion of the Incredibly Naughty Cafeteria Ladies from Outer Space: A Third Epic Novel, Blue Sky Press (New York, NY), 1999.

Captain Underpants and the Perilous Plot of Professor Poopypants: The Fourth Epic Novel, Blue Sky Press (New York, NY), 2000.

Captain Underpants and the Wrath of the Wicked Wedgie Woman: The Fifth Epic Novel, Blue Sky Press (New York, NY), 2001.

The Adventures of Super Diaper Baby: The First Graphic Novel by George Beard and Harold Hutchins, Blue Sky Press (New York, NY), 2002.

Captain Underpants and the Big, Bad Battle of the Bionic Booger Boy, Part I: The Night of the Nasty Nostril Nuggets: The Sixth Epic Novel, Blue Sky Press (New York, NY), 2003.

Captain Underpants and the Big, Bad Battle of the Bionic Booger Boy, Part II: The Revenge of the Ridiculous Robo-Boogers: The Seventh Epic Novel, Blue Sky Press (New York, NY), 2003.

"RICKY RICOTTA" SERIES

Ricky Ricotta's Giant Robot: An Epic Novel, illustrated by Martin Ontiveros, Blue Sky Press (New York, NY), 2000.

Ricky Ricotta's Giant Robot vs. the Mutant Mosquitoes from Mercury: An Adventure Novel, illustrated by Martin Ontiveros, Blue Sky Press (New York, NY), 2000.

Ricky Ricotta's Giant Robot vs. the Voodoo Vultures from Venus: The Third Robot Adventure Novel, illustrated by Martin Ontiveros, Blue Sky Press (New York, NY), 2001.

Ricky Ricotta's Giant Robot vs. the Mecha-Monkeys from Mars: The Fourth Robot Adventure Novel, illustrated by Martin Ontiveros, Blue Sky Press (New York, NY), 2002.

Ricky Ricotta's Giant Robot vs. the Jurassic Jackrabbits from Jupiter: The Fifth Robot Adventure Novel, illustrated by Martin Ontiveros, Blue Sky Press (New York, NY), 2002.

Ricky Ricotta's Giant Robot vs. the Stupid Stinkbugs from Saturn: The Sixth Robot Adventure Novel, illustrated by Martin Ontiveros, Blue Sky Press (New York, NY), 2003.

Ricky Ricotta's Giant Robot vs. the Uranium Unicorns from Uranus: The Seventh Robot Adventure Novel, illustrated by Martin Ontiveros, Blue Sky Press (New York, NY), 2005.

ILLUSTRATOR

Adolph J. Moser, *Don't Pop Your Cork on Mondays! The Children's Anti-Stress Book* (nonfiction), Landmark Editions, 1988.

Jerry Segal, *The Place Where Nobody Stopped* (fiction), Orchard Books (New York, NY), 1991.

Angela Johnson, *Julius* (picture book), Orchard Books (New York, NY), 1993.

Adaptations

The "Dumb Bunnies" books were adapted into an animated cartoon series for CBS television.

Work in Progress

Captain Underpants and the Preposterous Plight of the Purple Potty People, and *The Adventures of Super Diaper Baby 2: The Invasion of the Potty Snatchers by George Beard and Harold Hutchins.*

Sidelights

An author and illustrator of picture books, fiction, and nonfiction, Dav Pilkey is a versatile and prolific creator of books for children from preschool through the middle grades. Considered one of the most popular contemporary authors for readers in elementary school, he is also regarded as a talented artist and inventive humorist as well as a subtle moralist. Pilkey favors broad parodies and farces based on art, literature, and popular culture, and his books target everything from monster movies, super-hero comic books, and modern art to science fiction and classic folk tales. Sometimes to the chagrin of parents, he relishes the same lowbrow humor that appeals to his readers, and his stories include toilet jokes and plots that revolve around such subjects as the effects of dog breath and a school principal who, hypnotized into thinking he is a super hero, runs around in his underwear. A versatile writer, Pilkey is also the creator of sensitive, evocative mood pieces, and he underscores his works—even at their most outrageous—with a philosophy that emphasizes friendship, tolerance, and generosity and celebrates the triumph of the good-hearted. Featuring both human and animal characters, Pilkey characteristically depicts sweet but sometimes dim protagonists who are misunderstood but end up on top, as well as genuinely silly creatures who remain blithely unaffected by the stupid things they do.

Pilkey is perhaps best known for his "Captain Underpants," "Dumb Bunnies," "Big Dog and Little Dog," and "Dragon" book series. Geared for middle graders, the "Captain Underpants" stories describe how two mischievous fourth-graders—creators, like the young Pilkey, of their own comic books—use a 3-D Hypno-Ring to turn their mean principal into their own creation: the bumbling but valiant crusader Captain Underpants. The "Dumb Bunnies" books—published by Pilkey under the name Sue Denim, a play on the word "pseudonym"—depicts a family of roly-poly, buck-toothed rabbits who do everything backwards, while the "Dragon" books, containing simple stories directed to beginning readers, feature a childlike blue dragon whose innocent, well-meaning nature leads him into humorous situations. The "Big Dog and Little Dog" series is composed of board books for very young children that feature two canine friends whose playfulness gets them into scrapes.

As a literary stylist, Pilkey favors straightforward but lively narratives that are filled with wordplay, especially puns, and jokes; some of his books are even written in verse. As an illustrator, his style range from campy cartoons in bold, fluorescent colors to sumptuous, detailed paintings in muted tones. Pilkey works in a variety of mediums, including watercolor, colored pencil, acrylics, magic markers, collage, and, according to the artist, Hamburger Helper and Dijon mustard. Most of his art is light-hearted and reflects the humor of his books, although several of his illustrations are darker and more mystical and surreal. As with his texts, Pilkey's illustrations are full of allusions and include take-offs on well-known paintings by such artists as Leonardo da Vinci, Vincent Van Gogh, James McNeil Whistler, Grant Wood, and Edward Hopper as well as echoing the styles of Picasso, Rousseau, Miro, and Chagall, among others. While Pilkey's illustrations are often thought to outshine his texts, he is also praised as a writer who understands what appeals to children. Writing in the *New York Times Book Review,* James Howe wrote: "If it's been a while since you've heard a 5-year-old chortle, you owe it to yourself to think of Dav Pilkey when gift giving time rolls around."

Born in Cleveland, Ohio, to a steel salesman and a church organist, Pilkey recalled his early life in commentary on his home page, *Dav Pilkey's Extra-Crunch Web Site o' Fun:* "I don't remember much about my early childhood, except that I was almost always happy. My parents tell me that I used to laugh in my sleep all the time, even as an infant. When I wasn't laughing, I kept myself busy by drawing. When the other kids in the neighborhood were outside playing baseball and football, I was inside drawing animals, monsters, and super-hero guys. Life was pretty cool when I was little . . . and then school started." "I was never very good at following the rules," Pilkey further admitted to *SATA.* "My elementary years were spent in a strict parochial school where everyone was expected to be solemn, self-controlled, and obedient. Naturally, I was the class clown. I quickly became well-versed in the art of spitball shooting, paper airplane throwing, and rude noise-making. In first grade I held the classroom record for the number of crayons I could stick up my nose at one time (six)." After setting another school record—for the amount of time spent in the principal's office—Pilkey was diagnosed with Attention Deficit Disorder and severe hyperactivity (ADHD).

By second grade, Pilkey was spending so much time standing outside class in the hallway that his teacher moved a desk there just for him, and it remained in use for the next three years. "I was the only kid in the whole school with my own personal desk out in the hall, and I made good use of it," he recalled to *SATA.* Keeping the desk well stocked with pencils, paper, magic markers, and crayons, Pilkey spent his detention time immersed in drawing, with the result that "I became an artist."

Art was not the only skill Pilkey developed during his chronic hallway detentions. In an interview with Sally Lodge in *Publishers Weekly,* he stated, "I'd draw pictures to relieve my boredom. Then I began making

comic books, since they seemed to make my stories come alive." He stapled together sheets of paper to make his own books, which he filled with the adventures of a group of superheroes; one of these creations was Captain Underpants, who was destined to make an appearance in later years. As Pilkey once recalled in *SATA,* "These comic books were a real hit with my classmates, but not with my teachers. I remember one teacher who, after furiously ripping up one of my stories, told me I'd better start taking life more seriously, because I couldn't spend the rest of my days making silly books. Lucky for me, I wasn't a very good listener either."

After graduating from grade school, Pilkey attended a strict high school where his sense of humor continued to be unappreciated by his teachers. He wrote on his home page, "One day my principal took me out of class and said to me, 'I know you think you're special because you can draw, but let me tell you something: artists are a dime-a-dozen. You will *never* make a living as an artist!' Those words haunted me for many years. How delightful it was to prove him wrong."

In his senior year in high school, a life-altering event occurred that resulted in the loss of the last letter of Pilkey's first name. As he recalled on his home page: "I was a waiter at Pizza Hut. One day they were making a name tag for me, but the label-maker was broken. Instead of printing 'Dave', it printed 'Dav'. The name stuck!" It was thus, as Dav Pilkey, that he entered Kent State University as an art major in the fall of 1984. There his freshman English teacher complimented his creative writing skills and encouraged him to write books. Thinking that this was an idea with some merit, Pilkey created a children's book titled *World War Won,* and entered it in the "National Written and Illustrated By. . ." contest, a competition for students that was sponsored by Landmark Editions of Kansas City, Missouri. The winner of the contest was to have his or her book published. *World War Won* was awarded the grand prize and, at age nineteen, Pilkey became a published author. "It was the most exciting time in my life," he recalled on his home page.

A picture book written in verse, *World War Won* describes how the leaders of two animal kingdoms, fighting for power, stockpile weapons to use against each other. The result of their stockpiling is a "nuclear freeze" in which both piles of weapons are sprayed with water and then left at Icicle Springs, which is always frozen. "The moral, of course," according to *School Library Journal* contributor Susan Scheps, "is that peace comes only through understanding and cooperation." Scheps added that Pilkey's full-page colored-pencil cartoons "are of professional caliber" and that *World War Won* "provides a model for other hopeful young authors."

After the publication of his first book, Pilkey began to research the genre of children's literature more thoroughly. As he explained to *SATA,* "When I really got serious about writing children's books, I began reading everything I could by my favorite writers, Arnold Lobel, Cynthia Rylant, James Marshall, and Harry Allard. I read *Frog and Toad, Henry and Mudge, George and Martha,* and *The Stupids* over and over again, until I started to pick up rhythms and recognize patterns. Soon I began to see what really *worked* in these books—what made them great pieces of literature."

In 1991, Pilkey produced the first of his "Dragon" books: *A Friend for Dragon* and *Dragon Gets By.* In *A Friend for Dragon* the gentle creature is tricked by a snake into believing that an apple is his friend, and when a hungry walrus eats the apple, Dragon is crushed. However, in the spot where he buries the apple's remains, a tree grows up, bearing a crop of new "friends" for Dragon. In *Dragon Gets By* Dragon spends a day doing everything wrong: he reads an egg, then fries the morning paper before watering his bed and going to sleep on his plants. In subsequent volumes of the series, Dragon celebrates Halloween and Christmas in his own inimitable way and adopts a stray cat, learning by trial and error how to take care of it. Assessing *A Friend for Dragon* and *Dragon Gets By,* a critic in *Publishers Weekly* stated, "With his excellent vocabulary choices and crafty characterizations . . . Pilkey has created a positively precious prehistoric prototype." *Booklist* critic Carolyn Phelan, reviewing *Dragon's Fat Cat: Dragon's Fourth Tale,* noted that "the Dragon series is fast moving toward that pantheon of children's reading reserved for books that make kids laugh out loud. . . . Again and again, Pilkey delivers." In a review of *Dragon's Halloween: Dragon's Fifth Tale,* a critic for *Publishers Weekly* concluded that "Bright blue Dragon never disappoints; Pilkey's series hero is affability incarnate."

In 1994 Pilkey launched his "Dumb Bunnies" series under the nom de plume Sue Denim. An homage to Harry Allard and James Marshall, the creators of the "Stupids" books, the series features a family of clueless bunnies whose adventures are depicted in deadpan text and brightly colored cartoons. Pilkey parodies "The Three Bears" and "Little Red Riding Hood" in the first volume of the series, *The Dumb Bunnies,* as Little Red Goldilocks wreaks havoc until Baby Bunny flushes her down the toilet. Subsequent volumes continue the escapades of the loopy lapins, who confuse holiday customs in *The Dumb Bunnies' Easter,* visit the beach during a storm in *Make Way for Dumb Bunnies,* and cause a riot when they let the animals out of their cages in *The Dumb Bunnies Go to the Zoo.* In his review of *The Dumb Bunnies* for the *Bulletin of the Center for Children's Books,* Roger Sutton called Pilkey's floppy-eared heroes "the Stupids in pink fur." Mary Harris Veeder, writing in *Booklist,* noted of *The Dumb Bunnies' Easter* that "The Bunny family is a worthy successor to those all-time favorites the Stupids. . . . This is dumbness supreme and a real treat."

Mega-popular with young readers, *The Dumb Bunnies* was adapted as an animated series on CBS television in

Anyone unsure that author/illustrator Pilkey is a grown up who has never actually grown up has only to scan a page of his highly popular **The Adventures of Captain Underpants** *to have this fact confirmed.*

the late 1990s. At around the same time, Pilkey introduced a new series, the "Silly Gooses," which is akin to the "Dumb Bunnies" in its depiction of anthropomorphic animals that engage in backwards behavior. The books feature Mr. and Mrs. Goose and their goslings Ketchup and Mustard, named after their parents' favorite ice cream toppings.

In addition to creating his books, Pilkey spends time visiting schools in order to talk to children, and in his first presentations he explained how he found his calling while sitting in the hallway of his elementary school. As the author recalled to *Publishers Weekly,* "Inevitably, the name 'Captain Underpants' would come up, and though I cracked jokes throughout my presentation, the mention of this name would get by far the biggest laugh. And whenever I mentioned the title of one of my early Captain Underpants comic books, which involved talking toilets, the room would explode with laughter. That's when I knew I had to do a book about him."

The Adventures of Captain Underpants: An Epic Novel introduces two misbehaving fourth graders at Jerome Horwitz Elementary School who write their own comic books: introverted Harold Hutchins and extroverted George Beard, whom Pilkey described in *Publishers Weekly* as "kind of like the yin and yang of my personality." The boys' nemesis is crabby principal Mr. Krupp, and after they hypnotize him with a 3-D Hypno-Ring, the principal is transformed into one of the boys' comic-book creations, Captain Underpants, whenever he hears fingers snapped. Clad only in his tighty whities and a cape and carrying a roll of toilet paper, Captain Underpants stands for "Truth, Justice, and ALL that is Preshrunk and Cottony." The scantily clad crime fighter tackles criminals such as bank robbers and robot thieves by giving them wedgies, and even confronts a mad scientist, the evil Dr. Diaper, who is intent on controlling the world. Distracting the doctor with doggy-doo, the boys and Captain Underpants save the planet; Harold and George then de-hypnotize their principal and hustle him back into his street clothes.

Pilkey illustrates *The Adventures of Captain Underpants* with black-and-white cartoons, and even animates a chapter by means of what he calls "Flip-o-Rama," a device by which readers can flip the pages back and forth for an animation effect. Writing in *Booklist*, Stephanie Zvirin noted that while the silliness "goes overboard . . . and the many action-packed illustrations rob the plot of some of its zip by commanding more than their share of attention," nonetheless, Pilkey's "humor is on target for some kids in this age group." A critic in *Kirkus Reviews* added, "There'll be no silence in the library once readers get hold of this somewhat classier alternative to Barf-o-Rama."

The "Captain Underpants" saga continues with *Captain Underpants and the Attack of the Talking Toilets.* Drawing from the comic books he created as a youngster, Pilkey relates how George and Harold use the science project of school brain Melvin, a copying machine that changes images into matter, to reproduce their latest comic book. Inadvertently, the boys set loose an army of teacher-eating toilets led by the evil Turbo Toilet 2000. Captain Underpants—with the aid of Wedgie Power and his Incredible Robo-Plunger—saves the school, and George and Harold get to become principals for a day. In *Captain Underpants and the Invasion of the Incredibly Naughty Cafeteria Ladies from Outer Space* the two boys fool the cafeteria staff into baking cupcakes that flood Jerome Horwitz Elementary School with goo. After the staff quits, Principal Krupp mistakenly hires an alien trio to take their place. When the aliens begin turning the students into zombie nerds, Harold, George, and Captain Underpants are called into action and end up saving the world from an alien invasion. Reviewing *Captain Underpants and the Attack of the Talking Toilets, Booklist* critic John Peters wrote that the book is "destined to be as popular as the first book," while a reviewer in *Horn Book* called it "part graphic novel, part tongue-in-cheek parody, . . . very hip and funny."

In *Captain Underpants and the Perilous Plot of Professor Poopypants* the boys invoke the wrath of Professor Pippy P. Poopypants, a scientific genius who gets no respect because of his name. When chaos ensues, Captain Underpants dons his undies once again. The retirement of a despised teacher is pivotal in *Captain Underpants and the Wrath of the Wicked Wedgie Woman,* which finds Miss Ribble annoyed by George and Harold's uncharitable portrait of her in a comic book. Sent to Krupp's office, the boys orchestrate a pretend protestation of love from Krupp, angering the retiring teacher even more, until it is clear that Ribble must be calmed by a 3-D Hypno-Ring treatment. The two-part epic *Captain Underpants and the Big, Bad Battle of the Bionic Booger Boy* finds school smartypants Melvin accidentally transforming himself into a giant Bionic Booger Boy who produces robo-boogers in part one: *The Night of the Nasty Nostril Nuggets.* Although the robo-booger threat is eliminated in part two, *The Revenge of the Ridiculous Robo-Boogers,* it returns in the midst of a power shift that renders Captain Underpants useless while a school toilet is transformed into a time machine. Despite the complicated plot, *School Library Journal* reviewer JoAnn Jonas called *The Revenge of the Ridiculous Robo-Boogers* "witty, fun, and full of adventure."

Praising the "Captain Underpants" series as a whole, Tim Wadham wrote in *School Library Journal* that it is

Straight from the minds of middle-schoolers George Beard and Harold Hutchins, **The Adventures of Super Diaper Baby** *continues the comic-book stories that the boys' frustrated teachers continually try to force underground.*

"one of the best series to get reluctant readers reading." In the same periodical, Marlene Gawron noted that "the fun" of Pilkey's books "is in the reading, which is full of puns, rhymes, and nonsense along with enough revenge and wish fulfillment for every downtrodden fun-seeking kid who never wanted to read a book." Adding that the cartoon drawings and Flip-o-Rama pages make the work "so appealing that youngsters won't notice that their vocabulary is stretching," Gawron concluded: "Hooray for Captain Underpants!" Explaining the appeal of the books in *Time*, Pilkey said: "I think kids feel trapped just by being kids. You can't do anything when you're a kid. Adults are always trying to spoil your fun. . . . I think kids are drawn to these books because . . . George and Harold . . . get away with so much. They're always having great adventures, and the adults can't stop them. It's great escapism." Interestingly, although the "Captain Underpants" books are written primarily for boys, Pilkey has received an equal amount of fan mail from middle-grade girls.

As a spin-off of the "Captain Underpants" books, Pilkey penned *The Adventures of Super Diaper Baby: The First Graphic Novel by George Beard and Harold Hutchins*, the first volume of a series that follows a new creation by the imaginative duo. Punished with a writing assignment in which Captain Underpants may not appear, George and Harold spin a new tale about a baby that, doused in super power juice shortly after birth, begins his crime-fighting career by wadding up a villain in toilet paper. Presented as the work of the middle-schoolers themselves, *The Adventures of Super Diaper Baby* is "preposterously good-humored," according to a *Publishers Weekly* reviewer, while in *School Library Journal* Piper L. Nyman dubbed it "another goofy, gross-out selection from a popular author." Words of caution came from a *Kirkus Reviews* writer: "Adults will want to use this book as birdcage liner, and young readers with elementary senses of humor will revel in the . . . silliness."

Pilkey is also the creator of book series with roots in science fiction. In *Ricky Ricotta's Mighty Robot*, a lonely little mouse befriends a giant robot who takes on the school bullies, rescues the city from an evil rat scientist, and saves the world from an invasion of massive mosquitoes from Mercury. The series continues with titles that suggest a host of ridiculous plot conflicts: *Ricky Ricotta's Mighty Robot vs. the Mutant Mosquitoes from Mercury, Ricky Ricotta's Mighty Robot vs. the Jurassic Jackrabbits from Jupiter,* and *Ricky Ricotta's Mighty Robot vs. the Stupid Stinkbugs from Saturn.* In typical Pilkey form, the last-named volume finds mouse and robot forced to defend the planet from a scourge of stinky litterbugs who, led by Sergeant Stinkbug, plan to trash the planet for good. Noting the book's appeal to reluctant readers, Elaine E. Knight noted in *School Library Journal* that *Ricky Ricotta's Mighty Robot vs. the Stupid Stinkbugs from Saturn* contains a "short, easy-reading text [that] is highlighted by Pilkey's off-the-wall, deadpan humor."

Pilkey hands off illustration duties to Martin Ontiveros in his "Ricky Ricotta" series, which features the tantalizing Ricky Ricotta's Mighty Robot vs. the Stupid Stinkbugs from Saturn *as installment number six.*

In contrast to his humorous books, Pilkey has written and illustrated several picture books that showcase the full range of his talents as an illustrator and present young readers with more serious and meditative subjects. One book of this type, *The Paperboy,* was named a Caldecott Medal Honor Book for its illustrations in 1997. A young African-American boy, accompanied by his dog, rises before dawn on a Saturday morning to deliver his papers; after finishing their job, the pair go back to bed and dream about flying across the night sky. According to *School Library Journal* reviewer Wendy Lukehart, Pilkey "paints their shared experience with a graceful economy of language"; the critic concluded by calling *The Paperboy* a "totally satisfying story." Pilkey illustrates his book with acrylic paintings that, according to Carolyn Phelan in *Booklist*, "include beautifully composed landscapes and interiors."

With his "Big Dog and Little Dog" series, Pilkey also takes the silliness down a notch, this time focusing his attention on the toddler set. Using minimal text and large illustrations printed on thick cardboard, he introduces two devoted canine companions who go for walks, play in puddles, and snuggle together while demonstrating both the sweet and more fun-loving sides of their personalities. The sixth volume of the series, *Big Dog and Little Dog Making a Mistake,* describes what happens when the duo mistake a skunk for a kitten and then disrupt a party. Writing in *School Library Journal,* Maura Bresnahan predicted that babies and toddlers will find "the colorful illustrations appealing but the humor will be better appreciated by older children." The critic added that the simple sentence structure and repetitive text "makes this board book ideal for those just learning to read."

In addition to the books he has written and illustrated, Pilkey has provided the pictures for *Don't Pop Your Cork on Mondays! The Children's Anti-Stress Book,* a nonfiction handbook for children on the causes and effects of childhood stress by psychologist Adolph J. Moser; *The Place Where Nobody Stopped,* a folktale-like story by Jerry Segal about how a young Jewish man and his family change the life of a lonely Russian baker when they come to stay with him; and *Julius,* a humorous picture book by Angela Johnson that features an Alaskan pig who lives with an African-American family. Pilkey received special notice for his paintings for this last book, multimedia collages composed using fabrics and instant coffee as well as more traditional mediums. Writing in *Horn Book,* Ellen Fader noted that Pilkey's pictures "constitute an evolution from his more modest efforts," while *Bulletin of the Center for Children's Books* reviewer Betsy Hearne concluded that the artist's paintings "are a major factor in the hilarity. He translates a keen sense of the ridiculous into vivacious hues and wildly varied patterns without ever getting cluttered."

Pilkey once observed to *SATA:* "One of my biggest inspirations as an illustrator is the drawings of children. Children often send me pictures that they've drawn, and I'm always amazed at the way they present shape and color. Children are natural impressionists. They're not afraid to make their trees purple and yellow, and it's okay if the sky is green with red stripes. . . . When children are drawing, anything goes! Of course, you know that one day an art teacher is going to grab hold of these kids and turn them all into accountants, but while they are still fresh and naive, children can create some of the freshest and most beautiful art there is." He added on his home page, "When I was a kid making silly books out in the hall, I never dreamed that one day I'd be making silly books for a living. The coolest thing is that I used to get in trouble for being the class clown . . . and now it's my job."

Biographical and Critical Sources

BOOKS

Children's Literature Review, Volume 48, Thomson Gale (Detroit, MI), 1998, pp. 99-114.
Pilkey, Dav, *The Adventures of Captain Underpants: An Epic Novel,* Blue Sky Press (New York, NY), 1997.

PERIODICALS

Booklist, February 1, 1992, Carolyn Phelan, review of *Dragon's Fat Cat: Dragon's Fourth Tale,* p. 1029; February 1, 1995, Mary Harris Veeder, review of *The Dumb Bunnies' Easter,* p. 1009; March 1, 1996, Carolyn Phelan, review of *The Paperboy,* p. 1179; October 1, 1996, p. 1406; July 19, 1997, Stephanie Zvirin, review of *The Adventures of Captain Underpants: An Epic Novel,* p. 1819; May 1, 1999, John Peters, review of *Captain Underpants and the Attack of the Talking Toilets: Another Epic Novel.*
Bulletin of the Center for Children's Books, May, 1993, Betsy Hearne, review of *Julius,* p. 284; January, 1994, Roger Sutton, review of *The Dumb Bunnies,* p. 150; April, 1998, p. 292.
Horn Book, March-April, 1993, Ellen Fader, review of *Julius,* pp. 196-197; July-August, 1996, Mary M. Burns, review of *The Paperboy,* p. 453.
Kirkus Reviews, June 1, 1997, review of *The Adventures of Captain Underpants,* p. 678; December 15, 1997, p. 72; February 1, 2002, review of *The Adventures of Super Diaper Baby,* p. 187.
New York Times Book Review, November 8, 1992, James Howe, "Perchance to Dream," p. 57.
Publishers Weekly, December 21, 1990, review of *A Friend for Dragon* and *Dragon Gets By,* p. 56; September 20, 1993, review of *Dragon's Halloween,* p. 30; October 14, 1996, p. 82; February 22, 1999, Sally Lodge, "Dav Pilkey's Captain Underpants Wins a Starring Role," p. 32; January 28, 2002, review of *The Adventures of Super Diaper Baby,* p. 291; September 15, 2003, review of *Dragon's Halloween,* p. 67; September 29, 2003, review of *Kat Kong,* p. 66.
School Library Journal, March, 1988, Susan Scheps, review of *World War Won,* p. 174; March, 1996, Wendy Lukehart, review of *The Paperboy,* pp. 180-181; June, 1999, Maura Bresnahan, review of *Big Dog and Little Dog Make a Mistake,* p. 109, and Marlene Gawron, review of *Captain Underpants and the Attack of the Talking Toilets,* p. 136; October, 2001, Tim Wadham, review of *Captain Underpants and the Wrath of the Wicked Wedgie Woman,* p. 129; April, 2002, Elaine E. Knight, review of *Ricky Ricotta's Mighty Robot v. the Mecha-Monkeys from Mars,* p. 120; June, 2002, Piper L. Nyman, review of *The Adventures of Super Diaper Baby,* p. 108; January, 2004, Elaine E. Knight, review of *Ricky Ricotta's Mighty Robot vs. the Stupid Stinkbugs from Saturn,* p. 104; January, 2004, Kristina Aaronson, review of *Captain Underpants and the Big, Bad Battle of the Bionic Booger Boy,* p. 103; February, 2004, JoAnn Jonas, review of *Captain Underpants and the Big, Bad Battle of the Bionic Booger Boy,* p. 121; June, 2005, Jackie Parich, review of *Dav Pilkey's Extra-Crunchy Web site o' Fun,* p. 67.
Time, August 27, 2001, "A Hero in Briefs: The Zany Author of the Captain Underpants Books Has Written a New One, and Tries to Explain Their Appeal," p. F18.

ONLINE

Dav Pilkey's Extra-Crunch Web Site o' Fun, http://www. pilkey.com (December 1, 2005).*

PILKEY, David Murray, Jr.
See PILKEY, Dav

*   *   *

PLATT, Richard 1953-

Personal

Born April 15, 1953, in England; father a civil engineer, mother a pharmacist. *Education:* Studied engineering at University of Newcastle upon Tyne, 1972-73; Newcastle College of Art and Design, diploma in art, 1974; Leeds Polytechnic University, B.A. (first-class honors), 1977; attended Central School of Art.

Addresses

Agent—Patricia White, Rogers, Coleridge & White, 20 Powis Mews, London W11, 1JN, England.

Career

Worked as a photographer and teacher of photography, 1978-80; Camerawork Gallery, London, England, photographer, 1979-80; Marshall Cavendish, London, subeditor, 1980-82; Mitchell Beazley International, technical editor, 1982-83; affiliated with Applied Holographics PLC, 1984-85; freelance writer, 1985—.

Member

British Society of Authors.

Awards, Honors

Outsanding Science Trade Book designation, National Science Teachers Association and Children's Book Council, 2004, for *Eureka!;* Utah Children's Informational Book Award, 1994, for *Incredible Cross Sections;* Smarties Silver Medal, 2004, for *Pirate Diary.*

Writings

NONFICTION FOR CHILDREN

Stephen Biesty's Incredible Cross-Sections Book, illustrated by Biesty, Knopf (New York, NY), 1992.
Stephen Biesty's Cross-Sections Man-of-War, illustrated by Biesty, Dorling Kindersley (New York, NY), 1993.
Stephen Biesty's Cross-Sections Castle, illustrated by Biesty, Dorling Kindersley (New York, NY), 1994.
The Smithsonian Visual Timeline of Inventions, Dorling Kindersley (New York, NY), 1994.
In the Beginning: The Nearly Complete History of Almost Everything, illustrated by Brian Delf, Dorling Kindersley (New York, NY), 1995.
The Apartment Book: A Day in Five Stories, illustrated by Leo Hartas, Dorling Kindersley (New York, NY), 1995.

Richard Platt

Stephen Biesty's Incredible Explosions, illustrated by Biesty, Dorling Kindersley (New York, NY), 1996.
Stephen Biesty's Incredible Everything, illustrated by Biesty, Dorling Kindersley (New York, NY), 1997.
Disaster!, illustrated by Richard Bonson, Dorling Kindersley (New York, NY), 1997.
Great Events That Changed the World, illustrated by Brian Delf, Dorling Kindersley (New York, NY), 1997, published as *History: The Really Interesting Bits!,* 1998.
Inventions Explained: A Beginner's Guide to Technological Breakthroughs, Henry Holt (New York, NY), 1997.
Stephen Biesty's Incredible Body, illustrated by Biesty, Dorling Kindersley (New York, NY), 1998.
The Amazing Pop-up 3-D Time Scape, illustrated by Stephen Biesty, Dorling Kindersley (New York, NY), 1999.
Aztecs: The Fall of the Aztec Capital, illustrated by Peter Dennis, Dorling Kindersley (New York, NY), 1999.
DK Illustrated Book of Great Adventures, illustrated by George Sharp and others, Dorling Kindersley (New York, NY), 1999, published as *Illustrated Book of Great Adventures: Real-Life Tales of Danger and Daring,* Dorling Kindersley (London, England), 1999.
Plants Bite Back!, Dorling Kindersley (New York, NY), 1999.
Space Explorer Atlas, illustrated by Leo Hartas, Dorling Kindersley (New York, NY), 1999.
Everest: Reaching the World's Highest Peak, illustrated by Russell Barnet and John James, Dorling Kindersley (New York, NY), 2000.
Spies!, Dorling Kindersley (New York, NY), 2000.

Media and Communications, Marshall Cavendish (London, England), 2000.

Spiders' Secrets, Dorling Kindersley (New York, NY), 2001.

Technology and Communications, Silver Dolphin (San Diego, CA), 2001.

Stephen Biesty's Coolest Cross-Sections Ever, illustrated by Biesty, Dorling Kindersley (New York, NY), 2001.

Apes and Other Hairy Primates, Dorling Kindersley (New York, NY), 2001.

Explorers: Pioneers Who Broke New Boundaries, Dorling Kindersley (New York, NY), 2001.

Extreme Sports, Dorling Kindersley (New York, NY), 2001.

Julius Caesar: Great Dictator of Rome, illustrated by John James and Jim Robins, Dorling Kindersley (New York, NY), 2001.

Villains: Traitors, Tyrants, and Thieves, Dorling Kindersley (New York, NY), 2002.

Discovering Pirates, Red Kite (London, England), 2002.

Crime Scene: The Ultimate Guide to Forensic Science, Dorling Kindersley (New York, NY), 2003.

Eureka!: Great Inventions and How They Happened, Kingfisher (Boston, MA), 2003, published as *Eureka!: Great Inventors and Their Brilliant Brainwaves,* Kingfisher (London, England), 2003.

Fidel Castro, Raintree (Austin, TX), 2003, published as *Fidel Castro: From Guerrilla to World Statesman,* Watts (London, England), 2003.

The Vanishing Rainforest, illustrated by Rupert van Wyk, Frances Lincoln (London, England), 2003.

Communications: From Hieroglyphics to Hyperlink, Kingfisher (Boston, MA), 2004.

D-Day Landings: The Story of the Allied Invasion, Dorling Kindersley (New York, NY), 2004.

Discovering Egyptians, Red Kite (London, England), 2004.

Forensics, Kingfisher (New York, NY), 2005.

Experience Flight, Dorling Kindersley (New York, NY), 2006.

Pirates of the Caribbean Visual Guide, Dorling Kindersley (New York, NY), 2006.

"EYEWITNESS" SERIES

Film, Knopf (New York, NY), 1992.

Pirate, photographs by Tina Chambers, Knopf (New York, NY), 1994.

Spy, photographs by Geoff Dann and Steve Gorton, Knopf (New York, NY), 1996.

Shipwreck, photographs by Alex Wilson and Tina Chambers, Knopf (New York, NY), 1997, revised edition, 2005.

"DIARY" SERIES

Castle Diary: The Journal of Tobias Burgess, illustrated by Chris Riddell, Candlewick (Cambridge, MA), 1999.

Pirate Diary: The Journal of Jake Carpenter, Candlewick (Cambridge, MA), 2001.

Egyptian Diary: The Journal of Nakht, illustrated by David Parkins, Candlewick (Cambridge, MA), 2005.

FOR ADULTS

The Magic of Black and White, Time-Life (Alexandria, VA), 1985.

The Photographer's Idea Book: How to See and Take Better Pictures, Amphoto (New York, NY), 1985.

(With John Hedgecoe and Jack Tresidder) *The Art of Color Photography,* Simon & Schuster (New York, NY), 1989.

The Professional Guide to Photo Data, Beazley (London, England), 1989.

The Ultimate Photo Data Guide, Simon & Schuster (New York, NY), 1989.

The Ordnance Survey Guide to Smuggler's Britain, Cassell (London, England), 1991.

Also author of monthly column for *SLRCamera,* 1980-82; contributor to books and periodicals. Consulting editor, Michael Busselle, *The Complete 35mm Sourcebook,* Amphoto (New York, NY), 1988, revised edition, 1992.

Adaptations

Smugglers' Britain Web site, http://www.smuggling.co.uk, is based on Platt's book *The Ordnance Survey Guide to Smugglers' Britain.*

Sidelights

Richard Platt is the author of more than sixty informative books for young readers, and he also writes for innovative multimedia projects. Some of his most popular works have been collaborations with illustrator Stephen Biesty on the "Cross-Sections" series. After a failed attempt to forge a career as a photographer, Platt discovered that he had a knack for writing. "I started writing about photography: first magazine articles, then books," he explained on the *Walker Books Web site.* "I got a job editing children's books, then went on to write them."

In the 1990s, Platt teamed up with popular juvenile illustrator Biesty for several books, beginning with *Stephen Biesty's Incredible Cross-Sections Book,* published in 1992. The following year, a second volume in the series, *Stephen Biesty's Cross-Sections Man-of-War,* proved equally interesting for late-elementary-age readers, especially those enchanted by seventeenth-century battleships. Alongside Biesty's cutaway illustrations, Platt provides explanatory text that indicates the purpose and activities in each section of the ship. The hardships of life aboard such vessels for their often 800-member crews are not overlooked, either, and the drawings depict food rations crawling with maggots and a doctor's pail containing severed limbs. Ellen Mandel, writing for *Booklist,* asserted that Platt's "intriguing text" serves to make "this meticulously presented book a treasure of factual content and visual imagery."

For *Stephen Biesty's Incredible Everything,* Platt provides informative paragraphs to accompany the illustrations for many everyday products, such as athletic shoes and compact discs. Much of the text revolves around the manufacturing process. *Stephen Biesty's Incredible Body* is a lesson in human anatomy, with sections on each of the body's systems and several major organs; the digestive system alone takes up four pages. Platt has also worked with the illustrator on *Stephen Biesty's Cross-Sections Castle* and *Stephen Biesty's Incredible Explosions.*

Working with publisher Dorling Kindersley, Platt has authored several titles in their "Eyewitness" series, some of which have appeared in the United States under the Knopf/Borzoi imprint. *Pirate* details the world of corsairs, privateers, and crime on the high seas throughout history. A reviewer for *Science Books and Films,* Richard B. Woodbury, praised the work as "a veritable miniencyclopedia or minimuseum" and "a pleasure to look at." *Spy* chronicles the history of espionage and the decisive role intelligence-gathering triumphs have played in history. Of particular emphasis are the code-breaking endeavors by Allied intelligence networks during World War II. *Shipwreck,* also part of the "Eyewitness" series, investigates famous sea disasters and rescues. Like the other books in the popular series, *Shipwreck* is lavishly illustrated. Chris Stephenson, writing in *School Librarian,* called it "an excellent source of historical evidence and nautical information."

Platt has also written several books about inventions. His *The Smithsonian Visual Timeline of Inventions,* which appeared in 1994, won praise from reviewers for its comprehensiveness. Platt divides the development of technology throughout the ages into five sections, including agriculture, conquest, and communication. The timeline begins at 600,000 BCE, around the time humans likely began using fire, and includes predictions for innovations that may occur in the near future. Cathryn A. Camper, reviewing *The Smithsonian Visual Timeline of Inventions* for *School Library Journal,* praised Platt's skilled use of illustration and text, which the critic felt "teaches a sophisticated form of literacy similar to" that provided with multimedia learning tools—an area in which Platt already had a great deal of writing experience. "Readers will delight in the colorful pictures and the text, which gives just enough information to satisfy curiosity," opined *Voice of Youth Advocates* writer Christine Miller.

Platt has also written another work on essential technology, the 1997 work *Inventions Explained: A Beginner's Guide to Technological Breakthroughs.* In this work he explains, for elementary-age readers, some notable achievements throughout human history, and how they positively affected life. Platt begins with the first tools developed in primitive cultures, then moves on through eons of technological advancement all the way to computerization and other space-age technology. "The strength of the book is the way it conveys the global nature of inventions," noted a *Kirkus Reviews* assessment.

For young readers, Platt has penned some books on general history topics. With illustrator Brian Delf, he wrote *History: The Really Interesting Bits!,* which describes thirteen significant events that changed the course of history, including the construction of Egypt's Great Pyramid, the fall of the Roman Empire, the Russian Revolution, and World War II. Each is given a double-page spread, and Delf provides the illustrations and maps. In *Books for Keeps,* reviewer Clive Barnes commended the writing as "accurate," and further noted that "the design is clear, colourful and enticing." Nansi Taylor, writing for *School Librarian,* termed it "a book to pore over and learn from."

In *Castle Diary: The Journal of Tobias Burgess* Platt offers readers a glimpse into what life might have been like during the Middle Ages for an eleven-year-old boy who lives in a castle and works as a page, or a knight in training. Accompanied by illustrations by Chris Riddell, the 1999 title describes, in diary form, Tobias's daily life, his page friends, an illness in which he is "bled" as a cure, and a jousting tournament. Further information on medieval history is included at the back of the book. "Readers will enjoy the child's language and descriptions," stated Betsy Barnett in her *School Library Journal* review, and concluded by singling the

With a yo, ho, ho, readers of Platt's **Pirate Diary: The Journal of Jake Carpenter** *climb aboard in 1716 and join ten-year-old Jake as he lives the pirate code and survives the hardships of a scallywag's life at sea. (Illustration by Chris Riddell.)*

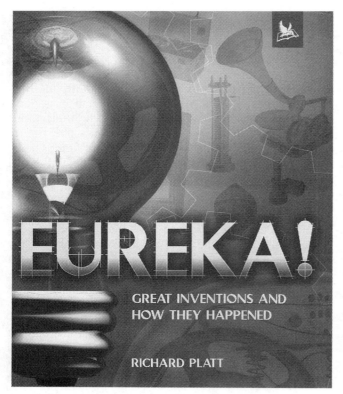

Platt takes a break from historical fiction to share his interest in the history of technology in this 2003 work, and shows that the "Eureka!" moment often comes after many years of effort. (Cover illustration by Mike Buckley.)

work out as a "fresh, appealing offering." *Booklist* contributor Carolyn Phelan commented on the book's educational value, noting that "readers will learn about the social structure of feudalism as well as life in and around the castle."

Castle Diary was the first of the diary books written by Platt. Discussing the series with Nikki Gamble in an online interview for the *Write Away* Web site, Platt noted that "the diary books are really midway between the two forms of writing; they are more like historical novels than conventional nonfiction." With *Pirate Diary: The Journal of Jake Carpenter,* Platt describes the realistic life of pirates from the perspective of nine-year-old Jake who is captured and then forced to work as part of the pirate crew. "While he does not romanticize piracy, the author displays a keen eye for the sort of gorier details that young buccaneers will relish," commented a *Publishers Weekly* reviewer. Shelle Rosenfeld, in *Booklist,* noted that Platt provides "a wealth of information in an entertaining, historical-fiction diary format." Anne Chapman Callaghan, writing for *School Library Journal,* commented that "kids looking for adventure will certainly find plenty of it here." *Egyptian Diary: The Journal of Nakht,* the third book of the series, reveals ancient Egypt from the perspective of a young scribe-in-training.

Platt's work in traditional nonfiction has continued alongside his production of further "Diary" books. *Ever-*

est: Reaching the World's Highest Peak* is "packed with information" about the quest to climb Mount Everest, according to Elizabeth Stumpf in *School Library Journal,* while his award-winning *Eureka!: Great Inventions and How They Happened* gives information on twenty-nine important inventions and is useful for both "report writers and browsers," according to Kathy Piehl, writing in *School Library Journal.*

In his *Write Away* online interview with Gamble, Platt discussed some of the recurring themes in his books, such as pirates and castles. "What engages me particularly about pirates is the mythology that has grown around them," he explained. "It's this clash between the reality of piracy and the myths that really interests me." About castles, he commented, "The medieval period is colourful and interesting, which is a reason that I've done more than one castle book. The other reason is that writers become stereotyped in publishing so that having written one castle book, there's a very good chance of being asked to write another." Platt confessed to Gamble that he is frightened of writing fiction, which made the "Diary" books particularly challenging for him. On the Walker Books Web site Platt explained some of what he loves about writing: "People pay me to find out all this fascinating stuff about strange, wacky and obscure subjects."

Biographical and Critical Sources

PERIODICALS

Booklist, October 1, 1993, Ellen Mandel, review of *Stephen Biesty's Cross-Sections Man-of-War,* p. 337; November 15, 1999, Carolyn Phelan, review of *Castle Diary: The Journal of Tobias Burgess, Page,* p. 627; October 15, 2001, Hazel Rochman, review of *Apes and Other Hairy Primates* and *Explorers: Pioneers Who Broke New Boundaries,* p. 420; December 15, 2001, Shelle Rosenfeld, review of *Pirate Diary: The Journal of Jake Carpenter,* p. 732; September 1, 2004, John Peters, review of *Communication: From Hieroglyphs to Hyperlinks,* p. 116.

Books for Keeps, November, 1996, review of *Spy,* p. 15; May, 1998, Clive Barnes, review of *History,* p. 25.

Bulletin of the Center for Children's Books, February, 2002, review of *Pirate Diary,* p. 216.

Kirkus Reviews, September 1, 1995, review of *In the Beginning,* p. 1286; December 15, 1997, review of *Inventions Explained,* p. 1838.

Library Journal, June 15, 2003, review of *Crime Scene: The Ultimate Guide to Forensic Science,* p. 89.

Library Media Connection, February, 2004, review of *Crime Scene,* p. 60.

Magpies, March, 1998, Lynne Babbage, review of *History,* p. 42; March, 2002, review of *Julius Caesar: Great Dictator of Rome,* p. 45.

Publishers Weekly, December 20, 1999, "Special Effects," p. 82; October 22, 2001, review of *Pirate Diary,* p. 77; August 25, 2003, review of *Castle Diary,* p. 67.

Reading Teacher, October, 2002, Nancy J. Johnson and Cyndi Giorgis, review of *Pirate Diary,* p. 201.

School Librarian, February, 1996, Nansi Taylor, review of *In the Beginning,* p. 35; spring, 1998, Nansi Taylor, review of *History,* p. 51, and Chris Stephenson, review of *Shipwreck,* p. 41; spring, 2002, review of *Pirate Diary,* p. 38.

School Library Journal, February, 1993, Judie Porter, review of *Film,* p. 103; February, 1995, Cathryn A. Camper, review of *Smithsonian Visual Timeline,* p. 110; June, 1997, Eldon Younce, review of *Spy,* p. 142; January, 1998, Eldon Younce, review of *Stephen Biesty's Incredible Everything,* p. 128; February, 1998, Anne Chapman Callaghan, review of *Inventions Explained,* p. 115; January, 1999, Christine A. Moesch, review of *Stephen Biesty's Incredible Body,* p. 151; December, 1999, Betsy Barnett, review of *Castle Diary: The Journal of Tobias Burgess,* p. 158; October, 2000, Elizabeth Stumpf, review of *Everest: Reaching the World's Highest Peak,* p. 180; December, 2001, Anne Chapman Callaghan, review of *Pirate Diary,* p. 142; March, 2004, Kathy Piehl, review of *Eureka!,* p. 241; November, 2004, Carol Wichman, review of *Communication,* p. 158.

Science Books and Films, November, 1995, Richard B. Woodbury, review of *Pirate,* p. 239; September, 2002, review of *Apes and Other Hairy Primates,* p. 520.

Voice of Youth Advocates, August, 1995, Christine Miller, review of *Smithsonian Visual Timeline,* p. 187

ONLINE

Write Away Web site, http://improbability.ultralab.net/writeaway/ (December 2, 2005), Nikki Gamble, interview with Platt.

* * *

PRATT, Pierre 1962-

Personal

Born February 1, 1962, in Montreal, Quebec, Canada; son of Marcel and Sylviane (Rouleau) Pratt. *Education:* Studied graphic design at the college level. *Hobbies and other interests:* Music, playing instruments, travel.

Addresses

Home—5976 rue Jeanne Mance, Montreal, Quebec H2V 4K8, Canada. *E-mail*—ppratt@mlink.net.

Career

Children's book author and illustrator. Began in magazine illustration.

Awards, Honors

Canadian Governor General's Award, and Mr. Christie Award for best illustration, both 1991, both for *Uncle Henry's Dinner Guests;* UNICEF-Bologna Book Fair Award, 1992; Golden Apple Award (Bratislava), for *Follow That Hat!;* Governor General's Award for Illustration, and Mr. Christie Book Award in French-language category, both for *My Dog Is an Elephant;* "Totem" for Best French Album in Montreuil, France, 1994, for *Marcel and Andre;* Governor General's Literary Award for Children's Literature (French) Illustration, 1998, for *Monsieur Ilétaitunefois,* by Rémy Simard.

Writings

SELF-ILLUSTRATED

Follow That Hat!, Firefly Books (Richmond Hill, Ontario, Canada), 1992.

Marcel & Andre, Gallimard (Paris, France), 1994.

Hippo Beach, Seuil Jeunesse (Paris, France), 1996, Firefly Books (Richmond Hill, Ontario, Canada), 1997.

Beaux dimanches, Seuil (Paris, France), 1996.

Léon sans son chapeau, Autrement (Paris, France), 1997.

Collection pied de nez, 4 volumes, Éditions Chouette (Montreal, Quebec, Canada), 1997.

La vie exemplaire de Martha et Paul, Seuil (Paris, France), 1998.

I See . . . My Mom; I See . . . My Dad, Annick Press (Toronto, Ontario, Canada), 2001.

I See . . . My Sister; I See . . . My Cat, Annick Press (Toronto, Ontario, Canada), 2001.

Le jour où Zoé zozota, Les 400 Coups (Montreal, Quebec, Canada), 2005.

SELF-ILLUSTRATED; "VERY BUSY LIFE OF OLAF AND VENUS" SERIES

Shopping, Candlewick Press (Cambridge, MA), 2000.

Park, Macmillan Children's Books (London, England), 2000, Candlewick Press (Cambridge, MA), 2001.

Home, Macmillan Children's Book (London, England), 2000, Candlewick Press (Cambridge, MA), 2001.

Car, Macmillan Children's Books (London, England), 2000, Candlewick Press (Cambridge, MA), 2001.

Series has been translated into French.

ILLUSTRATOR

Benedicte Froissant, *Les fantasies de l'oncle Henri,* 1990, translated by David Homel as *Uncle Henry's Dinner Guests,* Firefly Books (Richmond Hill, Ontario, Canada), 1990.

Rémy Simard, *Mon chien est un éléphant!,* Casterman, 1994, translated by David Homel as *My Dog Is an Elephant,* Firefly Books (Richmond Hill, Ontario, Canada), 1994.

Rémy Simard, *La bottine magique de Pipo,* [Paris, France], translated as *The Magic Boot,* Firefly Books (Richmond Hill, Ontario, Canada), 1995.

Hannah Roche, *Corey's Kite,* Stewart, Tabori & Chang (New York, NY), 1996.

Hannah Roche, *Sandra's Sun Hat,* Stewart, Tabori & Chang (New York, NY), 1996.

Hannah Roche, *Su's Snowgirl,* Stewart, Tabori & Chang (New York, NY), 1996.

Hannah Roche, *Pete's Puddles,* Stewart, Tabori & Chang (New York, NY), 1996.

Hannah Roche, *Soleil,* Hatier (Paris, France), 1996.

Hannah Roche, *Vent,* Hatier (Paris, France), 1996.

Hannah Roche, *Pluie,* Hatier (Paris, France), 1996.

Jacques Godbout, *Une leçon de chasse,* Boréal (Montreal, Quebec, Canada), 1997.

François Gravel, *Klonk* (novel), Hachette (Paris, France), 1997.

François Gravel, *Le cauchemar de Klonk* (novel), Québec/Amérique (Montreal, Quebec, Canada), 1997.

François Gravel, *Klonk et le Beatle mouillé* (novel), Québec/Amérique (Montreal, Quebec, Canada), 1997.

James Sage, *Sassy Gracie,* Dutton (New York, NY), 1998.

Rémy Simard, *Monsieur Ilétainunefois,* Annick Press (Toronto, Ontario, Canada), 1998, translated by David Homel as *Mister Once-upon-a-Time,* 1998.

Hannah Roche, *Have You Ever Seen a Chicken Hatch?,* Zero to Ten (New York, NY), 1998.

Hannah Roche, *Have You Ever Picked a Dandelion?,* Zero to Ten (New York, NY), 1998.

Joceline Sanschagrin, *Le cercle des magiciens,* La Courte Échelle (Montreal, Quebec, Canada), 1998.

Hannah Roche, *Have You Ever Seen a Frog Leap?,* Zero to Ten (New York, NY), 1999.

Hannah Roche, *Have You Ever Seen a Cat Purr?,* Zero to Ten (New York, NY), 1999.

Joceline Sanschagrin, *La marque du dragon,* La Courte Échelle (Montreal, Quebec, Canada), 1999.

François Gravel, *Klonk et le treize noir* (novel), Québec/Amérique (Montreal, Quebec, Canada), 1999.

Laurent Chabin, *La machine à manger des brocolis,* Boréal (Montreal, Quebec, Canada), 2000.

François Gravel, *Klonk et la queue du Scorpion* (novel), Québec/Amérique (Montreal, Quebec, Canada), 2000.

François Gravel, *David et le fantôme,* Dominique et Cie. (Saint-Lambert, Quebec, Canada), 2000.

Joceline Sanschagrin, *Le labyrinthe des rêves,* La Courte Échelle (Montreal, Quebec, Canada), 2000.

Joël des Rosiers, *Métropolis opéra: suivi de Tribu* (poetry), Triptyque (Montreal, Quebec, Canada), 2000.

Matthieu de Laubier, *Une joyeux Noël,* Bayard Jeunesse (Paris, France), 2000.

François Gravel, *David et les monstres de la forêt,* Dominique et Cie. (Saint-Lambert, Quebec, Canada), 2000.

François Gravel, *Coca-Klonk* (novel), Québec/Amérique (Montreal, Quebec, Canada), 2001.

François Gravel, *David et le précipice,* Dominique et Cie. (Saint-Lambert, Quebec, Canada), 2001.

Hannah Roche, *Une fleur est née!,* Millepages (Paris, France), 2001.

Hannah Roche, *Un poussin est né!,* Millepages (Paris, France), 2001.

Ron Hirsch, *No, No Jack!,* Dial Books for Young Children (New York, NY), 2002.

François Gravel, *David et la maison de la sorcière,* Dominique et Cie. (Saint-Lambert, Quebec, Canada), 2002.

François Gravel, *La racine carrée de Klonk* (novel), Québec/Amérique (Montreal, Quebec, Canada), 2002.

Jacques Godbout, *Mes petites fesses,* Les 400 Coups (Montreal, Quebec, Canada), 2002.

Dayle Ann Dodds, *Where's Pup?,* Dial Books (New York, NY), 2003.

François Gravel, *La testament de Klonk* (novel), Québec/Amérique (Montreal, Quebec, Canada), 2003.

François Gravel, *David et l'orage,* Dominique et Cie. (Saint-Lambert, Quebec, Canada), 2003.

Cynthia Zarin, *Albert, the Dog Who Liked to Ride in Taxis,* Atheneum (New York, NY), 2004.

François Gravel, *David et les crabes noirs,* Dominique et Cie. (Saint-Lambert, Quebec, Canada), 2004.

François Gravel, *Klonk contre Klonk* (novel), Québec/Amérique (Montreal, Quebec, Canada), 2004.

François Gravel, *David et le salon funéraire,* Dominique et Cie. (Saint-Lambert, Quebec, Canada), 2005.

Emily Jenkins, *That New Animal,* Farrar, Straus (New York, NY), 2005.

Halfdan Wedel Rasmussen, *The Ladder* (originally published as *Stigen*), translation by Marilyn Nelson, Candlewick Press (Cambridge, MA), 2005.

Marsha Diane Arnold, *Roar of a Snore,* Dial Books for Young Readers (New York, NY), 2006.

Sidelights

Quebec-based artist and author/illustrator Pierre Pratt creates exuberant, distinctive illustrations for children's books. In addition to producing images for the texts of predominately French-language authors such as Rémy Simard, Hannah Roche, and François Gravel, he has also paired his brightly colored illustrations with his own stories, and has produced a series of board books focusing on the adventures of Olaf the elephant and Venus the mouse. Praising Pratt's contribution to Dayle Ann Dodds's humorous rhyming picture book *Where's Pup?,* about a small dog who becomes mislaid by his circus-clown owner, *Horn Book* writer Betty Carter cited the artist's "near-sunshine palette" and added that Pratt's illustrations "provide context, offering a colorful, but uncluttered circus setting" that enhances Dodds's "engaging story." In *School Library Journal,* Linda M. Kenton dubbed the book "a visually exciting charmer for storytime."

Pratt decided on his career course as a child, when drawing was his favorite pastime. "As far back as I can remember, I always drew," the illustrator noted on the *Annick Press Web site.* "When my father took me to hockey games, I would go home and draw the players!" During his teen years, Pratt became a fan of "Tintin" comics and was inspired to write and illustrate his own comic strips; following high school he enrolled in college to study graphic design.

Pratt's first illustration project, a story by Benedicte Froissant published in English translation in 1990 as *Uncle Henry's Dinner Guests,* is a surreal fantasy in

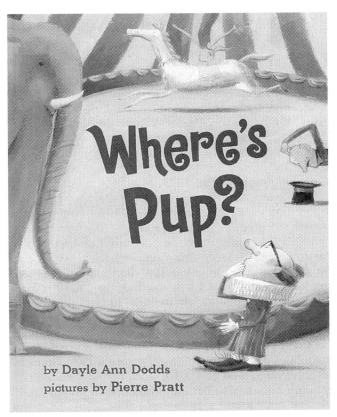

The search is on in this lighthearted collaboration between Pratt and Dayle Ann Dodds, as readers must search the colorful illustrations for a circus clown's missing puppy.

which the chickens pictured on Uncle Henry's shirt come alive during an otherwise quiet dinner, though only the children at the table seem to notice. Pratt's drawings are "zany and inventive," averred Anne Denoon in *Books in Canada;* "although his characters are pretty grotesque, they seem ideally suited to the strange goings-on at the dinner table." While *Quill & Quire* reviewer Frieda Wishinsky termed Froissant's story "nothing but silly," she called Pratt's illustrations "exaggerated but in a quirky, stylized manner. The colours are warm and inviting and the pages well designed." *Uncle Henry's Dinner Guests* earned Pratt two major illustration honors, and established him as a contender in the arena of children's book illustration.

Pratt teams up with children's author Rémy Simard in several books that have been noted for their absurdist tendencies. In *My Dog Is an Elephant,* for example, a boy tries to save an elephant from being sent back to the zoo by disguising the creature as a moose, a dinosaur, a butterfly, and finally, as the boy's father. "Both author and illustrator draw their jokes from within the fantasy they have created," Janet McNaughton observed in *Quill & Quire,* adding: "This state of serious silliness is a worthwhile achievement in a children's book." Although Lucinda Snyder Whitehurst, a contributor to *School Library Journal,* remarked that "most of the humor is rather mature" for the intended audience, and the illustrations are "bright, but not particularly attractive,"

other critics wrote that the quality of Simard's story equals that of Pratt's illustrations. As Diana Brebner commented in *Books in Canada,* "The high quality of the artwork" and the "delightful absurdity of the text" keeps the reader turning the pages until the unexpected ending.

For *The Magic Boot* Pratt and Simard create a picture book that explains why the land mass of Italy looks like a boot when viewed from above. Little Pipo's feet are too big for any boots made, so a good fairy gives him a pair of magic boots that will grow every time they are watered. After several mishaps occur, one of the boots gets tossed into the Mediterranean Sea. "The basic idea . . . is excellent," declared a reviewer in *Junior Bookshelf,* who added, however, that "somehow, we are left dissatisfied." Some critics faulted the book's narrative rather than its artwork; a *Publishers Weekly* contributor wrote that Pratt's illustrations "heighten the absurdity but don't deepen the story." *The Magic Boot* "isn't quite the tour de force that *My Dog Is an Elephant* was," McNaughton allowed, "but it proves that this pair is far from exhausting the creative potential of their partnership." Another collaboration, *Mister Once-in-a-Time,* won Pratt one of several Governor General awards for illustration he has received over his career.

Follow That Hat! marks Pratt's entry into children's literature in the role of writer. In the award-winning book, Leon chases his hat around the world, utilizing every form of transportation imaginable in the process. "Pratt's plot is admirable in its simplicity," McNaughton remarked in a *Quill & Quire* review. While Jane Robinson maintained in a *Canadian Review of Materials* appraisal that the story is "too 'clever' and too sophisticated for the younger reader," she added that experienced story-readers, if alerted, can sidestep "this pitfall and, that way, everyone could enjoy the work of this talented artist." Also expressing reservations about the story's text, Robin Baird Lewis wrote in *Canadian Children's Literature* that Pratt's illustrations, featuring "richly deep and textural colours, yummily scrumbled across black underpainting," more than compensate.

"I have lots of ideas, but sometimes it's difficult to get them out," Pratt noted on the Annick Press Web site, referring to the fact that his work sometimes requires him to tap into the visual inspiration behind other people's stories. "Once I start working, though, the ideas usually begin to flow," he added. Using oil pastel and acrylic paint in his works and incorporating heavy black lines, he often plays with perspective and draws on influences from Matisse to Edward Hopper to give his works an absurdist or sometimes merely silly slant. In fact, Pratt's illustrations are sometimes more successful with critics than the stories they accompany. "Pratt is undoubtedly one of the most original of the many gifted children's illustrators Quebec has given us in the last decade," remarked McNaughton in a 1992 *Quill & Quire* article, reflecting the award-winning artist's growing stature.

His lighthearted, quirky approach reflects the enjoyment Pratt takes in his work. In fact, he often incorporates musical interludes into his working day. "Often while I'm waiting for a painting to dry," he admitted, "I have fun playing the accordion, or the double bass, or the piano, or the guitar."

Biographical and Critical Sources

PERIODICALS

Booklist, January 1, 2002, Ilene Cooper, review of *No, No, Jack,* p. 864.

Books in Canada, April, 1991, Anne Denoon, review of *Uncle Henry's Dinner Guests,* p. 37; December, 1994, Diana Brebner, review of *My Dog Is an Elephant,* p. 55.

Canadian Children's Literature, number 72, 1993, Robin Baird Lewis, review of *Follow That Hat!,* pp. 80-81.

Canadian Review of Materials, January, 1991, Adele M. Fasick, review of *Uncle Henry's Dinner Guests,* p. 26; January, 1993, Jane Robinson, review of *Follow That Hat!,* p. 23.

Horn Book, March-April, 2003, Betty Carter, review of *Where's Pup?,* p. 201.

Junior Bookshelf, June, 1996, review of *The Magic Boot,* p. 103.

Kirkus Reviews, January 15, 2002, review of *No, No, Jack!,* p. 106; January 15, 2003, review of *Where's Pup?,* p. 141.

Publishers Weekly, August 28, 1995, review of *The Magic Boot,* p. 113; June 11, 2001, review of *Park, Shopping, Car,* and *Home,* p. 87; April 7, 2003, review of *Where's Pup?,* p. 69.

Quill & Quire, January, 1991, Frieda Wishinsky, review of *Uncle Henry's Dinner Guests,* p. 22; October, 1992, Janet McNaughton, review of *Follow That Hat!,* p. 33; September, 1994, Janet McNaughton, review of *My Dog Is an Elephant;* April, 2001, review of *I See . . . My Mom/I See . . . My Dad,* pp. 33-34.

School Library Journal, February, 1995, Lucinda Snyder Whitehurst, review of *My Dog Is an Elephant,* p. 82; November, 2001, Olga R. Kuharets, review of "Very Busy Life of Olaf and Venus" series, p. 133; July, 2003, Linda M. Kenton, review of *Where's Pup?,* p. 95.

Tribune Books (Chicago, IL), July 1, 2001, review of *Home,* p. 3.

ONLINE

Annick Press Web site, http://www.annickpress.com/ (December 1, 2005), "Pierre Pratt."*

PREISS, Byron 1953(?)-2005
(Byron Cary Preiss)

OBITUARY NOTICE—See index for *SATA* sketch: Born c. 1953, in New York, NY; died in a car accident July 9, 2005, in East Hampton, NY. Publisher and author. A pioneer in the area of digital publishing, Preiss was president of Byron Preiss Visual Publications and Ibooks, as well as an author of children's and adult books. With an early interest in education, he was an editor and writer for the television program *Electric Company* from 1972 to 1973, as well as an elementary school teacher in Pennsylvania. Graduating from the University of Pennsylvania in 1973, he completed a master's degree in communications at Stanford University in 1974. From there, he was hired as head writer for American Broadcasting Company television in San Francisco, worked as a movie writer and director during the mid-1970s, and was an editor for publisher Harcourt, Brace, Jovanovich from 1976 to 1977. Preiss then founded his own publishing house and quickly became a leader in publishing biographies, as well as books in other media besides print. His release of the audiobook *The Words of Gandhi* earned a 1985 Grammy award. Preiss, who enjoyed science fiction, fantasy, and mystery books, also became interested in graphic novels and later focused on digital publications, releasing books on CD-ROM and as e-books. An accomplished writer himself, he wrote lighthearted juvenile titles such as *The Silent "E's" from Outer Space* (1973) and *The First Crazy Word Book: Verbs* 1982), and authored genre fiction, such as the science-fiction novel *Starfawn* (1976) and the fantasy *Dragonworld* (1979), the latter which he coauthored with Michael Reaves.

OBITUARIES AND OTHER SOURCES:

PERIODICALS

New York Times, July 11, 2005, p. A19.

ONLINE

Publishers Newswire Online, http://www.publishersnewswire.com/ (July 11, 2005).

*   *   *

PREISS, Byron Cary
See PREISS, Byron

*   *   *

PROFESSOR SCRIBBLER
See HOLLINGSWORTH, Mary

R

RASCHKA, Chris 1959-
(Christopher Raschka)

Personal
Born March 6, 1959, in Huntingdon, PA; son of Donald F. (an historian) and Hedwig T. (a translator; maiden name, Raschka) Durnbaugh; married Lydie Olson (a teacher), August 4, 1984. *Education:* St. Olaf College, B.A., 1981. *Hobbies and other interests:* Yoga, walking, playing solitaire, playing viola and concertina, knitting.

Addresses
Office—310 Riverside Dr., No. 418, New York, NY 10025. *Agent*—c/o Author Mail, Atheneum, Simon & Schuster, 1230 Avenue of the Americas, New York, NY 10020.

Career
Writer, artist, and musician. Art teacher in St. Croix, Virgin Islands, 1985-86; freelance artist, cartoonist, and editorial illustrator, Ann Arbor, MI, 1987-89; freelance artist and children's book writer and illustrator, New York, NY, 1989—. Member, New York City School Volunteers Program; member, Ann Arbor Symphony Orchestra, Ann Arbor, 1982-84, 1986-89, and Flint Symphony Orchestra, Flint, MI, 1983-84. Also worked as an intern in an orthopedic clinic in Germany, 1981-82, and as a respite care worker in Ypsilanti, MI, 1982-84. *Exhibitions:* Artwork included in numerous exhibitions, including *From Sea to Shining Sea—An American Sampler: Children's Books from the Library of Congress,* Library of Congress, Washington, DC, 1998; *America Illustrated,* Bolzano, Padua, Rome, and Venice, Italy, 1998-2000; *The Art of the Book,* Grand Valley State University, Michigan, 1999; Katonah Museum of Art, Katonah, NY, 2001; *Charmed: The Art of Chris Raschka,* Thurber Center Gallery, Columbus, OH, 2003; and Padiglione Esprit Nouveau, Bolobna, Italy, 2005.

Member
Authors Guild, Authors League of America, Society of Children's Book Writers and Illustrators, Municipal Art Society, New York-New Jersey Trail Conference.

Awards, Honors
Best Books of the Year citation, *Publishers Weekly,* Notable Children's Book citation, American Library Association (ALA), and Pick of the Lists citation, American Booksellers Association, all 1992, all for *Charlie Parker Played Be Bop; New York Times* Best Illustrated Book of the Year inclusion, Caldecott Honor Book award, ALA, and U.S. winner of UNICEF-Ezra Jack Keats Award, all 1994, all for *Yo! Yes?*

Writings

FOR CHILDREN; SELF-ILLUSTRATED

(Under name Christopher Raschka) *R and R: A Story about Two Alphabets,* Brethren Press, 1990.
Charlie Parker Played Be Bop, Orchard (New York, NY), 1992.
Yo! Yes?, Orchard (New York, NY), 1993.
Elizabeth Imagined an Iceberg, Orchard (New York, NY), 1994.
Can't Sleep, Orchard (New York, NY), 1995.
The Blushful Hippopotamus, Orchard (New York, NY), 1995.
Mysterious Thelonious, Orchard (New York, NY), 1997.
Arlene Sardine, Orchard (New York, NY), 1998.
Like Likes Like, DK (New York, NY), 1999.
Moosey Moose, Hyperion (New York, NY), 2000.
Doggy Dog, Hyperion (New York, NY), 2000.
Goosey Goose, Hyperion (New York, NY), 2000.
Lamby Lamb, Hyperion (New York, NY), 2000.
Ring! Yo?, DK (New York, NY), 2000.
Sluggy Slug, Hyperion (New York, NY), 2000.
Snaily Snail, Hyperion (New York, NY), 2000.

Whaley Whale, Hyperion (New York, NY), 2000.

Wormy Worm, Hyperion (New York, NY), 2000.

Waffle, Atheneum (New York, NY), 2001.

Little Tree, based on a poem by e. e. cummings, Hyperion (New York, NY), 2001.

(With Vladimir Radunsky) *Table Manners: The Edifying Story of Two Friends Whose Discovery of Good Manners Promises Them a Glorious Future,* Candlewick (Cambridge, MA), 2001.

John Coltrane's Giant Steps, Atheneum (New York, NY), 2002.

Talk to Me about the Alphabet, Holt (New York, NY), 2003.

(With Vladimir Radunsky) *Boy Meets Girl; Girl Meets Boy,* Seuil Chronicle (San Francisco, CA), 2004.

New York Is English, Chattanooga Is Creek, Atheneum (New York, NY), 2005.

Five for a Little One, Atheneum (New York, NY), 2006.

ILLUSTRATOR

James H. Lehman, *The Saga of Shakespeare Pintlewood and the Great Silver Fountain Pen,* Brotherstone (Elgin, IL), 1990.

James H. Lehman, *Owl and the Tuba,* Brotherstone (Elgin, IL), 1991.

Phyllis Vos Wezeman and Colleen Aalsburg Wiessner, *Benjamin Brody's Backyard Bag,* Brethren Press (Elgin, IL), 1991.

George Dolnikowski, *This I Remember,* Brethren Press (Elgin, IL), 1994.

Nikki Giovanni, *The Genie in the Jar,* Holt (New York, NY), 1996.

Simple Gifts: A Shaker Hymn, Holt (New York, NY), 1998.

Margaret Wise Brown, *Another Important Book,* HarperCollins (New York, NY), 1999.

bell hooks, *Happy to Be Nappy,* Hyperion (New York, NY), 1999.

Sharon Creech, *Fishing in the Air,* HarperCollins (New York, NY), 2000.

Paul Janeczko, editor, *A Poke in the Eye,* Candlewick (Cambridge, MA), 2001.

bell hooks, *Be Boy Buzz,* Hyperion (New York, NY), 2002.

Claude Nougaro, *Armstrong,* Didier Jeunesse (Paris, France), 2002.

Francis Bellamy, *I Pledge Allegiance: The Pledge of Allegiance,* with commentary by Bill Martin, Jr., and Michael Sampson, Candlewick (Cambridge, MA), 2002.

Dylan Thomas, *A Child's Christmas in Wales,* Candlewick (Cambridge, MA), 2004.

bell hooks, *Skin Again,* Hyperion (New York, NY), 2004.

Agnès Grunelius-Hollard, *Petite fille et le loup,* Didier Jeunesse (Paris, France), 2004.

Paul B. Janeczko, editor, *A Kick in the Head,* Candlewick (Cambridge, MA), 2005.

Norton Juster, *The Hello, Good-bye Window,* Hyperion (New York, NY), 2005.

Sidelights

Caldecott Honor-winning author and illustrator Chris Raschka likes to take chances. Employing only thirty-four well-chosen words in his book *Yo! Yes?,* and artwork that *Publishers Weekly* contributor Diane Roback dubbed "brash, witty, and offbeat," Raschka manages to convey volumes about not only the process of making friends, but also about race relations and the subtle nuances of emotion. His *Charlie Parker Played Be Bop,* constructed like a jazz piece with its text forming the rhythm and cadence of be bop, "stretched the definition of picture book," according to Roback in another *Publishers Weekly* review. Raschka is a chance-taker in his private life as well: accepted to medical school in the early 1980s, he made an eleventh-hour decision to forego the financial security of a doctor's life for the risk and reward of being a freelance artist. It is a decision he has never regretted. Raschka credits Vladimir Radunsky, a picture book artist with whom he later collaborated, with having been the inspiration for moving to New York to be nearer opportunities to illustrate children's books.

Born in Pennsylvania, Raschka is the only one of his siblings not born abroad. His parents met while both were doing refugee work after World War II: his father is an American from Detroit, and his mother is from Vienna, Austria. "So I grew up with a little bit of both in me," the author/illustrator once told *SATA* in an interview. "My earliest stories were Viennese fairy tales and sagas of Vienna that my mother would tell me." Growing up speaking both German and English, Raschka attended first grade in Marburg, Germany, where his father, a seminary professor of church history, was on sabbatical. "At that time of my life, I actually forgot English," he said. "When I got back to the United States, I remember my first grade teacher, Mrs. Ericson, saying 'Do you understand, Christopher?' I thought this was strange." His entire childhood was not spent solely in distant locales, however. Living in suburban Chicago, "I played in the storm sewers and ditches," he also recalled. "They were the one interesting place in the whole bleak environment."

Though Raschka remembers some of the American cultural artifacts from his youth, such as the "Dick and Jane" readers, it is primarily the picture books from his mother's part of the world that informed his earliest imaginings and that still influence his own work. "I loved books such as *Die kleine Hexe* (*The Little Witch*) by [Otfried] Preussler," he explained to *SATA.* "Another all-time favorite is the illustrator Winnie Gebhardt Gayler and Wilhelm Busch with his 'Max and Moritz' stories. I even liked *Struwelpeter* when I was growing up. I know they are all pretty frightening, with horrific things happening to children who disobey their parents, but I think that kids are so used to seeing dangers all around them that they can deal with it. I was disturbed by some of the cruelty of the old German stories, but I loved the drawings and still do." Only as an adult did

Raschka "catch up" on the great illustrators known to British and American audiences.

Raschka was involved in art and music from an early age. As a child, he loved to draw, and also started studying the piano at age six. From the piano he went on to the recorder and then violin. "But I was such a bad violinist," Raschka said, "that the director of the junior high orchestra made me take up viola." He went on to play in both high school and college orchestras. "But all the while I planned to be a biologist. I just loved animals of all types, especially crocodiles and turtles. I also loved drawing and music, but never thought I could make a living at those." Raschka was a biology major at college, and after graduation he planned to work on a crocodile farm in India on a project to restore the crocodile population in the country's rivers, thereby reviving a limited harvesting of the animal. But when these plans were put on hold, he took a position as an intern in a children's orthopedic clinic in Germany instead. "I learned so much from those kids," Raschka said, "and I loved the work. It was after that experience that I decided to go to medical school." After studying for and passing the entrance tests, Raschka was ultimately admitted to medical school, but again he put his plans on hold while he and his new wife went to St. Croix, Virgin Islands.

"I had a lot of luck in St. Croix," Raschka recalled. "My wife and I both decided to try our art—we had met in an art class—and we had shows there. My work was in galleries and I began to get freelance work as an illustrator. It was there that I first realized I might be able to make it as an artist." But the time came to enter medical school, and Raschka and his wife returned to the United States and the University of Michigan in Ann Arbor. The very night of his orientation, Raschka decided not to go to school. Instead, he opted to work as an illustrator for various regional newspapers and magazines, doing everything from political cartoons to illustrations for legal text. Meanwhile, Raschka's wife trained as a Montessori teacher. "After a couple of years illustrating, I thought I would try a children's book," Raschka said. "That's how *R and R* came about."

Raschka's first picture book explores a theme he continues to develop: finding commonality in difference and allowing tolerance to bridge the gaps between people and peoples. "Actually the second 'R' in the title should be backwards, like in the Russian alphabet," Raschka once explained to *SATA*. "The book is a story that contrasts the English and Russian alphabets and the two letters are the main characters. It's a Russian-American friendship book and the text is both in English and Russian." With this first book, Raschka was already demonstrating the care and attention to detail that have become characteristic of his work. "My goal is to create a book where the entire book—text, pictures, shape of book—work together to create the theme. The placement of images and text on the page is crucial for me."

Raschka began painstaking work toward this goal with *R and R,* which he finished in only three weeks. Encouraged by a professor of children's literature at the University of Michigan, Raschka prepared a complete package with lettering, design, and layout all camera-ready, and submitted it to Trethren Press of Elgin, Illinois. "The idea was to get into print," Raschka told *SATA*. "The publishing house liked my work and this led to other illustration jobs." He worked on three picture books with text by other authors at this time. "It was all sort of my apprenticeship period," Raschka recalled. "It taught me the amount of work involved in creating a picture book and how to put books together. And most of all this work taught me to see the book as a whole work and not just one illustration after another."

Meanwhile, Raschka was still pursuing his second love: music. As a member of two professional symphony orchestras, he still held hope of a career as a viola player. New York City also began to beckon. "My wife and I spent a couple of summers in New York and it was a wonderful experience. For me, New York City is the best blend of two worlds. It has the feeling of a big European city." In 1989, with no job prospects, Raschka and his wife decided to make the leap. For Raschka, this was the point where he made the decision between art or music. All that summer he practiced on a new viola, hoping to audition for the big orchestras in the fall. He even experimented with a new hand position on the instrument, and then nature took over. "I developed this incredibly painful case of tendonitis," he related in his interview. "I simply couldn't play anymore. My decision was made for me."

It was this musical inclination that won Raschka his first big break. After struggling for a couple of years to find freelance illustration work, and creating a small body of work in children's books, Raschka felt he knew the children's book trade and was ready to take a chance with something really innovative. "I start work early every morning," Raschka said. "And I like to listen to the radio when I work. In New York there is this one show on morning radio that plays all the music of [jazz saxophone player] Charlie Parker. This is every morning, and the man who does the show, Phil Schaap, plays every last scrap of the music. I was caught up by his enthusiasm for Parker. That and my own love for the music convinced me I should do a book on him. Ultimately I dedicated my book to Schaap." Convinced that jazz will be the classical music of the next century, Raschka decided it was time kids learned something more about jazz greats like Parker than that their lives were messed up by drugs. "I wanted to write about Parker for the birth of be bop, and not for the downside of his life."

Initially planning to write a straightforward biography of the musician, Raschka's intention was derailed after the very first sentence of the book: "Charlie Parker played be bop," which also became the book's title. "I realized these words could fit one of the great be bop tunes of the time, 'Night in Tunisia,' by Dizzy Gillespie," Raschka recounted for *SATA*. "After these first words I put away the notion of a regular biography and decided to convey just two facts: that Parker played the saxophone and played be bop. The rest was like a be bop tune itself, based on a repeating stanza or motif, with pure nonsense stanzas in between—a simple line that gets modified over and over again." Raschka blended this text with art done in charcoal and watercolors, angular and skewed and quite humorous. The finished book was turned down by one publisher, and then an illustrator friend of Raschka's suggested he submit it to Richard Jackson at Orchard Books, who took an immediate interest in the project.

Doubts as to whether the public would understand what Raschka was trying to do with *Charlie Parker Played Be Bop* were quickly dispelled by reviews. "Rather than attempting to teach his young audience about Parker's music," *Booklist* contributor Bill Ott noted, "Raschka allows them to hear it—not with sounds but with words and pictures." Raschka's text sticks in the head like a persistent ditty: "Charlie Parker played *be bop*./ Charlie Parker played *saxophone*./ The music sounded like *be bop*./ Never leave your cat alone./ Be bop./ Fisk, fisk./ Lollipop./ Boomba, boomba./ Bus stop./ Zznnzznn./ Boppity, bibbitty, bop. BANG!" In addition, Raschka's artwork gives his figures "extraordinary energy; creating jaunty, fantastical creatures to move with the beat," explained a *Kirkus Reviews* critic. Roback, writing in *Publishers Weekly*, added that "even the typeface joins in the fun as italics and boldface strut and swing across the pages." Roback also noted the inside jokes Raschka plays, such as the birds which are used as decorative motifs on some pages—Parker's nickname was "Bird." Raschka "has created a memorable tribute" to Parker, wrote Elizabeth S. Watson in *Horn Book*, calling the work "one of the most innovative picture books of recent times." Jazz great Dizzy Gillespie himself praised the book in *Entertainment Weekly*. Comparing the text to scat singing, Gillespie liked the "drawings of Bird, too; they're funny. So was he. I think this book would make him laugh a lot. It will surely make kids laugh."

Like *Charlie Parker Played Be Bop, Mysterious Thelonious* is a tribute to a famous figure in jazz history; this time it is composer Thelonious Monk. And like *Charlie Parker Played Be Bop,* the text of *Mysterious Thelonious* mimics the music of its subject. Critics compared the text of the earlier book to the improvisational be-bop music it celebrates; in the latter book, the author/illustrator associates the placement and color of each page's illustration with placement of a note on the musical scale. Thus the book may be "played" as music to the tune of the composer's famous "Mysterioso." Watson, in another *Horn Book* review, remarked that while not all readers would be able to access this aspect of Raschka's tribute, those who could would find "Raschka's fresh, inventive use of color, rhythm, and melody will sing."

Returning to jazz with *John Coltrane's Giant Steps,* Raschka adapts one of Coltrane's songs to the printed page by representing each instrument with a "performer": a kitten representing the saxophone, snowflakes taking the part of the piano, raindrops as drums, and boxes for the bass. The characters depicting the instruments all refer to another number of Coltrane's, the jazz interpretation of the song "My Favorite Things." Raschka explained his goal with *John Coltrane's Giant Steps* to a writer for *Children's Literature Web site:* "The thing that I hoped to get across with this book was mostly a feeling of the potential for complexity that comes from a very simple layering of abstract things. Which is the case in Coltrane's music. It's more a visual experimentation to see what happens if you follow principles that are developed in music and try to translate them into graphic materials." While some reviewers noted that the book would be best accompanied by a recording of Coltrane playing "Giant Steps," most applauded Raschka's visual representation. "Raschka's transparent watercolors layer colors and shapes the way a musician would notes and harmonies," reported a *Publishers Weekly* critic. Wendy Lukehart in *School Library Journal* noted that "the sequential design and layering of the organic forms are a creative, joyful, and energetic match" for the original music.

The positive reception earned by *Charlie Parker Played Be Bop* encouraged Raschka to push ahead with another project that had started germinating about the same time as that book. "I was walking to the post office one day," Raschka recalled for *SATA,* "and was suddenly struck with how rich the street scene was. I've got a real interest in language and how words such as 'Yo' come into use. And so I began thinking about how language and culture and race all seem so big, but are actually small. They shouldn't really stand between people and keep us apart." With this germ of an idea—the interplay of language and race—Raschka started playing with story ideas. He wanted to talk about friendship, about the process of making friends. And he wanted to keep it simple and direct. "When I was a kid, my dad would play this little one-word game with us. We used to carry on whole dialogues with just one word back and forth." From these elements, *Yo! Yes?* was born.

With just thirty-four words Raschka portrays a potential racial stand-off that turns into friendship. On the left-hand page, an African-American boy, coolly outfitted in baggy shorts and unlaced sneakers, calls "Yo!" across the book to a shy white boy who seems to be inching off the right-hand page. From this beginning, the picture book progresses through one-word exchanges that show the white kid to be lonely for lack of friends, and culminates in the more outgoing black kid offering friendship, an offer accepted in an ecstatic high-five as the two join together on the final page and shout "Yow!" with joy. "Raschka exhibits an appreciation of the rhythms of both language and human exchange in his deceptively simple story," Maeve Visser Knoth wrote in

Horn Book. "The succinct, rhythmic text and the strong cartoon-like watercolor-and-charcoal illustrations are perfect complements," Judy Constantinides similarly commented in *School Library Journal.* Raschka's artwork and layout are "bold, spare and expressive," summarized a *Bulletin of the Center for Children's Books* reviewer, who concluded that "the language has the strength of a playground chant; the story is a ritual played out worldwide."

Named a Caldecott Honor Book, *Yo! Yes?* was a further step in Raschka's attempt to innovate the picture book: his placement of illustrations on the very bottom edge of the page is as important as the hand-lettered text. The structure of the book itself also adds to the story, as the two boys seem to be looking across, and eventually bridge, the actual seam between the book's left and right pages. The book is also a distillation of some of the kids Raschka plays basketball with in New York and of himself as the shy new white kid on the block. "Beneath it all," Raschka told *SATA,* "the black kid is shy too. It's a risk for him to offer friendship. I hope it's always a risk worth taking."

In *The Blushful Hippopotamus* Raschka offers up his signature combination of expressionistic depictions of characters and unusual, rhythmic text. Like the earlier *Yo! Yes?,* Raschka tells much of the story in *The Blushful Hippopotamus* visually, using the simple technique of rendering confident characters large and timid characters small. Roosevelt Hippopotamus is so overpowered by his sister's teasing that he practically slinks off the right-hand page while his sister looms so large that only part of her face and body can fit on the left-hand page. But, as Roosevelt's bird friend Lombard boosts his confidence, Roosevelt grows in stature (and his sister shrinks correspondingly). The book ends with a grateful embrace by the two friends. "Ah, the sweet balm of friendship," beamed a reviewer for *Publishers Weekly,* continuing: "its magic works as admirably on these pages as it does in real life." Raschka's *Like Likes Like* is another celebration of friendship with a story played out mainly in the author/illustrator's expressive drawings. This book "features Raschka at his most amenable," contended Julie Corsaro in *Booklist.*

Of *The Blushful Hippopotamus, School Library Journal* reviewer Barbara Kiefer predicted: "This simple story will comfort any child who's ever been teased unmercifully." Reviewers likewise praised Raschka's evident sympathy for the uncomfortable feelings of children that are demonstrated in *Can't Sleep. Horn Book* reviewer Mary M. Burns described Raschka's illustrations as "a minimum of detail but supercharged with emotion," depicting a small dog as he goes to bed and lies awake listening to the sounds of the rest of his family preparing for sleep. Burns singled out for praise the author's "brilliantly imaginative and completely childlike conclusion," in which the moon watches over the fearful child/dog at night so that, during the day, when the moon is asleep and the dog awake, the child can watch over the moon "and keep her safe."

Although much of Raschka's early works are considered innovative, none got the kind of reaction evoked by *Arlene Sardine.* In this book, Raschka chronicles the two-year life of Arlene, from her birth in a fjord among thousands of her kind, to her death on the deck of a fishing boat and, beyond death, to her processing in a sardine factory. Ilene Cooper observed that the sardine's short life and subsequent death "seems a dubious topic upon which to write a book for preschoolers," in a *Booklist* review. *School Library Journal* reviewer Carol Ann Wilson expressed a similar viewpoint while observing that "the graphic design [of the book] is masterful," and praising the touches of whimsy injected into the fact-based account of Arlene's life via the poetic rhythms and use of repetition in the text. Still, "Arlene's saga, like sardines, is an acquired taste," Wilson concluded. While Betsy Hearne, in the *Bulletin of the Center for Children's Books,* acknowledged the issues raised concerning the appropriateness of the book for its intended audience, she also praised *Arlene Sardine* by writing that "it's refreshing to have a visual storyteller trying innovative things." "One thing for sure," Hearne continued, "Raschka's work always surprises, challenges, and intrigues us one way or another."

Raschka explained the basis for his idea to create *Arlene Sardine* to Etta Wilson of *BookPage.com.* "One day, as he was putting away an assortment of food donations from the United States, he was struck by the amazing journey of a can of sardines," Wilson explained. Raschka wrote to sardine companies, curious about the process of transforming brisling fish into sardines, and he received responses from around the world, with his most valuable information coming from Norway. This curiosity led to a picture book in which, according to Wilson, although "the story may be hard to swallow for an adult . . . young readers will certainly like the interesting depiction."

After creating several titles about animals, including *Snaily Snail* and *Wormy Worm,* Raschka tells the story of a protagonist who cannot make up his mind in *Waffle.* Poor Waffle worries constantly, until he finally finds his inner strength and learns to fly. "Conceptually, and visually, the book is ingenious," praised Martha V. Parravano in *Horn Book,* although noting that "it's difficult to be as enthusiastic about the text." While other critics also noted the story's awkward cadences, Michael Cart wrote in *Booklist* that "Raschka's spare, alliterative text will be great fun to read aloud." According to a *Publishers Weekly* critic, Raschka "captures the essence of a mood with the merest hint of text and the briefest of brush strokes."

Raschka followed *Waffle* with *Little Tree,* a Christmas tale inspired by a poem by e. e. cummings. Creating text to expand upon cummings's original tale of a fir tree who wants to become a Christmas tree, Raschka delivers the story "with loads of repetition and an almost hypnotic rhythm," according to a *Kirkus Reviews* contributor. The picture book "embodies the warm sense of love and belonging that for many defines the true meaning of Christmas," wrote a reviewer for *School Library Journal.*

In 2001, Raschka collaborated with artist Vladimir Radunsky on *Table Manners: The Edifying Story of Two Friends Whose Discovery of Good Manners Promises Them a Glorious Future.* Chester and Dudunya ask questions about appropriate manners and give examples

In **Waffle** *a young boy who has earned the titular nickname through his worrying, stalling, and waiting, finally learns to deal with the fears that keep him actionless.*

of good restaurant conduct, as well as teaching readers to say "please" and "thank you" in six different languages. Commenting on the "free-spirited" illustration style, a *Publishers Weekly* reviewer found that, "together, these two [artists] are anything but uptight." Kathleen Whalin, writing in *School Library Journal,* called the collaboration "a funny, artistic creation on the subject of living well." In a second collaboration between Raschka and Radunsky, *Girl Meets Boy; Boy Meets Girl,* the words of the story are the same from right to left and from left to right, and are occasionally sprawled across the page upside-down. The experimental format "busts linear narrative to smithereens," according to a *Kirkus Reviews* contributor. A *Publishers Weekly* reviewer likened the story to "a Mobius strip that never stops."

A list of letters with attitude is the subject of *Talk to Me about the Alphabet,* Raschka's first alphabet book since his first self-illustrated title. A lumpy looking narrator demands to be told about the alphabet, going through the letters with his cat for company. Due to the lack of theme that tied *R and R* together, some critics, including a reviewer for *Publishers Weekly,* found "the end result is underwhelming." However, other critics, including GraceAnne A. DeCandido in *Booklist,* described Raschka's unconventional style as "quirky and satisfying." Marian Creamer noted, "The strength of the book lies in the vibrancy of the rhythmic text and ink-and-watercolor illustrations," in her *School Library Journal* review.

Raschka has also illustrated titles for such well-known writers as poet bell hooks and children's author Sharon Creech. When Raschka illustrated hooks's *Happy to Be Nappy,* he faced controversy as a white illustrator of black-themed books. "My own perspective is that bell hooks asked me to illustrate her lovely text and I said 'sure,' and that's the level on which I view it," he explained to a writer for *ChildrensLit.com.* Of his illustrations for hooks's *Be Boy Buzz,* a *Publishers Weekly* contributor commented on "Raschka's trademark visual haiku." On his work for *Skin Again,* also written by hooks, *Booklist* contributor Hazel Rochman wrote that Raschka's "art vividly celebrates history and the realism, fun, and fantasy inside each one of us."

Raschka's collaboration with Creech on *Granny Torrelli Makes Soup,* was considered by Maria B. Salvadore in *School Library Journal* to be "a meal that should not be missed." His illustrations have also adorned poetry collections, including *A Poke in the Eye* and *A Kick in the Head,* both edited by Paul B. Janeczko. Raschka "works in tandem with each poem's design," noted a *Publishers Weekly* critic in a review of the earlier anthology. A *Horn Book* reviewer wrote of *A Poke in the Eye* that "Raschka decorates rather than interprets, but he does so with strong, vertical lines and bold colors that add energy to the collection without overwhelming it."

Working with author bell hooks, Raschka creates vivid, colorful illustrations that pair well with hooks's simple, energetic text describing the antics of an active young boy.

Raschka generally has several projects going at once. "I may be finishing up one book while another one is in the early stages of artwork and still another one is just a few words scribbled onto a bit of scrap paper and left to ripen for a time," he said. "With my illustrations, I am working very close to the surface. Most of the information is right up front without great detail in the background. That's why I like to position them on the bottom of the page. To make them almost come out of the frame, to jump off the page. I work for young kids who want things close up and are immediate and tactile." As for content and theme, Raschka writes out of personal experience and necessity: "My books are my own thoughts about things that are important to me," he once explained to *SATA.* "I work through how I feel about such things as language, art, music, and friendship with these loose, colorful and slightly wild drawings."

"I hope that my books create an openness to the world," Raschka concluded in *SATA.* "An openness to cultural and racial differences. So far, I've looked at language and music and diversity. I want kids to be able to be positive toward these things. To enjoy difference and not be frightened by it."

Biographical and Critical Sources

PERIODICALS

Booklist, September 1, 1988, Ilene Cooper, review of *Arlene Sardine,* p. 126; June 15, 1992, Bill Ott, review of *Charlie Parker Played Be Bop,* p. 1843; April 1, 1999, Julie Corsaro, review of *Like Likes Like,* p. 1409; May 15, 2001, Michael Cart, review of *Waffle,* p. 1760; November 1, 2002, review of *Be Boy Buzz,* p. 508; April 1, 2003, Gillian Engberg, review of *John Coltrane's Giant Steps,* p. 1414; May 1, 2003, GraceAnne A. DeCandido, review of *Talk to Me about the Alphabet,* p. 1606; September 15, 2004, Hazel Rochman, review of *Skin Again,* p. 250.

Bulletin of the Center for Children's Books, April, 1993, review of *Yo! Yes?,* pp. 262-263; September, 1998, Betsy Hearne, review of *Arlene Sardine,* pp. 3-4.

Entertainment Weekly, October 9, 1992, Dizzy Gillespie, "What about Bop?," p. 70.

Horn Book, November-December, 1992, Elizabeth S. Watson, review of *Charlie Parker Played Be Bop,* pp. 718-719; May-June, 1993, Maeve Visser Knoth, review of *Yo! Yes?,* p. 323; March-April, 1996, Mary M. Burns, review of *Can't Sleep,* p. 191; January-February, 1998, Elizabeth S. Watson, review of *Mysterious Thelonious,* p. 68; May, 2001, Martha V. Parravano, review of *Waffle,* p. 315; July, 2001, review of *A Poke in the Eye,* p. 466.

Kirkus Reviews, July 1, 1992, review of *Charlie Parker Played Be Bop,* p. 853; August 15, 2001, review of *Little Tree,* p. 1210; October 1, 2001, review of *Table Manners,* p. 1431; July 1, 2003, review of *Granny Torrelli Makes Soup,* p. 908; August 1, 2004, review of *Girl Meets Boy; Boy Meets Girl,* p. 748.

Los Angeles Times Book Review, June 20, 1993, p. 3.

Publishers Weekly, October, 1992, Diane Roback, review of *Charlie Parker Played Be Bop,* p. 108; February 15, 1993, Diane Roback, review of *Yo! Yes?,* p. 236; December 13, 1993, Diane Roback, review of *Elizabeth Imagined an Iceberg,* p. 69; August 5, 1996, review of *The Blushful Hippopotamus,* p. 441; April 16, 2001, review of *Waffle,* p. 64; September 24, 2001, review of *Little Tree,* p. 49; October 29, 2001, review of *Table Manners,* p. 62; June 25, 2002, review of *John Coltrane's Giant Steps,* p. 55; August 26, 2002, review of *I Pledge Allegiance,* p. 68; September 30, 2002, review of *Be Boy Buzz,* p. 71; February 3, 2003, review of *Talk to Me about the Alphabet,* p. 74; December 22, 2003, review of *Charlie Parker Played Be Bop,* p. 63; August 30, 2004, review of *Boy Meets Girl; Girl Meets Boy,* p. 53.

School Library Journal, July 6, 1992, p. 54; May, 1993, Judy Constantinides, review of *Yo! Yes?,* p. 90; April, 1994, Kate McClelland, review of *Elizabeth Imagined an Iceberg,* p. 112; September, 1996, Barbara Kiefer, review of *The Blushful Hippopotamus,* pp. 117-118; September, 1998, Carol Ann Wilson, review of *Arlene Sardine,* p. 179; April, 2001, review of *Charlie Parker Played Be Bop* (audiobook), p. 92; October, 2001, review of *Little Tree,* p. 63; November, 2001, Kathleen Whalin, review of *Table Manners,* p. 134; July, 2002,

Wendy Lukehart, review of *John Coltrane's Giant Steps,* p. 97; December, 2002, Anna DeWind Walls, review of *Be Boy Buzz,* p. 97, and Krista Tokarz, review of *I Pledge Allegiance,* p. 127; February, 2003, Lee Bock, review of *Yo! Yes?,* p. 97; March, 2003, Kirsten Martindale, review of *John Coltrane's Giant Steps* (audiobook), p. 93; June, 2003, Marian Creamer, review of *Talk to Me about the Alphabet,* p. 113; August, 2003, Maria B. Salvadore, review of *Granny Torrelli Makes Soup,* p. 158; November, 2004, Marie Orlando, review of *Girl Meets Boy; Boy Meets Girl,* p. 116.

ONLINE

BookPage.com, http://www.bookpage.com/ (September, 1998), Etta Wilson, interview with Raschka.

ChildrensLit.com, http://www.childrenslit.com/ (December 1, 2005), "Chris Raschka."

Storyopolis Art Gallery Online, http://www.storyopolis.com/ (December 1, 2005).

* * *

RASCHKA, Christopher
See RASCHKA, Chris

* * *

REID, Desmond
See MOORCOCK, Michael

* * *

RIDDELL, Chris 1962-
(Christopher Barry Riddell)

Personal

Born April 13, 1962, in Capetown, South Africa; son of Morris Stroyan (an Anglican priest) and Pamela Aileen (Moyle) Riddell; married Joanna Kathleen Burroughes (an artist), November 7, 1987; children: William, Katy, Jack. *Education:* Attended Epsom School of Art and Design, 1980-81; Brighton Polytechnic, B.A. (first-class honours), 1984.

Addresses

Home—Brighton, England. *Agent*—c/o Author Mail, Andersen Press, 20 Vauxhall Bridge Rd., London SW1V 2SA, England.

Career

Freelance illustrator and writer. Political cartoonist for London periodicals, including *Economist,* 1988-95, *Independent, Independent on Sunday, Guardian,* and *Observer,* beginning 1995. Producer of cover art for *Literary Review,* beginning 1997, and *New Statesman.*

Awards, Honors

Kate Greenaway Medal special commendation, 1995, and UNESCO Prize, 1997, both for *Something Else;* Ragazza Prize honorable mention, Bologna Book Fair, and Kurt Maschler Award shortlist, both 1998, both for *The Swan's Stories;* Kate Greenaway Medal, 2002, for *Pirate Diary: The Journal of Jake Carpenter,* and 2004, for *Jonathan Swift's Gulliver;* (with Paul Stewart) Smarties Award, 2004, for *Fergus Crane.*

Writings

SELF-ILLUSTRATED

Ben and the Bear, Walker (New York, NY), 1985.
Mr. Underbed, Holt (New York, NY), 1986.
Bird's New Shoes, Holt (New York, NY), 1987.
The Fibbs, Walker (New York, NY), 1988.
The Trouble with Elephants, Walker (New York, NY), 1988.
When the Walrus Comes, Walker (New York, NY), 1989.
The Bear Dance, Simon & Schuster (New York, NY), 1990.
The Wish Factory, Walker (New York, NY), 1990.
The World of Zoom, Walker (New York, NY), 1993.
Platypus, Harcourt (San Diego, CA), 2001.
Platypus and the Lucky Day, edited by Karrie A. Oswald, Harcourt (San Diego, CA), 2002.
Platypus and the Birthday Party, Harcourt (Orlando, FL), 2003.

WITH PAUL STEWART; AND ILLUSTRATOR

Fergus Crane ("Far-Flung Adventures" series), Doubleday (London, England), 2004, David Fickling Books (New York, NY), 2006.
Corby Flood, Doubleday Children's (London, England), 2005.

"EDGE CHRONICLES"; WITH PAUL STEWART; AND ILLUSTRATOR

Beyond the Deepwoods, Doubleday (London, England), 1998, David Fickling Books (New York, NY), 2004.
Stormchaser, Doubleday (London, England), 1999, David Fickling Books (New York, NY) 2004.
Midnight over Sanctaphrax, Doubleday (London, England), 2000, David Fickling Books (New York, NY), 2004.
The Curse of the Gloamglozer, Doubleday (London, England), 2001, David Fickling Books (New York, NY), 2005.
The Last of the Sky Pirates, Doubleday (London, England), 2002, David Fickling Books (New York, NY), 2005.
Vox, Doubleday (London, England), 2003.
The Edge Chronicles Maps, Corgi (London, England), 2004.

Freeglader, Doubleday (London, England), 2004, David Fickling Books (New York, NY), 2006.
Winter Knights, Doubleday (London, England), 2005.

"BLOBHEADS" SERIES; ILLUSTRATOR

Invasion of the Blobs, Macmillan (London, England), 2000.
Talking Toasters, Macmillan (London, England), 2000.
School Stinks, Macmillan (London, England), 2000.
Beware of the Babysitter, Macmillan (London, England), 2000.
Garglejuice, Macmillan (London, England), 2000.
Silly Billy, Macmillan (London, England), 2000.
Naughty Gnomes, Macmillan (London, England), 2000.
Purple Alert!, Macmillan (London, England), 2000.
Blobheads (omnibus), Macmillan (London, England), 2003.
Blobheads Go Boing!, Macmillan (London, England), 2004.

"MUDDLE EARTH" SERIES; WITH PAUL STEWART; AND ILLUSTRATOR

Muddle Earth, Macmillan (London, England), 2003.
Here Be Dragons, Macmillan (London, England), 2004.
Dr. Cuddles of Giggle Glade, Macmillan (London, England), 2004.

"KNIGHT'S STORY" SERIES; WITH PAUL STEWART; AND ILLUSTRATOR

Free Lance and the Lake of Skulls, Hodder (London, England), 2003, published as *Lake of Skulls,* Simon & Schuster (New York, NY), 2004.
Free Lance and the Field of Blood, Hodder (London, England), 2004, published as *Joust of Honor,* Atheneum (New York, NY), 2005.
Free Lance and the Dragon's Hoard, Hodder (London, England), 2005, published as *Dragon's Hoard,* Atheneum (New York, NY), 2005.

ILLUSTRATOR

Sarah Hayes, reteller, *Gruesome Giants,* Derrydale Books (New York, NY), 1985.
Mary Hoffman, *Beware, Princess!,* Heinemann (London, England), 1986.
Ted Hughes, *Fangs the Vampire Bat and the Kiss of Truth,* Faber & Faber (Boston, MA), 1986.
Kate Andrew, *Beyond the Rolling River,* Collins (London, England), 1988.
J.M. Barrie, *Peter Pan,* Magnet, 1988.
Ted Hughes, *Moon-Whales,* revised edition, Faber & Faber (London, England), 1988.
Mary Hoffman, *Dracula's Daughter,* Heinemann (London, England), 1988, Barron's (New York, NY), 1989.
Robert McCrum, *The Dream Boat Brontosaurus,* Methuen (London, England), 1989.

Andrew Gibson, *Ellis and the Hummick,* Faber & Faber (Boston, MA), 1989.

Andrew Gibson, *The Abradizil,* Faber & Faber (Boston, MA), 1990.

Kate Andrew, *The Prism Tree,* Collins (London, England), 1990.

Kathryn Cave, *Henry Hobbs, Alien,* Viking (London, England) 1990.

Kathryn Cave, *Jumble,* Blackie (London, England), 1991.

Helen Cresswell, *Lizzie Dripping and the Witch,* BBC Books (London, England), 1991.

Andrew Gibson, *Jemima, Grandma, and the Great Lost Zone,* Faber & Faber (Boston, MA), 1991.

Kathryn Cave, *Out for the Count: A Counting Adventure,* Barron's (Hauppauge, NY), 1991.

Freida Hughes, *The Thing in the Sink,* Simon & Schuster (New York, NY), 1992.

Catherine Baker, editor, *An Armful of Bears* (poetry), Methuen (London, England), 1993.

Andrew Gibson, *The Amazing Witherspoon's Amazing Circus Crew,* Faber & Faber (London, England), 1993.

Kathryn Cave, *Something Else,* Viking (London, England), 1994, Mondo (Greenvale, NY), 1998.

Freida Hughes, *Rent-a-Friend,* Simon & Schuster (New York, NY), 1994.

Miles Gibson, *Say Hello to the Buffalo,* Heinemann (London, England), 1994.

Andrew Gibson, *Chegwith Skillett Escapes,* Faber & Faber (London, England), 1995.

Ted Hughes, *Collected Animal Poems,* Volume 1: *The Iron Wolf,* Faber & Faber (London, England), 1995.

Louise Howard, *Buddhism for Sheep,* St. Martin's Press (New York, NY), 1996.

Kathryn Cave, *The Emperor's Gruckle Hound,* Hodder & Stoughton (London, England), 1996.

Alan Durant, *Angus Rides the Goods Train,* Viking (London, England), 1996.

Hans Christian Andersen, *The Swan's Stories,* selected and translated by Brian Aldersen, Walker (New York, NY), 1997.

Roger McGough, *Until I Met Dudley: How Everyday Things Really Work,* Walker (New York, NY), 1997.

Philip Ridley, *Kasper in the Glitter,* Dutton (New York, NY), 1997.

Louise Howard, *Feng Shui for Cats,* Ebury Press (London, England), 1997.

Louise Howard, *Feng Shui for Dogs,* Ebury Press (London, England), 1997.

Freida Hughes, *The Tall Story,* Macdonald (London, England), 1997.

Kathryn Cave, *Horatio Happened,* Hodder & Stoughton (London, England), 1998.

Paul Stewart, *A Little Bit of Winter,* HarperCollins (New York, NY), 1998.

Kathryn Cave, *William and the Wolves,* Hodder & Stoughton (London, England), 1999.

Richard Platt, *Castle Diary: The Journal of Tobias Burgess,* Walker (New York, NY), 1999.

Claire Nielson, *Buddhism for Bears,* St. Martin's Press (New York, NY), 1999.

Paul Stewart, *The Birthday Presents,* Andersen Press (London, England), 1999, HarperCollins (New York, NY), 2000.

Paul Stewart, *Rabbit's Wish,* HarperCollins (New York, NY), 2001.

Claire Nielson, *The Tao For Babies,* Seastone (Berkeley, CA), 2001.

Richard Platt, *Pirate Diary: The Journal of Jake Carpenter,* Candlewick Press (Cambridge, MA), 2001.

Paul Stewart, *What Do You Remember?,* Random House (London, England), 2003.

Martin Jenkins, abridger, *Jonathan Swift's Gulliver,* Candlewick Press (Cambridge, MA), 2004.

Sidelights

Chris Riddell is an author and award-winning illustrator whose lively, color-filled books for young readers include *Ben and the Bear, The Wish Factory,* and *The Trouble with Elephants,* while work for older readers includdes coauthoring and illustrating the "Edge Chronicles" fantasy series with Paul Stewart. Known in particular as an illustrator, Riddell is credited with bringing to life texts by authors such as Kathryn Cave, Andrew Gibson, and Jonathan Swift. Of Riddell's work on *The Swan's Stories,* a collection of tales by Hans Christian Andersen, *Horn Book* contributor Ann A. Flowers described the "superb" illustrations as "a cross between [Arthur] Rackham and [E.H.] Shepard with a touch of Carl Larsson" and dubbed it "a beautiful book."

Riddell was born in 1962 in Capetown, South Africa, but moved to London as a child and attended British schools. He graduated from Brighton Polytechnic in 1984 with a honors degree in visual communications. His first published book, *Ben and the Bear,* appeared in 1985, the same year his illustrations began appearing in picture books by other authors.

The humorous *Ben and the Bear* was quickly followed by *Mr. Underbed* and *Bird's New Shoes,* the last in which Riddell pokes fun at the world of high fashion. Bird's latest fashion find, a pair of bright red shoes, causes Rat to covet a pair—or two—of his own. Of course, a new tie would set off the shoes, and when Rat parades around in his dashing new duds, Warthog simply must have not only the same shoes, but an equally snazzy tie as well. And so goes the one-upmanship in a book that a *Publishers Weekly* contributor called "a fun picture book with a simple story line." Particular praise was lavished on Riddell's vibrantly colored illustrations: a *Publishers Weekly* critic dubbed them "bright, busy, and cartoony," while in *School Library Journal* critic Lauralyn Persson added that "the animals are cleverly drawn" and reveal "lots of innate comic personality."

In *The Trouble with Elephants* a young girl's much-loved stuffed elephant causes her to imagine problems that living with real elephants might cause: pink rings in the bathtub, snoring at night, and terribly unfair games of see-saw and hide-and-go-seek. And never mind letting them ride on your bicycle, even once, or they'll squash it flat! Amid this litany of elephantine flaws scampers a herd of happy-go-lucky elephants whose demeanor is "sure to elicit grins," according to *School Library Journal* contributor Lori A. Janick. Phillis Wilson also praised *The Trouble with Elephants* in a review for *Booklist,* commenting that Riddell's "use of exaggeration is a delightful addition to the gently engaging narrative."

The Wish Factory again delves into a child's imagination while focusing on a child's bedtime. Here, young Oliver is taken to a magical place in the clouds called the Wish Factory, where he is given a wish to be used the next time a bad dream threatens to disturb his sleep. Called "a beautifully illustrated . . . picture book in nighttime colors" by *School Librarian* contributor Margaret Banerjee, *The Wish Factory* also received praise from critic Liz Waterland, who noted in her review for *Books for Keeps* that readers "will find [Riddell's] story straightforward and reassuring, especially if they're afraid of the dark."

In *Platypus* readers meet an interesting character who loves to collect special things, including a marble, an acorn, and a sneaker. Platypus feels his accumulation is not complete, however, and when he waddles to the seaside in search of a special something to complete his prized collection, he discovers a beautiful, curly shell. Tired after discovering this prize, he takes a quick nap, only to wake up and discover that the shell is gone! After a second shell disappears in a similar fashion, Platypus realizes a hermit crab had been living in the first shell and has made the second shell his new home. "Riddell conveys his message subtly and with good humor," wrote a *Kirkus Reviews* contributor, who also commented that the author/illustrator's "crisp watercolor illustration, finely accented in black ink, stands out against the stark white page." A *Publishers Weekly* reviewer pointed out that "Riddell's well-paced plotting makes the mystery and resolution equally enticing" for two-to-five-year-olds.

Platypus returns in both *Platypus and the Lucky Day* and *Platypus and the Birthday Party,* the last which finds the engaging hero planning a party for his favorite stuffed animal friend. In *Platypus and the Lucky Day,* Platypus is sure that this particular day will be his lucky day. When he goes outside to fly his kite, however, it gets stuck in a tree. When he tries to paint a picture, the wind blows it away, and then it begins to rain. When other not-so-fun things continue to happen, he decides that back in bed is the safest place to be, and the discovery of a lost toy under the covers inspires Platypus to give the day one more try. Describing Platypus as a "winsome character," a *Kirkus Reviews* contributor noted that Riddell's story is "comical in its own low-key way"; "what succeeds here," the critic added, "is the note of cheery hope."

In 1998 Riddell began a collaboration with neighbor and children's author Paul Stewart that has produced a number of unique books. Meeting as a result of the fact that their children attended the same school, the two also respected each other's work, and eventually became friends. The "Edge Chronicles" came about when Riddell drew a map and gave it to Stewart, who invented a story about the world Riddell had drawn. As reported by a *Bookseller* writer, Stewart explained that "Chris and I live so close that I just go down to his house and we usually work in his studio"—a converted coach house at the bottom of his garden. "We sit in two chairs, sometimes have red wine, and just make each other laugh. Sometimes he'll draw a picture and it'll be fantastic, so I'll have to come up with that character in the book. . . . By the end it's gone through so many conversations, back and forth, that it's often impossible to remember who came up with an idea first."

The creative collaboration between Riddell and Stewart has produced the "Edge Chronicles," a series of middle-grade novels that feature illustrations by Riddell. The first novel in the series, *Beyond the Deepwoods,* introduces Twig, a woodtroll who is shunned because he is taller and lankier than the other short, stout woodtrolls. When Twig's mother decides her son is old enough, she tells him that he is not really a woodtroll, but was found, abandoned, as a small infant. Realizing that he his an outsider in woodtroll society, Twig decides to leaves the beaten path and strike out on his own in the wider world. In search of his past as well as his destiny, he makes several friends, encounters all sorts of creatures, including Banderbears, shrykes, nightwaifs, halitoads, wigwigs, carnivorous Bloodoak trees, trogs, and the horrific, shapeshifting Gloamglozer before ultimately locating his father. In a review of *Beyond the Deepwoods* for *Green Man Review* online, Marian McHugh praised Riddell and Stewart for creating a story that allows readers to "make new friends as well as lose some that have become dear, but overall have a rollicking good time." McHugh also praised Riddell's "wonderful pen drawings" that "fully complement the story" and pointed out that "it is obvious . . . that both author and illustrator have worked closely together to produce this novel." Noting that the illustrations "create a strong sense of the believable, well-imagined" fantasy world, *Booklist* reviewer Carolyn Phelan called *Beyond the Deepwoods* "an inventive, promising start" to the series.

Other novels in the "Edge Chronicles" series include *Stormchaser, Midnight over Sanctaphrax, The Curse of the Gloamglozer,* and *The Last of the Sky Pirates.* In the flat Edge world creatures of all sorts live in floating cities and skyships. The first three novels follow Twig as he becomes a sky-pirate under the tutelage of his sky-pilot father and ultimately helps to save his world from the threat posed by the Guardians of the Night. *Midnight over Sanctaphrax,* in which Twig saves a floating city that is chained to the Edge and peopled by a group of highly competitive alchemists, apprentices, and scholars was described by *School Library Journal* critic

Lisa Prolman as "a good adventures story with a very Hobbit-like feel" in which the coauthors also address "issues of slavery and class structure."

In *The Curse of the Gloamglozer* Stewart and Riddell backtrack to the time before Twig's birth, and relate the adventures of the young sky-captain's father, Quint. Apprenticed to Sanctaphrax scholar Linius Pallitax, Quint studies by day and is sent on strange missions at night by his master. Eventually, with the help of Pallitax's daughter Maris (who becomes Twig's mother), Quint learns that the scholar is up to no good and sets about rescuing the floating city.

The Last of the Sky Pirates, Vox, and *Freeglader* take place fifty years in the future, as the Edge has become an even darker place. Apprentice scholar/knight Rook Barkwater is making a dangerous journey into the Deep-woods in a quest for knowledge when he comes upon Twig and joins the forces mounting against the Guardians of the Night. His master scholar, Vox Verlix, is up to no good, and Rook must thwart the evil academe's quest for power, a quest that threatens the entire Edge world. Noting that the series is best known for its "imaginative settings" and its wealth of imaginative— and sometimes ruthless—creatures, *School Library Journal* reviewer Jenna Miller noted that readers new to the "Edge Chronicles" will find *The Curse of the Gloamglozer* "complete and satisfying on its own." Citing the "icky monsters, profoundly rotten villains, and shiny striving heroes" in the series, Walter Minkel wrote in a *School Library Journal* review of *The Last of the Sky Pirates* that Riddell's "antique-style illustrations add to the fun."

Riddell and Stewart have also joined forces in several other heavily illustrated novel series, including "Knight's Story" and "Blobheads," both of which hold particular appeal among middle-grade boys due to their wacky humor and Riddell's illustrations. They have also produced several books for younger readers, featuring Stewart's text and Riddell's illustrations. Two of their most popular characters, Rabbit and Hedgehog, appeared in *A Little Bit of Winter, The Birthday Presents,* and *Rabbit's Wish.* In a review of *Rabbit's Wish* for *Booklist,* Helen Rosenberg wrote that Riddell's "soft, expressive watercolor illustrations are a good match for this story about friendship," a stor,y Rosenberg pointed out, that shares similarities with the popular "Frog and Toad" books by children's author Arnold Lobel. In *School Library Journal,* Ann Cook also praised Riddell's artistry, commenting that his "gentle" illustrations "underscore the joy these creatures share and the anxiety they feel when each thinks the other is in danger."

In addition to his work with Stewart, Riddell continues to illustrate books for other authors. His work for Richard Platt's *Pirate Diary: The Journal of Jake Carpenter,* about a nine-year-old boy who endures a brutal sea voyage on the ship of wicked Captain Nick, only to end up in the hands of much more easy-to-get-along-with

pirates, was praised by *Booklist* contributor Shelle Rosenfeld as "colorful" and "dynamic." Anne Chapman Callaghan, who reviewed *Pirate Diary* for *School Library Journal,* wrote that the "myriad ink-and-watercolor illustrations help illuminate the dramatic events" of the story. A *Publishers Weekly* contributor commented on the variety of drawings Riddell scatters throughout the text, including "spot illustrations, dramatic full-page and full-spread scenes, and a detailed cutaway of the ship." The reviewer concluded that "with verve and puckish humor, they easily transport readers to high times on the high seas."

Biographical and Critical Sources

PERIODICALS

Booklist, October 15, 1988, Phillis Wilson, review of *The Trouble with Elephants,* p. 413; October 15, 2001, Helen Rosenberg, review of *Rabbit's Wish,* p. 402; December 15, 2001, Shelle Rosenfeld, review of *Pirate Diary: The Journal of Jake Carpenter,* p. 732; July, 2004, Carolyn Phelan, review of *Beyond the Deepwoods,* p. 1844; November 1, 2005, Brian Wilson, review of *Beyond the Deepwoods* (audiobook), p. 68.

Books, autumn, 2001, review of *Platypus,* p. 18.

Bookseller, January 24, 2003, review of *Muddle Earth,* p. 29; July 18, 2003, "Briggs' Blooming Books," pp. 22-23.

Books for Keeps, March, 1988, Jill Bennett, review of *Mr. Underbed,* p. 17; November, 1992, Liz Waterland, review of *The Wish Factory,* p. 16.

Horn Book, November-December, 1997, Ann A. Flowers, review of *The Swan's Stories,* p. 689.

Kirkus Reviews, April 15, 2002, review of *Platypus,* p. 577; July 1, 2002, review of *Platypus and the Lucky Day,* p. 962; July 1, 2004, review of *Beyond the Deepwoods,* p. 637.

Observer (London, England), October 28, 2001, review of *Platypus,* p. 16.

Publishers Weekly, February 27, 1987, review of *Bird's New Shoes,* p. 164; June 4, 2001, review of *Rabbit's Wish,* p. 82; October 22, 2001, review of *Pirate Diary,* p. 77; April 15, 2002, review of *Platypus,* p. 62; July 8, 2002, review of *Platypus and the Lucky Day,* p. 51; June 16, 2003, review of *What Do You Remember?,* p. 73; August 25, 2003, review of *Castle Diary: The Journal of Tobias Burgess,* p. 67.

School Librarian, February, 1991, Margaret Banerjee, review of *The Wish Factory,* p. 20; winter, 2004, Irene Babsky, review of *Fergus Crane,* p. 204; spring, 2005, Robin Barlow, review of *Jonathan Swift's Gulliver,* p. 35; autumn, 2005, review of *Corby Flood,* p. 147.

School Library Journal, September, 1987, Lauralyn Persson, review of *Bird's New Shoes,* p. 169; March, 1989, Lori A. Janick, review of *The Trouble with Elephants,* pp. 168-69; July, 2001, Ann Cook, review of *Rabbit's Wish,* p. 89; December, 2001, Anne Chapman Callaghan, review of *Pirate Diary,* p. 142; June, 2002, Lisa Dennis, review of *Platypus,* p. 109; November, 2002, Bina Williams, review of *Platypus and the Lucky Day,* p. 134; December, 2003, Andrea Tarr, review of *Platypus and the Birthday Party,* p. 124; September, 2004, Erin Gray, review of *Lake of Skulls,* p. 218; October, 2004, Lisa Prolman, review of *Midnight over Sanctaphrax,* p. 178; February, 2005, Jenna Miller, review of *The Curse of the Gloamglozer,* p. 140; June, 2005, Walter Minkel, review of *The Last of the Sky Pirates,* p. 170; August, 2005, Walter Minkel, review of *Joust of Honor,* p. 136.

ONLINE

Edge Chronicles Web site, http://www.randomhouse.com/ kids/edgechronicles/ (December 24, 2005).

Green Man Review Online, http://www.greenmanreview. com/ (April 27, 2004), Marian McHugh, review of *Beyond the Deepwoods.**

*   *   *

RIDDELL, Christopher Barry
See RIDDELL, Chris

*   *   *

ROBINS, Deri 1958-

Personal

Born June 16, 1958, in Cardiff, Wales; daughter of Roy and Jean (a teacher; maiden name, Rhydderch) Cumberlidge; married James Robins (an illustrator), 1987; children: Ben, Tom, Nell. *Education:* University of London, B.A. (with honors), 1979; attended London College of Printing, 1985. *Politics:* "Leftish."

Addresses

Home—Bath, England. *Agent*—Clare Pearson, 22 Upper Grosvenor St., London W1Y 9PB, England.

Career

Charles Letts & Co., Sunderland, England, began as proofreader, became editor, 1980-82; Grisewood & Dempsey, London, England, began as assistant editor, 1983, became senior editor of children's nonfiction, 1985-88; freelance writer and editor, 1989—.

Writings

An A-Z Activity Book of Animal Fun, illustrated by Charlotte Stowell, Kingfisher (New York, NY), 1989.
(With Meg Sanders) *An A-Z Activity Book of Outdoor Fun,* illustrated by Charlotte Stowell, Kingfisher (New York, NY), 1989.

(Editor) *The Spies and Detectives Cut and Colour Book,* Kingfisher (New York, NY), 1989.
(Editor) *Flags and Uniforms,* Kingfisher (New York, NY), 1991.
(With Meg Sanders) *By Myself Book,* illustrated by Charlotte Stowell, Kingfisher (New York, NY), 1991.
Holiday Book, illustrated by Charlotte Stowell, Kingfisher (New York, NY), 1991.
Gardening Book, illustrated by Charlotte Stowell, Kingfisher (New York, NY), 1992.
(With Meg Sanders and Kate Crocker) *The Kids Can Do It Book,* illustrated by Charlotte Stowell, Kingfisher (New York, NY), 1993.
Making Prints, illustrated by husband, Jim Robins, Kingfisher (New York, NY), 1993.
Papier Mâché, illustrated by Jim Robins, Kingfisher (New York, NY), 1993.
Santa's Sackful of Best Christmas Ideas, illustrated by George Buchanan, Kingfisher (New York, NY), 1993.
The Kids' around the World Cookbook, illustrated by Charlotte Stowell, Kingfisher (New York, NY), 1994.
In Roman Times, illustrated by David Salariya and others, Kingfisher (New York, NY), 1994.
The Great Pirate Activity Book, illustrated by George Buchanan, Kingfisher (New York, NY), 1994.
Making Books, illustrated by Charlotte Stowell, Kingfisher (New York, NY), 1994.
Christmas Fun, illustrated by Maggie Downer, Kingfisher (New York, NY), 1995.
Easter Fun, illustrated by Maggie Downer, Kingfisher (New York, NY), 1996.
Birthday Fun, illustrated by Annabel Spenceley, Kingfisher (New York, NY), 1996.
Top Tips for Girls, Hippo (London, England), 1997.
Mystery of the Monster Party, illustrated by Anni Axworthy, Candlewick Press (Cambridge, MA), 1998.
The Stone in the Sword: The Quest for a Stolen Emerald, illustrated by Jim Robins, Candlewick Press (Cambridge, MA), 1998.
Spooky Time!, illustrated by Martin Chatterton, Scholastic (London, England), 1998.
Dinosaurs, Aladdin Books (London, England), 2000.
Smart Art, illustrations by David Mostyn, Robinson Children's Books (London, England), 2000.
Farm Animals, Aladdin Books (London, England), 2000.
Let's Start! Fabric Art, Design Eye Holdings, 2000.
(With Lianne South) *Creative Bracelets,* Tangerine Press (Lake Mary, FL), 2000.
A Smart Girl's Guide to Boys, illustrated by Kat, Red Fox (London, England), 2002.
Cartooning, QED (London, England), 2004.
Special Effects, QED (North Mankato, MN), 2004.
Painting, QED (North Mankato, MN), 2004.
Stencils and Prints, QED (North Mankato, MN), 2004.
Drawing and Sketching, QED (North Mankato, MN), 2004.
Cartooning, QED (North Mankato, MN), 2004.

Other books include *Brat Packs: Making Jewelry* and *Secret File for Girls,* Scholastic; *The Ultimate Activity Book, My Secret Personality Profile,* and *My Secret Astrology Profile,* all Robinson; *Learning with Ozmo,* ac-

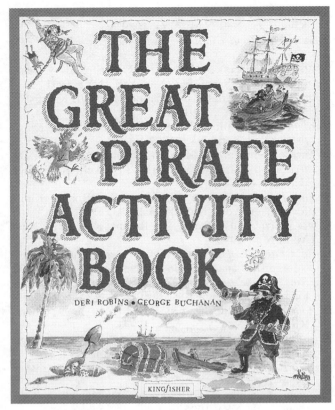

Fulfilling the fantasy of young swashbucklers everywhere, Robins's 1994 book serves up a wealth of adventure in the form of facts, games, crafts, and other activities. (Cover illustration by George Buchanan.)

tivity books for BBC Publications; *Action Packs: Friendship Bracelets,* Hat Trick; *Arts and Crafts for all Seasons,* Two-Can; and *Animals All Around: Farm Animals,* Reader's Digest. Contributor to *The Millennium Encyclopedia.* Contributor to magazines, including *Art Magic* and *Smart.*

Work in Progress

Research on young people in history, especially in medieval times, with publications expected to result.

Sidelights

Welsh author and editor Deri Robins has worked in the publishing world for much of her adult career. While she has produced several children's story books, such as *The Sword in the Sword: The Quest for a Stolen Emerald,* and *Mystery of the Monster Party,* most of Robins's books have been in the area of nonfiction. In addition to activity books such as *Easter Fun, The Spies and Detective Cut and Color Book,* and *Creative Bracelets,* Robins has also presented more focused books that discuss art techniques from painting to cartooning and textile design, and has also served up advice to young readers in *A Smart Girl's Guide to Boys.*

Robins once told *SATA:* "I became an author because, after fifteen years of editing other people's work, I decided I preferred the idea and writing side of publishing

to the job of dotting all the "i's' and crossing all the 't's.' (I was also very bad at administration and at chasing tardy authors and illustrators.) I still drift in and out of editorial work to pay the mortgage . . . , but I live by writing as and when I can. More by luck than design, I think I've become pigeonholed as a writer of craft, puzzle, and story books—this is something I never intended!"

Biographical and Critical Sources

PERIODICALS

Booklist, April, 1998, Carolyn Phelan, review of *The Stone in the Sword: The Quest for a Stolen Emerald,* p. 1322; November 1, 2004, Stephanie Zvirin, review of *Special Effects,* p. 497.
Reading Teacher, October, 1999, review of *The Stone in the Sword,* p. 180.
School Library Journal, July, 1998, p. 81; April, 2005, review of *Painting,* p. 126.

ONLINE

ChildrensLit.com, http://www.childrenslit.com/ (November 6, 2005), Barbara Youngblood, review of *Fabric Art.**

*   *   *

RYAN, Margaret 1950-

Personal

Born June 23, 1950, in Trenton, NJ; daughter of Thomas Michael (an accountant) and Anne (a secretary; maiden name, Jansen) Ryan; married Steven Lerner (a computer salesman), August 29, 1974; children: Emily Ryan. *Education:* University of Pennsylvania, B.A., 1972; Syracuse University, M.A., 1974; attended Columbia University, 1976.

Addresses

Home—250 W. 104th St., No. 63, New York, NY 10025. *Agent*—c/o Author Mail, Franklin Watts/Scholastic Library Publishing, P.O. Box 1795, 90 Sherman Tpke., Danbury, CT 06816.

Career

Ryan Business Writing, speechwriter and owner, 1976—. New York State Poets in Public Service, teacher, 1987-91. 92nd St. Y, New York, NY, poetry instructor.

Awards, Honors

College poetry prize, *Mademoiselle* magazine, 1972; Davidson Prize for Sonnets, Poetry Society of America, 1986; New York Foundation for the Arts fellowship, 1987, 1995.

Writings

NONFICTION; FOR CHILDREN

So, You Have to Give a Speech!, Franklin Watts (New York, NY), 1987, revised as *How to Give a Speech,* 1994.

Figure Skating, Franklin Watts (New York, NY), 1987.

How to Read and Write Poems, Franklin Watts (New York, NY), 1991.

How to Write a Poem, Franklin Watts (New York, NY), 1996.

Extraordinary Oral Presentations, Franklin Watts (New York, NY), 2005.

Extraordinary Poetry Writing, Franklin Watts (New York, NY), 2006.

POETRY; FOR ADULTS

Filling out a Life, Front Street Press (New York, NY), 1982.

Black Raspberries, Parsonage Press, 1988.

Sidelights

Poet and author Margaret Ryan has parlayed her experience teaching public speaking and creative writing in several books. *How to Write a Poem,* the second of three volumes she has authored on the art of versification, focuses on not only inspiration but also on form, meter, rhythm, and other literary devices used in writing verse. In her book's concluding chapters, Ryan also provides ideas for sharing one's poetry, from public readings to submitting works to contests and periodicals. Noting that Ryan's "breezy" text is "engaging, personal, and motivating," *Booklist* reviewer Anne O'Malley predicted that both poetry readers and beginning writers will "appreciate the advice." *How to Give a Speech,* a revision of an earlier work, discusses how to gather, organize, and share information in spoken form and features what *Booklist* reviewer Chris Sherman described as a "well written, clearly organized" text.

Ryan once told *SATA:* "I knew I wanted to be a writer from the time I was seven years old. We were asked to write a composition about spring during class; it was second grade. All my classmates struggled and chewed their pencils and thought and wrote and scratched out. I closed my eyes, and could see spring: a deep green lawn dotted with dandelions; lilacs in bloom at the edge of the lawn; a robin foraging for worms. I wrote down what I saw. My teacher read it out loud to the class . . . I liked the recognition of my talent; I was a shy child who rarely spoke in class, so it was nice to have a voice, finally, even if it was the teacher's voice reading my words. I knew then that I would be a writer.

"I began to write poems when I was in high school. I liked reading poems: Shakespeare's sonnets, e.e. cummings, Edna St. Vincent Millay, Ernest Downson, Edgar Allan Poe. So I began trying to write poems of my own when I was about fifteen. At that time, folk music was very popular, and there was an emphasis on the lyrics of popular songs, so writing poems seemed like a very natural thing to do. Again, I learned that I was good at it: I submitted works to my high school literary magazine, and they were published. It was a great pleasure to see my poems in print.

"In college, I was lucky to have a wonderful Latin teacher who taught Catullus and Ovid and Horace as poems, real living poems, not as artifacts of a dead language. Through him I learned much about the form of poetry, its structure and subtlety. For a time I thought I, too, would like to be a Latin teacher. But then when I was a senior in college, I won the *Mademoiselle* magazine poetry contest and I knew I only wanted to be a poet. So I went to graduate school in creative writing, in Syracuse.

"I met my husband there. We were married in 1974 and moved to New York City. Guess what? There were no jobs for poets! In fact, it was the middle of a recession, and there were very few jobs at all. I got work in an advertising agency that did ads and catalogs for art galleries in New York. I was chosen because I knew how to spell the word 'Renaissance,' and no one else applying for the job could spell it!

"Eventually, I found work as a speechwriter. It is in many ways like writing poetry: you are writing for the voice; it must be rhythmical and interesting to the ear; it has to tell a story and be convincing. You also have to learn a lot of interesting facts, which can then be used in poems.

"Here's how I came to write a book about writing poetry: from a poetry workshop I was in, I knew an editor at Franklin Watts. He knew I was also a speechwriter, and asked me to do a book about it for high school students. So I wrote *So, You Have to Give a Speech!*

"Later, they asked me if I would like to write a book about something else, and I suggested figure skating. I have loved skating since I was a child, and it's always nice to write about something you love. Then a new editor came to Franklin Watts, and wanted to do a book about poetry. He called me because on the jacket of the speech book it said I was also a poet.

"I had then been teaching children how to read and write poems for several years, through a program called Poets in Public Service. I taught in schools all around New York City: kindergartens and high schools, middle schools and grade schools, in the city and in the suburbs, and everywhere I saw how much children liked poetry if they could just read it without too much emphasis on 'what it meant.' I had my own daughter by then, too, and I knew that making things—poems, pictures, puppets, cookies, anything creative—made kids feel better about themselves. So I agreed to write the book.

"It was hard to do, because I love poetry so much and know so much about it. I had trouble deciding what was most important to say in five thousand words—which is hardly anything. I wanted to make sure I communicated some of the conventions of poetry, and the excitement of poetry, and answered the kinds of questions I had about poems when I was a child. Finding the pictures was fun. It was great to think up visual ways of representing ideas like repetition or metaphor.

"I still write poems and meet with a group of poets once a month or so to discuss what we've written. And I still write speeches for business executives. And I'm working on revising the first book I did for Franklin Watts, on giving speeches, to include some information on recent speeches, such as those given by Bill Clinton and George Bush during the [1992 presidential campaign].

"But poetry is my first love."

Biographical and Critical Sources

PERIODICALS

Booklist, April 15, 1987, p. 1270; February 1, 1988, p. 936; January 1, 1992, Hazel Rochman, review of *How to Read and Write Poems,* p. 828; June 1, 1995, Chris Sherman, review of *How to Give a Speech,* p 1743; February 1, 1997, Anne O'Malley, review of *How to Write a Poem,* p. 934.

Book Report, May, 1987, p. 56; March, 1988, p. 49.

Library Talk, May, 1993, p. 11.

School Library Journal, August, 1987, review of *So You Have to Give a Speech!,* p. 98; March, 1988, p. 209; January, 1992, Anette Curtis Klause, review of *How to Read and Write Poems,* p. 132; June, 1995, Kate Hegarty Bowman, review of *How to Give a Speech,* p. 140; January, 1997, Barbara Chatton, review of *How to Write a Poem,* p. 134.

Voice of Youth Advocates, August, 1987, review of *So You Have to Give a Speech!,* p. 139; August, 1995, review of *How to Give a Speech,* p. 186.

Wilson Library Journal, June, 1987, p. 65.

S-T

SALLEY, Coleen

Personal

Born in Baton Rouge, LA. *Education:* Attended Louisiana State University.

Addresses

Home—New Orleans, LA. *Agent*—c/o Author Mail, Harcourt Children's Books, 15 E. 26th St., New York, NY 10011.

Career

Writer, educator, and professional storyteller. Winthrop College for Women (now Winthrop University), librarian in laboratory school; University of New Orleans, New Orleans, LA, distinguished professor of children's literature for thirty years, became professor emerita. Visiting professor at Simmons College, University of Southern California, Los Angeles, University of Denver, George Peabody College, and Louisiana State University. Founder, Coleen Salley/Bill Morris Literacy Foundation, 2004. Storyteller on audio and video recordings, including *Louisiana Folk Tales, Texas Folk Tales,* and *Georgia Folk Tales,* all Gateway Productions; *Cajun Night before Christmas/Gaston the Green Nose Alligator* and *Cajun Night before Christmas/Cajun Night after Christmas,* both Pelican Publishing Company; *Tub People,* HarperCollins; *Read-aloud Riches, Eight Favorites,* and *Big Mama Makes the World,* all Candlewick; *Cocodrie Cajun Classics,* More than a Card Press; and *Three Classy Storytellers Read Three Classy Tales,* SeaStar.

Awards, Honors

Outstanding undergraduate teacher of the year award, University of New Orleans, 1972; distinguished faculty award, Louisiana State University Alumni Association, 1983; Essae M. Culver Service Award, Louisiana Library Association, 1989; Flicker Tale Children's Book Award (North Dakota), and children's book award,

Florida Reading Association, both 2004, Virginia Young Readers Award, 2005, and Book Sense 76 citation, Children's Choice Award, International Reading Association/Children's Book Council, Gold Award, Oppenheimer Toy Portfolio, Volunteer State Book Award (Tennessee), and Show Me Readers Award (Missouri), all for *Epossumondas.*

Writings

PICTURE BOOKS

Who's That Tripping over My Bridge?, illustrated by Amy Jackson Dixon, Pelican (Gretna, LA), 2002.
Epossumondas, illustrated by Janet Stevens, Harcourt (San Diego, CA), 2002.
Why Epossumondas Has No Hair on His Tail, illustrated by Janet Stevens, Harcourt (San Diego, CA), 2004.
Epossumondas Saves the Day, illustrated by Janet Stevens, Harcourt (San Diego, CA), 2006.

Sidelights

Coleen Salley was a storyteller for many years before she began turning her favorite stories into books. Her first picture book, *Who's That Tripping over My Bridge?,* takes the classic Norwegian fairy tale of the three billy goats Gruff and transplants it to her native Louisiana. "Salley spices up her retelling, giving it a dramatic sense of place and Louisiana flare," Shauna Yusko commented in *School Library Journal.* Plus, anyone who has ever heard the author tell the story live "will hear echoes of Salley's distinctive voice and delivery" in the text, commented a *Kirkus Reviews* critic. The story is set just north of Baton Rouge, Louisiana, in East Feliciana Parish. The three goats want to cross from that parish over Thompson Creek into West Feliciana Parish, where there are many nice hills full of green grass to eat, but a mean troll under the bridge threatens to eat anyone who tries to travel across the creek. The goats, however, are stubborn and smart, and they even-

Salley, a talented storyteller, relates an endearing tale about a young Southern-born possum who takes everything literally in **Epossumondas**. *(Illustration by Janet Stevens.)*

tually succeed in getting across, arriving in St. Francisville. As Salley explained to a *Publishers Weekly* interviewer, she began telling this story to school groups because "when I go to the west bank of New Orleans, those kids have never been across the river. They won't ever get to Norway, but they might get to St. Francisville. . . . Maybe one day, a kid will be sitting in the back of the car, and he'll see a sign that says 'Thompson Creek,' and he'll gasp and say, 'I know who lives under that bridge.'"

Epossumondas, Why Epossumondas Has No Hair on His Tail, Epossumondas Saves the Day all feature a diaper-wearing, none-too-bright baby possum. In his first picture-book outing, Epossumondas travels back and forth from his auntie's home to his mama's house with a series of gifts, but he manages to ruin each gift along the way. When his auntie gives him cake to carry home he smashes it, prompting his mama to tell him that cake should be carried under one's hat. Thus, next time, when he is carrying butter, he puts it under his hat—where it promptly melts and runs down his face. After each such mishap, Epossumondas's mama greets her son with the same refrain: "Epossumondas, you don't have the sense you were born with." Once again, Salley emphasizes her Louisiana setting, with alligators, nutrias, and armadillos featuring in the tale. Her "text rolls off the page (and off the tongue) easily," Jane

Marino commented in *School Library Journal,* and *Horn Book* reviewer Joanna Rudge Long also found the "well-honed text . . . just right for group sharing."

In *Why Epossumondas Has No Hair on His Tail* the possum's mama tells him a just-so story explaining why possums have hairless tails. Long ago, she explains, the ancestral Papapossum had a long, fluffy tail, just like the other animals. Then Papapossum and Hare team up to try to steal some persimmons from Bear, but everything does not go as planned. Papapossum finds himself grabbed by the tail by Bear, and in the ensuing tug-of-war all of the tail's hair is lost, never to return. Like *Epossumondas, Why Epossumondas Has No Hair on His Tail* was praised for its humor and read-aloud appeal. "Salley's a grand storyteller who makes the most of the twists and turns," Joanna Rudge Long wrote in *Horn Book,* while *School Library Journal* contributor Grace Oliff commented upon Salley's "colorful descriptions and amusing expressions."

Biographical and Critical Sources

BOOKS

Salley, Coleen, *Epossumondas,* illustrated by Janet Stevens, Harcourt (San Diego, CA), 2002.

PERIODICALS

Book, March-April, 2003, Kathleen Odean, review of *Epossumondas,* p. 36.

Booklist, August, 2002, GraceAnne A. DeCandido, review of *Epossumondas,* p. 1976; September 1, 2004, Julie Cummins, review of *Why Epossumondas Has No Hair on His Tail,* p. 135.

Bulletin of the Center for Children's Books, October, 2004, Timnah Card, review of *Why Epossumondas Has No Hair on His Tail,* p. 98.

Horn Book, November-December, 2002, Joanna Rudge Long, review of *Epossumondas,* p. 767; January-February, 2005, Joanna Ridge Long, review of *Why Epossumondas Has No Hair on His Tail,* p. 85.

Instructor, April, 2003, Judy Freeman, review of *Epossumondas,* p. 54.

Kirkus Reviews, April 15, 2002, review of *Who's That Tripping over My Bridge?,* p. 578; August 1, 2002, review of *Epossumondas,* p. 1142; August 1, 2004, review of *Why Epossumondas Has No Hair on His Tail,* p. 748.

Library Media Connection, April-May, 2005, Anne Hanson, review of *Why Epossumondas Has No Hair on His Tail,* p. 87.

Publishers Weekly, February 3, 1997, review of *The Tub People,* p. 46; March 18, 2002, review of *Who's That Tripping over My Bridge?,* p. 103, Jennifer M. Brown, "*PW* Talks with Coleen Salley," p. 103; June 17, 2002, review of *Epossumondas,* p. 63.

School Library Journal, May, 2002, Shauna Yusko, review of *Who's That Tripping over My Bridge?,* p. 144; September, 2002, Jane Marino, review of *Epossumondas,* p. 217; September, 2004, Grace Oliff, review of *Why Epossumondas Has No Hair on His Tail,* p. 179.

Tribune Books (Chicago, IL), December 1, 2002, review of *Epossumondas,* p. 5.

ONLINE

Balkin Buddies Web site, http://www.balkinbuddies.com/ (November 6, 2005), "The Coleen Salley/Bill Morris Literacy Foundation."

Coleen Salley Web site, http://www.coleensalley.com (November 6, 2005).

Woman's Day Online, http://www.womansday.com/ (November 6, 2005), review of *Epossumondas.*

* * *

SHRODE, Mary
See HOLLINGSWORTH, Mary

* * *

SINGLETON, Linda Joy 1957-
(L.J. Singleton, Jamie Suzanne, a house pseudonym)

Personal

Born October 29, 1957; daughter of Edwin D. (a computer technician) and Nina Jean (a square-dance caller;

Linda Joy Singleton

maiden name, Lowes) Emburg; married Corey L. Swaine, 1975 (divorced, 1980); married David G. Singleton (a crane operator), January 2, 1982; children: (second marriage) Melissa, Andrew. *Education:* Telephone Company, Sacramento, CA, operator, 1975, word processor, 1975-82, staff clerk, 1982. *Politics:* Democrat. *Hobbies and other interests:* Square dancing, boating, swimming, walking, reading, collecting series books, cats.

Addresses

Home—P.O. Box 155, Burson, CA 95225. *Agent*—Pesha Rubinstein, 1392 Rugby Rd., Teaneck, NJ 07666. *E-mail*—ljscheer@inreach.com.

Member

Romance Writers of America, Society of Children's Book Writers and Illustrators, Young Adult Writers Network, Sisters in Crime.

Awards, Honors

Romance Writers of America's Silver Diary Award; HOLT Contest finalist; first-place winner, MARA Contest; Young Adult Library Association Quick-Pick Choice, 2001, for "Regeneration" series; Eppie Award for best children book, 2003, for *Twin Again.*

Writings

Almost Twins, Willowisp Press, 1991.
Opposites Attract ("Sweet Dreams" series), Bantam (New York, NY), 1991.
(As Jamie Suzanne) *Barnyard Battle* ("Sweet Valley Twins" series), Bantam (New York, NY), 1992.
Almost Perfect ("Sweet Dreams" series), Bantam (New York, NY), 1992.
Love to Spare ("Sweet Dreams" series), Bantam (New York, NY), 1993.
Deep in My Heart ("Sweet Dreams" series), Bantam (New York, NY), 1994.
The Saturday Night Bash ("Pick Your Own Dream Date" series), Lowell House, 1994.
Spring Break! ("Pick Your Own Dream Date" series), Lowell House, 1994.
Dreamboat ("Sweet Dreams" series), Bantam (New York, NY), 1995.
Double Vision, Amber Quill Press, 2003.

Author of e-books, including *Mail-Order Monster* and *Melissa's Mission Impossible.* Contributor to *The Whispered Watchword.*

"MY SISTER THE GHOST" SERIES

Twin Again, Avon (New York, NY), 1995.
Escape from Ghostland, Avon (New York, NY), 1995.
Teacher Trouble, Avon (New York, NY), 1996.
Babysitter Beware, Avon (New York, NY), 1996.

"CHEER SQUAD" SERIES

Crazy for Cartwheels, Avon (New York, NY), 1996.
Spirit Song, Avon (New York, NY), 1996.
Stand up and Cheer, Avon (New York, NY), 1996.
Boys Are Bad News, Avon (New York, NY), 1997.
Spring to Stardom, Avon (New York, NY), 1997.
Gimme a C-A-M-P!, Avon (New York, NY), 1997.

"REGENERATION" SERIES; UNDER NAME L.J. SINGLETON

Regeneration, Berkley Jam (New York, NY), 2000.
The Search, Berkley Jam (New York, NY), 2000.
The Truth, Berkley Jam (New York, NY), 2000.
The Impostor, Berkley Jam (New York, NY), 2000.
The Killer, Berkley Jam (New York, NY), 2001.

Also author of *Cloned and Dangerous,* posted on *LJSingleton.com.*

"STRANGE ENCOUNTERS" SERIES

Oh, No! UFO!, Llewellyn (St. Paul, MN), 2004.
Shamrocked!, Llewellyn (St. Paul, MN), 2005.
Sea Switch, Llewellyn (St. Paul, MN), 2005.

"SEER" SERIES

Don't Die Dragonfly, Llewellyn (St. Paul, MN), 2004.
Last Dance, Llewellyn (St. Paul, MN), 2005.
Witch's Ball, Llewellyn (St. Paul, MN), 2006.
Sword Play, Llewellyn (St. Paul, MN), 2006.

Sidelights

A longtime collector of vintage juvenile novels in the "Nancy Drew," "Trixie Belden," "Judy Bolton," and other series, Linda Joy Singleton eventually translated all that reading into writing. Beginning her writing career penning middle-grade fiction, Singleton has contributed titles to the ongoing "Sweet Valley Twins," "Sweet Dreams," and "Pick Yourself a Dream Date" series. In 1994 her own series, the "My Sister the Ghost" books—which Singleton described on her home page as "a spooky series about twins"—was released and was followed by her "Cheer Squad" series. In 2000 Singleton shifted genres, moving to science fiction with her popular "Regeneration" books, and she has gone on to produce several other series as well as stand-alone books published both in print and e-book format. Discussing her preference for series novels with Patricia M. Newman in *California Kids!,* Singleton noted: "When you read a series, the characters become your friends. . . . It's nice when a book doesn't stop at the end."

In the "Regeneration" series, Singleton focuses on five children—Varina, Chase, Eric, Allison, and Sandee—who suddenly learn that each of them have been cloned from other individuals, strangers. Realizing that the scientist who created them wishes their destruction, the children team together, and soon they learn that each of them has been given a special power. Each of the "Regeneration" novels, which include *Regeneration, The Search,* and *The Killer,* follows one of the children as they grapple with their power and find adventure. Her "Seer" novels, which include *Don't Die Dragonfly* and *Last Dance,* move into the supernatural as they focus on sixteen-year-old psychic Sabine Rose, who tries to hide her ability to solve crimes but continues to become drawn into mystery.

In *Don't Die Dragonfly* Sabine is haunted by a vision about a girl with a dragonfly tattoo and becomes determined to find and warn her, while *Last Dance* finds her road trip with goth friend Opal veering off course when a restless ghost named Chloe begins to haunt her. Enthusiastic about Singleton's series, *Reviewer's Bookwatch* contributor Charisse Floyd wrote of *Don't Die Dragonfly* that "the surprising twists and page-turning cliffhangers literally pulsate with dramatic tension, and the novel's pace . . . runs full-throttle." While noting that the prose in *Last Dance* is standard genre fare, *School Library Journal* contributor Jessie Platt added that several "sections are quite poetic and help reinforce the eerie mood."

A psychic teen trying to help her ailing grandmother travels to California hoping to locate a book of family remedies and winds up in the middle of a generations-old mystery. (Cover illustration by Linda Novak.)

Singleton once told *SATA:* "I wrote my first two-hundred-page novel on blue-lined note paper when I was eleven years old. It was a romantic suspense called 'Holiday Terror,' and I was especially proud of the gruesome scene where a body is discovered. I was always reading and writing as a kid. Mostly, I would start a story, write several chapters, get bored with it, and begin a new story. I enjoyed reading my stories aloud to my mother—and I still do. When I was fourteen, I was too young to take a writing course at a college, so my father took it instead. He helped me submit some stories to *American Girl* magazine, which gave me my first rejection experiences. I've learned not to get too upset over rejections; instead I consider each one a step closer to my goal.

"A job, marriages, and two children filled my life until I was twenty-seven—that's when I renewed my childhood dream of writing. I joined Romance Writers of America, attended a weekly critique group, read avidly, and learned as much as I could from writing workshops. Then in 1988, my dream came true—I sold my first book to Willowisp Press! *Almost Twins* is a juvenile story about girls who pretend to be twins. I continued to sell books after that, mostly teen romances for Bantam's "Sweet Dreams" line. But it wasn't until 1994 that my BIGGEST dream came true.

"As a kid, I loved Nancy Drew, Judy Bolton, Penny Parker, and other girl series books. I even corresponded with Judy Bolton's author, Margaret Sutton. More than anything, I wanted a series of my own. And that happened in 1994 when my agent sold 'My Sister, the Ghost' to Avon books for publication in 1995, letting me add my own series books to the thousands of others in my collection." By 2005, according to Newman, Singleton had amassed over four thousand series books, several from the classic girls' series of the 1920s and 1930s.

"Wonderful things can happen if you work hard and hold onto your dreams," Singleton maintains, and she shares this optimistic attitude with others. "I love seeing the world through the heart of a child," she noted on her home page, "where magic is real and every day begins a new adventure. I hope to inspire [readers] . . . to reach for their dreams. Writing for kids is a gift, a responsibility, and an honor."

Biographical and Critical Sources

PERIODICALS

California Kids!, January, 2005, Patricia M. Newman, "Who Wrote That? Featuring Linda Joy Singleton."
Daily Times (Ottawa, IL), June 20, 2000, Julia Durango, interview with Singleton.
Kliatt, May, 2005, Sherry Hoy, review of *Don't Die Dragonfly,* p. 36.
Reviewer's Bookwatch, March, 2005, Charisse Floyd, review of *Don't Die, Dragonfly* and *Oh No! UFO!*
School Library Journal, July, 2005, Jessie Platt, review of *Last Dance,* p. 108.
Voice of Youth Advocates, August, 1992, p. 170.

ONLINE

Crescent Blues Web site, http://www.crescentblues.com/ (December 1, 2005), Lynne Marie Pisano, review of *Double Vision.*
FictionForum.net, http://www.fictionforum.net/ (November 25, 1005), Bob Rich, interview with Singleton.
Linda Joy Singleton Home Page, http://www.lindajoy singleton.com (December 1, 2005).

*   *   *

SINGLETON, L.J.
See SINGLETON, Linda Joy

STEFFENS, Bradley 1955-

Personal

Born February 10, 1955, in Waterloo, IA; son of Henry Wallace (a machinist) and Marcella Rose (a switchboard operator; maiden name, Krueger) Steffens; married Bonnie Rose Szumski (an editor), July 5, 1980 (marriage ended); children: Ezekiel, Tessa Rose. *Education:* Attended Macalester College (St. Paul, MN), 1973-74. *Religion:* Lutheran. *Hobbies and other interests:* Racquetball, golf, aerobics.

Addresses

Home—13628 Pomerado Rd., No. 36, Poway, CA 92064-3539. *Agent*—c/o Author Mail, KidHaven Press, 15822 Bernardo Center Dr., Ste. C, San Diego, CA 92127.

Career

Deluxe Check Printers, Inc., St. Paul, MN, copywriter, 1982-87; Gelbach Lee, St. Paul, copywriter, 1987-88; Mitchell International, San Diego, CA, copywriter, 1989-94. San Diego Book Awards Association, member of board and chairperson, 2000, president, 2004—.

Member

Society of Children's Book Writers and Illustrators.

Awards, Honors

Contemporary Writers Series awards, Depot Arts Center (Duluth, MN), 1985, 1987; winner of Emerging Voices competition, The Loft (Minneapolis, MN), 1987; poetry prizes from *Artemis, New Worlds Unlimited,* St. Paul Chapter of American Association of University Women, and White Bears Arts Council.

Writings

NONFICTION

(With Harry Nickelson) *Vietnam,* Lucent Books (San Diego, CA), 1989.
(With James House) *The San Francisco Earthquake,* Lucent Books (San Diego, CA), 1989.
Working Mothers, Greenhaven Press (San Diego, CA), 1989.
Animal Rights, Greenhaven Press (San Diego, CA), 1989.
Printing Press: Ideas into Type, Lucent Books (San Diego, CA), 1990.
The Children's Crusade, Lucent Books (San Diego, CA), 1991.
Photography: Preserving the Past, Lucent Books (San Diego, CA), 1991.
Free Speech: Identifying Propaganda Techniques, Greenhaven Press (San Diego, CA), 1992.

Phonograph: Sound on Disk, Lucent Books (San Diego, CA), 1992.
The Fall of the Roman Empire, Greenhaven Press (San Diego, CA), 1994.
Addiction: Distinguishing between Fact and Opinion, Greenhaven Press (San Diego, CA), 1994.
Censorship, Lucent Books (San Diego, CA), 1994.
Loch Ness Monster, Greenhaven Press, 1995.
Censorship, Lucent Books (San Diego, CA), 1996.
Emily Dickinson, Lucent Books (San Diego, CA), 1998.
(With Robyn M. Weaver) *Cartoonists,* Lucent Books (San Diego, CA), 2000.
(With Dan Woog) *Jesse Jackson,* Lucent Books (San Diego, CA), 2000.
(With Diane Saenger) *Life as a POW,* Lucent Books (San Diego, CA), 2001.
Furman v. Georgia: Fairness and the Death Penalty, Lucent Books (San Diego, CA), 2001.
Understanding Of Mice and Men, Lucent Books (San Diego, CA), 2002.
J.K. Rowling, Lucent Books (San Diego, CA), 2002.
(With Craig L. Staples) *The Trial of Charles Manson: California Cult Murders,* Lucent Books (San Diego, CA), 2002.
(Editor) *The Free Speech Movement,* Greenhaven Press (San Diego, CA), 2004.
Giants, KidHaven Press (San Diego, CA), 2005.
(With Don Nardo) *Cyclops,* KidHaven Press (San Diego, CA), 2005.

PLAYS

Pageant of the Masters (radio play), produced in Minneapolis, MN, 1979.
Last Stand, produced in Minneapolis, MN, 1979.
Virodha-Bhakti: A Sequence of Pageants, produced in Minneapolis, MN, 1980.
The Cursing of the Fig Tree, produced in Minneapolis, MN, 1982.

Contributor of poetry to periodicals, including *Crosscurrents, Bellingham Review, Stone Country, Bellowing Ark,* and *Loonfeather.* Contributor of commentaries and opinion pieces to periodicals, including *Los Angeles Times, Minnesota Literature,* and *San Diego Writer's Monthly.*

Sidelights

A former copywriter who also authored plays early in his career, Bradley Steffens has penned a number of nonfiction titles for young readers, his books ranging from a discussion of John Steinbeck's well-known novel *Of Mice and Men* and biographies of Emily Dickinson and Jesse Jackson to several volumes in KidHaven Press's "Monster" series. *Cartoonists,* which Steffens co-authored with Robyn M. Weaver, is part of Lucent's "History Makers" series. The book begins by providing readers with an in-depth history of cartoon art that includes discussions of the work of six high-profile artists: Charles Schulz, Chuck Jones, Garry Trudeau, Cathy

Guisewite, Matt Groening, and Scott Adams. "The writing is clear, unbiased, and interesting," commented Linda Wadleigh in *School Library Journal,* adding that *Cartooning* will likely inspire young readers to search out the works of "some of their favorite cartoonists."

Steffens contributes the volumes *Cyclops* and *The Loch Ness Monster* to the 'Monsters' series, which is designed to appeal particularly to middle-grade reluctant readers. The series, which seeks to educate readers on the mythology and history surrounding the origins of legendary creatures, explores literature, folklore and myth, toys, and most importantly, modern film to trace each creature's impact on human society. Discussing the series as a whole, Ginny Gustin praised the "Monsters" books as "clearly written and contain[ing] fascinating information that will satisfy both casual browsers and serious report writers." A monster of a different sort is the focus of *The Trial of Charles Manson: California Cult Murders,* which Steffens coauthored with Craig L. Staples. This examination of one of the most high-profile murder cases of the twentieth century—the Tate/LaBianca murders of 1969—includes trial excerpts, photographs, and a backdrop to the crime, victims, and murderers in a volume that *School Library Journal* reviewer Tracy Ansley cited as "useful to students writing reports as well as those interested in famous cases."

Steffens once told *SATA:* "I first thought about being a writer in eleventh grade. My creative writing teacher, James Malone, told our class to write something about the automobile culture of Los Angeles, where we lived. It could be anything, Malone said—an essay, a poem, a short story, the first chapter of a novel. Wanting to avoid homework, I dashed off a twenty-line poem in class and turned it in. The next day, Malone sat on the corner of his desk with a piece of paper in his hand. 'Someone has turned in the first assignment,' he said, 'and I want to share it with you.' He began to read my poem aloud. A trained actor, he read with sensitivity and passion. When he finished, the room was silent. He looked up from the page. 'That, boys and girls, is poetry,' he said. He walked over to my desk and laid the paper in front of me. 'Publish it this semester, and I'll give you an "A" in the course,' he promised. 'You won't have to do another thing.'

"That morning changed my life. I changed my high school major. I changed the college I planned to attend. I began to write in earnest. I sent the poem out, and kept sending it out after it was rejected. Two years later, that poem, 'Automobile,' was accepted by the editor of *River Bottom,* a small literary journal published in Eau Claire, Wisconsin. After that, I never considered doing anything but writing."

Biographical and Critical Sources

PERIODICALS

Booklist, February 15, 1995, Merri Monks, review of *The Loch Ness Monster,* p. 1074; February 15, 1996, Hazel Rochman, review of *Censorship,* p. 1004.

School Library Journal, May, 1992, p. 128; May, 1993, p. 135; February, 1995, Elaine E. Knight, review of *The Loch Ness Monster,* p. 102; June, 1998, Kate Foldy, review of *Emily Dickinson,* p. 170; August, 2000, Linda Wadleigh, review of *Cartoonists,* p. 208; September, 2002, Tracy Ansley, review of *The Trials of Charles Manson: California Cult Murders,* p. 252; October, 2002, Kathleen Simonetta, review of *J.K. Rowling,* p. 194; February, 2005, Carol Fazioli, review of *The Free Speech Movement,* p. 153; April, 2005, Ginny Gustin, review of *Cyclops,* p. 144.

ONLINE

LocalAuthors.com, http://www.localauthors.com/ (November 6, 2005), "Bradley Steffens."*

* * *

STIMPSON, Gerald
See MITCHELL, Adrian

* * *

STONE, David Lee 1978-

Personal

Born 1978, in Margate, Kent, England; son of Barbara Anne Stone and Henry Cooke. *Hobbies and other interests:* Role-playing games.

Addresses

Home—Kent, England. *Agent*—c/o Author Mail, Hodder Headline, 338 Euston Rd., London NW1 3BH, England.

Career

Novelist. Blockbuster Video, clerk, then assistant manager, 1999-2001; freelance writer.

Awards, Honors

Three Dover District Festival of Literature prizes, 1988.

Writings

The Ratastrophe Catastrophe ("Illmoor Chronicles"), Hodder Children's Books (London, England), 2003, Hyperion Books for Children (New York, NY), 2004.
The Yowler Foul-Up ("Illmoor Chronicles"), Hodder Children's Books (London, England), 2004.
The Shadwell Shenanigans ("Illmoor Chronicles"), Hodder Children's Books (London, England), 2005.

Contributor to periodicals, including *Xenos* and *SFX.* Short fiction included in anthology *Knights of Madness,* edited by Peter Haining, Souvenir Press, 1998.

Stone's books have been translated into other languages.

Adaptations

The Ratastrophe Catastrophe was adapted as an audiobook, read by Robert Llewellyn, Listening Library, 2004.

Sidelights

A fan of fantasy literature and role-playing games, British writer David Lee Stone knew that he wanted to be a writer from an early age, and was inspired by the works of Douglas Adams (his literary idol), Terry Pratchett, Mervyn Peake, and Fritz Leiber. Leaving secondary school at age sixteen after an admittedly irregular attendance record, he worked as a freelance writer for several years. He had several stories published in *Xenon* magazine, but became so discouraged with his novel-length efforts that he tossed away his second full-length manuscript. Thanks to his mother, who fished the manuscript out of the trash and mailed it to a literary agent, Stone has since become a published author: his first novel, *The Ratastrophe Catastrophe,* was published in 2003 as the first volume of Stone's "Illmoor Chronicles," a fantasy series that had been in the works for much of its author's life. Praising Stone's brand of fantasy in *Kliatt,* Michele Winship wrote that the novel serves up "a healthy dose of sarcasm and one-liners that fly by quickly."

The Ratastrophe Catastrophe introduces readers to the slightly askew city of Dullitch in the land of Illmoor.

Dullitch residents proudly engage in thievery in addition to other unethical modes of behavior, all guided by their egomaniacal duke. In addition to all its societal corruption, Dullitch also happens to be plagued by rats. Diek Wustapha, a young shepherd, seems to be the solution to the citizens' plight: he possesses a magical mouth organ that is able to lead the rats out of the city, much as did the legendary Pied Piper of Hamlin. However, after this particular de-ratting, when Diek goes to collect his payment due from the city council, his request is refused. In revenge, the angered young man plays a new tune, this time leading Dullitch children away into hidden caves and forests. Worried for the town's youth, Duke Modeset commissions the quick-witted and well-connected Jimmy Quickstint, along with a dwarf comrade, to track the children down, promising a healthy reward in return. Larry Cooperman commented in *School Library Journal* that "*The Ratastrophe Catastrophe* comes crackling to life with humor, danger, and adventure," while in *Horn Book* Anita L. Burkham called Stone's prose "lighthearted" and his protagonists "outsized and colorful."

The Ratastrophe Catastrophe was followed by *The Yowler Foul-Up* and *The Shadwell Shenanigans,* both of which continue to chronicle the events ongoing in and around Dullitch. In *The Yowler Foul-Up* a sect takes root in the corrupt city, making it even more unpleasant than ever. Rising to fight this growing menace are Jimmy Quickstint as well as a less-than-enthusiastic

In **The Ratastrophe Catastrophe** *Stone introduces his "Illmore Chronicles" fantasy series, about a Pied Piper-like boy who takes a Pied Piper-like revenge on a penny-pinching duke. (Illustration by Bob Lea.)*

Duke Modeset and a half-vampiric resident. Further events are covered in *The Shadwell Shenanigans,* as a pair of local looters run amuck while citizens demand that the duke take action. Remarking on his own long relationship with reading, Stone was quoted as remarking on the *British Literacy Trust Web site:* "Reading is fun and exciting, and there's nothing better than a really good book. Films allow you to explore other people's imaginations, but books allow you to explore YOUR OWN."

Biographical and Critical Sources

PERIODICALS

Booklist, November 1, 2004, Kay Weisman, review of *The Ratastrophe Catastrophe,* p. 486.

Bookseller, April 11, 2003, p. 11.

Bulletin of the Center for Children's Books, January, 2005, Timnah Card, review of *The Ratastrophe Catastrophe,* p. 228.

Horn Book, January-February, 2005, Anita L. Burkam, review of *The Ratastrophe Catastrophe,* p. 99.

Kirkus Reviews, September 15, 2004, review of *The Ratastrophe Catastrophe,* p. 921.

Kliatt, November, 2004, Michele Winship, review of *The Ratastrophe Catastrophe,* p. 11; May, 2005, Carol Reich, review of *The Ratastrophe Catastrophe,* p. 59.

Library Media Connection, February, 2005, Sherry Hoy, review of *The Ratastrophe Catastrophe,* p. 74.

M2 Best Books, March 26, 2003.

Publishers Weekly, November 8, 2004, review of *The Ratastrophe Catastrophe,* p. 56.

School Library Journal, January, 2005, Farida S. Dowler, review of *The Ratastrophe Catastrophe,* p. 137; February, 2005, Larry Cooperman, review of *The Ratastrophe Catastrophe,* p. 74.

Voice of Youth Advocates, December, 2004, review of *The Ratastrophe Catastrophe,* p. 410.

ONLINE

British Broadcasting Corporation Web site, http://www.bbc.co.uk/ (November 6, 2005), "David Lee Stone."

David Lee Stone Home Page, http://www.illmoorchronicles.com (November 6, 2005).

Infinity Plus Web site, http://www.infinityplus.co.uk/ (January 29, 2005), Caleb Woodbridge, review of *The Ratastrophe Catastrophe.*

Literacy Trust Web site, http://www.literacytrust.org.uk/ (November 6, 2005), "Reading Champions: David Lee Stone."

Write Away! Web site, http://www.improbability.ultralab.net/writeaway/ (April 8, 2005), Tom Costello, interview with Stone.

*   *   *

SUZANNE, Jamie
See SINGLETON, Linda Joy

THAYER, Jane
See WOOLLEY, Catherine

*   *   *

TURTLEDOVE, Harry 1949-
(Eric G. Iverson, Harry Norman Turtledove, H.N. Turtletaub)

Personal

Born June 14, 1949, in Los Angeles, CA; married Laura Frankos (a writer); children: Alison, Rachel, Rebecca. *Education:* University of California at Los Angeles, Ph.D. (Byzantine history), 1997.

Addresses

Agent—Scott Meredith, 845 3rd Ave., New York, NY 10022.

Career

Science-fiction novelist and short-story writer. Technical writer for Los Angeles County Office of Education, c. 1982-91.

Member

Science Fiction Writers of America (treasurer, 1986-87).

Awards, Honors

HOMer Award for Short Story, 1990, for "Designated Hitter"; John Esthen Cook Award for Southern Fiction, 1993, for *The Guns of the South: A Novel of the Civil War;* Hugo Award for best novella, 1994, for *Down in the Bottomlands;* Sidewise Award honorable mention, 1995, for *The Two Georges,* and 1996, for "Worldwar" series; Premio Italia, 1996, for *Worldwar: In the Balance;* Nebula Award and Hugo Award nominations, both 1996, both for "Must and Shall"; Sidewise Award for Long Form, 1997, and Nebula Award nomination, 1999, both for *How Few Remain; Publishers Weekly* Top Ten SF Books list, 1998, for *The Great War: American Front;* Hugo Award nomination, 2000, for "Forty, Counting Down"; Sidewise Award for Long Form, 2002, for *Ruled Britannia;* Golden Duck Hal Clement Award, 2004, for *Gunpowder Empire;* World Fantasy Award nomination, 2004, for *First Heroes.*

Writings

NOVELS

A Different Flesh, Congdon & Weed (New York, NY), 1988.

Noninterference, Ballantine (New York, NY), 1988.

A World of Difference, Ballantine (New York, NY), 1990.

The Guns of the South: A Novel of the Civil War, Ballantine (New York, NY), 1992.

The Case of the Toxic Spell Dump, Ballantine (New York, NY), 1994.

(With Richard Dreyfuss) *The Two Georges,* Tor (New York, NY), 1996.

Thessalonica, Baen (New York, NY), 1997.

Between the Rivers, St. Martin's Press (New York, NY), 1998.

(With Judith Tarr) *Household Gods,* Tor (New York, NY), 1999.

Sentry Peak, Baen (New York, NY), 2000.

Marching through Peachtree, Baen (New York, NY), 2001.

Ruled Britannia, New American Library (New York, NY), 2002.

Counting up, Counting Down, Del Ray (New York, NY), 2002.

Advance and Retreat, Baen (New York, NY), 2002.

In the Presence of Mine Enemies, New American Library (New York, NY), 2003.

Conan of Venarium, Tor (New York, NY), 2003.

Days of Infamy, New American Library (New York, NY), 2004.

End of the Beginning, New American Library (New York, NY), 2005.

FANTASY NOVELS; "GERIN THE FOX" SERIES

(As Eric G. Iverson) *Wereblood,* Belmont Tower, 1979.

(As Eric G. Iverson) *Werenight,* Belmont Tower, 1979.

Prince of the North, Baen (New York, NY), 1994.

King of the North, Baen (New York, NY), 1996.

Fox and Empire, Baen (New York, NY), 1998.

FANTASY NOVELS; "VIDESSOS CYCLE" SERIES

The Misplaced Legion, Ballantine (New York, NY), 1987.

An Emperor for the Legion, Ballantine (New York, NY), 1987.

The Legion of Videssos, Ballantine (New York, NY), 1987.

Swords of the Legion, Ballantine (New York, NY), 1987.

Krispos Rising, Ballantine (New York, NY), 1991.

Krispos of Videssos, Ballantine (New York, NY), 1991.

Krispos the Emperor, Ballantine (New York, NY), 1994.

The Stolen Throne, Ballantine (New York, NY), 1995.

Hammer and Anvil, Ballantine (New York, NY), 1996.

The Thousand Cities, Ballantine (New York, NY), 1997.

Videssos Besieged, Ballantine (New York, NY), 1998.

FANTASY NOVELS; "TIME OF TROUBLE" SERIES

The Time of Troubles I, Baen (Riverdale, NY), 2005.

The Time of Troubles II, Baen (Riverdale, NY), 2006.

FANTASY NOVELS; "DARKNESS" SERIES

Into the Darkness, Tor (New York, NY), 1999.

Darkness Descending, Tor (New York, NY), 2000.

Through the Darkness, Tor (New York, NY), 2001.

Rulers of the Darkness, Tor (New York, NY), 2002.

Jaws of Darkness, Tor (New York, NY), 2003.

Out of the Darkness, Tor (New York, NY), 2004.

FANTASY NOVELS; "CROSSTIME TRAFFIC" SERIES

Gunpowder Empire, Tor (New York, NY), 2003.

Curious Notions, Tor (New York, NY), 2004.

In High Places, Tor (New York, NY), 2006.

SCIENCE-FICTION NOVELS; "WORLDWAR" SERIES

Worldwar: In the Balance, Ballantine (New York, NY), 1994.

Worldwar: Tilting the Balance, Ballantine (New York, NY), 1995.

Worldwar: Upsetting the Balance, Ballantine (New York, NY), 1996.

Worldwar: Striking the Balance, Ballantine (New York, NY), 1996.

Colonization: Second Contact, Del Rey (New York, NY), 1999.

Colonization: Down to Earth, Del Rey (New York, NY), 2000.

Colonization: Aftershocks, Ballantine (New York, NY), 2001.

Homeward Bound, Ballantine (New York, NY), 2004.

SCIENCE-FICTION NOVELS; "GREAT WAR" SERIES

How Few Remain, Del Rey (New York, NY), 1997.

American Front, Del Rey (New York, NY), 1998.

Walk in Hell, Del Rey (New York, NY), 1999.

Breakthroughs, Del Rey (New York, NY), 2000.

SCIENCE-FICTION NOVELS; "AMERICAN EMPIRE" SERIES

Blood and Iron, Del Rey (New York, NY), 2001.

The Center Cannot Hold, Del Rey (New York, NY), 2002.

The Victorious Opposition, Del Rey (New York, NY), 2003.

SCIENCE-FICTION NOVELS; "SETTLING ACCOUNTS" SERIES

Settling Accounts: Return Engagement, Del Rey (New York, NY), 2004.

Drive to the East, Random House (New York, NY), 2005.

The Grapple, Random House (New York, NY), 2006.

SHORT-STORY COLLECTIONS

Agent of Byzantium, Congdon & Weed (New York, NY), 1987, revised edition, 1994.

Kaleidoscope, Ballantine (New York, NY), 1990.

Earthgrip, Ballantine (New York, NY), 1991.

Departures, Ballantine (New York, NY), 1993.

(Editor) *Alternate Generals,* Pocket Books (New York, NY), 1998.

(Editor with Martin H. Greenberg) *The Best Military Science Fiction of the Twentieth Century,* Ballantine (New York, NY), 2001.

(Editor with Martin H. Greenberg) *The Best Alternate History Stories of the Twentieth Century,* Del Rey (New York, NY), 2001.

(Editor) *Alternate Generals II,* Baen (Riverdale, NY), 2002.

3 x T (includes *Earthgrip, Noninterference,* and *Kaleidoscope*), Baen (Riverdale, NY), 2004.

(Compiler with Noreen Doyle) *The First Heroes: New Tales of the Bronze Age,* Tor (New York, NY), 2004.

(Editor with Martin H. Greenberg) *The Best Time-Travel Stories of the Twentieth Century,* Random House (New York, NY), 2005.

(Editor with Roland J. Green) *Alternate Generals III,* Baen (Riverdale, NY), 2005.

Contributor of short stories to anthologies, including *Worlds That Weren't,* Roc (New York, NY), 2002; contributor to periodicals, including *Magazine of Fantasy and Science Fiction* and *Analog.* Author of novella *Down in the Bottomlands.*

OTHER

(Translator) *The Chronicle of Theophanes: An English Translation of Anni Mundi 6095-9305 (A.D. 602-813),* University of Pennsylvania Press (Philadelphia, PA), 1982.

(As H.N. Turtletaub) *Justinian* (historical novel), Forge (London, England), 1998, Tor (New York, NY), 1999.

Also collaborated with Susan Schwartz, S.M. Stirling, and Judith Tar on "War World" series.

Adaptations

The Two Georges was optioned for film by Britain's Granada Television.

Sidelights

Harry Turtledove is "the standard-bearer for alternate history," according to Tom Squitieri writing in *USA Today.* A sub-genre of science fiction, alternate history gained popularity as a genre during the 1990s, and according to Russell Letson in *Locus,* Turtledove is considered the "best practitioner of the classic alternate-history story since L. Sprague de Camp domesticated it for American SF over a half-century ago." According to Letson, Turtledove's work, which includes novels in the "World War," "Colonization," "American Empire," and "Great War" series, as well as stand-alone titles such as *Ruled Britannia* and *Advance and Retreat,* is characterized by "meticulous research and thorough knowledge of his period, an understated but firm way with storytelling, and a sense of the exotic appeal of the past combined with a recognition of the ordinariness of ordinary life."

Turtledove has served up fantasy versions of the Roman Empire and Byzantium in his fictions, reworked the U.S. Civil War so that the Confederacy wins, allied Na-

zis and Jews against an unearthly reptilian power, constructed trench warfare in the United States, and rewritten the history of early man. Quite brazenly creating alternate universes, turning history on its head, and perennially making the reader ask the question, "What if?," Turtledove's alternate histories frequently span several volumes. His popular "Videssos Cycle," in which Caesar's legions are transported from ancient Gaul to a world of wizards, comprises eleven books; his "Worldwar" series began as a tetralogy and has since sprouted a further trilogy in the "Colonization" extension; his "Great War" series included four books before morphing in to the "American Empire" cycle; and "Darkness," set in a fantastical middle ages, concluded in six. Turtledove's breakthrough, however, was not in a series, but in the stand-alone title *The Guns of the South: A Novel of the Civil War,* his account of how the Civil War might have progressed if South African time travelers had handed over a modern arsenal to General Lee.

Turtledove and his coauthors posit sixteen scenarios in which readers discover what would happen in history if famous military leaders were put in charge of unfamiliar, and sometimes failed commands. (Cover illustration by Charles Keegan.)

As Turtledove told Jeremy Bloom for *SciFi.com,* "I use the standard SF technique. Because one of the things SF does is postulate—if we changed this, what happens next?—most of those changes are set in the present and then you examine the future, or set in the future and then you examine the farther future. I say, all right, what if we make that change and set it in the past? With as rigorous an extrapolation as I can make." Rigor is something Turtledove can appreciate in things historical: he earned a Ph.D. in Byzantine history from the University of California at Los Angeles (UCLA) before making his name among alternate history fans.

Born in Los Angeles, California, in 1949, Turtledove grew up in nearby Gardena; his parents, Romanian immigrants, first settled in Winnipeg, Canada, before making their permanent home on the U.S. West Coast. A major turning point in his life occurred at age fourteen, when he discovered a copy of L. Sprague de Camp's *Lest Darkness Fall* in a second-hand bookstore. "I read it," Turtledove told Bloom, "and thought 'This is so cool,' and started trying to find out what Sprague was making up and what was real. I was hooked."

History would become a passion, although Turtledove was slow to realize it. He began college as an engineering major at Cal Tech, but flunked out in his freshman year. Because a college deferment kept one out of Vietnam, Turtledove subsequently spent a year at California State in Los Angeles improving his grade-point average, and then entered UCLA where he ultimately—in 1977—earned a doctorate. His dissertation was titled *The Immediate Successors of Justinian,* a look at late sixth-century Byzantium. "If it hadn't been for Sprague I wouldn't have the degree I have—I wouldn't have gotten interested in Byzantine history any OTHER way," the author admitted. "I wouldn't have written a lot of what I've written, because I wouldn't know the things I happen to know."

With few jobs available to scholars of Byzantium, Turtledove turned to writing, publishing his first two novels, *Wereblood* and *Werenight,* in 1979 under the pseudonym Eric G. Iverson because his editor thought that no one would take his real name seriously. (He continued to publish as Iverson until 1985). In addition to fiction, he earned his living as a technical writer for the Los Angeles County Office of Education. It was not until 1991 that he was able to leave technical writing and devote himself full time to creating alternate history.

Turtledove's writing has included many genres. As he noted to Bloom, he has written pure science fiction as well as high-tech "hard sci-fi," and has also worked in the fantasy genre: "historically-based fantasy, high fantasy, funny fantasy." Ultimately, however, it is Turtledove's reworking of history that has produced his most notable work.

Turtledove began experimenting with his peculiar blending of fantasy and history right from the start. Both *Wereblood* and *Werenight,* part of his "Gerin the Fox" series, deal with an empire in decline. As Peter T. Garratt noted in the *St. James Guide to Fantasy Writers,* all the "Gerin the Fox" books deal with a theme and location that "resembles a cross between Rome and medieval Europe." The hero is a baron living in Elabon, a border province that remains aloof from central authority, paying no taxes, and when menaced by a powerful wizard, the province and its baron are left to defend themselves in a battle for survival. Turtledove returned to the series fifteen years after the first two titles, expanding on Gerin's life and his attempts to make peace for his people, and exploring the concept of a universe containing multiple gods. *Prince of the North, King of the North,* and *Fox and Empire* fill out the history of this mythical empire of Elabon.

In 1987 Turtledove began his ambitious "Videssos Cycle," which is comprised of three separate series of books, as well as a few short stories. The core of the cycle includes four books published in 1987: *The Misplaced Legion, An Emperor for the Legion, The Legion of Videssos,* and *Swords of the Legion.* The hero of this quartet is Marcus Scaurus, a well-educated Roman officer of the late republic era who receives a mysterious sword while campaigning near Gaul. During a battle with an enemy chieftain possessing an identical sword, the sword blades touch, and Scaurus, the chieftain, and all the Roman soldiers in their vicinity are magically transported to another world. This alternate world, the empire of Videssos, resembles eleventh-century Byzantium, and the enemy chieftain joins forces with the Romans to make contact with the locals. Meanwhile, Scaurus and his men also become involved in palace intrigue and adventures that almost bring about the downfall of the Videssian empire. According to Garratt, the second and third volumes of the tetralogy "are among the best things Turtledove has written." As the empire crumbles into chaos, Scaurus marries the widow of a powerful mercenary. Although he tries valiantly to bring civil wars within Videssos to an end, Scaurus's wife must choose between loyalty to her new husband or to her own kin, a long line of mercenaries.

Serving as a three-book prequel to the "Videssos Cycle" are the novels *Krispos Rising, Krispos of Videssos,* and *Krispos the Emperor.* Set several centuries before the main novel cycle, these books feature the protagonist Krispos, born a lowly farmer, but advancing to his destiny as emperor during the course of the trilogy. Turtledove returns to Videssos again in the four-volume "Time of Troubles" cycle.

Throughout his career Turtledove has written standalone works, one of the most popular being the 1987 *Agent of Byzantium,* a collection of seven inter-related stories about the adventures of secret agent Basil Argyros. The tales rest upon a tweaking of history: in Turtledove's cosmology, the young Mohammed is converted to Christianity by a Nestorian priest instead of founding his own powerful religion. Turtledove then follows the historical revisions that would follow upon such a change, one of them being the presence of still-powerful Byzantine and Persian empires in the early fourteenth century. Argyros figures at the center of the novel's plots and counter-plots, and introduces many inventions to the empire: the telescope, gunpowder, and printing among them. "The narrative carries the reader along," commented M. Hammerton in _Twentieth-Century Science-Fiction Writers,_ the critic adding that Turtledove's protagonist is portrayed as a fully fleshed out human being rather than a wooden figure. As Letson reported in _Locus,_ the "greatest pleasure in these stories . . . is the evocation of the past."

Other popular individual titles include the author's humorous take on the environment in _The Case of the Toxic Spell Dump,_ as well as another volume set in the same universe thirteen centuries earlier, titled _Thessalonica._ 1998's _Between the Rivers_ is related to _The Case of the Toxic Spell Dump_ due to the books' shared theme of henotheism: the belief that many gods exist and that their strength is based on the number of adherents and worshipers they attract. Set in a fantasy world similar to ancient Mesopotamia, the gods of this universe are not only manifold, but also manifest; their actions are all too visible as they constantly meddle in human affairs. A trio of protagonists scheme to cripple the power of some of these gods as Turtledove examines the classic SF theme of reason versus faith. A _Publishers Weekly_ critic wrote that the author "uses all of his historiographical and narrative skills, plus his inimitable wit, to elevate his version of [this] theme to the same high level occupied by (among others) L. Sprague de Camp." Jackie Cassada, writing in _Library Journal,_ noted that Turtledove's "cadenced prose imparts an epic feel to this tale of humanity's attempt to forge its own destiny," and a critic for _Kirkus Reviews_ called _Between the Rivers_ "historically intriguing, splendidly textured, and full of stimulating ideas."

Justinian is a straight history from Turtledove, who in this instance writes under the pen name H.N. Turtletaub. The choice of pseudonym was once again an editor's dictate, based on concerns that straight historical fiction would not sell well and might negatively affect Turtledove's future sales. In the event, his portrait of Justinian II, the wily Byzantine emperor, proved quite successful and saleable. _Booklist_ reviewer Flanagan called it an "artfully styled narrative," noting that the author's "painstaking attention to historical details" serves to "vivify this mesmerizing account of one of history's most remarkable rulers."

Focusing on Great Britain, Turtledove collaborated with actor Richard Dreyfuss on the speculative novel _The Two Georges,_ which focuses on a version of the American colonies in which England never lost control of its North American relatives. In _Ruled Britannia_ he moves even further back in time, this time to England during the age of William Shakespeare. In the novel, set in 1598, the Spanish Armada has proved victorious over British naval power and England is now under the sway

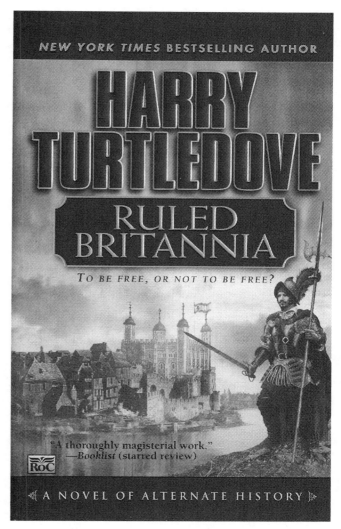

A decade after the Spanish Armada claims victory over Her Majesty's Navy, English playwright Will Shakespeare is drawn into a plot to save Queen Elizabeth I from the Tower of London and free England from the clutches of Spain in this well-received 2002 novel. (Cover illustration by Steve Stone.)

of both the Spanish government and the Vatican. With Queen Elizabeth I deposed and languishing in the Tower of London, Shakespeare has no patron, and his writings must reflect an ardent Catholicism or be prohibited. His creative abilities are ultimately put to the test when he is asked by the Resistance to author a play containing coded lines that will incite rebellion against the Spanish monarchy. Praising the novel for its compelling plot, Christine C. Menefee noted in _School Library Journal_ that _Ruled Britannia_ is a "complex tour de force" that brings Shakespeare's "work and times to life." In _Publishers Weekly,_ a reviewer echoed such praise, writing that "Turtledove has woven an intricate and thoroughly engrossing portrait of an era" that includes such individuals as Kit Marlowe, Robert Cecil, Lord Burghley, and others. Calling the novel one of Turtledove's "finest achievements," Ronald Green wrote in _Booklist_ that _Ruled Britannia_ stands as a "thoroughly magisterial work of alternate history."

Although other stand-alone novels by Turtledove have achieved success, *The Guns of the South,* published in 1992, first connected his name to the alternate-history genre and attracted the attention of both mainstream reviewers and the science-fiction community. The story begins in January, 1864, with Confederate General Robert E. Lee's troops suffering from shortages of both arms and supplies. Lee is despondent that the war may be lost, until he receives an interesting visitor. Andries Rhoodie, a time traveler who has come from South Africa together with several fellows, offers the general a supply of futuristic armaments, including the AK-47. When this weaponry allows the South to win the war, it also changes history, although not perhaps as Rhoodie might have wished. When the Confederacy subsequently begins to relax its slave laws, the South African becomes nervous; his purpose in helping Lee was to lay the foundation for a future white supremacist culture. As Lee continues his reforms, he and his men are suddenly faced with a new threat: Rhoodie and his soldiers.

Margaret Flanagan, reviewing *The Guns of the South* for *Booklist,* called Turtledove's re-creation an "exceptionally riveting and innovative narrative that successfully straddles the gulf between fact and fantasy." Discussing his own personal fascination with the Civil War period, as well as its popularity as a theme for alternate history, such as his standalone novels *Sentry Peak* and *Marching through Peachtree,* Turtledove told Bloom, "There is a general fascination with that period because it's a key period in the history of the United States. We are what we are now, for better and for worse, because of what happened during those four crowded years." In Turtledove's "Great War," "American Empire," and "Settling Accounts" series he also based his storyline on a United States torn by a civil war in which Confederate forced prevailed.

Containing a strong sci-fi element, the "Worldwar" series explores what might have happened had an external menace confronted Earth at the time of World War II. The series opens in late 1942 with *In the Balance.* Nazis are busy trying to eliminate Jews in Europe, while in the United States scientists are attempting to unlock the secrets of the atom. Suddenly, the skies overhead are filled with spaceships full of aliens. These reptilian invaders call themselves the Race, but earthlings name them the Lizards. Due to the invasion Earth-bound enemies must form odd alliances to battle this new and devastating menace, which seeks to enslave the people of this world.

Turtledove's canvas for his "Worldwar" epic is the planet Earth. The huge cast of characters includes real people from history, such as military generals Marshall and Patton, scientists Leo Szilard and Enrico Fermi, and political figures such as Churchill, Roosevelt, and Molotov. Settings include the United States, England, Germany, the Soviet Union, China, and Japan. Reviewing *In the Balance, Voice of Youth Advocates* reviewer Thomas Pearson called the series "promising," while

Booklist contributor Roland Green dubbed Turtledove "one of alternate history's authentic modern masters" and called the novel "engrossing." Letson, reviewing the initial title in *Locus,* commented that *In the Balance* delivers excitement "in the form of interesting characters responding to conditions both new and unchanged. . . . It is this ground-level . . . view of the world at war that I find gripping, the lives of individuals as they are affected by the macrohistorical military-economic-political forces represented by the wargames layer of the book." A reviewer for *Publishers Weekly* called the series opener an "intelligent speculative novel" which "gives a surprisingly convincing flavor to the time-worn story of warring nations uniting to repel extraterrestrials."

Turtledove continues his "Worldwar" saga with *Tilting the Balance,* in which Earthlings begin to fight back using ginger, a substance found to be addictive to the Lizards. Pearson commented in *Voice of Youth Advocates* that "real historical characters intermingle with Turtledove's fictional creatures in a wild 600 page blend of soap opera, carefully drawn character studies, and slam-bang action." *Upsetting the Balance* and *Striking the Balance* complete the tetralogy, ending with an uneasy truce declared between Earthlings and the Race. Reviewing the final volume, a critic for *Kirkus Reviews* said that Turtledove has created a huge opus: "A cast of thousands with a plot to match, well-drawn if unoriginal aliens, a wealth of fascinating speculation—and scope for any number of sequels."

Extending the "Worldwar" scenario, the "Colonization" series is set sixteen years after the end of the "Worldwar" books, and opens with the arrival of a flotilla of Lizard starships carrying a cargo of forty million sleep-frozen Lizard colonists. As the series continues, Lizards are integrated into human society, while alien technology has been mined by the major superpowers for use in weaponry advances in the ongoing war. *Colonization: Second Contact* is "outstanding entertainment," according to *Booklist* contributor Roberta Johnson. "In high fashion, the master of alternative SF launches a sequel series to his acclaimed 'Worldwar' tetralogy," wrote a reviewer for *Publishers Weekly,* adding that Turtledove, "with his fertile imagination running on overdrive . . . develops an exciting, often surprising story that will not only delight his fans but will probably send newcomers back to the 'Worldwar' saga to fill in the backstory." Reviewing the concluding "Colonization" novel, *Aftershocks, Booklist* critic Roberta Johnson dubbed the book "highly entertaining," and noted Turtledove's "trademark wry humor" in composing the Warren Commission of lizards charged with investigating the death of President Earl Warren. The entire "Worldwar" sequence concludes with *Homeward Bound,* in which a human spaceship travels to the Race's home planet, thus threatening the lizard's technological dominance and leaving Turtledove room for yet another sequel.

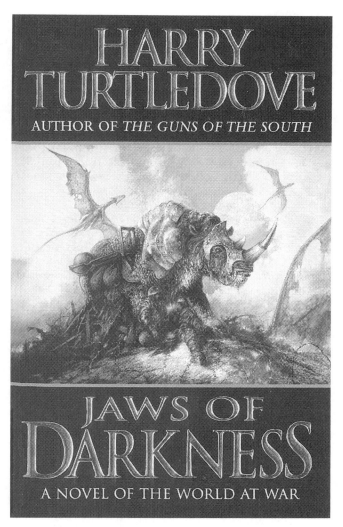

Turtledove's multi-part "Darkness" series includes this 2003 novel, which finds the Algarve laying siege to the continent of Derlavai with fantastical weapons that threaten to wipe out a civilization. (Cover illustration by Bob Eggleton.)

War on a global scale also serves as the backdrop for Turtledove's "Great War" series, which had its inception in the Civil War novel *How Few Remain*. This time, Turtledove tweaks history by having the Confederacy winning the Battle of Antietam and go on to victory after creating an alliance with the French and British. When the United States declares war on the Confederate States in 1881 over its purchase of northern territories from Mexico, the Confederacy again wins the conflict, again with the support of French and British troops. This is the setting for the alternate history Turtledove explores in subsequent novels about the First World War. *How Few Remain* "displays the compelling combination of rigorous historiography and robust storytelling that readers have come to expect from Turtledove," noted a reviewer for *Publishers Weekly,* who added that "Turtledove delivers his most gripping novel since 1992's *The Guns of the South.*"

In *The Great War: American Front* Turtledove roots his tale in the same historical world. It is 1914 and there is a world war between Germany, an ally of the United States, and the alliance comprising France, England, and the Confederate States. "Turtledove sustains high interest throughout the lengthy narrative," commented a reviewer for *Publishers Weekly.* "With shocking vividness, Turtledove demonstrates the extreme fragility of our modern world. . . . This is state-of-the-art alternate history, nothing less." Turtledove extends the saga in *The Great War: Walk in Hell,* which covers the year 1915 and includes a Negro rebellion in the Confederacy and a U.S. invasion of Canada where the horrors of trench warfare play out on the American continent instead of in Europe. According to Green, "This is not alternate history intended to give readers the warm fuzzies; it is a remorseless working out of the consequences of greater follies producing even worse results than the ones we may read about in actual history."

Throughout the "Great War" novels Turtledove follows the rise to power of Jake Featherstone, president of the Confederate States of America and a member of the radical Freedom Party. Featherstone's power base continues to grow in the "American Empire" and "Settling Accounts" novels, in which events unfold in North American that are analogous to those that actually transpired during World War II. With the World War over, beginning with *American Empire: The Center Cannot Hold,* the French have since restored their monarchy with Charles XI, and an economic depression has hit around the world. As World War II looms in the near future, a racial holocaust begins to unfold in the South. The militaristic Featherstone attempts to avert economic disaster by proposing War with the United States to his north, and the secession of Kentucky to the Confederacy and its racial policies may provide the spark. War ultimately breaks out in the "Settling Accounts" series, and Featherstone plays out as a native-born Hitler. Calling the concluding novel in the "American Empire" series, *The Victorious Opposition,* "the most powerful volume" in the "Great War" saga, Green added in *Booklist* that the novel showcases its author's "continuing mastery of historical fiction on the macrocosmic and the microcosmic levels." In *Publishers Weekly* a critic also praised the novel as "compelling," citing the entire "Great War" saga as "colossal and brilliant."

Turtledove's "Darkness" fantasy series utilizes technology of the 1930s and 1940s, but takes as its setting an imaginary world where technological advances are achieved through magic. *Into the Darkness,* the first novel in the series, opens in a fantasy world reminiscent of medieval Europe, Derlavai, where sorcery has been harnessed to create military power. This sprawling saga, which follows the armies of Algarve as they embark upon world conquest and gain power from the blood of their Kaunian foe while the Unkerlant seek to stop them, continues in *Darkness Descending, Through the Darkness Rulers of the Darkness, Jaws of Darkness,* and *Out of the Darkness.* In *Booklist* Green praised the series as "original and absorbing," while in *Library*

Journal Jackie Cassada deemed the novel sequence "a complex and richly detailed epic of war and magic."

While Turtledove's books are primarily geared for adult readers with a sophisticated knowledge of world history, his novels have also proven popular with young-adult readers. In his "Crosstime Traffic" series, which begins with 2003's *Gunpowder Empire*, the author addresses teen readers more directly by casting two teenagers as protagonists. In the story the Solter family is living in the twenty-first century, where alternative realities provide a means to escape the pollution and depleted planetary resources. While spending the summer in an alternative world where ancient Rome still rules, Jeremy Solter and his sister are left to fend for themselves when their mother must be rushed back to the hospital near the family's Southern California home. Unable to communicate with their parents due to technical problems, the stranded teens soon become aware that Lietuvan invaders are making strategic inroads into Roman lands, particularly in the city where the children are living. Hoping to survive the invasion with their status as time travelers undetected, the two West Coast teens are forced to rely on their wits. A *Publishers Weekly* reviewer described *Gunpowder Empire* as "a rousing story" in which Turtledove's teen characters are required to confront "moral choices and dilemmas that will . . . resonate with younger fans." The "Crosstime Traffic" series continues with *Curious Notions* and *In High Places.*

Turtledove, who is married to mystery writer Laura Frankos, spends much of his time writing. One interviewer estimated that Turtledove writes 350 days per year, hardly surprising given his prodigious output. In the 1990s alone he wrote over two dozen epics, while also serving as editor of several fiction anthologies. Summing up the difference between writing history and fiction, Turtledove explained to Bloom: "Fiction has to be plausible. All history has to do is happen."

Biographical and Critical Sources

BOOKS

The Encyclopedia of Science Fiction, edited by John Clute and Peter Nicholls, St. Martin's Press (New York, NY), 1993.
Reginald, Robert, *Science Fiction and Fantasy Literature, 1975-1991,* Thomson Gale (Detroit, MI), 1992.
St. James Guide to Fantasy Writers, edited by David Pringle, St. James Press (Detroit, MI), 1996, pp. 562-564.
Twentieth-Century Science-Fiction Writers, 3rd edition, edited by Noelle Watson and Paul E. Schellinger, St. James Press (Detroit, MI), 1991, pp. 809-810.

PERIODICALS

Booklist, February 15, 1987, p. 878; May 1, 1987, p. 1336; June 15, 1987, p. 1565; August, 1987, p. 1722; October 1, 1987, p. 222; May 1, 1990, p. 1688; May 15,
1990, p. 1785; November 1, 1992, Margaret Flanagan, review of *The Guns of the South: A Novel of the Civil War,* p. 490; January 1-15, 1996, p. 799; February 1, 1996, p. 899; August 19, 1998, Margaret Flanagan, review of *Justinian,* p. 1971; January 1, 1999, Roberta Johnston, review of *Colonization: Second Contact,* p. 842; March 1, 1999, p. 1104; June 1, 1999, Roland Green, review of *The Great War: Walk in Hell;* November 15, 2000, Roberta Johnson, review of *Colonization: Aftershocks,* p. 588; February 15, 2001, Roland Green, review of *Through the Darkness,* p. 1086; April 15, 2001, Roland Green, review of *Blood and Iron,* p. 1510; October 15, 2001, Ronald Green, review of *Marching through Peachtree,* p. 388; May 1, 2002, Roland Green, review of *The Center Cannot Hold,* p. 1445; July, 2002, John Mort, review of *Alternate Generals II,* p. 1831, and *Worlds That Weren't,* p. 1833; October 1, 2002, Ronald Green, review of *Ruled Britannia,* p. 276; November 15, 2002, Roland Green, review of *Advance and Retreat,* p. 584; February 15, 2003, Roland Green, review of *Jaws of Darkness,* p. 1019; May 15, 2003, Roland Green, review of *The Victorious Opposition,* p. 1619; August, 2003, Roland Green, review of *Conan of Venarium,* p. 1969; September 1, 2003, Roland Green, review of *In the Presence of Mine Enemies,* p. 9; December 1, 2003, Roland Green, review of *Gunpowder Empire,* p. 656; February 1, 2004, Roland Green, review of *Out of the Darkness,* p. 933; April 15, 2004, Roland Green, review of *The First Heroes,* p. 1432; July, 2004, Roland Green, review of *Return Engagements,* p. 1800; September 15, 2004, Roland Green, review of *Days of Infamy,* p. 180; October 15, 2004, Roland Green, review of *Homeward Bound,* p. 363, and *Curious Notions,* p. 395.
Kirkus Reviews, May 1, 1987, p. 682; March 15, 1988, p. 417; August 1, 1992, p. 947; January 1, 1995, p. 34; October 1, 1996, review of *Worldwar: Striking the Balance,* p. 1434; August 15, 1997, p. 1265; January 1, 1998, review of *Between the Rivers,* p. 28; June 15, 2003, review of *Conan of Venarium,* p. 840; July 1, 2004, review of *Return Engagement,* p. 605; November 1, 2004, review of *Homeward Bound,* p. 1032.
Kliatt, January, 2004, Sherry Hoy, review of *Worlds That Weren't,* p. 25; July, 2004, Sherry Hoy, review of *Alternate Generals II,* p. 33; March, 2005, Sherry Hoy, review of *Gunpowder Empire,* p. 29.
Library Journal, April 15, 1988, p. 98; September 1, 1992, p. 217; November 15, 1993, p. 102; December, 1995, p. 163; January, 1998, Jackie Cassada, review of *Between the Rivers,* p. 149; June 15, 1998, p. 110; January, 1999, p. 165; September 15, 2000, Jackie Cassada, review of *Sentry Peak,* p. 118; February 15, 2001, Jackie Cassada, review of *Colonization: Aftershocks,* p. 205; March 15, 2001, Jackie Cassada, review of *Through the Darkness,* p. 111; November 15, 2001, Jackie Cassada, review of *Marching through Peachtree,* p. 101; April 15, 2002, Jackie Cassada, review of *Rulers of the Darkness,* p. 128; July, 2002, Jackie Cassada, review of *The Center Cannot Hold,* p. 127; November 15, 2002, Jackie Cassada, review of *Ruled Britannia,* p. 105; June 15, 2003, Jackie Cassada, review of *The Victorious Opposition,* p. 106;

August, 2003, Jackie Cassada, review of *Conan of Venarium,* p. 142; December, 2003, Jackie Cassada, review of *Gunpowder Empire,* p. 173; March 15, 2004, Jackie Cassada, review of *Out of the Darkness,* p. 111; May 15, 2004, Jackie Cassada, review of *The First Heroes,* p. 119; August, 2004, Jackie Cassada, review of *Return Engagement,* p. 72; October 15, 2004, Jackie Cassada, review of *Days of Infamy,* p. 57; December 1, 2004, Jackie Cassada, review of *Homeward Bound,* p. 104.

Locus, June, 1990, p. 33; March, 1991, p. 60; October, 1991, pp. 31, 56; February, 1994, Russell Letson, review of *Worldwar: In the Balance,* pp. 31-32; April, 1994, Russell Letson, review of *Agent of Byzantium,* pp. 23-24.

Publishers Weekly, January 23, 1987, p. 66; May 22, 1987, p. 69; March 18, 1988, p. 76; March 16, 1990, p. 66; January 11, 1991, p. 98; August 24, 1992, p. 63; December 1, 1993, Roland Green, review of *Worldwar: In the Balance,* p. 678; December 6, 1993, review of *Worldwar: In the Balance,* p. 60; February 20, 1995, p. 200; January 22, 1996, p. 61; February 5, 1996, p. 80; August 16, 1997, review of *How Few Remain,* p. 390; January 26, 1998, review of *Between the Rivers,* p. 73; April 27, 1998, review of *The Great War: American Front,* p. 50; November 30, 1998, review of *Colonization: Second Contact,* p. 53; March 22, 1999, p. 74; August 23, 1999, p. 54; February 5, 2001, review of *Colonization: Aftershocks,* p. 72; February 19, 2001, review of *Through the Darkness,* p. 74; July 16, 2001, review of *American Empire,* p. 163; October 1, 2001, review of *The Best Alternate History Stories of the Twentieth Century,* p. 43; October, 21, 2002, review of *Ruled Britannia,* p. 59; November 25, 2002, review of *Advance and Retreat,* p. 47; March 10, 2003, review of *Jaws of Darkness,* p. 58; July 7, 2003, review of *The Victorious Opposition,* p. 57; October 20, 2003, review of *In the Presence of Mine Enemies,* p. 39; November 17, 2003, review of *Gunpowder Empire,* p. 49; February, 23, 2004, review of *Out of the Darkness,* p. 56; April 5, 2004, review of *The First Heroes,* p. 46; July 19, 2004, review of *Return Engagement,* p. 149; October 11, 2004, review of *Days of Infamy,* p. 60; November, 29, 2004, review of *Homeward Bound,* p. 27; March 28, 2005, review of *Alternate Generals III,* p. 61; June 6, 2005, review of *Drive to the East,* p. 44.

School Library Journal, March, 2002, Christine C. Menefee, review of *The Best Alternate History Stories of the Twentieth Century,* p. 261; May, 2003, Christine C. Menefee, review of *Ruled Britannia,* p. 180.

Science Fiction Chronicle, October, 1987, p. 41; January, 1988, p. 49; April, 1988, p. 52.

USA Today, October 13, 1998, Tom Squitieri, "Author Loves to Shake Up History."

Voice of Youth Advocates, June, 1992, p. 116; August, 1995, Thomas Pearson, review of *Worldwar: In the Balance,* pp. 160-161; August, 1996, Thomas Pearson, review of *Worldwar: Tilting the Balance,* p. 172; October, 1996, pp. 221-122.

Washington Post Book World, June 27, 1993, p. 12.

ONLINE

SciFi.com, http://www.sfsite.com/ (June 1, 2000), Jeremy Bloom, "Da Toastmaster Guest of Honor"; (December 1, 2005) Lisa DuMond, review of *Ruled Britannia,* and Steven Silver, reviews of *Conan of Venarium* and *Days of Infamy.**

*   *   *

TURTLEDOVE, Harry Norman
See TURTLEDOVE, Harry

*   *   *

TURTLETAUB, H.N.
See TURTLEDOVE, Harry

W-Y

WARNES, Tim 1971-
(Lily Moon, Timothy Warnes)

Personal

Born June 11, 1971, in London, England; son of Michael (a paper conservator) and Julia (Smith) Warnes; married Jane Chapman (an illustrator), April 16, 1994; children: Noah. *Education:* Kingston Polytechnic, diploma, 1990; Brighton University, B.A. (illustration; with honors), 1993. *Religion:* Christian. *Hobbies and other interests:* The natural world, photography, "walking, beachcombing, and going to the cinema, being a dad.

Addresses

Home—Somerset, England. *Agent*—c/o Author Mail, Little Tiger Press/Magi Publications, 1 The Coda Centre, 189 Munster Rd., London SW6 6AW, England.

Career

Freelance illustrator specializing in children's picture books, 1993—.

Member

Royal Society for the Protection of Birds, National Trust.

Awards, Honors

Nottinghamshire Children's Book Award, Benjamin Franklin award finalist, and Dutch Libraries Association's Children's Book Prize, all 1997, all for *I Don't Want to Go to Bed!;* Nottinghamshire Children's Book Award, 1998, for *I Don't Want to Take a Bath!;* Nottingham's Experian Big Three Book Award finalist, 2000, for *It Could Have Been Worse;* Sheffield Children's Book Award commended title, 2003, for *Scaredy Mouse.*

Writings

SELF-ILLUSTRATED, UNLESS OTHERWISE NOTED

Ollie's 123, Walker (London, England), 1999.
Ollie's Colours, Walker (London, England), 1999.
Ollie's ABC, Walker (London, England), 2000.
Ollie's Opposites, Walker (London, England), 2000.
Can't You Sleep, Dotty?, Tiger Tales (Wilton, CT), 2001.
Happy Birthday, Dotty!, Tiger Tales (Wilton, CT), 2003.
Mommy Mine, illustrated by wife, Jane Chapman, Harper-Collins (New York, NY), 2005.
Daddy Hug, illustrated by Jane Chapman, HarperCollins (New York, NY), 2007.

ILLUSTRATOR

Linda Jennings, *Tom's Tail,* Little, Brown, 1995.
Ragnhild Scamell, *Who Likes Wolfie?* Little, Brown, 1995.
Jane Chapman, *Peter and Pickle's Puzzling Presents,* Little Tiger Press (London, England), 1995.
Julie Sykes, *I Don't Want to Go to Bed!* Little Tiger Press (London, England), 1996.
A.H. Benjamin, *The Clumsy Elephant,* Golden Press, 1996.
Julie Sykes, *Sssh!,* Little Tiger Press (London, England), 1996.
Hiawyn Oram, *Counting Leopard's Spots: Animal Stories from Africa,* Orchard (London, England), 1996.
Julie Sykes, *I Don't Want to Take a Bath,* Little Tiger Press (London, England), 1997.
Christine Leeson, *Max and the Missing Mice,* Golden Press, 1997.
Christine Leeson, *Davy's Scary Journey,* Little Tiger Press (London, England), 1997.
Hiawyn Oram, *Not-so-Grizzly Bear Stories,* Orchard (London, England), 1997, Little Tiger Press (London, England), 1998.
Julie Sykes, *Hurry Santa!,* Little Tiger Press (London, England), 1998.
We Love Preschool, Millbrook Press (Brookfield, CT), 1998.

James Riordan, *Little Bunny Bobkin,* Little Tiger Press (London, England), 1998.

A.H. Benjamin, *It Could Have Been Worse . . . ,* Little Tiger Press (London, England), 1998.

Julie Sykes, *Little Tiger Goes to School,* Little Tiger Press (London, England), 1999.

Julie Sykes, *Santa's Busy Day!,* Little Tiger Press (London, England), 1999.

Julie Sykes, *Little Tiger's Big Surprise!,* Little Tiger Press (London, England), 1999, Tiger Tales (Wilton, CT), 2001.

Judy West, *Have You Got My Purr?,* Little Tiger Press (London, England), 1999.

Dick King-Smith, *Dinosaur School,* Puffin (Harmondsworth, England), 1999.

Michael Coleman, *You Noisy Monkey,* Rigby (London, England), 2000.

Michael Coleman, *George and Sylvia: A Tale of True Love,* Little Tiger Press (London, England), 2000.

Julie Sykes, *Wake up, Little Tiger,* Little Tiger Press (London, England), 2000.

Julie Sykes, *Time for Bed, Little Tiger,* Little Tiger Press (London, England), 2000.

Isobel Gamble, *Who's That?,* Barron's (Hauppauge, NY), 2001.

Julie Sykes, *Wait for Me, Little Tiger!,* Tiger Tales (Wilton, CT), 2001.

Julie Sykes, *That's Not Fair, Hare!,* Barron's Educational (Hauppauge, NY), 2001.

Dick King-Smith, *The Great Sloth Race,* Puffin (London, England), 2001.

Judith Nicholls, *Inky-Pinky Blot,* Ladybird (London, England), 2001.

Julie Sykes, *Careful, Santa!,* Tiger Tales (Wilton, CT), 2002.

Alan MacDonald, *Scaredy Mouse,* Tiger Tales (Wilton, CT), 2002.

Hiawyn Oram, *Pudge's Play,* Puffin (London, England), 2002.

Hiawyn Oram, *Pudge's House,* Puffin (London, England), 2002.

Julie Sykes, *Bless You, Santa!,* Tiger Tales (Wilton, CT), 2004.

Nicola Grant, *Don't Be So Nosy, Posy!,* Tiger Tales (Wilton, CT), 2004.

Julia Rawlinson, *A Surprise for Rosie,* Tiger Tales (Wilton, CT), 2005, published as *Rosie's Special Surprise,* Little Tiger Press (London, England), 2005.

Jesus Loves Me!, Simon & Schuster (New York, NY), 2005.

Ian Whybrow, *Say Hello to the Animals!,* Macmillan Children's (London, England), 2005.

David Bedford, *I've Seen Santa,* Tiger Tales (Wilton, CT), 2005.

Steve Smallman, *Bumbletum,* Tiger Tales (Wilton, CT), 2006.

Rise and Shine!, Simon & Schuster (New York, NY), 2006.

Gillian Lobell, *Little Honey Bear and the Smiley Moon,,* Tiger Tales (Wilton, CT), 2006.

Books illustrated by Warnes have been translated into seventeen languages.

ILLUSTRATOR, UNDER PSEUDONYM LILY MOON

Kenneth Steven, *The Bearer of Gifts,* Dial (New York, NY), 1998.

Kenneth Steven, *The Song of the Trees,* Little Tiger Press (London, England), 2002.

Adaptations

The "Little Tiger" series by Julie Sykes, featuring Warnes' illustrations, has been adapted into other books.

Sidelights

British artist and author Tim Warnes brings to life the works of a number of children's book authors through his vibrant, cartoon-like drawings and his whimsical take on life. Working with writers such as Julie Sykes, Judy West, Dick King-Smith, and Hiawyn Oram, Warnes has collaborated on several award-winning picture-book efforts, among them Sykes's humorous *I Don't Want to Go to Bed!* and *I Don't Want to Take a Bath!,* which reverberate with the adamant stance taken by children everywhere. Describing Oram's *Counting Leopard's Spots: Animal Stories from Africa* as a "handsome offering," *School Library Journal* contributor Tom S. Hurlburt noted that Warnes' "paintings . . . are expressive, nicely capturing the characters and their environs," and his "expressive, comical illustrations add even more whimsy" to Alan Macdonald's *Scaredy Mouse,* in the opinion of a *Kirkus Reviews* critic.

As his career has progressed, Warnes has taken on the role of author, creating texts for both self-illustrated books such as *Happy Birthday Dotty,* and stories such as *Mommy Mine* and *Daddy Hug,* which feature illustrations by Warnes' wife, artist Jane Chapman. Reviewing the couple's first collaboration, *Mommy Mine,* in *School Library Journal,* Linda M. Kenton praised the "creative wording and joyful imagery," while in *Kirkus Reviews* a contributor wrote that the "sing-song cadence" Warnes weaves into his rhyming text "is naturally suited for read-aloud sessions" and ranked the volume "high on the exuberance scale."

Born in London, England, in 1971, Warnes "used to spend hours drawing, making little illustrated books and cartoon strips," as he once revealed to *SATA;* consequently "my career is essentially a natural and happy progression of my main lifelong interest." Among his favorite illustrations were the cartoon characters featured in animated films, particularly those by Walt Disney, and his early training in drawing was gained by copying those characters. "I love reading 'The Making of . . .'-type books to major animated feature films; the process behind character and stylistic development is especially revealing and feeds my work probably more than any other one particular source."

For Warnes, developing well-defined characters is his favorite part of being a children's book illustrator. "When I come to a new project," he explained to *SATA,*

Mommies may come in all shapes and sizes, but the most beautiful mommy is always one's own, as Warnes proves in his rhythmic text for **Mommy Mine.** *(Illustration by Jane Chapman.)*

"I really enjoy researching picture reference for it, and I'm very proud of my extensive collection of reference material gleaned over years from various magazines and newspapers, etc! Without a source of reference I feel very out of my depth; as it is, each new project is always daunting."

Warnes begins each of his book projects by sketching page after page of character drawings, sometimes using photographs, "sometimes taking inspiration from people that I know, especially children, even if it is an elephant that I'm drawing!" He then reviews these drawings, picking out the ones that best fit the author's text. "At this stage I may make minor suggestions to the original text if I have a particular idea in mind, which may or may not be incorporated, and add my own incidental characters or actions."

The Christmastime book *Shhh!* is one of many collaborations between Warnes and author Sykes; others include *That's Not Fair, Hare!*, Sykes's "Little Tiger" picture-book series, and the "Santa" books *Hurry Santa, Bless You Santa!*, and *Santa's Busy Day*. In *Shhh!* the artist/illustrator wanted to provide something in each of his drawings for young readers to hunt for, so he drew a small mouse into every two-page illustration. "The publisher and [Sykes] developed this idea and gave me a voice on the last spread—now Mouse is as much a part of our Santa books as Santa himself," he told *SATA*. Praising Warnes' use of "bright colors" in *Shhh!*, a *School Library Journal* contributor commented of the finished product: The "lively illustrations show a round-faced, button-eyed Santa, . . . [whose] constant state of surprise and confusion . . . will delight young readers." Praising the artwork in *Hurry Santa!*, *Booklist* reviewer Ilene Cooper noted that Warnes "mixes the right amount of frenetic energy and laughs," creating art work that "attracts attention with its bright colors and cute characterizations." *That's Not Fair, Hare!* "strikes a nice bal-

ance between expressive illustrations and a read-aloud text," concluded Piper L. Nyman in a *School Library Journal* review.

Containing ten stories based on tales from around the world, Oram's *Not-so-Grizzly Bear Stories* reflects a wealth of tales with universal themes, such as the trickster tale. Reflecting these themes, Warnes' color-filled cartoon-like illustrations "represent an endearing array of animals from pandas to polar bears," commented Shelley Woods in her *School Library Journal* review of the work. Animals also feature prominently in Ragnhild Scamell's *Who Likes Wolfie?*, as a wolf tries to become more popular with the animals around him. Warnes' illustrations for Scamell's book successfully mirror Wolfie's dreams of popularity, "maintain[ing] a certain naive playfulness," according to a *Publishers Weekly* contributor. Commenting on the illustrator's technique, *Booklist* reviewer Ilene Cooper called Warnes' artwork "eye-catching . . . thick paintings with elements so well defined that at first glance" they apper"to be collage."

Although while in college Warnes worked primarily in black-and-white media, such as pen and ink, his more recent artwork has exhibited an increasingly sophisticated use of color. "In my first books I used a limited palette of just one red, one yellow, one blue and white," Warnes explained to *SATA*, "but now I actively enjoy seeking out new combinations of process colors. I work in acrylic paint, with oil pastel and pencil details and Chinese ink outlines (my Dad gave me the solid ink stone when I was thirteen, and I'm still using it today).

"Over the last few years, my work has seen a definite progression. Now working with water-soluble crayons and using acrylic-like watercolour to give more fluid, painterly artwork (this move in style encouraged by UK publisher Little Tiger Press). With this new technique, I am beginning to tackle atmosphere, light, and shade."

In addition to working under his own name, Warnes also coined the pseudonym Lily Moon, under which he illustrated the picture book *The Bearer of Gifts,* a story written by Kenneth Steven that retells the story of Santa Claus. Using a pseudonym "gives me a new identity and the freedom to express ideas . . . that wouldn't be possible in my usual style," Warnes once explained to *SATA.* "It has also fed my other work: the technique of using oil pastel on top of acrylic that was a distinguishing feature of my Lily Moon work has now crept into some of 'my own' work." As Lily Moon, Warnes has designed a number of greeting cards and Christmas cards, as well as illustrating *The Bearer of Gifts.* "I was delighted to receive this commission," Warnes explained of the 1998 picture book, "since it gave me the opportunity to express my [Christian] faith in my work; I also happen to love wintry landscapes which always seem so magical to me." Warnes' inspiration for *The Bearer of Gifts* was "largely drawn from my imagination, textiles, and primitive art, and any source of color reference that grabbed me, [among them] . . . my rug and a painting by Paul Klee," he told *SATA.* Praising the folk art-style and "deep, rich hues" apparent in Warnes' work, *Booklist* reviewer Lauren Peterson noted that the illustrations, "in a variety of sizes and shapes and with patterned borders and intriguing compositions, add interest."

Considering his future as an illustrator, Warnes looks forward to expanding his skills as an artist. "As time goes on, I would like to get to grips with portraying light and atmosphere," he admitted to *SATA.* "So far I have illustrated over twenty-five children's books with many foreign editions, but I still cannot grasp perspective!" In addition to the technical aspects of his job, he also has dreams of expanding his work beyond the printed page. "I suppose my ideal dream would be for something of mine to be properly animated as a feature, or to be involved in the character designs for such a film."

Biographical and Critical Sources

PERIODICALS

Booklist, March 15, 1995, p. 1334; April 15, 1996, Ilene Cooper, review of *Who Likes Wolfie?,* p. 1447; December 1, 1997, p. 644; May 15, 1998, p. 1629; September 1, 1998, Ilene Cooper, review of *Hurry Santa!,* p. 134; October 15, 1998, Lauren Peterson, review of *The Bearer of Gifts,* p. 429.
Child Education, June, 1996.
Independent, March 30, 1996, p. 9.
Junior, May-June, 1999, p. 111.
Kirkus Reviews, February 15, 2002, review of *Scaredy Mouse,* p. 261; February 15, 2005, review of *Mommy Mine,* p. 237.

Publishers Weekly, May 1, 1995, p. 58; April 8, 1996, review of *Who Likes Wolfie?,* p. 68; September 30, 1996, p. 89; August 17, 1998, p. 74; October 26, 1998, p. 65; December 21, 1998, p. 66; May 29, 2000, review of *Have You Got My Purr?,* p. 81; February 11, 2002, review of *Scaredy Mouse,* p. 186.
School Librarian, August, 1996.
School Library Journal, June, 1995, p. 88; April, 1996, Jacqueline Elsner, review of *Who Likes Wolfie?,* p. 117; October, 1996, review of *Shhh!,* p. 41; November, 1997, p. 91; December, 1998, Tom S. Hurlburt, review of *Counting Leopard's Spots: Animal Stories from Africa,* p. 112; April, 1999, Shelley Woods, review of *Not-so-Grizzly Bear Stories,* p. 106; February, 2002, Piper L. Nyman, review of *That's Not Fair, Hare!,* p. 114; April, 2003, Heather Miller, review of *Happy Birthday, Dotty!,* p. 142; June, 2002, Roxanne Burg, review of *Scaredy Mouse,* p. 102; July, 2005, Linda M. Kenton, review of *Mommy Mine,* p. 84.
Scotsman, November 28, 1998.

*   *   *

WARNES, Timothy
See WARNES, Tim

*   *   *

WHITELAW, Nancy 1933-

Personal

Born August 29, 1933, in New Bedford, MA; daughter of Joseph Eaton (a furniture store manager) and Mildred (a furniture store manager; maiden name, Pehrson) Eaton; married David Whitelaw (a farmer), 1955; children: Katherine Whitelaw-Barrett, Patricia Whitelaw-Drogue. *Education:* Tufts University, B.A., 1954; University of Buffalo, M.Ed., 1968. *Hobbies and other interests:* Grass-roots politics, volunteering in local mayor's office.

Addresses

Home—3212 Salisbury Rd., Jamestown, NY 14701. *Agent*—c/o Author Mail, *E-mail*—eio@netsync.net.

Career

Malden Schools, Malden, MA, elementary-grade teacher, 1954-55; Amerikan Kiz Koleji, Izmir, Turkey, teacher, 1955-58; Amherst public school system, Amherst, NY, teacher, 1968-88; Institute of Children's Literature, instructor, beginning 1988.

Member

Authors Guild, Authors League of America, American Society of Journalists and Authors, Society of Children's Book Writers and Illustrators.

Writings

NONFICTION

A Beautiful Pearl, Albert Whitman (Morton Grove, IL), 1990.

Charles de Gaulle, Dillon/Macmillan (New York, NY), 1991.

Theodore Roosevelt Takes Charge, Albert Whitman (Morton Grove, IL), 1992.

Joseph Stalin, Dillon/Macmillan (New York, NY), 1992.

Margaret Sanger: "Every Child a Wanted Child", Maxwell Macmillan International (New York, NY), 1994.

They Wrote Their Own Headlines: American Women Journalists, Morgan Reynolds (Greensboro, NC), 1995.

Grace Hopper: Programming Pioneer, illustrated by Janet Hamlin, Scientific American Books for Young Readers (New York, NY), 1995.

Mr. Civil Rights: The Story of Thurgood Marshall, Morgan Reynolds (Greensboro, NC), 1995, 2nd edition, 2003.

William Tecumseh Sherman: Defender and Destroyer, Morgan Reynolds (Greensboro, NC), 1996.

Nathaniel Hawthorne: American Storyteller, Morgan Reynolds, (Greensboro, NC), 1996, 2nd edition, 2003.

Clara Barton: Civil War Nurse, Enslow Publishers (Springfield, NJ), 1997.

More Perfect Union: The Story of Alexander Hamilton, Morgan Reynolds (Greensboro, NC), 1997, 2nd edition, 2003.

Lady Diana Spencer: Princess of Wales, Morgan Reynolds (Greensboro, NC), 1998.

Bram Stoker, Author of Dracula, Morgan Reynolds (Greensboro, NC), 1998, revised edition, 2004.

Let's Go! Let's Publish!: Katharine Graham and the Washington Post, Morgan Reynolds (Greensboro, NC), 1999.

Joseph Pulitzer and the New York World, Morgan Reynolds (Greensboro, NC), 2000.

William Randolph Hearst and the American Century, Morgan Reynolds (Greensboro, NC), 2000, revised edition, 2004.

The Shot Heard 'round the World: The Battles of Lexington and Concord, Morgan Reynolds (Greensboro, NC), 2001.

Andrew Jackson: Frontier President, Morgan Reynolds (Greensboro, NC), 2001.

Thomas Jefferson: Philosopher and President, Morgan Reynolds (Greensboro, NC), 2002.

Jimmy Carter: President and Peacemaker, Morgan Reynolds (Greensboro, NC), 2004.

Queen Isabella and the Unification of Spain, Morgan Reynolds (Greensboro, NC), 2005.

Queen Victoria and the British Empire, Morgan Reynolds (Greensboro, NC), 2005.

Catherine the Great and the Enlightenment in Russia, Morgan Reynolds (Greensboro, NC), 2005.

Catherine de' Medici and the Protestant Reformation, Morgan Reynolds (Greensboro, NC), 2005.

Victory in Destruction: The Story of William Tecumseh Sherman, Morgan Reynolds (Greensboro, NC), 2005.

Dark Dreams: The Story of Stephen King, Morgan Reynolds (Greensboro, NC), 2006.

The Homestead Steel Strike of 1892, Morgan Reynolds (Greensboro, NC), 2006.

Also of other works of nonfiction; contributor to newspapers and periodicals, including *Christian Science Monitor, USA Today,* and *Sail.*

Sidelights

The author of numerous biographies geared for a young-adult readership, Nancy Whitelaw embarked on her second career penning juvenile nonfiction following her retirement from teaching. Her books focus on a wide range of personalities—men and women who have gained renown in the arts and technology as well as those from the political and legal realms—and include the titles *Andrew Jackson: Frontier President, Mr. Civil Rights: The Story of Thurgood Marshall,* and *Let's Go! Let's Publish! Katharine Graham and the Washington Post.* Frequently praised for her clear prose and use of original source material in bringing her subject to life, Whitelaw was cited by *Booklist* contributor Carolyn Phelan for the "crisp writing style" used in *More Perfect Union: The Story of Alexander Hamilton,* while fellow *Booklist* critic Krista Hutley wrote in a review of *Dark Dreams: The Story of Stephen King* that Whitelaw "has a knack for sharing unusual details . . . and for showing how important historical events" affect her subject.

Whitelaw was inspired to begin writing when she visited a school to observe its reading program. A trained educator, she was astonished to find that the children were not reading books; instead, they read brief stories and articles printed on small cardboard cards, and when they finished they turned the cards over to answer questions printed on the back. After checking their answers, they took another card and continued. "They reminded me of supermarket cashiers who read prices, record numbers, make change, and then greet the next customer," Whitelaw once told *SATA.* "My disgust exploded in short angry bursts which became lines of a poem."

That first poem eventually found its way into publication in the pages of an educational journal, and when Whitelaw saw her byline in print, she was hooked. Soon she was submitting articles based on ideas she had gathered during her many years of teaching to educational magazines. After receiving thirty rejections in response, she decided to sign up for a series of writing courses, and "soaked up all the information I could get from other writers," as she recalled. Soon her articles began to sell, not only to the educational magazines, but also to more general magazine markets, such as *Christian Science Monitor, USA Today,* and *Sail.* Her experience writing on a variety of subjects for several different audiences has proved useful to Whitelaw since her focus has shifted to young-adult nonfiction.

In **Bram Stoker: Author of Dracula** *Whitelaw profiles the life of the nineteenth-century writer who introduced the forbidding Count Dracula to the world in his 1897 novel.*

Whitelaw's books are often part of more extensive series, such as the "European Queens" and "Notable Americans" series published by Morgan Reynolds. In *Queen Isabella and the Unification of Spain, Catherine the Great and the Enlightenment in Russia,* and *Catherine de' Medici and the Protestant Reformation,* Whitelaw tackles a significant moment in European history while also profiling a fascinating and influential woman. In her profile of Catherine the Great (1729-96), she follows the Russian empress from her childhood in Germany to her marriage to Grand Duke Peter, her rise to power following her husband's overthrow, and her ability to advance the scientific principles of French Enlightenment such as Rousseau while placating the powerful Russian Orthodox Church. Another Catherine receives a similar treatment in *Catherine de' Medici and the Protestant Reformation.* Queen to King Henri II of France, mother-in-law to Mary Queen of Scots, and mother to three monarchs who ruled during the religious wars waged between Protestants and Roman Catholics during the 1560s, Catherine de' Medici was a controversial figure. Exerting her influence behind the throne, she was ultimately implicated in the death of hundreds of Protestants during the bloody St. Bartholomew's Day Massacre, a reaction to the Protestant Reformation that took place in August of 1572. Re-

viewing *Catherine the Great and the Enlightenment in Russia* for *Booklist,* Gillian Engberg praised the book as "detailed" and "highly readable." *Andrew Jackson,* another Whitelaw biography that is part of the "Notable Americans" series, was praised by *Booklist* reviewer Roger Leslie as a "finely written, information-packed" account of the life of America's seventh president.

Biographical and Critical Sources

PERIODICALS

Booklist, September 1, 1995, Jeanne Triner, review of *Mr. Civil Rights: The Story of Thurgood Marshall,* p. 64; March 15, 1996, Susan Dove Lempke, review of *William Tecumseh Sherman: Defender and Destroyer,* p. 1250, and Kay Weisman, *Grace Hopper: Programming Pioneer,* p. 1260; July, 1997, Carolyn Phelan, review of *More Perfect Union: The Story of Alexander Hamilton,* p. 1817; March 15, 1998, Diane Janoff, review of *Clara Barton: Civil War Nurse,* p. 1243; August, 1998, Ilene Cooper, review of *Lady Diana Spencer: Princess of Wales,* p. 2002; October 1, 1998, Carolyn Phelan, review of *Bram Stoker: Author of Dracula,* p. 318; January 1, 1999, Anne O'Malley, review of *Let's Go! Let's Publish! Katharine Graham and the Washington Post,* p. 854; June 1, 1999, Shelle Rosenfeld, review of *Joseph Pulitzer and the New York World,* p. 1812; November 1, 2000, Roger Leslie, review of *Andrew Jackson: Frontier President,* p. 524; May 15, 2001, Carolyn Phelan, review of *The Shot Heard 'round the World: The Battles of Lexington and Concord,* p. 1749; December 15, 2003, Carolyn Phelan, review of *Jimmy Carter: President and Peacemaker,* p. 744; December 15, 2004, Gillian Engberg, review of *Catherine the Great and the Enlightenment in Russia,* p. 735; November 15, 2005, Krista Hutley, review of *Dark Dreams: The Story of Stephen King,* p. 36.

School Library Journal, February, 2001, Barbara Jo McKee, review of *Andrew Jackson,* p. 141; July, 2001, Ilene Abramson, review of *The Shot Heard 'round the World,* p. 133; March, 2002, Andrew Medlar, review of *Thomas Jefferson: Philosopher and President,* p. 259; December, 2004, Elizabeth Talbot, review of *Catherine the Great and the Enlightenment in Russia,* p. 172; January, 2005, Ann W. Moore, review of *Catherine de' Medici and the Protestant Reformation,* p. 157; February, 2005, Ann W. Moore, review of *Queen Isabella and the Unification of Spain,* p. 154; May, 2005, Patricia Ann Owens, review of *Victory in Destruction: The Story of William Tecumseh Sherman,* p. 162.

Voice of Youth Advocates, June, 2005, Pam Carlson, review of *Victory in Destruction,* p. 166.

ONLINE

Nancy Whitelaw Home Page, http://www.nancywhitelaw.com (December 1, 2005).

WILLIAMS, Charles
See COLLIER, James Lincoln

*   *   *

WILSON, Leslie 1952-

Personal

Born 1952, in Nottingham, England; married; children: Jo, Kathy. *Education:* Durham University, graduated. *Hobbies and other interests:* Gardening, photography, Chinese martial arts.

Addresses

Home—Berkshire, England. *Agent*—Sarah Molloy, A. M. Heath and Co. Ltd., 6 Warwick Ct., London WC1R 5DJ, England. *E-mail*—corneliuswilson@btinternet. com.

Career

Writer and writing tutor. Former translator.

Awards, Honors

London *Guardian* Children's Fiction Award shortlist, 2004, and Branford Boase Award, 2005, both for *Last Train to Kummersdorf.*

Writings

FOR ADULTS

Mourning Is Not Permitted, Women's Press, 1990.
Malefice, Pantheon Books (New York, NY), 1992.
The Mountain of Immoderate Desires, Weidenfeld & Nicolson (London, England), 1994.

FOR YOUNG ADULTS

Last Train from Kummersdorf, Faber & Faber (London, England), 2004.

Sidelights

One of British author Leslie Wilson's first awards came during childhood: a package of Cadbury creme eggs, won for the budding author's prize story about the origin of Easter eggs. In the years since, Wilson has balanced jobs in adult education and as a translator with her writing career. She published her first adult novel in 1990, and *Last Train from Kummersdorf,* her first book for young-adult readers, was released in 2005.

Inspired by the memories of Wilson's mother, *Last Train from Kummersdorf* brings readers back to 1945 Germany, during the days leading up to the end of World War II. In this highly acclaimed novel, two street-wise teens, sixteen-year-old Hanno and communist resistance-fighter Effi, meet while hiding in rural Germany and find themselves on the run as Hitler's Reich crumbles around them. With no family and no home, the teens rely on their wits and what the land will provide. In an amoral world full of desperate people, where laws no longer exist, they find that threats can lurk in the most unlikely places. As Geraldine Bedell noted in her review of the novel for the London *Observer,* Wilson's "beautifully written" novel brings to life the terror felt by "two teenagers who have lost almost everything, but hold on doggedly, somehow, to the exuberance and optimism of their youth."

Geared for older readers, Wilson's novel *Malefice* takes place in seventeenth-century England and follows the last days of a doomed woman who is ultimately executed for witchcraft by her fellow villagers. The narration alternates back and forth between Alice Slade as she sits in her jail cell and the thoughts of her friends, family and fellow villagers leading up to her dreary fate. "Wilson's lean, uncluttered prose evokes this distant era with the earthy resonance of folktales," commented a *Publishers Weekly* reviewer.

Biographical and Critical Sources

PERIODICALS

Observer (London, England), April 11, 2004, Geraldine Bedell, "Reality Check."
Publishers Weekly, April 12, 1993, review of *Malefice,* p. 48; October 31, 1994, review of *The Mountain of Immodest Desires,* p. 45.
School Librarian, spring, 2004, review of *Last Train to Kummersdorf,* p. 49.

ONLINE

Guardian Unlimited, http://books.guardian.co.uk/ (October 12, 2004), Claire Armitstead, review of *Last Train from Kummersdorf.*
Leslie Wilson Web site, http://www.lesliewilson.co.uk (December 11, 2005).

*   *   *

WISHINSKY, Frieda 1948-

Personal

Surname is pronounced "wish-in-ski"; born July 14, 1948, in Munich, West Germany (now Germany); immigrated to United States, 1949; immigrated to Canada, 1970s; daughter of Herman (originally a pastry chef; became a sculptor) and Mala (a homemaker) Reches;

married Solomon W. ("Bill") Wishinsky (a family doctor), 1971; children: David, Suzanne. *Education:* City University of New York, B.A., 1970; Ferkanf Graduate School, Yeshiva University, M.Sc., 1971. *Politics:* "Independent (but usually Democrat)." *Religion:* Jewish.

Addresses

Home and office—292 Horsham Ave., Willowdale, Ontario M2R 1G4, Canada. *E-mail*—wish@inforamp.net.

Career

Special education teacher in New York, NY, Israel, and Canada, for twenty-three years; York University, Toronto, Ontario, Canada, research assistant for one year; full-time freelance writer. Speaker at workshops on literature and writing for children.

Member

Society of Children's Book Writers and Illustrators, Canadian Association for Children's Writers and Performers, Canadian Writers' Union.

Awards, Honors

Pick of the List citation, American Bookseller, 1990, for *Oonga Boonga;* nominee, Governor General's Award, Canada Council, and Tiny Torgi Award for Print Braille Book of the Year, both 1999, both for *Each One Special;* 100 Best Canadian Children's Books citation, Toronto Public Library, for *No Frogs for Dinner;* outstanding book citation, Parents Council of the United States, 1999, for *The Man Who Made Parks;* Book of the Week citation, London *Sunday Times,* Best of Children's Fiction citation, Yorkshire Libraries, and Children's Choice citation, International Reading Association/Children's Book Council, 2001, all for *Nothing Scares Us;* Best Book of 2002 citation, *Resource Links,* 2003, for *Give Maggie a Chance;* Stockport Children's Book Award, and Sheffield Children's Book Award, both 2004, and Portsmouth Children's Book Award, all for *Jennifer Jones Won't Leave Me Alone;* Great Book Award, Canadian Toy Council, 2005, for *A Noodle up Your Nose.*

Writings

Queen of the Toilet Bowl (young-adult novel), Orca (Custer, WA), 2005.

FOR CHILDREN

Oonga Boonga, illustrated by Suçie Stevenson, Little, Brown (Boston, MA), 1990, illustrated by Carol Thompson, Dutton (New York, NY), 1998, illustrated by Michael Martchenko, Scholastic Canada (Richmond Hill, Ontario, Canada), 1998.

Why Can't You Fold Your Pants like David Levine?, illustrated by Jackie Snider, HarperCollins (Toronto, Ontario, Canada), 1993.

Jennifer Jones Won't Leave Me Alone, illustrated by Linda Hendry, HarperCollins (Toronto, Ontario, Canada), 1995, illustrated by Neal Layton, Carolrhoda Books (Minneapolis, MN), 2003.

Crazy for Chocolate, illustrated by Jock McRae, Scholastic Canada (Richmond Hill, Ontario, Canada), 1998.

Each One Special, illustrated by H. Werner Zimmermann, Orca Book Publishers (Victoria, British Columbia, Canada), 1998.

The Man Who Made Parks: The Story of Parkbuilder Frederick Law Olmsted, illustrated by Song Nan Zhang, Tundra Books (Toronto, Ontario, Canada), 1999.

No Frogs for Dinner, illustrated by Linda Hendry, Fitzhenry & Whiteside (Markham, Ontario, Canada), 1999.

Give Maggie a Chance, illustrated by Ann Iosa, ITP Nelson (Toronto, Ontario, Canada), 1999, illustrated by Dean Griffiths, Fitzhenry & Whiteside (Markham, Ontario, Canada), 2002.

Nothing Scares Us, illustrated by Neal Layton, Carolrhoda Books (Minneapolis, MN), 2000.

So Long Stinky Queen, illustrated by Linda Hendry, Fitzhenry & Whiteside (Markham, Ontario, Canada), 2000.

A Quest in Time, illustrated by Bill Slavin, Owl Books (Toronto, Ontario, Canada), 2000.

What's the Matter with Albert?: A Story of Albert Einstein, illustrated by Jacques Lamontagne, Maple Tree Press (Toronto, Ontario, Canada), 2002.

Manya's Dream: A Story of Marie Curie, illustrated by Jacques Lamontagne, Maple Tree Press (Toronto, Ontario, Canada), 2003.

Just Call Me Joe, Orca (Custer, WA), 2003.

A Bee in Your Ear, illustrated by Louise-Andréé Laliberté, Orca (Custer, WA), 2004.

Just Mabel, illustrated by Sue Heap, Kingfisher (Boston, MA), 2004.

A Noodle up Your Nose, illustrated by Louise-Andréé Laliberté, Orca (Custer, WA), 2004.

(With Janice Weaver) *It's Your Room: A Decorating Guide for Real Kids,* illustrated by Claudia Davila, Tundra Books (Toronto, Ontario, Canada), 2005.

Just Imagine ABC, illustrated by Christine Tripp, Scholastic Canada (Markham, Ontario, Canada), 2005.

Dimples Delight, illustrated by Louise-Andréé Laliberté, Orca (Custer, WA), 2005.

Albert Einstein, DK Publishing (New York, NY), 2005.

EDUCATIONAL

Airplanes, Teacher Created Materials, Inc., 1997.

Construction, Teacher Created Materials, Inc., 1997.

Farm, Teacher Created Materials, Inc., 1997.

Cars & Trucks, Teacher Created Materials, Inc., 1997.

Boats & Ships, Teacher Created Materials, Inc., 1997.

Nelson Language Arts 5, Supplementary Readings, ITP Nelson (Toronto, Ontario, Canada), 1998.

Nelson Language Arts 6: Going the Distance, Choosing Peace, Supplementary Readings, ITP Nelson (Toronto, Ontario, Canada), 1998.

Nelson Language Arts 3, Supplementary Readings, ITP Nelson (Toronto, Ontario, Canada), 1999.

My Dog Kam, Thomson Nelson (Toronto, Ontario, Canada), 2003.

Moving Away, Thomson Nelson (Toronto, Ontario, Canada), 2003.

Picnic Plans, Thomson Nelson (Toronto, Ontario, Canada), 2003.

Grandpa Moves In, Thomson Nelson (Toronto, Ontario, Canada), 2003.

First Day, Thomson Nelson (Toronto, Ontario, Canada), 2003.

A Trip by Train, Thomson Nelson (Toronto, Ontario, Canada), 2003.

Ten Blue Things, Thomson Nelson (Toronto, Ontario, Canada), 2003.

A Hat for Me, Thomson Nelson (Toronto, Ontario, Canada), 2003.

All about Miss Miller, Thomson Nelson (Toronto, Ontario, Canada), 2003.

My Little House, Thomson Nelson (Toronto, Ontario, Canada), 2004.

(With Sharon Siamon) *Canada Day,* Thomson Nelson (Toronto, Ontario, Canada), 2004.

Family Night, Thomson Nelson (Toronto, Ontario, Canada), 2004.

Around the World in a Day, Thomson Nelson (Toronto, Ontario, Canada), 2004.

The Worrywart, Thomson Nelson (Toronto, Ontario, Canada), 2004.

Breakfast in the Bathtub, Thomson Nelson (Toronto, Ontario, Canada), 2004.

David Thompson: Map-Maker, Pearson Education Canada (Don Mills, Ontario, Canada), 2005.

Alexander Graham Bell: Man of Ideas, Pearson Education Canada (Don Mills, Ontario, Canada), 2005.

OTHER

Contributor of reviews, features, and profiles to "Books for Young Readers" department, *Quill & Quire;* contributor to other periodicals, including *Books in Canada, Parentalk, Canadian Living, Owl Canadian Family,* and *Publishers Weekly.*

Work in Progress

A Frog in Your Throat.

Sidelights

Frieda Wishinsky found success as a children's book author with her first effort, the picture book *Oonga Boonga,* which earned positive reviews for its warmhearted depiction of the havoc wrought on a young family by a fussy baby. Nothing and no one seems able to make baby Louise happy until older brother Daniel steps in to whisper the magic words of the title, bringing smiles all around. The author "adeptly captures the ordinary but magical relationship between an older and younger sibling," commented Theo Hersh in *Quill & Quire,* praising the "rhythmic cadence" of Wishinsky's prose. *School Library Journal* contributor Ellen Fader observed that the story's elevation of the older sibling to the role of hero would be a comfort to those feeling pushed out of the way by the birth of a new family member, and called the book "fun for all who enjoy the warmth and sweetness of a family story touched by just the right sense of silliness."

For early readers, Wishinsky wrote *Why Can't You Fold Your Pants like David Levine?,* a humorous tale about a boy who feels unappreciated at home because his mother always compares his accomplishments unfavorably with those of a neighborhood boy. When the harried child runs away from home, however, he quickly meets up with another boy, who is fleeing his mother for the same reason. The two decide to switch places, whereupon they discover that their parents really do miss them. Wishinsky returns to the picture-book genre with *Jennifer Jones Won't Leave Me Alone!,* in which a little girl's love for a little boy provides ample fodder for teasing from the boy's friends. When Jennifer goes away for a while, the boy discovers he misses her after all, and decides to show his true feelings to Jennifer, despite what his friends might say. The book's "message about friendship and feelings is implicit rather than explicit, and the book remains light and funny," remarked Gwyneth Evans in *Quill & Quire.* Indeed, Carolyn Cutt declared in *Resource Links,* this "delightful story, written in rhyme, will make every reader smile."

Crazy for Chocolate is an amusing adventure novel for young readers in which Anne Banks travels back through time with the help of a magical CD-ROM given to her by a local librarian in order to research a school assignment. With the help of her computer mouse, Anne clicks in and out of fun and sometimes frightening countries and historical eras in her quest for information on the history of chocolate. "Although the text of the novel is extremely simple, readers will be engaged and intrigued by the situations and difficulties Anne encounters," attested Sheree Haughian in *Quill & Quire.* The inclusion of Anne's report at the end of the book provides appropriate closure for Wishinsky's imaginative story.

Wishinsky is also the author of *Each One Special,* a picture-book story about young Ben, whose friend Harry the baker is laid off from his job. Harry quickly falls into depression until he and Ben start a new venture molding sculptures out of clay. "As a work portraying 'special' talents and warm relationships between generations, the book succeeds," concluded Mary Beaty in *Quill & Quire. Nothing Scares Us,* another picture book, tells the story of two seemingly fearless friends, Lucy and Lenny. As they play, they fight make-believe aliens, alligators, pirates, and monsters without batting an eye, yet they both share one fear: admitting to the other that there are real-life things that scare them. In Lenny's case, he is afraid of spiders, while Lucy avoids watching scary television shows like Lenny's favorite, *The Creature*. "The story successfully illustrates that it is normal to have some fears, and that it's OK to share them with your friends," Sheilah Kosco noted in *School Library Journal*. Wishinsky also manages to "inject a heavy dose of humor into a common childhood anxiety," concluded a *Publishers Weekly* reviewer.

In *Give Maggie a Chance* the title character is a shy little kitten who is just starting school. Maggie is good at reading and wants to prove that to her teacher, Mrs. Brown, but every time she stands up in front of the class to read she freezes. Meanwhile, unkind schoolmate Kimberly jumps up and reads with no problem at all; in fact, Kimberly can read while teasing Maggie at the same time! Only when Kimberly turns her mean streak on another student and refocuses her verbal torments does Maggie find the confidence to stand up to the bully. "*Give Maggie a Chance* would be a great opening to a discussion about bullying or teamwork with a primary class," noted *Resource Links* reviewer Joanne de Groot.

Wishinsky draws on her childhood love of science and scientists with the books *What's the Matter with Albert?: A Story of Albert Einstein* and *Manya's Dream: A Story of Marie Curie*. Both books contain stories about the struggles these two famous scientists faced as children and had to overcome in order to make their great discoveries. In Einstein's case, he struggled to overcome others' opinions of him as stupid: he learned to talk relatively late, causing some people to think he was not bright, and was labeled a poor student because of his tendency to daydream. For Marie Curie, born Maria "Manya" Sklodowska, the challenge was learning a new language and adapting to life as an immigrant after she moved from Poland to France as a young woman. "Both of these books are very reader friendly for a young person who is just beginning to be interested in reading biographies," Karen MacKinnon commented in a *Resource Links* review of *Manya's Dream*. In both cases, the scientists' stories are framed with those typical of children who are struggling with similar issues, helping young readers to draw the connections between these famous people and their own lives. "Perhaps the most important aspect of the whole book," MacKinnon wrote in her review of *What's the Matter with Albert?*, "is that it encourages the reader to believe in himself as Einstein himself did even when others found him to be rather odd."

A Bee in Your Ear is another beginning chapter book. In this title, Kate is stressed out over an upcoming school spelling bee. She thinks she can win, but she struggles with homonyms; her friend Jake, also a good speller, has trouble with silent vowels. They start studying together, but their newfound competitiveness strains their friendship, and in a moment of frustration Kate

In Manya's Dream *Wishinsky recounts the life of Marie Curie, the Polish-born and French-educated physicist who became the first woman to receive the Nobel Prize for her work in isolating radium. (Illustration by Jacques Lamontagne.)*

yells at Jake. Now, Kate thinks, she has lost her friend, and she has nobody to partner with to beat Violet, the school bully and another spelling bee challenger. Reviewers praised the realism of this story; Carolyn Phelan wrote in *Booklist,* that "most children will feel right at home in the elementary-school setting realistically depicted here," while *Resource Links* contributor Carolyn Cutt commented that "the dialogue is natural and flows easily. The conversations and thoughts ring true of any student."

Queen of the Toilet Bowl is written for a slightly older audience than many of Wishinsky's works. This book tells the story of Renata, a ninth grader and Brazilian immigrant. Renata's new best friend, Liz, convinces Renata to audition for the school's upcoming production of *The Sound of Music,* and to shy Renata's surprise she is cast as Maria Von Trapp—the lead. However, Karin, a bully accustomed to being the center of attention, is jealous and sets out to make Renata miserable. Her plan to frame Renata for stealing her watch fails, but Karin then succeeds in striking a harsh, humiliating blow, posting on the Internet a picture of Renata's mother, who works as a maid, cleaning a toilet. Somehow, Renata must overcome her embarrassment and have enough confidence in herself to show her face in school and on stage. "The straightforward, uncomplicated plot is told in short chapters, moving the story along at a fast clip" and helping to make it a good choice for reluctant readers, Amanda MacGregor noted in *Kliatt.*

"I love writing probably because I've always loved reading," Wishinsky once told *SATA.* "As an only child, books were some of my best companions. Many of my happiest memories are heading home from the library laden with six books (the maximum you could take out at one time) and opening each one like a treasure. Then would come the hard part; deciding which book to read first. The choice was all mine.

"As a child I had few choices. I had to make my bed, go to school, learn multiplication tables, and do my homework. What to read, on the other hand, was up to me. My parents, immigrants from Europe, never censored my reading and so I read everything: fiction, travel books, history. I especially loved books about magic, adventure, and biographies. The 'Mary Poppins' series was a particular favorite and as for biographies, I loved reading about scientists who changed the world: people like Louis Pasteur or Madame Curie. In my fantasies, I dreamed about becoming a scientist and perhaps discovering a cure for cancer or a new vaccine. (That all changed when I realized I liked the romance of science a lot more than the reality).

"Aside from the pleasure I derived from reading, I soon discovered that I liked writing, too. In seventh grade I had a teacher who introduced us to some exciting literature and gave lots of creative writing assignments. Re-reading some of them now, I realize they were full of

In **Just Call Me Joe** *Wishinsky tells the story of a Jewish immigrant who is determined to embrace his new country, despite the difficulties he encounters after arriving in New York Harbor. (Illustration by Stephen McCallum.)*

flowery phrases and elaborate sentences, but my teacher saw beyond that. On one paper he wrote: 'You know how to use words effectively. Therefore you should attempt to read and write poetry, stories, and essays in order to develop your writing talent.' His words have stayed with me all these years.

"I majored in international relations in university. I loved history and political science and still do, but right before entering graduate school I realized that it wasn't what I wanted to do with my life. So I started to hunt for a job. I stumbled into an excellent M.S. program in special education and before I could fully think it through, I was headed in an entirely new area. I earned my degree and began teaching. Since then I've taught in three countries and with every age group. Teaching has been rewarding and generally a pleasure. It's also led me back into writing.

"About ten years ago, when I taught in a high school for students with very low reading abilities, I began to search for books at their reading level that would also be fun. At that time, 'high-interest/low-vocabulary books' had hit the market, but the kids and I found the stories boring. So I started to introduce them to picture books that I liked and felt were suited for any age. These books delighted me and my students. They were funny and touching and always universal in feeling. I began buying picture books and early novels with a school library budget that had never been used because no one thought these kids would ever read. Soon I was adopted as an honorary librarian by the head librarian of the school board and was invited on buying trips. On those trips, I discovered Arnold Lobel, James Marshall, Jean Fritz, Katherine Patterson, the "Narnia" books, *The Secret Garden,* and *Tom's Midnight Garden.* And then, when I was on a two-month sabbatical with my husband in Eugene, Oregon (where he was doing a family medicine rotation), I started to write. I haven't stopped since.

"Throughout these years of writing, I've learned that publishing is an iffy business, but I've also learned I'm persistent and that there's nothing more satisfying to me than writing for children. It's just what I want to do."

Biographical and Critical Sources

PERIODICALS

Booklist, March 1, 1990, pp. 1350-1351; January 1, 2003, Carolyn Phelan, review of *What's the Matter with Albert?: A Story of Albert Einstein,* p. 886; December 15, 2003, Hazel Rochman, review of *Manya's Dream: A Story of Marie Curie,* p. 750; March 15, 2005, Carolyn Phelan, review of *A Bee in Your Ear,* p. 1296.

Children's Book News, summer-fall, 1999, p. 7.

Kirkus Reviews, April 15, 1990, p. 588; May 1, 1999; December 15, 2002, review of *Jennifer Jones Won't Leave Me Alone,* p. 1860.

Kliatt, July, 2005, Amanda MacGregor, review of *Queen of the Toilet Bowl* p. 27.

Publishers Weekly, February 23, 1990, Diane Roback, review of *Oonga Boonga,* p. 216; November 6, 2000, review of *Nothing Scares Us,* p. 90; December 2, 2002, review of *Jennifer Jones Won't Leave Me Alone,* p. 51.

Quill & Quire, September, 1990, Theo Hersh, review of *Oonga Boonga,* p. 20; January, 1994, review of *Why Can't You Fold Your Pants like David Levine?,* p. 37; March, 1995, Gwyneth Evans, review of *Jennifer Jones Won't Leave Me Alone!,* p. 77; May, 1998, Sheree Haughian, review of *Crazy for Chocolate,* p. 34; September, 1998, Mary Beaty, review of *Each One Special,* p. 66.

Resource Links, April, 2000, review of *Each One Special,* p. 51; October, 2000, review of *Quest in Time,* p. 12; December, 2000, review of *So Long Stinky Queen,* p. 15; February, 2001, review of *Nothing Scares Us,* p. 51; October, 2002, Joanne de Groot, review of *Give Maggie a Chance,* p. 10; December, 2002, Karen

MacKinnon, review of *What's the Matter with Albert?,* p. 43; December, 2003, Karen MacKinnon, review of *Manya's Dream,* p. 35; April, 2004, Carolyn Cutt, review of *Jennifer Jones Won't Leave Me Alone,* p. 56; June, 2004, Linda Irvine, review of *A Noodle up Your Nose,* p. 11; December, 2004, Carolyn Cutt, review of *A Bee in Your Ear,* p. 24.

School Arts, December, 1999, Ken Marantz, review of *The Man Who Made Parks: The Story of Park Builder Frederick Law Olmstead,* p. 48.

School Library Journal, May, 1990, Ellen Fader, review of *Oonga Boonga,* p. 93; November, 2000, Sheilah Kosco, review of *Nothing Scares Us,* p. 138; November, 2002, Dona Ratterree, review of *What's the Matter with Albert?,* p. 151; December, 2002, Linda M. Kenton, review of *Give Maggie a Chance,* p. 113; February, 2003, Susan Marie Pitard, review of *Jennifer Jones Won't Leave Me Alone,* p. 124; May, 2004, Christine E. Carr, review of *Just Call Me Joe,* p. 127; October, 2005, Lynn Evarts, review of *Queen of the Toilet Bowl,* p. 178.

Toronto Star, October 17, 1999.

Yes Mag, March-April, 2004, review of *Manya's Dream,* p. 28.

ONLINE

Canadian Association for Children's Writers and Performers Web site, http://www.canscaip.org/ (May 28, 2005), "Frieda Wishinsky."

Canadian Review of Materials Online, http://www.umanitoba.ca/cm/ (October 3, 2003), review of *What's the Matter with Albert?;* (November 6, 2005) Dave Jenkinson, "Profile: Frieda Wishinsky."

Transatlantic Literary Agency Web site, http://www.tla1.com/ (November 6, 2005), "Frieda Wishinsky."

*   *   *

WOODING, Chris 1977-

Personal

Born February 28, 1977, in Leicester, Leicestershire, England. *Education:* Attended University of Sheffield. *Hobbies and other interests:* Watching movies, backpacking in foreign countries, touring with his band.

Addresses

Home—London, England. *Agent*—Carolyn Whitaker, London Independent Books, 26 Chalcot Crescent, London NW1 8YD, England.

Career

Full-time writer.

Awards, Honors

Smarties Book Prize, 2001, *Horn Book* Notable Book designation, *School Library Journal* Best Books designation, and American Library Association Best Book

For Teens designation, all 2004, all for *The Haunting of Alaizabel Cray;* Lancashire Children's Book of the Year Award, and Dracula Society Children of the Night Award for best gothic novel, both 2004, and Children's Book Council Outstanding International Book Award, 2005, all for *Poision.*

Writings

YOUNG-ADULT NOVELS

Crashing, Scholastic (London, England), 1998, Scholastic/Push (New York, NY), 2003.
Catchman, Scholastic (London, England), 1998.
Kerosene, Scholastic (London, England), 1999.
Endgame, Scholastic (London, England), 2000.
The Haunting of Alaizabel Cray, Scholastic (London, England), 2001, Orchard (New York, NY), 2004.
Poison, Scholastic (London, England), 2003, Orchard Books (New York, NY), 2005.
Storm Thief, Orchard (New York, NY), 2006.

"BROKEN SKY" SERIES; FANTASY; FOR CHILDREN

Broken Sky: Part One, illustrated by Steve Kyte, Scholastic (London, England), 1999.
Broken Sky: Part Two, illustrated by Steve Kyte, Scholastic (London, England), 1999.
Broken Sky: Part Three, illustrated by Steve Kyte, Scholastic (London, England), 1999.
Broken Sky: Part Four, illustrated by Steve Kyte, Scholastic (London, England), 1999.
Broken Sky: Part Five, illustrated by Steve Kyte, Scholastic (London, England), 1999, published as *Defy It,* Scholastic (New York, NY), 2000.
Broken Sky: Part Six, illustrated by Steve Kyte, Scholastic (London, England), 1999.
Broken Sky: Part Seven, illustrated by Steve Kyte, Scholastic (London, England), 2000.
Broken Sky: Part Eight, illustrated by Steve Kyte, Scholastic (London, England), 2000.
Broken Sky: Part Nine, illustrated by Steve Kyte, Scholastic (London, England), 2000.

"BRAIDED PATH" SERIES; FANTASY; FOR ADULTS

The Weavers of Saramyr, Gollancz (London, England), 2003.
The Skein of Lament, Gollancz (London, England), 2004.
The Ascendancy Veil, Gollancz (London, England), 2005.

OTHER

Halflight (adult fantasy novel), Gollancz (London, England), 2006.

Work in Progress

The screenplays *Nursery,* a horror film, for director Michael Radford, and *Fusion,* a cartoon series for Canada's Nelvana television; *Pandemonium,* a graphic novel, for Scholastic's Grafix imprint, due 2008.

Sidelights

Chris Wooding achieved success as an author at a very young age. His first novel, *Crashing,* was written and accepted for publication while he was still a teenager, and by the time he graduated from college at age twenty-one he was making a living as a full-time writer. Being published so young "was brilliant, obviously," Wooding told a *Push* online interviewer, "but more because I had finally achieved what I'd been trying for all my life up till then. I had a frighteningly sharp focus on what I wanted to do and be ever since I can remember."

Wooding's first few books, including *Crashing* and *Kerosene,* are realistic novels about teenagers struggling with love and bullies. In *Crashing,* protagonist Jay is a teenager at the end of his last year of high school. His parents have gone out of town, giving him the chance to throw a party for his friends to celebrate the end of exams and have one last get-together before they all head off into adulthood. He also hopes that the party will give him a chance to get closer to Jo, a girl on whom he has long had his eye. However, things do not go as planned, and Jay and his friends soon find the party devolving into a clash with a drunken lout named Stew and Stew's gang of buddies. The book "captures

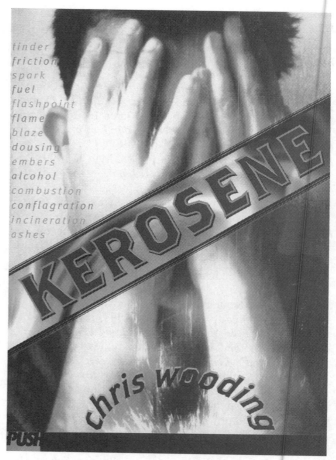

Feeling like a misfit in high school, sixteen-year-old Cal compensates by starting fires, but as the social pressures mount, no fire seems big enough in Wooding's 1999 debut novel. (Cover design by Steve Scott.)

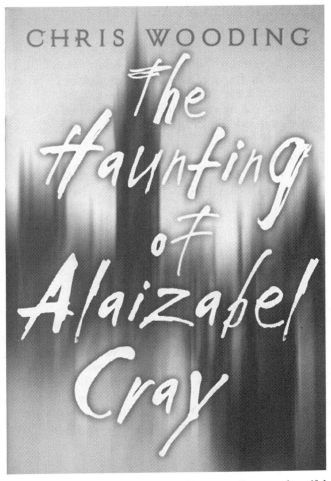

CHRIS WOODING
the Haunting of Alaizabel Cray

A seventeen-year-old witch hunter and his mentor discover a beautiful but possessed woman wandering the streets of a Victorian London where demons are as common as rats in Wooding's 2001 page-turner. (Cover design by Steve Scott.)

the essence of being a high school boy, yearning for first love, and wanting to impress your friends," Sarah Applegate wrote in *Kliatt,* while a *Publishers Weekly* contributor concluded that "the character study of friends on the verge of adulthood has a pleasing, cinematic energy."

Kerosene is the story of Cal, an almost pathologically shy sixteen-year-old boy. Two of the popular girls at his school, Emma and Abby, team up to torture Cal just for fun, and to cope with his frustration he begins setting fires—first small ones, then larger and larger blazes. Although some reviewers were unhappy with the book's resolution, *School Library Journal* contributor Sharon Rawlins noted that Cal's "feelings of alienation and inadequacy are believably portrayed." "Although Cal himself realistically suffers from being overwrought, the story is not, but rather is a gripping and insightful psychological adventure," Francisca Goldsmith noted in *Kliatt.*

The Haunting of Alaizabel Cray differs from Wooding's earlier works. This supernatural novel, which won the prestigious British Smarties Book Prize, is set in an al-

ternate London full of magic and strange monsters. Most people in this city fear that if they go out at night they will be in danger from the wyches, but some, including seventeen-year-old Thaniel Fox, bravely set out to hunt the creatures instead. While out hunting one night, Thaniel finds Alaizabel Cray, a half-mad, seemingly possessed young woman whom the wyches find strangely attractive. "This is dark fare, often graphically violent," Jennifer Mattson noted in *Booklist,* adding that "Wooding delivers characters to care about." Reviewers praised many aspects of *The Haunting of Alaizabel Cray.* A *Kirkus Reviews* contributor commented on the "complex plotting and structure[, which] combine with rich, atmospheric world-building in a fast-paced, tension-filled read." Another critic, writing in *Publishers Weekly,* wrote that "the tactile quality of the prose will make readers feel as if they can touch and smell the dank sewers of the city." Wooding "fuses together his best storytelling skills—plotting, atmosphere, shock value—to create a fabulously horrific and ultimately timeless underworld," Hillias J. Martin concluded in *School Library Journal.*

Biographical and Critical Sources

PERIODICALS

Booklist, July, 2002, Todd Morning, review of *Kerosene,* p. 1838; August, 2004, Jennifer Mattson, review of *The Haunting of Alaizabel Cray,* p. 1925.

Bookseller, December 7, 2001, "Three Take Gold Smarties," p. 6; February 4, 2005, review of *The Ascendancy Veil,* p. 32.

Girls' Life, October-November, 2004, review of *The Haunting of Alaizabel Cray,* p. 42.

Horn Book, November-December, 2004, Anita L. Burkam, review of *The Haunting of Alaizabel Cray,* p. 719.

Kirkus Reviews, August 15, 2004, review of *The Haunting of Alaizabel Cray,* p. 815.

Kliatt, July, 2002, Francisca Goldsmith, review of *Kerosene,* p. 26; May, 2004, Sarah Applegate, review of *Crashing,* p. 25; July, 2004, Michele Winship, review of *The Haunting of Alaizabel Cray,* p. 13.

Publishers Weekly, February 18, 2002, review of *Kerosene,* p. 98; December 15, 2003, review of *Crashing,* p. 75; September 13, 2004, review of *The Haunting of Alaizabel Cray,* p. 80.

School Librarian, autumn, 1999, review of *Kerosene,* p. 158; winter, 2000, review of *Endgame,* p. 215; autumn, 2001, review of *The Haunting of Alaizabel Cray,* p. 161; autumn, 2003, review of *Poison,* p. 161.

School Library Journal, July, 2002, Sharon Rawline, review of *Kerosene,* p. 128; August, 2004, Hillias J. Martin, review of *The Haunting of Alaizabel Cray,* p. 132; April, 2005, review of *The Haunting of Alaizabel Cray,* p. 72.

Voice of Youth Advocates, June, 2004, Ed Sullivan, review of *Crashing,* p. 138.

ONLINE

British Broadcasting Corporation Web site, http://www.bbc.co.uk/blast/ (November 6, 2005), "Blast: Chris Wooding."

Chris Wooding Home Page, http://www.chriswooding.com (November 6, 2005).

Fantastic Fiction Web site, http://www.fantasticfiction.co.uk/ (November 6, 2005), "Chris Wooding Bibliography."

Push Web site, http://www.thisispush.com/ (November 6, 2005), interview with Wooding.

ScifiDimensions.com, http://www.scifidimensions.com/ (November 6, 2005), Chris Coppeans, review of *The Skein of Lament.*

*   *   *

WOOLLEY, Catherine 1904-2005
(Jane Thayer)

OBITUARY NOTICE— See index for *SATA* sketch: Born August 11, 1904, in Chicago, IL; died July 23, 2005, in Truro, MA. Author. Woolley was a prolific author of children's books written under her name and the pseudonym Jane Thayer. A 1927 graduate of the University of California at Los Angeles, she worked as an advertising copywriter and freelance writer in New York City during the late 1920s and early 1930s. From 1933 to 1940, she was a copywriter and worked in publicity for the American Radiator & Standard Corporation. She found a job as a desk editor for the *Architectural Record* and as a production editor for the *Society of Automotive Engineers Journal* in the early 1940s. By the time Woolley had advanced to the position of public relations writer for the National Association of Manufacturers in New York City, she had also begun writing and publishing children's books. Her debut, *I Like Trains,* was released in 1944. The author went on to pen over eighty books, and she was so prolific that her editor suggested she publish some of her works under a pen name. Woolley wrote picture books under the name of Thayer, while her books for older children were published under her own name. She left her public relations job in 1947 to concentrate full time on writing, though she occasionally taught classes and led writing workshops. Included among her many books under her own name are the "Ginny" and "Cathy" series, and, as Thayer, such books as *Sandy and the Seventeen Balloons* (1955), *Quiet on Account of Dinosaur* (1964), and *Mr. Turtle's Magic Glasses* (1971). Her last book for children is *The Popcorn Dragon* (1989). This was followed by the nonfiction title *Writing for Children* (1989). Woolley was honored by her hometown in 1996 when the Truro library named its children's reading room after her.

OBITUARIES AND OTHER SOURCES:

PERIODICALS

Los Angeles Times, July 29, 2005, p. B11.
New York Times, July 28, 2005, p. C19.
Washington Post, July 30, 2005, p. B6.

YAMANAKA, Lois-Ann 1961-

Personal

Born September 7, 1961, in Ho'olchua, Moloka'i, HI; daughter of Harry (a taxidermist) and Jean (a primary school teacher); married John Inferrera (a teacher); children: John. *Education:* University of Hawaii at Manoa, B.Ed., 1983, M.Ed., 1987.

Addresses

Home—Honolulu, HI. *Agent*—c/o Author Mail, Farrar, Straus & Giroux, 19 Union Square W., New York, NY 10001.

Career

Writer. Hawaii Department of Education, language arts resource teacher and English teacher.

Awards, Honors

National Endowment for the Humanities grant, 1990; Pushcart Prize for Poetry, 1993, for "Saturday Night at the Pahala Theatre"; Elliot Cades Award for Literature, 1993; Carnegie Foundation grant, 1994; National Endowment for the Arts creative writing fellowship, 1994; Pushcart Prize XIX, 1994, for "Yarn Wig"; Rona Jaffe Award for Women Writers, 1996; Lannan Literary Award, 1998; Asian-American Studies National Book Award, 1998.

Writings

Saturday Night at the Pahala Theatre (verse novellas), Bamboo Ridge Press (Honolulu, HI), 1993.
Wild Meat and the Bully Burgers (novel), Farrar, Straus (New York, NY), 1996.
Blu's Hanging (novel), Farrar, Straus (New York, NY), 1997.
Heads by Harry (novel), Farrar, Straus, (New York, NY), 1999.
Name Me Nobody (young-adult novel), Hyperion (New York, NY), 1999.
Father of the Four Passages (novel), Farrar, Straus (New York, NY), 2001.
The Heart's Language (picture book), illustrated by Aaron Jasinski, Hyperion (New York, NY), 2005.
Behold the Many (novel), Farrar, Strauss (New York, NY), 2006.

Contributor to books, including *Transnational Asia Pacific: Gender, Culture, and the Public Sphere,* edited by Shirley Geok-lin Lim and others, University of Illinois Press (Urbana, IL), 1999.

Sidelights

One of Hawaii's most noted novelists, Lois-Ann Yamanaka depicts life on the islands through an Asian-American perspective. In addition to penning several novels for adults, such as the trilogy including *Wild Meat and the Bully Burgers, Blu's Hanging,* and *Heads by Harry,* she has also authored the short-story collection *Saturday Night at the Pahala Theatre,* a picture book titled *The Heart's Language,* and the young-adult novel *Name Me Nobody.* Young, working-class Japanese Americans living in Hawaii, Yamanaka's adolescent protagonists struggle with universal teen problems, such as sexual development and peer acceptance while also coming to terms with their cultural identity as the descendants of Japanese immigrant laborers. Most notably, in her writing Yamanaka validates the use of pidgin, or Hawaii Creole English—a dialect developed by immigrants to Hawaii from China, the Philippines, Japan and other countries—thereby giving voice to a segment of the Hawaiian population that had previously been little represented in literature.

Yamanaka grew up in Pahala, a sugar-plantation town on Hawaii's big island, and is one of four daughters. "My youngest sister and I were very much like our mother," Yamanaka told Valerie Takahama in the *Orange County Register,* describing her childhood. "Talk too much, wore strange clothes, did strange things. We always thought things that we shouldn't have been thinking or said things that we shouldn't have been saying." Through her use of pidgin in a school system that disproved of the dialect, and her unusual upbringing, Yamanaka found it "very painful not being able to fit in with what was middle class-class Japanese."

Later attending the University of Hawaii at Manoa, Yamanaka earned a master's degree in education. After college she enrolled in a writing class that exposed her to books by African-American women writers who were writing in their own dialect. "That's when I came to terms that pidgin was not an ignorant language, that I was speaking a dialect and that my feelings and thoughts were so connected to the language that in order for me to write truthfully, I needed to write in that voice," Yamanaka further commented to Takahama. Working her authentic voice into short fiction, she published *Saturday Night at the Pahala Theatre* in 1993. Composed of four verse novellas focusing on and narrated by working-class Hawaiian teenagers, the book explores ethnic identity, sexual awakening, drug use, and abusive relationships. Marilyn Kallet, writing in the *American Book Review,* praised the work, commenting that Yamanaka's "characters speak in dramatic monologues as tight and fierce as anything Browning might have dreamed of, but their voices hold true to the idiomatic language of tough, vulnerable preteen girls holding private talks."

While *Saturday Night at the Pahala Theatre* earned Yamanaka critical praise and awards, it also elicited concern from Hawaiian educators who criticized both the author's use of pidgin English and her inclusion of strong doses of profanity. Suddenly Yamanaka was considered a controversial writer, and teachers were urged not to use her work in classes. While Yamanaka's adult

Hawaiian teen Lovey Nariyoshi straddles between two worlds in Yamanaka's debut novel; while images of American culture permeate her life, Lovey's haole neighbors keep her family at a distance by putting up invisible walls. (Cover illustration by Cora Yee.)

novels have continued to create a measure of controversy, her work for younger readers has managed to elicit praise while still focusing attention on the tension of growing up and living between cultures.

In Yamanaka's young-adult tale, *Name Me Nobody,* middle-grader Emi-Lou Kaya is overweight, and is given nicknames like Emi-Lump and Emi-Loser. An outcast at school and raised by her cloistered grandmother, Emi-Lou's sole contact to the mainstream world of school is her best friend, Yvonne, who tries to get her friend into playing softball with the Hilo Astros, or else cheerleading. Yvonne also encourages Emi-Lou to lose weight, and even steals diet pills for her friend, before suddenly abandoning the cause due to a crush on Babes, the catcher for the Astros. Emi-Lou, now slimming down, is desperate to get her best friend back and make Yvonne be 'normal' again. Meanwhile, the newly slim Emi-Lou begins to attract the attention of two boys, one who has genuine feelings for her and the other who wants to use her. Ultimately, grandmother comes to the rescue, helping the girl realize that the only person she has control over is herself.

In the *Honolulu Star-Bulletin,* Cynthia Oi noted that, in writing for younger readers, Yamanaka "doesn't dumb down her writing"; instead, in addition to allowing her characters to speak pidgin, the author "maintain[s] . . . the lyric style and imagery of her adult works, but keep[s] . . . it simple." Reviewing *Name Me Nobody,*

Booklist contributor Hazel Rochman wrote that teen readers "will recognize the outsider story, the vicious name-calling . . . as well as the elemental drama of friendship, betrayal, and love." In *Horn Book* a critic compared the novel to Yamanaka's "notable works for adults," and concluded that the author's "is a welcome new YA voice noteworthy for its complexity and richness." While noting the novel's slow pace, a *Publishers Weekly* contributor dubbed the book "rich in atmosphere and bold in its themes."

While frequently featuring teen characters, Yamanaka's adult novels are more suitable for mature readers. *Wild Meat and the Bully Burgers, Blu's Hanging*, and *Heads by Harry* comprise a coming-of-age trilogy that also deals with larger issues, such as class and ethnicity. Composed of a series of vignettes, *Wild Meat and the Bully Burgers* is narrated by Lovey Nariyoshi, a Japanese-American teen who struggles with self-consciousness and dreams of a better life. While Lauren Belfer wrote in the *New York Times Book Review* that Yamanaka's use of pidgin is sometimes impenetrable, *Wild Meat and the Bully Burgers* contains "moments of stinging clarity," in which the author weaves "haunting images as she sketches Lovey's search for a spiritual home." A *Publishers Weekly* reviewer noted that the harsh, realistic view of life presented in the book is balanced by images of "the bonds of love and understanding that can create poignant, epiphanic moments of reconciliation." Alice Joyce, writing in *Booklist,* dubbed *Wild Meat and the Bully Burgers* "vibrant," adding that "Yamanaka's voice demands to be heard."

Focusing on thirteen-year-old narrator Ivah Ogata, Ivah's brother, Blu, and her younger sister, Maisie, *Blu's Hanging* finds the children trying to deal with their mother's death and the dismal realities of a life of poverty. In particular, Ivah has a difficult choice to make when she realizes that she must decide between her own future and the ongoing job of caring for her siblings. "In presenting issues of race, violence and neglect through the filtered lenses of these children," a *Publishers Weekly* reviewer noted, the author presents "a textured picture" of a family in trouble. Writing in *People,* Lan N. Nguyen called the novel "a touching tale of an impoverished family's disintegration in spite of their love for each other," while Jessica Hagedorn wrote in *Harper's Bazaar* that all is not dark; the "scrappy characters" in *Blu's Hanging* "endure poverty, racism, and sexual and emotional abuse, but never lose their capacity for humor."

Yamanaka continues her coming-of-age trilogy with *Heads by Harry,* a story set in a Hilo taxidermist shop that is run by Harry and Mary Alice Yangyuu. Oldest daughter Toni, something of a misfit, often accompanies her father on his hunting expeditions, while younger sister Bunny manipulates her parents through her good looks. Meanwhile, flamboyantly gay brother Sheldon is a constant thorn in the side of his macho taxidermist father. Again employing pidgin to tell her tale, Ya-

As if being a teen isn't bad enough, in this thought-provoking yet humorous coming-of-age tale Toni must cope with a gay older brother, a sister who is perfect in every way, and a taxidermist father whose plans for her future don't jibe with Toni's hopes and dreams. (Cover illustration by Barbara Lambase.)

manaka creates what a *Publishers Weekly* reviewer dubbed a "frank and tragicomic novel" wherein "the potency and honesty of Yamanaka's view of Hawaiian life achieves the haunting force of myth." While some critics found the book to be derivative of the author's earlier books, *Library Journal* reviewer Shirley N. Quan called Yamanaka's prose "emotionally gripping and filled with harsh realism," while also "liberally sprinkled with sensitivity and humor."

More recently Yamanaka has adjusted her literary focus; "I got tired of being the pidgin poster girl," she explained to a *Time* writer. In *Father of the Four Passages* she also addresses a challenge she herself shares: parenting an autistic child. In the novel, streetwise single mother Sonia Kurisu struggles to raise her child, Sonny Boy, while also coming to terms with a past that included addiction and three prior abortions. In parallel stories, Yamanaka recounts Sonia's early life, including her abandonment by both parents and her wish to establish an emotional truce with her father. Sonia's search for absolution is answered, ironically, by the developmental problems Sonny Boy begins to exhibit. In *Publishers Weekly* a reviewer called *Father of the Four Passages* "an uncompromising story of the tenaciousness of motherly love amid the chaos of drugs and dysfunction," while Joseph Dewey noted in the *Review of Contemporary Fiction* that Sonia is a challenging yet "compelling" protagonist who is brought to life by Yamanaka in "pitch-perfect prose that is earthy and convincing."

Yamanaka also expresses her relationship with her son in a less-weighty medium: the picture book *The Heart's Language*. In this work, illustrated by Aaron Jasinksi, a young child is able to communicate with trees, birds, and other creatures from the heart; his parents must also learn to understand this expression of love because the child cannot master human speech.

Biographical and Critical Sources

BOOKS

Contemporary Novelists, 7th edition, St. James Press (Detroit, MI), 2001.

PERIODICALS

American Book Review, September 11, 1995, Marilyn Kallet, review of *Saturday Night at the Pahala Theatre,* p. 11.
Atlantic Monthly, February, 1999, Jamie James, "This Hawaii Is Not for Tourists," pp. 90-92.
Booklist, December 1, 1995, Alice Joyce, review of *Wild Meat and the Bully Burgers,* p. 611; January 1, 1999, Donna Seaman, review of *Heads by Harry,* p. 835; August, 1999, Hazel Rochman, review of *Name Me Nobody,* p. 2045; December 1, 2000, Donna Seaman, review of *Father of the Four Passages,* p. 694.
Christian Science Monitor, January 19, 1996, p. 14.
Harper's Bazaar, April, 1997, Jessica Hagedorn, review of *Blu's Hanging,* p. 164.

Honolulu Star Bulletin, April 8, 1997, Nadine Kam, review of *Blu's Hanging;* June 25, 1999, Cynthia Oi, review of *Name Me Nobody.*
Horn Book, July, 1999, review of *Name Me Nobody,* p. 476.
Library Journal, November 15, 1995, p. 101; March 1, 1997, Anna Quan Leon, review of *Blu's Hanging,* p. 105; February 1, 1999, Shirley N. Quan, review of *Heads by Harry,* p. 124; October 15, 2000, Shirley N. Quan, review of *Father of the Four Passages,* p. 105.
Los Angeles Times, July 23, 1998, p. E1.
Ms., July-August, 1996, p. 85.
Nation, March 1, 1999, Mindy Pennybacker, review of *Heads by Harry,* pp. 28-29.
Newsweek, August 17, 1998, p. 63.
New Yorker, March 19, 2000, p. 152.
New York Times, February 8, 1999, p. E1.
New York Times Book Review, December 31, 1995, Lauren Belfer, review of *Wild Meat and the Bully Burgers,* p. 11; May 4, 1997, p. 21; March 14, 1999, p. 23.
Orange County Register, February 28, 1996, Valerie Takahama, "Hawaiian Writer Lois-Ann Yamanaka Draws Praise, Criticism for Her Novel Using Pidgin English."
People, May 26, 1997, Lan N. Nguyen, "Hawaiian Eye-Opener: Talking with Lois-Ann Yamanaka," p. 42.
Publishers Weekly, August 21, 1995, p. 35; October 2, 1995, review of *Wild Meat and the Bully Burgers,* p. 51; February 24, 1997, review of *Blu's Hanging,* p. 62; December 21, 1998, review of *Heads by Harry,* p. 54; June 28, 1999, review of *Name Me Nobody,* p. 81; October 30, 2000, review of *Father of the Four Passages,* p. 45.
Review of Contemporary Fiction, fall, 1999, Brian Evenson, review of *Heads by Harry,* p. 160; summer, 2001, Joseph Dewey, review of *Father of the Four Passages,* p. 159.
School Library Journal, May, 2005, Kathleen Kelly MacMillan, review of *The Heart's Language,* p. 105.
Time, February 5, 2001, "Black and Blue Hawaii," p. 78.
Voice Literary Supplement, December, 1993, Lawrence Chu, review of *Saturday Night at the Pahala Theatre,* pp. 7-8.
Women's Review of Books, July, 1996, Kiana Davenport, review of *Saturday Night at the Pahala Theatre,* p. 37.*